Tenth Edition

Human Communication

The Basic Course

Joseph A. DeVito

Hunter College of the
City University of New York

Boston New York San Francisco
Mexico City Montreal Toronto London Madrid Munich Paris
Hong Kong Singapore Tokyo Cape Town Sydney

Executive Editor: Karon Bowers
Senior Editor: Brian Wheel
Editorial Assistant: Heather Hawkins
Development Editor: Kristen Desmond LeFevre
Senior Marketing Manager: Mandee Eckersley
Editorial Production: Nesbitt Graphics, Inc.
Composition Buyer: Linda Cox
Manufacturing Buyer: JoAnne Sweeney
Cover Administrator: Joel Gendron
Text Design: Nesbitt Graphics, Inc.
Photo Research: Julie Tesser
Text Composition: Nesbitt Graphics, Inc.

For related titles and support materials, visit our online catalog at www.ablongman.com.

Library of Congress Cataloging-in-Publication Data

DeVito, Joseph A.
Human communication : the basic course / Joseph A. DeVito.—10th ed.
p. cm.
Includes bibliographical references and index.
ISBN 0-205-42849-5 (pbk.)
1. Communication. I. Title.

P90.D485 2005
302.2—dc22

2004062684

Printed in the United States of America

10 9 8 7 6 5 4 3 2 1—VHP—08 07 06 05

Brief Contents

CD-ROM Units

These sections are included on the CD-ROM with bonus units, which is available to be packaged with this book. Some restrictions apply.

CONTENTS

CD-ROM Units

These sections are included on the CD-ROM with bonus units, which is available to be packaged with this book. Some restrictions apply.

Specialized Contents

Ask the Researcher

Understanding Theory and Research

Building Communication Skills

Media Watch

Self-Tests

Communication@Work

Reflections on Ethics

Public Speaking Sample Assistant

Welcome to

Human Communication

The Basic Course

It's an extraordinary pleasure to write a preface to a book that is going into its tenth edition. Here I'd like to introduce (1) the general nature of the text, (2) the book's major features and some of the ways in which this edition differs from the previous edition, and (3) the supplements and ancillaries that are available with this text.

The Book (In Brief)

Human Communication: The Basic Course is designed for the introductory college course that covers the major areas and skills of the broad field of communication. After a thorough coverage of the fundamentals of communication in Part 1 (preliminaries, principles of communication, culture, perception, listening, the self, and verbal and nonverbal messages), Parts 2 and 3 focus on interpersonal and small group communication (five units) and public speaking (five units). The text covers classic approaches and new developments; it covers research and theory but gives coordinate attention to communication skills.

This book is addressed to students who have little or no prior background in communication. If this will be your only communication course, *Human Communication* will provide you with a thorough foundation in the theory, research, and skills of this essential liberal art. For those of you who will take additional and advanced courses or who are beginning a major in communication, it will provide the essential foundation for more advanced and specialized study.

Major Features of *Human Communication*

The tenth edition builds on the successful features of previous editions but also incorporates much that is new. Consequently, I'd like to explain the major features of the text (especially those new to this edition) as well as the changes specific to this edition.

Balance of Theory/Research and Skills

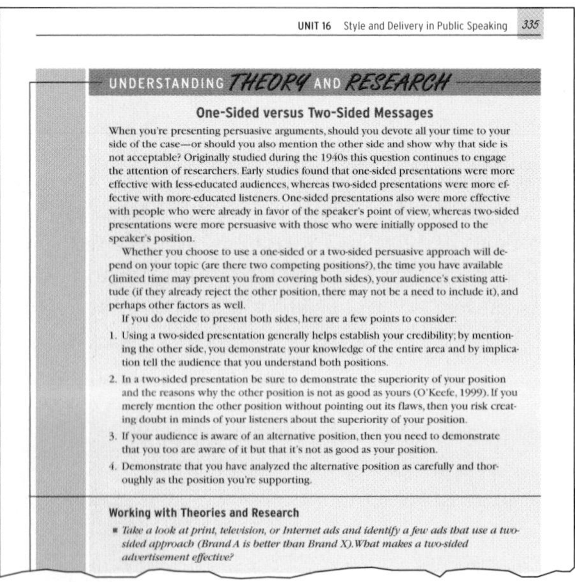
UNIT 16 Style and Delivery in Public Speaking 335

UNDERSTANDING THEORY AND RESEARCH

One-Sided versus Two-Sided Messages

When you're presenting persuasive arguments, should you devote all your time to your side of the case—or should you also mention the other side and show why that side is not acceptable? Originally studied during the 1940s this question continues to engage the attention of researchers. Early studies found that one-sided presentations were more effective with less-educated audiences, whereas two-sided presentations were more effective with more-educated listeners. One-sided presentations also were more effective with people who were already in favor of the speaker's point of view, whereas two-sided presentations were more persuasive with those who were initially opposed to the speaker's position.

Whether you choose to use a one-sided or a two-sided persuasive approach will depend on your topic (are there two competing positions?), the time you have available (limited time may prevent you from covering both sides), your audience's existing attitude (if they already reject the other position, there may not be a need to include it), and perhaps other factors as well.

If you do decide to present both sides, here are a few points to consider:

1. Using a two-sided presentation generally helps establish your credibility; by mentioning the other side, you demonstrate your knowledge of the entire area and by implication tell the audience that you understand both positions.
2. In a two-sided presentation be sure to demonstrate the superiority of your position and the reasons why the other position is not as good as yours (O'Keefe, 1999). If you merely mention the other position without pointing out its flaws, then you risk creating doubt in minds of your listeners about the superiority of your position.
3. If your audience is aware of an alternative position, then you need to demonstrate that you too are aware of it but that it's not as good as your position.
4. Demonstrate that you have analyzed the alternative position as carefully and thoroughly as the position you're supporting.

Working with Theories and Research

- *Take a look at print, television, or Internet ads and identify a few ads that use a two-sided approach (Brand A is better than Brand X). What makes a two-sided advertisement effective?*

The tenth edition continues the pattern of the previous edition in giving coordinate emphasis to research and theory, on the one hand, and practical communication skills, on the other. To highlight theory and research, 38 **Understanding Theory and Research** boxes appear throughout the text and provide just a small sampling of the many theories and research findings in communication. These boxes explain how we know what we know about communication, describe how researchers go about expanding our knowledge of communication in all its forms, and introduce numerous interesting theories and research findings. In addition, theories and research are discussed throughout the text. A complete list of these Understanding Theory and Research boxes appears in the Specialized Contents on page ix.

To emphasize communication skills, 36 **Building Communication Skills** boxes appear throughout the text and offer you opportunities to practice important skills in human communication. In addition, skills implications are discussed throughout the text. A complete list of these Building Communication Skills boxes appears in the Specialized Contents on pages ix–x.

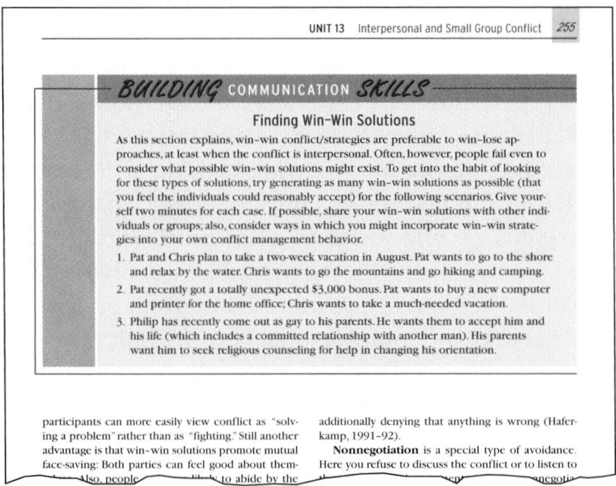

UNIT 13 Interpersonal and Small Group Conflict 255

BUILDING COMMUNICATION SKILLS

Finding Win-Win Solutions

As this section explains, win-win conflict/strategies are preferable to win-lose approaches, at least when the conflict is interpersonal. Often, however, people fail even to consider what possible win-win solutions might exist. To get into the habit of looking for these types of solutions, try generating as many win-win solutions as possible (that you feel the individuals could reasonably accept) for the following scenarios. Give yourself two minutes for each case. If possible, share your win-win solutions with other individuals or groups; also, consider ways in which you might incorporate win-win strategies into your own conflict management behavior.

1. Pat and Chris plan to take a two-week vacation in August. Pat wants to go to the shore and relax by the water. Chris wants to go the mountains and go hiking and camping.
2. Pat recently got a totally unexpected $3,000 bonus. Pat wants to buy a new computer and printer for the home office; Chris wants to take a much-needed vacation.
3. Philip has recently come out as gay to his parents. He wants them to accept him and his life (which includes a committed relationship with another man). His parents want him to seek religious counseling for help in changing his orientation.

participants can more easily view conflict as "solving a problem" rather than as "fighting." Still another advantage is that win-win solutions promote mutual face-saving: Both parties can feel good about them-

additionally denying that anything is wrong (Haferkamp, 1991–92).

Nonnegotiation is a special type of avoidance. Here you refuse to discuss the conflict or to listen to

For this new edition I have revised many of these boxes—not only to make them shorter and more clearly focused but also to update them. The skill boxes, in particular, I've revised to encourage specific communication responses. And I've added a variety of new theory/research and skills boxes. For example, new Understanding Theory and Research boxes include "Styles of Leadership" (Unit 12) and "Balance Theories" (Unit 18), and the discussions of systematic desensitization and performance visualization have been recast as Understanding Theory and Research boxes (Unit 14). New Building Communication Skills boxes include "Regulating Your Listening Style" (Unit 5); "Confirming, Rejecting, or Disconfirming" (Unit 7); "Formulating Excuses" (Unit 9); "Repairing Relationships" (Unit 10); "Using Cultural Beliefs as Assumptions" (Unit 14); and "Constructing Conclusions and Introductions" (Unit 15).

A third and related feature, new to this tenth edition of *Human Communication* and called **Ask the Researcher,** is designed to combine the text's two major emphases: theory/research and skills. In Ask the Researcher, nationally and internationally known theorists and researchers respond to questions typical of students' queries about the practical applications of human communication. You'll find the experts' responses—18 in all (one per unit)—most interesting. A complete list of these Ask the Researcher items appears in the Specialized Contents on page ix.

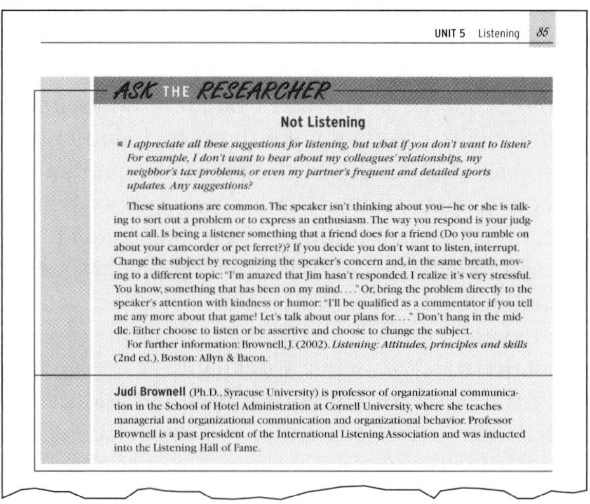

UNIT 5 Listening 85

ASK THE RESEARCHER

Not Listening

- *I appreciate all these suggestions for listening, but what if you don't want to listen? For example, I don't want to hear about my colleagues' relationships, my neighbor's tax problems, or even my partner's frequent and detailed sports updates. Any suggestions?*

These situations are common. The speaker isn't thinking about you—he or she is talking to sort out a problem or to express an enthusiasm. The way you respond is your judgment call. Is being a listener something that a friend does for a friend (Do you ramble on about your camcorder or pet ferret?)? If you decide you don't want to listen, interrupt. Change the subject by recognizing the speaker's concern and, in the same breath, moving to a different topic: "I'm amazed that Jim hasn't responded. I realize it's very stressful. You know, something that has been on my mind. . . ." Or, bring the problem directly to the speaker's attention with kindness or humor: "I'll be qualified as a commentator if you tell me any more about that game! Let's talk about our plans for. . . ." Don't hang in the middle. Either choose to listen or be assertive and choose to change the subject.

For further information: Brownell, J. (2002). *Listening: Attitudes, principles and skills* (2nd ed.). Boston: Allyn & Bacon.

Judi Brownell (Ph.D., Syracuse University) is professor of organizational communication in the School of Hotel Administration at Cornell University, where she teaches managerial and organizational communication and organizational behavior. Professor Brownell is a past president of the International Listening Association and was inducted into the Listening Hall of Fame.

The photo captions, which go beyond traditional textbook captions and are called **ViewPoints**, also focus on this dual concern; approximately half the ViewPoints focus primarily on theory and research and half on skills.

Website Integration

One of the most interesting developments in textbooks today is integration with the World Wide Web. This edition comes with an extensive website that complements the material presented in the text (and in the typical introductory communication course). As you'll see, the text website is extensive; it is not intended that every student read both the text and the entire website. Rather, the website offers extra avenues for pursuing topics raised in the text that will interest a wide variety of students and meet many course objectives. One student and one course might focus on the public speaking sections, another on the skill exercises, and still another on the self-tests. The textbook provides the essential foundation for all students; the website provides an efficient means for learning more about specific areas that interest you.

Specifically, the website for this text—www.ablongman.com/devito—contains the following materials:

- **Self-Tests:** Numerous self-tests that are not presented in the text are available on the website. These Web self-tests include tests measuring cultural awareness, lying, self-disclosure, shyness, self-monitoring, politeness, directness, conversational and group apprehension, conversational satisfaction, beliefs about relationships, the type of relationship you prefer, romanticism, commitment, individualism, assertiveness, argumentativeness, and more.
- **Skill Building Exercises:** A wide variety of skill building exercises on the website complement those offered in the text's Building Communication Skills boxes. Among those included on the website are exercises dealing with communication channels, contradictory messages, communication in relationships, culture and gender, cultural beliefs, perception, listening, self-awareness and self-disclosure, conversational effectiveness, nonverbal messages, relationships, small group effectiveness, and public speaking.
- **Extensions and Elaborations:** Additional material on a variety of topics is included on the website. For example, there are additional approaches to friendship, love, and family as well as elaborations of communication apprehension, assertiveness, and the influence of culture and gender on friendships and love. Similarly, the motivated sequence; questions of fact, value, and policy; and the speech of introduction receive more extended coverage on the website. Also included on the website are 13 skeletal outlines for a wide variety of speeches to help guide initial attempts at developing a public speech.

In addition, the website contains flash-card exercises to test your knowledge of the key terms, practice tests, and lots more.

Additional Units

Four complete units that do not appear in the printed text are available on CD-ROM.

- The **Mass Media** discusses the functional and dysfunctional effects of the media and shows how you can become a more critical (and active) consumer of mass media.
- **Emotional Communication** provides a concentrated focus on this one form of interpersonal communication. The unit covers emotions and emotional messages, obstacles in communicating emotions, and guidelines for communicating emotions effectively.
- **Criticism in the Public Speaking Classroom** addresses ways and means to criticize classroom speeches effectively and covers the nature and values of criticism, cultural differences in criticism, and standards and principles of criticism.
- **Developing Special Occasion Speeches** presents thorough coverage of a variety of special occasion speeches: speeches of introduction, presentation, and acceptance; speeches aimed at securing goodwill; and speeches of tribute. In addition, the unit considers some cultural influences on the special occasion speech.

Comprehensive Coverage of Human Communication

The tenth edition of *Human Communication* offers comprehensive coverage of the fundamentals of human communication, including perception, listening, the self, and verbal and nonverbal messages (Units 1-8); interpersonal and small group communication (Units 9-13); and public speaking (Units 14-18). Two organizational changes should be noted here. First, because some courses cover interviewing but others do not, the interviewing material formerly included in the textbook is now a separate pamphlet, *Interviewing and Human Communication*. Available free with this text, the pamphlet is a revised and expanded version of the ninth edition's interviewing unit. Second, the interpersonal conflict unit now discusses both interpersonal and small group conflict, in light of the fact that the two conflict types and the relevant conflict management skills are more similar than different. This rewritten unit, "Interpersonal and Small Group Conflict," now follows the units on interpersonal and small group communication.

Thorough Coverage of Public Speaking

The book devotes five full units to public speaking. The first three of these units cover the 10 essential steps for preparing and presenting a public speech.

Unit 14, "Public Speaking Topics, Audiences, and Research," introduces the study of public speaking, shows you how to manage your fear, and explains the first three steps for speech preparation: selecting the topic and purpose, analyzing the audience, and researching the topic.

Unit 15, "Supporting and Organizing Your Speech," covers the next four steps: formulating the thesis and main points; supporting the main points; organizing the speech; and constructing the conclusion, introduction, and transitions.

Unit 16, "Style and Delivery in Public Speaking," covers the remaining three steps: wording the speech, rehearsing the speech, and presenting the speech.

The next two units (Units 17, "The Informative Speech," and Unit 18, "The Persuasive Speech") cover informative and persuasive speeches in detail—the types of speeches and the strategies for informing and persuading an audience. In addition, two entire units on public speaking, "Developing Special Occasion Speeches" and "Criticism in the Public Speaking Classroom," are available on CD-ROM.

New to the public speaking units is the **Public Speaking Sample Assistant,** a series of boxes presenting sample speeches and outlines with suggestions for critical analysis. In all, the Public Speaking Sample Assistant boxes occur eight times in these units, featuring two poorly constructed speeches to illustrate what to avoid and six extremely well constructed examples of both informative and persuasive speeches and outlines. The aim of this feature is to provide specific examples of what you should do and what you should avoid.

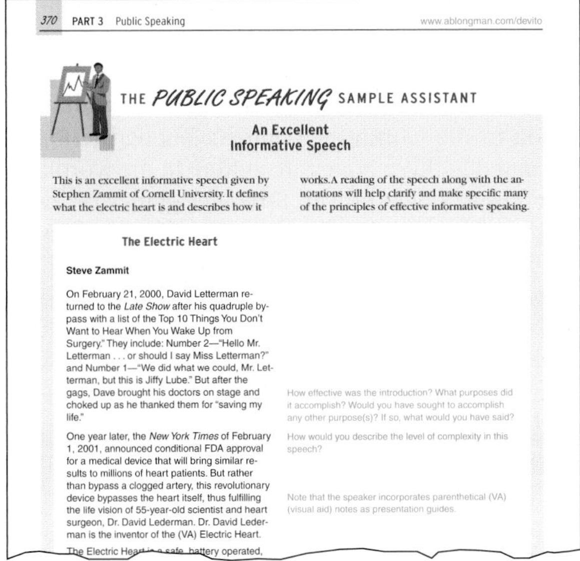

370 PART 3 Public Speaking www.ablongman.com/devito

THE *PUBLIC SPEAKING* SAMPLE ASSISTANT

An Excellent Informative Speech

This is an excellent informative speech given by Stephen Zammit of Cornell University. It defines what the electric heart is and describes how it works. A reading of the speech along with the annotations will help clarify and make specific many of the principles of effective informative speaking.

The Electric Heart

Steve Zammit

On February 21, 2000, David Letterman returned to the *Late Show* after his quadruple bypass with a list of the Top 10 Things You Don't Want to Hear When You Wake Up from Surgery." They include: Number 2—"Hello Mr. Letterman . . . or should I say Miss Letterman?" and Number 1—"We did what we could, Mr. Letterman, but this is Jiffy Lube." But after the gags, Dave brought his doctors on stage and choked up as he thanked them for "saving my life."

How effective was the introduction? What purposes did it accomplish? Would you have sought to accomplish any other purpose(s)? If so, what would you have said?

One year later, the *New York Times* of February 1, 2001, announced conditional FDA approval for a medical device that will bring similar results to millions of heart patients. But rather than bypass a clogged artery, this revolutionary device bypasses the heart itself, thus fulfilling the life vision of 55-year-old scientist and heart surgeon, Dr. David Lederman. Dr. David Lederman is the inventor of the (VA) Electric Heart.

How would you describe the level of complexity in this speech?

Note that the speaker incorporates parenthetical (VA) (visual aid) notes as presentation guides.

The Electric Heart is a safe, battery operated,

Emphasis on Cultural Issues

Like the previous edition, this edition reflects the growing importance of culture and intercultural interactions in all forms of human communication. There are few communications that are not influenced by culture in some way. Thus, a cultural consciousness is essential in any communication text. In this tenth edition this cultural consciousness and coverage takes several forms.

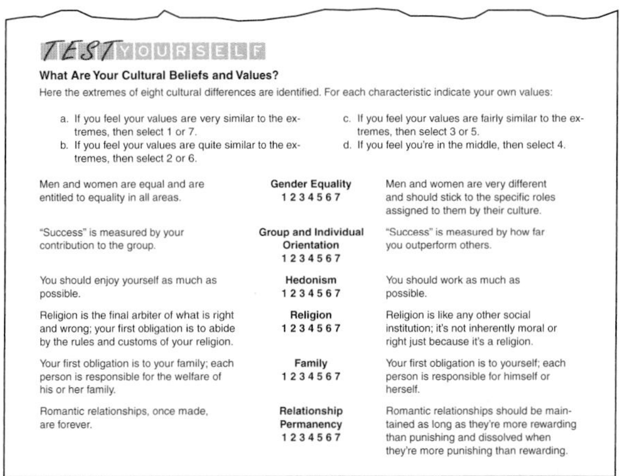

TEST YOURSELF

What Are Your Cultural Beliefs and Values?

Here the extremes of eight cultural differences are identified. For each characteristic indicate your own values:

a. If you feel your values are very similar to the extremes, then select 1 or 7.
b. If you feel your values are quite similar to the extremes, then select 2 or 6.
c. If you feel your values are fairly similar to the extremes, then select 3 or 5.
d. If you feel you're in the middle, then select 4.

Men and women are equal and are entitled to equality in all areas.	**Gender Equality** 1 2 3 4 5 6 7	Men and women are very different and should stick to the specific roles assigned to them by their culture.
"Success" is measured by your contribution to the group.	**Group and Individual Orientation** 1 2 3 4 5 6 7	"Success" is measured by how far you outperform others.
You should enjoy yourself as much as possible.	**Hedonism** 1 2 3 4 5 6 7	You should work as much as possible.
Religion is the final arbiter of what is right and wrong; your first obligation is to abide by the rules and customs of your religion.	**Religion** 1 2 3 4 5 6 7	Religion is like any other social institution; it's not inherently moral or right just because it's a religion.
Your first obligation is to your family; each person is responsible for the welfare of his or her family.	**Family** 1 2 3 4 5 6 7	Your first obligation is to yourself; each person is responsible for himself or herself.
Romantic relationships, once made, are forever.	**Relationship Permanency** 1 2 3 4 5 6 7	Romantic relationships should be maintained as long as they're more rewarding than punishing and dissolved when they're more punishing than rewarding.

- An entire unit (Unit 3, "Culture and Communication") explains the nature of culture, some of the ways in which cultures differ from one another and the influences these differences have on communication, and some of the ways you can improve your own intercultural communication.
- Cultural issues also are integrated throughout the text. Here are major examples:
  - Unit 1 establishes the central role of the cultural context in all forms of communication.
  - Unit 2 considers the role of culture and gender differences in the principles of communication.
  - Unit 3 focuses entirely on culture, as already noted.
  - Unit 4 considers the role of cultural scripts and of culture in implicit personality theory and in uncertainty.
  - Unit 5 considers cultural and gender differences in listening.
  - Unit 6 discusses culture's role in our self-concept and its influence in self-disclosure.
  - Unit 7 looks at cultural and gender rules in verbal messages (e.g., "rules" about directness and politeness); at sexist, heterosexist, and racist language; and at the cultural identifiers people prefer.
  - Unit 8 looks at cultural influences on nonverbal communication channels such as facial expression, color, touch, silence, and time.
  - Unit 9 examines cultural influences on conversational rules, cultural sensitivity as a general conversational skill, and cultural differences in turn taking and in the qualities of conversational effectiveness.
  - Unit 10 looks at cultural influences on the stages of interpersonal relationships and on re-

lationship rules and the cultural bias in relationship research.

- Unit 11 examines the small group as a culture, looks at the role of norms in small group communication, and examines the distinctions between high- and low-power-distance groups.
- Unit 12 looks at small group membership and leadership in cultural perspective.
- Unit 13 discusses the influence of cultural and gender differences on interpersonal and small group conflict and conflict resolution strategies, and at the importance of face-saving in different cultures.
- Unit 14 covers cultural sensitivity and speech topics, the role of culture and gender in audience analysis, and secular and sacred cultures.
- Unit 15 discusses cultural considerations in speech organization (high- and low-context cultures), cultural sensitivity in presentation aids, and culture shock (in a sample PowerPoint speech).
- Unit 16 covers the role of culture in emotional display and provides a sample speech outline whose topic is culture shock.
- Unit 17 discusses the cultural implications of the "knowledge gap" hypothesis.
- Unit 18 explains some of the cultural differences in the ways people use and respond to persuasive strategies.

People with disabilities also may be viewed from a cultural perspective, and four special tables in this edition offer suggestions for improving communication between people with and people without disabilities. These tables provide tips for communicating between blind and sighted people (Unit 1), between people with and people without disabilities (e.g., people who have cerebral palsy or who use wheelchairs) (Unit 3), between deaf and hearing people (Unit 5), and between people with and people without speech or language disorders (Unit 9).

Finally, a great deal of material on the website deals with cultural issues. For example, there are skill building exercises on the relationship of culture and gender, on cultural beliefs as influences, and on gift giving in different cultures. There are discussions of culture, gender, and friendship; culture, gender and love; and the role of culture in conflict. And among the self-tests are quizzes dealing with intercultural communication, cultural awareness, and individualistic orientation.

Coverage of Workplace Communication

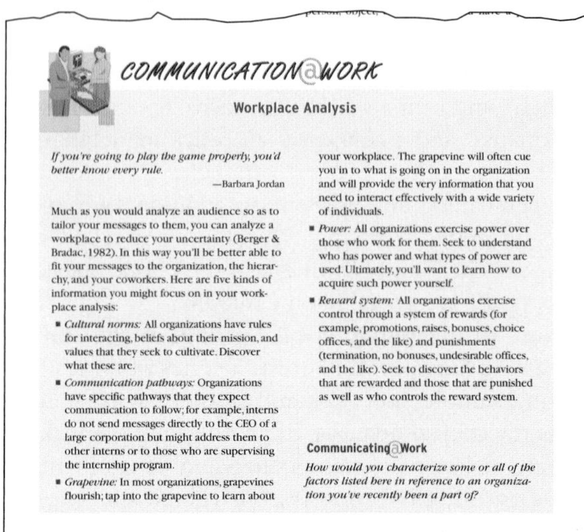

COMMUNICATION@WORK

Workplace Analysis

If you're going to play the game properly, you'd better know every rule.

—Barbara Jordan

Much as you would analyze an audience so as to tailor your messages to them, you can analyze a workplace to reduce your uncertainty (Berger & Bradac, 1982). In this way you'll be better able to fit your messages to the organization, the hierarchy, and your coworkers. Here are five kinds of information you might focus on in your workplace analysis:

- *Cultural norms:* All organizations have rules for interacting, beliefs about their mission, and values that they seek to cultivate. Discover what these are.
- *Communication pathways:* Organizations have specific pathways that they expect communication to follow; for example, interns do not send messages directly to the CEO of a large corporation but might address them to other interns or to those who are supervising the internship program.
- *Grapevine:* In most organizations, grapevines flourish; tap into the grapevine to learn about your workplace. The grapevine will often cue you in to what is going on in the organization and will provide the very information that you need to interact effectively with a wide variety of individuals.
- *Power:* All organizations exercise power over those who work for them. Seek to understand who has power and what types of power are used. Ultimately, you'll want to learn how to acquire such power yourself.
- *Reward system:* All organizations exercise control through a system of rewards (for example, promotions, raises, bonuses, choice offices, and the like) and punishments (termination, no bonuses, undesirable offices, and the like). Seek to discover the behaviors that are rewarded and those that are punished as well as who controls the reward system.

Communicating@Work

How would you characterize some or all of the factors listed here in reference to an organization you've recently been a part of?

New to the ninth edition and continued here is the feature emphasizing workplace communication—the application of the principles of human communication to the workplace. References to the workplace are integrated throughout the text. In addition, **Communication@Work** boxes (one per unit)—all revised for this tenth edition—address specific workplace issues and apply the general skills of communication to the workplace context. Among the topics discussed in these boxes are culture in the worplace, first impressions, power listening, grapevine communication, romance in the workplace, and sexual harassment. A new **Communication@Work** box, "Workplace Analysis," appears in Unit 14. Each of these boxes also contains a series of questions that encourage you to apply the content of the box to your own communicating at work. A complete list of these **Communication@Work** features appears in the Specialized Contents on page xi.

Coverage of Mass Media

This edition of *Human Communication* continues the ninth edition's inclusion of mass media in two ways. First, there are **Media Watch** boxes—all revised for this edition—in all units; these features integrate mass media with other areas of communication and sensitize you to the ever-present, ever-influential media. They also connect the concepts of interpersonal, small group, and public speaking with the concepts and theories of the media. These Media Watch boxes cover three major areas (discussions new to this edition appear in italics):

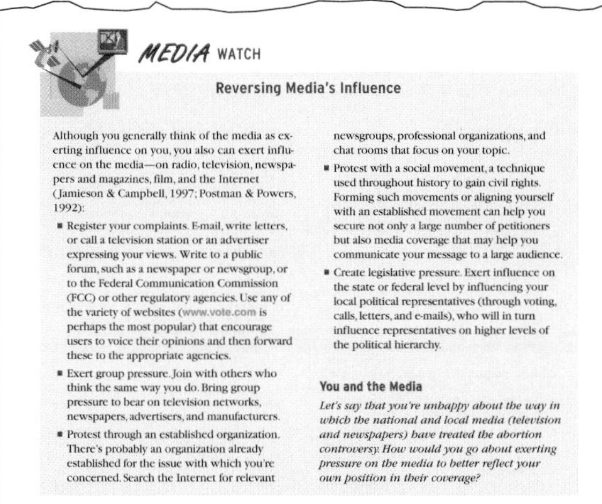

MEDIA WATCH

Reversing Media's Influence

Although you generally think of the media as exerting influence on you, you also can exert influence on the media—on radio, television, newspapers and magazines, film, and the Internet (Jamieson & Campbell, 1997; Postman & Powers, 1992):

- Register your complaints. E-mail, write letters, or call a television station or an advertiser expressing your views. Write to a public forum, such as a newspaper or newsgroup, or to the Federal Communication Commission (FCC) or other regulatory agencies. Use any of the variety of websites (www.vote.com is perhaps the most popular) that encourage users to voice their opinions and then forward these to the appropriate agencies.
- Exert group pressure. Join with others who think the same way you do. Bring group pressure to bear on television networks, newspapers, advertisers, and manufacturers.
- Protest through an established organization. There's probably an organization already established for the issue with which you're concerned. Search the Internet for relevant newsgroups, professional organizations, and chat rooms that focus on your topic.
- Protest with a social movement, a technique used throughout history to gain civil rights. Forming such movements or aligning yourself with an established movement can help you secure not only a large number of petitioners but also media coverage that may help you communicate your message to a large audience.
- Create legislative pressure. Exert influence on the state or federal level by influencing your local political representatives (through voting, calls, letters, and e-mails), who will in turn influence representatives on higher levels of the political hierarchy.

You and the Media

Let's say that you're unhappy about the way in which the national and local media (television and newspapers) have treated the abortion controversy. How would you go about exerting pressure on the media to better reflect your own position in their coverage?

- **Media theories:** *theories of media influence* (Unit 1), uses and gratifications theory (Unit 2); cultural imperialism (Unit 3), cultivation theory (Unit 4); spiral of silence (Unit 9); *the third-person effect* (Unit 11); agenda-setting theory (Unit 12); diffusion of innovations (Unit 14), and the knowledge gap hypothesis (Unit 17).
- **Central concepts:** gatekeeping (Unit 5), outing (Unit 6); hate speech (Unit 7), violence and the media (Unit 13), and *reversing the media's influence* (Unit 18).
- **Types and forms of media**: legible clothing (Unit 8); parasocial relationships (Unit 10); public relations (Unit 15), and advertising (Unit 16).

In addition, an entire unit on the mass media is available on CD-ROM and covers:

- The functional and dysfunctional media
- Helping, playing, relating, informing, influencing
- Becoming a critical consumer of media
- Learn how the media work, make use of a variety of media, question the credibility of the media, exercise critical thinking, talk back

Integration of Technology

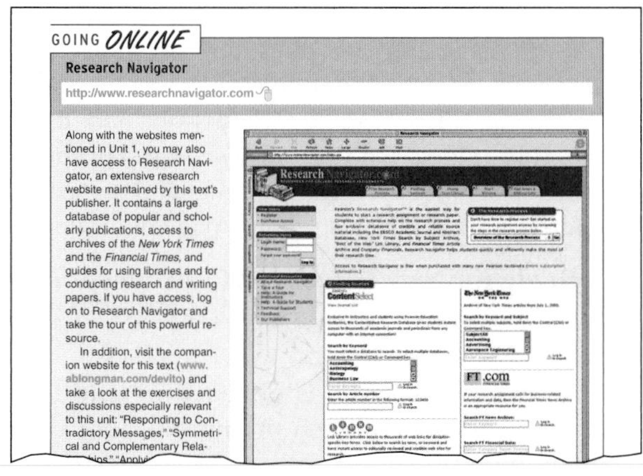

GOING ONLINE

Research Navigator

http://www.researchnavigator.com

Along with the websites mentioned in Unit 1, you may also have access to Research Navigator, an extensive research website maintained by this text's publisher. It contains a large database of popular and scholarly publications, access to archives of the *New York Times* and the *Financial Times*, and guides for using libraries and for conducting research and writing papers. If you have access, log on to Research Navigator and take the tour of this powerful resource.

In addition, visit the companion website for this text (www.ablongman.com/devito) and take a look at the exercises and discussions especially relevant to this unit: "Responding to Contradictory Messages," "Symmetrical and Complementary Rela-

The integration of technology continues to be a special goal of *Human Communication*. The text addresses this goal in a variety of ways. First, numerous sections throughout the text cover communication via computer. Examples: the ways in which online communication and face-to-face communication are similar and different; the role of technology in easing intercultural communication; the ease of misperception in Internet interactions; self-disclosure on the Internet; politeness (netiquette) on the Net; e-mail as a form of conversation; the advantages and disadvantages of online relationships; how online and face-to-face relationships differ; listservs and chat groups as small groups; leadership on the Internet; online conflicts; how to conduct research using e-mail, newsgroups, and the Web and how to evaluate Internet material; and computer-assisted presentations in public speaking.

In addition, special **Going Online** features appear throughout the text. These items will introduce you to websites that can help you learn about and master the skills of human communication. Some of these websites are academic—for example, the websites of the National Communication Association and the International Listening Association—and will help illustrate the breadth and depth of the study of human communication. Others, such as the publisher's websites for varied areas of communication and for research, are more clearly aimed at providing you with opportunities to develop and improve your communication knowledge and skills.

Finally, most of the ancillaries and supplements that are available with this text are electronic and/or focus on technology (see below).

Coverage of Ethical Issues

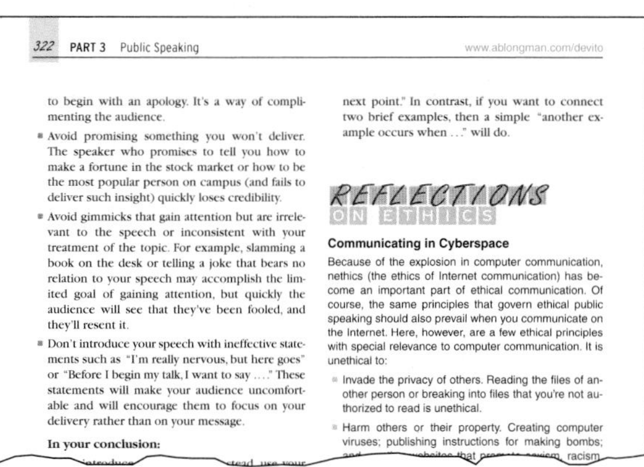

322 PART 3 Public Speaking www.ablongman.com/devito

to begin with an apology. It's a way of complimenting the audience.

- Avoid promising something you won't deliver. The speaker who promises to tell you how to make a fortune in the stock market or how to be the most popular person on campus (and fails to deliver such insight) quickly loses credibility.
- Avoid gimmicks that gain attention but are irrelevant to the speech or inconsistent with your treatment of the topic. For example, slamming a book on the desk or telling a joke that bears no relation to your speech may accomplish the limited goal of gaining attention, but quickly the audience will see that they've been fooled, and they'll resent it.
- Don't introduce your speech with ineffective statements such as "I'm really nervous, but here goes" or "Before I begin my talk, I want to say . . . ." These statements will make your audience uncomfortable and will encourage them to focus on your delivery rather than on your message.

In your conclusion:

next point." In contrast, if you want to connect two brief examples, then a simple "another example occurs when . . ." will do.

REFLECTIONS ON ETHICS

Communicating in Cyberspace

Because of the explosion in computer communication, nethics (the ethics of Internet communication) has become an important part of ethical communication. Of course, the same principles that govern ethical public speaking should also prevail when you communicate on the Internet. Here, however, are a few ethical principles with special relevance to computer communication. It is unethical to:

- Invade the privacy of others. Reading the files of another person or breaking into files that you're not authorized to read is unethical.
- Harm others or their property. Creating computer viruses; publishing instructions for making bombs;

The **Reflections on Ethics** boxes, introduced in the previous edition, are continued in this tenth edition; these sections appear at the end of each unit. These "reflections" discussions raise ethical principles and pose ethical dilemmas. The purpose of these features is to connect ethical issues with the various topics of human communication and to encourage you to think about your own ethical system. Among the ethical issues considered are censoring messages and interactions; making ethical choices; listening, speaking, and criticizing ethically; the ethics of lying, gossip, and emotional appeals; ethics on the job; and the leader's ethical responsibility. New to this edition are ethics boxes on the obligation you have to reveal yourself, the ethics of conflict, and the ethics of communicating in cyberspace. A complete list of these Reflections on Ethics boxes appears in the Specialized Contents on page xi.

Interactive Pedagogy

As in previous editions, *Human Communication* continues to emphasize new and useful pedagogical aids, especially those that are interactive, to help you better understand the theory and research and to enable you to effectively build and polish your communication skills.

- **Boxed interactives:** The Reflections on Ethics discussions, the Media Watch boxes, the Communication@Work boxes, and the Understanding Theory and Research boxes throughout the text contain interactive experiences designed to encourage you to interact with the concepts and to relate these insights to your own everyday communication.
- **Self-tests:** Interactive self-tests called "Test Yourself" appear throughout the text and are designed to help personalize the material. I have revised many of these tests for this edition (generally to make them more focused and somewhat shorter) and have added a new test on ethnocentrism in Unit 3. Each of these self-tests ends with a two-part discussion: *How did you do?* (which contains the scoring instructions and often general norms) and *What will you do?* (which asks about the appropriate course of action that might be taken, given the insight the test provided). A list of these self-tests appears in the Specialized Contents on pages x–xi.
- **Critical thinking questions:** These questions, appearing at the end of each unit, now focus more clearly on the central concepts and skills of the unit. You can use these questions to expand on, evaluate, and apply the concepts, theories, and research findings discussed in the text and to stimulate lively classroom discussion.
- **Key terms and glossaries:** A list of key terms at the end of each unit will help you review the major terms discussed in the unit. In addition, two glossaries appear at the back of the book: (1) a traditional glossary of communication concepts, which provides brief definitions of the significant concepts in the study of human communication, and (2) a glossary of communication skills.

132 PART 1 Foundations of Human Communication www.ablongman.com/devito

THINKING CRITICALLY ABOUT

Verbal Messages

1. When researchers asked men and women what they would like to change about the communication style of the opposite sex, most men said they wanted women to be more direct and most women said they wanted men to stop interrupting and offering advice (Noble 1994). What one change would you like to see in the communication style of the opposite sex? Of your own sex?
2. Visit any of the electronic dictionaries (use your favorite search engine and look for "dictionary") and browse through the terms and definitions. How is an online dictionary different from a print dictionary? What would a connotative dictionary look like?
3. One theory of politeness claims that you are most polite with friends and considerably less polite with both strangers and intimates (Wolfson, 1988; Holmes, 1995). Do you find this theory a generally accurate representation of your own level of politeness in different types of relationships?
4. What cultural identifiers do you prefer to use to describe yourself? Have these preferences changed over time? How can you let other people know the designations that you prefer and those that you don't? An interesting exercise—especially in a large and multicultural classroom—is for each stu-

wanted to reduce this type of listening, how would you do it?

6. A widely held assumption in anthropology, linguistics, and communication is that the importance of a concept to a culture can be measured by the number of words the language has for talking about the concept. So, for example, in English there are lots of words for money or for transportation or communication. With this principle in mind, consider the findings of Julia Stanley, for example, who researched terms indicating sexual promiscuity. Stanley found 220 English-language terms referring to a sexually promiscuous woman but only 22 terms for a sexually promiscuous man (Thorne, Kramarae, & Henley, 1983). What does this suggest about cultural attitudes and beliefs about promiscuity in men and women?
7. Consider this situation: An instructor at your school persists in calling the female students girls, refers to gay men and lesbians as queers, and refers to various racial groups with terms that most people would consider inappropriate. To the objection that these terms are offensive, the instructor claims the right to free speech and argues that to prevent instructors from using such terms would be a restriction on free speech, which would be a far greater wrong than being culturally or politically incorrect. How would you comment on this argument?

- **Unit openers:** The opening paragraph of each unit identifies the major topics covered in the unit and the learning goals (both theory and skills) you should be able to achieve.
- **Summary statements:** At the end of each unit, a summary reviews the essential concepts and principles covered in the unit.
- **Photo ViewPoints:** All photo captions also ask for your active involvement; for example, they may ask you to apply theoretical concepts or to develop specific communication skills.

Ancillaries/Supplementary Materials

Instructor Supplements

Print Supplements

- **Instructor's Manual/Test Bank** by Melissa Sherbert, Northampton Community College.

  This Instructor's Manual/Test Bank includes unit objectives, unit outlines, a wealth of thought-provoking discussion questions, and activities. The Test Bank contains hundreds of challenging multiple-choice, true-false, short answer, and essay questions along with an answer key. The questions closely follow the text units and are cross-referenced with corresponding page numbers.

- **A Guide for New Teachers of Introduction to Communication, 2/e,** by Susanna G. Porter, Kennesaw State University.

  This instructor's guide is designed to help new teachers effectively teach the introductory communication course.

- **A Guide for New Public Speaking Teachers: Building toward Success, 3/e,** by Calvin L. Troup, Duquesne University.

  This guide is designed to help new teachers prepare their introductory public speaking course effectively, covering topics such as preparation for the term, planning and structuring the course, evaluating speeches, using the textbook, and integrating technology into the classroom. The third edition includes a brief guide on teaching students for whom English is a second language.

- **The Blockbuster Approach: Teaching Interpersonal Communication with Video, 3/e,** by Thomas E. Jewell, Marymount College.

  This guide provides lists and descriptions of commercial videos that you can use in the classroom to illustrate interpersonal concepts and complex interpersonal relationships. Sample activities are included.

- **Great Ideas for Teaching Speech (GIFTS), 13/e,** by Raymond Zeuschner, California Polytechnic State University.

  This book provides descriptions of and guidelines for assignments successfully used by experienced public speaking instructors in their classrooms.

Electronic Supplements

- **VideoWorkshop for Introduction to Communication, Version 2.0,** by Kathryn Dindia, University of Wisconsin.

  VideoWorkshop is a way to bring video into your course for maximized learning. This total teaching and learning system includes quality video footage on an easy-to-use CD-ROM plus a Student Learning Guide and an Instructor's Teaching Guide—both with textbook-specific Correlation Grids. The result? A program that brings textbook concepts to life with ease and helps your students to understand, analyze, and apply the objectives of the course. Visit www.ablongman.com/videoworkshop for more details.

- **Computerized Test Bank**

  The printed Test Bank is also available electronically through our computerized testing system, TestGen EQ. The fully networkable test-generating software is now available on a multiplatform CD-ROM. The user-friendly interface enables you to view, edit, and add questions; transfer questions to tests; and print tests in a variety of fonts. Search and sort features allow you to locate questions quickly and arrange them in a preferred order.

- **Allyn & Bacon Digital Media Archive for Communication, Version 3.0**

  This CD-ROM contains electronic images of charts, graphs, maps, tables, and figures, along with media elements such as video, audio clips, and related weblinks. These media assets are fully customizable to use with our preformatted PowerPoint outlines or to import into your own lectures (Windows and Mac).

- **PowerPoint Presentation Package for *Human Communication*, 10/e** (available on the Web at http://suppscentral.ablongman.com/) by Dan Cavanaugh.

  This text-specific package consists of a collection of lecture outlines and graphic images keyed to every chapter in the text.

- **Allyn & Bacon PowerPoint Presentation for Introduction to Communication** (available on the Web at http://suppscentral.ablongman.com/).

  This PowerPoint presentation includes approximately 50 slides that cover a range of communication topics: public speaking, interpersonal communication, group communication, mass media, and interviewing.

- **Allyn & Bacon Student Speeches Video Library**

  Instructors have their choice of one video from a collection of seven videos that includes three 2-hour American Forensic Association videos of award-winning student speeches and four videos with a range of student speeches delivered in the classroom. Contact your Allyn & Bacon representative for ordering information. Some restrictions apply.

- **Allyn & Bacon Public Speaking Key Topics Video Library**

  This library contains three videos that address core topics covered in the classroom: Critiquing Student Speeches, Speaker Apprehension, and Addressing Your Audience. Contact your Allyn & Bacon representative for ordering information. Some restrictions apply.

- **Allyn & Bacon Public Speaking Video**

  This video includes excerpts of classic and contemporary public speeches and student speeches to illustrate the public speaking process. One speech is delivered two times under different circumstances by the same person to illustrate the difference between effective and ineffective delivery based on appearance, nonverbal cues, and verbal style. Contact your Allyn & Bacon representative for ordering information. Some restrictions apply.

- **Allyn & Bacon Student Speeches Video III**

  This video introduces a variety of student speakers who speak about a variety of topics designed to illustrate the principles of the public speaking process. The video contains informative, persuasive, after-dinner, and special topic speeches. A User's Guide for the video provides instructors with discussion questions, speech critiques, outlines, and complete manuscripts for all of the speeches on the video. Contact your Allyn & Bacon representative for ordering information. Some restrictions apply.

- **Allyn & Bacon Interpersonal Communication Videos**

  Allyn & Bacon offers three Interpersonal Videos ranging from 30 to 50 minutes that contain scenarios illustrating key concepts in interpersonal communication. Accompanying user guides feature transcripts, teaching activities, and class discussion questions for the episodes. Contact your Allyn & Bacon representative for ordering information. Some restrictions apply.

- **Allyn & Bacon Communication Video Library**

  This library is a collection of communication videos produced by Films for the Humanities and Sciences. Topics include, but are not limited to: Business Presentations, Great American Speeches, and Conflict Resolution. Contact your local Allyn & Bacon representative for ordering information. Some restrictions apply.

- **CourseCompass for Introduction to Communication**

  CourseCompass, powered by Blackboard and hosted nationally, is the most flexible online course management system on the market today. By using this powerful suite of online tools in conjunction with Allyn & Bacon's preloaded textbook and testing content, you can create an online presence for your course in under 30 minutes. The Introduction to Communication course features preloaded content such as quiz questions, video clips, instructor's manuals, PowerPoint presentations, still images, course preparation, VideoWorkshop for Introduction to Communication, weblinks, and much more! Log on at www.coursecompass.com and find out how you can get the most out of this dynamic teaching course. The content is also compatible with Blackboard and WebCT.

- **Allyn & Bacon Classic and Contemporary Speeches DVD**

  This DVD presents a collection of over 120 minutes of video footage in an easy-to-use DVD format. Each speech is accompanied by a biographical and historical summary that helps students to understand the context and motivation behind each speech. Contact your Allyn & Bacon representative for additional details and ordering information.

Student Supplements

Print Supplements

- ***Interviewing and Human Communication,*** by Joseph A. DeVito.

  This booklet introduces students to the process of interviewing, including the job résumé and the letters that are an essential part of the entire interview process. It also provides worksheets for preparing for both the information-gathering interview and the employment interview. Listening, ethical, and power issues as they relate to interviewing are included in boxes, as are skill development exercises to help students work actively with the concepts discussed here. Skills topics include practicing interviewing skills, displaying communication confidence in the employment interview, and responding to unlawful questions. Scenarios asking students to apply their interview skills in different situations, quotations to highlight different perspectives, ideas for exploring online materials, and invitations to use our online Research Navigator tool to learn more about interviewing are included in the margins. In addition, to make it easier for students to use the interviewing preparation guides in the booklet, these guides are also available on the website at www.ablongman.com/devito and may be downloaded for students to complete and submit to their instructor, or to keep in their personal records. This product is available FREE when packaged with this text. For a complete table of contents, go to the website at www.ablongman.com/devito. Contact your Allyn & Bacon representative for ordering information. Some restrictions apply.

- **Research Navigator Guide for Speech Communication,** by Terrence Doyle, Northern Virginia Community College, and Linda R. Barr, University of the Virgin Islands.

  This resource guide is designed to teach students how to conduct high-quality online research and document it properly. The guide provides access to Research Navigator (www.researchnavigator.com), which contains exclusive databases of credible and reliable source material, including EBSCO's ContentSelect Academic Journal Database and the New York Times Search by Subject Archive. This product is available FREE when packaged with this text. Contact your Allyn & Bacon sales representative for ordering information. Some restrictions apply.

- **Preparing Visual Aids for Presentations, 4/e,** by Dan Cavanaugh.

  This booklet provides ideas to improve presentations, including suggestions for planning a presentation, guidelines for designing visual aids, storyboarding, and a PowerPoint presentation walk-through.

- **Public Speaking in the Multicultural Environment, 2/e,** by Devorah A. Lieberman, Portland State University.

  This booklet helps students learn to analyze cultural diversity within their audiences and adapt their presentations accordingly. Contact your Allyn & Bacon representative for ordering information. Some restrictions apply.

- **Speech Preparation Workbook** by Jennifer Dreyer and Gregory H. Patton, San Diego State University.

  This workbook takes students through the various stages of speech creation—from audience analysis to writing the speech—and provides supplementary assignments and tear-out forms. Contact your Allyn & Bacon representative for ordering information. Some restrictions apply.

- **Outlining Workbook** by Reeze L. Hanson and Sharon Condon, Haskell Indian Nations University.

  This workbook includes activities, exercises, and answers to help students develop and master the critical skill of outlining. Contact your Allyn & Bacon representative for ordering information. Some restrictions apply.

- **Brainstorms** by Joseph A. DeVito.

  This is a guide to thinking more creatively about communication, or anything else. Students will find 19 practical, easy-to-use creative thinking techniques along with insights into the creative thinking process. Contact your Allyn & Bacon representative for ordering information. Some restrictions apply.

Electronic Supplements

- **DeVito, *Human Communication*, 10/e, Student CD-ROM with Bonus Units**

  This CD-ROM contains four additional units that are not available anywhere else: The Mass Media, Emotional Communication, Criticism in the Public Speaking Classroom, and Developing Special Occasion Speeches. Available on request in a special package with a **new textbook.** Contact your Allyn & Bacon representative for ordering information. Some restrictions apply.

- **Interactive Speechwriter Software, Version 1.1 (Windows and Mac)** by Martin R. Cox.

  This interactive software package for student purchase provides supplemental material, writing templates (for the informative, persuasive, and motivated sequence speeches, as well as for outlines), sample student speeches (text only), and more! This program enhances students' understanding of key concepts discussed in the text and is available for Windows and Mac. Contact your Allyn & Bacon representative for ordering information. Some restrictions apply.

- **Speech Writer's Workshop CD-ROM 2.0**

  This interactive software will assist students with speech preparation and will enable them to write better speeches. The software includes four separate features: (1) a speech handbook with tips for researching and preparing speeches, plus information about grammar, usage, and syntax; (2) a speech workshop that guides students through the speech-writing process and includes a series of questions at each stage; (3) a topics dictionary containing hundreds of speech ideas—all divided into subcategories to help students with outlining and organization; and (4) a citation database that formats bibliographic entries in MLA and APA style. Contact your Allyn & Bacon representative for ordering information. Some restrictions apply.

- **Companion Website Plus with Online Practice Tests** (http://www.ablongman.com/devito) by Joseph A. DeVito and Elizabeth A. Lindsey, New Mexico State University.

  This site includes unit objectives, self-tests, skill building exercises, and extensions and elaborations on the text. The website also includes an online study guide with practice tests and weblinks.

- **VideoWorkshop for Introduction to Communication, Version 2.0,** by Kathryn Dindia, University of Wisconsin.

  VideoWorkshop includes quality video footage on an easy-to-use CD-ROM plus a Student Learning Guide with textbook-specific Correlation Grids. The result? A program that brings textbook concepts to life with ease and helps students to understand, analyze, and apply the objectives of the course. Visit www.ablongman.com/videoworkshop for more details.

- **Allyn & Bacon Communication Studies Website,** by Terrence Doyle, Northern Virginia Community College, and Tim Borchers, Minnesota State University at Moorhead, and **Allyn & Bacon Public Speaking Website,** by Nan Peck, Northern Virginia Community College.

  These websites contain modules built with enrichment materials, weblinks, and interactive activities designed to enhance students' understanding of key concepts. The Communication Studies Website includes interpersonal, small group communication, and public speaking topics. Access this site at www.ablongman.com/commstudies. The Public Speaking Website, updated for 2004, helps students build, organize, and research speeches while learning about the process of public speaking. Access this website at www.ablongman.com/pubspeak.

- **Communication Tutor Center (access code required),** www.aw.com/tutorcenter.

  The Tutor Center provides students with free, one-on-one interactive tutoring from qualified public speaking instructors on all material in the text. The Tutor Center offers students help with understanding major communication principles as well as methods for studying. In addition, students have the option of submitting self-taped speeches for review and critique by Tutor Center instructors to help prepare for and improve their speech assignments. Tutoring assistance is offered by phone, fax, Internet, and e-mail during Tutor Center hours. For more details and ordering information, contact your Allyn & Bacon sales representative.

- **Allyn & Bacon Classic and Contemporary Speeches DVD**

  This DVD presents a collection of over 120 minutes of video footage in an easy-to-use DVD format. Each speech is accompanied by a biographical and historical summary that helps students to understand the context and motivation behind each speech. Contact your local Allyn & Bacon sales representative for additional details and ordering information.

Acknowledgments

There are three groups of people I want to thank.

First, my thanks to my colleagues for taking time from their busy schedules and responding to the Ask the Researcher questions. Thank you for making this undertaking enjoyable for me—your e-mails were always interesting and stimulating—and for helping to illustrate the practical skills that can be derived from theory and research. I thank you for your contributions to communication and for your willingness to contribute to this feature. Thank you (in order of appearance):

Mark Hickson III
Pam Shockley-Zalabak
Melbourne S. Cummings
Ann Bainbridge Frymier
Judi Brownell
Sandra Metts
Richard A. Fiordo
Don W. Stacks
Gust A. Yep
Walid A. Afifi
Carole A. Barbato
Katherine Hawkins
Charles J. Wigley III
Virginia P. Richmond
Bruce E. Gronbeck
Joseph Chesebro
Timothy P. Mottet
Jon F. Nussbaum

Thank you to the following reviewers who have shared insights and classroom experiences with me and have commented on the previous editions. Your suggestions have helped me improve this text significantly. Thank you: Cynthia Graham, University of Wisconsin, Superior; Rachel C. Prioleau, University of South Carolina, Spartanburg; Charles V. Roberts, East Tennessee State University; Jill Tyler, University of South Dakota; and Alan Zaremba, Northeastern University.

Thank you to Allyn & Bacon and all the people who worked to turn my manuscript into the great-looking book you now hold. Thank you:

Brian Wheel, editor; Heather Hawkins, editorial assistant; Kristen Desmond LeFevre, developmental editor; Mandee Eckersley, marketing manager; Julie Tesser, photo researcher; Jay Howland, copy editor; and Susan McIntyre of Nesbitt Graphics, project manager. All contributed significantly to the finished book.

Joseph A. DeVito
jadevito@earthlink.net

PART 1 Foundations of Human Communication

UNIT

Preliminaries to Human Communication

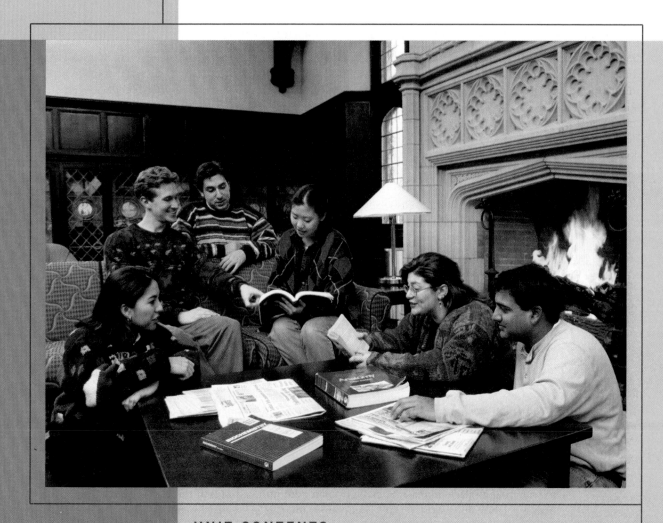

UNIT CONTENTS

Of all the knowledge and skills you have, those concerning communication will prove the most important and the most useful. They will always influence and play a crucial part in how effectively you live your personal and professional lives. And so it's vital to your success to learn how communication works and how you can master its most essential skills. In this first unit you'll learn:

- what communication is, the purposes it serves, And the forms it takes
- how understanding the way communication works can help you achieve a variety of personal and professional purposes

Your communication knowledge and skills are among your most important assets. They will help you achieve a wide variety of personal, professional, and social goals. In many situations, communication skills will make the difference between success and failure.

You use your communication knowledge and skills in just about everything you do—asking for directions, discussing an issue in a chat room, interviewing for a job, listening to others, or surfing the Net. Communication abilities also play a significant part (perhaps the most significant part) in all your interactions—from making friends and lifelong partners, to resolving inevitable conflicts, to networking for professional advantage, to working on a team solving a problem, to informing and persuading large groups.

In short, your communication knowledge and skills will prove of value in all your interactions with other people, whether you're speaking or listening.

Elements of Human Communication

Communication occurs when one person (or more) sends and receives messages that are distorted by noise, occur within a context, have some effect, and provide some opportunity for feedback. This introductory unit explains the various parts of this definition and identifies the purposes and types of human communication. Throughout this explanation—and, in fact, throughout this book—the text makes reference to both face-to-face and electronic communication. No matter how sophisticated, electronic communication is still very similar to ordinary face-to-

ASK THE RESEARCHER

The Value of a Human Communication Course

- *I'm taking this course in human communication. I am not certain what practical uses this course will have for me. Why should I be taking this course?*

You interact with others every day in a variety of contexts. In most contexts, you have a purpose in mind: To learn or to persuade. In the job interview, you need to know what factors the employer is seeking in nonverbal behavior, language use, attitude, level of knowledge, amount of enthusiasm, and personal motivation. In learning situations, you need to know when to ask a question as well as how to frame your question. As a manager of other people, you need to know what kinds of messages will motivate your subordinates to perform at their highest levels. Human communication is significant for every aspect of your life from learning at school to obtaining positions in a corporation to soliciting a salary increase. Socially, human communication is at the core of what makes relationships work or fail. This course and this book may be among the most important instruments in developing you as a more sensitive and effective person.

For further information: Hickson, M., III, Stacks, D. W., & Padgett-Greely, M. (1998). *Organizational communication in the personal context: From interview to retirement.* Boston: Allyn & Bacon.

Mark Hickson, III (Ph.D., Southern Illinois University) is professor of communication studies at the University of Alabama at Birmingham. He teaches courses in communication theory, nonverbal communication, and organizational communication.

face interactions. For example, electronic communication allows for the same types of communication as does face-to-face interaction, whether interpersonal, small group, or public. In Internet communication you put your thoughts into words that you type on your keyboard and send via modem or cable; similarly, in speech you put your thoughts into spoken words and send your sounds through the air.

Two-person, or interpersonal, communication can occur face-to-face or on the phone or through e-mail or snail mail. Similarly, you engage in interpersonal communication in chat groups when you "whisper" or single out just one person to receive your message instead of the entire group. In chat groups you can talk with a small group of others in ways similar to the way you'd talk around a table in the cafeteria or in a business organization or in a telephone or video conference. In newsgroups posting a message for members to read is in many ways similar to the way you express your thoughts in delivering a public speech to an audience. Of course, there are also differences between face-to-face and electronic communications, which we'll discuss as we consider the various forms of human communication throughout the text.

Before reading about the elements of human communication, think about your beliefs about communication by taking the self-test below.

TEST YOURSELF

What Do You Believe about Communication?

Respond to each of the following statements with T (true) if you believe the statement is usually true and F (false) if you believe the statement is usually false.

____ **1.** Good communicators are born, not made.

____ **2.** The more a couple communicates, the better their relationship will be.

____ **3.** When two people are in a close relationship for a long period of time, one person should not have to communicate his or her needs and wants; the other person should know what these are.

____ **4.** Complete openness should be the goal of any meaningful interpersonal relationship.

____ **5.** Interpersonal or group conflict is a reliable sign that the relationship or group is in trouble.

____ **6.** Like good communicators, leaders are born, not made.

____ **7.** Fear of speaking in public is detrimental and must be eliminated.

HOW DID YOU DO? As you may have figured out, all seven statements are generally false. As you read this text, you'll discover not only why these beliefs are false but also the trouble you can get into when you assume they're true. Briefly, here are some of the reasons why each of the statements is generally false:

1. Effective communication is a learned skill; although some people are born brighter or more extroverted, all can improve their abilities and become more effective communicators.
2. If you practice bad communication habits, you're more likely to grow less effective than to become more effective; consequently, it's important to learn and follow the principles of effectiveness.
3. This assumption is at the heart of many interpersonal difficulties—people aren't mind readers, and to assume that they are merely sets up barriers to open and honest communication (Unit 10).
4. Although you may feel ethically obligated to be totally honest, this is generally not an effective strategy. In fact, "complete" anything is probably a bad idea.
5. Interpersonal conflict does not have to involve a winner and a loser; both people can win, as demonstrated in Unit 13.
6. Leadership, like communication and listening, is a learned skill that you'll develop as you learn the principles of human communication in general and of group leadership in particular (Unit 12).
7. Most speakers are nervous; managing, not eliminating, the fear will enable you to become effective regardless of your current level of fear (Unit 14).

WHAT WILL YOU DO? Consider how these beliefs about communication influence the way you communicate. Then, as you read this book and participate in class discussions and activities, reexamine your beliefs about communication and consider how new beliefs would influence the way you communicate. The theories and research discussed in this text will help you reconsider your own beliefs about communication, and the skill building activities will help you practice new ways of communicating. Three excellent websites containing a variety of self-tests on emotional intelligence, personality, knowledge, relationships, careers, and more are http://www.allthetests.com, www.queendom.com/tests and http://www.psychologytoday.com.

Figure 1.1 on page 4 illustrates the elements present in all communication acts, whether intrapersonal, interpersonal, small group, public speaking, or mass communication—or whether face-to-face, by telephone, or over the Internet: (1) context,

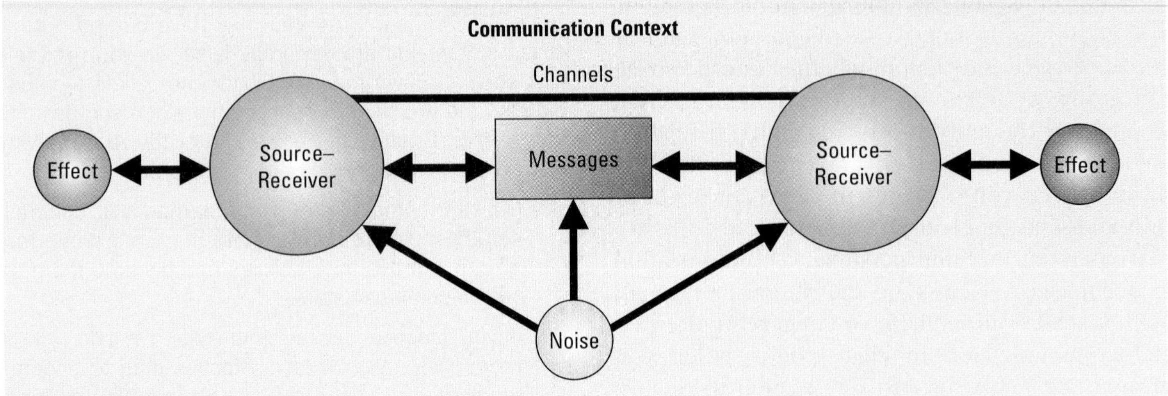

Figure 1.1

The Elements of Human Communication

This is a simplified view of the elements of human communication and their relationship to one another. Messages (including feedforward and feedback) are sent simultaneously through a variety of channels from one source–receiver to another. The communication process takes place in a context (physical, cultural, social–psychological, and temporal) and is subjected to interference by noise (physical, psychological, and semantic). The interaction of messages with each source–receiver leads to some effect.

(2) sources-receivers, (3) messages, (4) channels, (5) noise, (6) effects, and (7) ethics.

Communication Context

All communication takes place in a context that has at least four dimensions: (1) physical, (2) social-psychological, (3) temporal, and (4) cultural. The *physical context* is the tangible or concrete environment in which communication takes place—the room or hallway or park. This *physical context* exerts some influence on the content of your messages (what you say) as well as on the form (how you say it).

The *social-psychological context* includes, for example, the status relationships among the participants, the roles and the games that people play, and the cultural rules of the society in which people are communicating. It also includes the friendliness or unfriendliness, formality or informality, and seriousness or humorousness of the situation. Communication that would be permitted at a graduation party might not be considered appropriate at a funeral.

The *temporal (or time) context* includes the time of day as well as the time in history in which the communication takes place. For many people, the morning is not a time for communication. For others, the morning is ideal. Historical context is no less important—because the appropriateness and impact of messages depend, in part, on the time in which they're uttered. Consider, for example, how messages on racial, sexual, or religious attitudes and values would be differently framed and responded to in different times in history.

Still another aspect of time is how a message fits into the sequence of communication events. For example, consider the varied meanings a "simple" compliment paid to a friend would have depending on whether you said it immediately after your friend paid you a compliment, immediately before you asked your friend for a favor, or during an argument.

The *cultural context* has to do with your (and others') *culture:* the beliefs, values, and ways of behaving that are shared by a group of people and passed down from one generation to the next. Cultural factors affect every interaction and influence what you say and how you say it. As you'll see throughout this book, the communication strategies and principles that work with members of one culture may not work with members of other cultures. And this is why intercultural communication is so difficult and why culture is so crucial to communication. In fact, research shows that you lose more information in an intercultural situation (approximately 50 percent) than in an intracultural situation (approximately 25 percent) (Li, 1999).

These dimensions of context interact with one another. For example, arriving late for an appointment (temporal context) might violate a cultural rule, which might lead to changes in the social-psychological context, perhaps creating tension and unfriendliness, which in turn might lead to changes in the physical context—for example, choosing a less intimate restaurant for your lunch meeting.

Sources-Receivers

The compound term *sources-receivers* emphasizes that each person involved in communication is both a **source** (or speaker) and a **receiver** (or listener). You send messages when you speak, write, gesture, or smile. You receive messages in listening, reading, smelling, and so on. As you send messages, however, you're also receiving messages. You're receiving your own messages (you hear yourself, you feel your own movements, you see many of your own gestures), and you're receiving the messages of the other person—visually, aurally, or even through touch or smell. As you assign meaning to these verbal and nonverbal signals, you're performing receiving functions.

Source-Receiver Encoding-Decoding

The act of producing messages—for example, speaking or writing—is called **encoding.** By putting your ideas into sound waves or into a computer program you're putting these ideas into a **code,** hence encoding. The act of receiving messages—for example, listening or reading—is called **decoding.** By translating sound waves or words on a screen into ideas you take them out of code, hence decoding. Thus, speakers or writers are called **encoders,** and listeners or readers, **decoders.**

As with sources-receivers, the compound term *encoding-decoding* emphasizes that you perform these functions simultaneously, at least in face-to-face communication. As you speak (encoding), you're also deciphering the responses of the listener (decoding). In computer communication this simultaneous exchange of messages occurs only sometimes. In e-mail (as well as snail mail) and newsgroup communication, for example, the sending and receiving may be separated by several days or much longer. In chat groups and instant messaging, on the other hand, communication takes place in real time; the sending and receiving take place (almost) simultaneously.

UNDERSTANDING *THEORY* AND *RESEARCH*

Communication Theories

A **theory** is a generalization that explains how something works—for example, gravity, blood clotting, interpersonal attraction, or communication. In academic writing the term "theory" is usually reserved for a well-established system of knowledge about how things work or how things are related. It is still fundamentally a generalization, but it's often supported by research findings and other well-accepted theories.

The theories you'll encounter in this book try to explain how communication works—for example, how you accommodate your speaking style to your listeners, how communication works when relationships deteriorate, how friends self-disclose, how problem-solving groups communicate, how speakers influence audiences, and how the media affect people. As you can see from even these few examples, theories provide general principles that help you understand an enormous number of specific events.

One great value of communication theories is that they help you predict future events. Because theories summarize what's been found, they can offer reasonable predictions for events that you've never encountered. For example, theories of persuasion will help you predict what kinds of emotional appeals will be most effective in persuading a specific audience. Or theories of conflict resolution will enable you to predict what strategies would be effective or ineffective in resolving differences.

Working with Theories and Research

- *Develop your own generalization or theory about what verbal and nonverbal cues would lead you to assume someone was lying. (Don't be deceived by the seeming simplicity of this task; it will actually prove quite difficult.) After you propose your theory, take a look at the Understanding Theory and Research box "Cues to Lying," on page 86.*

Source-Receiver Competence

The term **communication competence** refers to your knowledge of the social aspects of communication (Rubin, 1982, 1985; Spitzberg & Cupach, 1989). Communication competence includes knowledge of such factors as the role of context in influencing the content and form of communication messages—for example, the knowledge that in certain contexts and with certain listeners one topic is appropriate and another is not. Knowledge about the rules of nonverbal behavior—for example, the appropriateness of touching, vocal volume, and physical closeness—is also part of communication competence. The term *communication competence* is also taken to include your ability to apply this knowledge in communicating. So when you read about communication competence, realize that it includes both an understanding of how communication works and the ability to use this understanding in communicating effectively. Keep in mind, however, that communication competence is culture specific; the way communication works and the elements that make it effective differ from one culture to another.

Messages

Communication **messages** take many forms. You send and receive messages through any one or any combination of sensory organs. Although you may customarily think of messages as being verbal (oral or written), you also communicate nonverbally. For example, the clothes you wear and the way you

COMMUNICATION@WORK

Communication in the Workplace

Organizations are almost entirely determined by communication techniques.

—Chester Barnard

Workplace communication consists of the many kinds of messages sent and received within an organization, including messages involved in giving directions; counseling workers; interviewing new employees; evaluating personnel; motivating workers; analyzing problems; resolving conflicts; and establishing, participating, and leading work groups. These communications rely on the skills of interpersonal, small group, and public communication discussed throughout this text—skills that are considered essential in just about every area of work (Morreale, Osborn, & Pearson, 2000).

Workplace communication may be either formal or informal. Formal communications are those that are sanctioned by the organization itself and deal with the workings of the organization, with productivity, and with the various jobs done throughout the organization: memos, policy statements, press releases, and employee newsletters. Other types of formal organizational communication take place between one organization and another or between the organization and the public—for example, in advertising and in public relations.

Informal communications, on the other hand, follow no formal structure and may deal with the activities of the organization—as would be the case in grapevine communication (see the Communication@Work box, "Grapevine Communication," in Unit 9)—or with more personal activities such as celebrating birthdays, discussing family problems, planning joint vacations, and communicating in the process of developing friendship and romantic relationships.

Because your communication effectiveness in the workplace has significant consequences—from getting a job, to working comfortably and effectively with colleagues, to rising in the organization—workplace communication is given special prominence in this text. The skills that form the bases for effectiveness in all communication are covered throughout the text, but special Communication@Work boxes in each unit further emphasize the connection between the theories and skills discussed in the text and the world of work.

Communicating@Work

Trace a day in the life of someone in the profession you hope to be working in, say five years from now. What types of communication will you engage in during, say, one week of work?

walk, shake hands, cock your head, comb your hair, sit, and smile all communicate messages. Everything about you communicates.

In face-to-face communication the actual message signals (the movements in the air) are evanescent; they fade almost as they're uttered. Some written messages, especially computer-mediated messages such as those sent via e-mail, are unerasable. E-mails that are sent among employees in a large corporation, for example, are often stored on disk or tape. Currently, much litigation is using as evidence racist or sexist e-mails that senders thought were erased, but weren't.

Two special types of messages need to be explained more fully; these are feedback (the messages you send that are reactions to other messages) and feedforward (the messages you send as preface to your "main" messages). Both feedback and feedforward are **metamessages**—messages that communicate about other messages. Such communication about communication, or **metacommunication,** may be verbal ("I agree with you" or "Wait until you hear this one") or nonverbal (a smile or a prolonged pause). Or, as is most often the case, it's some combination of verbal and nonverbal signals.

Feedback Messages

Throughout the listening process, a listener gives a speaker **feedback**—messages sent back to the speaker reacting to what is said. Feedback tells the speaker what effect he or she is having on the listener(s). This can take many forms: A frown or a smile, a yea or a nay, a pat on the back or a punch in the mouth are all types of feedback. Sometimes feedback is easy to identify, but sometimes it isn't (Skinner, 2002). Part of the art of effective communication is the ability to discern feedback and to adjust messages on the basis of that feedback. For example, on the basis of feedback, a speaker may adjust messages by strengthening, deemphasizing, or changing the content or form of the messages. These adjustments then serve as feedback to the receiver—who, in response, readjusts his or her feedback messages. The process is a circular one, with one person's feedback serving as the stimulus for the other person's feedback, just as any message serves as the stimulus for another person's message.

Another type of feedback is the feedback you get from listening to yourself: You hear what you say, you feel the way you move, you see what you write. On the basis of this self-feedback you adjust your messages; for example, you may correct a mispronunciation, shorten your story, or increase your volume.

You can view feedback in terms of five important dimensions: positive-negative, person-focused-message-focused, immediate-delayed, low-monitored-high-monitored, and supportive-critical.

Positive-Negative. **Positive feedback** (smiles, applause, and head nods signifying approval) tells the speaker that the message is being well received and that he or she should continue speaking in the same general mode. **Negative feedback** (frowns, boos, puzzled looks, gestures signifying disapproval) tells the speaker that something is wrong and that some adjustment needs to be made.

Person-Focused-Message-Focused. Feedback may center on the person ("You're sweet," "You've got a great smile") or on the message ("Can you repeat

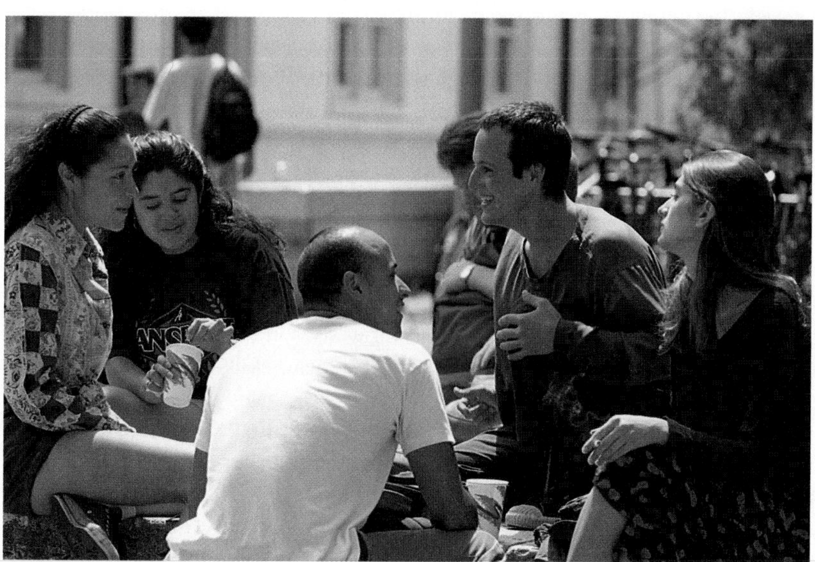

VIEWPOINT

The "feedback theory of relationships" holds that in satisfying friendships or romantic relationships, feedback tends to be positive, person focused, immediate, low monitoring, and supportive—whereas in unsatisfying relationships, feedback is often negative, self-focused, nonimmediate, high monitoring, and critical. How effective do you find this theory? That is, how well does the theory explain relationships with which you're familiar?

BUILDING COMMUNICATION SKILLS

Giving Feedback

For any one or two of the following situations, *(a)* indicate the kind of feedback that you would consider appropriate (positive or negative? person focused or message focused? immediate or delayed? low monitoring or high monitoring? supportive or critical?), and *(b)* write one or two sentences in which you express feedback that has the qualities you identified in *(a)*.

1. A neighbor—whom you like but don't have romantic feelings for—asks you for a date.
2. A colleague persists in talking explicitly about sex despite your frequent objections.
3. A homeless person smiles at you on the street and asks for some change.

that phone number?" "Your argument is a good one").

Immediate-Delayed. In interpersonal situations feedback is most often conveyed immediately after the message is received. In other communication situations, however, the feedback may be delayed; for example, feedback from an interview may come weeks after the interview took place. In media situations some feedback comes immediately—for example, through Nielsen ratings; other feedback comes much later, through consumers' viewing and buying patterns.

Low-Monitored-High-Monitored. Feedback varies from the spontaneous and totally honest reaction (low-monitored feedback) to the carefully constructed response designed to serve a specific purpose (high-monitored feedback). In most interpersonal situations you probably give feedback spontaneously; you allow your responses to show without any monitoring. At other times, however, you may be more guarded, as when your boss asks you how you like your job or when your grandmother asks what you think of her holiday fruitcake.

Supportive-Critical. Supportive feedback confirms the worth of the person and what that person says; it occurs when, for example, you console another or when you encourage the other to talk; it often involves **affirmation** of the person's self-definition. Critical feedback, on the other hand, is evaluative. When you give critical feedback you judge another's performance—as in, for example, evaluating a speech or coaching someone learning a new skill.

Each feedback opportunity, then, presents you with choices along at least these five dimensions. To use feedback effectively you need to make educated choices along these dimensions. Realize that these categories are not exclusive. Feedback does not have to be either critical or supportive; it can be both. Thus, in teaching someone how to become a more effective interviewer, you might critically evaluate a specific interview but you might also express support for the effort. Similarly, you might respond to a friend's question immediately and then after a day or two elaborate on your response.

Feedforward Messages

Feedforward is information you provide before sending your primary messages; it reveals something about the messages to come (Richards, 1951). Feedforward includes such diverse examples as the preface or the table of contents in a book, the opening paragraph of a chapter, movie previews, magazine covers, and introductions in public speeches. Feedforward has four major functions: (1) to open the channels of communication, (2) to preview the message, (3) to altercast, and (4) to disclaim.

To Open the Channels of Communication. Often we preface our messages with comments whose only function is to open the channels of communication (Malinowski, 1923; Lu, 1998). The infamous "opening line" ("Do you come here often?" or "Haven't we met before?") is a clear example of this type of feedforward. In fact, when such feedforward messages don't precede an initial interaction, you sense that something is wrong and may conclude that the speaker lacks the basic skills of communication.

To Preview Future Messages. Feedforward messages frequently preview other messages. Feedforward may, for example, preview the content ("I have news for you"), the importance ("Listen to this be-

BUILDING COMMUNICATION SKILLS

Giving Feedforward

In each of the following situations, you may want to preface your main message with feedforward. For any one or two of the following situations, *(a)* identify the specific purpose you hope to achieve with your feedforward, and *(b)* write a brief feedforward message that helps you achieve the purpose you identified in *(a)*.

1. You see an attractive person in one of your classes and would like to get to know the person a bit more, with the possible objective of a date.
2. You just saw the posted grades for the midterm; your close friend failed, but you did extremely well. In the cafeteria you meet your friend, who asks, "How'd I do on the midterm?"
3. You have a reputation for proposing outlandish ideas in the midst of otherwise formal and boring discussions. This time, however, you want to offer a proposal that you fear will seem to be one of your standard outlandish notions but is actually an idea that you think could work. You want to assure your group that this idea is worthy of their serious attention.

fore you make a move"), the form or style ("I'll be brief"), or the positive or negative quality of subsequent messages ("You're not going to like this, but here's what I heard").

To Altercast. The type of feedforward known as altercasting asks the receiver to approach your message in a particular role or even as someone else (McLaughlin, 1984; Weinstein & Deutschberger, 1963; Johnson, 1993; Pratkanis, 2000). For example, you might ask a friend, "As a single mother, what do you think of the new child care proposals?" This question casts your friend into the role of single mother (rather than that of teacher, Democrat, or Baptist, for example). It asks your friend to assume a particular perspective.

To Disclaim. A *disclaimer* is a statement that aims to ensure that your message will not reflect negatively on you. Disclaimers entice the listener to hear your message as you wish it to be heard rather than through some assumption that might reflect negatively on you (Hewitt & Stokes, 1975). For example, to ensure that people listen to you fairly, you might disclaim any thought that you're biased against one gender: "I'm no sexist, but . . . ." The disclaimer is discussed in greater detail in Unit 9.

Channels

The communication **channel** is the medium through which the message passes. Communication rarely takes place over only one channel; you may use two, three, or four different channels simultaneously. For example, in face-to-face interactions you speak and listen (vocal channel), but you also gesture and receive signals visually (visual channel). In chat groups you type and read words and use various symbols and abbreviations to communicate the emotional tone of the message. If your computer system is especially sophisticated, you may communicate via the Internet through audio and visual means as well. In addition, in face-to-face communication you emit and detect odors (olfactory channel). Often you touch another person, and this too communicates (tactile channel).

At times, one or more channels may be damaged. For example, in blind individuals the visual channel is impaired, and so adjustments have to be made. Table 1.1 on page 10 gives you an idea of how such adjustments between blind and sighted persons can make communication more effective.

Noise

Noise is any interference or **barrier to communication**—anything that distorts the message, anything that prevents the receiver from receiving the message fully. At one extreme, noise may prevent a message from getting from source to receiver at all. A roaring noise or line static can block entire phone messages. At the other extreme, with virtually no noise interference, the message sent and the message received are almost identical. Most often, however, noise distorts some portion of the message a source sends as it travels to a receiver. Noise may be physical (others talking

Table 1.1
Interpersonal Communication Tips

Between Blind and Sighted People
People vary greatly in their visual abilities; some people are totally blind, some are partially sighted, and some have unimpaired vision. Ninety percent of individuals who are "legally blind" have some vision. All of us, however, have the same need for communication and information. Here are some tips for making communication between blind and sighted people more effective.

If you're the sighted person and are talking with a blind person:

1. *Identify yourself.* Don't assume the blind person will recognize your voice.
2. *Face your listener; you'll be easier to hear.* At the same time, don't shout. People who are visually impaired are not hearing impaired. Speak at your normal volume.
3. Because your gestures, eye movements, and facial expressions cannot be seen by the visually impaired listener, *encode into speech all the meanings—both verbal and nonverbal—that you wish to communicate.*
4. *Use audible turn-taking cues.* When you pass the role of speaker to a person who is visually impaired, don't rely on nonverbal cues; instead, say something like "Do you agree with that, Joe?"
5. *Use normal vocabulary, and discuss the same kinds of topics you would discuss with sighted people.* Don't avoid terms like "see" or "look" or even "blind." Don't avoid discussing a television show, or a painting, or the way your new car looks; these are normal conversational topics for all people.

If you are a visually impaired person and are interacting with a sighted person:

1. *Help the sighted person meet your special communication needs.* If you want your surroundings described, ask. If you want the person to read the road signs, ask.
2. *Be patient with the sighted person.* Many people are nervous talking with people who are visually impaired for fear of offending. Put them at ease in a way that also makes you more comfortable.

These suggestions were drawn from http://www.cincyblind.org/what_do_you_do_.htm and http://www.rnib.org/uk/ (both accessed October 23, 2004).

loudly, cars honking, illegible handwriting, "garbage" on your computer screen), physiological (hearing or visual impairment, articulation disorders), psychological (preconceived ideas, wandering thoughts), or semantic (misunderstood meanings). Table 1.2 identifies these four types of noise in more detail.

Because messages may be visual as well as spoken, noise too may be visual. Thus, sunglasses that prevent someone from seeing the nonverbal messages from your eyes would be considered noise, as would blurred type on a printed page.

All communications contain noise. Noise cannot be totally eliminated, but its effects can be reduced. Making your language more precise, sharpening your skills for sending and receiving nonverbal messages, and improving your listening and feedback skills are some ways to combat the influence of noise.

Communication Effects

Communication always has some **effect** on one or more persons involved in the communication act. For every communication act, there is some consequence. For example, you may gain knowledge or learn how to analyze, synthesize, or evaluate something. These are intellectual or cognitive effects. Or you may acquire or change your attitudes, beliefs, emotions, or feelings. These are affective effects. You may even learn new bodily movements, such as throwing a ball or painting a picture, as well as appropriate verbal and nonverbal behaviors. These are psychomotor effects.

Ethics

Because communication has consequences, it also involves questions of **ethics,** of right and wrong (Bok, 1978; Jaksa & Pritchard, 1994). For example, while it might be (temporarily) effective to exaggerate or even lie in order to sell a product or get elected, it would not be ethical to do so.

The ethical dimension of communication is complicated because ethics is so interwoven with your personal philosophy of life and the culture in which

Table 1.2
Four Types of Noise

One of the most important skills in communication is an ability to recognize the types of noise and to develop ways to combat them. Consider, for example, what kinds of noise occur in the classroom. What kinds of noise occur in your family communications? What kinds occur at work? What can you do to combat these kinds of noise?

Types of Noise	Definition	Example
Physical	Interference that is external to both speaker and listener; interferes with the physical transmission of the signal or message	Screeching of passing cars, hum of computer, sunglasses
Physiological	Physical barriers within the speaker or listener	Visual impairments, hearing loss, articulation problems, memory loss
Psychological	Cognitive or mental interference	Biases and prejudices in senders and receivers, closed-mindedness, inaccurate expectations, extreme emotionalism (anger, hate, love, grief)
Semantic	Assignment of different meanings by speaker and listener	People speaking different languages, use of jargon or overly complex terms not understood by listener, dialectical differences in meaning

you were raised that it's difficult to propose general guidelines for specific individuals. Nevertheless, ethical responsibilities need to be considered as integral to any communication act. The decisions you make concerning communication must be guided by what you consider right as well as by what you consider effective. To emphasize this important dimension of communication, each unit of this text concludes with a Reflections on Ethics discussion designed to highlight the relevance of ethics, to raise ethical issues, and to ask you to consider how you'd respond to specific ethical dilemmas.

The Elements in Transaction

Communication is **transactional,** which means that the elements in communication are interdependent. Each person in the communication act is both speaker and listener; each person is simultaneously sending and receiving messages (see Figure 1.2 on page 12) (Barnlund, 1970; Watzlawick, 1977, 1978; Watzlawick, Beavin, & Jackson, 1967; Wilmot, 1987).

There are several implications and ramifications of this transactional view. First, "transactional" nature means that communication is an ever changing **process.** It's an ongoing activity; all the elements of communication are in a state of constant change. You're constantly changing, the people with whom you're communicating are changing, and your environment is changing. Nothing in communication ever remains static.

In any transactional process, each element relates integrally to every other element; each exists in relation to the others. For example, there can be no source without a receiver. There can be no message without a source. There can be no feedback without a receiver. Because of this interdependence, a change in any one element of the process produces changes in the other elements. For example, you're talking with a group of your friends when your mother enters the group. This change in "audience" will lead to other changes. Perhaps you or your friends will adjust what you're saying or how you say it. The new situation may also influence how often certain people talk, and so on. Regardless of what change is introduced, other changes will be produced as a result.

Also, each person in a communication transaction acts and reacts on the basis of the present situation—but this present situation, your immediate context, is influenced by your history, past experiences, attitudes, cultural beliefs, self-image, future expectations, emotions, and a host of related issues. One implication of this is that actions and reactions in communication are determined not only by what is said, but also by the way each person interprets

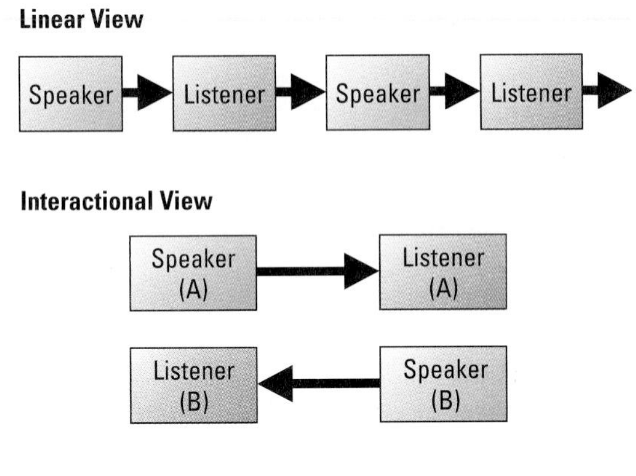

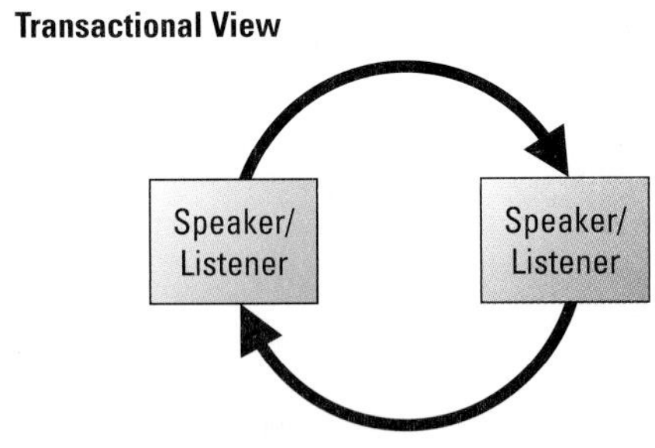

Figure 1.2

Three Views of Communication

The top diagram represents a linear view of communication, in which the speaker speaks and the listener listens. The middle diagram represents an interactional view, in which speaker and listener take turns speaking and listening; A speaks while B listens, then B speaks while A listens. The bottom diagram represents a transactional view. This is the view that most communication theorists hold. In the transactional view, each person serves simultaneously as speaker and listener; at the same time that you send messages, you're also receiving messages from your own communications and also from the messages of the other person(s).

what is said. Your responses to a movie, for example, don't depend solely on the words and pictures in the film but also on your previous experiences, present emotions, knowledge, physical well-being, and other factors.

Another implication is that two people listening to the same message will often derive two very different meanings. Although the words and symbols are the same, each person interprets them differently.

Purposes of Human Communication

The purposes of human communication may be conscious or unconscious, recognizable or unrecognizable. And, although communication technologies are changing rapidly and drastically—we send electronic mail, work at computer terminals, and telecommute, for example—the purposes of communication are likely to remain essentially the same throughout the computer revolution and whatever revolutions follow. Five general purposes of communication can be identified: To discover, to relate, to help, to persuade, and to play (see Figure 1.3). Purposes of the media—following this same fivefold classification—are presented in Unit 20 on the CD-ROM.

To Discover

One of the major purposes of communication concerns personal discovery. When you communicate with another person, you learn about yourself as well as about the other person. In fact, your self-perceptions result largely from what you've learned about yourself from others during communications, especially your interpersonal encounters.

Much as communication gives you a better understanding of yourself and of the person with whom you're communicating, it also helps you discover the external world—the world of objects, events, and other people. Today, you rely heavily on the various communications media for information about entertainment, sports, war, economic developments, health and dietary concerns, and new products to buy. Much of what you acquire from the media interacts with what you learn from your interpersonal interactions. You get information from the media, discuss it with other people, and ultimately learn or internalize the material as a result of the interaction between these two sources.

To Relate

One of our strongest motivations is to establish and maintain close relationships with others. The vast majority of people want to feel loved and liked, and in turn want to love and like others. You probably spend much of your communication time and energy establishing and maintaining social relationships. You communicate with your close friends in school, at work, and probably on the phone. You talk with your parents, children, and brothers and sisters. You interact with your relational partner. All told, this takes a great deal of your time and attests to the importance of this purpose of communication.

Of course, you may also use communication to distance yourself from others, to argue and fight with friends or romantic partners, and even to dissolve relationships.

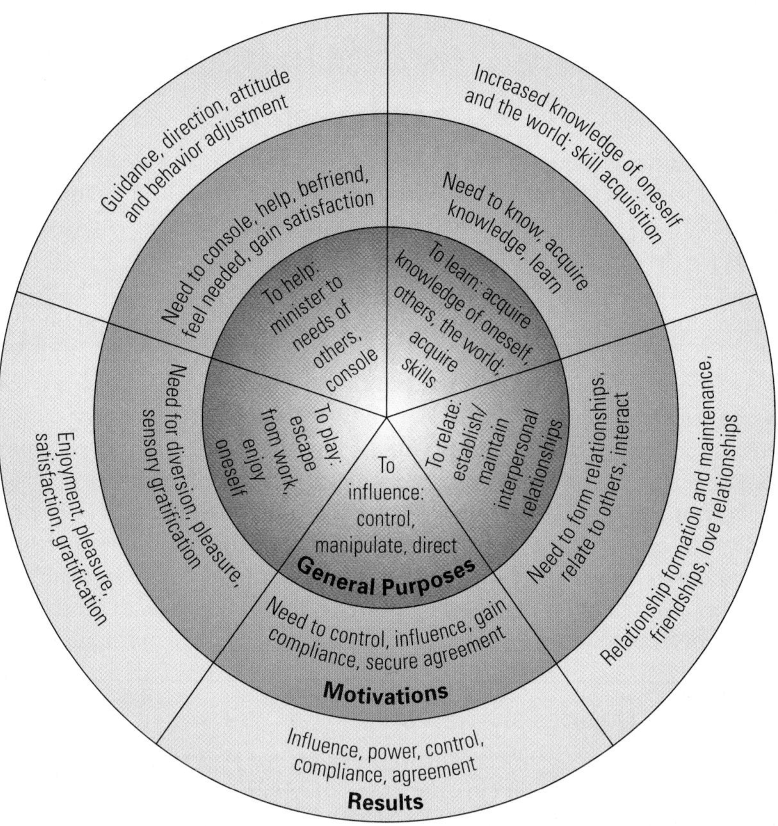

Figure 1.3

The Multipurposeful Nature of Human Communication

Shown here are the five general purposes of communication—but the aims of communication also can be looked at from at least two other perspectives. First, purposes may be seen as motives for engaging in communication. That is, you engage in communication to satisfy your need for knowledge or to form relationships. Second, these purposes may be viewed in terms of the results you want to achieve. That is, you engage in interpersonal communication to increase your knowledge of yourself and others or to exert influence or power over others. Any communication act serves a unique combination of purposes, is prompted by a unique combination of motives, and can produce a unique combination of results. A similar typology of purposes comes from research on motives for communicating. In a series of studies, Rubin and her colleagues (Rubin & Martin, 1998; Rubin, Fernandez-Collado, & Hernandez-Sampieri, 1992; Rubin & Martin, 1994; Rubin, Perse, & Barbato, 1988; Rubin & Rubin, 1992; Graham, 1994; Graham, Barbato, & Perse, 1993) have identified six primary motives for communication: pleasure, affection, inclusion, escape, relaxation, and control. How do these compare to the five purposes discussed here?

To Help

Therapists, counselors, teachers, parents, and friends are just a few categories of those who often—though not always—communicate in order to help. As is the case with therapists and counselors, entire professions are built around this communication function. But there are few professions that don't make at least some significant use of this helping function. You also use this function when you constructively criticize, express empathy, work with a group to solve a problem, or listen attentively and supportively to a public speaker. Not surprisingly, obtaining and giving help are among the major functions of Internet communication and among the major reasons people use it (Meier, 2000, 2002).

To Persuade

People spend a great deal of their time in persuasion, both as sources and as receivers. In your everyday interpersonal and group encounters, you try to change the attitudes and behaviors of others. You try to get them to vote a particular way, try a new diet, buy a particular item, see a movie, read a book, take a specific course, believe that something is true or false, value or devalue some idea, and so on. In interviews you may try to persuade a company to hire you, or in public speaking to persuade your audience that you should be elected. The list is endless. Some researchers, in fact, would argue that all communication is persuasive and that all our communications seek some persuasive goal. Some examples (Canary, Cody, & Manusov, 2000):

UNDERSTANDING *THEORY* AND *RESEARCH*

Theories and Truth

Despite their many values, theories don't reveal truth in any absolute sense. Rather, theories reveal some degree of accuracy, some degree of truth. In the natural sciences (such as physics and chemistry), theories are extremely high in accuracy. If you mix two parts of hydrogen to one part of oxygen, you'll get water—every time you do it. In social and behavioral sciences such as communication, sociology, and psychology, the theories are far less accurate in describing the way things work and in predicting how things will work.

This failure to reveal truth, however, does not mean that theories are useless. In increasing your understanding and your ability to predict, theories are extremely helpful. Theories often have practical implications for developing your own communication skills. For example, theories of interpersonal attraction offer practical insights into how to make yourself more attractive to others; theories of leadership offer practical advice on how you can more effectively exert your own leadership. This interrelationship between theories and skills is a theme you'll find throughout this book. The more you know about how communication works (that is, the theories and research), the more likely you'll be able to use it effectively (that is, build your communication skills).

Working with Theories and Research

- *If you have access, log on to Research Navigator (www.researchnavigator.com) and browse through issues of* Quarterly Journal of Speech, Communication Monographs, *or* Communication Theory *(or scan similar journals in your own field of study); you'll be amazed at the breadth and depth of academic research and theory.*

- Self-presentation goals: You communicate to give others the image you want them to have of you.
- Relationship goals: You communicate to form the relationships that will meet your needs.
- Instrumental goals: You communicate to get others to do something for you.

To Play

You probably also spend a great deal of your communication behavior on play. Communication as play includes motives of pleasure, escape, and relaxation (Barbato & Perse, 1992; Rubin, Perse, & Barbato, 1988). For example, you often listen to comedians—as well as friends—largely because it's fun, enjoyable, and exciting. You tell jokes, say clever things, and relate interesting stories largely for the pleasure it gives to you and your listeners. Similarly, you may communicate because it relaxes you, allowing you to get away from pressures and responsibilities.

Popular belief and recent research both agree that men and women use communication for different purposes. Generally, men seem to communicate more for information, while women seem to communicate more for relationship purposes (Shaw & Grant, 2002). Gender differences also occur in computer communication. For example, women ICQ users chat more for relationship reasons, while men chat more to play and to relax (Leung, 2001).

Types of Human Communication

Human communication is a vast field and ranges from talking to yourself, to talking with one person or a small group, to speaking in public to an audience of hundreds, to mass communication in which you talk to millions (see Table 1.3).

Table 1.3
Human Communication

This table identifies and arranges the forms of communication in terms of the number of persons involved, from one (in intrapersonal communication) to thousands and millions (in mass communication). It also previews (in general) the progression of topics in this book.

Areas of Human Communication	Some Common Purposes	Some Theory-Related Concerns	Some Skills-Related Concerns
Intrapersonal: communication with the self 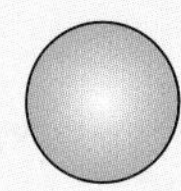	To think, reason, analyze, reflect	How does a person's self-concept develop? How does the self-concept influence communication? How can problem-solving and analyzing abilities be improved and taught? What is the relationship between personality and communication?	Enhancing self-esteem, increasing self-awareness, improving problem-solving and analyzing abilities, increasing self-control, reducing stress, managing intrapersonal conflict
Interpersonal: communication between two persons 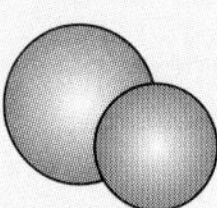	To discover, relate, influence, play, help	What is interpersonal effectiveness? Why do people develop relationships? What holds friends, lovers, and families together? What tears them apart? How can relationships be repaired?	Increasing effectiveness in one-to-one communication, developing and maintaining effective relationships (friendship, love, family), improving conflict resolution abilities
Small group: communication within a small group of persons 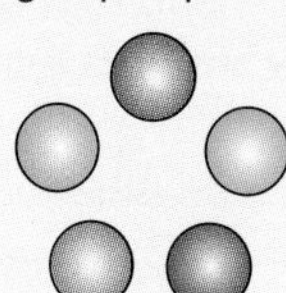	To share information, generate ideas, solve problems, help	What makes a leader? What type of leadership works best? What roles do members play in groups? What do groups do well, and what do they fail to do well? How can groups be made more effective?	Increasing effectiveness as a group member, improving leadership abilities, using groups to achieve specific purposes (for example, solving problems, generating ideas)
Public: communication of speaker with audience 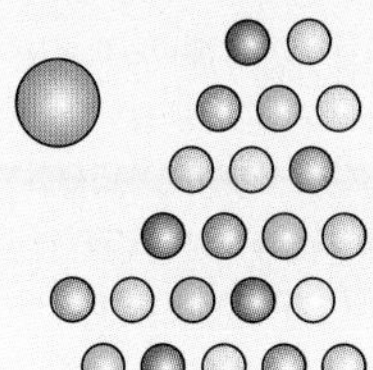	To inform, persuade, entertain	What kinds of organizational structure work best in informative and persuasive speaking? How can audiences be most effectively analyzed and adapted to? How can ideas be best developed for communication to an audience?	Communicating information more effectively; increasing persuasive abilities; developing, organizing, styling, and delivering messages with greater effectiveness
Mass: communication addressed to an extremely large audience, mediated by audio and/or visual means 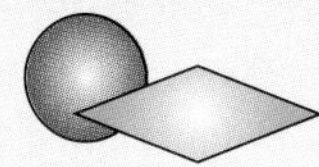	To entertain, persuade, and inform	What functions do the media serve? How do the media influence us? How can we influence the media? In what ways is information censored by the media for the public? How does advertising work?	Improving our ability to use the media to greater effectiveness, increasing our ability to control the media, avoiding being taken in by advertisements and tabloid journalism

GOING *ONLINE*

Allyn & Bacon's Communication Studies Website

www.ablongman.com/commstudies

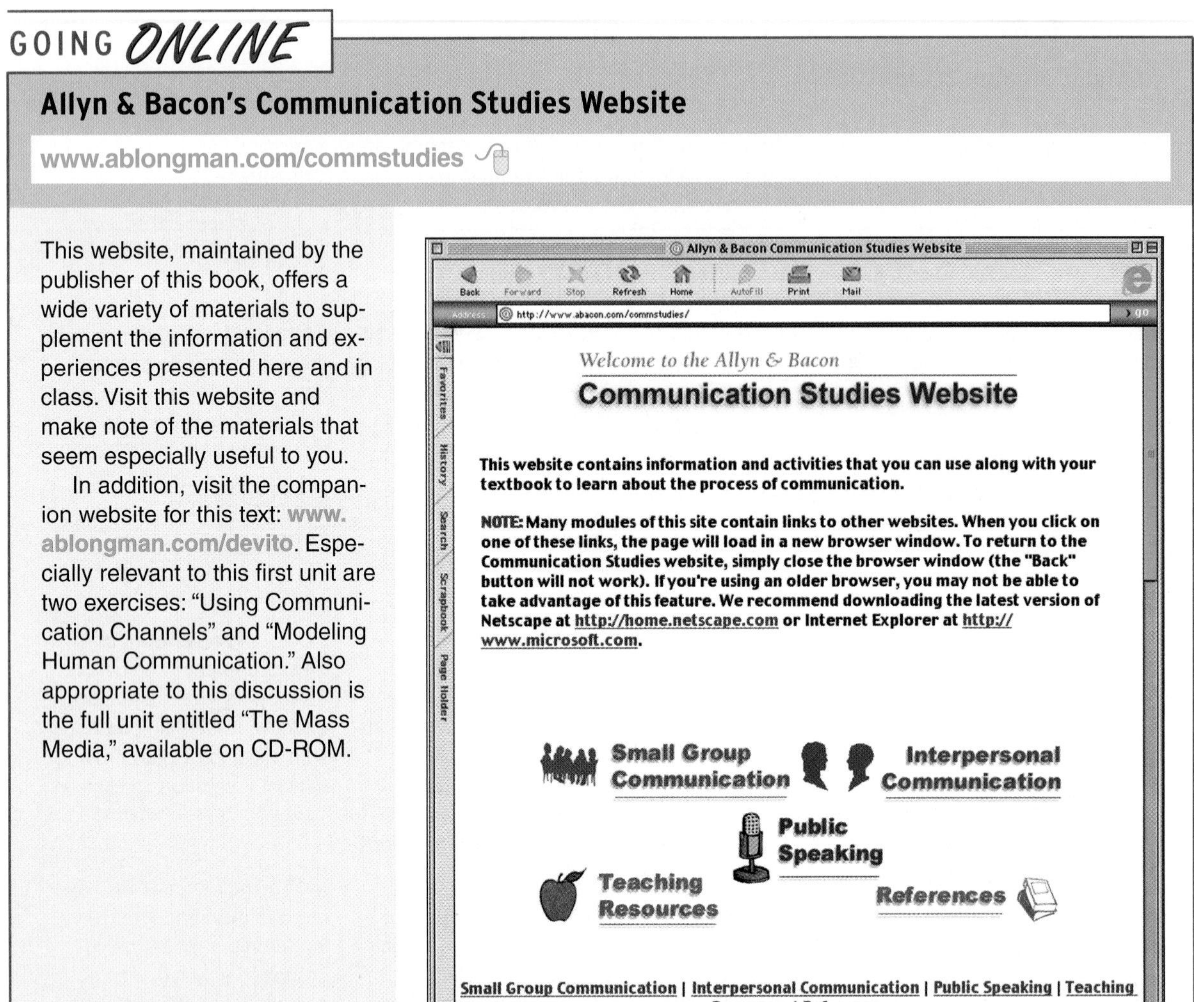

This website, maintained by the publisher of this book, offers a wide variety of materials to supplement the information and experiences presented here and in class. Visit this website and make note of the materials that seem especially useful to you.

In addition, visit the companion website for this text: www.ablongman.com/devito. Especially relevant to this first unit are two exercises: "Using Communication Channels" and "Modeling Human Communication." Also appropriate to this discussion is the full unit entitled "The Mass Media," available on CD-ROM.

In **intrapersonal communication** you talk with yourself. You learn about and evaluate yourself, persuade yourself of this or that, reason about possible decisions to make, and rehearse messages you intend to send to others.

Through **interpersonal communication** you interact with others, learn about them and about yourself, and reveal yourself to others. Whether with new acquaintances, old friends, lovers, or family members, it's through interpersonal communication that you establish, maintain, and sometimes destroy (and sometimes repair) your personal relationships.

In **small group communication** you interact with others, solving problems, developing new ideas, and sharing knowledge and experiences. From the employment interview to the executive board meeting, from the informal social group having coffee to the formal meeting discussing issues of international concern, your work life and social life are lived largely in small groups.

Through **public communication** others inform and persuade you. And you in turn inform and persuade others—to do, to buy, or to think in a particular way, or to change an attitude, opinion, or value.

Through **mass communication** you are entertained, informed, and persuaded by the media—movies, television, radio, newspapers, and books. Also, through your viewing habits and buying patterns, you in turn influence the media's form and content.

All forms of communication except intrapersonal communication may be **intercultural communication,** in which you communicate with members of other cultures; that is, people who follow different customs, roles, and rules. Through intercultural communication you come to understand new ways of thinking and new ways of behaving and begin to see the tremendous variety in human thought and experience.

This book, then, is about these types of communication and about your personal communication. Its major goal is to explain the concepts and principles,

MEDIA WATCH

Theories of Media Influence

Media messages have effects on readers, listeners, and viewers. Some messages seek to influence people in obvious ways; for example, the advertisements on television or on the Internet and the editorials in newspapers. Other media messages influence indirectly; for example, dramas and sitcoms that influence our views of family, of work and workplace relationships, and of friendship and love.

An early theory, called the one-step theory, argued that the influence of the media was direct and immediate and occurred in one step—from the media to you. You read a newspaper or watched television and were persuaded by what they said (Schramm & Porter, 1982). This theory saw audience members as relatively passive, as targets that could hardly resist being influenced.

A more sophisticated explanation visualizes media influence as a two-step process: First, the media influence opinion leaders (step 1), and second, these opinion leaders influence the rest of the people (step 2). A more current and complicated approach, the multistep theory, claims that media interact with interpersonal channels. So, for example, the media may influence you on a specific issue; then you interact interpersonally with others who influence you to alter your newly formed opinions. You then attend to more media, and they influence you in other directions. In this view, media influence combines with interpersonal influence to affect your thinking.

You and the Media

Can you identify specific ways in which the media have influenced you? For example, have media messages influenced your buying habits, your view of relationships, or your attitudes toward the opposite sex? What theory seems to best explain how the media influence you?

the theory and research central to these varied areas of human communication. Another goal is to give you the foundation and direction for learning the skills of human communication and for increasing your own communication competency.

Among the skills you'll learn are:

- *Self-presentation skills* to enable you to present yourself as a confident, likable, approachable, and credible person. Incidentally, it is also largely

VIEWPOINT A recent study finds that 80 percent of young adult women consider a husband who can communicate his feelings more desirable than a spouse who earns a good living (www.gallup.com/poll/releases/pr010627b.asp, accessed June 27, 2001). How important, compared to all the other factors you might take into consideration in choosing a partner, is the ability to communicate? What specific communication skills would you consider "extremely important" in a life partner?

through self-presentation that you display negative qualities as well.

- *Relationship skills* to help you build friendships, enter into love relationships, work with colleagues, and family members. These are the skills for initiating, maintaining, repairing, and (sometimes) dissolving relationships of all kinds—the skills that make you or break you as a relationship partner.
- *Interviewing skills* to enable you to interact to gain information, to present yourself successfully to get the job you want, and to engage effectively in a wide variety of other interview situations. (This topic is covered in a separate pamphlet, *Interviewing and Human Communication*.)
- *Group interaction and leadership skills* to help you participate effectively in relationship and task groups—informative, problem-solving, and brainstorming groups, at home or at work—as a member and as a leader.
- *Presentation skills* to enable you to communicate information to and influence the attitudes and behaviors of small and large audiences.

Approaching Ethics

In thinking about the ethics of communication, you can take the position that ethics is objective or that it's subjective.

- In an *objective view* you'd claim that the morality of an act—say, a communication message—is absolute and exists apart from the values or beliefs of any individual or culture. This objective view holds that there are standards that apply to all people in all situations at all times. If lying, advertising falsely, using illegally obtained evidence, and revealing secrets, for example, are considered unethical, then they'd be considered unethical regardless of the circumstances surrounding them or of the values and beliefs of the culture in which they occur.
- In a *subjective view* you'd claim that the morality of an act depends on the culture's values and beliefs as well as on the particular circumstances. Thus, from a subjective position you would claim that the end might justify the means—a good result can justify the use of unethical means to achieve that result. You would further argue that lying is wrong to win votes or sell cigarettes, but that lying can be ethical if the end result is positive (such as trying to make someone who is unattractive feel better by telling them they look great, or telling a critically ill person that they'll feel better soon.)

WHAT WOULD YOU DO? At work, you see a colleague repeatedly take home computer parts. When you confront him, he says that because he's so underpaid and was recently denied promotion because of prejudice, he feels justified in taking this additional compensation. You agree that he is underpaid and that he probably was denied promotion because of prejudice. He asks you if you think his behavior is unethical. What would you say if you took an objective view of ethics? What would you say if you took a subjective view?

SUMMARY

This unit explained the elements, purposes, and types of human communication that we'll focus on throughout the rest of this book.

1. Communication is the act, by one or more persons, of sending and receiving messages that are distorted by noise, occur within a context, have some effect (and some ethical dimension), and provide some opportunity for feedback.
2. The universals of communication—the elements present in every communication act—are context, culture, source–receiver, message, channel, noise, sending or encoding processes, receiving or decoding processes, feedback and feedforward, effect, and ethics.
3. The communication context has at least four dimensions: physical, social–psychological, temporal, and cultural.
4. Culture consists of the collection of beliefs, attitudes, values, and ways of behavior shared by a group of people and passed down from one generation to the next.
5. Communication competence is knowledge of the elements and rules of communication, which vary from one culture to another.
6. Feedback is information or messages that are sent back to the source. It may come from the source itself or from the receiver and may be characterized along such dimensions as positive and negative,

person-focused and message-focused, immediate and delayed, low-monitored and high-monitored, and supportive and critical.

7. Feedforward messages preface other messages and may be used to open the channels of communication, to preview future messages, to disclaim, and to altercast.
8. Communication messages may be of varied forms and may be sent and received through any combination of sensory organs. The communication channel is the medium through which the messages are sent.
9. Noise is anything that distorts a message; it's present to some degree in every communication transaction and may be physical, physiological, psychological, or semantic in origin.
10. Communication always has an effect. Effects may be cognitive, affective, or psychomotor.
11. Ethics in communication consists of the rightness or wrongness—the morality—of a communication transaction. Ethics is integral to every communication transaction.
12. Communication is a transactional process in which each person simultaneously sends and receives messages.
13. Communication is multipurposeful; we use communication to discover, relate, help, persuade, and play.
14. The major types of human communication are intrapersonal, interpersonal, small group, public, mass, and intercultural communication.
15. The major skills to be learned here include self-presentation, relationships, interviewing, group interaction and leadership, and presentation.

Key Terms

communication context
sources–receivers
encoders–decoders
encoding–decoding
communication competence
message
channel
feedback
feedforward
altercasting
disclaimer
noise
communication effects
ethics
intrapersonal communication
interpersonal communication
small group communication
public communication
mass communication
intercultural communication

Thinking Critically About

Preliminaries to Human Communication

1. In what ways do your college courses integrate a multicultural perspective? How is this perspective reflected in your textbooks? What do you think about this issue?
2. What additional advice would you offer for improving communication between blind and sighted persons?
3. Based on your own experiences, do you find that instructors who accurately read student feedback are better liked than instructors who can't read feedback as accurately? Is there a relationship between the ability to read feedback and the ability to communicate information or to motivate or persuade an audience?
4. What kinds of feedforward can you find in this textbook? What specific functions do these feedforwards serve?
5. Assume you're in a conversation in your present surroundings. What kinds of noise can you identify?
6. Do you agree that men and women use communication for different purposes? Can you offer specific examples from your own experience?
7. In what specific ways are e-mail and whispering in chat groups similar to interpersonal conversation? How are chat room communications similar to face-to-face small group communication? How are newsgroup postings similar to public speeches? What are the differences?

8. Will the new communication technologies (for example, electronic mail, working at computer terminals, and telecommuting) change the basic purposes of communication identified here?
9. In what ways would the skills of self-presentation, relationship, interviewing, group interaction, and presentation be of value to you in both your social and professional lives?
10. What noted personality would you nominate for the "Communication Competence Hall of Fame"? Why?
11. What is the single communication skill that you most admire in others? What is the single communication behavior of others that most irritates you?

MEDIA WATCH

Uses and Gratifications Theory

Using media requires effort. The amount of effort you'll have to expend to use the media will depend upon the availability of different media, the ease with which you may use them, and the expense. For example, there's less effort required—less expense, less time lost—in watching television than in going to a movie. There's less effort in watching a movie than in reading a book.

Uses and gratifications theory—originally developed in the 1940s and currently receiving renewed emphasis as it is applied to electronic media (Wimmer & Dominick, 2003; Ruggiero, 2000)—argues that in making media choices, you're more likely to select media that provide great rewards while requiring little effort. Conversely, you're less likely to select media that promise small rewards and require great effort. According to this theory, media (movies, television, the Internet, books, newspapers, magazines, radio) compete with one another, as well as with other sources (for example, interpersonal interaction) to provide the rewards people want while requiring as little effort as possible.

Rewards can be both immediate and delayed. So, for example, you may watch a particular television program because it satisfies your immediate need for information or entertainment. Or you may read a book because it contributes to satisfying a delayed need you have to become a writer.

You and the Media

Can you use this theory of uses and gratifications to explain your own media choices? Can you use this theory to explain the changes that Internet service providers, search engines, and websites generally have made over the last several years?

Communication Involves Content and Relationship Dimensions

Communications, to a certain extent at least, refer to the real world, to something external to both speaker and listener. At the same time, however, communications also refer to the relationships between the parties (Watzlawick, Beavin, & Jackson, 1967). In other words, communication has both **content and relationship dimensions.**

For example, an employer may say to a worker, "See me after the meeting." This simple message has a content aspect and a relational aspect. The **content message** refers to the behavioral responses expected—namely, that the worker see the employer after the meeting. The **relationship message** tells how the communication is to be dealt with. For example, the use of the simple command says that there's a status difference between the two parties: The employer can command the worker. This aspect is perhaps seen most clearly if you imagine the worker giving this command to the employer; to do so would be awkward and out of place, because it would violate the expected communications between employer and worker.

In any communication situation the content dimension may stay the same but the relationship aspect may vary. Or the relationship aspect may be the same while the content is different. For example, the employer could say to the worker either "You had better see me after the meeting" or "May I please see you after the meeting?" In each case the content is essentially the same; that is, the message being communicated about the behaviors expected is the same. But the relationship dimension is very different. The first example signifies a definite superior–inferior relationship and even a put-down of the worker. In the second, the employer signals a more equal relationship and shows respect for the worker.

Similarly, at times the content may be different but the relationship essentially the same. For example, a teenager might say to his or her parents, "May I go away this weekend?" and "May I use the car tonight?" The content of the two messages is clearly very different. The relationship dimension, however, is essentially the same. It clearly denotes a superior–inferior relationship in which permission to do certain things must be secured.

VIEWPOINT

What implications do the principle of adjustment and the theory of communication accommodation have for communication between adults and children? For communication between students and teachers? For communication between members of different races or religions?

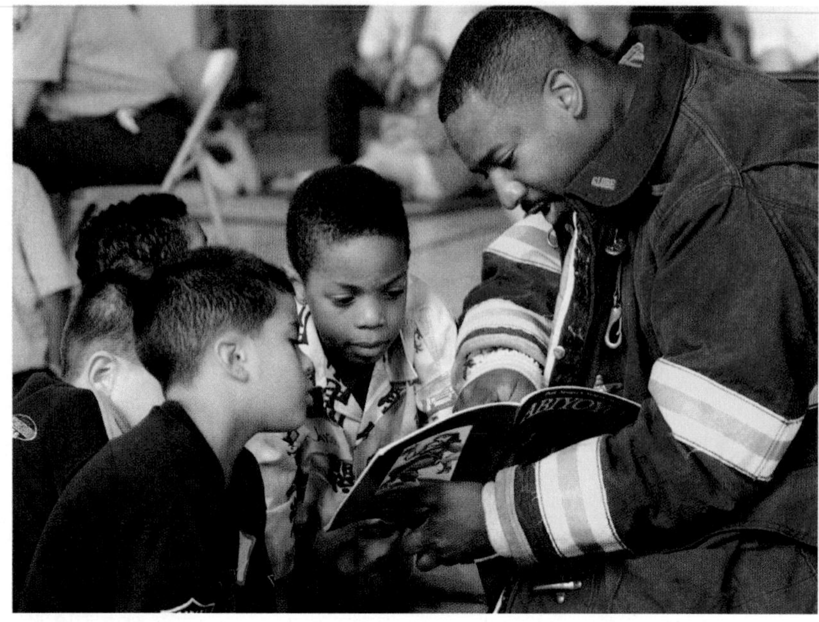

Ignoring Relationship Dimensions

Problems may arise when the distinction between the content and relationship levels of communication is ignored. Consider a couple arguing over the fact that Pat made plans to study with friends during the weekend without first asking Chris if that would be all right. Probably both would have agreed that to study over the weekend was the right choice to make. Thus the argument is not at all related to the content level. The argument centers on the relationship level. Chris expected to be consulted about plans for the weekend. Pat, in not doing so, rejected this definition of the relationship.

Let me give you a personal example. My mother came to stay for a week at a summer place I had. On the first day she swept the kitchen floor six times, though I had repeatedly told her that it did not need sweeping: I would be tracking in dirt and mud from outside, so all her effort would be wasted. But she persisted in sweeping, saying that the floor was dirty and should be swept. On the content level, we were talking about the value of sweeping the kitchen floor. But on the relationship level we were talking about something quite different. We were each saying, "This is my house." When we realized this (though only after considerable argument), I stopped complaining about the relative usefulness of sweeping a floor that did not need sweeping and she stopped sweeping it. Consider the following interchange:

Thom: I'm going bowling tomorrow. The guys at the plant are starting a team. [He focuses on the content and ignores any relational implications of the message.]

Sofia: Why can't we ever do anything together? [She responds primarily on a relational level, ignoring the content implications of the message and expressing her displeasure at being ignored in his decision.]

Thom: We can do something together anytime; tomorrow's the day they're organizing the team. [Again, he focuses almost exclusively on the content.]

This example reflects research findings that show that men tend to focus more on content messages, whereas women focus more on relationship messages (Pearson, West, & Turner, 1995). Once we recognize this gender difference, we may be able to develop increased sensitivity to the opposite sex.

Recognizing Relationship Dimensions

Here's essentially the same situation but with added sensitivity to relationship messages:

Thom: The guys at the plant are organizing a bowling team. I'd sure like to be on the team. Do you mind if I go to the organizational meeting tomorrow? [Although he focuses on content, he shows awareness of the relational dimensions by asking if this would be a problem. He also shows this in expressing his desire rather than his decision to attend this meeting.]

SOFIA: That sounds great, but I'd really like to do something together tomorrow. [She focuses on the relational dimension but also acknowledges his content message. Note too that she does not respond as if she has to defend herself or her emphasis on relational aspects.]

THOM: How about your meeting me at Luigi's for dinner after the organizational meeting? [He responds to the relational aspect without abandoning his desire to join the bowling team—and seeks to incorporate it into his communications. He attempts to negotiate a solution that will meet both Judy's and his needs and desires.]

SOFIA: Perfect. I'm dying for spaghetti and meatballs. [She responds to both messages, approving of both his joining the team and their dinner date.]

Arguments over content are relatively easy to resolve. You can look something up in a book or ask someone what actually took place. Arguments on the relationship level, however, are much more difficult to resolve, in part because you (like me in the example with my mother) may not recognize that the argument is in fact about your relationship.

Communication Is Ambiguous

Ambiguous messages are messages with more than one potential meaning. Sometimes this **ambiguity** occurs because we use words that can be interpreted differently. Informal time terms offer good examples; *soon, right away, in a minute, early, late,* and similar terms often mean different things to different people. The terms are ambiguous. A more interesting type of ambiguity is grammatical ambiguity. You can get a feel for this type of ambiguity by trying to paraphrase—rephrase in your own words—the following sentences:

1. What has the cat in its paws?
2. Visiting relatives can be boring.
3. They are flying planes.

You can interpret and paraphrase each of these in at least two different ways:

1. What monster has the cat in its paws? What does the cat have in its paws?
2. To visit relatives is boring. Relatives who visit are boring.
3. Those people are flying planes. Those planes are for flying.

Although these examples are particularly striking—and are the work of linguists, or specialists who analyze language—some degree of ambiguity exists in all communication; all messages are ambiguous to some degree. In other words, when you express an idea, you never communicate your meaning exactly and totally; rather, you communicate your meaning with some reasonable accuracy—enough to give the other person a reasonably clear sense of what you mean. Sometimes, of course, you're less accurate than you anticipated: Your listener "gets the wrong idea," or "gets offended" when you only meant to be humorous, or "misunderstands your emotional meaning." Because of this inevitable uncertainty, you may qualify what you're saying, give an example, or ask "Do you know what I mean?" These tactics help the other person understand your meaning and reduce uncertainty (to some degree).

Similarly, all relationships contain uncertainty. Consider a close relationship of your own and ask yourself the following questions. Answer on a scale ranging from 1 (completely or almost completely uncertain) to 6 (completely or almost completely certain). How certain are you about:

- what you can or cannot say to each other in this relationship?
- whether or not you and your partner feel the same way about each other?
- how you and your partner would describe this relationship?
- the future of the relationship?

Very likely you were not able to respond to all four questions with 6s, and it's equally likely that your relationship partner would be unable to respond with all 6s. These questions from a relationship uncertainty scale (Knoblock & Solomon, 1999)—and other similar tests—illustrate that you probably experience some degree of uncertainty about the norms that govern your relationship communication (question 1), the degree to which each of you sees the relationship in similar ways (question 2), the definition of the relationship (question 3), and the relationship's future (question 4).

By developing the skills of communication presented in this text, you can often reduce ambiguity and make your meanings as unambiguous as possible.

Communication Sequences Are Punctuated

Communication events are continuous transactions. There's no clear-cut beginning or ending. As a participant in or an observer of the communication act, you *engage in punctuation:* You divide up this continuous, circular process into causes and effects, or **stimuli** and **responses**. That is, you segment this continuous stream of communication into smaller pieces. You label some of these pieces causes or stimuli and others effects or responses.

Consider an example: The students are apathetic; the teacher does not prepare for classes. Figure 2.1(a) illustrates the sequence of events, in which there's no absolute beginning and no absolute end. Each action (the students' apathy and the teacher's lack of preparation) stimulates the other. But there's no initial stimulus. Each of the events may be regarded as a stimulus and each as a response, but there's no way to determine which is which.

Consider how the teacher might divide up this continuous transaction. Figure 2.1(b) illustrates the teacher's perception of the situation. From this point of view, the teacher sees the students' apathy as the stimulus for his or her lack of preparation, and the lack of preparation as the response to the students' apathy. In Figure 2.1(c) we see how the students might divide up the transaction. The students might

Figure 2.1

The Sequence of Events

Try using this three-part figure, discussed in the text, to explain what might go on when Pat complains about Chris's nagging and Chris complains about Pat's avoidance and silence.

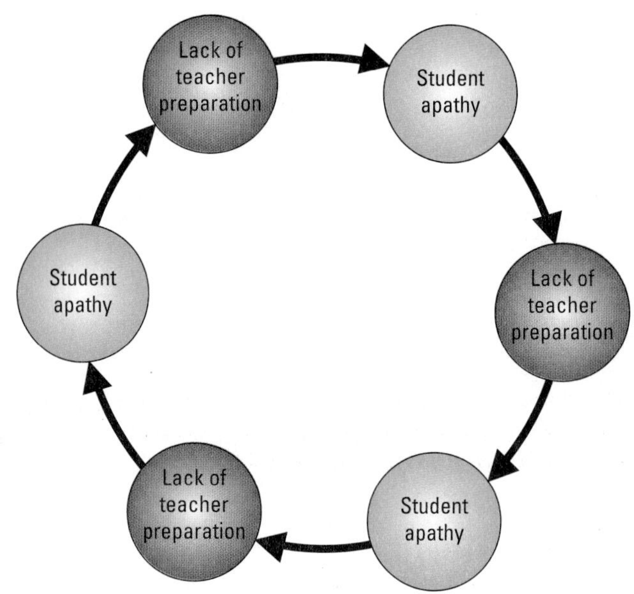

(a) The sequence of events as it exists in reality

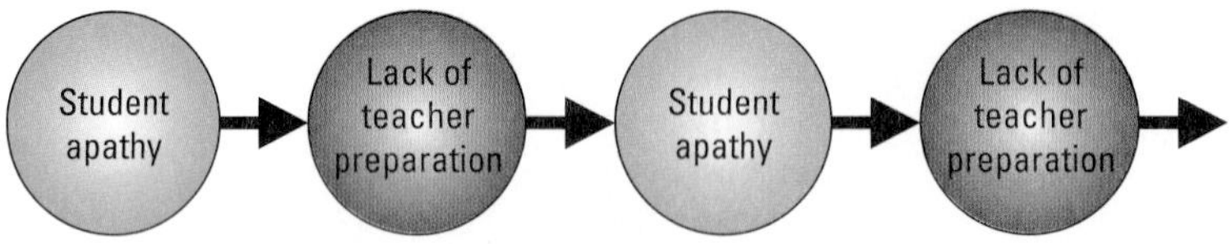

(b) The sequence of events punctuated by the teacher

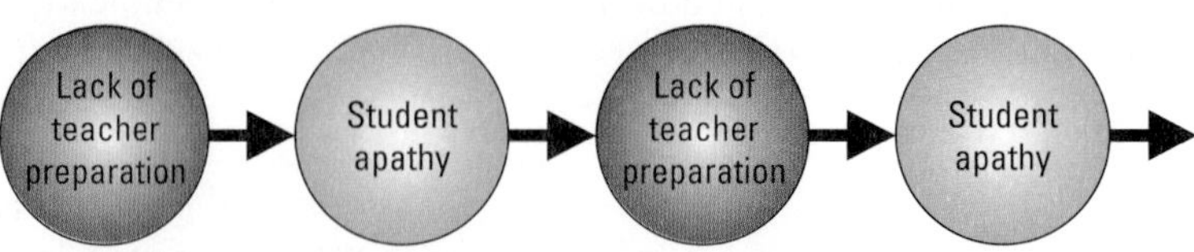

(c) The sequence of events punctuated by the students

BUILDING COMMUNICATION SKILLS

Describing Relationships

How would you use the principles discussed in this unit to describe what is happening in any one or two of the following situations? What advice would you give the individuals in these scenarios to improve their interpersonal interactions?

1. A couple, together for 20 years, argues constantly about the seemingly most insignificant things—who takes the dog out, who does the shopping, who decides where to go to dinner, and so on. It has gotten to the point where they rarely have a day without argument; both are considering separating.
2. In the heat of argument, Harry said he didn't ever want to see Peggy's family again: "They don't like me and I don't like them." Peggy reciprocated and said she felt the same way about his family. Now, weeks later, there remains tension between them, especially when they are with one of the families.
3. Sandra supervises a team of 12 workers, but she has very little influence on what they do. They just go about their business as if she were not in charge. Sandra wants to become more persuasive.

see this "same" sequence of events as beginning with the teacher's lack of preparation as the stimulus (or cause) and their own apathy as the response (or effect).

Take another example: Pat cooks; Chris criticizes the cooking. Pat begins to exert less effort, Chris criticizes more, Pat exerts still less effort, Chris continues to criticize, and so on. Pat may see the argument as beginning with Chris's negative comments—the criticism is the cause and exerting less effort is the effect. Chris may see the argument as beginning with Pat's lousy cooking—lack of effort is the cause and justifiable criticism is the effect.

This tendency to divide up the various communication transactions in sequences of stimuli and responses is referred to as **punctuation of communication** (Watzlawick, Beavin, & Jackson, 1967). People punctuate the continuous sequences of events into stimuli and responses for ease of understanding and remembering. And, as both the preceding examples illustrate, people punctuate communication in ways that allow them to look good and that are consistent with their own self-image.

If communication is to be effective, if you're to understand what another person means from his or her point of view, then you have to see the sequence of events as punctuated by the other person. Further, you have to recognize that your punctuation does not reflect what exists in reality. Rather, it reflects your own unique but fallible perception.

Communication Involves Symmetrical and Complementary Transactions

Relationships can be described as either symmetrical or complementary (Watzlawick, Beavin, & Jackson, 1967). In a **symmetrical relationship** the two individuals mirror each other's behavior. The behavior of one person is reflected in the behavior of the other. If one member nags, the other member responds in kind. If one member expresses jealousy, the other member expresses jealousy. If one member is passive, the other member is passive. The relationship is one of equality, with the emphasis on minimizing the differences between the two individuals.

Note, however, the problems that can arise in this type of relationship. Consider the situation of a husband and wife, both of whom are aggressive. The aggressiveness of the husband fosters aggressiveness in the wife; the anger of the wife arouses anger in the husband. As this escalates, the aggressiveness can no longer be contained, and the relationship is consumed by aggression.

In a **complementary relationship** the two individuals engage in different behaviors. The behavior of one serves as the stimulus for the complementary behavior of the other. In complementary relationships the differences between the parties are maximized.

ASK THE RESEARCHER

Practical Principles

- *The principles of communication are interesting, but—and forgive me for seeming so mercenary—can they help me get a job, get promoted, or otherwise help me earn a living?*

The principles of communication can be directly related to career success. Interviewing skills help us describe our competencies to a prospective employer and seek information about employment opportunities. Today's organization needs individuals with strong interpersonal skills who can work in diverse groups and situations. Problem-solving and decision-making skills, team and group communication expertise, presentation capabilities, conflict management competencies, and the ability to do organizational communication analysis all are related to job and career advancement. Studies in the United States and internationally have described both human and technological communication as the key to excellence in the twenty-first century. Numerous employer surveys have found that accurately processing large volumes of information within companies, although necessary, is not sufficient for excellence; organizations need employees who take personal responsibility for building relationships that contribute to trust, quality communication, innovation, and change.

For further information: Shockley-Zalabak, P. (2004). *Fundamentals of organizational communication* (6th ed.). Boston: Allyn & Bacon.

Pam Shockley-Zalabak (Ph.D., University of Colorado) is a professor of communication and chancellor at the University of Colorado at Colorado Springs. She conducts research on organizational trust and teaches organizational communication classes.

One partner acts as the superior and the other as the inferior, one is passive and the other active, one strong and the other weak. At times cultures establish such relationships—as, for example, the complementary relationship between teacher and student or between employer and employee.

Early marriages are likely to be complementary relationships in which each person tries to complete himself or herself. When these couples separate and form new partnerships, the new relationships are likely to be symmetrical and to involve a kind of reconfirmation of each partner's own identity (Prosky, 1992). Generally, research finds that complementary couples have a lower marital adjustment level than do symmetrical couples (Main & Oliver, 1988; Holden, 1991; McCall & Green, 1991).

A problem in complementary relationships—familiar to many college students—is the situation created by extreme rigidity. Whereas the complementary relationship between a nurturing and protective mother and a dependent child is at one stage vital and essential to the life of the child, a **rigid complementarity** when the child is older can become a handicap to further development, if the change so essential to growth is not allowed to occur.

Communication Is Inevitable, Irreversible, and Unrepeatable

Communication is a process that is inevitable, irreversible, and unrepeatable. Communication messages are always being sent (or almost always), can't be reversed or uncommunicated, and are always unique and one-time occurrences. Let's look at these qualities in more detail.

Inevitability

In many instances communication takes place even though one of the individuals does not think he or she is communicating or does not want to communicate. Consider, for example, the student sitting in the back of the classroom with an expressionless face, perhaps staring out the window. Although the

COMMUNICATION@WORK

Communication Networks

If an organization is to work effectively, the communication should be through the most effective channel regardless of the organization chart.

—David Packard

Organizations use a variety of different communication networks—configurations of channels through which messages pass from one person to another. The five types of networks shown in Figure 2.2 are among the most commonly used organizational communication patterns. These networks are defined by the exchange of messages, which may be transmitted face-to-face or via telephone, e-mail, intranet, teleconferencing, informal memos, or formal reports.

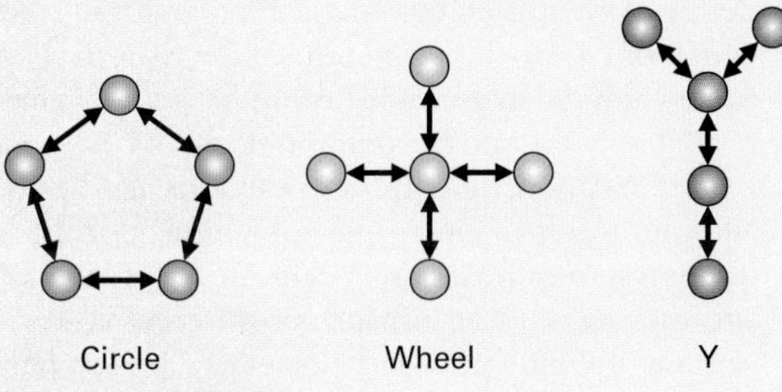

Figure 2.2
Five Network Structures

- In the *circle,* members may communicate with the two members on either side. The circle has no leader; all members have exactly the same authority or power to influence the group.
- In the *wheel,* all messages must go through the central position or leader. Members may not communicate directly with each other.
- In the *Y,* the messages pass mainly to the third person from the bottom and to a lesser extent to the person second from the bottom.
- In the *chain,* messages may be sent only to the person next to you. In this pattern there are some power differences; the middle positions receive more messages than the end positions.
- In the *all-channel* or *star* pattern, each member may communicate with any other member, allowing for the greatest member participation. All members, as in the circle, have the same power to influence others.

Communicating@Work

If you were the manager of a complex organization, what pattern of communication channels would you establish if you had to get simple repetitive tasks done quickly and efficiently? What pattern would you use if you wanted to increase the morale of the workers? What pattern would you use if you had a few experienced people but the vast majority of others were inexperienced?

student might claim not to be communicating with the teacher, the teacher may derive any of a variety of messages from this behavior; for example, that the student lacks interest, is bored, or is worried about something. In any event, the teacher is receiving messages even though the student may not intend to communicate. In an interactional situation, you can't avoid communicating (Watzlawick, Beavin, & Jackson, 1967); communication is inevitable. This principle of **inevitability** does not mean, of course,

VIEWPOINT
How would you apply the concepts and the skills of inevitability, irreversibility, and unrepeatability to participation (and let's assume a strong desire to win) in a reality television show such as *Survivor*? How about on a first date with the person who seems exactly what you've been looking for all your life?

that all behavior is communication. For example, if the student looked out the window and the teacher failed to notice this, no communication would have taken place.

Further, when you're in an interactional situation you can't avoid responding to the messages of others. For example, if you notice someone winking at you, you must respond in some way. Even if you don't respond actively or openly, that lack of response is itself a response, and it communicates. Again, if you don't notice the winking, then obviously communication has not occurred.

Irreversibility

Notice that you can reverse the processes of only some systems. For example, you can turn water into ice and then the ice back into water. And you can repeat this reversal process as many times as you wish. Other systems, however, are irreversible. You can turn grapes into wine, but you can't turn the wine back into grapes—the process can go in only one direction. Communication is such an irreversible process. Once you say something, once you press the send key on your e-mail, you can't uncommunicate it. You can of course try to reduce the effects of your message by saying, for example, "I really didn't mean what I said" or "I was so angry I couldn't think straight." But regardless of how you try to negate or reduce the effects of a message, the message itself, once it has been sent and received, can't be reversed.

Because of **irreversibility** (and unerasability), be careful not to say things you may be sorry for later. Especially in conflict situations, when tempers run high, avoid saying things you may later wish to withdraw. Commitment messages—"I love you" messages and their variants—also need to be monitored. And in group and public communication situations, when messages are received by many people, it's crucial to recognize their irreversibility. Similarly, online messages that could be interpreted as sexist, racist, homophobic, or ageist, which you thought were private or erased from your computer, may later be recalled and retrieved by others, creating all sorts of problems for you and your organization.

As a result of the differences between the permanency of electronic communication and the evanescence of face-to-face communication, you may wish to be cautious in your electronic messages. E-mail is probably your most common form of computer communication, though these cautions also apply to all other forms of electronic communication, including newsgroup postings, instant messages, and website messages. In an organizational context, it's important to find out what the e-mail policy of the company is. According to one survey, 75 percent of companies have written e-mail policies, but less than half of all companies train their workers in e-mail policies (Coombes, 2003).

- E-mails are difficult to destroy. Often e-mails you think you deleted will remain on servers and workstations and may be retrieved by a clever hacker.
- E-mails can readily be made public; the ease of forwarding e-mails to others or of posting your comments on websites makes it especially important that you consider carefully what you write. The message that you intend for one person may actually be received by many others, too.
- E-mails are not privileged communication and can easily be used against you, especially in the workplace. Criticizing a colleague may one day leave you open to accusations of discrimination. Passing along sexist, racist, homophobic, or ageist "jokes" to a friend may one day fuel accusations of a hostile working environment and cost your employer millions, as such "jokes" cost Chevron a few years ago.
- E-mails provide permanent records: They make it impossible for you to say, for example, "That's not exactly what I said," because exactly what you said will be there in black and white.

UNDERSTANDING *THEORY* AND *RESEARCH*

Evaluating Communication Research

In evaluating communication research (or any kind of research), ask yourself three questions:

Are the results reliable? Reliability, a measure of the extent to which research findings are consistent, is always important to consider when you evaluate research findings. In investigating reliability, you ask if another researcher, using the same essential tools, would find the same results. Would the same people respond in the same way at other times? If the answer to such questions is yes, then the results are reliable. If the answer is no, then the results may be unreliable.

Are the results valid? Validity is a measure of the extent to which a measuring instrument measures what it claims to measure. For example, does your score on an intelligence test really measure what we think of as intelligence? Does your score on a test of communication apprehension measure what most people think of as constituting apprehension?

Do the results justify the conclusion? Results and conclusions are two different things. Results are objective findings such as "men scored higher than women on this test of romanticism." Conclusions are the researcher's (or reader's) interpretation of the results and might include, for example, "Men are more romantic than women."

Working with Theories and Research

- *If you have access, log on to Research Navigator (*www.researchnavigator.com*) and search the general interest or the* New York Times *database for an article that summarizes or popularizes a scientific research study. Then, using the relevant academic database (such as communication, psychology, sociology, or business), locate an original research article on a similar topic and compare the two presentations. What are the major differences?*

- E-mail files may be accessed by others, such as a nosy colleague at the next desk or a visiting neighbor, and can then be sent to additional outsiders.

Unrepeatability

The reason for the **unrepeatability** of communication is simple: Everyone and everything is constantly changing. As a result, you can never recapture the exact same situation, frame of mind, or relationship dynamics that defined a previous communication act. For example, you can never repeat meeting someone for the first time, making a first impression in an interview, or resolving a specific group problem.

You can, of course, try again, as when you say, "I'm sorry I came off so forward, can we try again?" But even after you say this, you have not erased the initial impression. Instead you try to counteract this initial and perhaps negative impression by going through the motions again.

Censoring Messages and Interactions

In all aspects of human communication, censors may intervene and regulate both the content and the relationship messages you receive.

- The content messages you receive from television and newspapers are censored by programmers and editors. Teachers, authors, and newsgroup moderators censor the information you receive in the classroom, in books, and online.
- Relationships and relationship messages also are censored; censors encourage certain relationships and discourage or even prevent other relationships. Religions are powerful relationship censors in that

many faiths attempt to censor relationships between their members and people of other religions—for example, by blessing intrareligious relationships and not blessing or even condemning interreligious relationships. Parents and friends also function as censors. Parents, for example, often encourage their children to play and become friends with children from the same racial or national group and religion, but discourage friendships with children from different cultures. Your friends also may exert pressure on you to date one person and not another, to associate with some people but not others.

WHAT WOULD YOU DO? John is interested in Colleen and so approaches Jennifer (her best friend) to ask if Colleen would go out with him. John's been charged with physically abusing his former girlfriend, and rumor has it that he's still married. Even so, Colleen is extremely vulnerable and would probably be tempted by John's fast talk. Jennifer, convinced that John would be bad for Colleen, tells him that Colleen would not date him and says nothing to Colleen. Was Jennifer ethical in lying to John? Was she ethical in concealing John's interest from Colleen? If you were Colleen's best friend, what would you do in this situation?

SUMMARY

In this unit we looked at some of the principles of human communication, principles that explain what communication is and how it works in a wide variety of situations and contexts.

1. Communication is normally a package of signals, each reinforcing the other. Opposing communication signals from the same source result in contradictory messages.
2. The double bind, a special kind of contradictory message, may be created when contradictory messages are sent simultaneously.
3. Communication is a process of adjustment and takes place only to the extent that the communicators use the same system of signals.
4. Communication involves both content dimensions and relationship dimensions.
5. Communication is ambiguous and often can be interpreted in different ways.
6. Communication sequences are punctuated for processing. Different people divide up the communication sequence into stimuli and responses differently.
7. Communication involves symmetrical and complementary transactions.
8. In any interactional situation, communication is inevitable; you can't avoid communicating, nor can you not respond to communication.
9. Communication is irreversible. You can't uncommunicate.
10. Communication is unrepeatable. You can't duplicate a previous communication act.

KEY TERMS

transaction
adjustment
content messages
relationship messages
punctuation of communication
symmetrical relationship
complementary relationship
inevitability
irreversibility
unrepeatability

THINKING CRITICALLY ABOUT

The Principles of Human Communication

1. For a good illustration of contradictory messages (sometimes called double-bind messages), consider the interaction between a therapist and a client with disabilities: Often, each seems to send contradictory messages that create "double binds" for the other (Esten & Wilmott, 1993). The client communicates both the desire to focus on the disability and the desire to disregard it. What does the therapist do? If the therapist focuses on the disability, it's in violation of the client's desire to ignore it—but if the therapist ignores it, it's in violation of the client's desire to concentrate on it. Regardless of how the therapist responds, the response will violate one of the client's preferences. What guidelines would you offer the therapist or the client, based on your understanding of contradictory messages?
2. Do you accommodate to the communication styles of those with whom you interact? Do teachers and students or lawyers and witnesses or doctors and patients accommodate to each other's communication styles? In what direction is there likely to be greater accommodation? For example, is the teacher or the student more likely to accommodate the other? Do you find that men and women accommodate differently? If so, in what ways?
3. Some researchers (for example, Beier, 1974) argue that the impulse to communicate two different feelings (for example, "I love you" and "I don't love you") creates messages in which the nonverbal contradicts the verbal message. Do you think this idea has validity? What other explanations might you offer to account for contradictory messages?
4. With very good intentions, you say to your partner, "I guess you'll just never learn how to dress." To your surprise your partner becomes extremely offended. Although you know you can't take the statement back (communication really is irreversible), you want to lessen its negative tone and its effect on your partner. What do you say?

UNIT

3

Culture and Communication

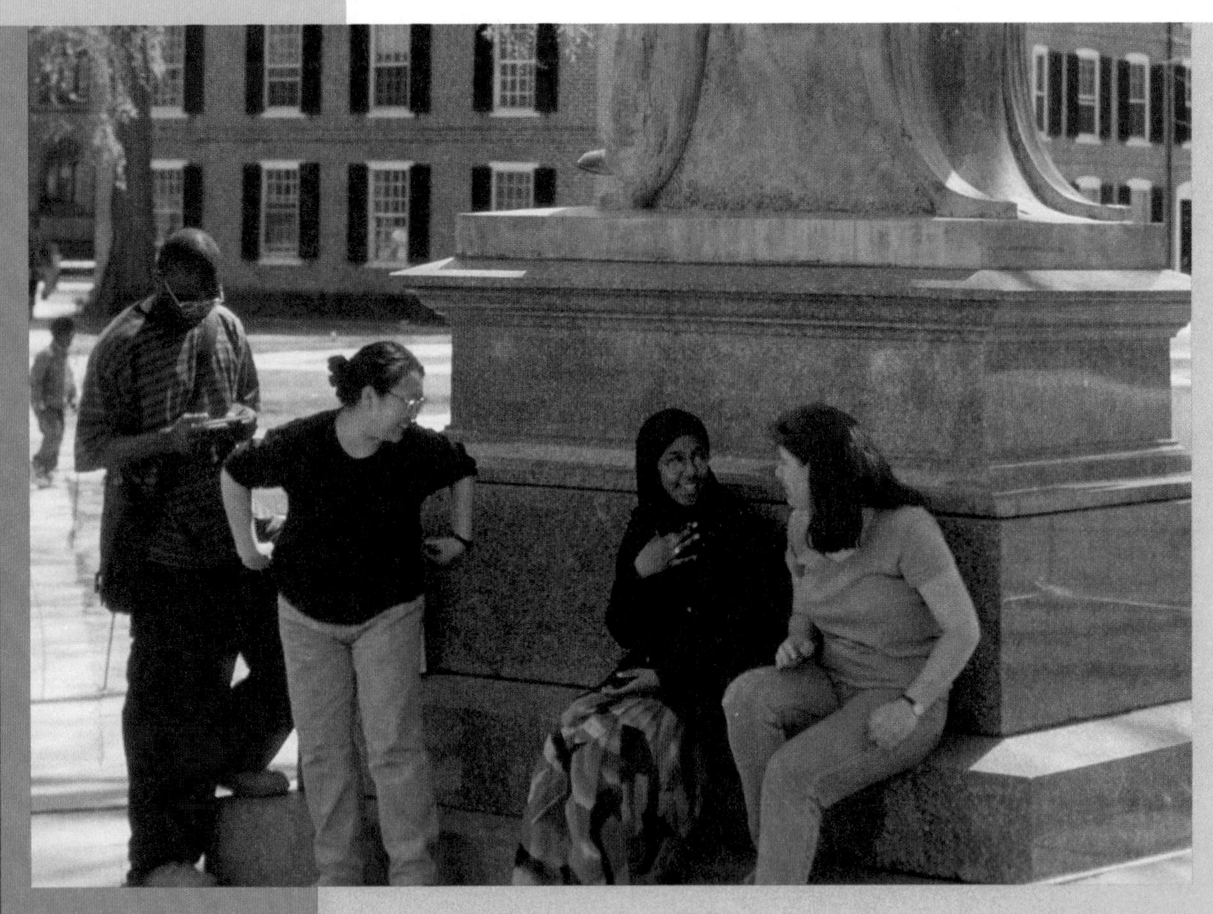

UNIT CONTENTS

When you speak or listen, you're doing so as a member of a particular and unique culture—you're greatly influenced by the teachings of your religion, racial and national history, the social expectations for your gender, and a host of other factors. In this unit you'll learn

- what culture is and how it influences communication
- how you can communicate more effectively in a world that's becoming increasingly multicultural

What Is Culture?

Culture (introduced briefly in Unit 1) consists of the relatively specialized lifestyle of a group of people: their values, beliefs, artifacts, ways of behaving, and ways of communicating. Included in a social group's "culture" is everything that members of that group have produced and developed—their language; ways of thinking; art; laws; religion; and, of course, communication theories, styles, and attitudes.

Culture is passed on from one generation to the next through communication, not through genes. Thus, the term *culture* does not refer to color of skin or shape of eyes, as these are passed on through genes, not communication. Because members of a particular race or country are often taught similar beliefs, attitudes, and values, this similarity makes it possible to speak of "Hispanic culture" or "African American culture." But it's important to realize that within any large culture—especially a culture based on race or nationality—there will be enormous differences. The Kansas farmer and the Wall Street executive may both be, say, German American, but may differ widely in their attitudes, beliefs, and lifestyles. In some ways the Kansas farmer may be closer in attitudes and values to a Chinese farmer than to the New York financier.

Gender—although it is transmitted genetically and not by communication—is considered a cultural variable largely because cultures teach boys and girls different attitudes, beliefs, values, and ways of communicating and relating to one another. Thus, you act like a man or a woman in part because of what your culture has taught you about how men

UNDERSTANDING *THEORY* AND *RESEARCH*

Cultural Theories

Consider two very different theories of culture: cultural evolution and cultural relativism. The theory of *cultural evolution* (often called social Darwinism) holds that much as the human species evolved from lower life forms to *Homo sapiens,* cultures also evolve. Consequently, some cultures may be considered advanced and others primitive. Most contemporary scholars reject this view, because the judgments that distinguish one culture from another have no basis in science and are instead based on individual values and preferences as to what constitutes "advanced" and what constitutes "primitive."

The *cultural relativism* approach, on the other hand, holds that all cultures are different but that no culture is either superior or inferior to any other (Berry, Poortinga, Segall, & Dasen, 1992). This view is generally accepted today and guides the infusion of cultural materials into contemporary textbooks on all academic levels (Jandt, 2004). But this position does not imply that all cultural practices are therefore equal or that you have to accept all cultural practices equally. As noted in the text, there are many cultural practices popular throughout the world that you may find, quite logically and reasonably, unacceptable.

Working with Theories and Research

- *If you have access, log on to Research Navigator (www.researchnavigator.com) and investigate these two positions further. What do you think of these positions? What arguments could you advance in support of or against each of these theories?*

and women should act. This does not, of course, deny that biological differences also play a role in the differences between male and female behavior. In fact, research continues to uncover biological roots of male/female differences we once thought were entirely learned (McCroskey, 1997).

Culture is transmitted from one generation to another through **enculturation,** the process by which you learn the culture into which you're born (your native culture). Parents, peer groups, schools, religious institutions, and government agencies are the main teachers of culture.

A different process of learning culture is **acculturation,** the process by which you learn the rules and norms of a culture different from your native culture. In acculturation your original or native culture is modified through direct contact with or exposure to a new and different culture. For example, when immigrants settle in the United States (the host culture), their own culture becomes influenced by the host culture. Gradually, the values, ways of behaving, and beliefs of the host culture become more and more a part of the immigrants' culture. At the same time, of course, the host culture changes too as it interacts with the immigrants' culture. Generally, however, the culture of the immigrant changes more. The reasons for this are that the host country's members far outnumber the immigrant group and that the media are largely dominated by and reflect the values and customs of the host culture (Kim, 1988).

New citizens' acceptance of the new culture depends on many factors (Kim, 1988). Immigrants who come from cultures similar to the host culture will become acculturated more easily. Similarly, those who are younger and better educated become acculturated more quickly than do older and less well educated people. Personality factors also play a part. Persons who are risk takers and open-minded, for example, have greater acculturation potential. Also, persons who are familiar with the host culture before immigration—through interpersonal contact or through media exposure—will be acculturated more readily.

Before exploring further the role of culture in communication, consider your own cultural values and beliefs by taking the self-test below. This test illustrates how your own cultural values and beliefs may influence your interpersonal, small group, and public communications—both the messages you send and the messages you listen to.

TEST YOURSELF

What Are Your Cultural Beliefs and Values?

Here the extremes of eight cultural differences are identified. For each characteristic indicate your own values:

a. If you feel your values are very similar to the extremes, then select 1 or 7.
b. If you feel your values are quite similar to the extremes, then select 2 or 6.
c. If you feel your values are fairly similar to the extremes, then select 3 or 5.
d. If you feel you're in the middle, then select 4.

Men and women are equal and are entitled to equality in all areas.	**Gender Equality** 1 2 3 4 5 6 7	Men and women are very different and should stick to the specific roles assigned to them by their culture.
"Success" is measured by your contribution to the group.	**Group and Individual Orientation** 1 2 3 4 5 6 7	"Success" is measured by how far you outperform others.
You should enjoy yourself as much as possible.	**Hedonism** 1 2 3 4 5 6 7	You should work as much as possible.
Religion is the final arbiter of what is right and wrong; your first obligation is to abide by the rules and customs of your religion.	**Religion** 1 2 3 4 5 6 7	Religion is like any other social institution; it's not inherently moral or right just because it's a religion.
Your first obligation is to your family; each person is responsible for the welfare of his or her family.	**Family** 1 2 3 4 5 6 7	Your first obligation is to yourself; each person is responsible for himself or herself.
Romantic relationships, once made, are forever.	**Relationship Permanency** 1 2 3 4 5 6 7	Romantic relationships should be maintained as long as they're more rewarding than punishing and dissolved when they're more punishing than rewarding.

People should express their emotions openly and freely.	**Emotional Expression** **1 2 3 4 5 6 7**	People should not reveal their emotions, especially those that may reflect negatively on them or others or make others feel uncomfortable.
Money is extremely important and should be a major consideration in just about any decision you make.	**Money** **1 2 3 4 5 6 7**	Money is relatively unimportant and should not enter into life's really important decisions, such as what relationship to enter or what career to pursue.

HOW DID YOU DO? This test was designed to help you explore the possible influence of your cultural beliefs and values on communication. If you visualize communication as involving choices, then your beliefs will influence the choices you make and thus how you communicate and how you listen and respond to the communications of others. For example, your beliefs and values about gender equality will influence the way in which you communicate with and about the opposite sex. Your group and individual orientation will influence how you perform in work teams and how you deal with your peers at school and at work. Your degree of hedonism will influence the kinds of communications you engage in, the books you read, and the television programs you watch. Your religious beliefs will influence the ethical system you follow in communicating. Review the entire list of characteristics and try to identify one specific way in which each characteristic influences your communication.

WHAT WILL YOU DO? Are you satisfied with your responses? If not, how might you get rid of your unproductive or unrealistic beliefs? What beliefs would you ideally like to substitute for these?

The Relationship between Culture and Communication

There are lots of reasons for the current cultural emphasis in the field of communication. Here are several of the more important reasons.

Demographic Changes

Most obvious, perhaps, are the vast demographic changes taking place throughout the United States. Whereas at one time the United States was largely a country populated by northern Europeans, it's now a country greatly influenced by the enormous number of new citizens from Central and South America, Africa, and Asia. And the same is true to an even greater extent on college and university campuses throughout the United States. With these changes have come different customs and the need to understand and adapt to new ways of looking at communication (see Figure 3.1 on page 40).

Cultural Sensitivity

As a people we've become increasingly sensitive to cultural differences. American society has moved from an assimilationist perspective (which holds that people should leave their native culture behind and adapt to their new culture) to a perspective that values cultural diversity (which holds that people should retain their native cultural ways). And, with some notable exceptions—hate speech, racism, sexism, homophobia, and classism come quickly to mind—we're more concerned with communicating respectfully and ultimately with developing a society where all cultures can coexist and enrich each other. At the same time, the ability to interact effectively with members of other cultures often translates into financial gain and increased employment opportunities and advancement prospects.

Economic Interdependency

Today most countries are economically dependent on one another. Our economic lives depend on our ability to communicate effectively across different cultures. Similarly, our political well-being depends in great part on that of other cultures. Political unrest in any part of the world—South Africa, eastern Europe, or the Middle East, to take a few examples—affects our security in the United States. Following the World Trade Center and Pentagon attacks, it became especially clear that intercultural communication and understanding are now more crucial than ever.

Communication Technology and Competence

The rapid spread of communication technology has brought foreign and sometimes very different cultures right into our living rooms. News from foreign countries is commonplace. You see nightly—in vivid color—what is going on in remote countries. Technology has made intercultural communication easy,

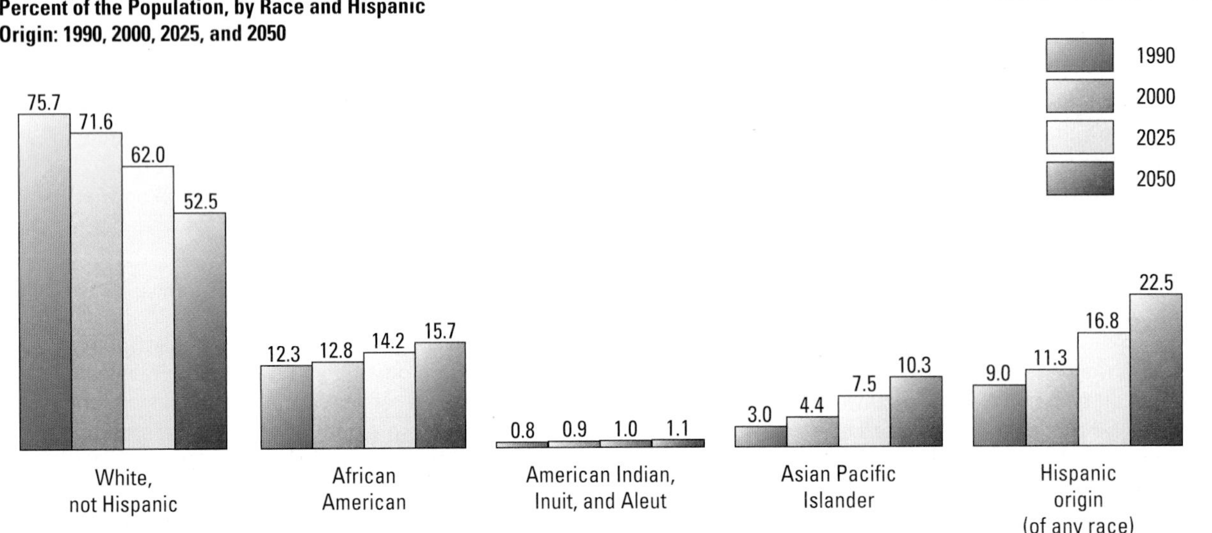

Figure 3.1

The Faces of the Nation

This figure shows the percentages of the U.S. population made up of various ethnic groups in 1990 and 2000 and the projections for the years 2025 and 2050 (U.S. Bureau of the Census, 2001). It's important to realize that within each group there are also wide cultural variations. Whites from Sweden are culturally quite different from whites from Greece or Russia, and Asians from Japan are culturally quite different from those from China or Korea. To complicate matters even further, not all Japanese or all Chinese or all Koreans are culturally similar. There are wide variations within each country, just as there are cultural differences between whites from, say, Manhattan and rural Tennessee. Visit one of the population websites and examine the cultural makeup of your state or county (www.census.gov). How do the figures for your state or county compare to those presented here for the country as whole?

practical, and inevitable. Daily the media bombard you with evidence of racial tensions, religious disagreements, sexual bias, and all the other problems caused when intercultural communication fails. And, of course, the Internet has made intercultural communication as easy as writing a note on your computer. You can now communicate by e-mail just as easily with someone in Europe or Asia, for example, as with someone in another city or state.

Communication competence is specific to a given culture; what proves effective in one culture may be ineffective in another. For example, in the United States corporate executives get down to business during the first several minutes of a meeting. In Japan, however, business executives interact socially for an extended period and try to find out something about one another. Thus, the communication principle influenced by U.S. culture would advise participants to get down to the meeting's agenda during the first five minutes. The principle influenced by Japanese culture would advise participants to avoid dealing with business until everyone has socialized sufficiently and feels well enough acquainted to begin negotiations. Each principle seems effective within its own culture and ineffective outside its own culture. For example, Asians often find that the values they have learned—values that discourage competitiveness and assertiveness—work against them in Western cultures that endorse competition and outspokenness (Cho, 2000).

The Aim of a Cultural Perspective

Because culture permeates all forms of communication, it is necessary to understand its influences if you are to understand how communication works and master its skills. As illustrated throughout this text, culture influences communications of all types (Moon, 1996). It influences what you say to yourself and how you talk with friends, lovers, and family in everyday conversation. It influences how you interact in groups and how much importance you place on the group versus the individual. It influences the topics you talk about and the strategies you use in communicating information or in persuading. And it

COMMUNICATION@WORK

Culture in the Workplace

The inherent preferences of organizations are clarity, certainty, and perfection. The inherent nature of human relationships involves ambiguity, uncertainty, and imperfection.

—Richard Tanner Pascale and Anthony G. Athos

Each organization, much like any culture, has its own rituals, norms, and rules for communicating. These rules—whether in an interview situation or in a friendly conversation—delineate appropriate and inappropriate verbal and nonverbal behavior, specify rewards (or punishments for breaking the rules), and tell you what will help you get the job and what won't. For example, the general advice given throughout this text is to emphasize your positive qualities, to highlight your abilities, and to minimize any negative characteristics or failings. But in some organizations—especially in collectivist cultures such as those of China, Korea, and Japan—workers are expected to show modesty (Copeland & Griggs, 1985). If you stress your own competencies too much, you may be seen as arrogant, brash, and unfit to work in an organization where teamwork and cooperation are emphasized.

In collectivist organizational cultures great deference is to be shown to managers, who represent the company. If you don't treat managers with respect, you may appear to be disrespecting the entire company. In the individualist cultures that prevail in many U.S. companies, on the other hand, too much deference may make you appear unassertive, unsure of yourself, and unqualified to assume a position of authority. Not surprisingly, research finds that Japanese managers emphasize cooperation and exert influence through appeals to personal motives. American managers, on the other hand, emphasize individualism and exert influence through the control of rewards and punishments (Hirokawa & Miyahara, 1986; Hirokawa & Wagner, 2004).

Communicating@Work

Can you identify at least one rule or norm that operated in a place in which you worked? How did you learn this rule? What happened when it was violated?

influences how you use the media and the credibility you attribute to them.

A cultural emphasis helps distinguish what is universal (true for all people) from what is relative (true for people in one culture but not for people in other cultures) (Matsumoto, 1994). The principles for communicating information and for changing listeners' attitudes, for example, will vary from one culture to another. If you are to understand communication, then you need to know how its principles vary and how the principles must be qualified and adjusted on the basis of cultural differences.

And of course this cultural understanding is necessary to communicate effectively in a wide variety of intercultural situations. Success in communication—on your job and in your social life—will depend on your ability to communicate effectively with persons who are culturally different from yourself.

As demonstrated throughout this text, cultural differences exist across the communication spectrum—from the way you use eye contact to the way you develop or dissolve a relationship (Chang & Holt, 1996). But these should not blind you to the great number of similarities that also exist among even the most widely separated cultures. Close interpersonal relationships, for example, are common in all cultures, though they may be entered into for very different reasons by members of different cultures. Further, when reading about cultural differences, remember that these are usually matters of degree. Thus, most cultures value honesty, but not all value it to the same degree. Also, advances in media and technology and the widespread use of the Internet are influencing cultures and cultural change and are perhaps homogenizing cultures to some extent, lessening the differences and increasing the similarities. They are also tending to Americanize different cultures, because the dominant values and customs evidenced in the media and on the Internet are in large part American, a product of current U.S. dominance in both media and technology.

An emphasis on cultural awareness does not imply that you should accept all cultural practices or that all cultural practices are equal (Hatfield & Rapson,1996). For example, cockfighting, foxhunting, and bullfighting are parts of the culture of some Latin American countries, England, and Spain, but you need not find these activities acceptable or equal to cultural practices in which animals are treated kindly. Further, a cultural emphasis does not imply that you have to accept or follow even the practices of your own culture. For example, even if the majority in your culture finds cockfighting acceptable, you need not agree with or follow the practice. Similarly, you can reject your culture's values and beliefs; its religion or political system; or its attitudes toward the homeless, the handicapped, or the culturally different. Of course, going against your culture's traditions and values is often very difficult. But it is important to realize that although culture influences you, it does not determine your values or behavior. Often, for example, personality factors (such as your degree of assertiveness, extroversion, or optimism) will prove more influential than culture (Hatfield & Rapson, 1996).

How Cultures Differ

There are at least four major ways in which cultures differ that are especially important for communication. Following Hofstede (1997) and Hall and Hall (1987), we'll consider (1) collectivism and individu-

MEDIA WATCH

Cultural Imperialism

The theory of cultural imperialism affords an interesting perspective on the influence of media, especially the impact of Western media on the cultures of developing countries (Becker & Roberts, 1992; DeZoysa & Newman, 2002). The theory argues that media from developed countries such as those of North America and Western Europe dominate the cultures of countries importing such media. This cultural dominance is also seen in computer communication, in which the United States and the English language dominate.

Media products from the United States emphasize the country's dominant attitudes and values—for example, the preference for competition, the emphasis on individual expression, the advantages of capitalism and democracy, and the quest for financial success. An extreme form of the theory of cultural imperialism argues that the attitudes and values of the dominant media culture will eventually become the attitudes and values of the rest of the world.

Television programs, films, and music from the United States and Western Europe are so popular and so in demand in developing countries that they may actually inhibit the growth of the native culture's own talent. So, for example, instead of creating their own vision in an original television drama or film, native writers in developing countries may find it easier to work as translators for products from more developed countries. And native promoters may find it more lucrative to sell, say, U.S. rock groups' CDs than to cultivate native talent. Similarly, the popularity of U.S. and Western European media may also lead artists in developing countries to imitate Western cultural artifacts rather than developing their own styles—styles more consistent with their native culture.

From another perspective, however, some people might argue that media products from the United States are superior to those produced elsewhere and hence serve as a standard for quality work throughout the world. Also, it might be argued that such products introduce new trends and perspectives and hence enrich the importing cultures.

You and the Media

What do you think of the influence that media from the United States and Western Europe are having on native cultures throughout the world? How do you evaluate this trend? Do you see advantages? Disadvantages?

alism, (2) high and low context, (3) power distances, and (4) masculine and feminine cultures.

Individual and Collective Orientation

Cultures differ in the way in which they promote individualist and collectivist thinking and behaving. An **individualist culture** teaches members the importance of individual values such as power, achievement, hedonism, and stimulation. A **collectivist culture** teaches members the importance of group values such as benevolence, tradition, and conformity. Americans generally have a preference for individualist values; in contrast, many Asian cultures have a preference for collectivist values (Kapoor, Wolfe, & Blue, 1995; Hofstede, 1997).

One of the major differences between these two orientations is the extent to which an individual's goals or the group's goals are given greater importance. Of course, these goals are not mutually exclusive; you probably have both individualist and collectivist tendencies. For example, you may compete with other members of your basketball team for the most baskets or most valuable player award (and thus emphasize individual goals). At the same time, however, you will—in a game—act in a way that will benefit the entire team (and thus emphasize group goals). In actual practice both individual and collective tendencies will help you and your team each achieve your goals. Yet most people and most cultures have a dominant orientation; they're more individually oriented or more collectively oriented in most situations, most of the time. In an individualist culture members are responsible for themselves and perhaps their immediate family. In a collectivist culture members are responsible for the entire group.

In some instances these tendencies may come into conflict. For example, do you shoot for the basket and try to raise your own individual score, or do

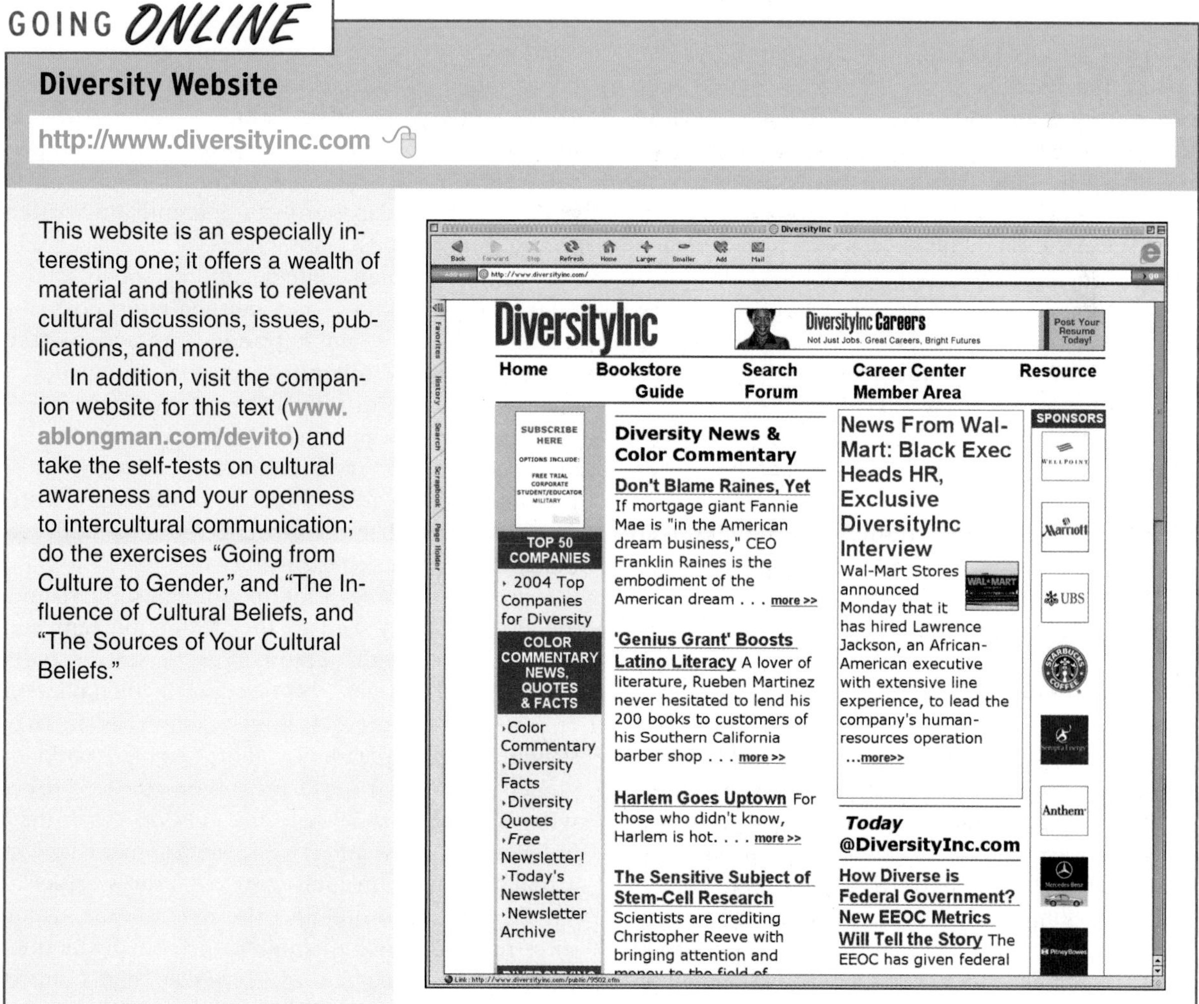

you pass the ball to another player who is better positioned to score and thus benefit your team? You make this distinction in popular talk when you call someone a team player (collectivist orientation) or an individual player (individualist orientation).

Success, in an individualist culture, is measured by the extent to which you surpass other members of your group; you take pride in standing out from the crowd. And your heroes—in the media, for example—are likely to be those who are unique and who stand apart. In a collectivist culture success is measured by your contribution to the achievements of the group as a whole; you take pride in your similarity to other members of your group. Your heroes are more likely to be team players who don't stand out from the rest of the group's members.

In an individualist culture you're responsible to your own conscience, and responsibility is largely an individual matter; in a collectivist culture you're responsible to the rules of the social group, and responsibility for an accomplishment or a failure is shared by all members. Competition is fostered in individualist cultures, whereas cooperation is promoted in collectivist cultures. In small group settings in an individualist culture, you may compete for leadership; there will likely be a very clear distinction between leaders and members. In a collectivist culture leadership will often be shared and rotated; there will likely be little distinction between leader and members. These orientations also influence the kinds of communication members consider appropriate in an organizational context. For example, individualist organization members favor clarity and directness; in contrast, collectivists favor "face-saving" and the avoidance of hurting others or arousing negative evaluations (Kim & Sharkey, 1995).

Distinctions between in-group members and out-group members are extremely important in collectivist cultures. In individualistic cultures, which prize each person's individuality, the distinction is likely to be less important.

High- and Low-Context Cultures

Cultures also differ in the extent to which information is made explicit, on the one hand, or is assumed to be in the context or in the persons communicating, on the other. In a **high-context culture** much of the information in communication is in the context or in the person—for example, information that was shared through previous communications, through assumptions about each other, and through shared experiences. The information is thus known by all participants but it is not explicitly stated in the verbal message.

In a **low-context culture** most of the information is explicitly stated in the verbal message. In formal transactions it will be stated in written (or contract) form.

To appreciate the distinction between high and low context, consider giving directions ("Where's the voter registration center?") to someone who knows the neighborhood and to a newcomer to your city. With someone who knows the neighborhood (a high-context situation), you can assume that the person knows the local landmarks. So you can give directions such as "next to the laundromat on Main Street" or "the corner of Albany and Elm." With a newcomer (a low-context situation), you cannot assume that the person shares any information with you. So you have to use only those directions that even a stranger will understand; for example, "Make a left at the next stop sign" or "Go two blocks and then turn right."

High-context cultures are also collectivist cultures (Gudykunst, Ting-Toomey, & Chua, 1988; Gudykunst & Kim, 1992). These cultures (Japanese, Arabic, Latin American, Thai, Korean, Apache, and Mexican are examples) place great emphasis on personal relationships and oral agreements (Victor, 1992). Low-context cultures are also individualist cultures. These cultures (German, Swedish, Norwegian, and American are examples) place less emphasis on personal relationships and more emphasis on verbalized, explicit explanation—for example, on written contracts in business transactions.

Members of high-context cultures spend lots of time getting to know one another interpersonally and socially before any important transactions take place. Because of this prior personal knowledge, a great deal of information is shared by the members and therefore does not have to be explicitly stated. Members of low-context cultures spend a great deal less time getting to know one another and hence don't have that shared knowledge. As a result everything has to be stated explicitly.

A frequent source of intercultural misunderstanding that can be traced to the distinction between high- and low-context cultures can be seen in **face-saving** (Hall & Hall, 1987). People in high-context cultures place a great deal more emphasis on face-saving. For example, they're more likely to avoid argument for fear of causing others to lose face, whereas people in low-context cultures (with their individualist orientation) will use argument to win a point. Similarly, in high-context cultures criticism should take place only in private. Low-context cultures may not make this public–private distinction. Low-context managers who criticize high-context workers in public will find that their criticism causes

UNDERSTANDING *THEORY* AND *RESEARCH*

Language and Thought

The linguistic relativity hypothesis claims that (1) the language you speak influences the thoughts you have, and (2) therefore, people speaking widely differing languages will see the world differently and will think differently.

Theory and research, however, have not been able to find much support for this claim. A more modified hypothesis currently seems supported: The language you speak helps you to talk about what you see and perhaps to highlight what you see. For example, if you speak a language that is rich in color terms (English is a good example), you will find it easier to talk about nuances of color than will someone from a culture that has fewer color terms (some cultures, for example, distinguish only two, three, or four parts of the color spectrum). But, this doesn't mean that people see the world differently, only that their language helps (or doesn't help) them to talk about certain variations in the world and may make it easier (or more difficult) for them to focus their thinking on such variations.

Nor does it mean that people speaking widely differing languages are doomed to misunderstand one another. Translation enables you to understand a great deal of the meaning in any foreign language message. And, of course, you have your communication skills; you can ask for clarification, for additional examples, for restatement. You can listen actively, give feedforward and feedback, use perception checking, and employ a host of other skills you'll encounter throughout this course.

Language differences don't make for very important differences in perception or thought. Difficulties in intercultural understanding are due more often to ineffective communication than to differences in languages.

Working with Theories and Research

- *Based on your own experience, how influential do you find language differences to be in perception and thought? Can you recall any misunderstandings that might be attributed to a particular language's leading its speakers to see or interpret things differently?*

interpersonal problems—and does little to resolve the difficulty that led to the criticism in the first place (Victor, 1992).

Members of high-context cultures are reluctant to say *no* for fear of offending and causing the person to lose face. So, for example, it's necessary to understand when the Japanese executive's yes means yes and when it means no. The difference is not in the words used but in the way in which they're used. It's easy to see how the low-context individual may interpret this reluctance to be direct—to say no when you mean no—as a weakness or as an unwillingness to confront reality.

Power Distances

In some cultures power is concentrated in the hands of a few, and there's a great difference between the power held by these people and the power of the ordinary citizen. These are called **high-power-distance cultures;** examples are Mexico, Brazil, India, and the Philippines (Hofstede, 1997). In **low-power-distance cultures,** power is more evenly distributed throughout the citizenry; examples include Denmark, New Zealand, Sweden, and to a lesser extent the United States. These differences impact communication in numerous ways. For example, in high-power-distance cultures there's a great power distance between students and teachers; students are expected to be modest, polite, and totally respectful. In low-power-distance cultures (and you can see this clearly in U.S. college classrooms) students are expected to demonstrate their knowledge and command of the subject matter, participate in discussions with the teacher, and even challenge the teacher—something many high-power-distance culture members wouldn't even think of doing.

Friendship and dating relationships will also be influenced by the power distance between groups (Andersen, 1991). In India, for example, such relationships are expected to take place within your cultural class. In Sweden a person is expected to select friends and romantic partners on the basis not of class or culture but of individual factors such as personality, appearance, and the like.

In low-power-distance cultures you're expected to confront a friend, partner, or supervisor assertively; there is in these cultures a general feeling of equality that is consistent with assertive behavior (Borden, 1991). In high-power-distance cultures, direct confrontation and assertiveness may be viewed negatively, especially if directed at a superior.

Masculine and Feminine Cultures

Especially important for self-concept is the culture's attitude about gender roles; that is, about how a man or woman should act. In fact, a popular classification of cultures is in terms of their masculinity and femininity (Hofstede, 1997, 1998). When denoting cultural orientations, the terms *masculine* and *feminine,* and used by G. Hofstede (1997) to describe this cultural difference, should be taken not as perpetuating stereotypes but as a reflecting some of the commonly held assumptions of a sizable number of people throughout the world. In a highly **masculine culture,** people value male aggressiveness, material success, and strength. Women, on the other hand, are valued for their modesty, focus on the quality of life, and tenderness. A highly **feminine culture** values modesty, concern for relationships and the quality of life, and tenderness in both men and women. On the basis of Hofstede's (1997, 1998) research, the 10 countries with the highest masculinity score are (beginning with the highest) Japan, Austria, Venezuela, Italy, Switzerland, Mexico, Ireland, Jamaica, Great Britain, and Germany. The 10 countries with the highest femininity score are (beginning with the highest) Sweden, Norway, Netherlands, Denmark, Costa Rica, Yugoslavia, Finland, Chile, Portugal, and Thailand. Of the 53 countries ranked, the United States ranks 15th most masculine.

Masculine cultures emphasize success and so socialize their members to be assertive, ambitious, and competitive. For example, members of masculine cultures are more likely to confront conflicts directly and to fight out any differences competitively; they're more likely to emphasize win–lose conflict strategies. Feminine cultures emphasize the quality of life and so socialize their members to be modest and to highlight close interpersonal relationships. Feminine cultures, for example, are more likely to utilize compromise and negotiation in resolving conflicts; they're more likely to seek win–win solutions.

Similarly, organizations can be viewed as masculine or feminine. Masculine organizations emphasize competitiveness and aggressiveness. They stress the

BUILDING COMMUNICATION SKILLS

Confronting Intercultural Difficulties

How might you deal with any one or two of the following obstacles to intercultural communication? If you have the opportunity, share responses with others in your class. You'll gain a wealth of practical insights.

1. Karla, a close friend, is really an open-minded person. But she has the habit of referring to members of other racial and ethnic groups and to gay men and lesbians with the most derogatory language. You decide to tell her how you feel about her way of talking.
2. Your parents persist in holding stereotypes about other religious, racial, and ethnic groups. These stereotypes come up in all sorts of conversations. You're really embarrassed by these attitudes and feel you must tell your parents how incorrect you think these stereotypes are.
3. George, a colleague at work, recently underwent a religious conversion. He now persists in trying to get everyone else—you included—to undergo this same religious conversion. You decide to tell him that you find this behavior offensive.

bottom line and reward their workers on the basis of their contribution to the organization. Feminine organizations are less competitive and less aggressive. They emphasize worker satisfaction and reward their workers on the basis of need; those who have large families, for example, may get better raises than single people, even if they haven't contributed as much to the organization.

Improving Intercultural Communication

An understanding of the role of culture in communication is an essential foundation for understanding intercultural communication as it occurs interpersonally, in small groups, in public speaking, or in the media—and for appreciating the principles of effective intercultural communication. As discussed in Unit 1, the term *intercultural communication* refers to communication between persons who have different cultural beliefs, values, or ways of behaving. The model in Figure 3.2 illustrates this concept. The larger circles represent the culture of the individual communicators. The inner circles identify the communicators (the sources-receivers). In this model each communicator is a member of a different culture. In some instances the cultural differences are relatively slight—say, between persons from Toronto and New York. In other instances the cultural differences are great—say, between persons from Borneo and Germany, or between persons from rural Nigeria and industrialized England.

All messages originate from within a specific and unique cultural context, and that context influences their content and form. You communicate as you do largely as a result of your culture. Culture (along with the processes of enculturation and acculturation) influences every aspect of your communication experience.

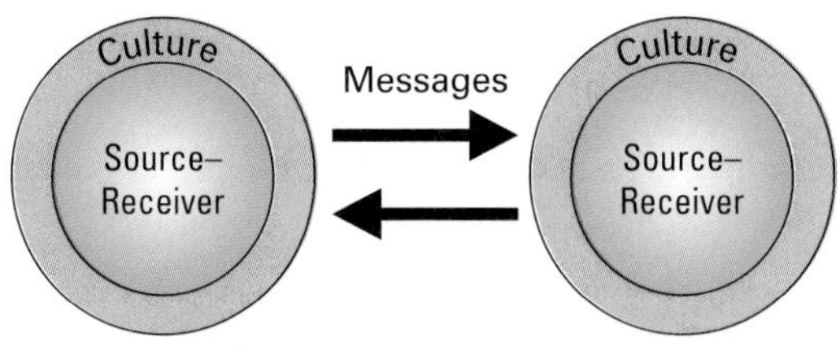

Figure 3.2

A Model of Intercultural Communication

This basic model of intercultural communication is designed to illustrate that culture is a part of every communication transaction, What other ways can you think of to illustrate the process of intercultural communication?

You receive messages through the filters imposed by your cultural context. That context influences what you receive and how you receive it. For example, people in some cultures rely heavily on television or newspapers and trust them implicitly. Others rely on face-to-face interpersonal interactions, distrusting many of the mass communication systems.

Here then are a variety of principles for increasing intercultural communication effectiveness—in conversation, on the job, and in friendly and romantic relationships. These guidelines are based on the intercultural research of a wide variety of researchers (Barna, 1985; Ruben, 1985; Gudykunst & Kim, 1992; Hofstede, 1997, 1998).

Recognize and Reduce Ethnocentrism

As you learn your culture's ways, you develop an **ethnic identity**—that is, a commitment to the beliefs and philosophy of your culture (Chung & Ting-Toomey, 1999). The degree to which you identify with your cultural group can be measured by your responses to such questions as the following (from Ting-Toomey, 1981). Using a scale ranging from 1 (strongly disagree) to 5 (strongly agree), indicate how true of you the following statements are:

- I am increasing my involvement in activities with my ethnic group.
- I involve myself in causes that will help members of my ethnic group.
- It feels natural being part of my ethnic group.
- I have spent time trying to find out more about my own ethnic group.
- I am happy to be a member of my ethnic group.
- I have a strong sense of belonging to my ethnic group.
- I often talk to other members of my group to learn more about my ethnic culture.

High scores (say 5s and 4s) indicate a strong commitment to your culture's values and beliefs; low numbers (1s and 2s) indicate a relatively weak commitment.

A different type of cultural identification is ethnocentrism. Before reading about this important concept, examine your own cultural thinking by taking the self-test on pages 48–49.

ASK THE RESEARCHER

Talking about Culture

■ *I'm going to work abroad in a firm where most of the people are members of a culture very different from mine. I know culture is important; what I don't know is when it's appropriate to discuss cultural differences and when it's not. Any general guidelines I could follow? I don't want to do anything stupid, at least not during my first few weeks.*

Your recognizing that culture is important is the first sign that you'll do well abroad. Intercultural communication as an academic discipline developed because of our (American's) oblivion to other people's cultures, even as guests in their country.

We earned the "ugly American" title because we assumed that American culture was superior to other's, and that despite where we visited or worked, people from the host culture had to acquiesce to our desires. Before you move to a foreign country, learn as much about its culture and people as you can; it will help you accept, appreciate, and respect difference.

Talking about cultural difference is inevitable. It's how you do it. When you notice difference, ask, respectfully, about it, for example, "I noticed that your head is always covered, I've never seen your hair. Is there some cultural or religious reason for it?" Instead of, "Why don't you take that scarf off your head, I get tired of looking at it".

For further information: Calloway-Thomas, C., Cooper, P. J., & Blake, C. (1999). *Intercultural communication: Roots and routes*. Boston: Allyn & Bacon. And Samovar, L. A., & Porter, R. E. (2003). *Intercultural communication: A reader* (10th ed.). Belmont, CA: Wadsworth.

Melbourne S. Cummings (Ph.D., University of California, Los Angeles) is professor of communication at Howard University and teaches courses in African American communication, nonverbal communication, and intercultural communication.

TEST YOURSELF

How Ethnocentric Are You?

Here are 18 statements representing your beliefs about your culture. For each statement indicate how much you agree or disagree, using the following scale: Strongly agree = 5, agree = 4, neither agree nor disagree = 3, disagree = 2, strongly disagree = 1.

____ **1.** Most cultures are backward compared to my culture.

____ **2.** My culture should be the role model for other cultures.

____ **3.** Lifestyles in other cultures are just as valid as those in my culture.

____ **4.** Other cultures should try to be like my culture.

____ **5.** I'm not interested in the values and customs of other cultures.

____ **6.** People in my culture could learn a lot from people in other cultures.

____ **7.** Most people from other cultures just don't know what's good for them.

____ **8.** I have little respect for the values and customs of other cultures.

____ **9.** Most people would be happier if they lived like people in my culture.

____ **10.** People in my culture have just about the best lifestyles of anywhere.

____ **11.** Lifestyles in other cultures are not as valid as those in my culture.

____ **12.** I'm very interested in the values and customs of other cultures.

____ **13.** I respect the values and customs of other cultures.

____ **14.** I do not cooperate with people who are different.

____ **15.** I do not trust people who are different.

____ **16.** I dislike interacting with people from different cultures.

____ **17.** Other cultures are smart to look up to my culture.

____ **18.** People from other cultures act strange and unusual when they come into my culture.

HOW DID YOU DO? This test was presented to give you the opportunity to examine some of your own cultural beliefs, particularly those cultural beliefs that contribute to ethnocentrism. The person who is low in ethnocentrism would have high scores (4s and 5s) for items 3, 6, 12, and 13, and low scores (1s and 2s) for the other items. The person who is high in ethnocentrism would have low scores for items 3, 6, 12, and 13, and high scores for the other items.

WHAT WILL YOU DO? Use this test to bring to consciousness your own cultural beliefs so that you can examine those beliefs logically and objectively. Ask yourself if your beliefs are productive; will they help you achieve your professional and social goals? Or are they counterproductive; will they actually hinder your achieving your goals?

Source: This test is taken from James W. Neuliep, Michelle Chaudoir, and James C. McCroskey (2001). A cross-cultural comparison of ethnocentrism among Japanese and United States college students. *Communication Research Reports, 18* (Spring), 137–146. Used with permission of Eastern Communication Association.

VIEWPOINT

How would you describe your own ethnocentrism immediately after the events of September 11, 2001, and over the next several months? For example, did you become more ethnocentric after these events? Less ethnocentric? How would you describe your current level of ethnocentrism? How do political and social events influence your level of ethnocentrism?

As you've probably gathered from taking this test, **ethnocentrism** is the tendency to see others and their behaviors through your own cultural filters, often as distortions of your own behaviors. It's the tendency to evaluate the values, beliefs, and behaviors of your own culture as more positive, superior, logical, and natural than those of other cultures. So although ethnocentrism may give you pride in your own culture and its achievements and encourage you to sacrifice for that culture, it also may lead you to see other cultures as inferior and may foster an unwillingness to profit from the contributions of other cultures. For example, recent research shows a "substantial relationship" between ethnocentrism and homophobia (Wrench & McCroskey, 2003).

Ethnocentrism exists on a continuum. People are not either ethnocentric or not ethnocentric; rather, most are somewhere between these polar opposites. And, of course, your degree of ethnocentrism varies depending on the group on which you focus. For example, if you're Greek American you may have a low degree of ethnocentrism when dealing with Italian Americans but a high degree when dealing with Turkish Americans or Japanese Americans. Your degree of ethnocentrism (and we're all ethnocentric to at least some degree) will influence your communication in all its forms, an influence illustrated throughout this text.

Confront Your Stereotypes

Stereotypes, especially when they operate below the level of conscious awareness, can create serious communication problems. Originally, *stereotype* was a printing term that referred to the plate that printed the same image over and over. A sociological or psychological **stereotype** is a fixed impression of a group of people. Everyone has attitudinal stereotypes—of national groups, religious groups, or racial groups, or perhaps of criminals, prostitutes, teachers, or plumbers. Consider, for example, if you have any stereotypes of, say, bodybuilders, the opposite sex, a racial group different from your own, members of a religion very different from your own, hard drug users, or college professors. It is very likely that you have stereotypes of several or perhaps all of these groups. Although we often think of stereotypes as negative ("They're lazy, dirty, and only interested in getting high"), they may also be positive ("They're smart, hardworking, and extremely loyal").

If you have these fixed impressions, you might, upon meeting a member of a particular group, see that person primarily as a member of that group. Initially, a stereotype may provide you with some helpful orientation. However, it creates problems when you apply to a person all the characteristics you assign to members of that person's group without examining the unique individual. If you meet a politician, for example, you may tend to apply to the person a series of stereotypical "politician" images. To complicate matters further, you may see in the person's behavior the manifestation of various characteristics that you would not see if you did not know that this person was a politician. In online communication, because there are few visual and auditory cues, it's not surprising to find that people form impressions of their online communication partner with a heavy reliance on stereotypes (Jacobson, 1999).

Consider another kind of stereotype: You're driving along a dark road and are stopped at a stop sign. A car pulls up beside you and three teenagers jump out and rap on your window. There may be a variety of reasons for this: They may need help, they may want to ask directions, or they may be planning a carjacking. Your self-protective stereotype may help you decide on "carjacking" and may lead you to pull away and into the safety of a busy service station. In doing that, of course, you may have escaped being carjacked, or you may have failed to help innocent people who needed your help.

Stereotyping can lead to two major barriers. First, you will fail to appreciate the multifaceted nature of all people and all groups. The tendency to group a person into a class and to respond to that person primarily as a member of that class can lead you to perceive that a person possesses those qualities (usually negative) that you believe characterize the group to which he or she belongs. For example, consider your stereotype of a high computer user. Very likely it's quite different from the research findings—which show that such users are as often female as male and are as sociable, popular, and self-assured as their peers who are not into heavy computer use (Schott & Selwyn 2000).

Second, stereotyping also can lead you to ignore the unique characteristics of an individual; you therefore fail to benefit from the special contributions each person can bring to an encounter.

Be Mindful

Being mindful rather than mindless (a distinction considered in Unit 9) is generally helpful in intercultural communication situations (Burgoon, Berger, & Waldron, 2000). When you're in a mindless state, you behave on the basis of assumptions that would not normally pass intellectual scrutiny. For example, you know that cancer is not contagious, and yet you may still avoid touching cancer patients. You know that people who are blind generally don't have hearing problems, yet you may use a louder voice when talking to persons without sight. When the discrepancies between behaviors and available evidence are pointed out and your mindful state is awakened, you quickly realize that these behaviors are not logical or realistic.

You can look at this textbook and your course in human communication as means of awakening your mindful state about the way you engage in interpersonal, group, and public communication. After completing this course you should be much more mindful and much less mindless about all your communication behavior.

Face Fears

Another factor that stands in the way of effective intercultural communication is fear (Stephan & Stephan, 1985; Gudykunst, 1994). You may fear for your self-esteem. You may become anxious about your ability to control the intercultural situation, or you may worry about your own level of discomfort. You may fear that you'll be taken advantage of by the member of the other culture. Depending on your own stereotypes, you may fear being lied to, financially duped, or made fun of. You may fear that members of this other group will react to you negatively. They may not like you or may disapprove of your attitudes or beliefs or may even reject you as a person. Conversely, you may fear negative reactions from members of your own group. They might, for example, disapprove of your socializing with people who are culturally different.

These fears—coupled with the greater effort that intercultural communication takes and the ease with which we all communicate with those who are culturally similar—can easily create sufficient anxiety to make some people give up.

Recognize Differences

When you assume that all people are similar and ignore the differences between yourself and culturally different persons, your intercultural efforts are likely to fail. This is especially true in the area of values, attitudes, and beliefs. It's easy to see and accept different hairstyles, clothing, and foods. But when it comes to values and beliefs, it's easier to assume (mindlessly) that deep down we're all similar. We aren't. Henry may be a devout Baptist, Carol may be an atheist, and Jan may be a Muslim. Because of the differences in their religious views, each person sees his or her own life as having a very different meaning. When you assume similarities and ignore differences, you may implicitly communicate to others that you feel your ways are right and their ways are wrong. The result is confusion and misunderstanding on both sides.

Be especially alert to differences within cultural groups. Within every cultural group there are wide and important differences. Just as we know that all Americans are not alike (think of the various groups found in your city or even within your own school), so neither are all Jamaicans, Koreans, Mexicans, and so on. Within each culture there are many smaller cultures. These smaller cultures differ from one another and from the majority culture. Further, members of one smaller culture may share a great deal with members of that same smaller culture in another part of the world. Farmers in Indiana may have more in common with farmers in Borneo than with bankers in Indianapolis. For example, all will be concerned with weather conditions, crop rotation, and soil composition. Of course, these farmers, so similar when it comes to farming, may differ drastically on such issues as sales techniques, community governance, and the rights of women.

Avoid Overattribution

Overattribution is the tendency to attribute too much of a person's behavior or attitudes to one of that person's characteristics (she thinks that way because she's a woman; he believes that because he was raised as a Catholic). In intercultural communication situations, overattribution appears in two ways. First, it's the tendency to see too much of what a person believes or does as caused by the person's cultural identification. Second, it's the tendency to see a person as a spokesperson for his or her particular culture—to assume that because a person is, say, African American, he or she is therefore knowledgeable about the entire African American experience; or that the person's thoughts are always focused on African American issues. People's ways of thinking and ways of behaving are influenced by a wide variety of factors; culture is just one of them.

Recognize Differences in Meaning

Meaning does not exist solely in the words we use. Rather, it exists mainly in the person using the words. This principle is especially important in intercultural communication. Consider the differences in meaning that might exist for the word *woman* to an American and an Iranian. What about religion to a Christian fundamentalist and to an atheist, or *lunch* to a Chinese rice farmer and a Wall Street executive? Or consider the meanings of the words *security, future,* and *family* when used by a New England prep school student and by a homeless teenager in Los Angeles.

When it comes to nonverbal messages, the potential differences are even greater. Thus, the over-the-head clasped hands that signify victory to an Ameri-

BUILDING COMMUNICATION SKILLS

Facilitating Intercultural Communication

For any one or two of the following scenarios, which involve people from different cultural orientations, *(a)* identify at least one difference between the two extremes that might cause communication difficulties, and *(b)* identify at least one thing the individuals can do to prevent this difference from obstructing effective communication.

1. A couple (one from an individualist and one from a collectivist culture) see two children fighting in the street; no other adults are around, and the passersby worry that the children may hurt themselves.
2. A group of new advertising executives (three from a high-context culture and three from a low-context culture) prepare to interact for the first time.
3. Two businesspeople (one from a high-context culture and one from a low-context culture) negotiate a contract for a jointly owned restaurant.
4. At work one female colleague (with a highly "masculine" cultural style) tells another woman (with a highly "feminine" cultural style) that she has chronic fatigue syndrome and is awaiting results of her blood tests.

can may signify friendship to a Russian. To an American, holding up two fingers to make a V signifies victory. To certain South Americans, however, it's an obscene gesture that corresponds to our extended middle finger. Tapping the side of your nose will signify that you and the other person are in on a secret in England or Scotland, but that the other person is nosy in Wales. A friendly wave of the hand will prove insulting in Greece, where the wave of friendship must show the back rather than the front of the hand.

Avoid Violating Cultural Rules and Customs

Each culture has its own rules and customs for communicating. These **cultural rules** identify what is appropriate and what is inappropriate. Thus, for example, if you lived in a middle-class community in Connecticut, you would follow the rules of the culture and call the person you wished to date three or four days in advance. If you lived in a different culture, you might be expected to call the parents of your future date weeks or even months in advance. In this same Connecticut community, you might say, as a courteous remark to people you don't ever want to see again, "Come on over and pay us a visit." In other cultures, this comment would be sufficient to cause these people to visit at their convenience.

In some cultures people show respect by avoiding direct eye contact with the person to whom they're speaking. In other cultures this same eye avoidance would signal lack of interest. In some Mediterranean cultures men walk arm in arm. Other cultures consider this inappropriate.

A good example of a series of rules for an extremely large and important culture that many people don't know appears in Table 3.1.

Avoid Evaluating Differences Negatively

Be careful not to evaluate negatively the cultural differences you perceive. That is, avoid falling into the trap of ethnocentric thinking, evaluating your culture positively and other cultures negatively. For example, many Americans of northern European descent evaluate negatively the tendency of many Hispanics and southern Europeans to use the street for a gathering place, for playing dominoes, and for just sitting on a cool evening. Whether you like or dislike using the street in this way, recognize that neither attitude is logically correct or incorrect. This street behavior is simply adequate or inadequate for members of the culture.

Remember that you learned your behaviors from your culture. The behaviors are not natural or innate. Therefore, try viewing these variations nonevaluatively. See them as different but equal.

Recognize That Culture Shock Is Normal

The term **culture shock** refers to the psychological reaction you experience at being in a culture very different from your own (Furnham & Bochner, 1986). Culture shock is normal; most people experience it when entering a new and different culture.

VIEWPOINT

In what ways will intercultural communication figure into your professional life? Your social and personal life? Are there intercultural communication situations that you feel less comfortable in than you'd like to?

Table 3.1
Interpersonal Communication Tips

Between People with and without Disabilities
The suggestions offered here are considered appropriate in the United States, though not necessarily in other cultures. For example, although most people in the United States accept the phrase "person with mental retardation," it's considered offensive to many in the United Kingdom (Fernald, 1995).

If you're the one without such a disability:

1. *Avoid negative terms and terms that define the person as disabled such as "the disabled man" or "the handicapped child."* Instead say "person with a disability," always emphasizing the person rather than the disability. Avoid terms that describe the person with a disability as abnormal; for example, when you refer to people without disabilities as "normal," you in effect say that a person with a disability isn't normal.
2. *Treat assistive devices such as wheelchairs, canes, walkers, or crutches as the personal property of the user.* Be careful not to move these out of your way; they're for the convenience of the person with the disability. Avoid leaning on a person's wheelchair, for example; it's similar to leaning on a person.
3. *Shake hands with the person with the disability if you shake hands with others in a group.* Don't avoid shaking hands if an individual's hand is crippled, for example.
4. *Avoid talking about the person with a disability in the third person.* For example, avoid saying, "Doesn't he get around beautifully with the new crutches." Always direct your comments directly to the individual.
5. *Don't assume that people who have a disability are intellectually impaired.* Slurred speech—such as may occur with people who have cerebral palsy or cleft palate—should never be taken as indicating a low-level intellect. Be especially careful not to talk down to such people as, research shows, many people do (Unger, 2001).
6. *When you're not sure of how to act, ask.* For example, if you're not sure if you should offer walking assistance, ask: "Would you like me to help you into the dining room?" And, even more important, accept the person's response. If he or she says no, then that means no; don't insist.
7. *Maintain similar eye level.* If a person is in a wheelchair, for example, it might be helpful for you to sit down or kneel down to get onto the same eye level.

If you're the one with a disability:

1. *Let the other person know if he or she can do anything to assist you in communicating.* For example, if you want someone to speak in a louder voice, ask. If you want to relax and have someone push your wheelchair, say so.
2. *Be patient and understanding.* Many people mean well but may simply not know how to act or what to say. Put them at ease as best you can.
3. *Demonstrate your own comfort.* If you detect discomfort in the other person, you might talk a bit about your disability to show that you're not uncomfortable and that you understand that others may not know how you feel. But don't feel this is something you should or have to do; you're under no obligation to educate the public.

These suggestions are based on a wide variety of sources; for example, http://www.empowermentzone.com/etiquet.txt (the website for the National Center for Access Unlimited), http://www.dol.gov/dol/top/disability/index.htm, http://www.dissvcs.uga.edu/com-peodis.html, and http://www.ucpa.org/ ucp_generaldoc.cfm (all accessed October 23, 2004).

Nevertheless, it can be unpleasant and frustrating and can sometimes lead to a permanently negative attitude toward this new culture. Understanding the normalcy of culture shock will help lessen any potential negative implications.

Part of culture shock results from your feelings of alienation, conspicuousness, and difference from everyone else. When you lack knowledge of the rules and customs of the new society, you can't communicate effectively. You're apt to blunder frequently and seriously. The person experiencing culture shock may not know some very basic things:

- how to ask someone for a favor or pay someone a compliment
- how to extend or accept an invitation for dinner
- how early or how late to arrive for an appointment or how long to stay

- how to distinguish seriousness from playfulness and politeness from indifference
- how to dress for an informal, formal, or business function
- how to order a meal in a restaurant or how to summon a server

Anthropologist Kalervo Oberg (1960), who first used the term *culture shock,* notes that it occurs in stages. These stages are useful for examining many encounters with the new and the different. Going away to college, getting married, or joining the military, for example, can all result in culture shock.

At the first stage, the *honeymoon,* there's fascination, even enchantment, with the new culture and its people. You finally have your own apartment. You're your own boss. Finally, on your own! Among people who are culturally different, the early (and superficial) relationships of this stage are characterized by cordiality and friendship. Many tourists remain at this stage because their stay in foreign countries is so brief.

At stage two, the *crisis stage,* the differences between your own culture and the new one create problems. In the new apartment example, no longer do you find dinner ready for you unless you do it yourself. Your clothes are not washed or ironed unless you do them yourself. Feelings of frustration and inadequacy come to the fore. This is the stage at which you experience the actual shock of the new culture. In one study of foreign students from more than 100 countries studying in 11 different countries, it was found that 25 percent of the students experienced depression (Klineberg & Hull, 1979).

During the third period, *recovery,* you gain the skills necessary to function effectively. You learn how to shop, cook, and plan a meal. You find a local laundry and figure you'll learn how to iron later. You learn the language and ways of the new culture. Your feelings of inadequacy subside.

At the final stage, *adjustment,* you adjust to and come to enjoy the new culture and the new experiences. You may still experience periodic difficulties and strains, but on the whole the experience is pleasant. Actually, you're now a pretty decent cook. You're even coming to enjoy it. You're making a good salary, so why learn to iron?

Simply spending time in a foreign country is not sufficient for the development of positive attitudes; in fact, limited contact with nationals often leads to the development of negative attitudes. Rather, friendships with nationals are crucial for satisfaction with the new culture. Contacts only with other expatriates or sojourners are not sufficient (Torbiorn, 1982).

People may also experience culture shock when they return to their original culture after living in a foreign culture—a kind of reverse culture shock (Jandt, 2000). Consider, for example, Peace Corps volunteers who have been working in a rural and economically deprived area. Upon returning to Las Vegas or Beverly Hills, they too may experience culture shock. Sailors who serve long periods aboard ship and then return to an isolated farming community may also experience culture shock. In these cases, however, the recovery period is shorter and the sense of inadequacy and frustration is less.

Culture and Ethics

Throughout history there have been numerous cultural practices that most people today would judge unethical and even illegal. Sacrificing virgins to the gods and sending children to fight wars are obvious examples. And even today there are practices woven deep into the fabric of different cultures that many Americans would find unethical. Consider just a few of these:

- Some cultures support bronco-riding events at which the bull's testicles are tied so that it will experience pain and try to throw off the rider.
- Some cultures support clitoridectomy, the practice of cutting a young girl's genitals so that she can never experience sexual intercourse without pain; the goal is to keep the girl a virgin until marriage.
- Some cultures support and enforce the belief that a woman must be subservient to her husband's will.
- Some cultures support the practice of wearing fur. In some cases this means catching wild animals in extremely painful traps; in others it involves raising captive animals so they can be killed when their pelts are worth the most money.

WHAT WOULD YOU DO? Imagine that you're on a television talk show dealing with the topic of cultural differences and diversity. During the discussion one or another of the panelists expresses approval of each of the above practices, arguing that each culture has a right to its own practices and beliefs and that no one has the right to object to cultural traditions. Given your own beliefs about these issues and about cultural diversity in general, what ethical obligations do you have as a member of this panel?

SUMMARY

This unit introduced the study of culture and its relationship to communication and considered how cultures differ and some of the theories developed to explain how culture and communication affect each other. In addition, the unit introduced the study of intercultural communication and its nature and principles.

1. Culture consists of the relatively specialized lifestyle of a group of people—their values, beliefs, artifacts, ways of behaving, and ways of communicating—that is passed on from one generation to the next through communication rather than through genes.
2. Enculturation is the process by which culture is transmitted from one generation to the next.
3. Acculturation involves the processes by which one culture is modified through contact with or exposure to another culture.
4. Cultures differ in terms of individualist or collectivist orientations, high and low context, high and low power distance, and masculinity and femininity.
5. Individualist cultures emphasize individual values such as power and achievement, whereas collectivist cultures emphasize group values such as cooperation and responsibility to the group.
6. In high-context cultures much information is in the context or the person, whereas in low-context cultures information is expected to be made explicit.
7. In high-power-distance cultures there are large differences in power between people; in low-power-distance cultures power is more evenly distributed throughout the population.
8. Masculine cultures emphasize assertiveness, ambition, and competition; feminine cultures emphasize compromise and negotiation.
9. Ethnocentrism, which exists on a continuum, is our tendency to evaluate the beliefs, attitudes, and values of our own culture positively and those of other cultures negatively.
10. Stereotyping is the tendency to develop and maintain fixed, unchanging impressions of groups of people and to use these impressions to evaluate individual members of these groups, ignoring unique individual characteristics.
11. Intercultural communication is communication among people who have different cultural beliefs, values, or ways of behaving.
12. Among guidelines for more effective intercultural communication are: recognize and reduce your ethnocentrism, confront your sterotypes, be mindful, face fears, recognize differences, avoid overattribution, recognize differences in meaning in verbal and nonverbal messages, avoid violating cultural rules and customs, avoid evaluating differences negatively, and recognize that culture shock is normal.

KEY TERMS

culture
enculturation
acculturation
individualist and collectivist cultures
high-context culture
low-context culture
high- and low-power-distance cultures
masculine culture
feminine culture
ethnocentrism
culture shock

THINKING CRITICALLY ABOUT

Culture and Communication

1. Cultural differences underlie some of the most hotly debated topics in the news today. For example, consider the following questions. How would you answer these? How do your cultural attitudes, beliefs, and values influence your responses?

- Should Christian Science parents be prosecuted for preventing their children from receiving life-saving medical procedures such as blood transfusions? Some states, such as Connecticut and Arizona, grant Christian Scientists special rights in this regard. Should this special treatment be adopted by all states? Should it be eliminated?

- Should cockfighting be permitted or declared illegal in all states as "cruelty to animals"? Some Latin Americans have argued that cockfighting is a part of their culture and should be permitted even though it's illegal in most of the United States. In five states and Puerto Rico, cockfighting is legal.
- Should same-sex marriages be legalized?
- Should safe sex practices be taught in elementary schools, or is this a matter for the home?
- Should those who commit hate or bias crimes be given harsher sentences?
- Should doctor-assisted suicide be legalized?
- Should the race of adopting parents and that of the child be a relevant issue in adoption decisions?

2. The U.S. Department of Education has issued guidelines (recommendations that are not legally binding on school boards) covering the types of religious communications and activities public schools may permit (*New York Times,* August 26, 1995, Section A, pp. 1, 8). Among the permitted activities are: student prayer, student-initiated discussions of religion, saying grace, proselytizing that would not be considered harassment, and the wearing of religious symbols and clothing. Among the forbidden activities are: prayer endorsed by teachers or administrators, invitations to prayer that could constitute harassment, teaching of a particular religion (rather than about religion), encouraging (officially or through teaching) either religious or antireligious activity, and denying school facilities to religious groups if these same facilities are provided to nonreligious groups. What do you think of these guidelines? If you were a member of a local school board, would you vote to adopt or reject these guidelines? How do your cultural beliefs influence your view of these guidelines?

3. In this age of multiculturalism, how do you feel about Article II, Section 1, of the U.S. Constitution? The relevant section reads: "No person except a natural-born citizen, or a citizen of the United States at the time of the adoption of this Constitution, shall be eligible to the office of President."

4. How do you feel about the Boy Scouts' being allowed to exclude gay boys from joining and gay men from serving as troop leaders? How do you feel about large corporations (Merrill Lynch, for example) that support the Boy Scouts?

5. Some years ago, the Emma Lazarus poem on the Statue of Liberty was changed. The words "the wretched refuse of your teeming shore" were deleted, and the poem now reads:

   Give me your tired, your poor,
   Your huddled masses yearning to breathe free, . . .
   Send these, the homeless, tempest-tost to me:
   I lift my lamp beside the golden door.

   Harvard zoologist Stephen Jay Gould, commenting on this change, notes that with the words omitted, the poem no longer has balance or rhyme and, more important, no longer represents what Lazarus wrote (Gould, 1995). "The language police triumph," notes Gould, "and integrity bleeds." On the other hand, it can be argued that calling immigrants "wretched refuse" is insulting and degrading and that if Lazarus were writing today, she would not have used that phrase. How do you feel about this? Would you have supported the deletion of this line?

6. With the growth of the Internet, the question of a universal language that would be understood worldwide has become a hot topic. In many ways—and largely because of the Internet—English is now the world's universal language. What do you think of English as a universal language? Would you propose a different language? What arguments for and against English as a universal language would you see as crucial in this debate (Kramarae, 1999)?

7. Do you agree with the assumption that everyone is ethnocentric to some degree? If so, where would you place yourself on the ethnocentric continuum when the "other" is a person of the opposite sex? A person of a different affectional orientation? A person of a different race? A person of a different religion?

8. Research shows that differences in power distance are significantly related to the style of leadership found in businesses and to the frequency of disagreements in the workplace (Offerman & Hellman, 1997; Smith, Dugan, Peterson, & Leung, 1998). What relationships do you think were found? For example, what type of leadership style would be more frequent in high-power-distance cultures? What style would be more frequent in low-power-distance cultures? In which cultural group would workplace disagreements be more frequent?

9. What additional advice would you offer for improving communication between people who have and who do not have disabilities?

UNIT

Perception

UNIT CONTENTS

You speak or listen on the basis of the way you perceive yourself, other people, and the world in general. You don't, for example, communicate with friends and enemies in the same way; nor do you see yourself in the same way that others do. In this unit you'll learn

- how the processes of perception influence your communication
- how you can increase your perceptual accuracy and hence your communication efficiency and effectiveness

The Process of Perception

Perception is the process by which you become aware of objects, events, and, especially, people through your senses: sight, smell, taste, touch, and hearing. Your perceptions result from what exists in the world *and* from your own experiences, desires, needs and wants, loves and hatreds. Among the reasons why perception is so important in communication is that it influences your communication choices. The messages you send and listen to will depend on how you see the world, on how you size up specific situations, on what you think of the people with whom you interact.

Perception is a continuous series of processes that blend into one another. *For convenience of discussion* we can separate these processes into five stages: (1) You sense some kind of stimulation; (2) you organize the stimuli in some way; (3) you interpret and evaluate what you perceive; (4) you store it in memory; and (5) you retrieve it when needed.

Stage 1: Stimulation

At this first stage, your sense organs are stimulated—you hear a new CD, you see a friend, you smell someone's perfume, you taste an orange, you feel another's sweaty palm. Naturally, you don't perceive everything; rather, you engage in **selective perception,** a general term that includes selective attention and selective exposure. In **selective attention** you attend to those things that you anticipate will fulfill your needs or will prove enjoyable. For example, when daydreaming in class, you don't hear what the instructor is saying until your name is called. Your selective attention mechanism focuses your senses on your name.

Through **selective exposure** (see also Unit 18) you expose yourself to people or messages that will confirm your existing beliefs, contribute to your objectives, or prove satisfying in some way. For example, after you buy a car, you're more apt to read and listen to advertisements for the car you just bought, because these messages tell you that you made the right decision. At the same time, you will tend to avoid advertisements for the cars that you considered but eventually rejected, because these messages would tell you that you made the wrong decision.

You're also more likely to perceive stimuli that are greater in intensity than surrounding stimuli and those that have novelty value. For example, television commercials normally play at a greater intensity than regular programming to ensure that you take special notice. You're also more likely to notice the coworker who dresses in a novel way than you are to notice the colleague who dresses like everyone else.

Stage 2: Organization

At the second stage, you organize the information your senses have picked up. You organize perceptions in three ways: by rules, by schemata, and by scripts.

Organization by Rules

Rules of perception lead you to see connections among elements that may or may not be present in reality. For example, following the rule of **physical closeness** or **proximity,** you'd perceive messages uttered in succession as a unit. Following a **temporal** rule, you'd perceive people who are often together as constituting a unit, such as "a couple" or "best friends."

Following the rule of **similarity,** you'd perceive things that are physically alike or have other similarities as belonging together and forming a unit. For example, you'd see people who dress alike as belonging together. Similarly, you might assume that people who work at the same jobs, who are of the same religion, who live in the same building, or who talk with the same accent belong together. The rule of **contrast** is the opposite of similarity: When items (people or messages, for example) are very different from one another, you conclude that they don't belong together; they're too different to be part of the same unit. If you're the only one who shows up at an informal gathering in a tuxedo, you'll be seen as not belonging to the group, because you contrast too much with other members.

Organization by Schemata

Another way you organize material is by creating **schemata**—mental templates or structures. Schemata help you organize the millions of items of information you come into contact with every day as

The National Communication Association and The International Communication Association

http://www.natcom.org and http://www.icahdq.org

These are websites for two of the largest professional organizations concerned with communication. Both organizations are extremely broad in scope and have divisions and activities focusing on all the areas of communication covered in this text. Visit one or both of these websites. What benefits might you derive from these websites?

In addition, visit the companion website for this text (www.ablongman.com/devito) and take a look at some relevant exercises: "Perceiving Yourself," "Perceiving Your Many Intelligences," "Perceiving Others," "Taking Another's Perspective," "Barriers to Accurate Perception," and "Paraphrasing."

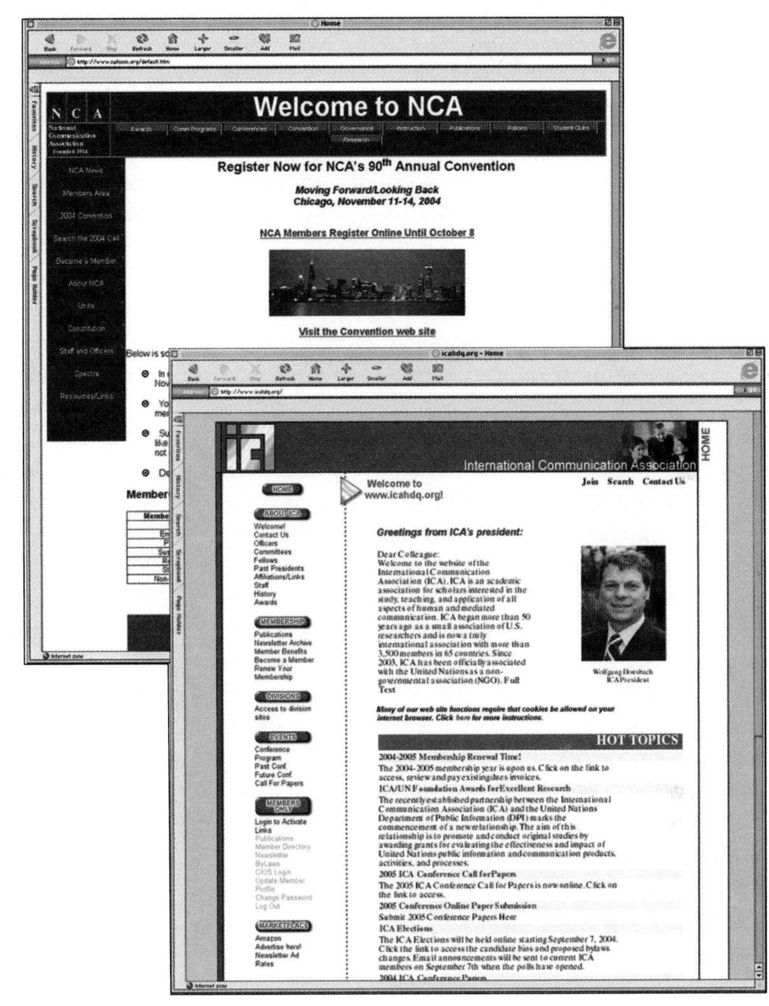

well as those items you already have in memory. Schemata may thus be viewed as general ideas about people (about Pat and Chris, about Japanese people, about Baptists, about New Yorkers), yourself (your qualities, abilities, and even liabilities), or social roles (what's a police officer, professor, or multibillionaire CEO like). (The word *schemata* is the plural of *schema* and is preferred to the alternative plural *schemas*.)

You develop schemata from your experiences—from actual experiences as well as from television, reading, and hearsay. Thus, for example, you might have a schema for college athletes; it might include perceptions that athletes are strong, ambitious, academically weak, and egocentric. And, of course, you have probably developed schemata for different religious, racial, and national groups; for men and women; and for people of different affectional orientations. Each group with which you have some familiarity will be represented in your mind in some kind of schema. Schemata help you organize your perceptions by allowing you to classify millions of people into a manageable number of categories or classes.

Organization by Scripts

A **script** (a type of schema) is a general idea of how some event should play out or unfold; it's the rules governing events and their sequence. For example, you probably have a script for eating in a restaurant with the actions organized into a pattern something like this: Enter, take a seat, review the menu, order from the menu, eat your food, ask for the bill, leave a tip, pay the bill, exit the restaurant. Similarly, you probably have scripts for how you do laundry, how an interview is to be conducted, the stages you go through in introducing someone to someone else, and the way you ask for a date.

Stage 3: Interpretation–Evaluation

At this stage you give your perceptions meaning; you draw conclusions about what you're seeing or smelling, for example. This step is inevitably subjective and is greatly influenced by your experiences, needs, wants, values, beliefs about the way things are or should be, expectations, physical and emotional state, and so on. Your interpretation–evaluation will be influenced by your rules, schemata, and scripts as well as by your gender; for example, women have been found to view others more positively than men (Winquist, Mohr, & Kenny, 1998).

For example, on meeting Ben Williams, who is introduced to you as a football player, you will apply your schema to Ben and view him as strong, ambitious, academically weak, and egocentric. You will, in other words, see this person through the filter of your schema and evaluate him according to your schema for athletes. Similarly, when viewing someone performing some series of actions (say, eating in a restaurant), you will apply your script to this event and view the event through the script. You'll then interpret the actions of the diner as appropriate or inappropriate depending on the script you had for this behavior and the ways in which the diner performed the sequence of actions.

Stage 4: Memory

Your perceptions and their interpretations–evaluations are put into memory; they're stored so that you may retrieve them at some later time. So, for example, you have in memory your schema for athletes and the fact that Ben is a football player. Ben is then stored in memory with "cognitive tags" that tell you that he's strong, ambitious, academically weak, and egocentric. Now, despite the fact that you've not witnessed Ben's strength or ambitions and have no idea of his academic record or his psychological profile, you still may store your memory of Ben along with the qualities that make up your schema for "athletes."

Schemata act as filters or gatekeepers; they allow certain information to get stored in relatively objective form, much as you heard or read it, but may distort other information or prevent it from getting stored. Let's say, for example, that at different times you hear that Ben failed Spanish I (normally an A or B course at your school), that Ben got an A in chemistry (normally a tough course), and that Ben is transferring to Harvard as a theoretical physics major. Each of these three items of information about Ben is likely to get stored very differently in your memory.

For example, you might readily store the information that Ben failed Spanish, because it's consistent with your schema; it fits neatly into the template you have for college athletes. Information such as this is consistent with your schema and so will strengthen your schema and make it more resistant to change (Aronson, Wilson, & Akert, 1999). Depending on the strength of your schema, you may also store in memory, even though you didn't hear it, a perception that Ben did poorly in other courses as well; this seems logical enough, given that he failed an extremely easy course. The information that Ben got an A in chemistry, because it contradicts your schema (it just doesn't seem right), may easily be distorted or lost. The information that Ben is transferring to Harvard, however, is a bit different. This information is so drastically inconsistent with your existing schema that you may begin to look at this mindfully and may even begin to question the logic of your schema. Or perhaps you'll view Ben as an exception to the general rule (and continue to entertain your original schema about athletes). In either case, you're going to etch Ben's transferring to Harvard very clearly in your mind.

Stage 5: Recall

At some later date, you may want to recall or access the information you have stored in memory. Let's say you want to retrieve your information about Ben because he's the topic of discussion among you and a few friends. You may, however, recall it with a variety of inaccuracies. For example, you're likely to

- recall information that is consistent with your schema; in fact, you may not even recall the specific information (about Ben) but may actually just recall your schema (which contains the information about college athletes and, because of this, also about Ben)
- fail to recall information that is inconsistent with your schema; you have no place to put that information, because it just doesn't fit into your existing schema, so you lose it or forget it
- recall information that drastically contradicts your schema, because it forces you to think (and perhaps rethink) about your schema and its accu-

racy; it may even force you to revise your schema for athletes in general

Reflections on the Model of Perception

This five-stage model has several important implications for your own perceptions:

1. Everyone relies heavily on shortcuts; rules, schemata, and scripts, for example, are all useful shortcuts to simplify your understanding, remembering, and recalling information about people and events. If you didn't have these shortcuts, you'd have to treat every person, role, or action differently from each other person, role, or action. This would make every experience a new one, totally unrelated to anything you already know. If you didn't use these shortcuts, you'd be unable to generalize, draw connections, or otherwise profit from previously acquired knowledge.
2. Shortcuts, however, may mislead you; they may contribute to your remembering things that are consistent with your schemata (even if they didn't occur) and distorting or forgetting information that is inconsistent.
3. What you remember about a person or an event isn't an objective recollection but is more likely heavily influenced by your preconceptions or your schemata about what belongs and what doesn't belong, what fits into the templates in your brain and what doesn't fit. Your reconstruction of an event or person contains a lot of information that was not in the original sensory experience and may omit a lot that was in this experience.
4. Judgments about members of other cultures are often ethnocentric. Because your schemata and scripts are created on the basis of your own cultural beliefs and experiences, you can easily (but inappropriately) apply these to members of other cultures. So it's easy to infer that when members of other cultures do things that conform to your scripts, they're right, and when they do things that contradict your scripts, they're wrong—a classic example of ethnocentric thinking. This tendency can easily contribute to intercultural misunderstandings.
5. A similar problem arises when you base your scripts for different cultural groups on stereotypes that you may have derived from television or movies. So, for example, you may have a script for religious Muslims that you derived from the stereotypes presented in the media. If you apply that script to all Muslims, you will tend to see only the behaviors that conform to your script; you will be likely to distort or fail to see the behaviors that do not conform to your script.
6. Memory is especially unreliable when the information can be interpreted in different ways—when it's ambiguous. Thus, for example, consider the statement that "Ben didn't do as well in his other courses as he would have liked." If your schema for Ben was "brilliant," then you may "remember" that Ben got Bs in those other courses. But if, as in our example, your schema was of the academically weak athlete, you may "remember" that Ben got Ds. Conveniently, but unreliably, schemata reduce ambiguity.

Influences on Perception

Between the occurrence of the stimulus (the uttering of the message, the presence of the person, the smile or wink of the eye) and the evaluation or interpretation of that stimulus, perception is influenced by several significant psychological processes. Before reading about these processes, take the following self-test to analyze your own customary ways of perceiving others. Regardless of what form of communication you're engaged in—interpersonal, small group, public speaking, or mass communication—the ways in which you perceive the people involved will influence your communications and your communication effectiveness. The self-test below will give you an idea of the factors that make for accuracy in perception.

TEST YOURSELF

How Accurate Are You at People Perception?

Respond to each of the following statements with T (true) if the statement is usually or generally accurate in describing your behavior, or F (false) if the statement is usually or generally inaccurate in describing your behavior.

____ **1.** When I know some things about another person, I can pretty easily fill in what I don't know.

____ **2.** I make predictions about people's behaviors that generally prove to be true.

____ **3.** Generally my expectations are borne out by what I actually see; that is, my later perceptions usually match my initial expectations.

____ **4.** I base most of my impressions of people on the first few minutes of our meeting.

____ **5.** I generally find that people I like possess positive characteristics and people I don't like possess negative characteristics.

____ **6.** I generally attribute people's attitudes and behaviors to their most obvious physical or psychological characteristic.

HOW DID YOU DO? This brief perception test was designed to raise questions to be considered in this chapter, not to provide you with a specific perception score. All statements refer to perceptual processes that we're likely to use but that often get us into trouble, leading us to form inaccurate impressions. The questions refer to the processes to be discussed below: implicit personality theory (1), self-fulfilling prophecy (2), perceptual accentuation (3), primary–recency (4), and consistency (5). Statement (6) refers to overattribution, one of the problems that beset our attempts to attribute motives to other people's—and even our own—behaviors.

WHAT WILL YOU DO? As you read this chapter, think about these processes and consider how you might prevent them from getting in the way of accurate and reasonable people perception. At the same time, recognize that situations vary widely. Can you identify situations in which you actually should go ahead and engage in each one of these perceptual processes?

Here we discuss some of the major processes that influence your perception of others (Cook, 1971; Rubin & McNeil, 1985): (1) implicit personality theory, (2) the self-fulfilling prophecy, (3) perceptual accentuation, (4) primacy-recency, (5) consistency, and (6) attribution. Each of these processes also contains potential barriers to accurate perception that can significantly distort your perceptions and your communication interactions.

Implicit Personality Theory

Each person has an **implicit personality theory,** a subconscious or implicit system of rules that says which characteristics of an individual go with other characteristics. To see how this works, choose the word in parentheses that you think best completes each of the following sentences:

1. Carlo is energetic, eager, and (intelligent, stupid).
2. Kim is bold, defiant, and (extroverted, introverted).
3. Joe is bright, lively, and (thin, heavy).
4. Eve is attractive, intelligent, and (likable, unlikable).
5. Susan is cheerful, positive, and (outgoing, shy).
6. Angel is handsome, tall, and (friendly, unfriendly).

What makes some of these choices seem right and others wrong is your implicit personality theory. Your theory may, for example, have told you that a person who is energetic and eager is also intelligent, even though there is no logical reason why a stupid person could not be energetic and eager.

The widely documented **halo effect** is a function of the implicit personality theory. If you believe an individual has certain positive qualities (for example, is kind, generous, and friendly), you make the inference that she or he also has other positive qualities (for example, is supportive or empathic). The "reverse halo effect" operates in a similar way. If you know a person has certain negative qualities, you're likely to infer that the person also has other negative qualities.

As might be expected, the implicit personality theories that people hold differ from culture to culture, from group to group, and even from person to person. For example, the Chinese have a concept, *shi gu*, which refers to "someone who is worldly, devoted to his or her family, socially skillful, and somewhat reserved" (Aronson, Wilson, & Akert, 1999, p. 190). This concept is not easily encoded in English, as you can tell by trying to find a general concept that covers this type of person. In English, on the other hand, we have a concept of the "artistic type," a generalization that is absent in Chinese. Thus, although it's easy for speakers of English or Chinese to refer to specific descriptive concepts—such as "socially skilled" or "creative"—each language creates its own generalized categories. In Chinese the qualities that make up *shi gu* are more seen as going together easily than they might be for an English speaker; they're part of the implicit personality theory of more Chinese than English speakers.

Similarly, consider the different personality theories that graduate students and blue-collar high school dropouts might have for "college students." Likewise, one individual may have had great experiences with doctors and so may have a very positive personality theory of "doctors," whereas another person may have had negative experiences with doctors and may have developed a very negative personality theory.

Potential Barriers with Implicit Personality Theories

Two serious barriers to accurate perception can occur when you use implicit personality theories.

First, your tendency to develop personality theories and to perceive individuals as confirming your theory can lead you to perceive qualities in an individual that your theory tells you should be present when they actually are not. For example, you may see "goodwill" in the "charitable" acts of a friend when a tax deduction may be the real motive. Conversely you may see "tax deduction" as the motive of the enemy when altruism may have been the motive. Because you remember information that is consistent with your implicit theories more easily than you recall inconsistent information, you're unlikely to revise or modify your theories even when you come upon contradictory evidence (Cohen, 1983). Second, implicit personality theories can also lead you to ignore or distort qualities or characteristics that don't conform to your theory. You may ignore (simply not see) negative qualities in your friends that you would easily see in your enemies.

Both of these perceptual inaccuracies are more likely to occur when you have few perceptual cues and know little of the other person. Thus, you're more likely to make these errors when interacting with someone on the Internet than when thinking about someone you've known a while and know a lot about.

The Self-Fulfilling Prophecy

A **self-fulfilling prophecy** occurs when you make a prediction or formulate a belief that comes true because you made the prediction and acted on it as if it were true (Insel & Jacobson, 1975; Merton, 1957; Darley & Oleson, 1993). There are four basic steps in the self-fulfilling prophecy:

1. You make a prediction or formulate a belief about a person or a situation. For example, you predict that Pat will be awkward in interpersonal situations.
2. You act toward that person or situation as if your prediction or belief were true. You act toward Pat as if Pat were awkward.
3. Because you act as if the belief were true, it becomes true. Because of the way you act toward Pat, Pat becomes tense and manifests awkwardness.
4. You observe your effect on the person or the resulting situation, and what you see strengthens your beliefs. You observe Pat's awkwardness, and this reinforces your belief that Pat is in fact awkward.

If you expect people to act in a certain way or if you make a prediction about the characteristics of a situation, your predictions will frequently come true because of the self-fulfilling prophecy. This has been demonstrated in widely different areas; for example, in leadership, athletic coaching, military training, business, and effective stepfamilies (Eden, 1992; Solomon et al., 1996; Einstein, 1995; McNatt, 2001).

The self-fulfilling prophecy is significant in all forms of communication. Consider, for example, the group member who believes that other members will not give his or her proposals a fair hearing and so doesn't put forth the persuasive effort required to sell the proposal; or consider the public speaker who thinks the audience doesn't want to hear his or her speech and so doesn't rehearse or expend any energy in delivering the speech. Invariably, these people will be proved right, because (according to the self-fulfilling prophecy) they act in ways that encourage people to respond negatively. Such people fulfill their own prophecies.

Potential Barriers with the Self-Fulfilling Prophecy

The self-fulfilling prophecy may create two potential barriers to accurate perception. First, your tendency to fulfill your own prophecies can lead you to influence another's behavior so that it confirms your prophecy. Thus, if students believe that Professor Crawford is a boring teacher and so pay no attention and give no feedback, they may actually help create a boring lecturer.

The self-fulfilling prophecy also distorts your perception by influencing you to see what you predicted rather than what is really there. For example, it can lead you to see yourself as a failure because you've made this prediction rather than because of any actual setbacks. It can lead you to see someone's behavior as creative because you are expecting this person to act creatively.

Perceptual Accentuation

When researchers showed poor and rich children pictures of coins and later asked them to estimate the coins' size, the poor children's size estimates were much greater than the rich children's. Similarly, experiments show that hungry people need fewer visual cues to perceive food objects and food terms than do people who are not hungry (Wispé & Drambarean, 1953). These findings demonstrate the process called **perceptual accentuation,** which leads you to see what you expect or want to see. You see people you like as better looking and smarter than those you don't like. You magnify or accentuate what will satisfy your needs and desires: The thirsty person a mirage of water, the sexually deprived person a mirage of sexual satisfaction.

UNDERSTANDING THEORY AND RESEARCH

The Pygmalion Effect

A widely known example of the self-fulfilling prophecy is the Pygmalion effect (Rosenthal & Jacobson, 1992). The effect is named after Pygmalion, a sculptor in Greek mythology who created a statue of a beautiful woman and then fell in love with it. Venus, the goddess of love, rewarded Pygmalion for his artistry and love by making the statue come to life as a real woman, Galatea. George Bernard Shaw used this idea for his play *Pygmalion,* the story of a poor, uneducated London flower vendor who is taught "proper speech" and enters society's upper class. The musical *My Fair Lady* was in turn based on Shaw's play.

In a classic research study, experimenters told teachers that certain pupils were expected to do exceptionally well—that they were late bloomers (Rosenthal & Jacobson, 1968, 1992). And although the experimenters actually selected the "late bloomers" at random, the students who were labeled "late bloomers" actually did perform at higher levels than their classmates. Like the beautiful statue, these students became what their teachers thought they were. The expectations of the teachers may have caused them to pay extra attention to the students, and this may have positively affected the students' performance. More recently, the Pygmalion effect has been studied in such varied contexts as the courtroom, the clinic, the work cubicle, management practices, leadership, athletic coaching, and stepfamilies (Eden, 1992; Solomon et al., 1996; Einstein, 1995; McNatt, 2001; Rosenthal, 2002).

Working with Theories and Research

- *Findings such as those cited above have led one researcher to suggest that companies apply the Pygmalion effect as a way to improve worker productivity by creating in supervisors positive attitudes about employees and by helping employees to feel that their supervisors and the organization as a whole value them highly (McNatt, 2001). In what ways might this Pygmalion effect be applied at your own workplace?*

Potential Barriers with Perceptual Accentuation

Perceptual accentuation can create a variety of barriers. Your tendency to perceive what you want or need can lead you to distort your perceptions of reality—to see what you need or want to see rather than what is really there. At the same time it can lead you to fail to perceive what you don't want to perceive. For example, people frequently perceive a salesperson's politeness and friendliness as demonstrating personal liking for them, not as a persuasive strategy. Similarly, you may not perceive that you're about to fail your chemistry course because you focus on what you want to perceive.

Accentuation can influence you to filter out or distort information that might damage or threaten your self-image (for example, criticism of your writing or speaking) and thus can make self-improvement difficult. It can also lead you to perceive in others the negative characteristics or qualities you have yourself, a defense mechanism psychoanalysts refer to as **projection.**

In addition, accentuation can influence you to perceive and remember positive qualities more strongly than negative ones (the "Pollyanna effect") and thus can distort your perceptions of others. In one study, for example, students who liked and who disliked Madonna viewed her video "Open Your Heart." Those who liked Madonna saw the performance as the story of a dancer and her son. Those who disliked Madonna saw it as the story of sexual attraction between a young boy and an older woman (Brown & Schulze, 1990).

Misperception due to accentuation is something that is likely to occur frequently in Internet communication. Consider, for example, entering a chat room hoping to meet someone for a date. Because you expect and want to meet someone, you may read into another person's ambiguous cues a wonderful personality and a desire to meet you. The more you expect or want something to happen and the fewer the unambiguous cues you have to go on, the more likely you are to misperceive the cues you do have. So, for example, because of perceptual accentuation you might perceive relatively neutral comments from a chat room member to be a lot more positive and perhaps romantically slanted than the person intended. Or you might perceive a person who has expressed an interest in you to have a lot more positive qualities (and a lot fewer negative qualities) than you might have glimpsed if this person had not expressed this positive attitude toward you.

Primacy-Recency

Consider the following situation: You have been taking a course in which half the classes were extremely dull and half were extremely exciting. It's now the end of the semester, and you're reflecting on the course and the instructor. Will your evaluation be more favorable if the dull classes came during the first half of the semester and the exciting classes during the second half, or if the order is reversed? Similarly, would you evaluate a chat room member more favorably if your initial experiences were positive or if your most recent experiences were positive? If what comes first exerts the most influence on perception, the result is a **primacy effect.** If what comes last (or is the most recent) exerts the most influence, the result is a **recency effect.**

In an early study on the effects of **primacy–recency** in perception, a researcher read a list of adjectives describing a person to a group of students (Asch, 1946). Not surprisingly, the order in which the adjectives were read influenced the students' perceptions of the person. A person described as "intelligent, industrious, impulsive, critical, stubborn, and envious" was evaluated more positively than a person described as "envious, stubborn, critical, impulsive, industrious, and intelligent." This finding suggests that you use early information to provide yourself with a general idea of what a person is like. You use later information to make this general idea

COMMUNICATION@WORK

First Impressions

Manage every second of a first meeting. Do not delude yourself that a bad first impression can be easily corrected. Putting things right is a lot harder than getting them right the first time.

—David Lewis

Whether in a job interview, in the early days on a new job, or in meeting new colleagues, first impressions are especially important—because they're so long lasting and so powerful in influencing future impressions and interactions (Parsons, Liden, & Bauer, 2001). Here are a few guidelines that will help you make a good first impression on the job.

- Dress appropriately, even on "casual Friday." Any drastic deviation from the standard dress for your position is likely to be perceived negatively and may communicate that you somehow don't fit in.
- Both verbally and nonverbally, express positive attitudes toward the organization, the job, and your colleagues. Avoid negative talk and sarcasm (even in your humor); it's often perceived as an attack on others.
- Be open and friendly; be available and helpful as appropriate. Be cooperative, and share rather than monopolizing.
- Avoid stereotyping and talk that might be considered racist, sexist, heterosexist, or ageist. Otherwise, you're sure to offend someone.
- Be time conscious, and be respectful of other people's time.
- Discover what the organization's cultural rules and norms are and avoid violating them.
- Be a good listener; good listeners are invariably among the most popular people anywhere, and the workplace is no exception.

Communicating@Work

What type of first impressions do you usually make? Are you pleased with these first impressions? How might you go about improving these early impressions?

ASK THE RESEARCHER

Making a Great First Impression

- *I'm planning on becoming a teacher and want to draw on the insights of this course to be a better (no, a sensational) teacher. For starters, how can I make a great first impression on high school students?*

The first thing to keep in mind is that your students will have a great deal of uncertainty on the first day. They will be trying to figure out who you are and what kind of teacher you'll be. Students will be interpreting both your verbal and nonverbal messages, so make sure your verbal messages give them information that they need in order to meet your expectations and to succeed. Your nonverbal messages need to communicate that you like them, want to know them as individuals, and want them to succeed. Specific nonverbal behaviors that communicate liking (also referred to as immediacy) are smiling, making eye contact, and moving about the classroom so that you are physically close (but not too close) to as many students as possible. Immediacy and enthusiasm tend to be reciprocated, so make the first move and show your students how much you like them and how enthusiastic you are about the course.

For additional information: Frymier, A. B., & Houser, M. (2000). The teacher–student relationship as an interpersonal relationship. *Communication Education, 49,* 207–219. And Richmond, V. P. (2002). Teacher nonverbal immediacy: Uses and outcomes. In J. L. Chesebro & J. C. McCroskey (Eds.), *Communication for teachers* (pp. 65–82). Boston: Allyn & Bacon.

Ann Bainbridge Frymier (Ed.D., West Virginia University) is an associate professor at Miami University in Oxford, Ohio, and teaches courses in instructional communication, persuasion, interpersonal communication, and research methods. Her research examines how communication functions in the classroom to enhance student learning (frymierab@muohio.edu).

more specific. The obvious practical implication of primacy-recency is that the first impression you make—interpersonally, in small groups, or in public speaking—is likely to be the most important. Through this first impression, people will filter additional information to formulate a picture of who they perceive you to be.

Potential Barriers with Primacy-Recency

Primacy-recency may lead to two major types of barriers. Your tendency to give greater weight to early information and to interpret later information in light of these early impressions can lead you to form a "total" picture of an individual on the basis of initial impressions that may not be typical or accurate. For example, perhaps you form an image of someone as socially ill at ease. If this impression was based on watching the person at a stressful job interview, it's likely to be wrong. But because of primacy you may fail to see accurately the person's later comfortable behavior.

Primacy may even lead you to discount or distort later perceptions to avoid disrupting your initial impressions. For instance, you may fail to see signs of deceit in someone who made a good first impression because of the tendency to avoid disrupting or revising initial impressions.

Consistency

People have a strong tendency to maintain balance or consistency among their perceptions. **Consistency** represents people's need to maintain balance among their attitudes. You expect certain things to go together and other things not to go together.

Consider your own attitudes in terms of consistency by responding to the following sentences; note the word in parentheses that you feel best represents your attitudes.

1. I expect a person I like to (like, dislike) me.
2. I expect a person I dislike to (like, dislike) me.
3. I expect my friend to (like, dislike) my friend.
4. I expect my friend to (like, dislike) my enemy.
5. I expect my enemy to (like, dislike) my friend.
6. I expect my enemy to (like, dislike) my enemy.

According to most consistency theories, your expectations would be as follows: You would expect a person you liked to like you (1) and a person you disliked to dislike you (2). You would expect a friend to like a friend (3) and to dislike an enemy (4). You would expect your enemy to dislike your friend (5) and to like your other enemy (6). Further, you would expect someone you liked to have characteristics you liked or admired. And you'd expect your enemies not to possess characteristics you liked or admired. Conversely, you'd expect persons you liked to lack unpleasant characteristics and persons you disliked to have unpleasant characteristics. All these expectations seem intuitively right. But are they?

Potential Barriers with Consistency

Consistency can create two major barriers to accuracy in perception. Your tendency to see consistency in an individual can lead you to ignore or distort your perceptions of behaviors that are inconsistent with your picture of the whole person. For example, you may misinterpret Karla's unhappiness because your image of Karla is "happy, controlled, and contented."

Your desire for consistency may also lead you to perceive specific behaviors as emanating from positive qualities in the people you like and from negative qualities in the people you dislike. You therefore fail to see the positive qualities in the people you dislike and the negative qualities in the people you like.

Attribution

Attribution is the process through which you try to discover why people do what they do and even why

BUILDING COMMUNICATION SKILLS

Perceiving Others' Perceptions

For any one or two of the following situations, explain how each of the persons identified might view the situation. What one principle of perception can you derive from this brief experience?

1. Pat is a single parent with two children, ages 7 and 12. The kids often lack some of the important things children their age should have, such as school supplies, sneakers, and toys, because Pat can't afford them. Yet Pat smokes two packs of cigarettes a day.

   Pat sees ...
   The 12-year-old daughter sees ...
   The children's teacher sees ...

2. Chris has extremely high standards, feels that getting all A's in college is an absolute necessity, and would be devastated with even one B. In fear of earning that first B (after three and a half years of college), Chris cheats on an examination in a course on family communication and gets caught by the instructor.

   Chris sees ...
   The instructor sees ...
   The average B-student sees ...

3. Pat, a supervisor in an automobile factory, has been ordered to increase production or be fired. In desperation Pat gives a really tough message to the workers—many of whom are greatly insulted and, as a result, slow down rather than increasing their efforts.

   Pat sees ...
   The average worker sees ...
   Pat's supervisor sees ...

you do what you do (Fiske & Taylor, 1984; Jones & Davis, 1965; Kelley, 1979). One way we try to answer this question (in part) is to ask if the person acts this way because of who the person is (personality) or because of the situation. That is, your task is to determine whether the cause of the behavior is internal (due to who the person really is) or external (due to extenuating circumstances).

Internal causes for behaviors involve the person's personality or some enduring trait. In this case you might hold the person responsible for his or her behaviors, and you would judge the behaviors and the person in light of this responsibility. External causes for behaviors, on the other hand, have to do with situational factors. In this case you might not hold the person responsible for his or her behaviors.

Consider an example. A teacher has given 10 students F's on a cultural anthropology examination. In attempting to discover what this behavior (assignment of the 10 F's) reveals about the teacher, you have to determine whether the teacher was responsible for the behavior (the behavior was internally caused) or not (the behavior was externally caused). If you discover that a faculty committee made up the examination and that the committee set the standards for passing or failing, you cannot attribute any particular motives to the teacher. You have to conclude that the behavior was externally caused. In this case, it was caused by the department committee in conjunction with each student's performance on the examination.

On the other hand, assume that this teacher made up the examination and set the standards for passing and failing. Now you will be more apt to attribute the 10 F's to internal causes. You will be strengthened in your belief that something within this teacher (some personality trait, for example) led to this behavior if you discover that (1) no other teacher gave nearly as many F's, (2) this particular teacher frequently gives F's in cultural anthropology, (3) this teacher frequently gives F's in other courses as well, and (4) this teacher is free to give grades other than F. These four bits of added information may lead you to conclude that something in this teacher motivated the behavior. According to **attribution theory,** each of these new items of information represents one of the principles you use in making causal judgments, or attributions: principles known as (1) consensus, (2) consistency, (3) distinctiveness, and (4) controllability.

Consensus

When you focus on the principle of **consensus,** you ask, "Do other people behave the same way as the person on whom I am focusing?" That is, does this person act in accordance with the general consensus? If the answer is no, you're more likely to attribute the behavior to some internal cause. In the previous example, you were strengthened in your belief that the teacher's behavior had an internal cause when you learned that other teachers did not follow this behavior—there was low consensus.

Consistency

When you focus on **consistency** in making attributions, you ask whether a person repeatedly behaves the same way in similar situations. If the answer is yes, there's high consistency, and you're likely to attribute the behavior to internal motivation. The fact that the teacher frequently gives F's in cultural anthropology leads you to attribute the cause to the teacher rather than to outside sources.

Distinctiveness

When you focus on the principle of **distinctiveness,** you ask if a person acts in similar ways in different situations. If the answer is yes, you're likely to conclude that the behavior has an internal cause. A finding of "low distinctiveness" indicates that this person acts in similar ways in different situations; it indicates that this situation is not distinctive.

Consider the alternative—high distinctiveness. Assume that this teacher gave all high grades and no failures in all his or her other courses (that is, that the cultural anthropology class situation was distinctive). Then you would probably conclude that the motivation for the failures was unique to this class and was external to the teacher.

Controllability

The term **controllability** refers to the degree to which you think a person was in control of his or her behavior. Let's say, for example, that you invite your friend Desmond to dinner for seven o'clock and he arrives at nine. Consider how you will respond to the reasons he may give you for his lateness:

> *Reason 1:* Oh, I got to watching this old movie and I wanted to see the end.
>
> *Reason 2:* On my way here I witnessed a robbery and felt I had to report it. At the police station the phones were all tied up.
>
> *Reason 3:* I got in a car accident and was taken to the hospital.

Assuming you believe all three explanations, you will attribute very different motives to Desmond's behavior. With reasons 1 and 2, you will conclude that Desmond was in control of his behavior; with

BUILDING COMMUNICATION SKILLS

Making Attributions

Consider how you would explain the following cases in terms of attribution theory. Do you think that in each scenario the individual's behavior was due to internal causes (for example, personality characteristics or various personal motives) or external causes (for example, the particular situation, the demands of others who might be in positions of authority, or the behaviors of others)? The behavior in question appears in italics. As you analyze these situations, consider the information contained in the brief background descriptions and try to make judgments concerning (1) consensus, (2) consistency, (3) distinctiveness, and (4) controllability. What combination of these principles would lead you to conclude that a behavior was internally motivated? What combination would lead you to conclude that the behavior was externally motivated?

1. *Mita's performance in the race was disappointing.* For the last few days Mita had to tend to her sick grandfather and got too little sleep.
2. *Peter quit his job.* No one else that you know who has had this same job has ever quit.
3. *Karla failed her chemistry test.* Many other students (in fact, some 40 percent of the class) also failed the test. Karla has never failed a chemistry test before and, in fact, has never failed any other test in her life.

reason 3, you will conclude that Desmond was not in control of his behavior. Further, you will probably respond negatively to reason 1 (Desmond was selfish and inconsiderate) but positively to reason 2 (Desmond did his duty as a responsible citizen). Because Desmond was not in control of his behavior in reason 3, you will probably not attribute either positive or negative motivation to Desmond's behavior. Instead you will probably feel sorry that he had an accident on the way to your house.

Consider your own tendency to make similar judgments based on controllability in a variety of situations. How would you respond to such situations as the following?

- Doris fails her midterm history exam.
- Sidney's car is repossessed because he failed to make the payments.
- Margie is 150 pounds overweight and is complaining that she feels awful.
- Thomas's wife has just filed for divorce and he is feeling depressed.

Very probably you'd be sympathetic to each of these people if you felt they were not in control of what happened—for example, if the examination was unfair, if Sidney lost his job because of employee discrimination, if Margie has a glandular problem, and if Thomas's wife is leaving him for a wealthy drug dealer. On the other hand, you might blame these people for their problems if you felt that they were in control of the situation—for example, if Doris partied instead of studying, if Sidney gambled his payments away, if Margie ate nothing but junk food and refused to exercise, and if Thomas had been repeatedly unfaithful and his wife finally gave up trying to change him.

Low consensus, high consistency, low distinctiveness, and high controllability lead to an attribution of internal causes. As a result, you praise or blame the person for his or her behaviors. High consensus, low consistency, high distinctiveness, and low controllability lead to an attribution of external causes. As a result, you may consider this person lucky or unlucky.

Potential Barriers with Attribution

Of course, the obvious problem with attribution is that we can only make guesses about another person's behaviors. Can we really know if Doris deserved to pass or fail the history exam? Can we really know if Sidney deserved to have his car repossessed? When you realize that such judgments are often based on guesses, you'll be more apt to seek further information before acting as if attributions were facts. In addition, the attribution process is often subject to different kinds of bias and error.

The Self-Serving Bias. The self-serving bias is another perceptual barrier and is generally designed to

UNDERSTANDING *THEORY* AND *RESEARCH*

The Just World Hypothesis

Many people believe that the world is just: that good things happen to good people and bad things happen to bad people (Aronson, Wilson, & Akert, 1999; Hunt, 2000). Put differently, the *just world hypothesis* suggests that you'll get what you deserve! Even if you mindfully dismiss this assumption, you may use it mindlessly when perceiving and evaluating other people. Consider a particularly vivid example: In certain cultures (for example, in Bangladesh, Iran, or Yemen), a woman who is raped is considered by many (though certainly not all) to have disgraced her family and to be deserving of severe punishment—in many cases, even death. Although most people reading this book will claim that this is unjust and unfair, it's quite common even in Western cultures to blame the victim. Much research, for example, shows that people often blame the victim for being raped (Bell, Kuriloff, & Lottes, 1994). In fact, defense attorneys routinely attack the rape victim in court for dressing provocatively. And it's relevant to note that only two states—New York and Florida—currently forbid questions about the victim's clothing.

This belief that the world is just creates perceptual distortions by leading us to deemphasize the influence of situational factors and to overemphasize the influence of internal factors in our attempts to explain the behaviors of other people or even our own behaviors.

Another way in which the belief in a just world distorts perception is through the *egocentric fairness bias*: People who have strong beliefs in a just world see their own behaviors as fairer and more moral than those of others (Tanaka, 1999). The reasoning goes like this:

- *If* I am fairer and more moral than others,
- *then* I will experience more good than bad,
- *because* the world is just.

Working with Theories and Research

- *If you have access, log on to Research Navigator (www.researchnavigator.com), using the psychology, sociology, and communication databases, and search for "just world." Scan some of the articles. What can you add to the discussion presented here?*

preserve or raise our own self-esteem as we engage in **self-attribution.** When you evaluate your own behaviors by taking credit for the positive and denying responsibility for the negative, you're demonstrating the **self-serving bias.** You're more likely to attribute your own negative behaviors to uncontrollable factors. For example, you're more likely to attribute getting a D on an exam to the difficulty of the test than to your failure to prepare adequately for it. And you're more likely to attribute your positive behaviors to controllable factors—to your own strength or intelligence or personality. For example, after getting an A on an exam, you're more likely to attribute it to your ability or hard work than to luck or the ease of the test (Bernstein, Stephan, & Davis, 1979).

The Fundamental Attribution Error. Perhaps the major difficulty in making accurate attributions is the **fundamental attribution error:** the tendency to conclude that people do what they do because that's the kind of people they are, not because of the situation they are in. When Pat is late for an appointment, we're more likely to conclude that Pat is inconsiderate or irresponsible than to attribute the lateness to the bus breaking down or to a traffic accident. When we commit the fundamental attribution error, we overvalue the contribution of internal factors and undervalue the influence of external factors.

When we explain our own behavior, we also favor internal explanations, although not to as great an extent as we do when explaining the behaviors of others. In one study, managers who evaluated their own performance and the performance of their subordinates used more internal explanations when evaluating the behavior of their subordinates than when evaluating their own (Martin & Klimoski, 1990). One reason we tend to give greater weight to external factors in explaining our own behavior than in explaining the behavior of others is that we know the situation surrounding our own behavior. We know, for example, what's going on in our love life, and we know our financial condition; so we naturally see the influence of these factors. But we rarely know as much about others, so we're more likely to give less weight to the external factors in their cases.

This fundamental attribution error is at least in part culturally influenced. For example, Americans are likely to explain behavior by saying that people did what they did because of who they are. But when Hindus in India were asked to explain why their friends behaved as they did, they gave greater weight to external factors than did people in the United States (Miller, 1984; Aronson, Wilson, & Akert, 1999). Further, Americans have little hesitation in offering causal explanations of a person's behavior ("Pat did this because . . ."). Hindus, on the other hand, are generally reluctant to explain a person's behavior in causal terms (Matsumoto, 1994).

Overattribution. Another problem is **overattribution**—attributing everything a person does to one or two obvious characteristics, as when we attribute a person's behavior to alcoholic parents or to being born blind or possessing great wealth. For example, "Sally has difficulty forming meaningful relationships because she grew up in a home of alcoholics," "Alex overeats because he's blind," or "Shandra is irresponsible because she never had to work for her money." Most behaviors and personality characteristics are the product of a wide variety of factors, however; it's almost always a mistake to select one factor and attribute everything to it.

VIEWPOINT

Some people feel that media portrayals of cultural groups often perpetuate stereotypes. Thus, for example, *The Sopranos*, the HBO series pictured here, has been accused of perpetuating the stereotype of Italian Americans as gangsters or of gangsters as Italian. How do you feel about media portrayals of your own cultural groups? For example, do the media create and perpetuate stereotypes? If so, are they basically positive or negative?

Accuracy in Perception

Successful communication depends largely on the accuracy of your perceptions—perceptions of people, of problems and solutions, of events. We've already identified the potential barriers that can arise with each of the seven perceptual processes; for example, our tendency to see what we expect or want instead of what is and our vulnerability to the self-serving bias. There are, however, additional useful guidelines for improving your **interpersonal perception** skills.

Analyze Your Perceptions

When you are aware of your perceptions, you are able to subject them to logical analysis and to critical thinking. Here are two suggestions.

- Recognize your own role in perception. Your emotional and physiological state will influence the meaning you give to your perceptions. A movie may seem hysterically funny when you're in a good mood but just plain stupid when you're in a bad mood or when you're preoccupied with family problems. Beware of your own biases. Know when your evaluations are unduly influenced by your biases—for example, your tendency to perceive only the positive in people you like and only the negative in people you don't like. Even your gender will influence your perceptions.

Women consistently evaluate other people more positively than do men on such factors as agreeableness, conscientiousness, and emotional stability (Winquist, Mohr, & Kenny, 1998).

- Avoid coming to conclusions early. On the basis of your observations of behaviors, formulate hypotheses to test against additional information and evidence rather than drawing conclusions you then look to confirm. Delay formulating conclusions until you have had a chance to process a wide variety of cues. Similarly, avoid the one-cue conclusion. Look for a variety of cues pointing in the same direction. The more cues point to the same conclusion, the more likely your conclusion will be correct. Be especially alert to contradictory cues—data that refute your initial hypotheses. It's relatively easy to perceive cues that confirm your hypotheses but more difficult to acknowledge contradictory evidence. At the same time, seek validation from others. Do others see things in the same way you do? If not, ask yourself if your perceptions may be in some way distorted.

Check Your Perceptions

Perception checking is another way to reduce uncertainty and to make your perceptions more accurate. The goal of perception checking is not to prove that your initial perception is correct but to explore further the thoughts and feelings of the other person. With this simple technique, you lessen your chances of misinterpreting another's feelings. At the same time, you give the other person an opportunity to elaborate on his or her thoughts and feelings. In its most basic form, perception checking consists of two steps:

- Describe what you see or hear, recognizing that even descriptions are not really objective but are heavily influenced by who you are, your emotional state, and so on. At the same time, you may wish to describe what you think is happening. Again, try to do this as descriptively (not evaluatively) as you can. Sometimes you may wish to offer several possibilities:
  - You've called me from work a lot this week. You seem concerned about whether everything is all right at home.
  - You haven't wanted to talk with me all week. You say that my work is fine, but you don't seem to want to give me the same responsibilities that other editorial assistants have.
- Avoid "mind reading"; that is, avoid trying to read other people's thoughts and feelings merely by observing their behaviors. Regardless of how many behaviors you observe and how carefully you examine them, you can only *guess* what is going on in someone's mind. A person's motives are not open to outside inspection; you can only make assumptions based on overt behaviors. So seek confirmation. Ask the other person if your description is accurate. Be careful that your request for confirmation does not sound as though you already know the answer. Avoid phrasing

VIEWPOINT

Consider how you might use perception checking in such situations as these: (1) A colleague offers a proposal you think is ridiculous; (2) a neighbor expresses fear of being robbed; (3) your friend says he wants to drop out of college; (4) your cousin hasn't called you in several months, though you've called her at least six times. What would you say in each case?

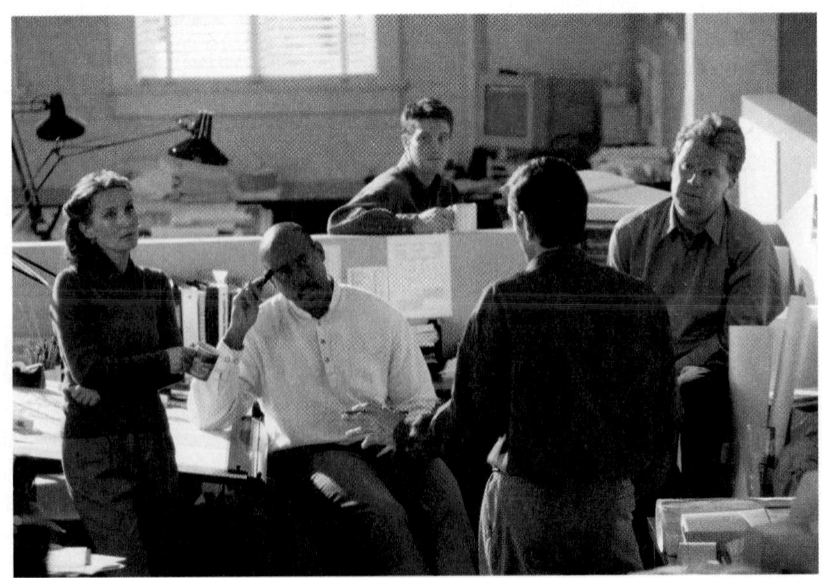

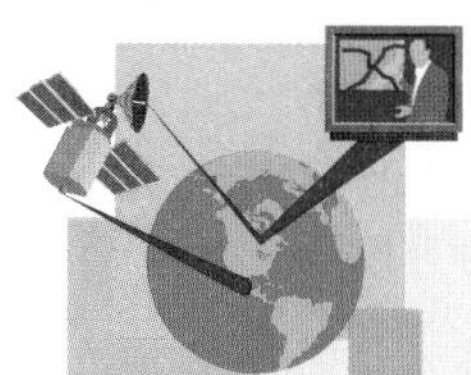

MEDIA WATCH

Cultivation Theory

According to cultivation theory, the media, especially television, are the primary means by which you form your perceptions of your society and your culture (Gerbner, Gross, Morgan, & Signorielli, 1980). What you watch and how often you watch it will influence your perception of the world and of people (Signorielli & Lears, 1992; Shanahan & Morgan, 1999; Vergeer, Lubbers, & Scheepers, 2000).

Cultivation theory argues that heavy television viewers form an image of reality that is inconsistent with the facts (Potter, 1986; Potter & Chang, 1990). For example:

- Heavy TV viewers see their chance of being a victim of a crime to be 1 in 10. In reality it's 1 in 50.
- Heavy TV viewers think that 20 percent of the world's population lives in the United States. In reality it's 6 percent.
- Heavy TV viewers believe that the percentage of workers in managerial or professional jobs is 25 percent. It's actually 5 percent.
- Heavy TV viewers in the United States are more likely to believe that "hard work yields rewards" and that "good wins over evil" than are light viewers.
- Heavy TV sports program viewers are more likely to believe in the values of hard work and good conduct.
- Heavy TV soap opera viewers are more likely to believe that "luck is important" and that "the strong survive" than are light viewers.
- Heavy TV viewers may be more materialistic than light viewers (Harmon, 2001).

You and the Media

In what ways do you think that cultivation theory might apply to you? What might you do to lessen such influence?

your questions defensively; for example, don't say, "You really don't want to go out, do you? I knew you didn't when you turned on that lousy television." Instead, ask for confirmation in as supportive a way as possible:

- Would you rather watch TV?
- Are you worried about me or the kids?
- Are you displeased with my work? Is there anything I can do to improve?

Reduce Your Uncertainty

Reducing uncertainty enables you to achieve greater accuracy in perception. Not surprisingly, many people find greater communication satisfaction when uncertainty is reduced (Neuliep & Grohskopf, 2000). In large part each of us learns about uncertainty and how to deal with it from our culture. In weak-uncertainty-avoidance cultures, people do little to avoid uncertainty and have little anxiety about not knowing what will happen next. Uncertainty to them is a normal part of life and is accepted as it comes. Members of these cultures don't feel threatened by unknown situations. Examples of such cultures include Singapore, Jamaica, Denmark, Sweden, Hong Kong, Ireland, Great Britain, Malaysia, India, Philippines, and the United States. In contrast, people in strong-uncertainty-avoidance cultures tend to avoid uncertainty and experience anxiety when they do not know what will happen next. In these cultures uncertainty is seen as threatening and as something that must be counteracted. Examples of such cultures include Greece, Portugal, Guatemala, Uruguay, Belgium, El Salvador, Japan, Yugoslavia, Peru, France, Chile, Spain, and Costa Rica (Hofstede, 1997).

The potential for communication problems can be great when people come from cultures with different attitudes toward uncertainty. For example, managers from cultures with weak uncertainty avoidance will accept employees who work only when they have to and will not get too upset when employees are late. Managers from cultures with strong uncertainty avoidance will expect employees to be busy at all times and will have little tolerance for lateness.

Because weak-uncertainty-avoidance cultures have great tolerance for ambiguity and uncertainty, they minimize the importance of rules governing communication and relationships (Hofstede, 1997; Lustig & Koester, 1999). People who don't follow the same rules as the cultural majority are readily tolerated. Cultures with weak uncertainty avoidance may even encourage different approaches and perspectives. Strong-uncertainty-avoidance cultures, however, create very clear-cut communication rules that must not be broken.

Students from weak-uncertainty-avoidance cultures value freedom in education and prefer vague assignments without specific timetables. These students will want to be rewarded for creativity and will easily accept the instructor's (sometimes) lack of knowledge. Students from strong-uncertainty-avoidance cultures prefer highly structured experiences in which there is little ambiguity; they prefer specific objectives, detailed instructions, and definite timetables. These students expect to be judged on the basis of the right answers and expect the instructor to have all the answers all the time (Hofstede, 1997).

A variety of uncertainty reduction **strategies** can help reduce uncertainty (Berger & Bradac, 1982; Gudykunst, 1994):

- Observing another person while he or she is engaged in an active task (preferably interacting with others in informal social situations) will often reveal a great deal about the person—because people are less apt to monitor their behaviors and more likely to reveal their true selves in informal situations.
- You can manipulate the situation so as to observe the person in more specific and more revealing contexts. Employment interviews, theatrical auditions, and student teaching are examples of situations structured to let one person observe how another individual might act and react and hence to reduce uncertainty about that individual.
- When you log on to an Internet chat group for the first time and then lurk, reading the exchanges between the other group members before saying anything yourself, you can learn about the people in the group and about the group itself and thus reduce uncertainty. Having reduced uncertainty, you're more likely to make contributions that will be appropriate to the group and less likely to violate any of the group's norms; in short, you're more likely to communicate effectively.
- Another way to reduce uncertainty is to collect information about a person by asking others. You might inquire of a colleague if a third person finds you interesting and might like to have dinner with you.
- And of course you can interact with the individual. For example, you can ask questions: "Do you enjoy sports?" "What did you think of that computer science course?" "What would you do if you got fired?" You also gain knowledge of another by disclosing information about yourself. Your self-disclosure will help to create an environment that encourages disclosures from the person about whom you wish to learn more.

Increase Your Cultural Awareness

Recognizing and being mindful of cultural differences will help increase your accuracy in perception. For example, Russian or Chinese artists such as ballet dancers will often applaud their audience by clapping. Americans may easily interpret this as egotistical—as if the performers are clapping for themselves. Similarly, a German man will enter a restaurant before the woman in order to see if the place is respectable enough for the woman to enter. This simple custom can easily be interpreted as rude when viewed by members of cultures in which it's considered courteous for the woman to enter first (Axtell, 1993). Not surprisingly, there are also large differences in the ways people from different cultures negotiate in business. Negotiation strategies, the influence of status in negotiated decisions, and the way information is presented may differ greatly from one culture to another (Hui & Luk, 1997; Shiraev & Levy, 2001).

Recall that within every cultural group, there are wide and important differences. As not all Americans are alike, neither are all Indonesians, Greeks, Mexicans, and so on. When you make assumptions that all people of a certain culture are alike, you're thinking in stereotypes.

Cultural awareness also helps counteract the difficulty most people have in understanding the nonverbal messages of people from other cultures. For example, it is easier to decode the emotions communicated facially by members of your own culture than to read the expressions of members of other cultures (Weathers, Frank, & Spell, 2002). This "ingroup advantage" will assist your perceptional accuracy for members of your own culture but will often hinder your accuracy for members of other cultures (Elfenbein & Ambady, 2002).

REFLECTIONS ON ETHICS

Information Ethics

The approach to ethics taken in this book from its first edition has been in keeping with this view of *information ethics*. This position argues that people have the right to information relevant to the choices they need to make. In fact, without such information, accurate perception of people, events, and the world in general would be impossible. From this basic premise several corollaries follow:

- Communications are ethical when they facilitate people's freedom of choice by presenting them with accurate information. Communications are unethical when they interfere with people's freedom of choice by preventing them from securing such information, or by giving them false or misleading information that will lead them to make choices they would not make if they had more accurate information.
- To make wise choices for yourself, you must have the right to information about yourself that others possess and that may influence your decisions. Thus, for example, you have the right to face your accusers, to know the witnesses who will testify against you, to see your credit rating, and to know what Social Security benefits you'll receive. On the other hand, you do not have the right to information that is none of your business—such as information about whether your neighbors are happy, or argue a lot, or receive food stamps.
- To facilitate the choices of others, you have an obligation to reveal information you possess that bears on the choices of other people and of your society. Thus, for example, you have an obligation to identify wrongdoing that you witness, to identify someone in a police lineup, to report criminal activity, and to testify at a trial when you possess pertinent information. This information is essential if society is to accomplish its purposes and make its legitimate choices.

WHAT WOULD YOU DO? Your best friend's husband is currently having an extramarital affair with a 17-year-old girl. Your friend suspects this is going on and asks if you know anything about it. Would it be ethical for you to lie and say you know nothing, or are you obligated to tell your friend what you know? Are you obligated to tell the police? What would you do in this situation?

SUMMARY

In this unit we explored the process of perception, the processes influencing perception, and recommendations for making perception more accurate.

1. Perception is the process through which you become aware of the many stimuli impinging on your senses.
2. The process of perception consists of five stages: sensory stimulation occurs; sensory stimulation is organized; sensory stimulation is interpreted–evaluated; information is stored in memory; and information is retrieved from memory.
3. The following processes influence perception: (1) implicit personality theory, (2) self-fulfilling prophecy, (3) perceptual accentuation, (4) primacy–recency, (5) consistency, and (6) attribution.
4. The concept of implicit personality theory has to do with the private personality theories that individuals hold and that influence how they perceive other people.
5. The self-fulfilling prophecy occurs when you make a prediction or formulate a belief that comes true because you've made the prediction and acted on it as if it were true.
6. Perceptual accentuation leads you to see what you expect and what you want to see.
7. The phenomenon of primacy–recency involves the relative influence of stimuli in relation to the order in which you perceive them. If what occurs first exerts the greatest influence, you're influenced by the primacy effect. If what occurs last exerts the greatest influence, you're experiencing a recency effect.
8. The principle of consistency describes your tendency to perceive that which enables you to achieve psychological balance or comfort among various attitude objects and their interconnections.
9. Attribution is the process through which you try to understand your own and others' behaviors and the motivations for these behaviors. In this process you utilize four types of data: data about consensus, consistency, distinctiveness, and controllability. Errors such as the self-serving bias, the fundamental attribution error, and overattribution can interfere with accuracy in attribution.
10. To increase accuracy in perception, analyze your perceptions, check your perceptions, reduce uncertainty, and increase your cultural awareness.

Key Terms

perception
implicit personality theory
self-fulfilling prophecy
perceptional accentuation
primacy–recency
consistency
stereotyping
attribution
consensus
distinctiveness
controllability
self-serving bias
fundamental attribution error
overattribution
uncertainty reduction strategies

Thinking Critically About

Perception

1. For the next several days, record all examples of people perception—all instances in which you drew a conclusion about another person. Try to classify these in terms of the processes identified in this unit, such as implicit personality theory, stereotyping, or attribution. Record also the specific context in which each instance occurred. After you've identified the various processes, share your findings in groups of five or six or with the entire class. As always, disclose only what you wish to disclose. What processes do you use most frequently? Do these processes lead to any barriers to accurate perception?
2. In the early 1990s one study of stereotypes on British television found that gender stereotypes hadn't changed much over 10 years and that these stereotypes were comparable to those found on North American television (Furnham & Bitar, 1993). Other research suggested that these stereotypes had changed and that television depictions of men and women were erasing older stereotypes (Vernon, Williams, Phillips, & Wilson, 1990). How would you update this research? What do you find to be the current gender stereotypes on television? How many can you identify?
3. In making evaluations of events or people, it would seem logical that we would first think about the event or person and then make the evaluation. Some research claims, however, that we really don't think before assigning any perception a positive or negative value. This research argues that all perceptions have a positive or negative value attached to them and that these evaluations are most often automatic and involve no conscious thought. That is, immediately on perceiving a person, idea, or thing, we attach a positive or negative value (*New York Times*, August 8, 1995, pp. C1, C10). What do you think of this? One bit of evidence against this position would be the ability to identify three or four or five things, ideas, or people about which you feel *completely* neutral. Can you do it?
4. Racial profiling (the practice whereby the police focus on members of specific races as possible crime suspects) has been widely reported and widely condemned as racist. In the aftermath of the attacks on the World Trade Center and the Pentagon on September 11, 2001, many people saw racial profiling—of Muslims and those who looked "Arab"—as necessary in preventing further acts of terrorism. How do you feel about racial profiling?
5. As your relationship with another person becomes closer and more intimate, you generally reduce your uncertainty about each other; you become more predictable to each other. Do you think high predictability makes a relationship more stable or less stable? More enjoyable or less enjoyable?
6. How would you explain the operation of primacy and recency in students' perceptions of instructors and instructors' perceptions of students?
7. How do the schemata of college students and, say, people in their 60s and 70s differ for "Japanese people," "gay men and lesbians," or "single mothers"?

UNIT

Listening

UNIT CONTENTS

There can be little doubt that you listen a great deal. Upon awakening you listen to the radio. On the way to school you listen to friends, people around you, screeching cars, singing birds, or falling rain. In school you listen to the teacher, to other students, and to yourself. You listen to friends at lunch and return to class to listen to more teachers. You arrive home and again listen to family and friends. Perhaps you listen to CDs, radio, or television. All in all, you listen for a good part of your waking day. In this unit you'll learn

- how listening works and the types of listening you can engage in
- how you can improve your own listening abilities

The Importance and Benefits of Listening

If you measured the importance of an activity by the time you spent on it, then—according to numerous research studies—listening would be your most important communication activity. Studies conducted from 1929 to 1980 showed that listening was the most often used form of communication, followed by speaking, reading, and writing (Rankin, 1929; Werner, 1975; Barker, Edwards, Gaines, Gladney, & Holley, 1980; Steil, Barker, & Watson, 1983; Wolvin & Coakley, 1982). This was true of high school and college students as well as of adults from a wide variety of fields. With the widespread use of the Internet today, these studies have become dated and their findings of limited value. Your communication patterns are very different from those of someone raised and educated before the widespread use of home computers. However, anecdotal evidence, although not conclusive in any way, still suggests that listening is probably the most used communication activity. Just think of how you spend your day; listening probably occupies a considerable amount of time.

It's also interesting to note that, according to research, the effective listener is more likely to emerge as a group leader, a more effective salesperson, a more attentive health care worker, and a more effective manager (Johnson & Bechler, 1998; Kramer, 1997; Castleberry & Shepherd, 1993; Lauer, 2003; Stein & Bowen, 2003). In recent years medical educators, claiming that doctors are not trained to listen to their patients, have introduced what they call "narrative medicine" to teach doctors how to listen to their patients—and how to recognize that their perceptions of their patients are influenced by their own emotions (Smith, 2003).

Another way to appreciate the importance of listening is to consider its many benefits. Here are some, built around the purposes of human communication identified in Unit 1:

- *Learning:* Listening enables you to acquire knowledge of others, the world, and yourself, so as to avoid problems and make better-informed decisions. For example, hearing Peter tell about his travels to Cuba will help you learn more about Peter and about life in another country. Listening to the difficulties of your sales staff may help you offer more pertinent sales training.
- *Relating:* Through attentive and supportive listening you can gain social acceptance and popularity. Others will increase their liking of you once they see your genuine concern for them.
- *Influencing:* Listening can help you change the attitudes and behaviors of others. For example, workers are more likely to follow your advice once they feel you've really listened to their insights and concerns.
- *Playing:* Listening can be enjoyable, letting you share pleasurable thoughts and feelings. Hearing the anecdotes of coworkers will allow you to balance the world of work and the world of play.
- *Helping:* Listening often is vital in efforts to assist others. For example, listening to your child's complaints about her teacher will increase your ability to help your child cope with school and her teacher.

The Process of Listening

Before reading about the process of listening, examine your own listening habits and tendencies by taking the self-test below.

TEST YOURSELF

How Do You Listen?

Respond to each question with the following scale: 1 = always, 2 = frequently, 3 = sometimes, 4 = seldom, and 5 = never.

____ **1.** I listen actively, communicate acceptance of the speaker, and prompt the speaker to further explore his or her thoughts.

____ **2.** I listen to what the speaker is saying and feeling; I try to feel what the speaker feels.

____ **3.** I listen without judging the speaker.

____ **4.** I listen to the literal meanings that a speaker communicates; I don't look too deeply into hidden meanings.

____ **5.** I listen without active involvement; I generally remain silent and take in what the other person is saying.

____ **6.** I listen objectively; I focus on the logic of the ideas rather than on the emotional meaning of the message.

____ **7.** I listen critically, evaluating the speaker and what the speaker is saying.

____ **8.** I look for the hidden meanings: the meanings that are revealed by subtle verbal or nonverbal cues.

HOW DID YOU DO? These statements focus on the ways of listening discussed in this unit. All of these ways are appropriate at some times but not at other times. It depends. So the only responses that are really inappropriate are "always" and "never." Effective listening is listening that is tailored to the specific communication situation.

WHAT WILL YOU DO? Consider how you might use these statements to begin to improve your listening effectiveness. A good way to start is to review these listening behaviors and try to identify situations in which each behavior would be appropriate and situations in which each behavior would be inappropriate.

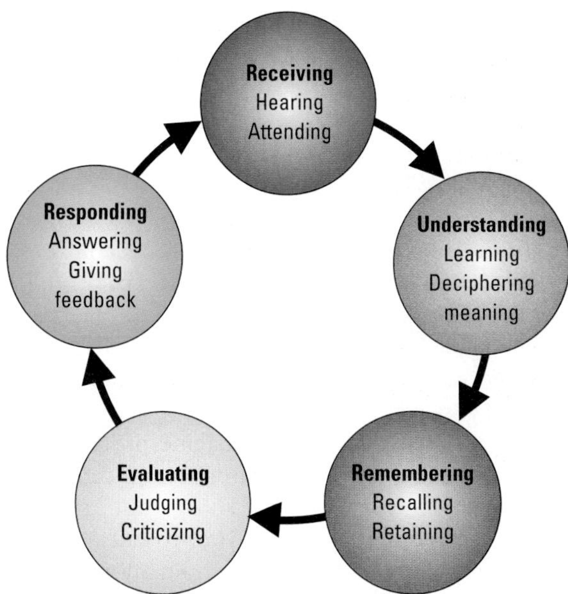

Figure 5.1

A Five-Stage Model of Listening

At each stage of listening there will be lapses. Thus, for example, at the receiving stage, a listener receives part of the message but because of noise (and perhaps for other reasons) fails to receive other parts. Similarly, at the stage of understanding, a listener understands part of the message but because of the inability to share another's meanings exactly (see Unit 7 for more on this) fails to understand other parts. The same is true for remembering, evaluating, and responding. This model draws on a variety of previous models that listening researchers have developed (e.g., Alessandra, 1986; Barker & Gaut, 2002; Brownell, 1987; Steil, Barker, & Watson, 1983).

The process of **listening** can be described as a series of five steps: (1) receiving, (2) understanding, (3) remembering, (4) evaluating, and (5) responding. The process is visualized in Figure 5.1. Note that the listening process is circular. The responses of person A serve as the stimuli for person B, whose responses in turn serve as the stimuli for person A, and so on. As will become clear in the following discussion of the five steps, listening is not a process of transferring an idea from the mind of a speaker to the mind of a listener. Rather, it is a process in which speaker and listener work together to achieve a common understanding.

Receiving

Unlike listening, hearing begins and ends with this first stage—receiving. Hearing is something that just happens when you open your ears or when you get within earshot of auditory stimuli.

Listening is quite different. Listening begins, but does not end, with receiving messages the speaker sends. In listening you receive both the verbal and the nonverbal messages—not only the words but also the gestures, facial expressions, variations in volume and rate, and lots more, as you'll discover when we discuss messages in more detail in Units 7 and 8. For improved reception:

- Focus **attention** on the speaker's verbal and nonverbal messages, on both what is said and what is not said.
- Look for feedback in response to previous messages as well as feedforward (Unit 1), which can reveal how the speaker would like his or her message viewed.
- Avoid distractions in the environment and focus attention on the speaker rather than on what you'll say next.

MEDIA WATCH

Gatekeepers

The concept of "gatekeeping," introduced by Kurt Lewin in his *Human Relations* (1947), involves two aspects: *the process* by which a message passes through various gates, as well as *the people or groups* that allow the message to pass (gatekeepers).

Gatekeeping, as you can imagine, prevents you from listening to (or reading or seeing) certain messages.

As you were growing up, your parents—your first gatekeepers—gave you certain information and withheld other information. For example, depending on the culture in which you were raised, you may have been told about Santa Claus and the Tooth Fairy but not about cancer or mutual funds. When you went to school, your teachers served a similar gatekeeping function. They taught you about certain historical events but not about others. Textbook authors serve a similar gatekeeping function (Robinson, 1993). Editors of newspapers, popular and scholarly periodicals, and publishing houses also are gatekeepers, as are those who regulate and monitor Internet messages (Lewis, 1995; Bodon, Powell, & Hickson, 1999).

The media, usually on the basis of their own codes and sometimes because of legal regulations, censor what gets through to viewers. Thus, for example, one Madonna video was rejected because of its depiction of group sex, and one David Bowie video was rejected because of a nude beach scene (Banks, 1995). Often, of course, media engage in gatekeeping so as to increase profits; for example, they emphasize (open the gates for) stories of celebrities, violence, and sex because these sell. At the same time, they deemphasize (close the gates on) reports on minority issues, classical drama, or issues that reflect negatively on their own biases.

You and the Media

Describe how one, two, or three of the following people function as gatekeepers in your ability to acquire information: the editor of your local or college newspaper, Oprah Winfrey, your romantic partner (past or present), the president of the United States, network news shows, or the advertising department of a large corporation.

- Maintain your role as listener and avoid interrupting the speaker until he or she is finished.

In this brief discussion of receiving (and in this entire chapter on listening), the unstated assumption is that both individuals can receive auditory signals without difficulty. But for the many people who have hearing impairments, listening presents a variety of problems. Table 5.1 provides tips for communication between deaf and hearing people.

Understanding

Understanding is the stage at which you learn what the speaker means. This understanding must take into consideration both the thoughts that are expressed and the emotional tone that accompanies them—the urgency or the joy or sorrow expressed in the message. For improved understanding:

- Relate new information to what you already know.
- See the speaker's messages from the speaker's point of view. Avoid judging the message until you've fully understood it—as the speaker intended it.
- Ask questions to clarify or to secure additional details or examples if necessary.
- Rephrase (paraphrase) the speaker's ideas in your own words.

Remembering

Messages that you receive and understand need to be remembered for at least some period of time. In some small group and public speaking situations, you can augment your memory by taking notes or by tape-recording the messages. In most interpersonal communication situations, however, such note taking would be considered inappropriate—although you often do write down a phone number, an appointment, or directions.

Table 5.1
Interpersonal Communication Tips

Between Deaf and Hearing People

People differ greatly in their hearing ability: Some are totally deaf and can hear nothing; others have some hearing loss and can hear some sounds; still others have impaired hearing but can hear most speech. Although people with profound hearing loss can speak, their speech may appear labored and may be less clear than the speech of those with unimpaired hearing. Here are some suggestions for more effective communication between deaf and hearing people.

If you have unimpaired hearing:

1. *Set up a comfortable context.* Reduce the distance between yourself and the person with a hearing impairment. Reduce the background noise. Turn off the television or even the air conditioner.
2. *Avoid interference.* Make sure the visual cues from your speech are clearly observable; for example, face the person squarely and avoid smoking, chewing gum, or holding your hand over your mouth. Make sure the lighting is adequate.
3. *Speak at an adequate volume.* But avoid shouting, which can distort your speech and may insult the person. Be careful to avoid reducing volume at the ends of your sentences.
4. *Phrase ideas in different ways.* Because some words are easier to lip-read than others, it often helps if you rephrase your ideas in different ways.
5. *Avoid overlapping speech.* In group situations only one person should speak at a time. Similarly, don't talk to a person with a hearing impairment through a third party; direct your comments to the person himself or herself. Elementary school teachers, for example, have been found to direct fewer comments to deaf children than to hearing students (Cawthon, 2001).
6. *Ask for additional information.* Ask the person if there is anything you can do to make it easier for him or her to understand you.
7. *Don't avoid common terms.* Use terms like "hear," "listen," "music," or "deaf" when they're relevant to the conversation. Trying to avoid these common terms will make your speech sound artificial.
8. *Use nonverbal cues.* These can help communicate your meaning; gestures indicating size or location and facial expressions indicating emotions and feelings are often helpful.

If you have impaired hearing:

1. *Do your best to eliminate background noise.*
2. *Move closer to the speaker if this helps you hear better.* Alert the speaker that this closer distance will help you hear better.
3. *Ask for adjustments.* If you feel the speaker can make adjustments to ease your comprehension, ask. For example, ask the speaker to repeat a message, to speak more slowly or more distinctly, or to increase his or her volume.
4. *Position yourself for best reception.* If you hear better in one ear than another, position yourself accordingly; if necessary, clue the speaker in to this fact.
5. *Ask for additional cues.* If necessary, ask the speaker to write down certain information, such as phone numbers or website addresses. Carrying a pad and pencil will prove helpful for this and in the event that you wish to write something down for others.

These suggestions were drawn from a variety of sources: *Tips for Communicating with Deaf People* (Rochester Institute of Technology, National Technical Institute for the Deaf, Division of Public Affairs), http://www.his.com/~lola/deaf.html, http://www.zak.co.il/deaf-info/old/comm_strategies.html, and http://www.agbell.org/information/brochures_communication.cfm (all websites accessed October 23, 2004).

You can improve your message memory by:

- identifying the central ideas in a message and the major support advanced for them
- summarizing the message in a more easily retained form, being careful not to ignore crucial details or qualifications

UNDERSTANDING THEORY AND RESEARCH

Reconstructing Memory

When you remember a message, do you remember it as it was spoken, or do you remember what you think you heard? The commonsense response, of course, would be that you remember what was said. But before accepting this simple explanation, try to memorize the list of 12 words presented below, which come from an actual research study (Glucksberg & Danks, 1975). Don't worry about the order of the words; only the number of words remembered counts. Take about 20 seconds to memorize as many words as possible. Then close the book and write down as many words as you can remember.

bed	comfort	night
rest	sound	eat
dream	awake	slumber
wake	tired	snore

Don't read any farther until you've tried to memorize and reproduce the list of words.

If you're like most people, you not only remembered a good number of the words on the list but also "remembered" at least one word that was not on the list: *sleep*. Most people recall the word *sleep* as being on the list (whether they read the list as you've done here or hear it spoken)—but, as you can see, it wasn't. What happens is that in remembering you don't simply reproduce the list; you reconstruct it. In this case you gave the list meaning, and part of that meaning included the word *sleep*. Memory for speech, then, is not reproductive—you don't simply reproduce in your memory what the speaker said. Rather, memory is reconstructive: You reconstruct the messages you hear into a system that makes sense to you but, in the process, often remember distorted versions of what was said.

Working with Theories and Research

- *If you have access, log on to Research Navigator* (www.researchnavigator.com) *and search for articles dealing with false memory. In what types of situations is false memory found? What are some of its implications for communication?*

- repeating names and key concepts to yourself or, if appropriate, aloud
- asking questions when in doubt

Evaluating

Evaluating consists of judging messages in some way. At times you may try to evaluate the speaker's underlying intent. Often this evaluation process goes on without much conscious thought. For example, Elaine tells you that she is up for a promotion and is really excited about it. You may then try to judge her intention. Does she want you to use your influence with the company president? Is she preoccupied with her accomplishment and thus telling everyone about it? Is she looking for a pat on the back? Generally, if you know the person well, you'll be able to identify the intention and therefore be able to respond appropriately.

In other situations, evaluation is more in the nature of critical analysis. For example, in listening to proposals advanced in a business meeting, you will at this stage evaluate them. Is there evidence to show that these proposals are practical and will increase productivity? Is there contradictory evidence? Are there alternative proposals that would be more practical and more productive?

In evaluating, try to

- resist evaluation until you fully understand the speaker's point of view
- assume that the speaker is a person of goodwill; give the speaker the benefit of any doubt by asking for clarification on issues that you feel you

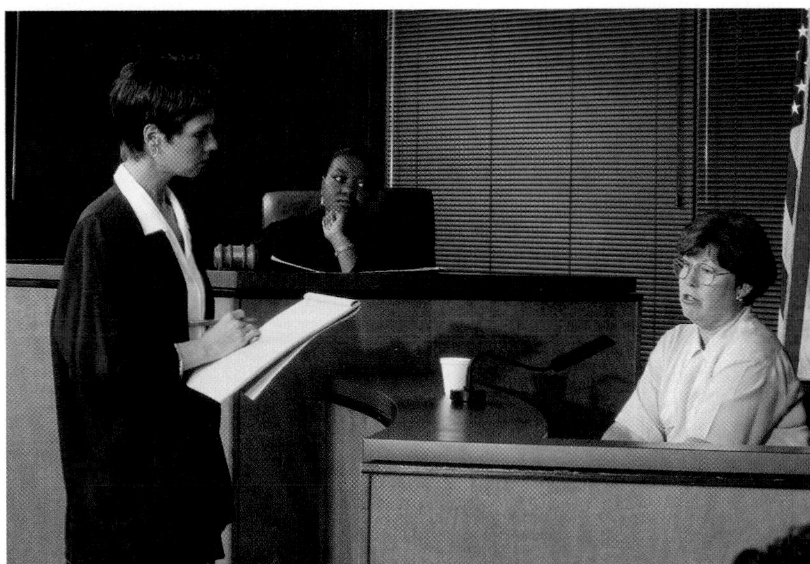

VIEWPOINT

The term *false memory syndrome* refers to a theory explaining the tendency to remember a past experience that never actually occurred. Most studies on false memory syndrome have centered on people's recollections of abuse and other traumatic experiences. Often these false memories turn out to have been implanted by therapists and interviewers, whose persistent questioning over a period of time creates such a realistic scenario that individuals may come to believe these things actually occurred (Porter, Brit, Yuille, & Lehman, 2000). In what other, less dramatic ways can false memory syndrome occur?

must object to (are there any other reasons for accepting this new proposal?)

- distinguish facts from inferences (see Unit 7), opinions, and personal interpretations by the speaker
- identify any biases, self-interests, or prejudices that may lead the speaker to slant unfairly what is presented

Responding

Responding occurs in two phases: (1) responses you make while the speaker is talking and (2) responses you make after the speaker has stopped talking. These responses are feedback—information that you send back to the speaker and that tells the speaker how you feel and think about his or her messages. Responses made while the speaker is talking should be supportive and should acknowledge that you're listening. These include what researchers on nonverbal communication call **backchanneling cues:** "I see," "yes," "uh-huh," and similar signals that let the speaker know you're attending to the message.

Responses made after the speaker has stopped talking are generally more elaborate and might include expressing empathy ("I know how you must feel"), asking for clarification ("Do you mean that this new health plan is to replace the old one, or will it just be a supplement?"), challenging ("I think your evidence is weak here"), and agreeing ("You're absolutely right on this, and I'll support your proposal when it comes up for a vote"). For effective responding:

- Be supportive of the speaker throughout the speaker's talk by using and varying backchanneling cues; using only one backchanneling cue—for example, saying "uh-huh" throughout—may make it appear that you're not really listening.
- Express support for the speaker in your final responses.
- Be honest; the speaker has a right to expect honest responses, even if these express anger or disagreement.
- State your thoughts and feelings as your own, using I-messages. For example, say "I think the new proposal will entail greater expense than you outlined" rather than "Everyone will object to the plan for costing too much."

Table 5.2 on page 84 identifies some types of difficult listeners—listeners who don't follow the suggestions for each of the five listening stages—and their problem-causing ways of responding.

Listening, Culture, and Gender

Listening is difficult, in part, because of the inevitable differences in the communication systems between speaker and listener. Because each person has had a unique set of experiences, each person's communication and meaning system is going to be different from each other person's. When speaker and listener come from different cultures or are of different genders, the differences and their effects are naturally so much greater. Let's look first at culture.

Table 5.2
Some Problem-Causing Ways of Responding in Listening

Review this table and try to see if it includes some of your own listening behaviors.

Listener Type	Listening (Responding) Behavior	(Mis)interpreting Thoughts
The static listener	Gives no feedback, remains relatively motionless, reveals no expression	Why isn't she reacting? Am I not producing sound?
The monotonous feedback giver	Seems responsive, but the responses never vary; regardless of what you say, the response is the same	Am I making sense? Why is he still smiling? I'm being dead serious.
The overly expressive listener	Reacts to just about everything with extreme responses	Why is she so expressive? I didn't say anything that provocative. She'll have a heart attack when I get to the punch line.
The reader/writer	Reads or writes while "listening" and only occasionally glances up	Am I that boring? Is last week's student newspaper more interesting than me?
The eye avoider	Looks all around the room and at others but never at you	Why isn't he looking at me? Do I have spinach on my teeth?
The preoccupied listener	Listens to other things at the same time, often with headphones turned up so loud that the sound interferes with your own thinking	When is she going to shut that music off and really listen? Am I so boring that my talk needs background music?
The waiting listener	Listens for a cue to take over the speaking turn	Is he listening to me or rehearsing his next interruption?
The thought-completing listener	Listens a little and then finishes your thought	Am I that predictable? Why do I bother saying anything? He already knows what I'm going to say.

Listening and Culture

In a global environment in which people from very different cultures work together, it's especially important to understand the ways in which cultural differences can influence listening.

Language and Speech

Even when speaker and listener speak the same language, they speak it with different meanings and different accents. No two speakers speak exactly the same language. Speakers of the same language will, at the very least, have different meanings for the same terms because they have had different experiences.

Speakers and listeners who have different native languages and who may have learned English as a second language will have even greater differences in meaning. Translations are never precise and never fully capture the meaning in the other language. If your meaning for "house" was learned in a culture in which everyone lived in their own house with lots of land around it, then talking about houses with someone whose meaning was learned in a neighborhood of high-rise tenements is going to be difficult. Although you'll each hear the same word, the meanings you'll each develop will be drastically different. In adjusting your listening—especially in an intercultural setting—understand that the speaker's meanings may be very different from yours even though you're speaking the same language.

In many classrooms throughout this country, there will be a wide range of **accents.** Those whose native language is a tonal one such as Chinese (in which differences in pitch signal important meaning differences) may speak English with variations in pitch that may seem puzzling to their hearers. Those whose native language is Japanese may have trouble distinguishing *l* from *r*, as Japanese does not include this distinction. The native language acts as a filter and influences the accent given to the second language.

ASK THE RESEARCHER

Not Listening

- *I appreciate all these suggestions for listening, but what if you don't want to listen? For example, I don't want to hear about my colleagues' relationships, my neighbor's tax problems, or even my partner's frequent and detailed sports updates. Any suggestions?*

These situations are common. The speaker isn't thinking about you—he or she is talking to sort out a problem or to express an enthusiasm. The way you respond is your judgment call. Is being a listener something that a friend does for a friend (Do you ramble on about your camcorder or pet ferret?)? If you decide you don't want to listen, interrupt. Change the subject by recognizing the speaker's concern and, in the same breath, moving to a different topic: "I'm amazed that Jim hasn't responded. I realize it's very stressful. You know, something that has been on my mind. . . ." Or, bring the problem directly to the speaker's attention with kindness or humor: "I'll be qualified as a commentator if you tell me any more about that game! Let's talk about our plans for. . . ." Don't hang in the middle. Either choose to listen or be assertive and choose to change the subject.

For further information: Brownell, J. (2002). *Listening: Attitudes, principles and skills* (2nd ed.). Boston: Allyn & Bacon.

Judi Brownell (Ph.D., Syracuse University) is professor of organizational communication in the School of Hotel Administration at Cornell University, where she teaches managerial and organizational communication and organizational behavior. Professor Brownell is a past president of the International Listening Association and was inducted into the Listening Hall of Fame.

Nonverbal Behaviors

Speakers from different cultures have different display rules—cultural rules that govern which nonverbal behaviors are appropriate and which are inappropriate in a public setting. As you listen to other people, you also "listen" to their nonverbal cues. If these are drastically different from what you expect on the basis of the verbal message, you may see them as a kind of noise or interference or even as contradictory messages. Also, of course, different cultures may give very different meanings to the same nonverbal gesture; for example, the thumb and forefinger forming a circle means "OK" in most of the United States, but it means "money" in Japan, "zero" in some Mediterranean countries, and "I'll kill you" in Tunisia.

Feedback

Members of some cultures give very direct and honest feedback. Speakers from these cultures—the United States is a good example—expect the feedback to be a forthright reflection of what their listeners are feeling. In other cultures—Japan and Korea are good examples—it's more important to be positive than to be truthful, so people may respond with positive feedback (say, in commenting on a business colleague's proposal) even though they don't actually feel positive. Listen to feedback, as you would all messages, with a full recognition that various cultures view feedback very differently.

Credibility

What makes a speaker credible, or believable, also will vary from one culture to another. In some cultures people would claim that competence is the most important factor in, say, the choice of a teacher for their preschool children. In other cultures the most important factor might be the goodness or morality of the teacher. Similarly, members of different cultures may perceive the credibility of various media very differently. For example, members of a repressive society in which the government controls television news may come to attribute little credibility to such broadcasts. After all, these listeners might reason, television news is simply what the government wants you to know. This reaction may be hard to understand or even recognize for someone raised in the United States, for example, where traditionally

UNDERSTANDING THEORY AND RESEARCH

Cues to Lying

In listening you normally assume that the speaker is telling the truth and seldom even ask yourself if the speaker is lying. When you do wonder about a speaker's truthfulness, research shows, it may be because the speaker exhibits behaviors that often accompany lying. Here are some verbal and nonverbal behaviors that are associated with lying (Knapp & Hall, 1997; O'Hair, Cody, Goss, & Krayer, 1988; Bond & Atoum, 2000; Al-Simadi, 2000; Burgoon & Bacue, 2003). As you review these behaviors, ask yourself if you use these cues in making assumptions about whether or not people are telling the truth. Be careful that you don't fall into the trap of thinking that just because someone emits these cues, he or she is therefore lying; these cues are often used by truth-tellers as well and are not 100 percent reliable in indicating lying. In fact, in one study participants who held stereotypical views of how liars behave (for example, liars don't look at you, or liars fidget) were *less* effective in detecting lying than were those who did not hold such beliefs (Vrij & Mann, 2001). Generally, however, research finds that liars

- smile less
- respond with shorter answers, often simple "yes" or "no" responses
- use fewer specifics and more generalities; for example, "we hung out"
- shift their posture more
- use more self-touching movements
- use more and longer pauses
- avoid direct eye contact with listener and blink more often than normal
- appear less friendly and attentive
- make more speech errors

Working with Theories and Research

- *Can you recall a situation in which you made the assumption that someone was lying on the basis of such cues (or others)? What happened? Should you want to learn more about lying, if you have access, log on to Research Navigator* (www.researchnavigator.com) *and search for "lying," "deception," and similar terms. It's a fascinating subject of study.*

the media have been largely free of such political control.

Listening and Gender

Deborah Tannen opens her chapter on listening in her best-selling *You Just Don't Understand: Women and Men in Conversation* (1990) with several anecdotes illustrating that when men and women talk, men lecture and women listen. The lecturer is positioned as the superior: as the teacher, the expert. The listener is positioned as the inferior: as the student, the nonexpert.

Women, according to Tannen, seek to build rapport and establish a closer relationship, and so use listening to achieve these ends. For example, women use more listening cues (such as interjecting "yeah," or "uh-uh," nodding in agreement, or smiling) to let the other person know they're paying attention and are interested. Women also make more eye contact when listening than do men, who are more apt to look around and often away from the speaker (Brownell, 2002). Men not only use fewer listening cues but interrupt more, and they will often change the topic to a subject they know more about or that is less relational or people oriented or that is more factual, such as sports statistics, economic developments, or political problems. Men, research shows, tend to play up their expertise, emphasize it, and use it in dominating the conversation. Women often play down their expertise.

Now, you might be tempted to conclude from this that women play fair in conversation and that men don't; for example, that men consistently seek

GOING *ONLINE*

The International Listening Association

http://www.listen.org

The International Listening Association is a group of people concerned with the study and teaching of effective listening. Visit this website and check out the "Listening Resources." What can you add to the discussion presented in this unit?

In addition, visit the companion website for this text (www.ablongman.com/devito) and take a look at the self-test "[When] Is Lying Unethical?" and the exercises "Passing Information from One Person to Another," "Listening Like a Man and a Woman," "Reducing Listening Barriers," "Practicing Active Listening," and "Listening."

International Listening Association

Back Forward Stop Refresh Home Larger Smaller Add Mail

Address http://www.listen.org/

Home About Convention Resources Quotations Members Only Site

International Listening Association

. . . the professional organization whose members are dedicated to learning more about the impact that listening has on all human activity.

The International Listening Association promotes the study, development, and teaching of listening and the practice of effective listening skills and techniques.

lis·ten·ing n (ILA, 1996): the process of receiving, constructing meaning from, and responding to spoken and/or nonverbal messages

- **26th Annual Convention - The Power of Listening.** April 13-17, 2005, Minneapolis, MN (USA). Call for Papers. New
- Join ILA
- Give the Gift of Listening
- About the ILA
- Membership Directory
- **Members Only:** Promote listening & the ILA by displaying an ILA Member logo & link at your website. New logos for members, life members, and founding members.
- **Members Only:** Committee Members Announced. Join an ILA Committee
- MarketPlace — do your usual online shopping by coming through this website first, and ILA will earn a percentage of your purchases.
- Public Service Announcements
- ILA Young Professionals, the Online Community for Student Members New
- Quotations about Listening
- Listening Resources Includes Listening Exercises, Listening Tests & Assessments, Listening Factoids, Convention Paper Resource Center and more
- Books by ILA Authors
- "The Listener Wins" by 2nd VP Michael Purdy (featured in the Monster.com Career Center)
- "Listening is the hardest of the 'easy' tasks" by syndicated writer and author Harvey Mackay
- Irritating Listening Habits
- ILA Official Calendar **Updated**
- Join Listen-2, the Internet discussion group devoted to listening.
- What's New at the ILA Website Updated

Send a link to this site to a friend. Bookmark this site.

to put themselves in a position superior to women. But that may be too simple an explanation. Research shows that men communicate this way not only with women but with other men as well. Men are not showing disrespect for their female conversational partners but are simply communicating as they normally do. Women, too, communicate as they do not only with men but also with other women.

Tannen argues that the goal of a man in conversation is to be accorded respect. Therefore, a man seeks to display his knowledge and expertise, even if to do this he has to change the topic to one he knows a great deal about. Women, on the other hand, seek to be liked; so they express agreement, rarely interrupt in order to take their turn as speaker, and give lots of cues (verbally and nonverbally) to indicate that they are listening.

There's no evidence to show that these differences represent any negative motives—for example, motives on the part of men to prove themselves superior or on the part of women to ingratiate themselves. Rather, these differences in listening are largely the result of the ways in which men and women have been socialized.

It should be mentioned that not all researchers agree that there is sufficient evidence to make the claims that Tannen and others make about gender differences in listening (Goldsmith & Fulfs, 1999). Gender differences are changing in today's world, and it's best to take generalizations about gender as starting points for investigation and not as airtight conclusions.

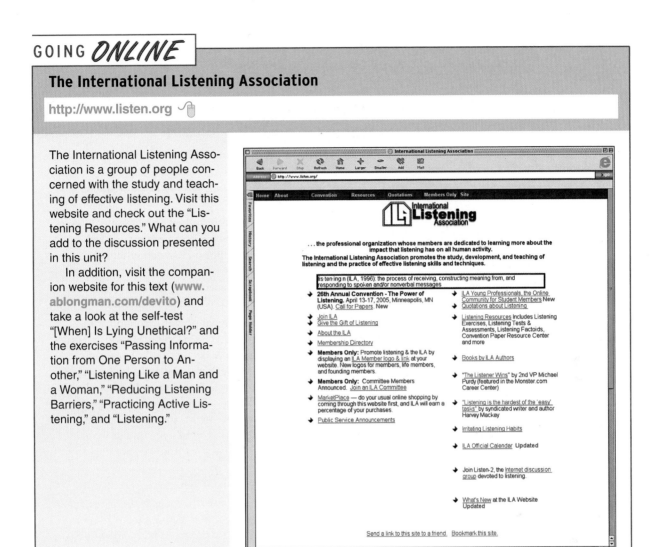

Styles of Effective Listening

As stressed throughout this chapter, listening is situational; the type of listening that is appropriate will vary with the situation, and each situation will call

COMMUNICATION@WORK

Power Listening at Company Meetings

Big people monopolize the listening. Small people monopolize the talking.

—David Schwartz

Much as you communicate power and authority with words and nonverbal expression, you can also communicate power through listening:

- Respond visibly, but in moderation. Too little response says you aren't listening, and too much response says you aren't listening critically. Backchanneling cues—head nods and brief oral responses that say you're listening—are especially helpful in communicating power.
- Avoid "adaptors"—behaviors such as playing with your hair or a pencil or drawing pictures on a Styrofoam cup. Adaptors signal discomfort and hence a lack of power. The absence of adaptors, on the other hand, makes you appear in control of the situation and comfortable in the role of listener.
- Maintain an open posture. When around a table or in an audience, resist covering your face, chest, or stomach with your hands. These postures are often interpreted to signal defensiveness or vulnerability and hence powerlessness.
- Take modest notes when appropriate. Taking too many notes may communicate a lack of ability to distinguish between what is and what is not important. Taking too few notes may communicate a lack of serious purpose or a reluctance to deal with the material.
- You also can signal power through *visual dominance* behavior (Exline, Ellyson, & Long, 1975; Burgoon & Bacue, 2003). For example, the average speaker maintains a high level of eye contact while listening and a lower level while speaking. When you want to signal dominance, you might reverse this pattern—maintain a high level of eye contact while talking but a lower level while listening.

Communicating@Work

Can you recall these listening behaviors in people you've seen at meetings? In what ways do you see these behaviors communicating power?

for a somewhat different combination of listening styles. The art of effective listening largely consists of making appropriate choices along the following four dimensions:

- empathic and objective listening
- nonjudgmental and critical listening
- surface and depth listening
- active and inactive listening

Let's take a look at each of these dimensions.

Empathic and Objective Listening

To understand what a person means and feels, listen with **empathy** (Rogers, 1970; Rogers & Farson, 1981). To empathize with others is to feel with them, to see the world as they see it, to feel what they feel. Empathy will enable you to understand other people's meanings, and it will also enhance your relationships (Barrett & Godfrey, 1988; Snyder, 1992).

Empathic listening is the preferred mode of responding in most communication situations, but there are times when you need to go beyond it to measure meanings and feelings against some objective reality. It's important to listen to Peter tell you how the entire world hates him and to understand how Peter feels and why he feels this way. But then you need to look more objectively at Peter and perhaps see the paranoia or the self-hatred behind his complaints. Sometimes, in other words, you have to put your empathic responses aside and listen with objectivity and detachment.

In adjusting your empathic and objective listening focus, keep the following recommendations in mind:

- *Punctuate from the speaker's point of view* (Unit 2). If you want to understand the speaker's perspective, see the sequence of events as the speaker does, and try to figure out how this can influence what the speaker says and does.

BUILDING COMMUNICATION SKILLS

Expressing Empathy

For any one or two of the following situations, indicate—in a sentence or two—how you'd respond with empathy to each comment. Assume that all three people are your peers.

1. I've never felt so alone in my life. Chris left last night and said it was all over. We were together for three years and now—after a 10-minute argument—everything is lost.
2. I just got $20,000 from my aunt's estate. She left it to me! Twenty thousand! Now I can get that car and buy some new clothes!
3. A Camry! My parents bought me a Camry for graduation. What a bummer. They promised me a Lexus.

- *Engage in equal, two-way conversation.* To encourage openness and empathy, try to eliminate any physical or psychological barriers to equality (for example, step out from behind the large desk separating you from your employee). Avoid interrupting the speaker—a sign that what you have to say is more important.
- *Seek to understand both thoughts and feelings.* Don't consider your listening task finished until you've understood what the speaker is feeling, as well as thinking.
- *Avoid "offensive listening,"* the tendency to listen to bits and pieces of information that will enable you to attack the speaker or find fault with something the speaker has said.
- *Strive especially to be objective in listening to friends and foes alike.* Be aware that your attitudes may lead you to distort messages—for example, to block out positive messages about a foe or negative messages about a friend. Guard against "expectancy hearing," in which you fail to hear what the speaker is really saying and instead hear what you expect.

Nonjudgmental and Critical Listening

Effective listening includes both nonjudgmental and critical responses. Listen nonjudgmentally (with an open mind and with a view toward understanding) and listen critically (with a view toward making some kind of evaluation or judgment). Listen first for understanding; only when you understand should you be willing to evaluate or judge the messages.

Listening with an open mind will help you understand messages better; listening with a critical mind will help you analyze and evaluate the messages. In adjusting your nonjudgmental and critical listening, focus on the following guidelines:

- *Keep an open mind.* Avoid prejudging. Delay your judgments until you fully understand the intention and the content the speaker is communicating. Avoid both positive and negative evaluation until you have a reasonably complete understanding.
- *Avoid filtering out or oversimplifying difficult or complex messages.* Similarly, avoid filtering out undesirable messages. Clearly, you don't want to hear that something you believe in is untrue, that people you care for are unkind, or that ideals you hold are self-destructive. Yet it's important that you reexamine your beliefs by listening to such messages.
- *Recognize your own biases.* These may interfere with accurate listening and cause you to distort message reception through the process of **assimilation**—the tendency to integrate and interpret what you hear or think you hear to conform to your own biases, prejudices, and expectations. For example, are your ethnic, national, or religious biases preventing you from appreciating a speaker's point of view?
- *Avoid uncritical listening when you need to make evaluations and judgments.* Recognize and resist the normal tendency to sharpen—a process in which one or two aspects of a message become highlighted, emphasized, and perhaps embellished. Often the concepts that are sharpened are incidental remarks that somehow stand out from the rest of the message.

Surface and Depth Listening

In Shakespeare's *Julius Caesar,* Marc Antony, in giving the funeral oration for Caesar, says: "I come to bury Caesar, not to praise him. / The evil that men do lives after them; / The good is oft interred with their bones." And later: "For Brutus is an honourable man; / So are they all, all honourable men." But if we listen beyond the surface of Marc Anthony's words, we can see that he does indeed come to praise Caesar, and to convince the crowd that Brutus was dishonorable—despite the fact that at first glance his words seem to say quite the opposite.

In most messages there's an obvious meaning that you can derive from a literal reading of the words and sentences. But there's often another level of meaning. Sometimes, as in these famous lines from *Julius Caesar,* the deeper level is the opposite of the literal meaning. At other times it seems totally unrelated. In reality, most messages have more than one level of meaning. For example, suppose Carol asks you how you like her new haircut. On one level, the meaning is clear: Do you like the haircut? But there's also another, perhaps a more important level: Carol is asking you to say something positive about her appearance. In the same way, the parent who complains about working hard at the office or in the home may, on a deeper level, be asking for an expression of appreciation. The child who talks about the unfairness of the other children in the playground may be asking for comfort and love, for some expression of caring.

To appreciate these other meanings, engage in depth listening. If you respond only to the surface-level communication (the literal meaning), you miss the opportunity to make meaningful contact with the other person's feelings and needs. If you say to the parent, "You're always complaining. I bet you really love working so hard," you fail to respond to the call for understanding and appreciation. In regulating your surface and depth listening, consider the following guidelines:

- *Focus on both verbal and nonverbal messages.* Recognize both consistent and inconsistent "packages" of messages, and use these as guides for drawing inferences about the speaker's meaning. Ask questions when in doubt. Listen also to what is omitted. Remember that speakers communicate by what they leave out as well as by what they include.
- *Listen for both content and relational messages.* The student who constantly challenges the instructor is, on one level, communicating disagreement over content. However, on another level—the relationship level—the student may be voicing objections to the instructor's authority or authoritarianism. The instructor needs to listen and respond to both types of messages.
- *Make special note of statements that refer back to the speaker.* Remember that people inevitably talk about themselves. Whatever a person says is, in part, a function of who that person is. Attend carefully to those personal, self-reference messages.
- *Don't disregard the literal meaning of messages in trying to uncover the more hidden meanings.* Balance your listening between surface and the underlying meanings. Respond to the different levels of meaning in the messages of others, as you would like others to respond to yours—sensitively but not obsessively, readily but not overambitiously.

VIEWPOINT
What one listening skill do you wish your friends, family, romantic partners, or work associates would cultivate and practice more faithfully?

Active and Inactive Listening

One of the most important communication skills you can learn is active listening. Consider the following interaction. You say: "I can't believe I have to redo this entire budget report. I really worked hard on this project, and now I have to do it all over again." To this, you get three different responses.

ANDY: That's not so bad; most people find they have to redo their first reports. That's the norm here.

CONNIE: You should be pleased that all you have to do is a simple rewrite. Peggy and Michael both had to completely redo their entire projects.

GREG: You have to rewrite that report you've worked on for the last three weeks? You sound really angry and frustrated.

All three listeners are probably trying to make you feel better. But they go about it in very different ways—and surely with very different results. Andy tries to lessen the significance of the rewrite. This well-intended and extremely common response does little to promote meaningful communication and understanding. Connie tries to give the situation a positive spin. In their responses, however, both Andy and Connie are also suggesting that you should not be feeling the way you do; they're saying that your feelings are not legitimate and should be replaced with more logical feelings.

Greg's response, however, is different from the others. Greg uses active listening. **Active listening** owes its development to Thomas Gordon (1975), who made it a cornerstone of his P.E.T. (parent effectiveness training) technique. It is a process of sending back to the speaker what you as a listener think the speaker meant—both in content and in feelings. Active listening, then, is not merely repeating the speaker's exact words, but rather putting together into some meaningful whole your understanding of the speaker's total message. And, incidentally, when combined with empathic listening, it proves the most effective mode for success as a salesperson (Comer & Drollinger, 1999).

Active listening helps you check your understanding of what the speaker said and, more importantly, of what he or she meant. Reflecting back perceived meanings to the speaker gives the speaker an opportunity to offer clarification and correct any misunderstandings. Active listening also lets the speaker know that you acknowledge and accept his or her feelings. In the sample responses given above, Greg listened actively and reflected back what he thought you meant while accepting what you were feeling. Note too that he also explicitly identified the feelings ("You sound angry and frustrated"), allowing you the opportunity to correct his interpretation. Still another function of active listening is that it stimulates the speaker to explore feelings and thoughts. Greg's response encourages you to elaborate on your feelings and perhaps to understand them better as you talk them through.

Three simple techniques may help you master the process of active listening: paraphrasing the speaker's meaning, expressing understanding, and asking questions.

- *Paraphrase the speaker's meaning.* Stating in your own words what you think the speaker means and feels helps ensure understanding and demonstrates your interest. Paraphrasing gives the speaker a chance to extend what was originally said. In paraphrasing, be objective; be especially careful not to lead the speaker in the direction you think he or she should go. Also, don't overdo paraphrasing. Paraphrase when you feel there's a chance for misunderstanding or when you want to express support for the other person and keep the conversation going.
- *Express understanding of the speaker's feelings.* In addition to paraphrasing the content, echo the feelings the speaker expressed or implied ("You must have felt horrible"). This expression of feelings will help you further check your perception of the speaker's feelings and will allow the speaker to see his or her feelings more objectively (especially helpful when they're feelings of anger, hurt, or depression) and the opportunity to elaborate on these feelings.
- *Ask questions.* Asking questions ensures your own understanding of the speaker's thoughts and feelings and secures additional information ("How did you feel when you read your job

BUILDING COMMUNICATION SKILLS

Regulating Your Listening Style

With specific reference to the four dimensions of effective listening discussed here, what styles would you use in each of the following situations? What types of listening would be obviously inappropriate in each situation?

1. Your steady dating partner for the last five years tells you that spells of depression are becoming more frequent and more long lasting.
2. Your history instructor lectures on the contributions of the ancient Greeks to modern civilization.
3. Your brother tells you he's been accepted into Harvard's MBA program.
4. Your supervisor explains the new computerized mail system.
5. A newscaster reports on a recent Arab-Israeli meeting.

appraisal report?"). Ask questions to provide just enough stimulation and support so that the speaker feels he or she can elaborate on these thoughts and feelings.

REFLECTIONS ON ETHICS

Listening Ethically

As a listener, you share not only in the success or failure of any communication but also in the moral implications of the communication exchange. Two major principles govern ethical listening:

- Give the speaker an ***honest hearing.*** Avoid prejudging the speaker before hearing her or him. Try to put aside prejudices and preconceptions so you can evaluate the speaker's message fairly. At the same time, try to empathize with the speaker. You don't have to agree with the speaker, but try to understand emotionally as well as intellectually what the speaker means. Then accept or reject the speaker's ideas on the basis of the information offered, not on the basis of some bias or prejudice or incomplete understanding.
- Give the speaker ***honest responses*** and feedback. In a learning environment such as a communication class, this means giving honest and constructive criticism to help the speaker improve. It also means reflecting honestly on the questions speakers raise. Much as the listener has a right to expect an active speaker, the speaker has the right to expect a listener who will actively deal with, rather than just passively hear, the message.

WHAT WOULD YOU DO? You're teaching a class in communication. In the public speaking segment, one of your students, a sincere and devout Iranian Muslim, gives a speech on "why women should be subservient to men." After the first two minutes of the speech, half the class walks out. During the next class you plan to give a lecture on the ethics of listening. What do you say?

SUMMARY

This unit discussed the process of listening, the influence of culture and gender on the way people listen, and the principles for listening more effectively.

1. Effective listening yields a wide variety of benefits, including more effective learning, relating, influencing, playing, and helping.
2. Listening is a five-part process that begins with receiving and continues through understanding, remembering, evaluating, and responding.
3. Receiving consists of hearing the verbal signals and seeing the nonverbal signals.
4. Understanding involves learning what the speaker means, not merely what the words mean.
5. Remembering involves retaining the received message, a process that involves considerable reconstruction.
6. Evaluating consists in judging the messages you receive.
7. Responding involves giving feedback while the speaker is speaking and taking your turn at speaking after the speaker has finished.
8. Listening is influenced by a wide range of cultural factors, such as differences in language and speech, nonverbal behaviors, credibility criteria, and feedback approaches.
9. Listening is influenced by gender: Men and women seem to view listening as serving different purposes.
10. Effective listening involves adjusting our behaviors on the basis of at least four dimensions: empathic and objective listening, nonjudgmental and critical listening, surface and depth listening, and active and inactive listening.
11. The empathic–objective dimension involves the degree to which the listener focuses on feeling what the speaker is feeling versus grasping the objective message.
12. The nonjudgmental–critical dimension involves the degree to which the listener evaluates what is said.
13. The surface–depth dimension has to do with the extent to which the listener focuses on the literal or obvious meanings versus the hidden or less obvious meanings.
14. The active–inactive dimension involves the extent to which the listener reflects back and expresses support for the speaker.

KEY TERMS

listening
receiving
understanding
remembering
evaluating
responding
empathic and objective listening
nonjudgmental and critical listening
surface and depth listening
active and inactive listening
paraphrase

THINKING CRITICALLY ABOUT

Listening

1. Using the four dimensions of listening effectiveness discussed here (empathic–objective, nonjudgmental–critical, surface–depth, and active–inactive), how would you describe yourself as a listener when listening in class? When listening to your best friend? When listening to a romantic partner? When listening to your parents? When listening to your superiors at work?

2. What would be an appropriate active listening response for each of these situations?
   - Your friend Phil has just broken up a love affair and is telling you about it. "I can't seem to get Chris out of my mind," he says. "All I do is daydream about what we used to do and all the fun we used to have."
   - A young nephew tells you that he can't talk with his parents. No matter how hard he tries, they just don't listen. "I tried to tell them that I can't play baseball and I don't want to play baseball," he confides. "But they ignore me and tell me that all I need is practice."
   - Your mother has been having a difficult time at work. She was recently passed up for a promotion and received one of the lowest merit raises given in the company. "I'm not sure what I did wrong," she tells you. "I do my work, mind my own business, don't take my sick days like everyone else. How could they give that promotion to Helen who's only been with the company for two years? Maybe I should just quit."

3. Would you find it difficult to listen to friends who were complaining that the insurance premium on their Rolls-Royce was going up? Would you find it difficult to listen to friends complain that their rent was going up and that they feared becoming homeless? If there is a difference, why?

4. Researchers have argued that effective listening skills are positively associated with salespeople's effectiveness in selling (Castleberrry & Shepherd, 1993). Can you think of examples from your own experience that would support this positive association between effective listening and effective selling?

5. Here are a few situations in which you might want to use paraphrasing to ensure that you understand the speaker's thoughts and feelings. For each situation: *(a)* identify the thoughts you feel the speaker is expressing, *(b)* identify the feelings you think the speaker is experiencing, and *(c)* put these thoughts and feelings into a paraphrase.
   - Did you hear I got engaged to Jerry? Our racial and religious differences are really going to cause difficulties for both of us. But we'll work it through.
   - I got a C on that paper. That's the worst grade I've ever received. I just can't believe that I got a C. This is my major. What am I going to do?
   - That rotten, inconsiderate pig just up and left. He never even said goodbye. We were together for six months and after one small argument he leaves without a word. And he even took my bathrobe—that expensive one he bought for my last birthday.

6. Consider this dialogue and note the active listening techniques used throughout:

   Pat: That jerk demoted me. He told me I wasn't an effective manager. I can't believe he did that, after all I've done for this place.

   Chris: I'm with you. You've been manager for three or four months now, haven't you?

   Pat: A little over three months. I know it was probationary, but I thought I was doing a good job.

   Chris: Can you get another chance?

   Pat: Yes, he said I could try again in a few months. But I feel like a failure.

Chris: I know what you mean. It sucks. What else did he say?

Pat: He said I had trouble getting the paperwork done on time.

Chris: You've been late filing the reports?

Pat: A few times.

Chris: Is there a way to delegate the paperwork?

Pat: No, but I think I know now what needs to be done.

Chris: You sound as though you're ready to give that manager's position another try.

Pat: Yes, I think I am, and I'm going to let him know that I intend to apply in the next few months.

7. What additional suggestions would you offer for improving communication between deaf and hearing people?

UNIT 6

The Self in Human Communication

UNIT CONTENTS

Of all the elements in communication, the most important is the self. Who you are and how you perceive yourself and others greatly influence your communications and your responses to the communications of others. In this unit you'll learn

- how self-concept, self-awareness, self-esteem, and self-disclosure work in communication
- how you can use this knowledge to communicate more effectively with others and even with yourself

Self-Concept

Your **self-concept** is your image of who you are. It's how you perceive yourself: your feelings and thoughts about your strengths and weaknesses and your abilities and limitations. Self-concept develops from the image that others have of you and reveal to you; the comparisons you make between yourself and others; your cultural experiences in the realms of race, ethnicity, gender, and gender roles; and your evaluation of your own thoughts and behaviors.

Others' Images of You

If you wished to see how your hair looked, you would probably look in a mirror. But what would you do if you wanted to see how friendly or how assertive you were? According to the concept of the **looking-glass self** (Cooley, 1922), you would look at the image of yourself that others reveal to you through their behaviors and especially through the way they treat you and react to you.

Of course, you would not look to just anyone. Rather, you would look to those who are most important in your life—to your significant others. As a child you would look to your parents and then to your elementary school teachers, for example. As an adult you might look to your friends and romantic partners. If these significant others think highly of you, you'll see a positive image reflected in their behaviors; if they think little of you, you'll see a more negative image.

Comparisons with Others

Another way you develop your self-concept is to compare yourself with others, to engage in what are called **social comparison processes** (Festinger, 1954). Again, you don't choose just anyone. Rather, when you want to gain insight into who you are and how effective or competent you are, you look to your peers; generally to those who are distinctly similar to you (Miller, Turnbull, & McFarland, 1988) or who have approximately the same level of ability as you do (Foddy & Crundall, 1993). For example, after an examination you probably want to know how you performed relative to the other students in your class. This gives you a clearer idea as to how effectively you performed. If you play on a baseball team, it's important to know your batting average in comparison with the batting averages of others on the team. Your absolute scores on the exam or your batting average alone may be helpful in telling you something about your performance, but you gain a different perspective when you see your score in comparison with those of your peers.

When comparing yourself to others, be careful of what's called the "false consensus effect": our tendency to overestimate the degree to which others share our attitudes and behaviors. For example, college students who smoked marijuana and took amphetamines were more likely to assume other students did likewise than were students who were not users (Wolfson, 2000). Overestimating commonality tends to validate our own attitudes and behaviors: "If others are like me, then I must be pretty normal."

Cultural Teachings

Through your parents, your teachers, and the media, your culture instills in you a variety of beliefs, values, and attitudes—about success (how you define it and how you should achieve it); about the relevance of your religion, race, or nationality; and about the ethical principles you should follow in business and in your personal life. These teachings provide benchmarks against which you can measure yourself. For example, achieving what your culture defines as success will contribute to a positive self-concept. Failure to achieve what your culture encourages (for example, being married by the time you're 30) will contribute to a negative self-concept.

When you demonstrate the qualities that your culture (or your organization) teaches, you'll see yourself as a cultural success and will be rewarded by other members of the culture (or organization). Seeing yourself as culturally successful and being rewarded by others will contribute positively to your self-concept. When you fail to demonstrate such qualities, you're more likely to see yourself as a cultural failure and to be punished by other members of the culture, an effect that will contribute to a more negative self-concept.

GOING *ONLINE*

Psychology Today

http://www.psychologytoday.com/HTDocs/prod/ptoselftest/self_test.asp

The popular psychology magazine *Psychology Today* maintains a wonderful website devoted to many of the topics covered in this unit. Of special interest are the self-tests, which can help you learn more about yourself. Log on to this website and take one or more of these self-tests. Other websites containing self-tests include All the Tests (http://www.allthetests.com) and Queendom.com (http://www.queendom.com).

In addition, visit the companion website for this text (www.ablongman.com/devito) and take the self-tests "How Shy Are You?" and "How Much Do You Self-Monitor?" Also try working with the exercises "Increasing Self-Awareness," "Giving and Receiving Compliments," "Timing Self-Disclosure," and "Responding to Self-Disclosures."

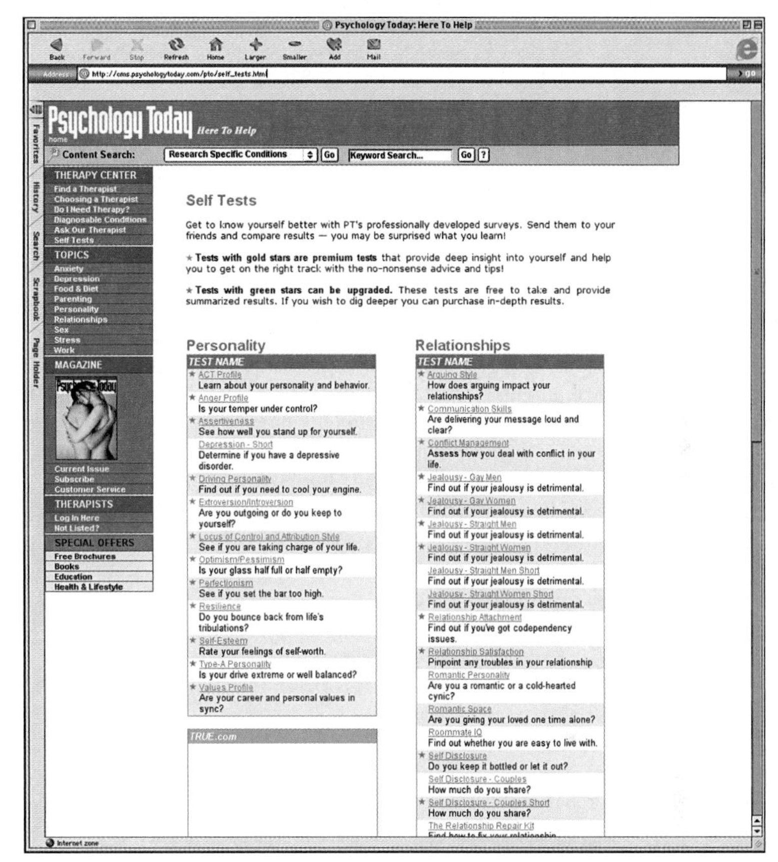

Your Own Interpretations and Evaluations

You also react to your own behavior; you interpret it and evaluate it. These interpretations and evaluations contribute to your self-concept. For example, let's say you believe that lying is wrong. If you lie, you'll probably evaluate this behavior in terms of your internalized beliefs about lying and will react negatively to your own behavior. You might, for example, experience guilt as a result of your behavior's contradicting your beliefs. On the other hand, let's say that you pull someone out of a burning building at great personal risk. You will probably evaluate this behavior positively; you will feel good about this behavior and, as a result, about yourself.

The more you understand why you view yourself as you do, the better you'll understand who you are. You can gain additional insight into yourself by looking more closely at self-awareness, and especially at the Johari model of the self.

Self-Awareness

If you listed some of the qualities you wanted to have, **self-awareness** would surely rank high. Self-awareness is eminently practical: The more you understand yourself, the more you'll be able to control your thoughts and behaviors (Wilson & Hayes, 2000).

	Known to self	Not known to self
Known to others	**Open self** Information about yourself that you and others know	**Blind self** Information about yourself that you don't know but that others do know
Not known to others	**Hidden self** Information about yourself that you know but others don't know	**Unknown self** Information about yourself that neither you nor others know

Figure 6.1
The Johari Window

Note that a change in any one of the quadrants produces changes in the other quadrants. Visualize the size of the entire window as constant, and the size of each quadrant as variable—sometimes small, sometimes large. As you communicate with others, information is moved from one quadrant to another. So, for example, if you reveal a secret, you shrink the hidden self and enlarge the open self. These several selves, then, are not separate and distinct from one another. Rather, each depends on the others.

Source: From *Group Processes: An Introduction to Group Dynamics*, Third Edition, by Joseph Luft. Copyright © 1984, 1970, 1963 by Joseph Luft. Used with permission of The McGraw-Hill Companies.

The Four Selves

Figure 6.1 explains self-awareness in terms of the **Johari window** (Luft, 1969, 1984). The window is broken up into four basic areas or quadrants, each of which contains a somewhat different self. Let's assume that this window and the four selves represent you.

The Open Self

The open self represents all the information, behaviors, attitudes, feelings, desires, motivations, ideas, and so on that you know about yourself and that others also know. The information included here might range from your name, skin color, and gender to your age, political and religious affiliations, and job title. Your open self will vary in size depending on the individuals with whom you're dealing. Some people probably make you feel comfortable and support you. To them, you open yourself wide. To others you may prefer to leave most of yourself closed.

The size of the open self also varies from person to person. Some people tend to reveal their innermost desires and feelings. Others prefer to remain silent about both significant and insignificant details. Most of us, however, open ourselves to some people about some things at some times.

The Blind Self

The blind self represents information about yourself that others know but you don't. This may vary from relatively insignificant quirks—using the expression "you know," rubbing your nose when you get angry, or having a peculiar body odor—to something as significant as defense mechanisms, fight strategies, or repressed experiences.

Communication depends in great part on both parties' having the same basic information about themselves and each other. Where blind areas exist, communication will be difficult. Yet blind areas will always exist for each of us. Although we may be able to shrink our blind areas, we can never eliminate them.

The Unknown Self

The unknown self represents those parts of yourself about which neither you nor others know. This is the information that is buried in your unconscious or that has somehow escaped notice.

You gain insight into the unknown self from a variety of different sources. Sometimes this area is revealed through temporary changes brought about by drug experiences, special experimental conditions such as hypnosis or sensory deprivation, or various projective tests or dreams. The exploration of the unknown self through open, honest, and empathic interaction with trusted and trusting others—parents, friends, counselors, children, lovers—is an effective way of gaining insight.

The Hidden Self

The hidden self contains all that you know of yourself but keep hidden from others. This area includes all your successfully kept secrets about yourself and others. At the extremes of this quadrant are overdisclosers and underdisclosers. Overdisclosers tell all, keeping nothing hidden about themselves or others. They will tell you their family history, sexual problems, financial status, goals, failures and successes, and just about everything else. Underdisclosers tell nothing. They will talk about you but not about themselves.

Very likely you fall somewhere between these two extremes; you keep certain things hidden and you disclose other things. Likewise, you disclose to some people and not to others. You are, in effect, a selective discloser.

Growing in Self-Awareness

Embedded in the foregoing discussion are suggestions on how to increase your own self-awareness. Some of these may now be made explicit.

ASK THE RESEARCHER

Increasing Popularity

- *Quite honestly, I'm not very popular with my peers, but I really want to be. Any suggestions that can help?*

When we say someone is "popular" what we probably mean is that he or she is a likeable person and therefore included in activities. Being liked and included is a common goal that scholars call "positive face need." How do we achieve this goal?

Self-Reflection: Honest and thorough assessment of how you appear to others.

- Do you express appreciation for other people by talking about topics of interest to them?
- Do your nonverbal responses make other people comfortable?
- Are you aware of and willing to respond to the conversational goals of others or more interested in your own agenda?

Social Action: Invest the effort it takes to develop relationships.

- Be aware that small talk is not small—it shows that you are interesting and interested in the other person.
- Initiate plans and activities. Don't always wait to be asked.
- Demonstrate your integrity by respecting the private information that others share with you.

For more information: Cupach, W. R., & Metts, S. (1994). *Facework.* Newbury Park, CA: Sage. And Metts, S., & Grohskopf, E. (2003). Impression management: Goals, strategies, and skills. In J. O. Greene & B. R. Burleson (Eds.), *Handbook of communication and social interaction skills*. Mahwah, NJ: Erlbaum.

Sandra Metts (Ph.D., University of Iowa) is a professor in the Department of Communication at Illinois State University, where she teaches courses in communication theory, interpersonal communication, and language. Her research interests include emotional experience and expression, and the role of communication in close relationships, particularly the roles of communication in securing forgiveness after a relational transgression and in negotiating first sexual involvement in dating couples (smmetts@ilstu.edu).

Dialogue with Yourself

No one knows you better than you do. The problem is that you probably seldom ask yourself about yourself. It can be interesting and revealing. Consider what you know by taking the "Who Am I?" test (Bugental & Zelen, 1950). Head a piece of paper "Who Am I?" and write 10, 15, or 20 times, "I am . . . ." Then complete each of the sentences. Try not to give only positive or socially acceptable responses; respond with what comes to mind first. On another piece of paper, make two columns; head one column "Strengths" or "Virtues" and the other column "Weaknesses" or "Vices." Fill in each column as quickly as possible.

Remember, too, that you're constantly changing. Consequently, your self-perceptions and goals also change, often in drastic ways. Update them at regular and frequent intervals.

Listen

You can learn about yourself from seeing yourself as others do. Conveniently, others are constantly giving you the very feedback you need to increase self-awareness. In every interpersonal interaction, people comment on you in some way—on what you do, what you say, how you look. Sometimes these comments are explicit: "You really look washed-out today." Most often they're only implicit, such as a stare or averted eyes. Often they're "hidden" in the way others look, what they talk about, and the focus of their interest.

Reduce Your Blind Self

Actively seek information to reduce your blind self. People will reveal information they know about you when you encourage them to do so. Use some of the situations that arise every day to gain self-information: "Do you think I came down too hard on the instructor today?" "Do you think I was assertive enough when I asked for the raise?" Don't, of course, seek this information constantly—if you did, your friends would quickly find others with whom to interact. But you can make use of some situations—perhaps those in which you're particularly unsure of what to do or how you appear—to reduce your blind self and increase self-awareness.

See Your Different Selves

To each of your friends and relatives, you're a somewhat different person. Yet you're really all of these. Try to see yourself as do the people with whom you interact. For starters, visualize how you're seen by your mother, your father, your teacher, your best friend, the stranger you sat next to on the bus, your employer, and your neighbor's child. Because you are, in fact, a composite of all of these views, it's important that you see yourself through the eyes of many people.

Increase Your Open Self

Self-awareness generally increases when you increase your open self. When you reveal yourself to others, you learn about yourself at the same time. You bring into clearer focus what you may have buried within. As you discuss yourself, you may see connections that you had previously missed. In receiving feedback from others, you gain still more insight.

Further, by increasing your open self, you increase the likelihood that a meaningful and intimate dialogue will develop. It's through such interactions that you best get to know yourself.

Self-Esteem

Personal **self-esteem** has to do with the way you feel about yourself—how much you like yourself, how valuable a person you think you are, how competent you think you are. These feelings reflect the value you place on yourself; they're a measure of your self-esteem.

VIEWPOINT

Popular psychology and many television talk shows (especially *Oprah*) emphasize the importance of self-esteem. The self-esteem camp has come under attack from critics, however (for example, Bushman & Baumeister, 1998; Baumeister, Bushman, & Campbell, 2000; Bower, 2001; Coover & Murphy, 2000; Hewitt, 1998). Much current thinking holds that high self-esteem is not desirable: It does nothing to improve academic performance, it does not predict success, and it even may lead to antisocial (especially aggressive) behavior. On the other hand, it's difficult to imagine how a person would function successfully without positive self-feelings. How do you feel about the benefits or liabilities of self-esteem? Would you have included this topic in this text?

There's also **group self-esteem,** or your evaluation of yourself as a member of a particular cultural group (Porter & Washington, 1993). Personal self-esteem is influenced by your group self-esteem. If you view your racial or ethnic group membership negatively, then it's especially difficult to develop high positive self-esteem. Conversely, if you view your membership positively, then you are more likely to develop high positive self-esteem. Pride in a group (racial, ethnic, religious, or gender, for example) and a supportive community contribute to group self-esteem and, consequently, to personal self-esteem.

There are also significant cultural differences in the way we're taught to view ourselves (Gudykunst & Ting-Toomey, 1988). For example, in the United States, Australia, and western Europe, people are encouraged to be independent. Members of these cultures are taught to get ahead, to compete, to win, to achieve their goals, to realize their unique potential,

UNDERSTANDING *THEORY* AND *RESEARCH*

The Value of Self-Esteem

Anecdotal evidence strongly favors the importance of self-esteem. Popular books and magazine articles regularly provide you with ways to raise your self-esteem. When you feel good about yourself—about who you are and what you're capable of doing—you perform more effectively. When you think you're a success, you're more likely to act like a success. When you think you're a failure, you're more likely to act like a failure. And success (or failure), in turn, raises (or lowers) your self-esteem.

Increasing your self-esteem is thus seen as a way to help you function more effectively in school, in your interpersonal relationships, and in your career. But the scientific evidence on that connection is not conclusive. For example, many people who have extremely low self-esteem have become quite successful in all fields. And a surprisingly large number of criminals and delinquents are found to have extremely high self-esteem (Johnson, 1998).

Working with Theories and Research

- *If you have access, log on to Research Navigator (*www.researchnavigator.com*) and search both the scholarly and the popular databases for "self-esteem." Do you find the popular articles adequately reflect the conclusions of research scientists?*

to stand out from the crowd. In many Asian and African cultures, on the other hand, people are taught to value an interdependent self. Members of these cultures are taught to get along, to help others, and not to disagree, stand out, or be conspicuous. Although self-esteem depends largely on achieving your goals, your culture seems to select the specific goals.

Here we consider a few suggestions for increasing your self-esteem: (1) Attack beliefs that are self-destructive, (2) seek out people who'll be nurturing, (3) secure affirmation, and (4) work on projects that will prove successful. Let's elaborate a bit on each.

Attack Self-Destructive Beliefs

Self-destructive beliefs are those beliefs that damage your self-esteem and prevent you from building meaningful and productive relationships. They may be about yourself ("I'm not creative," "I'm boring"), your world ("The world is an unhappy place," "People are out to get me"), and/or your relationships ("All the good people are already in relationships," "If I ever fall in love, I know I'll be hurt"). Identifying these beliefs will help you examine them critically and see that they're both illogical and self-defeating. A useful way to view self-destructive beliefs is given in the Building Communication Skills box entitled "Attacking Self-Defeating Drivers."

Seek Out Nurturing People

Seek out positive, optimistic people who make you feel good about yourself. Avoid those who find fault with just about everything. Seek to build a network of supportive others (Brody, 1991). At the same time, however, realize that you do not have to be loved by everyone. Many people believe that everyone should love them. This belief traps you into thinking you must always please others so they will like you.

Secure Affirmation

Proponents of building self-esteem frequently recommend that you remind yourself of your successes—that you focus on your good acts; your good deeds; your positive qualities, strengths, and virtues; and your productive and meaningful relationships with friends, loved ones, and relatives (Aronson, Cohen, & Nail, 1998; Aronson, Wilson, & Akert, 1999). There are plenty of people around to remind you of your failures and of your weaknesses, so your job is to engage in self-affirmation.

The idea behind this advice is that the way you talk to yourself will influence what you think of yourself. If you talk positively about yourself, you will come to feel more positive about yourself. If you tell yourself that you're a success, that others like you, that you will succeed on the next test, that you will be welcomed when asking for a date, you will soon come to feel positive about yourself. Self-affirmations such as the following often are recommended:

- I'm a worthy person, though there's room for improvement.
- I'm generally responsible and can be depended upon.
- I'm capable of loving and being loved.
- I deserve good things to happen to me.
- I can forgive myself for mistakes and misjudgments.
- I deserve to be treated with respect.

However, not all researchers agree with this advice. Some critics argue that such affirmations—although extremely popular in self-help books—may not be very helpful; these critics contend that if you have low self-esteem, you're not going to believe yourself, because you don't have a very high opinion of yourself to begin with (Paul, 2001). The alternative to engaging in self-affirmation is seeking to secure affirmation from others. You can do this by, for example, becoming more interpersonally competent and by interacting with more positive people. In this way you'll get more positive feedback from others. And positive feedback, according to this view, is more helpful than self-talk in raising self-esteem.

Work on Projects That Will Result in Success

Try to select projects that you can complete successfully. Success builds self-esteem. Each success makes achieving the next one a little easier. Remember, too, that the failure of a project is not the failure of you as a person; failure is something that happens, not something inside you. Everyone faces defeat somewhere along the line. Successful people are those who know how to deal with setbacks. Further, one defeat does not mean you'll fail the next time. Put failure in perspective, and don't make it an excuse for not trying again.

Another activity that has been shown to contribute to self-esteem is exercise. In a study of adults between the ages of 60 and 75, those who exercised—and it didn't matter what exercise it was—increased their self-esteem. The exercise seems to have made the individuals feel better physically; this gave them a feeling of increased physical strength and hence control over their environment (McAuley, Blissmer, Katula, Duncan, & Mihalko, 2000).

Self-Disclosure

Self-disclosure is communication in which you reveal information about yourself. Because self-disclo-

---

BUILDING COMMUNICATION SKILLS

Attacking Self-Defeating Drivers

Another approach to unrealistic beliefs is to focus on what Pamela Butler (1981) calls *drivers*—beliefs that may motivate you to act in ways that are self-defeating. These drivers set unrealistically high standards and therefore almost always ensure failure. As a result, you may develop a negative self-image, seeing yourself as someone who constantly fails. How would you restate each of these five drivers as realistic and productive beliefs?

1. The drive *to be perfect* impels you to try to perform at unrealistically high levels at work, school, and home; anything short of perfection is unacceptable.
2. The drive *to be strong* tells you that weakness and any of the more vulnerable emotions like sadness, compassion, or loneliness are wrong.
3. The drive *to please* others leads you to seek approval from others; you assume that if you gain the approval of others, then you're a worthy and deserving person—and that if others disapprove of you, then you're worthless and undeserving.
4. The drive *to hurry up* compels you to do things quickly, to try to do more than can be reasonably expected in any given amount of time.
5. The drive *to try hard* makes you take on more responsibilities than any one person can be expected to handle.

COMMUNICATION@WORK

Criticism

People ask you for criticism, but they only want praise.

—Somerset Maugham

In the workplace you'll often be asked to evaluate others, to render some kind of judgment, to criticize and to praise. Both criticism and praise are difficult tasks and will significantly affect the self-esteem of the individuals. Here are a few suggestions.

- State criticism positively, if possible. Rather than saying, "You look terrible in black," say, "You look much better in bright colors." If you do express criticism that seems too negative, it may be helpful to offer a direct apology or to disclaim any harmful intentions (Baron, 1990). Resist criticizing someone who is just learning the new skills; if you must criticize, end your comments with a reaffirmation of the person (Blanchard, 1992; Metts & Grohskopf, 2003). In giving praise, make sure your facial expressions communicate your positive feelings.
- Own your thoughts and feelings. Instead of saying, "Your report was unintelligible," say, "I had difficulty following your ideas." Similarly, avoid trying to read the other person's mind. Instead of saying, "You didn't give enough attention to detail," consider saying, "I would have liked to see more detailed examples." Use I-messages when praising as well; instead of saying, "The report was good," say, "I liked your report."
- Focus on the event or the behavior rather than on personality. In your focus on the event, be constructive and specific; explain specifically what could be done to make it better: "I'd like a more detailed abstract on the first page of the report and an itemized summary at the end." Similarly, in praising be specific. Instead of saying "That was good," say, "I thought your introductory story about economizing was great."
- Express criticism face-to-face (rather than by letter, memo, e-mail, or even phone) and in private, whenever possible. Privacy is especially important when you are dealing with members of cultures in which public criticism could result in a serious loss of face. Culture is also important when you are praising; some Asians, for example, feel uncomfortable when praised, because praise is often taken as a sign of veiled criticism (Dresser, 1996).

Communicating@Work

What are the major characteristics or qualities of the criticism that you find easiest to accept? Why?

sure is a type of communication, it includes not only overt statements but also, for example, slips of the tongue and unconscious nonverbal signals. It varies from whispering a secret to a best friend to making a public confession on a television talk show (Jourard, 1968, 1971a, b; Petronio, 2000).

Although by definition *self-disclosure* may refer to any information about the self, the term is most often used to refer to information that you normally keep hidden rather than simply to information that you have not previously revealed.

Before reading further about self-disclosure, its rewards and dangers, and the guidelines to consider before disclosing, explore your own willingness to disclose by taking the following self-test.

TEST YOURSELF

How Willing to Self-Disclose Are You?

Respond to each statement below by indicating the likelihood that you would disclose such items of information to, say, other members of this class. Use the following scale: 1 = would definitely self-disclose; 2 = would probably self-disclose; 3 = don't know; 4 = would probably not self-disclose; and 5 = would definitely not self-disclose.

1. My attitudes toward different nationalities and races
2. My sexual fantasies
3. My drinking and/or drug-taking behavior
4. My personal goals

5. My major weaknesses
6. My feelings about the people in this group

HOW DID YOU DO? There are, of course, no right or wrong answers to this self-test. By considering these topics, however, you may be able to pinpoint more precisely the areas about which you're willing to disclose and the areas about which you aren't willing to disclose. How would your answers have differed if the question had asked you to indicate the likelihood of your self-disclosing to your best friend?

WHAT WILL YOU DO? This test, and ideally its discussion with others who also complete it, should get you started thinking about your own self-disclosing behavior and especially the factors that influence it. Can you identify what factors most influence your willingness to disclose or not to disclose each of these items of information?

Factors Influencing Self-Disclosure

The most important factors influencing self-disclosure are who you are, who your listeners are, and the topic of the impending self-disclosure.

Yourself

Age influences self-disclosure. Researchers have found that people self-disclose more when they talk with those who are approximately the same age (Collins & Gould, 1994). For example, the level of intimacy seems to be more similar in similar-age dyads (groups of two people) than in differing-age dyads.

People who are competent and high in self-esteem disclose more than do those who are less competent and lower in self-esteem, perhaps because they're more confident and have more positive things to disclose than do less competent people (McCroskey & Wheeless, 1976).

MEDIA WATCH

Outing

In self-disclosure, as already noted, you reveal information about yourself to others. Although at times you may be forced to disclose, normally you control what you reveal to others. There is, however, another type of disclosure—the disclosure that occurs when someone else takes information from your hidden self and makes it public. Although this third-party disclosure can concern any aspect of your hidden self, the media have made a special case out of revealing information about affectional orientation, or "outing."

Outing as a media process began in a relatively obscure gay magazine *Outweek*. *Outweek's* article on "The Secret Gay Life of Malcolm Forbes" made public the homosexuality of one of the world's richest men; it "outed" him (Gross, 1991; Johansson & Percy, 1994). On March 3, 1995, the *Wall Street Journal* ran a front-page story on Jann Wenner, the multimillionaire owner and publisher of *Rolling Stone, Us, Men's Journal,* and *Family Life*. The story was basically financial and focused on the possible effects Wenner's marital breakup would have on his media empire. Somewhat casually noted in the article—without Wenner's permission and against his wishes (Rotello, 1995)—was the fact that the new person in Wenner's life was a man. This article, although not the first to discuss Wenner's gay relationship, has been singled out because of the prestige of the *Wall Street Journal* and because of the many issues this type of forced disclosure raises.

Outing raises a privacy issue that is not easy to resolve. If Wenner had been dating a woman, the media would have mentioned it, but few would have raised the privacy issue because he's a public figure, and divorce was a relevant issue that would likely affect his financial empire. However, if the media reported only on heterosexual extramarital relationships, it would imply that homosexual relationships are illegitimate and not to be spoken of openly.

You and the Media

How do you feel about outing? What guidelines should the media follow in dealing with issues that individuals wish to keep private? At what point should the media be allowed to consider a person a public figure and hence without the right to privacy?

Naturally enough, highly sociable and extroverted people disclose more than those who are less sociable and more introverted. People who are apprehensive about talking in general also disclose less than do those who are more comfortable in oral communication (Dolgin, Meyer, & Schwartz, 1991).

Culture also influences disclosures. People in the United States, for example, disclose more than do those in Great Britain, Germany, Japan, or Puerto Rico (Gudykunst, 1983). And among the Kabre of Togo, secrecy is a major part of everyday interaction (Piot, 1993). American students also disclose more than do students from nine different Middle East countries (Jourard, 1971a). Similarly, American students self-disclose more on a variety of controversial issues and self-disclose to more different types of people than do Chinese students (Chen, 1992).

Generally, women self-disclose more than men (Naifeh & Smith, 1984; Rosenfeld, 1979). Women seem more willing to disclose their feelings with their best friends than men. This gender difference is most pronounced with the negative emotions: Women are more apt to disclose their anxiety, apathy, depression, and fear. Males, on the other hand, rarely disclose such emotions to either same-sex or opposite-sex friends (Kiraly, 2000).

The gender role that a person plays is probably even more influential than is biological sex (Pearson, 1980; Shaffer, Pegalis, & Cornell, 1992). "Masculine women" disclose less than do women who score low on masculinity, and "feminine men" disclose more than do men who score low on femininity scales (Pearson, 1980). Both men and women resist self-disclosure for fear of projecting an unfavorable image. Men also avoid disclosing because they fear appearing inconsistent, losing control over the other person, and threatening the relationship. Women, on the other hand, avoid disclosing because they fear revealing information that may be used against them, giving others the impression that they are emotionally disturbed, or hurting their relationships (Rosenfeld, 1979).

Your Listeners

Self-disclosure is more likely to occur between people who like and trust each other than between those who don't. People you like are probably more supportive and positive, qualities that encourage self-disclosure (Derlega, Winstead, Wong, & Greenspan, 1987; Wheeless & Grotz, 1977; Petronio & Bantz, 1991). Interestingly, not only do you disclose to those you like; you probably also come to like those to whom you disclose (Berg & Archer, 1983).

Your relationship with the listener also will influence disclosure. At times self-disclosure is more likely to occur in temporary than in permanent

UNDERSTANDING *THEORY* AND *RESEARCH*

The Dyadic Effect

The phrase *dyadic effect* refers to the process whereby one person behaves in ways similar to the way another person has behaved. This effect is especially clear in self-disclosure, in which the dyadic effect takes a spiral form—each self-disclosure prompts self-disclosure by the other person, which in turn prompts still more self-disclosure, and so on. It's interesting to note that disclosures made in response to the disclosures of others are generally more intimate than those that are not the result of the dyadic effect (Berg & Archer, 1983).

This dyadic effect is not universal across all cultures, however. For example, Americans are likely to be susceptible to the dyadic effect and reciprocate with explicit, verbal self-disclosure, but Koreans aren't (Won-Doornink, 1985). As you can appreciate, this difference can easily cause intercultural misunderstandings; for example, an American may be insulted if his or her Korean counterpart doesn't reciprocate with self-disclosures that are similar in depth.

Working with Theories and Research

- *In what types of situations (for example, when first meeting someone, when visiting a childhood friend, when on a date) do you find the dyadic effect most influential? In what types of situations does the dyadic effect seem weak or not to operate at all? Are men and women equally likely to respond in accordance with the dyadic effect?*

relationships—for example, between strangers on a train or plane, a kind of "in-flight intimacy" (McGill, 1985). In this situation two people often establish an intimate self-disclosing relationship during some brief travel period, knowing that they will never see each other again. In a similar way, you might set up a relationship with one or several people on the Internet and engage in significant disclosure. Perhaps knowing that you'll never see these other people, and that they will never know where you live or work or what you look like, makes it a bit easier. Some research indicates that self-disclosure occurs more quickly and at higher levels of intimacy online than in face-to-face situations (Joinson, 2001; Levine, 2000). Other research, however, finds that people experience greater closeness and self-disclosure in face-to-face groups than in Internet chat groups (Mallen, Day, & Green, 2003).

Self-disclosure occurs more in small groups than in large groups. Dyads are the most hospitable setting for self-disclosure. With one listener, you can attend carefully to the person's responses. On the basis of this support or lack of support, you can monitor your disclosures, continuing if the situation is supportive and stopping if it's not.

You are also more likely to disclose to in-group members than to members of groups of which you are not a member. For example, people from the same race are likely to disclose more to one another than to members of another race, and people with disabilities are more likely to disclose to others with disabilities than to those without disabilities (Stephan, Stephan, Wenzel, & Cornelius, 1991).

Your Topic

If you're like the people studied by researchers, you're more likely to disclose about some topics than about others. For example, you're more likely to self-disclose information about your job, hobbies, interests, attitudes, and opinions on politics and religion than about your sex life, financial situation, personality, or interpersonal relationships (Jourard, 1968, 1971a). These topic differences have been found for people from Great Britain, Germany, the United States, and Puerto Rico (Jourard, 1971a). You're likely also to disclose favorable information more readily than unfavorable information. Generally, the more personal and the more negative the topic, the less likely you are to self-disclose—and this is true for both men and women (Nakanishi, 1986; Naifeh & Smith, 1984). Further, you're more likely to disclose information that reflects positively on the other person than information that reflects negatively (Shimanoff, 1985).

Deciding about Self-Disclosure

Because self-disclosure and its effects can be so significant, think carefully before deciding to disclose or not to disclose; weigh both the potential rewards and the potential dangers.

The Rewards of Self-Disclosure

One reason why self-disclosure is so significant is that its rewards are great. Self-disclosure may increase (1) self-knowledge, (2) coping abilities, (3) communication efficiency, and (4) relationship depth.

Self-Knowledge. When you disclose, you gain a new perspective on yourself and a deeper understanding of your own behavior. In therapy, for example, often the insight comes while the client is self-disclosing. He or she may recognize some previously unknown facet of behavior or relationship. Through self-disclosure, then, you also may come to understand yourself more thoroughly.

Coping Abilities. Self-disclosure may help you deal with your problems, especially guilt. One of the great fears many people have is that they will not be accepted because of some deep, dark secret, because of something they have done, or because of some feeling or attitude they have. By disclosing such feelings and receiving support rather than rejection, you may become better able to deal with any such guilt and perhaps reduce or even eliminate it (Pennebaker, 1991).

Communication Efficiency. Self-disclosure may help improve communication. You understand the messages of others largely to the extent that you understand the senders of those messages. You can understand what someone says better if you know that individual well. You can tell what certain nuances mean; when the person is serious and when joking; when the person is being sarcastic out of fear and when out of resentment. Self-disclosure is an essential condition for getting to know another individual and for the process of adjustment we considered in Unit 2.

Relational Depth. Self-disclosure is often helpful for establishing a meaningful relationship between two people. Research has found, for example, that marital satisfaction is greater for couples who are mid- to high self-disclosers and significantly less in low-disclosing relationships (Rosenfeld & Bowen, 1991). Further, within a sexual relationship, self-disclosure increases sexual rewards and general relationship satisfaction; these two benefits, in turn, increase sexual satisfaction (Byers & Demmons, 1999). Without self-disclosure, relationships of any meaningful depth seem difficult if not impossible. By self-disclosing in **dyadic communication** (communication between two people), you tell others that you trust them, respect them, and care enough about them and your relationship to reveal yourself to them. This in turn leads the other individual to self-disclose and forms at least the start of a meaningful relationship: a relationship that is honest and open and goes beyond surface trivialities.

The Dangers of Self-Disclosure

In March 1995 television talk show host Jenny Jones did a show on self-disclosing your secret crushes. One panelist, Scott Amedure, disclosed his crush on another man, Jonathan Schmitz. Three days after the taping of the show—a show that was never aired—Scott Amedure was shot in his home. The police arrested Schmitz and charged him with murder (*New York Times,* March 19, 1995, Section 4, p. 16). Although this is an extreme demonstration of the dangers of self-disclosure, there are many everyday risks to self-disclosing (Bochner, 1984). Remember too that self-disclosure, like any communication, is irreversible (see Unit 2). Regardless of how many times you may try to "take it back," once something is said it can't be withdrawn. Nor can you erase the conclusions and inferences listeners have made on the basis of your disclosures. Here, then, are a few potential dangers to keep in mind when you consider disclosing.

Personal and Social Rejection. Usually you self-disclose to someone you trust to be supportive. Sometimes, however, the person you think will be supportive may turn out to reject you. Parents, normally the most supportive of all in interpersonal relations, have frequently rejected children who self-disclosed their homosexuality, their plans to marry someone of a different race, or their belief in another faith. Your best friends and your closest intimates may reject you for similar self-disclosures.

Material Loss. Sometimes, self-disclosures result in material losses. Politicians who disclose inappropriate relationships with staff members may later find that their own political party no longer supports them and that voters are unwilling to vote for them. Professors who disclose former or present drug-taking behavior or cohabitation with students may find themselves denied tenure, forced to teach undesirable schedules, and eventually let go because of "budget cuts." In the corporate world, self-disclosures of alcoholism or drug addiction are often met with dismissal, demotion, or transfer.

Intrapersonal Difficulties. When other people's reactions are not as expected, intrapersonal difficulties may result. When you're rejected instead of supported, when your parents say that you disgust them instead of hugging you, or when your friends ignore you at school rather than seeking you out as before, you're in line for some intrapersonal difficulties.

Loss of Power. The more you reveal about yourself to others, the more areas of your life you expose to possible attack. Especially in the competitive context of work (or even romance), the more others know about you, the more they'll be able to use against you, and the more power they will have over you. This simple fact has prompted one power watcher (Korda, 1975, p. 302) to advise that you "never reveal all of yourself to other people, [but] hold something back in reserve so that people are never quite sure if they really know you." This advice is not to suggest that you necessarily be secretive; rather, it advocates "remaining slightly mysterious, as if [you] were always capable of doing something surprising and unexpected."

Guidelines for Self-Disclosure

Because self-disclosure is so important and so delicate a matter, here are guidelines for (1) deciding whether and how to self-disclose, (2) facilitating and responding to the disclosures of others, and (3) resisting pressure to self-disclose.

Deciding about Whether and How to Self-Disclosure. In addition to weighing the potential rewards and dangers of self-disclosure already discussed, consider the following guidelines; they will help raise the right questions before you make what must be *your* decision.

- *Consider your motivation for self-disclosure.* Self-disclosure should be motivated by a concern for the relationship, for the others involved, and for oneself. Some people self-disclose out of a desire to hurt the listener. Persons who tell their parents that they never loved them or that the parents hindered their emotional development may be disclosing out of a desire to hurt and perhaps punish rather than to improve the relationship. Neither, of course, should you use self-disclosure to punish yourself, perhaps because of some guilt feeling or unresolved conflict. Self-disclosure should serve a useful and productive function for all persons involved.
- *Consider the appropriateness of the self-disclosure.* Self-disclosure should be appropriate to the context and to the relationship between you and

your listener. Before making any significant self-disclosure, ask whether this is the right time and place. Could a better time and place be arranged? Ask, too, whether this self-disclosure is appropriate to the relationship. Generally, the more intimate the disclosures, the closer the relationship should be. It's probably best to resist intimate disclosures (especially negative ones) with casual acquaintances or in the early stages of a relationship.

- *Consider the disclosures of the other person.* During your disclosures, give the other person a chance to reciprocate with his or her own disclosures. If reciprocal disclosures are not made, reassess your own self-disclosures. The absence of reciprocity may be a signal that for this person at this time and in this context, your disclosures are not welcome or appropriate. So it's generally best to disclose gradually and in small increments. When you disclose too rapidly and all at once, you can't monitor your listener's responses and retreat if they're not positive enough. Further, you prevent the listener from responding with his or her own disclosures and thereby upset the natural balance that is so helpful in this kind of communication exchange.
- *Consider the possible burdens self-disclosure might entail.* Carefully weigh any potential problems that you may incur as a result of your disclosure. Can you afford to lose your job if you disclose your prison record? Are you willing to risk relational difficulties if you disclose your infidelities? Also, ask yourself whether you're making unreasonable demands on the listener. For example, consider the person who swears his or her mother-in-law to secrecy and then self-discloses having an affair with a neighbor. This disclosure places an unfair burden on the mother-in-law, who is now torn between breaking her promise of secrecy and allowing her child to believe a lie. Parents often place unreasonable burdens on their children by self-disclosing relationship problems, financial difficulties, or self-doubts—not realizing that the children may be too young or too emotionally involved to deal effectively with this information.

Facilitating and Responding to the Self-Disclosures of Others When someone discloses to you, it's usually a sign of trust and affection. In serving this most important receiver function, keep the following guidelines in mind. These guidelines will also help you facilitate the disclosures of another person.

- *Practice the skills of effective and active listening.* The skills of effective listening (Unit 5) are especially important when you are listening to self-disclosures: listen actively, listen for different levels of meaning, listen with empathy, and listen with an open mind. Paraphrase the speaker so that you can be sure you understand both the thoughts and the feelings communicated. Express an understanding of the speaker's feelings to allow the speaker the opportunity to see his or her emotions more objectively and through the eyes of another. Ask ques-

BUILDING COMMUNICATION SKILLS

Deciding about Self-Disclosure

For any one or two of the following instances of impending self-disclosure, indicate whether you think the person should self-disclose and why. In making your decisions, consider each of the guidelines identified in this unit.

1. Cathy has fallen in love with another man and wants to end her relationship with Tom, a coworker. She wants to call Tom on the phone, break the engagement, and disclose her new relationship.
2. Gregory plagiarized a term paper in anthropology. He's sorry, especially since the plagiarized paper only earned a grade of C+. He wants to disclose to his instructor and redo the paper.
3. Roberto, a college sophomore, has just discovered he is HIV positive. He wants to tell his parents and his best friends, but fears their rejection. In his Mexican American culture, information like this is rarely disclosed, especially by men. He wants the support of his friends and family and yet doesn't want them to reject him or treat him differently.

tions to ensure your own understanding and to signal your interest and attention.

- *Support and reinforce the discloser.* Express support for the person during and after the disclosures. Try to refrain from evaluation. Concentrate on understanding and empathizing with the discloser. Allow the discloser to choose the pace; don't rush the discloser with too-frequent "So how did it all end?" responses. Make your supportiveness clear to the discloser through your verbal and nonverbal responses: Maintain eye contact, lean toward the speaker, ask relevant questions, and echo the speaker's thoughts and feelings.
- *Be willing to reciprocate.* When you make relevant and appropriate disclosures of your own in response to the other person's disclosures, you're demonstrating your understanding of the other's meanings and at the same time a willingness to communicate on this meaningful level.
- *Keep the disclosures confidential.* When a person discloses to you, it's because she or he wants you to know the feelings and thoughts that are communicated. If you reveal these disclosures to others, negative effects are inevitable. Revealing what was said will probably inhibit future disclosures by this individual in general and to you in particular, and it's likely that your relationship will suffer considerably. But most importantly, betraying a confidence is unfair; it debases what could be and should be a meaningful interpersonal experience.

  It's interesting to note that one of the "netiquette" rules of e-mail is that you shouldn't forward mail to third parties without the writer's permission. This rule is a useful one for self-disclosure generally: Maintain confidentiality; don't pass on disclosures made to you to others without the person's permission.
- *Don't use the disclosures against the person.* Many self-disclosures expose some kind of vulnerability or weakness. If you later turn around and use disclosures against the person, you betray the confidence and trust invested in you. Regardless of how angry you may get, resist the temptation to use the disclosures of others as weapons—the relationship is sure to suffer and may never fully recover.

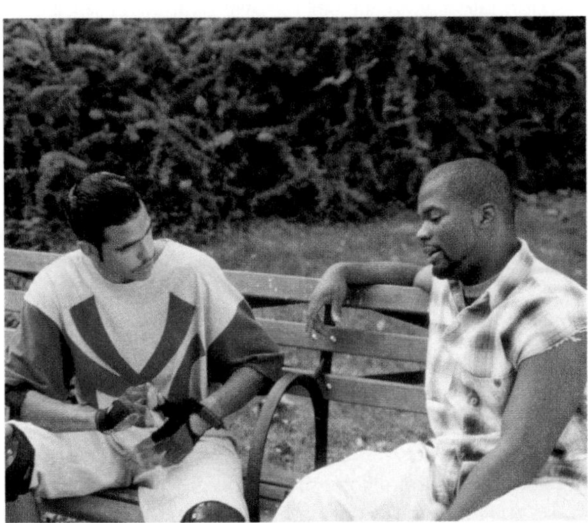

VIEWPOINT
What one principle or skill do you find most important in self-disclosure? What do you find to be the single most common error people make in self-disclosing or in listening to the disclosures of others?

Resisting Pressure to Self-Disclose You may, on occasion, find yourself in a position in which a friend, colleague, or romantic partner is pressuring you to self-disclose. In such situations you may wish to weigh the pros and cons of self-disclosure, then make your decision as to whether and what you'll disclose. If your decision is to not disclose and you're still being pressured, then you need to say something. Here are a few suggestions.

- *Don't be pushed.* Although there may be certain legal or ethical reasons for disclosing, generally, if you don't want to disclose, you don't have to. Don't be pushed into disclosing because others are doing it or because someone asks you to. Realize that you're in control of what you reveal, and to whom and when you reveal it. Self-disclosure has significant consequences, so if you're not sure you want to reveal something—at least not until you've had additional time to think about it—then don't.
- *Be indirect and move to another topic.* Avoid the question that seeks disclosure and change the subject. This can be a polite way of saying, "I'm not talking about it," and may be the preferred choice in certain situations and with certain people. Most often people will get the hint and will understand your refusal to disclose. If they don't, then you may have to be more direct and assertive.
- *If necessary, be assertive in your refusal to disclose.* Say, very directly, "I'd rather not talk about that now" or "Now is not the time for this type of discussion."

REFLECTIONS ON ETHICS

Your Obligation to Reveal Yourself

At some point in any close relationship, an ethical issue arises as to your obligation to reveal information about yourself. After all, people in a close relationship have considerable impact on each other, so you may have an obligation to reveal certain things about yourself. Conversely, you may feel that the other person—because he or she is so close to you—has an ethical obligation to reveal certain information to you.

WHAT WOULD YOU DO? At what point—if any—do you feel you have an ethical obligation to reveal each of the 10 items of information listed here? Record your answers for romantic relationships in the first column and for friendship relationships in the second column. Use numbers from 1 to 10 to indicate at what point you would feel your romantic partner or friend has a right to know this information about you by visualizing a relationship as existing on a continuum from initial contact (1) to extreme intimacy (10). If you feel you would never have the obligation to reveal this information, use 0. As you respond to these items, consider what gives one person the right to know personal information about another person.

Partner	Friend	At what point do you have an ethical obligation to reveal:
_______	_______	1. Age
_______	_______	2. History of family genetic disorders
_______	_______	3. HIV status
_______	_______	4. Past sexual experiences
_______	_______	5. Marital history
_______	_______	6. Annual salary and net financial worth
_______	_______	7. Affectional orientation
_______	_______	8. Race and nationality
_______	_______	9. Religion and religious beliefs
_______	_______	10. Past criminal activity or incarceration

SUMMARY

In this unit we looked at several aspects of the self: self-concept, self-awareness, self-esteem, and self-disclosure.

1. Self-concept is the image you have of yourself. It's developed from the image of you that others have and reveal, the comparisons you make between yourself and others, cultural teachings, and the ways you evaluate your own thoughts and behaviors.
2. In the Johari window model of the self, there are four major areas: the open self, the blind self, the hidden self, and the unknown self.
3. To increase self-awareness, ask yourself about yourself, listen to others to see yourself as others do, reduce your blind self, actively seek information from others about yourself, see yourself from different perspectives, and increase your open self.
4. Self-esteem has to do with the way you feel about yourself, the value you place on yourself, and the positive–negative evaluations you make of yourself. You can boost your self-esteem by attacking your self-destructive beliefs, seeking out nurturing people, securing affirmation, and working on projects that will result in success.
5. Self-disclosure is a form of communication in which information about the self (usually information that is normally kept hidden) is communicated to another person.
6. Self-disclosure is more likely to occur when the potential discloser is with one other person, when the discloser likes or loves the listener, when the two people are approximately the same age, when the listener also discloses, when the discloser feels competent, when the discloser is highly sociable and extroverted, and when the topic of disclosure is relatively impersonal and positive.
7. The rewards of self-disclosure include increased self-knowledge, a better ability to cope with difficult situations and guilt, more efficient communication, and a better chance for a meaningful relationship.
8. The dangers of self-disclosure include personal and social rejection, material loss, intrapersonal difficulties, and loss of power.
9. Before self-disclosing, consider the motivation and appropriateness of the self-disclosure, the opportunity available for open and honest responses, the disclosures of the other person, and the possible burdens that your self-disclosure might impose on you and your listeners.

10. When listening to disclosures, practice the skills of effective and active listening, support and reinforce the discloser, keep the disclosures confidential, and don't use the disclosures as weapons against the person.

11. Resisting self-disclosure is often a reasonable response. When appropriate resist by refusing to be pushed, being indirect or moving to another topic, or stating assertively that you'd rather not disclose.

KEY TERMS

self-concept	self-awareness	self-affirmation
looking-glass self	unknown self	self-disclosure
social comparison processes	self-esteem	outing
Johari window	self-destructive beliefs	dyadic effect

THINKING CRITICALLY ABOUT

The Self in Communication

1. Do you operate with the uniqueness bias when you compare yourself to others? Do you see advantages and disadvantages to this bias?
2. Take the self-test "How Shy Are You?" at www.ablongman.com/devito. In what ways is your shyness related to your self-concept?
3. What effect would you predict Internet communication to have on the self-esteem of adolescents? Would you make the same prediction about people in their 60s and 70s?
4. Have you self-disclosed more in close relationships, in casual relationships, or in temporary acquaintanceships? What accounts for these differences?
5. As a parent, would you share with your children your financial and personal worries? The answer, it seems, would depend at least in part on your socioeconomic status and on whether you were a single parent or one of two parents (McLoyd & Wilson, 1992). Research finds that members of middle-class two-parent families avoid sharing financial problems with their offspring, preferring to shelter the children from some of life's harsher realities. Low-income single mothers, however, feel that sharing their troubles with their youngsters will protect them, because the children will know how difficult life is and what they're up against. The researchers argue, however, that this practice actually creates problems for children such as aggressiveness, difficulties in concentrating on learning in school, and anxiety disorders. What would your general advice be to parents about disclosing personal and financial difficulties?
6. What do you think of people's self-disclosing publicly on, say, television talk shows? Would you go on such a show? What topics would you be willing to discuss? What topics would you be unwilling to discuss?
7. How would you compare disclosures made in chat groups with disclosures made face-to-face?
8. How open are you in communicating with members of different cultures? For example, would you have a "best friendship" with someone who is of a different race, religion, or nationality from you? Are there races, religions, or nationalities that might disqualify a person from "best friendship" status? Would you answer similarly for "long-term romantic relationship"?
9. To what extent are you willing to manipulate the image of yourself that you present to other people? For example, would you be willing to deceive people by being friendly when you really dislike them? Or, consider this situation: You're anxious to date a particular person. You know the kind of person your hoped-for date likes, and you have the ability to give the impression that you are this kind of person. Would it be ethical for you to do this? What if the situation were at a job interview? Would it be ethical for you to present an image of yourself that the interviewer wants but that isn't really you? How authentic must you be to be ethical?

UNIT

Verbal Messages

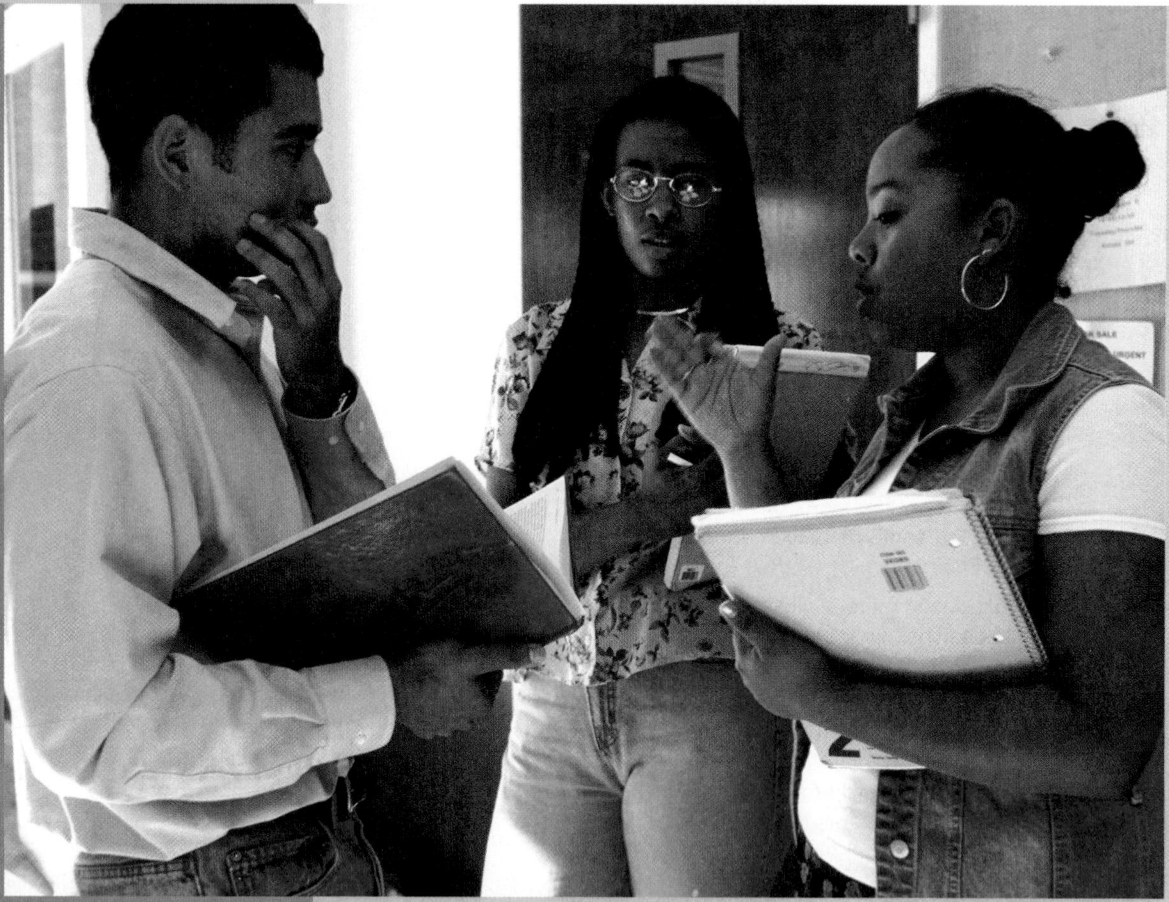

UNIT CONTENTS

You can use language to communicate your thoughts and feelings and to create meaningful and lasting relationships. But you can just as easily use language to distort and prevent meaningful dialogue and destroy relationships. In this unit you'll learn

- how language works
- how you can use it to communicate effectively and at the same time avoid the pitfalls that create misunderstanding

As you communicate, you use two major signal systems—the verbal and the nonverbal. This unit focuses on the verbal system (the next will examine the nonverbal system) and discusses the principles of verbal messages, the concepts of confirmation and disconfirmation, and the ways you can use verbal messages most effectively.

Principles of Verbal Messages

As you grew up, you learned the language spoken by the people around you. You learned its phonological, or sound, system; its semantic system, or system of word meanings; and its syntactic system, which enabled you to put words into meaningful sentence patterns. Our concern in this unit is not with the grammatical structure of language (that's the linguist's job) but with the verbal messages you speak and hear. These verbal messages, of course, rely on the rules of grammar; you can't just make up sounds or words or string words together at random and expect to be understood. But, as we'll see, following the rules of grammar is not enough to achieve effective communication. For this we need to understand five key principles of verbal messages; we'll now explore these principles one by one.

Meanings Are in People

If you wanted to know the meaning of the word *love*, you'd probably turn to a dictionary. There you'd find a definition such as Webster's: "the attraction, desire, or affection felt for a person who arouses delight or admiration or elicits tenderness, sympathetic interest, or benevolence." But where would you turn if you wanted to know what Pedro means when he says, "I'm in love"? Of course, you'd ask Pedro to discover his meaning. It's in this sense that meanings are not in words but in people. Consequently, to uncover meaning, you need to look into people and not merely into words.

Also recognize that as you change, you also change the meanings you created out of past messages. Thus, although the message sent may not have changed, the meanings you created from it yesterday and the meanings you create today may be quite different. Yesterday, when a special someone said, "I love you," you created certain meanings. But today, when you learn that the same "I love you" was said to three other people, or when you fall in love with someone else, you drastically change the meanings you perceive from those three words.

As already noted in Unit 3, this principle is especially important in intercultural communication, as meanings for the same words are often drastically different between members of different cultures. This became especially obvious after the tragedy of the World Trade Center attack: Terms like *justice, suicide*, and *terrorism* were given totally different meanings by many in Afghanistan and in the United States.

The Case of Bypassing

A failure to recognize this important principle is at the heart of a common pattern of miscommunication called bypassing. Bypassing is "the miscommunication pattern which occurs when the sender (speaker, writer, and so on) and the receiver (listener, reader, and so forth) miss each other with their meanings" (Haney, 1973).

Bypassing can take either of two forms. One type of bypassing occurs when two people use different words but give them the same meaning; on the surface there's disagreement, but at the level of meaning there's agreement. The two people actually agree but assume, because they use different words (some of which may actually never be verbalized), that they disagree. Here's an example:

Pat: I'm not interested in one-night stands. I want a permanent relationship. [Meaning: I want an exclusive dating relationship.]

Chris: I'm not ready for that. [Meaning: I'm not ready for marriage.]

The second type is more common and occurs when two people use the same words but give the words different meanings. On the surface it looks like the two people agree (simply because they're using the same words). But if you look more closely, you see that the apparent agreement masks real disagreement, as in this example:

Pat: I don't really believe in religion. [Meaning: I don't really believe in God.]

Chris: Neither do I. [Meaning: I don't really believe in organized religions.]

COMMUNICATION@WORK

Upward and Downward Communication

It's sad but true that the further up you get in an organization, the less likely it is that people will tell you what you ought to hear.

—Donald C. Cook

In any hierarchical organization, communication flows both upward and downward. **Upward communication** consists of messages sent from the lower levels of a hierarchy to the upper levels—for example, line worker to manager or faculty member to dean. This type of communication usually is concerned with job-related activities and problems; ideas for change and suggestions for improvement; and feelings about the organization, work, other workers, or similar issues.

Upward communication is vital to the growth of any organization. It provides management with feedback on worker morale and possible sources of dissatisfaction and offers leaders the opportunity to acquire new ideas from workers. At the same time, it gives subordinates a sense of belonging to and being a part of the organization. Among the guidelines for improving upward communication are:

- Set up a nonthreatening system for upward communication that is acceptable to the cultural norms of the workforce.
- Be open to hearing worker comments, and eliminate unnecessary gatekeepers that prevent important messages from traveling up the organizational hierarchy (Callan, 1993).
- Be willing to listen to these messages even when they're critical.

Downward communication consists of messages sent from the higher levels to the lower levels of the hierarchy; for example, messages sent by managers to workers or by deans to faculty members. Common forms of downward communication include orders; explanations of procedures, goals, and changes; and appraisals of workers. Among the guidelines for effective downward communication are:

- Use a vocabulary known to the workers. Keep technical jargon to a minimum, especially with workers who are not native speakers of the managers' language.
- Provide workers with sufficient information for them to function effectively but avoid information overload.
- When criticizing, be especially careful not to damage the image or face of those singled out.

Communicating@Work

What other suggestions would you offer for upward and downward communication in organizations?

Here Pat and Chris assume that they agree but actually they disagree. At some later date the implications of these differences may well become crucial.

Numerous other examples could be cited. Couples who say they're "in love" may mean very different things; one person may be thinking about "a permanent and exclusive commitment," whereas the other may be referring to "a sexual involvement." "Come home early" may mean one thing to an anxious parent and quite another to a teenager.

Because of bypassing it is a mistake to assume that when two people use the same word, they mean the same thing, or that when they use different words, they mean different things. Words in themselves don't have meaning; meaning is in the people who use those words. Therefore, people can use different words but mean the same thing or use the same words but mean different things.

Meanings Depend on Context

Verbal and nonverbal communications exist in a context, and that context to a large extent determines the meaning of any verbal or nonverbal behavior. The same words or behaviors may have totally different meanings when they occur in different contexts. For example, the greeting "How are you?" means "Hello" to someone you pass regularly on the street but means "Is your health improving?" when said to a friend in the hospital. A wink to an attractive person on a bus means something completely different from a wink that says "I'm kidding."

Similarly, the meaning of a given signal depends on the other behavior it accompanies or is close to in time. Pounding a fist on the table during a speech in support of a politician means something quite different from that same gesture in response to news of a friend's death. Focused eye contact may signify openness and honesty in one culture and defiance in another. In isolation from the context, it's impossible to tell what meaning was intended by merely examining the signals. Of course, even if you know the context in detail, you still may not be able to decipher the meaning of the message.

Messages Are Culturally Influenced

As noted in the introductory passage above, verbal messages must follow, in large part, the rules or grammar of the language. Another set of rules is cultural, however. *Cultural rules* (see Unit 3) focus on the customs and values that your culture considers important. When you follow these principles in communicating, you're seen as a properly functioning member of the culture. When you violate the rules, you risk being seen as deviant or perhaps as insulting. Let's consider how these cultural principles or maxims work in verbal communication.

The Principle of Cooperation

In much of the United States we operate under the principle of **cooperation:** the assumption that in any communication interaction, both parties will make an effort to help each other understand each other. That is, we assume cooperation. This general principle has four subprinciples or maxims. As you read down the list, ask yourself how you follow these maxims in your everyday conversation:

- *The maxim of quality:* Say what you know or assume to be true, and do not say what you know to be false.
- *The maxim of relation:* Talk about what is relevant to the conversation.
- *The maxim of manner:* Be clear, avoid ambiguities (as much as possible), be relatively brief, and organize your thoughts into a meaningful pattern.
- *The maxim of quantity:* Be as informative as necessary to communicate the information.

Note that this last maxim, of quantity, is frequently violated in e-mail communication. Here are three ways in which e-mail often violates the maxim of quantity and some suggestions on how to avoid these violations:

1. Chain e-mails often violate the maxim of quantity by sending people information they don't really need or want. Some people maintain lists of e-mail addresses and send the same information to everyone on their lists. But it's highly unlikely that everyone on every list needs or wants to read the latest joke. Suggestion: Avoid chain e-mail, at least most of the time. When something comes along that you think someone you know would like to read, then send it on to a specific person or to two or three specific people.
2. Chain e-mails often contain the e-mail addresses of everyone on the chain. These extensive headers clog the system and also reveal e-mail addresses that some people may want to keep private or to share at their own discretion. Suggestion: When you do send chain e-mails (and in some situations, they serve useful purposes), conceal the e-mail addresses of your recipients by using some general description such as "undisclosed recipients."
3. Lengthy attachments take time to download and often create problems when people have incompatible equipment. Not everyone wants to see every single photo from your last vacation. Suggestion: Use attachments in moderation; find out first who would like to receive photos and who would not.

Cultural Conversational Maxims

Of course, not all of the maxims followed in the United States are the same as maxims that prevail in other parts of the world. Here are three maxims that are especially important in other cultures. Do you follow these maxims as well as those belonging to the principle of cooperation?

- *The maxim of peaceful relations:* Keep peace in relationship communication, even to the point of agreeing with someone when you really disagree (Midooka, 1990).
- *The maxim of face-saving:* Never embarrass anyone, especially in public. Always allow people to save face, even if this means avoiding the truth—as when you tell someone he or she did good work although the job was actually poorly executed.
- *The maxim of self-denigration:* Avoid taking credit for accomplishments and minimize your abilities or talents in conversation (Gu, 1997).

Politeness

One maxim that seems universal across all cultures is that of **politeness** (Brown & Levinson, 1988).

Cultures differ, however, in how they define politeness and in how important politeness is compared with, say, openness or honesty. Cultures also differ in the rules for expressing politeness and in the punishments for violating the accepted rules of politeness (Mao, 1994; Strecker, 1993). Asian cultures, especially Chinese and Japanese, are often singled out because they emphasize politeness more and mete out harsher social punishments for violations than would most people in the United States and western Europe (Fraser, 1990). When this politeness maxim operates, it may actually override other maxims. For example, the maxim of politeness may require that you not tell the truth, a situation that would violate the maxim of quality.

Politeness is important in all forms of interaction, including online as well as face-to-face interactions. Not surprisingly, researchers find that people view polite e-mail users more positively than impolite users (Jessmer & Anderson, 2001). In general, politeness seems to vary with the type of relationship. One researcher, for example, has proposed that politeness varies among strangers, friends, and intimates as depicted in Figure 7.1.

Politeness and Gender. There are also large gender differences—as well as some similarities—in the expression of politeness (J. Holmes, 1995). Generally, studies from various different cultures show that women's speech is more polite than men's speech, even on the telephone (Brown, 1980; Wetzel, 1988; J. Holmes, 1995; Smoreda & Licoppe, 2000). Women seek areas of agreement in conversation and in conflict situations more often than men do. Similarly, young girls are more apt to try to modify disagreements, whereas young boys are more apt to express more "bald disagreements" (J. Holmes, 1995). Women also use more polite speech when seeking to gain another person's compliance than men do (Baxter, 1984).

There are also gender similarities. For example, in both the United States and New Zealand, men and women seem to pay compliments in similar ways (Manes & Wolfson, 1981; J. Holmes, 1995), and both men and women use politeness strategies when communicating bad news in an organization (Lee, 1993).

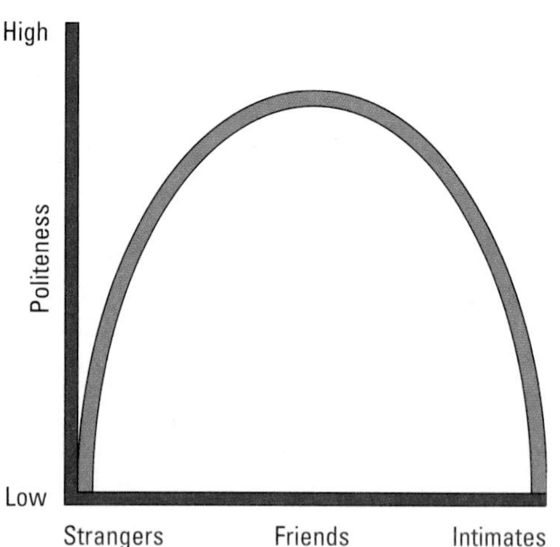

Figure 7.1

Wolfson's Bulge Model of Politeness

This figure depicts a proposed relationship between levels of politeness and degrees of intimacy. Politeness, according to this inverted U model, is greatest with friends and significantly less with strangers and intimates. Can you build a case for an opposite theory—that politeness is especially high with both strangers and intimates and least with friends?

Politeness on the Net: The Rules of Netiquette. Not surprisingly, politeness has its own rules in Internet culture. The rules of netiquette are the rules for communicating politely over the Internet. Much as the rules of etiquette provide guidance for communicating in social situations, the rules of netiquette provide guidance for communicating over the Net. These rules, as you'll see, are helpful for making Internet communication easier and more pleasant, facilitating greater personal efficiency, and putting less strain on the system and on other users. Here are several guidelines suggested by computer researchers (Shea, 1994; James & Weingarten, 1995; Barron, 1995; *Time* [special issue], Spring 1995). A helpful website to help you pursue this topic, with lots of links to a variety of netiquette-related websites, is www.albion.com/netiquette.

- *Read the FAQs.* Before asking questions about the system, read the Frequently Asked Questions; your question has probably been asked before, and you'll put less strain on the system.
- *Don't shout.* WRITING IN CAPS IS PERCEIVED AS SHOUTING. It's okay to use caps occasionally to achieve emphasis. If you wish to give emphasis without "shouting," underline like _this_ or *like this*.
- *Lurk before speaking.* Lurking is reading the posted notices and the conversations without contributing anything; in computer communication, lurking is good, not bad. Lurking will help you learn the rules of the particular group and will help you avoid saying things you'll want to take back.
- *Don't contribute to traffic jams.* Try connecting during off-hours whenever possible. If you're unable to connect, try again later, but not immedi-

UNDERSTANDING *THEORY* AND *RESEARCH*

Theories of Gender Differences

Throughout this text, gender differences are discussed in a wide variety of contexts. Holmes (1995) distinguishes three perspectives on gender differences in communication:

- Gender differences are due to innate biological differences. Thus, gender differences in communication, such as differences in politeness or in listening behavior, are the result of these biological differences.
- Gender differences are due to different patterns of socialization, which lead to different forms of communication. Thus, the gender differences that you observe are due to the different ways boys and girls are raised and taught.
- Gender differences are due to the inequalities in social power. For example, because of women's lesser social power, they're more apt to communicate with greater deference and politeness than are men.

Working with Theories and Research

- *If you have access, log on to Research Navigator (*www.researchnavigator.com*) and look up "gender differences" in the communication, psychology, and sociology databases. Can you identify the perspective supported by contemporary research? What perspective seems to be supported by your own experiences and observations?*

ately. Trying immediately only puts added strain on the system, and you're likely still to be unable to connect. To secure information, try local sources before trying more distant sources; it requires fewer connections and less time. And be economical in using files that may tie up lines for long periods of time, such as photographs.

- *Be brief.* Follow the maxim of quantity by communicating only the information that is needed; follow the maxim of manner by communicating clearly, briefly, and in an organized way.
- *Treat newbies kindly.* You once were new to the Internet yourself.

Language Is Both Denotative and Connotative

Denotation refers to the meaning you'd find in a dictionary; it's the meaning that members of the culture assign to a word. **Connotation** refers to the emotional meaning that specific speakers–listeners give to a word. Words have both kinds of meaning. Take as an example the word *death*. To a doctor this word might mean (or denote) the time when brain activity ceases. This is an objective description of a particular event. In contrast, when a mother is informed of her child's death, the word means (or connotes) much more. It recalls her child's youth, ambition, family, illness, and so on. To her it's a highly emotional, subjective, and personal word. These emotional, subjective, or personal reactions are the word's connotative meaning.

Semanticist S. I. Hayakawa (Hayakawa & Hayakawa, 1990) coined the terms "snarl words" and "purr words" to clarify further the distinction between denotative and connotative meaning. **Snarl words** are highly negative ("She's an idiot," "He's a pig," "They're a bunch of losers"). Sexist, racist, and heterosexist language and hate speech provide lots of other examples. **Purr words** are highly positive ("She's a real sweetheart," "He's a dream," "They're the greatest"). Although they may sometimes seem to have denotative meaning and refer to the "real world," snarl and purr words are purely connotative in meaning. They don't describe people or events; rather, they reveal the speaker's feelings about these people or events.

Language Varies in Directness

Direct speech communicates your meaning explicitly and leaves little doubt as to the thoughts and feelings you want to convey. **Indirect speech**, on the other hand, communicates your meaning in a roundabout way. You don't really say what you mean, but you imply it. Indirect messages have both advantages and disadvantages.

One of the advantages of indirect speech is that it allows you to express a desire without insulting or offending anyone; it allows you to observe the rules of polite interaction. So instead of saying, "I'm bored with this group," you say, "It's getting late and I have to get up early tomorrow," or you look at your watch and pretend to be surprised by the time. In this way you state a preference but express it indirectly so as to avoid offending someone. Sometimes indirect messages allow you to ask for compliments in a socially acceptable manner; for example, a person who says, "I was thinking of getting a nose job" may hope to get a response such as "A nose job? You? Your nose is perfect."

Indirect messages can also create problems, however. For example, meanings that are expressed too indirectly may be misunderstood; the other person may simply not grasp your implied meaning. When this happens, you may come to resent the other person for not seeing beneath the surface—and yourself for not being more up-front. Another disadvantage is that you may be seen as manipulative; that is, as trying to get someone to do something without really saying it. For example, you might tell a friend, "I really could use a loan until payday, but I really don't want to ask anyone."

A popular stereotype in the United States holds that women tend to be indirect in making requests and in giving orders (e.g., Kramarae, 1981). This indirectness is thought to communicate women's powerlessness and discomfort with their own authority. Men, the stereotype continues, generally use direct speech, sometimes to the point of being blunt or rude. This directness communicates power and comfort with one's own authority.

Deborah Tannen (1994b) provides an interesting perspective on these stereotypes. She agrees that women are more indirect in giving orders and are more likely to say, for example, "It would be great if these letters could go out today" rather than "Have these letters out by three." But Tannen (1994b, p. 84) argues that "issuing orders indirectly can be the prerogative of those in power" and in no way shows powerlessness. Power, to Tannen, is the ability to choose your own style of communication.

Men, however, are also indirect—but in different situations (Rundquist, 1992). According to Tannen (1994b), men are more likely to use indirectness when they express weakness, reveal a problem, or admit an error. Men are more likely to speak indirectly in expressing emotions other than anger. Men are also more indirect when they refuse expressions of increased romantic intimacy. Men are thus indirect, the theory goes, when they're saying something that goes against the masculine stereotype.

Many Asian and Latin American cultures value indirectness, largely because it enables a person to avoid appearing criticized or contradicted and thereby losing face. A somewhat different kind of indirectness is seen in the greater use of intermediaries to resolve conflict among the Chinese than among North Americans, for example (Ma, 1992). In most of the United States, you're taught that directness is the preferred style. "Be up-front" and "Tell it like it is" are commonly heard communication guidelines.

Disconfirmation and Confirmation

The terms *confirmation* and *disconfirmation* refer to the extent to which you acknowledge another person. Consider this situation. You've been living with someone for the last six months and you arrive home late one night. Your partner, let's say Pat, is angry and complains about your being so late. Which of the following is most likely to be your response?

1. Stop screaming. I'm not interested in what you're babbling about. I'll do what I want, when I want. I'm going to bed.
2. What are you so angry about? Didn't you get in three hours late last Thursday when you went to that office party? So knock it off.
3. You have a right to be angry. I should have called to tell you I was going to be late, but I got involved in a serious debate at work, and I couldn't leave until it was resolved.

In response 1, you dismiss Pat's anger and even indicate dismissal of Pat as a person. In response 2, you reject the validity of Pat's reasons for being angry but do not dismiss either Pat's feelings of anger or Pat as a person. In response 3, you acknowledge Pat's anger and the reasons for it. In addition, you provide some kind of explanation and, in doing so, show that both Pat's feelings and Pat as a person are important and that Pat has the right to know what happened. The first response is an example of disconfirmation, the second of rejection, and the third of confirmation.

Psychologist William James once observed that "no more fiendish punishment could be devised, even were such a thing physically possible, than that one should be turned loose in society and remain absolutely unnoticed by all the members thereof." In this often-quoted observation, James identifies the essence of disconfirmation (Watzlawick, Beavin, &

Jackson, 1967; Veenendall & Feinstein, 1995). **Disconfirmation** is a communication pattern in which we ignore someone's presence as well as that person's communications. We say, in effect, that this person and what this person has to say are not worth serious attention or effort—that this person and this person's contributions are so unimportant or insignificant that there is no reason to concern ourselves with her or him. The Amish community practices an extreme form of disconfirmation called "shunning," in which the community members totally ignore a person who has violated one or more of their rules. The specific aim of shunning is to get the person to repent and to reenter the community of the faithful. But it seems that all cultures practice some form of exclusion for those who violate important cultural rules.

Note that disconfirmation is not the same as **rejection.** In rejection, you disagree with the person; you indicate your unwillingness to accept something the other person says or does. In disconfirming someone, however, you deny that person's significance; you claim that what this person says or does simply does not count.

Confirmation is the opposite communication pattern. In confirmation you not only acknowledge the presence of the other person but also indicate your acceptance of this person, of this person's self-definition, and of your relationship as defined or viewed by this other person.

Disconfirmation and confirmation may be communicated in a wide variety of ways. Table 7.1 shows just a few examples.

You can gain insight into a wide variety of offensive language practices by viewing them as types of disconfirmation—as language that alienates and separates and prevents effective communication. Four common practices are (1) sexism, (2) heterosexism, (3) racism, and (4) ageism. Let's discuss each in turn.

Table 7.1
Confirmation and Disconfirmation

As you review this table, try to imagine a specific illustration for each of the ways of communicating disconfirmation and confirmation (Pearson, 1993; Galvin, Bylund, & Brommel, 2004).

Confirmation

1. Acknowledge the presence and the contributions of the other by either supporting or taking issue with what the other says.
2. Make nonverbal contact by maintaining direct eye contact, touching, hugging, kissing, or otherwise demonstrating acknowledgment of the other; engage in dialogue—communication in which both persons are speakers and listeners, both are involved, and both are concerned with each other.
3. Demonstrate understanding of what the other says and means and reflect these feelings to demonstrate your understanding.
4. Ask questions of the other concerning both thoughts and feelings and acknowledge the questions of the other, return phone calls, and answer e-mail and letters.
5. Encourage the other to express thoughts and feelings, and respond directly and exclusively to what the other says.

Disconfirmation

1. Ignore the presence and the messages of the other person; ignore or express (nonverbally and verbally) indifference to anything the other says.
2. Make no nonverbal contact; avoid direct eye contact; avoid touching the other person; engage in monologue—communication in which one person speaks and one person listens, there is no real interaction, and there is no real concern or respect for each other.
3. Jump to interpretation or evaluation rather than working at understanding what the other means; express your own feelings, ignore the feelings of the other, or give abstract, intellectualized responses.
4. Make statements about yourself; ignore any lack of clarity in the other's remarks; ignore the other's requests; and fail to answer questions, return phone calls, or answer e-mails and letters.
5. Interrupt or otherwise make it difficult for the other to express him- or herself; respond only tangentially or by shifting the focus in another direction.

BUILDING COMMUNICATION SKILLS

Confirming, Rejecting, or Disconfirming

Here are three practice situations. For each situation, *(a)* write the three potential responses as indicated; then, *(b)* after completing all three situations, indicate what effects each type of response is likely to generate.

1. Enrique receives this semester's grades in the mail; they're a lot better than previous semesters' grades but are still not great. After opening the letter, Enrique says: "I really tried hard to get my grades up this semester." Enrique's parents respond:

   With disconfirmation
   With rejection
   With confirmation

2. Elizabeth, who has been out of work for the past several weeks, says: "I feel like such a failure; I just can't seem to find a job. I've been pounding the pavement for the last five weeks and still nothing." Elizabeth's friend responds:

   With disconfirmation
   With rejection
   With confirmation

3. Candi's colleague at work comes to her overjoyed and tells her that she was just promoted to vice president of marketing, skipping three steps in the hierarchy and tripling her salary. Candi responds:

   With disconfirmation
   With rejection
   With confirmation

Sexism

Sexist language is language that puts down someone because of her or his gender. Usually, the term refers to language that denigrates women, but it can also legitimately refer to language that denigrates men. Usually sexist language is used by one sex against the other, but it need not be limited to these cases; women can be sexist against women and men can be sexist against men. The National Council of Teachers of English has proposed guidelines for nonsexist (gender-free, gender-neutral, or sex-fair) language. These concern the use of generic *man,* the use of generic *he* and *his,* and sex-role stereotyping (Penfield, 1987).

Generic *Man*. The word *man* refers most clearly to an adult male. To use the term to refer to both men and women emphasizes "maleness" at the expense of "femaleness." Similarly, the terms *mankind* and *the common man* and even *cavemen* imply a primary focus on adult males. Gender-neutral terms can easily be substituted. Instead of *mankind,* you can say *humanity, people,* or *human beings.* Instead of *the common man,* you can say *the average person* or *ordinary people.* Instead of *cavemen,* you can say *prehistoric people* or *cave dwellers.*

Similarly, the use of terms such as *policeman* and *fireman* and other terms that presume maleness as the norm and femaleness as a deviation from this norm are clear and common examples of sexist language. Using nonsexist alternatives for these and similar terms (for example, *police officer* and *firefighter* instead of *policeman* and *fireman*) and making these alternatives a part of your active vocabulary will include the female sex as "normal" in such professions. Similarly, using "female forms" such as *actress* or *stewardess* is considered sexist; these derivations of *actor* and *steward,* again, emphasize that the male form is the norm and the female is the deviation from the norm.

Generic *He* and *His*. The use of the masculine pronoun to refer to any individual regardless of sex is certainly declining. But as recently as 1975 all college textbooks, for example, used the masculine pronoun as generic. There is no legitimate reason why the feminine pronoun can't alternate with the masculine pronoun in referring to hypothetical individuals, or why terms such as *he and she* or *her and him* can't be used instead of just *he* or *him*. Perhaps the best solution is to restructure your sentences to eliminate any reference to gender. Here are a few examples from the NCTE Guidelines (Penfield, 1987):

Sexist	**Gender-Free**
The average student is worried about his grades.	The average student is worried about grades.
Ask the student to hand in his work as soon as he is finished.	Ask students to hand in their work as soon as they are finished.

Sex-Role Stereotyping. The words we use often reflect a sex-role bias—the assumption that certain roles or professions belong to men and others belong to women. To eliminate sex-role stereotyping, avoid, for example, making the hypothetical elementary school teacher female and the college professor male. Avoid referring to doctors as male and nurses as female. Avoid noting the sex of a professional with terms such as *female doctor* or *male nurse*. When you are referring to a specific doctor or nurse, the person's sex will become clear when you use the appropriate pronoun: "Dr. Smith wrote the prescription for her new patient" or "The nurse recorded the patient's temperature himself."

Heterosexism

A close relative of sexism is heterosexism, a relatively new addition to the list of linguistic prejudices. As the term implies, **heterosexist language** is language used to disparage gay men and lesbians. As with racist language, we see heterosexism in derogatory terms used for lesbians and gay men as well as in more subtle forms of language usage. For example, when you qualify a profession—as in *gay athlete* or *lesbian doctor*—you are in effect stating that athletes and doctors are not normally gay or lesbian. Further, you are highlighting the affectional orientation of the athlete and the doctor in a context in which it may have no relevance, in the same way that gender or racial distinctions often have no relevance to the issue at hand.

Still another instance of heterosexism—and perhaps the most difficult to deal with—is the presumption of heterosexuality. Usually, people assume that the person they are talking to or about is heterosexual. They are usually correct, because most people are heterosexual. At the same time, however, this assumption denies the lesbian and gay identity a certain legitimacy. The practice is similar to the presumptions of whiteness and maleness that we have made significant inroads in eliminating. Here are a few suggestions for avoiding heterosexist, or what some call homophobic, language.

- Avoid offensive nonverbal mannerisms that parody stereotypes when talking about gays and lesbians.
- Avoid "complimenting" gay men and lesbians by saying that "they don't look it." To gays and lesbians, this is not a compliment. Similarly, expressing disappointment that a person is gay—often thought to be a compliment, as in comments such as "What a waste!"—is not a compliment.
- Avoid the assumption that every gay or lesbian knows what every other gay or lesbian is thinking. It's very similar to asking a Japanese person why Sony is investing heavily in the United States or, as one comic put it, asking an African American, "What do you think Jesse Jackson meant by that last speech?"
- Avoid denying individual differences. Comments such as "Lesbians are so loyal" or "Gay men are so open with their feelings," which ignore the reality of wide differences within any group, are potentially insulting to all groups.
- Avoid overattribution—the tendency, in this case, to attribute just about everything a person does, says, and believes to his or her being gay or lesbian. This tendency helps to recall and perpetuate stereotypes (see Unit 3).
- Remember that relationship milestones are important to all people. Ignoring anniversaries or birthdays of, say, a relative's partner is resented by everyone.

Racism

According to Andrea Rich (1974), "any language that, through a conscious or unconscious attempt by the user, places a particular racial or ethnic group in an inferior position is racist." **Racist language** expresses racist attitudes. It also contributes to the development of racist attitudes in those who use or hear the language. This effect, of course, is similar to the way sexist and heterosexist language perpetuates sexist and heterosexist attitudes. Even when racism is subtle, unintentional, or even unconscious, its effects are systematically damaging (Dovidio, Gaertner, Kawakami, & Hodson, 2002).

Members of one culture use racist terms to disparage members of other cultures, their customs, or their accomplishments and to establish and maintain power over other groups. Racist language emphasizes differences rather than similarities and separates rather than unites members of different cultures. The social consequences of racist language in terms of employment, education, housing opportunities, and general community acceptance are well known.

It has often been pointed out (Bosmajian, 1974; Davis, 1973) that there are aspects of language that may be inherently racist. For example, one examination of English found 134 synonyms for *white.* Of these, 44 had positive connotations (for example, *clean, chaste,* and *unblemished*) and only 10 had negative connotations (for example, *whitewash* and *pale*). The remaining terms were relatively neutral. Of the 120 synonyms for *black,* 60 had unfavorable connotations (*unclean, foreboding,* and *deadly*) and none had positive connotations.

Consider the following expressions:

- the Korean doctor
- the Chicano prodigy
- the African American mathematician
- the white health aide

Often, people use these identifiers to emphasize that the combination of race and occupation (or talent or accomplishment) is rare and unexpected, that this member of a given ethnic group is an exception. Using racial identifiers also implies that racial factors are somehow important in the context. In some cases, of course, a racial identifier is in fact relevant to the conversation. For example, in commenting on changes in Hollywood films, you might say, "This is the first year that both best acting awards were won by African Americans." In the vast majority of cases, however, identifiers of these types are best left unused.

Ageism

Ageism is discrimination based on age. One researcher offers a more comprehensive definition: "any attitude, action, or institutional structure which subordinates a person or group because of age or any assignment of roles in society purely on the basis of age" (Traxler, 1980, p. 14). In the United States and throughout much of the industrialized world, ageism signifies discrimination against the old and against aging in general. But ageism can also involve prejudice against other age groups. For example, if you describe all teenagers as selfish and undependable, you're discriminating against a group purely because of their age and thus are ageist in your statements. In some cultures—some Asian and some African cultures, for example—the old are revered and respected. Younger people seek them out for advice on economic, ethical, and relationship issues.

Popular language is replete with examples of ageist phrases; *little old lady, old hag, old-timer, over the hill, old coot,* and *old fogy* are just some examples. As with sexism or racism, qualifying a description of someone in terms of his or her age demonstrates ageism. For example, if you refer to "a quick-witted 75-year-old" or "an agile 65-year-old" or "a responsible teenager," you are implying that these qualities are unusual in people of these ages and thus need special mention. You are saying that "quick-wittedness" and "being 75" do not normally go together; you imply the same abnormality for "agility" and "being 65" and for "responsibility" and "being a teenager." The problem with this kind of stereotyping is that it's simply wrong. There are many 80-year-olds who are extremely quick witted (and many 30-year-olds who aren't).

You also communicate ageism when you speak to older people in overly simple words or explain things that don't need explaining. Nonverbally, you demonstrate ageist communication when, for example, you avoid touching an older person but touch others, or when you avoid making direct eye contact with the older person but readily do so with others. Also, it's a mistake to speak to an older person at an overly high volume; this suggests that all older people have hearing difficulties, and it tends to draw attention to the fact that you are talking down to the older person.

Of course, the media perpetuate ageist stereotypes by depicting older people as unproductive, complaining, and unromantic. Rarely, for example, do television shows or films show older people working productively, being cooperative and pleasant, and engaging in romantic and sexual relationships.

One useful way to avoid ageism is to recognize and avoid the illogical stereotypes that ageist language is based on.

- Avoid talking down to a person because he or she is older. Older people are not mentally slow; most people remain mentally alert well into old age.
- Don't assume you have to refresh an older person's memory each time you see the person. Older people can and do remember things.
- Avoid implying that relationships are no longer important. Older people continue to be interested in relationships.
- Don't speak at an abnormally high volume or maintain overly close physical distances. Being older does not mean being hard of hearing or being unable to see; most older people hear and see quite well, sometimes with hearing aids or glasses.
- Engage older people in conversation as you would wish to be engaged. Older people are interested in the world around them.

Even though you want to avoid ageist communication, there are times when you may wish to make adjustments when talking with someone who does have language or communication difficulties. The American Speech and Hearing Association offers several useful suggestions (http://www.asha.org/public/speech/development/communicating-better-with-older-people.htm, accessed January 31, 2003):

- Reduce as much background noise as you can.
- Ease into the conversation by beginning with casual topics and then moving into more familiar topics. Stay with each topic for a while; avoid jumping too quickly from one topic to another.
- Speak in relatively short sentences and questions.
- Give the person added time to respond, and resist showing impatience. Some older people react more slowly and need extra time.
- Listen actively. Practice the skills of active listening discussed in the previous unit.

Sexist, Heterosexist, Racist, and Ageist Listening

Just as racist, sexist, heterosexist, and ageist attitudes will influence your language, they can also influence your listening. In this type of listening you hear what the speaker is saying through the stereotypes you hold. It occurs when you listen differently to a person because of his or her gender, race, affectional orientation, or age even though these characteristics are irrelevant to the message.

Sexist, racist, heterosexist, and ageist listening can occur in a wide variety of situations. For example, when you dismiss a valid argument—or attribute validity to an invalid argument—because the speaker is of a particular gender, race, affectional orientation, or age, you're listening with prejudice.

ASK THE RESEARCHER

Cultural Differences

- *I'm in a serious romantic relationship with someone who is my cultural opposite. We differ in race, religion, and nationality. Our problem, however, is not with us; rather, it is with our families. Both of our families are narrow-minded, bigoted, and culturally insensitive. What can we do to get our families to accept our relationship and to demonstrate some cultural sensitivity?*

Your complex question may yield no solution that satisfies you fully. However, you have opportunities available. If your families are important to you, how you communicate with them becomes significant. With intercultural challenges in your romantic relationship, fear in numerous forms may surface; for example, fear of your inability to mold the intercultural situation you desire. You may not be prepared to deal efficiently with family resistance to you as a culturally opposite romantic couple. If family resistance offers you a starting rather than stopping point, how you resist their narrow-mindedness may yield beneficial consequences. If you are passionate and caring about all, you will be more likely triumph over the limitations of your families. To proceed with wisdom on this sensitive matter, you would do well to collaborate with your families rather than avoid them or clash aggressively with them.

For additional information: Knowles, E. S., & Linn, J. A. (Eds.). (2004). *Resistance and persuasion.* Mahwah, NJ: Erlbaum. Also Wilmot, W. W., & Hocker, J. L. (2001). *Interpersonal conflict* (6th ed.). New York: McGraw-Hill. And Fiordo, R. A. (in press). The mindful dialectic and adolescence: Inviting collaboration. *Medicine, Mind, and Adolescence: International Journal of Adolescentology.*

Richard A. Fiordo (Ph.D. University of Illinois–Urbana) is professor of communication at the University of North Dakota, where he teaches courses in organizational communication, conflict and collaboration, and film/television narratives. He serves at UND as an advisor to PRSSA and the Ad Club, is developing a special interest group in sales and sales management for communication and marketing students, and is working on a project to enhance safety for women on campus. Fiordo (richard.fiordo@und.nodak.edu) is also a board member for the Society of Adolescentology out of Ambrosiana University in Milan, Italy (www.adolescence.it).

But there also are many instances when these characteristics are relevant and pertinent to your evaluation of the message. For example, the sex of a person who is talking about pregnancy, fathering a child, birth control, or surrogate motherhood is, most would agree, probably relevant to the message. So in these cases it is not sexist listening to take the sex of the speaker into consideration. It is, however, sexist listening to assume that only one sex can be an authority on a particular topic or that one sex's opinions are without value. The same is true in relation to listening through a person's race or affectional orientation.

Cultural Identifiers

Perhaps the best way to develop nonsexist, nonheterosexist, nonracist, and nonageist language is to examine the preferred cultural identifiers to use in talking to and about members of different groups. Remember, however, that preferred terms frequently change over time, so keep in touch with the most current preferences. The preferences and many of the specific examples identified here are drawn largely from the findings of the Task Force on Bias-Free Language of the Association of American University Presses (Schwartz, 1995).

Generally, the term *girl* should be used only to refer to very young females and is equivalent to *boy.* Neither term should be used for people older than say 13 or 14. *Girl* is never used to refer to a grown woman, nor is *boy* used to refer to people in blue-collar positions, as it once was. *Lady* is negatively evaluated by many because it connotes the stereotype of the prim and proper woman. *Woman* or *young woman* is preferred. *Older person* is preferred

MEDIA WATCH

Hate Speech

Hate speech is speech that is hostile, offensive, degrading, or intimidating to a particular group of people. Women, African Americans, Muslims, Jews, Asians, Hispanics, and gay men and lesbians are among the major targets in the United States.

Hate speech occurs in all forms of human communication. For example, it may occur when:

- people utter insults to someone passing by
- posters and fliers degrade specific groups
- radio talk shows denigrate members of certain groups
- computer games are reconfigured to target members of minority groups
- websites insult and demean certain groups and at the same time encourage hostility toward members of these groups

Because the media are so powerful in influencing opinions, and because the media reach so many people, the issue of hate speech in the media takes on special importance (Ruscher, 2001).

One of the difficulties in attacking hate speech is that it's often difficult to draw a clear line between speech that is protected by the First Amendment right to freedom of expression but is simply at odds with the majority viewpoint and speech that is designed to denigrate and encourage hostility against members of certain cultural groups.

Some colleges are instituting hate speech codes—written statements that spell out what constitutes hate speech as well as the penalties for hate speech. Proponents of such codes argue that they teach students that hate speech is unacceptable, is harmful to all people (but especially to minority members who are the targets of such attacks), and may be curtailed in the same way as other undesirable acts such as child pornography or rape). Opponents argue that such codes do not address the underlying prejudices and biases that give rise to hate speech, that they stifle free expression, and that they may be used unfairly by the majority to silence minority opinion and dissent.

You and the Media

If you have access, use the communication, business, and New York Times *databases of Research Navigator (*www.researchnavigator.com*) to look up "hate speech" and "campus codes." After reading about hate speech and the codes that have been developed, formulate your own position on campus codes for hate speech. What reasons can you develop in support of your position?*

to *elder, elderly, senior,* or *senior citizen* (which technically refers to someone older than 65).

Generally, *gay* is the preferred term to refer to a man who has an affectional preference for other men and *lesbian* is the preferred term for a woman who has an affectional preference for other women (Lever, 1995). (*Lesbian* means "homosexual woman," so the term *lesbian woman* is redundant.) *Homosexual* refers to both gays and lesbians, but more often to a sexual orientation to members of one's own sex. *Gay* and *lesbian* refer to a lifestyle and not just to sexual orientation. *Gay* as a noun, although widely used, may prove offensive in some contexts, as in "We have two gays on the team." Because most scientific thinking holds that sexuality is not a matter of choice, the terms *sexual orientation* and *affectional orientation* are preferred to *sexual preference* or *sexual status* (which is also vague).

Generally, most African Americans prefer *African American* to *black* (Hecht, Collier, & Ribeau, 1993), although *black* is often used with *white,* as well as in a variety of other contexts (for example, Department of Black and Puerto Rican Studies, the *Journal of Black History,* and Black History Month). The American Psychological Association recommends that both terms be capitalized, but the *Chicago Manual of Style* (the manual used by most newspapers and publishing houses) recommends using lowercase. The terms *Negro* and *colored,* although used in the names of some organizations (for example, the United Negro College Fund and the National Association for the Advancement of Colored People), are not used outside these contexts.

White is generally used to refer to those whose roots are in European cultures and usually does not include Hispanics. Analogous to *African American* (which itself is based on a long tradition of terms such as *Irish American* and *Italian American*) is the phrase *European American.* Few European Americans, however, call themselves that; most prefer their national origins emphasized, as in, for example, *German American* or *Greek American.* This preference may well change as Europe moves toward becoming a more cohesive and united entity. *People of color*—a more literary-sounding term appropriate perhaps to public speaking but awkward in most conversations—is preferred to *nonwhite,* which implies that whiteness is the norm and nonwhiteness is a deviation from that norm. The same is true of the term *non-Christian:* It implies that people who have other beliefs deviate from the norm.

Generally, the term *Hispanic* refers to anyone who identifies himself or herself as belonging to a Spanish-speaking culture. *Latina* (female) and *Latino* (male) refer to persons whose roots are in one of the Latin American countries, such as Haiti, the Dominican Republic, Nicaragua, or Guatemala. *Hispanic American* refers to United States residents whose ancestry is in a Spanish culture; the term includes Mexican, Caribbean, and Central and South Americans. In emphasizing a Spanish heritage, however, the term is really inaccurate, because it leaves out the large numbers of people in the Caribbean and in South America whose origins are African, Native American, French, or Portuguese. *Chicana* (female) and *Chicano* (male) refer to persons with roots in Mexico, although it often connotes a nationalist attitude (Jandt, 2004) and is considered offensive by many Mexican Americans. *Mexican American* is generally preferred.

Inuk (plural, *Inuit*), also spelled with two *n*'s (*Innuk* and *Innuit*), is preferred to *Eskimo* (a term

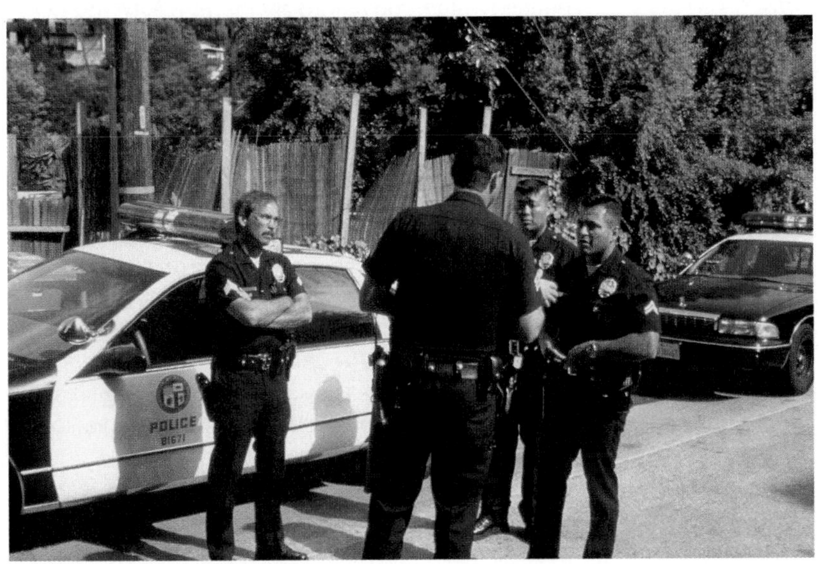

VIEWPOINT

Many people feel that it's permissible for members of a group or subculture to refer to themselves with terms that if said by outsiders would be considered, for example, racist or sexist. Some critics warn that using these terms may actually reinforce negative stereotypes: By using these words, group members may come to accept the labels and their negative connotations. Others would argue that voluntarily using such terms makes them less negative. What effects, if any, do you think such self-talk has?

the United States Census Bureau uses), which was applied to the indigenous peoples of Alaska and Canada by Europeans and literally means "raw meat eaters."

The word *Indian* technically refers only to someone from India, not to members of other Asian countries or to the indigenous peoples of North America. *American Indian* or *Native American* is preferred, even though many Native Americans do refer to themselves as *Indians* and *Indian people.* In Canada indigenous people are called *first people* or *first nations.* The term *native American* (with a lowercase *n*) is most often used to refer to persons born in the United States. Although technically the term could refer to anyone born in North or South America, people outside the United States generally prefer more specific designations such as *Argentinean, Cuban,* or *Canadian.* The term *native* describes an indigenous inhabitant; it is not used to indicate "someone having a less developed culture."

Muslim (rather than the older *Moslem*) is the preferred form to refer to a person who adheres to the religious teachings of Islam. *Quran* (rather than *Koran*) is the preferred term for the scriptures of Islam. *Jewish people* is often preferred to *Jews,* and *Jewess* (a Jewish female) is considered derogatory.

When history was being written from a European perspective, Europe was taken as the focal point and the rest of the world was defined in terms of its location relative to that continent. Thus, Asia became the East or the Orient, and Asians became *Orientals*—a term that is today considered inappropriate or "Eurocentric." Thus, people from Asia are *Asians,* just as people from Africa are *Africans* and people from Europe are *Europeans.*

Using Verbal Messages Effectively

A chief concern in using verbal messages is to recognize what critical thinking theorists call "conceptual distortions"; that is, mental mistakes, misinterpretations, or reasoning fallacies. Avoiding these distortions and substituting a more critical, more realistic analysis is probably the best way to improve your own use of verbal messages (DeVito, 1974). Let's look at several principles of language that are often ignored or misunderstood along with the conceptual distortions that result from such misunderstandings (Korzybski, 1933).

Language Symbolizes Reality (Partially)

Language symbolizes reality; it's not the reality itself. Of course, this is obvious. But consider: Have you ever reacted to the way something was labeled or described rather than to the actual item? Have you ever bought something because of its name rather than because of the actual object? If so, you were probably responding as if language were the reality, a distortion called intensional orientation.

Intensional Orientation

Intensional orientation (the s in *intensional* is intentional) is the tendency to view people, objects, and events according to way they're talked about—the way they're labeled. For example, if Sally were labeled "uninteresting," you would, responding intensionally, evaluate her as uninteresting even before listening to what she had to say. You'd see Sally through a filter imposed by the label "uninteresting." **Extensional orientation**, on the other hand, is the tendency to look first at the actual people, objects, and events and only afterwards at their labels. In this case, it would mean looking at Sally without any preconceived labels, guided by what she says and does, not by the words used to label her.

To avoid intensional orientation, extensionalize. Labels should never be given greater attention than the actual thing. Give your main attention to the people, things, and events in the world as you see them and not as they're presented in words. For example, when you meet Jack and Jill, observe and interact with them. Then form your impressions. Don't respond to them as "greedy, money-grubbing landlords" because Harry labeled them this way. Don't respond to George as "lazy" just because Elaine told you he was.

Allness

A related distortion is **allness:** forgetting that language symbolizes only a portion of reality, never the whole. When you assume that you can know all or say all about anything, you're into allness. In reality, you never can see all of anything. You never can experience anything fully. You see a part, then conclude what the whole is like. You have to draw conclusions on the basis of insufficient evidence (because you always have insufficient evidence). A useful **extensional device** to help combat the tendency to think that all can or has been said about anything is to end each statement mentally with **et cetera**—a reminder that there's more to learn, more to know, and more to say and that every statement is inevitably incomplete. Of course, some people overuse the "et cetera." They use it not as a mental reminder but as a substitute for being specific. This obviously is to be avoided and merely adds to the conversational confusion.

To avoid allness, recognize that language symbolizes only a part of reality, never the whole. Whatever someone says—regardless of what it is or how extensive it is—represents only part of the story.

UNDERSTANDING THEORY AND RESEARCH

The Verb "To Be"

The theory of E-prime (or E′) argues that if you wrote and spoke English without the verb *to be,* you'd describe events more accurately (Bourland, 1965–1966; Wilson, 1989; Klein, 1992). For example, when you say, "Johnny is a failure," the verb *is* implies that "failure" is *in* Johnny rather than in your observation or evaluation of Johnny. The verb *to be* (in forms such as *is, are,* and *am*) also implies permanence; the implication is that because failure is *in* Johnny, it will always be there; Johnny will always be a failure. A more accurate and descriptive statement might be "Johnny failed his last two math exams."

Consider this theory as applied to your thinking about yourself. When you say, for example, "I'm not good at public speaking" or "I'm unpopular" or "I'm lazy," you imply that these qualities are *in* you. But these are simply evaluations that may be incorrect or, if at least partly accurate, may change (Joyner, 1993).

Working with Theories and Research

- *Do you find the E-prime approach to language a useful one? Does it seem applicable to your own evaluations—of yourself and of others?*

Language Expresses Both Facts and Inferences

Language enables you to form statements of both facts and inferences without making any linguistic distinction between the two. Similarly, in speaking and listening you often don't make a clear distinction between statements of fact and statements of inference. Yet there are great differences between the two. Barriers to clear thinking can be created when inferences are treated as facts, a tendency called **fact–inference confusion.**

For example, you can say, "She's wearing a blue jacket," and you can say, "He's harboring an illogical hatred." Although the sentences have similar structures, they're different. You can observe the jacket and its color, but how do you observe "illogical hatred"? Obviously, this is not a **factual statement** but an **inferential statement.** It's a statement you make on the basis not only of what you observe, but of what

VIEWPOINT

When asked what they would like to change about the communication style of the opposite sex, men often said they wanted women to be more direct and women often said they wanted men to stop interrupting and offering advice (Noble, 1994). What one change would you like to see in the communication system of the opposite sex? Of your own sex?

GOING *ONLINE*

Institute of General Semantics

http://www.time-binding.org

General semantics is an approach to language that emphasizes the connection between the way you speak (on the one hand) and the way you think and behave (on the other). This unit's discussion of "Using Verbal Messages Effectively" rests on the principles of general semantics. Visit this website and learn more about how language works.

In addition, visit the text's companion website (www.ablongman.com/devito) for self-tests that measure how confirming, polite, and direct you are—and for a variety of exercises and discussions on verbal messages ("Men and Women Talking," "Talking with the Grief Stricken," "Integrating Verbal and Nonverbal Messages," "Using the Abstraction Ladder as a Creative Thinking Tool," "Varying Directness," "Identifying the Barriers to Communication," and "'Must Lie' Situations." An entire unit on "Emotional Communication" is available on CD-ROM.

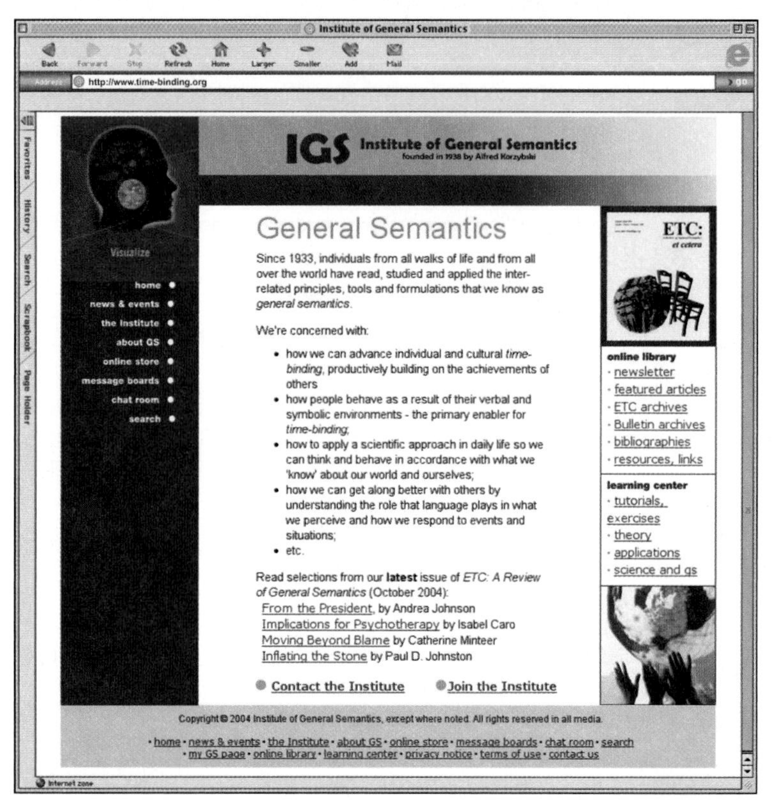

you infer. For a statement to be considered factual, it must be made by the observer after observation and must be limited to what is observed (Weinberg, 1958).

There is nothing wrong with making inferential statements. You must make them in order to talk about much that is meaningful to you. The problem arises when you act as if those inferential statements were factual. You can test your ability to distinguish facts from inferences by taking the fact-inference self-test below (based on the tests constructed in Haney, 1973).

TEST YOURSELF

Can You Distinguish Facts from Inferences?

Carefully read the following report and the observations based on it. Indicate whether you think the observations are true, false, or doubtful on the basis of the information presented in the report. Write T if the observation is definitely true, F if the observation is definitely false, and ? if the observation may be either true or false. Judge each observation in order. Don't reread the observations after you've indicated your judgment, and don't change any of your answers.

A well-liked college teacher had just completed making up the final examinations and had turned off the lights in the office. Just then a tall, broad figure with dark glasses appeared and demanded the examination. The professor opened the drawer. Everything in the drawer was picked up and the individual ran down the corridor. The dean was notified immediately.

____ **1.** The thief was tall and broad and wore dark glasses.

____ **2.** The professor turned off the lights.

____ **3.** A tall figure demanded the examination.

____ **4.** The examination was picked up by someone.

____ **5.** The examination was picked up by the professor.

____ **6.** A tall, broad figure appeared after the professor turned off the lights in the office.

____ **7.** The man who opened the drawer was the professor.

____ **8.** The professor ran down the corridor.

____ **9.** The drawer was never actually opened.

____ **10.** Three persons are referred to in this report.

HOW DID YOU DO? Number 3 is true, number 9 is false, and all the rest are "?" Review your answers by referring back to the story. To get you started, consider: Is there necessarily a thief? Might the dean have demanded to see the instructor's examination (statement 1)? Did the examination have to be in the drawer (statements 4 and 5)? How do you know it was the professor who turned off the lights (statement 6)? Need the professor have been a man (statement 7)? Do the instructor and the professor have to be the same person (statement 10)?

WHAT WILL YOU DO? Again, recognize that there's nothing wrong with making inferences. When you hear inferential statements, however, treat them as inferences and not as facts. Be mindful of the possibility that such statements may prove to be wrong. As you read this chapter, try to formulate specific guidelines that will help you distinguish facts from inferences.

To avoid fact-inference confusion, phrase inferential statements in such a way as to show that they are tentative. Inferential statements should leave open the possibility of alternatives. If, for example, you treat the statement "Our biology teacher was fired for poor teaching" as factual, you eliminate any alternatives. But if you preface your statement with, say, "Pat told me . . ." or "I'm wondering if . . .," the inferential nature of your statement will be clear. Be especially sensitive to this distinction when you're listening. Most talk is inferential. Beware of the speaker who presents everything as fact. Analyze closely and you'll uncover a world of inferences.

Language Is Relatively Static

Language changes only very slowly, especially when compared to the rapid change in people and things. **Static evaluation** is the tendency to retain evaluations without change while the reality to which they refer is changing. Often a verbal statement you make about an event or person remains static ("That's the way he is; he's always been that way") while the event or person may change enormously. Alfred Korzybski (1933) used an interesting illustration. In a tank you have a large fish and many small fish, the natural food for the large fish. Given freedom in the tank, the large fish will eat the small fish. If you partition the tank, separating the large fish from the small fish by a clear piece of glass, the large fish will continue to attempt to eat the small fish but will fail, knocking instead into the glass partition.

Eventually, the large fish will learn the futility of attempting to eat the small fish. If you now remove the partition, the small fish will swim all around the big fish, but the big fish will not eat them. In fact, the large fish will die of starvation while its natural food swims all around. The large fish has learned a pattern or "map" of behavior, and even though the actual territory has changed, the map remains static.

The mental **date** is an extensional device that helps you keep your language (and your thinking) up to date and helps you guard against static evaluation. The procedure is simple: date your statements and especially your evaluations. Remember that Pat Smith$_{1992}$ is not Pat Smith$_{2005}$; academic abilities $_{2001}$ are not academic abilities$_{2005}$. T. S. Eliot, in *The Cocktail Party*, said, "What we know of other people is only our memory of the moments during which we knew them. And they have changed since then . . . at every meeting we are meeting a stranger." In listening, look carefully at messages that claim that what was true still is. It may or may not be. Look for change.

Language Can Obscure Distinctions

Language can obscure distinctions among people or events that are covered by the same label but are really quite different (indiscrimination); it can also make it easy to focus on extremes rather than on the vast middle ground between opposites (polarization).

Indiscrimination

Indiscrimination is the failure to distinguish between similar but different people, objects, or events. It occurs when you focus on categories or classes and fail to see that each phenomenon is unique and needs to be looked at individually.

Everything is unlike everything else. Our language, however, provides you with common nouns, such as *teacher, student, friend, enemy, war, politician*, and *liberal*. These lead you to focus on similarities—to group together all teachers, all students, and all politicians. At the same time, the terms divert attention away from the uniqueness of each person, each object, and each event.

This misevaluation is at the heart of stereotyping on the basis of nationality, race, religion, sex, and

BUILDING COMMUNICATION SKILLS

Talking about the Middle

Fill in the word that would logically go where the question mark appears, a word that is the opposite of the term on the left.

hot ______________________________ ?
high ______________________________ ?
good ______________________________ ?
popular ______________________________ ?
sad ______________________________ ?

Filling in these opposites was probably easy—the words you supplied were probably short, and, if various different people supplied opposites, you'd probably find a high level of agreement among them.

Now fill in the middle positions with words meaning, for example, "midway between hot and cold," "midway between high and low." Do this before reading further.

You probably had greater difficulty here. You probably took more time to think of these middle terms, and you also probably used multiword phrases. Further, you would probably find less agreement among different people completing this same task. Although most things, people, and events fall between extremes, the common tendency is to concentrate on the extremes and ignore the middle. From this brief experience what implications can you draw about polarization?

affectional orientation. A stereotype, you'll remember from Unit 3, is a fixed mental picture of a group that is applied to each individual in the group without regard to his or her unique qualities. Whether stereotypes are positive or negative, they create the same problem: They provide you with shortcuts that are often inappropriate.

A useful antidote to indiscrimination (and stereotyping) is another extensional device called the index. This mental subscript identifies each individual as an individual even though both may be covered by the same label. Thus, politician_1 is not politician_2, teacher_1 is not teacher_2. The index helps you to discriminate among without discriminating against. Although the label ("politician," for example) covers all politicians, the index makes sure that each is thought about as an individual.

Polarization

Another way in which language can obscure differences is in its preponderance of extreme terms and its relative lack of middle terms, a characteristic that often leads to polarization. **Polarization** is the tendency to look at the world in terms of opposites and to describe it in extremes—good or bad, positive or negative, healthy or sick, intelligent or stupid. Polarization is often referred to as the fallacy of "either/or" or "black or white." Most people exist somewhere between the extremes. Yet there's a strong tendency to view only the extremes and to categorize people, objects, and events in terms of polar opposites.

Problems are created when opposites are used in inappropriate situations. For example, "So-and-so is either for us or against us." These options don't include all possibilities. The person may be for us in some things and against us in other things, or may be neutral.

To correct this polarizing tendency, beware of implying (and believing) that two extreme classes include all possible classes—that an individual must be one or the other, with no alternatives ("Are you pro-choice or pro-life?"). Most people, most events, most qualities exist between polar extremes. When others imply that there are only two sides or alternatives, look for the middle ground.

Lying

Lying occurs when you send messages designed to make others believe what you know to be untrue (Ekman, 1985; Burgoon & Hoobler, 2002). You can lie by commission (making explicitly false statements or deliberately being evasive or misleading) or by omission (omitting relevant information and thus allowing others to draw incorrect inferences). Similarly, you can lie verbally (in speech or writing) or nonverbally (with an innocent facial expression despite the commission of some wrong or a knowing nod instead of the honest expression of ignorance) (O'Hair, Cody, & McLaughlin, 1981). Lies may range from "white lies" and truth stretching to lies that form the basis of infidelity in a relationship, libel, and perjury. And, not surprisingly, lies have ethical implications.

- Some lies are considered innocent, acceptable, and ethical, such as lying to a child to protect a fantasy belief in Santa Claus or the Tooth Fairy or publicly agreeing with someone to enable the person to save face.
- Some lies may be considered not merely ethical but required, such as lying to protect someone from harm or embarrassment.
- Other lies are considered unacceptable and unethical such as lying to defraud investors or making false accusations.

WHAT WOULD YOU DO? You've been asked to serve as a witness in the trial for a robbery of a local grocery store. You really don't want to get involved; in fact, you're afraid to get involved. Yet, you wonder if you can ethically refuse and say you didn't see anything (although you did). There are other witnesses and your testimony is not likely to make a significant difference. What would you do?

SUMMARY

This unit focused on verbal messages, and specifically on the nature of language and the ways language works; the concept of disconfirmation and how it relates to sexism, heterosexism, and racist language; and the ways in which language can be used more effectively.

1. Meanings are in people, not in things.
2. Meanings are context based; the same message in a different context will likely mean something different.
3. Meanings are culturally influenced; each culture has its own rules identifying the ways in which language should be used.
4. Language is both denotative (objective and generally easily agreed upon) and connotative (subjective and generally highly individual in meaning).
5. Language varies in directness; through language you can state exactly what you mean or you can hedge and state your meaning very indirectly.
6. Disconfirmation is the process of ignoring the presence and the communications of others. Confirmation is accepting, supporting, and acknowledging the importance of the other person.
7. Sexist, heterosexist, racist, and ageist language puts down and negatively evaluates various cultural groups.
8. Using language effectively involves eliminating conceptual distortions and substituting more accurate assumptions about language, the most important of which are:
    - Language symbolizes reality; it's not the reality itself.
    - Language can express both facts and inferences, and distinctions need to be made between them.
    - Language is relatively static; because reality changes so rapidly, you need to constantly revise the way you talk about people and things.
    - Language can obscure distinctions in its use of general terms and in its emphasis on extreme rather than middle terms.

KEY TERMS

language
bypassing
netiquette
connotation
denotation
confirmation
disconfirmation
sexist language
heterosexist language
racist language
intensional orientation
extensional orientation
allness
fact–inference confusion
static evaluation
indiscrimination
polarization
lying

THINKING CRITICALLY ABOUT

Verbal Messages

1. When researchers asked men and women what they would like to change about the communication style of the opposite sex, most men said they wanted women to be more direct and most women said they wanted men to stop interrupting and offering advice (Noble 1994). What one change would you like to see in the communication style of the opposite sex? Of your own sex?
2. Visit any of the electronic dictionaries (use your favorite search engine and look for "dictionary") and browse through the terms and definitions. How is an online dictionary different from a print dictionary? What would a connotative dictionary look like?
3. One theory of politeness claims that you are most polite with friends and considerably less polite with both strangers and intimates (Wolfson, 1988; Holmes, 1995). Do you find this theory a generally accurate representation of your own level of politeness in different types of relationships?
4. What cultural identifiers do you prefer to use to describe yourself? Have these preferences changed over time? How can you let other people know the designations that you prefer and those that you don't? An interesting exercise—especially in a large and multicultural classroom—is for each student to write anonymously his or her preferred cultural identification on an index card and have them all read aloud.
5. Do you find the ideas expressed in the discussion of sexist, heterosexist, racist, and ageist listening reasonable? If not, how would you define this type of "-ist" listening? Do you find this a useful concept in understanding effective communication? Do you find these types of listening operating in your classes? In your family? In your community? If you wanted to reduce this type of listening, how would you do it?
6. A widely held assumption in anthropology, linguistics, and communication is that the importance of a concept to a culture can be measured by the number of words the language has for talking about the concept. So, for example, in English there are lots of words for money or for transportation or communication. With this principle in mind, consider the findings of Julia Stanley, for example, who researched terms indicating sexual promiscuity. Stanley found 220 English-language terms referring to a sexually promiscuous woman but only 22 terms for a sexually promiscuous man (Thorne, Kramarae, & Henley, 1983). What does this suggest about cultural attitudes and beliefs about promiscuity in men and women?
7. Consider this situation: An instructor at your school persists in calling the female students girls, refers to gay men and lesbians as queers, and refers to various racial groups with terms that most people would consider inappropriate. To the objection that these terms are offensive, the instructor claims the right to free speech and argues that to prevent instructors from using such terms would be a restriction on free speech, which would be a far greater wrong than being culturally or politically incorrect. How would you comment on this argument?
8. In one research study only 45 percent of the women actually objected to sexist comments. And, of these, only 15 percent responded directly. Among the reasons for such lack of confrontation are the social norms that teach us that it's best not to say anything, the pressure to be polite, and the concern about a prolonged confrontation (Swim & Hyers, 1999). Do you generally challenge sexist remarks? Are you equally likely to challenge racist and heterosexist remarks? Do you think things have changed since 1999, when this study was published?

UNIT

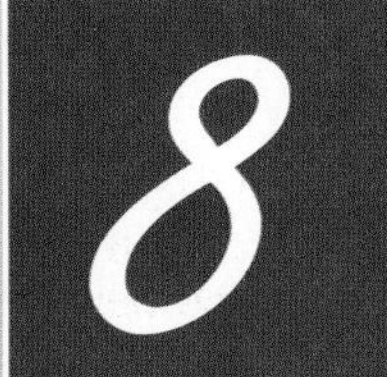

Nonverbal Messages

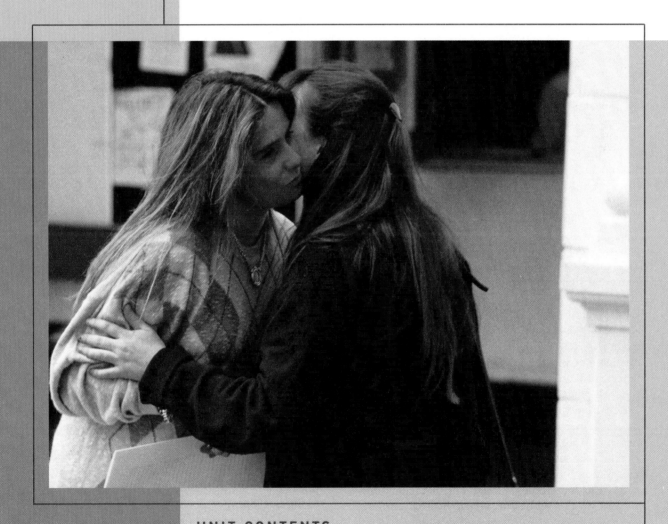

UNIT CONTENTS

When you smile, nod your head in agreement, or wave your hand to someone, you're communicating nonverbally. In fact, some researchers argue that you actually communicate more information nonverbally than you do with words. In this unit we explore this nonverbal communication system; here you'll learn

- how nonverbal communication works and the various forms it takes
- how you can use these nonverbal channels to communicate your thoughts and feelings more effectively

Nonverbal communication is communication without words. You communicate nonverbally when you gesture, smile or frown, widen your eyes, move your chair closer to someone, wear jewelry, touch someone, raise your vocal volume, or even say nothing. The crucial aspect of nonverbal communication is that the message you send is in some way received by one or more other people. If you gesture while alone in your room and no one is there to see you, then, most theorists would argue, communication has not taken place. The same, of course, is true of verbal messages; if you recite a speech and no one hears it, then communication has not taken place.

Using nonverbal communication effectively can yield two major benefits (Burgoon & Hoobler, 2002). First, the greater your ability to send and receive nonverbal signals, the higher your attraction, popularity, and psychosocial well-being are likely to be. Second, the greater your nonverbal skills, the more successful you're likely to be at influencing (or deceiving) others. Skilled nonverbal communicators are highly persuasive, and this persuasive power can be used to help or support another or it can be used to deceive and fool.

Research shows that of the two genders, women are the better senders and receivers of nonverbal messages (Hall, 1998; Burgoon & Hoobler, 2002). Although this superiority does not hold in all contexts, it does hold in most. For example, in a review of 21 research studies, 71 percent of the findings showed women to be superior nonverbal senders. And in a review of 61 studies on decoding, 84 percent showed women to be superior receivers (Hall, 1998).

The Functions of Nonverbal Communication

Let's consider the functions of nonverbal communication by looking at (1) the ways in which nonverbal messages are integrated with verbal messages and (2) the functions that researchers have focused on most extensively.

Integrating Nonverbal and Verbal Messages

In face-to-face communication you blend verbal and nonverbal messages to best convey your meanings. While speaking, you also smile, frown, or gesture, for example. It's this combination of verbal and nonverbal signals that communicates your meanings. Here are six ways in which nonverbal messages interact with verbal messages: (1) accenting, (2) complementing, (3) contradicting, (4) regulating, (5) repeating, and (6) substituting (Knapp & Hall, 1997):

- Nonverbal communication often serves to *accent* or emphasize some part of the verbal message. You might, for example, raise your voice to underscore a particular word or phrase; bang your fist on the desk to stress your commitment; or look longingly into someone's eyes when saying, "I love you."
- Nonverbal communication may *complement* or add nuances of meaning not communicated by your verbal message. Thus, you might smile when telling a story (to suggest that you find it humorous) or frown and shake your head when recounting someone's deceit (to suggest your disapproval).
- You may deliberately *contradict* your verbal messages with nonverbal movements—for example, by crossing your fingers or winking to indicate that you're lying.
- Movements may be used to *regulate*—to control or indicate your desire to control—the flow of verbal messages, as when you purse your lips, lean forward, or make hand gestures to indicate that you want to speak. You might also put up your hand or vocalize your pauses (for example, with "um" or "ah") to indicate that you have not finished and are not ready to relinquish the floor to the next speaker.
- You can *repeat* or restate the verbal message nonverbally. You can, for example, follow your verbal "Is that all right?" with raised eyebrows and a questioning look, or motion with your head or hand to repeat your verbal "Let's go."
- You may also use nonverbal communication to *substitute for* or take the place of verbal messages. For instance, you can signal "OK" with a hand gesture. You can nod your head to indicate yes or shake your head to indicate no.

COMMUNICATION@WORK

Communicating Power Nonverbally

The body says what words cannot.

—Martha Graham

If you want to signal your power nonverbally, try these suggestions (Lewis, 1989; Burgoon & Bacue, 2003).

- *Walk slowly and deliberately.* To appear hurried is to seem as without power, as if you were rushing to meet the expectations of those who have power over you.
- *Use facial expressions and gestures as appropriate;* these help you express your concern for the other person as well as your comfort and control of the situation.
- Other things being equal, *dress relatively conservatively* if you want to influence others; conservative clothing is associated with power and status.
- To *communicate dominance with your handshake,* exert more pressure than usual and hold the grip a bit longer than normal.
- *Use consistent packaging;* be careful that your verbal and nonverbal messages do not contradict each other, as this is a signal of uncertainty and a lack of conviction.
- Be sure to *respond in kind to another's eyebrow flash* (raising the eyebrow as a way of acknowledging another person).
- *When you break eye contact, direct your gaze downward;* otherwise you'll communicate a lack of interest.

Communicating@Work

Do you recognize these nonverbal cues in the communications of those in power? Do you recognize these nonverbal cues in your own behaviors?

Researching Nonverbal Communication Functions

Although nonverbal communication serves the same functions as verbal communication, nonverbal researchers have singled out several specific functions as especially significant (Burgoon, Buller, & Woodall, 1996; Burgoon & Hoobler, 2002).

Impression Formation and Management

It is largely through the nonverbal communications of others that you form impressions of them. Based on a person's body size, skin color, and dress as well as on the way the person smiles, maintains eye contact, and expresses himself or herself facially, you form impressions—you judge who the person is and what the person is like. One nonverbal researcher argues that these impressions may be grouped into four categories (Leathers, 1992):

- credibility, or how competent and believable you find the person
- likability, or how much you like or dislike the person
- attractiveness, or how attractive you find the person
- dominance, or how powerful the individual is

And, of course, you reveal yourself largely through the same nonverbal signals you use to size up others. But not only do you communicate your true self nonverbally; you also strive to manage the impression that you give to others. For example, you may do your best to appear brave when you're really scared or happy when you're really sad.

Form and Define Relationships

Much of your relationship life is lived nonverbally: Largely through nonverbal signals, you communicate your relationship to another person and that person communicates to you. Holding hands, looking longingly into each other's eyes, and even dressing alike are ways in which you communicate closeness in your interpersonal relationships.

You also use nonverbal signals to communicate your relationship dominance and status (Knapp & Hall, 1997). The large corner office with the huge desk communicates high status, just as the basement cubicle communicates low status.

Structuring Conversation and Social Interaction

When you're in conversation, you give and receive cues—to speak, to listen, to comment on what the speaker just said. Turn-taking cues regulate and structure the interaction. These turn-taking cues may be verbal (as when you say, "What do you think?"), but most often they're nonverbal—a nod of the head in the direction of someone else, for example, signals that you're ready to give up your speaking turn and want this other person to say something.

You also show that you're listening and that you want the conversation to continue (or that you're not listening and want the conversation to end) largely through nonverbal signals.

Influence

Much as you influence others by what you say, you also influence others by your nonverbal signals. A focused glance that says you're committed, gestures that further explain what you're saying, and appropriate dress signaling that "I'll easily fit in with this company," are a few examples of how you influence others with nonverbal signals.

And, of course, with the ability to influence comes the ability to deceive—to lie, to mislead another person into thinking something is true when it's false or that something is false when it's true. Using your eyes and facial expressions to communicate a liking for other people when you're really just interested in gaining their support for your promotion is an often-seen example of nonverbal deception. Not surprisingly, you also use nonverbal signals to detect deception in others. For example, you may well suspect a person of lying if he or she avoids eye contact, fidgets, or sends verbal and nonverbal messages that are inconsistent.

Emotional Expression

Although people often explain and reveal emotions verbally, nonverbal expressions communicate a great part of emotional experience. It is largely through facial expressions that you reveal your level of happiness or sadness or confusion, for example. Of course, you also reveal your feelings by posture (for example, whether tense or relaxed), gestures, and eye movements and even by the extent to which your pupils dilate.

Nonverbal messages often serve to communicate unpleasant messages—messages you might feel uncomfortable saying in words (Infante, Rancer, & Womack, 2002). For example, you might avoid eye contact and maintain large distances between yourself and someone with whom you don't want to interact, or with whom you want to decrease the intensity of your relationship.

The Channels of Nonverbal Communication

Nonverbal communication is probably most easily explained in terms of the various channels through which messages pass. Here we'll survey 10 channels: (1) body, (2) face, (3) eye, (4) space, (5) artifactual, (6) touch, (7) paralanguage, (8) silence, (9) time, and (10) smell.

The Body

Two areas of the body are especially important in communicating messages. First, the movements you make with your body communicate; second, the general appearance of your body communicates.

Body Movements

Researchers in **kinesics,** or the study of nonverbal communication through face and body movements, identify five major types of movements: emblems, illustrators, affect displays, regulators, and adaptors (Ekman & Friesen, 1969; Knapp & Hall, 1997).

Emblems are body gestures that directly translate into words or phrases; for example, the OK sign, the thumbs-up for "good job," and the V for victory. You use these consciously and purposely to communicate the same meaning as the words. But emblems are culture specific, so be careful when using your culture's emblems in other cultures. For example, when President Nixon visited Latin America and gestured with the OK sign, intending to communicate something positive, he was quickly informed that this gesture was not universal. In Latin America the gesture has a far more negative meaning. Here are a few cultural differences in the emblems you may commonly use (Axtell, 1993):

- In the United States, to say "hello" you wave with your whole hand moving from side to side, but in a large part of Europe that same signal means "no." In Greece such a gesture would be considered insulting.
- The V for victory is common throughout much of the world; but if you make this gesture in England with the palm facing your face, it's as insulting as the raised middle finger is in the United States.
- In Texas the raised fist with little finger and index finger held upright is a positive expression of

support, because it represents the Texas longhorn steer. But in Italy it's an insult that means "Your spouse is having an affair with someone else." In parts of South America it's a gesture to ward off evil, and in parts of Africa it's a curse: "May you experience bad times."

- In the United States and in much of Asia, hugs are rarely exchanged among acquaintances; but among Latins and southern Europeans, hugging is a common greeting gesture, and failing to hug someone may communicate unfriendliness.

Illustrators enhance (literally "illustrate") the verbal messages they accompany. For example, when referring to something to the left, you might gesture toward the left. Most often you illustrate with your hands, but you can also illustrate with head and general body movements. You might, for example, turn your head or your entire body toward the left. You might also use illustrators to communicate the shape or size of objects you're talking about. Research points to an interesting advantage of illustrators: They increase your ability to remember. In one study people who illustrated their verbal messages with gestures remembered some 20 percent more than those who didn't gesture (Goldin-Meadow, Nusbaum, Kelly, & Wagner, 2001).

Affect displays are movements of the face (smiling or frowning, for example) but also of the hands and general body (body tension or relaxation, for example) that communicate emotional meaning. Often affect displays are unconscious; you smile or frown, for example, without awareness. At other times, however, you may smile consciously, trying to convey your pleasure or satisfaction. Not surprisingly, people who smile spontaneously are judged to be more likable and more approachable than people who don't smile or people who pretend to smile (Gladstone & Parker, 2002).

Regulators are behaviors that monitor, control, coordinate, or maintain the speaking of another individual. When you nod your head, for example, you tell the speaker to keep on speaking; when you lean forward and open your mouth, you tell the speaker that you would like to say something.

Adaptors are gestures that satisfy some personal need, such as scratching to relieve an itch or moving your hair out of your eyes. **Self-adaptors** are self-touching movements (for example, rubbing your nose). **Alter-adaptors** are movements directed at the person with whom you're speaking, such as removing lint from someone's jacket or straightening a person's tie or folding your arms in front of you to keep others a comfortable distance from you. **Object-adaptors** are gestures focused on objects, such as doodling on or shredding a Styrofoam coffee cup.

Body Appearance

Your general body appearance also communicates. Height, for example, has been shown to be significant in a wide variety of situations. Tall presidential candidates have a much better record of winning the election than do their shorter opponents. Tall people seem to be paid more and are favored by interviewers over shorter applicants (Keyes, 1980; Guerrero, DeVito, & Hecht, 1999; Knapp & Hall, 1997).

Your body also reveals your race (through skin color and tone) and may also give clues as to your more specific nationality. Your weight in proportion to your height will also communicate messages to others, as will the length, color, and style of your hair.

Your general **attractiveness** is also a part of body communication. Attractive people have the advantage in just about every activity you can name. They get better grades in school, are more valued as friends and lovers, and are preferred as coworkers (Burgoon, Buller, & Woodall, 1996). Although we normally think that attractiveness is culturally determined—and to some degree it is—research seems to indicate that definitions of attractiveness are becoming universal (Brody, 1994). A person rated as attractive in one culture is likely to be rated as attractive in other cultures—even in cultures whose people are widely different in appearance.

Facial Communication

Throughout your interactions, your face communicates various messages, especially your emotions. Facial movements alone seem to communicate the degree of pleasantness, agreement, and sympathy felt; the rest of the body doesn't provide any additional information. But for other emotional messages—for example, the intensity with which an emotion is felt—both facial and bodily cues send messages (Graham, Bitti, & Argyle, 1975; Graham & Argyle, 1975).

So important are these cues in communicating your full meaning that graphic representations are now commonly used in Internet communication. In graphic user interface chat groups, buttons are available to help you encode your emotions graphically. Table 8.1 on page 138 identifies some of the more common "emoticons," icons that communicate emotions.

Some researchers in nonverbal communication claim that facial movements may express at least the following eight emotions: happiness, surprise, fear,

Table 8.1
Some Popular Emoticons

Here are a few of the many popular emoticons used in computer communication. The first six are popular in the United States; the last three are popular in Japan and illustrate how culture influences such symbols. That is, because Japanese culture considers it impolite for women to show their teeth when smiling, the emoticon for a woman's smile shows a dot signifying a closed mouth. Two excellent websites that contain extensive examples of smileys, emoticons, acronyms, and shorthand abbreviations are http://www.netlingo.com/smiley.cfm and http://www.netlingo.com/ emailsh.cfm.

Emoticon	Meaning	Emoticon	Meaning
:-)	Smile; I'm kidding	*This is important*	Substitutes for underlining or italics
:-(	Frown; I'm feeling down	<G>	Grin; I'm kidding
*	Kiss	<grin>	Grin; I'm kidding
{}	Hug	^.^	Woman's smile
{*****}	Hugs and kisses	^_^	Man's smile
This is important	Gives emphasis, calls special attention to	^ o ^	Happy

anger, sadness, disgust, contempt, and interest (Ekman, Friesen, & Ellsworth, 1972). Facial expressions of these emotions are generally called primary affect displays: They indicate relatively pure, single emotions. Other emotional states and other facial displays are combinations of these various primary emotions and are called affect blends. You communicate these blended feelings with different parts of your face. Thus, for example, you may experience both fear and disgust at the same time. Your eyes and eyelids may signal fear, and movements of your nose, cheek, and mouth area may signal disgust.

Facial Management

As you learned your culture's nonverbal system of communication, you also learned certain **facial management techniques** that enable you to communicate your feelings to achieve the effect you want—for example, ways to hide certain emotions and to emphasize others. Consider your own use of such techniques. As you do so, think about the types of interpersonal situations in which you would use each of the following facial management techniques (Malandro, Barker, & Barker, 1989; Metts & Planalp, 2002). Would you

- *Intensify?* For example, would you exaggerate surprise when friends throw you a party to make your friends feel better?
- *Deintensify?* Would you cover up your own joy about a successful outcome in the presence of a friend who didn't receive such good news?
- *Neutralize?* Would you cover up your sadness to keep from depressing others?
- *Mask?* Would you express happiness in order to cover up your disappointment at not receiving the gift you expected?
- *Simulate?* Would you express an emotion you don't feel?

These tactics of facial management help you display emotions in socially acceptable ways. For example, when someone gets bad news in which you may secretly take pleasure, the cultural display rule dictates that you frown and otherwise nonverbally signal your displeasure. If you place first in a race and your best friend barely finishes, the display rule requires that you minimize your expression of pleasure in winning and avoid any signs of gloating. If you violate these display rules, you'll seem insensitive. So although facial management techniques may be deceptive, they're also expected—in fact required—by the rules of polite interaction.

Encoding-Decoding Accuracy

One popular question concerns the accuracy with which people can encode and decode emotions through facial expressions. One problem confronting us as we try to answer this question is that it's difficult to separate the ability of the encoder from the ability of the decoder. Thus, a person may be quite adept at communicating emotions nonverbally, but the receiver may prove insensitive. On the other hand, the receiver may be good at deciphering emo-

UNDERSTANDING *THEORY* AND *RESEARCH*

Expressions and Attitudes

The **facial feedback hypothesis** holds that your facial expressions influence physiological arousal (Lanzetta, Cartwright-Smith, & Kleck, 1976; Zuckerman, Klorman, Larrance, & Spiegel, 1981). In one study, for example, participants held a pen in their teeth to simulate a sad expression and then rated a series of photographs. Results showed that mimicking sad expressions actually increased the degree of sadness the subjects reported feeling when viewing the photographs (Larsen, Kasimatis, & Frey, 1992). Further support for this hypothesis comes from a study that compared (1) participants who felt emotions such as happiness and anger with (2) participants who both felt and expressed these emotions. In support of the facial feedback hypothesis, people who felt *and* expressed the emotions became emotionally aroused faster than did those who only felt the emotion (Hess, Kappas, McHugo, & Lanzetta, 1992).

Generally, research finds that facial expressions can produce or heighten feelings of sadness, fear, disgust, and anger. But this effect does not occur with all emotions; smiling, for example, doesn't seem to make us feel happier (Burgoon & Bacue, 2003). Further, it has not been demonstrated that facial expressions can eliminate one feeling and replace it with another. So if you're feeling sad, smiling will not eliminate the sadness and replace it with gladness. A reasonable conclusion seems to be that your facial expressions can influence some feelings but not all (Burgoon & Bacue, 2003).

Working with Theories and Research

- *What effect do you observe when you express your emotions? Do they get stronger? Weaker?*

tions, but the sender may be inept. For example, introverts are not as accurate at decoding nonverbal cues as are extroverts (Akert & Panter, 1986).

Research in 11 different countries shows that women are better than men at both encoding and decoding nonverbal cues (Rosenthal & DePaulo, 1979). It may be argued that because men and women play different roles in society, they've learned different adaptive techniques and skills to help them perform these roles. Thus, in most societies women are expected to be more friendly, nurturing, and supportive and so learn these skills (Eagly & Crowley, 1986).

Accuracy also varies with the emotions themselves. Some emotions are easier to encode and decode than others. In one study, for example, people judged facial expressions of happiness with an accuracy ranging from 55 to 100 percent, surprise from 38 to 86 percent, and sadness from 19 to 88 percent (Ekman, Friesen, & Ellsworth, 1972).

Eye Communication

Research on the messages communicated by the eyes (a study known technically as oculesis) shows that these messages vary depending on the duration, direction, and quality of the eye behavior. For example, in every culture there are strict, though unstated, rules for the proper duration for eye contact. In U.S. culture the average length of gaze is 2.95 seconds. The average length of mutual gaze (two persons gazing at each other) is 1.18 seconds (Argyle & Ingham, 1972; Argyle, 1988). When eye contact falls short of this amount, you may think the person is uninterested, shy, or preoccupied. When the appropriate amount of time is exceeded, you may perceive the person as showing unusually high interest.

The direction of the eye also communicates. In much of the United States, you're expected to glance alternately at the other person's face, then away, then again at the face, and so on. The rule for the public speaker is to scan the entire audience, not focusing for too long on or ignoring any one area of the audience. When you break these directional rules, you communicate different meanings—abnormally high or low interest, self-consciousness, nervousness over the interaction, and so on. The quality of eye behavior—how wide or how narrow your eyes get during interaction—also communicates meaning, especially interest level and such emotions as surprise, fear, and disgust.

The Functions of Eye Contact and Eye Avoidance

Eye contact can serve a variety of functions. One such function is to seek feedback. In talking with someone, we look at her or him intently, as if to say, "Well, what do you think?" As you might predict, listeners gaze at speakers more than speakers gaze at listeners. In public speaking, you may scan hundreds of people to secure this feedback.

A second function is to inform the other person that the channel of communication is open and that he or she should now speak. You see this regularly in conversation, when one person asks a question or finishes a thought and then looks to you for a response. And one study found that eye contact was the most frequently noted nonverbal behavior used to tell library users that the librarian was approachable (Radford, 1998).

Eye movements may also signal the nature of a relationship, whether positive (an attentive glance) or negative (eye avoidance). You can also signal your power through **visual dominance** behavior (Exline, Ellyson, & Long, 1975). The average speaker, for example, maintains a high level of eye contact while listening and a lower level while speaking. When people want to signal dominance, they may reverse this pattern—maintaining a high level of eye contact while talking but a much lower level while listening.

By making eye contact you psychologically lessen the physical distance between yourself and another person. When you catch someone's eye at a party, for example, you become psychologically close though physically far apart.

Eye avoidance can also serve several different functions. When you avoid eye contact or avert your

GOING *ONLINE*

Nonverbal Behavior/Nonverbal Communication

http://www3.usal.es/~nonverbal/introduction.htm

This is one of the best websites devoted to nonverbal communication. Here you'll find hotlinks to just about any topic dealing with things nonverbal. Other useful websites include ComResources Online (http://www.natcom.org/ctronline/nonverb.htm), Nonverbal Communication Research (http://www.geocities.com/marvin_hecht/nonverbal.html), and Exploring Nonverbal Communication (http://nonverbal.ucsc.edu/).

In addition, visit the companion website for this text (www.ablongman.com/devito) for a variety of exercises in nonverbal communication: "Making Faces," "Making Eye Contact," "Giving Gifts in Different Cultures," "Expressing Meanings with Color," and "Interpersonal Interactions and Space."

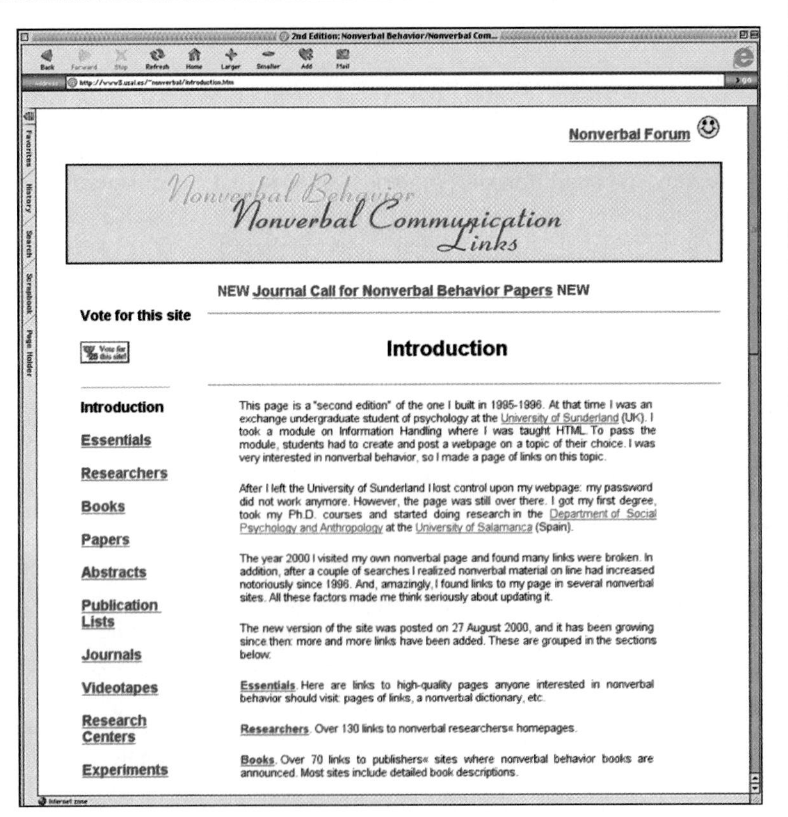

glance, you may help others maintain their privacy. For example, you may do this when you see a couple arguing in public. You turn your eyes away (though your eyes may be wide open) as if to say, "I don't mean to intrude; I respect your privacy," a behavior referred to as **civil inattention** (Goffman, 1971).

Eye avoidance can also signal lack of interest—in a person, a conversation, or some visual stimulus. At times, too, you may hide your eyes to block out unpleasant stimuli (a particularly gory or violent scene in a movie, for example) or close your eyes to block out visual stimuli and thus heighten other senses. For example, you may listen to music with your eyes closed. Lovers often close their eyes while kissing, and many prefer to make love in a dark or dimly lit room.

Pupil Dilation

In the fifteenth and sixteenth centuries, Italian women put drops of belladonna (which literally means "beautiful woman") into their eyes to enlarge the pupils so that they would look more attractive. Contemporary **pupillometrics** research supports the intuitive logic of these women; dilated pupils are judged more attractive than constricted ones (Hess, 1975; Marshall, 1983). In one study, researchers retouched photographs of women; in half they enlarged the pupils, and in the other half they made them smaller (Hess, 1975). Men were then asked to judge the women's personalities from the photographs. The photos of women with small pupils drew responses such as "cold," "hard," and "selfish"; those with dilated pupils drew responses such as "feminine" and "soft." Interestingly, the male observers could not verbalize the reasons for their different perceptions. Pupil dilation and our reactions to changes in the pupil size of others may function below the level of conscious awareness.

Pupil size also reveals your interest and level of emotional arousal. Your pupils enlarge when you're interested in something or when you are emotionally aroused. When homosexuals and heterosexuals were shown pictures of nude bodies, the homosexuals' pupils dilated more when they viewed same-sex bodies, whereas the heterosexuals' pupils dilated more when they viewed opposite-sex bodies (Hess, Seltzer, & Schlien, 1965). These pupillary responses are also observed in persons with profound mental retardation (Chaney, Givens, Aoki, & Gombiner, 1989). Perhaps we judge dilated pupils as more attractive because we respond to them as indicative of a person's interest in us. And that may be the reason why both models and fuzzy beanbag toys have exceptionally large pupils.

Space Communication

Space is an especially important factor in interpersonal communication, although we seldom think about it. Edward T. Hall (1959, 1963, 1976) pioneered the study of spatial communication and called this research area **proxemics**. We can examine this broad area by looking at (1) proxemic distances and (2) territoriality.

Proxemic Distances

Edward Hall (1959, 1963, 1976) distinguishes four **proxemic distances:** types of **spatial distances** that define the types of relationships between people and the types of communication in which they are likely to engage (see Table 8.2 on page 142). In **intimate distance,** ranging from actual touching to 18 inches, the presence of the other individual is unmistakable. Each person experiences the sound, smell, and feel of the other's breath. You use intimate distance for lovemaking, comforting, and protecting. This distance is so short that most people don't consider it proper in public.

Personal distance refers to the protective "bubble" that defines your personal space, ranging from 18 inches to 4 feet. This imaginary bubble keeps you protected and untouched by others. You can still hold or grasp another person at this distance, but only by extending your arms; this allows you to take certain individuals such as loved ones into your protective bubble. At the outer limit of personal distance, you can touch another person only if both of you extend your arms. This is the distance at which you conduct most of your interpersonal interactions; for example, talking with friends and family.

At **social distance,** ranging from 4 to 12 feet, you lose the visual detail you have at personal distance. You conduct impersonal business and interact at a social gathering at this social distance. The more distance you maintain in your interactions, the more formal they appear. In offices of high officials, the desks are positioned so the official is assured of at least this distance from clients.

Public distance, from 12 to more than 25 feet, protects you. At this distance you could take defensive action if threatened. On a public bus or train, for example, you might keep at least this distance from a drunken passenger. Although at this distance you lose fine details of the face and eyes, you're still close enough to see what is happening.

The specific distances that we maintain between ourselves and other people depend on a wide variety of factors (Burgoon, Buller, & Woodall, 1996; Burgoon & Bacue, 2003). Among the most significant are *gender* (in same-sex dyads women sit and stand

Table 8.2
Relationships and Proxemic Distances

Note that these four distances can be further divided into close and far phases and that the far phase of one level (say, personal) blends into the close phase of the next level (social). Do your relationships also blend into one another? Or are, say, your personal relationships totally separate from your social relationships?

Relationship	Distance
Intimate relationship	Intimate distance 0 —— 18 inches close phase — far phase
Personal relationship	Personal distance 1 —— 4 feet close phase — far phase
Social relationship	Social distance 4 —— 12 feet close phase — far phase
Public relationship	Public distance 12 —— 25+ feet close phase — far phase

closer to each other than do men, and people approach women more closely than they approach men), *age* (people maintain closer distances with similarly aged others than they do with those much older or much younger), and *personality* (introverts and highly anxious people maintain greater distances than do extroverts). Not surprisingly, we maintain shorter distances with people we're familiar with than with strangers and with people we like than with those we don't like.

Territoriality

One of the most interesting concepts in ethology (the study of animals in their natural surroundings)

BUILDING COMMUNICATION SKILLS

Choosing a Seat

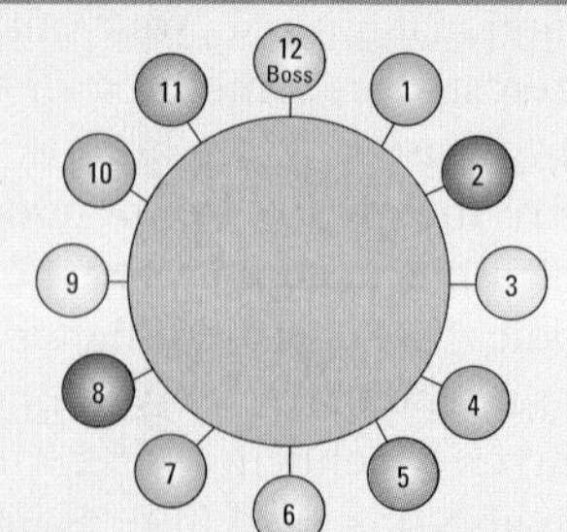

Look at the diagram here, which represents a table with 12 chairs, one of which is already occupied by the "boss." Below are listed five messages you might want to communicate. For each of these messages, indicate *(a)* where you would sit to communicate the desired message, and *(b)* any other messages that your seating position will make it easier for you to communicate.

1. You want to polish the apple and ingratiate yourself with your boss.
2. You aren't prepared and want to be ignored.
3. You want to challenge your boss on a certain policy that will come up for a vote.
4. You want to be accepted as a new (but important) member of the company.
5. You want to get to know the person already seated at position number 5.

is **territoriality,** a possessive or ownership reaction to an area of space or to particular objects. Two interesting dimensions of territoriality are territory-types and territorial markers.

Territory Types. Three types of territory are often distinguished: primary, secondary, and public (Altman, 1975). **Primary territories** are your exclusive preserve: your desk, room, house, or backyard, for example. In these areas you're in control. The effect is similar to the **home field advantage** that a sports team has when playing in its own ballpark. When you're in these home territories, you generally have greater influence over others than you would in someone else's territory. For example, in their own home or office people generally take on a kind of leadership role; they initiate conversations, fill in silences, assume relaxed and comfortable postures, and maintain their positions with greater conviction. Because the territorial owner is dominant, you stand a better chance of getting your raise approved, your point accepted, or a contract resolved in your favor if you're in your own primary territory (home, office) rather than in someone else's (Marsh, 1988).

Secondary territories, although they don't belong to you, are associated with you—perhaps because you've occupied them for a long time or they were assigned to you. For example, your desk in a classroom may become a secondary territory if it is assigned to you or if you regularly occupy it and others treat it as yours. Your neighborhood turf, a cafeteria table where you usually sit, or a favorite corner of a local coffee shop may be secondary territories. You feel a certain "ownership-like" attachment to the place, even though it's really not yours in any legal sense.

Public territories are areas that are open to all people, such as a park, movie house, restaurant, or beach. European cafés, food courts in suburban malls, and the open areas in large city office buildings are public spaces that bring people together and stimulate communication.

The electronic revolution, however, may well change the role of public space in stimulating communication (Drucker & Gumpert, 1991; Gumpert & Drucker, 1995). For example, home shopping clubs make it less necessary for people to go downtown or to the mall, and shoppers consequently have less opportunity to run into other people and to talk and exchange news. Similarly, electronic mail permits us to communicate without talking and without leaving the house to mail a letter. Perhaps the greatest change is telecommuting (Giordano, 1989), in which workers can go to work without leaving their homes. The face-to-face communication that normally takes place in an office is replaced by communication via computer.

Territoriality is closely linked to **status.** Generally, the size and location of your territories signal your status within your social group. For example,

UNDERSTANDING THEORY AND RESEARCH

Space Violations

Expectancy violations theory, developed by Judee Burgoon, explains what happens when you increase or decrease the distance between yourself and another person in an interpersonal interaction (Burgoon, 1978; Burgoon & Bacue, 2003). Each culture has certain expectancies for the distance that people are expected to maintain in their conversations. And, of course, each person has certain idiosyncrasies. Together, these determine *expected distance*. If you violate the expected distance to a great extent (small violations most often go unnoticed), the relationship itself comes into focus; the other person begins to turn attention away from the topic of conversation to you and to your relationship with him or her.

If this other person perceives you positively—for example, if you're a high-status person or you're particularly attractive—then you'll be perceived even more positively if you violate the expected distance. If, on the other hand, you're perceived negatively and you violate the norm, you'll be perceived even more negatively.

Working with Theories and Research

- *Do your own experiences support this theory of space expectancy violations? What do you see happening when space expectations are violated?*

male animals will stake out a particular territory and consider it their own. They will allow prospective mates to enter but will defend the territory against entrance by others, especially by other males of the same species. The larger the animal's territory, the higher the status of animal within the herd. The size and location of human territories also say something about status (Mehrabian, 1976; Sommer, 1969). An apartment or office in midtown Manhattan or downtown Tokyo, for example, is extremely high-status territory. The cost of the territory restricts it to those who have lots of money.

Territorial Markers. Much as animals mark their territory, humans mark theirs with three types of **markers:** central markers, boundary markers, and earmarkers (Hickson, Stacks, & Moore, 2003). **Central markers** are items you place in a territory to reserve it. For example, you place a drink at the bar, books on your desk, or a sweater over the chair to let others know that these territories belong to you.

Boundary markers set boundaries that divide your territory from "theirs." In the supermarket checkout line, the bar placed between your groceries and those of the person behind you is a boundary marker. Similarly, the armrests separating your seat from those of the people on either side at a movie theater and the molded plastic seats on a bus or train are boundary markers.

Earmarkers—a term taken from the practice of branding animals on their ears—are those identifying marks that indicate your possession of a territory or object. Trademarks, nameplates, and initials on a shirt or attaché case are all examples of earmarkers.

Artifactual Communication

Artifactual communication is communication via objects made by human hands. Thus, color, clothing, jewelry, and the decoration of space would be considered artifactual. Let's look at each of these briefly.

Color Communication

There is some evidence that colors affect us physiologically. For example, respiratory movements increase with red light and decrease with blue light. Similarly, eye blinks increase in frequency when eyes are exposed to red light and decrease when exposed to blue. These responses seem consistent with our intuitive feelings about blue being more soothing and red more arousing. When a school changed the color of its walls from orange and white to blue, the blood pressure of the students decreased and their academic performance increased (Ketcham, 1958; Malandro, Barker, & Barker, 1989).

Color communication also influences perceptions and behaviors (Kanner, 1989). People's acceptance of a product, for example, is largely determined by its packaging, especially its color. In one study the very same coffee taken from a yellow can was described as weak, from a dark brown can as too strong, from a red can as rich, and from a blue can as mild. Even your acceptance of a person may depend on the colors he or she wears. Consider, for example, the comments of one color expert (Kanner, 1989): "If you have to pick the wardrobe for your defense lawyer heading into court and choose anything but blue, you deserve to lose the case." Black is so powerful it could work against the lawyer with the jury. Brown lacks sufficient authority. Green would probably elicit a negative response.

Clothing and Body Adornment

People make inferences about who you are, at least in part, from the way you dress. Whether these inferences are accurate or not, they will influence what people think of you and how they react to you. Your socioeconomic class, your seriousness, your attitudes (for example, whether you're conservative or liberal), your concern for convention, your sense of style, and perhaps even your creativity will all be judged in part by the way you dress (Molloy, 1975, 1977, 1981; Burgoon, Buller, & Woodall, 1996; Knapp & Hall, 1997). Similarly, college students will perceive an instructor dressed informally as friendly, fair, enthusiastic, and flexible; they will see the same instructor dressed formally as prepared, knowledgeable, and organized (Malandro, Barker, & Barker, 1989).

The way you wear your hair says something about your attitudes—from a concern about being up to date to a desire to shock to perhaps a lack of interest in appearances. Men with long hair will generally be judged as less conservative than those with shorter hair. Your jewelry also communicates about you. Wedding and engagement rings are obvious examples that communicate specific messages. College rings and political buttons likewise communicate specific messages. If you wear a Rolex watch or large precious stones, others are likely to infer that you're rich. Men who wear earrings will be judged differently from men who don't. What judgments are made will depend on who the receiver is, the communication context, and all the factors identified throughout this text.

Body piercings are now common, especially among the young. Nose, nipple, tongue, and belly button jewelry (among other piercings) send a variety of messages. Although people wearing such jewelry may wish to communicate positive meanings,

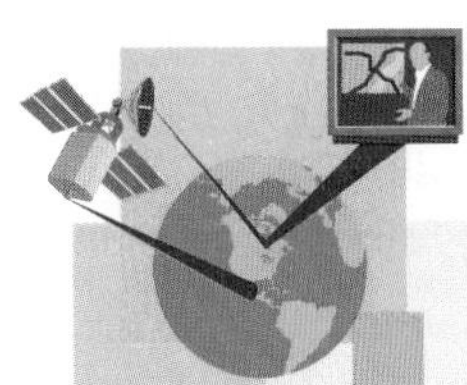

MEDIA WATCH

Legible Clothing

Legible clothing is anything that you wear that displays some verbal message; it's clothing that literally can be read. In some instances the message proclaims status; it tells others that you are, for example, rich or stylish or youthful. The Gucci or Louis Vuitton logos on your luggage communicate your financial status. In a similar way your sweatshirt with the word "Bulls" or "Pirates" emblazoned across it communicates your interest in sports and your favorite team.

Legible clothing is being bought and worn in record numbers. Many designers and manufacturers have their names integrated into the design of the clothing: DKNY, Calvin Klein, Armani, L. L. Bean, the Gap, and Old Navy are just a few examples. At the same time that you're paying extra to buy the brand name, you're also providing free advertising for the designer.

T-shirts and sweatshirts are especially popular as message senders. One study surveyed 600 male and female students as to the types of T-shirt messages they preferred (Sayre, 1992). Four messages were cited most often:

- Affiliation messages, such as a club or school name, communicate that you're a part of a larger group.
- Trophy names, such as those of a high-status concert or perhaps a ski lodge, say that you were in the right place at the right time.
- Metaphorical expressions, such as pictures of rock groups or famous athletes, reveal that you're part of a current trend.
- Personal messages, such as statements of beliefs or philosophies, tell others that you're willing to express your beliefs publicly.

You and the Media

Affiliation messages may create problems when they identify the wearer as a member of a gang, because wearing gang colors can contribute to violence, especially in schools (Burke, 1993; Zimmerman, 2000). How do you feel about these and other provocative types of clothing messages? Do you feel that some clothing messages should be prohibited? If so, which ones? Or do you feel that such messages should be protected by the first amendment to the Constitution guaranteeing freedom of speech?

research indicates that those interpreting these messages seem to infer that the wearer is communicating an unwillingness to conform to social norms and a willingness to take greater risks than people without such piercings (Forbes, 2001). It's worth noting that in a study of employers' perceptions, applicants with eyebrow piercings were rated and ranked significantly lower than those without such piercings (Acor, 2001). And, in another study, nose-pierced job candidates were scored lower on measures of credibility such as character and trust as well as sociability and hirability (Seiter & Sandry, 2003).

Tattoos, whether temporary or permanent, likewise communicate a variety of messages—often the name of a loved one or some symbol of allegiance or affiliation. Tattoos also communicate to the wearers themselves. For example, tattooed students see themselves (and perhaps others do as well) as more adventurous, creative, individualistic, and risk-prone than those without tattoos (Drews, Allison, & Probst, 2000).

Space Decoration

The way you decorate your private spaces also communicates about you. The office with a mahogany desk and bookcases and oriental rugs communicates your importance and status within an organization, just as a metal desk and bare floor indicate a worker much farther down in the hierarchy.

Similarly, people will make inferences about you based on the way you decorate your home. The expensiveness of the furnishings may communicate your status and wealth; their coordination may convey your sense of style. The magazines may reflect your interests, and the arrangement of chairs around a television set may reveal how important watching television is to you. The contents of bookcases lining the walls reveal the importance of reading in your life. In fact, there's probably little in your home that would not send messages from which others would draw inferences about you. Computers, wide-screen televisions, well-equipped kitchens, and oil paintings of great grandparents, for example, all say something about the people who live in the home.

Similarly, the absence of certain items will communicate something about you. Consider what messages you'd get from a home where no television, phone, or books could be seen.

People will also make judgments as to your personality on the basis of room decorations. Research finds, for example, that people will make judgments about your openness to new experiences (distinctive decorating usually communicates this, as would different types of books and magazines and travel souvenirs) and even about your conscientiousness, emotional stability, degree of extroversion, and agreeableness. Not surprisingly, bedrooms prove more revealing of personality than offices (Gosling, Ko, Mannarelli, & Morris, 2002).

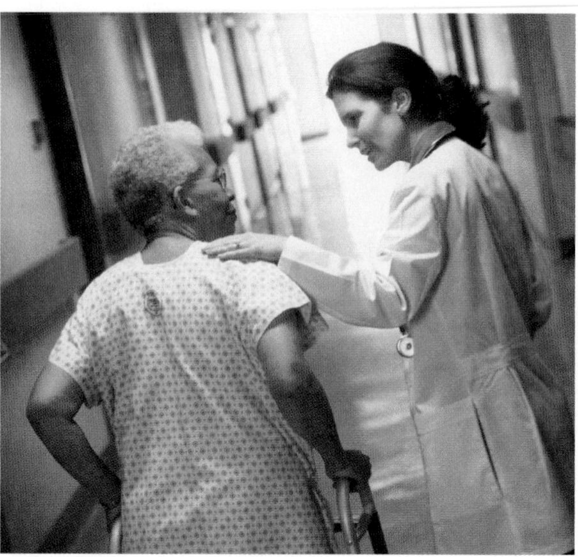

VIEWPOINT

Consider, as Nancy Henley suggests in her *Body Politics* (1977), who would touch whom—say, by putting an arm around the other person's shoulders or by putting a hand on the other person's back—in the following dyads: teacher and student, doctor and patient, manager and worker, minister and parishioner, business executive and secretary. Do your answers reveal that the higher-status person initiates touch with the lower-status person? Henley further argues that in addition to indicating relative status, touching demonstrates the assertion of male power, dominance, and superior status over women. When women touch men, Henley suggests, the interpretation that it designates a female-dominant relationship is not acceptable (to men)—and so the touching is interpreted as a sexual invitation. What do you think of this argument?

Touch Communication

The study of **touch communication,** technically referred to as **haptics,** suggests that touch is perhaps the most primitive form of communication (Montagu, 1971). Developmentally, touch is probably the first sense to be used. Even in the womb the child is stimulated by touch. Soon after birth the child is fondled, caressed, patted, and stroked. In turn, the child explores its world through touch. In a short time the child learns to communicate many different meanings through touch.

The Meanings of Touch

Touch communicates a wide range of messages (Jones & Yarbrough, 1985). Here are five major types of messages that will illustrate this great variety.

- Touch communicates positive feelings; for example, support, appreciation, inclusion, sexual interest or intent, composure, immediacy, affection, trust, similarity and quality, and informality (Jones & Yarbrough, 1985; Burgoon, 1991). Touch also stimulates self-disclosure (Rabinowitz, 1991).
- Touch often communicates your intention to play, either affectionately or aggressively.
- Touch may control the behaviors, attitudes, or feelings of other people. To obtain compliance, for example, you touch a person to communicate "move over," "hurry," "stay here," or "do it." You might also touch a person to gain his or her attention, as if to say "look at me" or "look over here."

  In some situations touching can even amount to a kind of **nonverbal dominance** behavior. Touch even seems to increase a waitperson's tips. Researchers found that people who were touched by a female waitperson on the hand or shoulder tipped more than those who weren't touched (Crusco & Wetzel, 1984; Stephen & Zweigenhaft, 1986).
- Ritualistic touching centers on greetings and departures; examples are shaking hands to say "hello" or "good-bye," hugging, kissing, or putting your arm around another's shoulder when greeting or saying farewell.
- Task-related touching is associated with the performance of some function, as when you remove a speck of dust from another person's coat, help someone out of a car, or check someone's forehead for fever.

Touch Avoidance

Much as you have a need and desire to touch and be touched, you also have a tendency to avoid touch from certain people or in certain circumstances (Andersen & Leibowitz, 1978). You may wish to examine your own **touch avoidance** tendency by taking the self-test below.

TEST YOURSELF

Do You Avoid Touch?

This test is composed of 18 statements concerning how you feel about touching other people and being touched. Please indicate the degree to which each statement applies to you according to the following scale: 1 = strongly agree; 2 = agree; 3 = undecided; 4 = disagree; and 5 = strongly disagree.

____ **1.** A hug from a same-sex friend is a true sign of friendship.

____ **2.** Opposite-sex friends enjoy it when I touch them.

____ **3.** I often put my arm around friends of the same sex.

____ **4.** When I see two friends of the same sex hugging, it revolts me.

____ **5.** I like it when members of the opposite sex touch me.

____ **6.** People shouldn't be so uptight about touching persons of the same sex.

____ **7.** I think it is vulgar when members of the opposite sex touch me.

____ **8.** When a member of the opposite sex touches me, I find it unpleasant.

____ **9.** I wish I were free to show emotions by touching members of the same sex.

____ **10.** I'd enjoy giving a massage to an opposite-sex friend.

____ **11.** I enjoy kissing a person of the same sex.

____ **12.** I like to touch friends that are the same sex as I am.

____ **13.** Touching a friend of the same sex does not make me uncomfortable.

____ **14.** I find it enjoyable when my date and I embrace.

____ **15.** I enjoy getting a back rub from a member of the opposite sex.

____ **16.** I dislike kissing relatives of the same sex.

____ **17.** Intimate touching with members of the opposite sex is pleasurable.

____ **18.** I find it difficult to be touched by a member of my own sex.

HOW DID YOU DO? To score your touch avoidance questionnaire:

1. Reverse your scores for items 4, 7, 8, 16, and 18. Use these reversed scores in all future calculations.
2. To obtain your same-sex touch avoidance score (the extent to which you avoid touching members of your sex), total the scores for items 1, 3, 4, 6, 9, 11, 12, 13, 16, and 18.
3. To obtain your opposite-sex touch avoidance score (the extent to which you avoid touching members of the opposite sex), total the scores for items 2, 5, 7, 8, 10, 14, 15, and 17.
4. To obtain your total touch avoidance score, add the subtotals from steps 2 and 3.

The higher the score, the higher the touch avoidance—that is, the greater your tendency to avoid touch. In studies by Andersen and Leibowitz (1978), who constructed this test, average opposite-sex touch avoidance scores were 12.9 for males and 14.85 for females. Average same-sex touch avoidance scores were 26.43 for males and 21.70 for females. How do your scores compare with those of the college students in Andersen and Leibowitz's study? Is your touch avoidance likely to be higher when you are interacting with persons who are culturally different from you? Can you identify types of people and types of situations in which your touch avoidance would be especially high? Especially low?

WHAT WILL YOU DO? Are you satisfied with your score? Would you like to change your touch avoidance tendencies? What might you do about them?

Source: From "Development and Nature of the Construct Touch Avoidance" by Peter Andersen and Ken Leibowitz in *Environmental Psychology and Nonverbal Behavior,* Vol. 3, 1978, pp. 89–106. Used with permission of Plenum Publishing Corporation.

Researchers using the self-test presented here have found several interesting connections between touch avoidance and other factors (Andersen & Liebowitz, 1978). For example, touch avoidance is positively related to communication apprehension. If you have a strong fear of oral communication, then you probably also have strong touch avoidance tendencies. Touch avoidance is also high in those who self-disclose less.

Both touch and self-disclosure are intimate forms of communication. People who are reluctant to get close to another person by self-disclosing also seem reluctant to get close by touching.

Older people avoid touch with opposite-sex persons more than younger people do. As people get older they're touched less by members of the opposite sex; this decreased frequency of touching may lead them to avoid touching.

Not surprisingly, touch also varies with your relationship stage. In early stages you touch little, in intermediate stages (involvement and intimacy) you touch a great deal, and at stable or deteriorating stages you again touch little (Guerrero & Andersen, 1991, 1994).

Paralanguage: The Vocal Channel

Paralanguage is the vocal but nonverbal dimension of speech. It has to do not with what you say but with how you say it. A traditional exercise students use to increase their ability to express different emotions, feelings, and attitudes is to repeat a sentence while accenting or stressing different words. One popular sentence is, "Is this the face that launched a thousand ships?" Significant differences in meaning are easily communicated depending on where the speaker places the stress. Consider the following variations:

- Is *this* the face that launched a thousand ships?
- Is this the *face* that launched a thousand ships?
- Is this the face that *launched* a thousand ships?
- Is this the face that launched a *thousand ships?*

Each sentence communicates something different; in fact, each asks a different question, even though the words are exactly the same. All that distinguishes the sentences is stress, one aspect of paralanguage. In addition to stress and **pitch** (highness or lowness), paralanguage includes such **voice qualities** as **rate** (speed), **volume** (loudness), rhythm, and pauses or hesitations as well as the vocalizations you make in crying, whispering, moaning, belching, yawning, and yelling (Trager, 1958, 1961; Argyle, 1988). A variation in any of these features communicates. When you speak quickly, for example, you communicate something different from when you speak slowly. Even though the words may be the same, if the speed (or volume, rhythm, or pitch) differs, the meanings people receive will also differ.

Judgments about People

Paralanguage cues are often used as a basis for judgments about people; for example, evaluations of their emotional state or even their personality. A listener can accurately judge the emotional state of a speaker from vocal expression alone if both speaker and listener speak the same language. Paralanguage cues are not so accurate when used to communicate emotions to those who speak a different language (Albas, McCluskey, & Albas, 1976). Also, some emotions are easier to identify than others; it's easy to distinguish between hate and sympathy but more difficult to distinguish between fear and anxiety. And, of course, listeners vary in their ability to decode, and speakers in their ability to encode emotions (Scherer, 1986).

Judgments about Communication Effectiveness

In one-way communication (when one person is doing all or most of the speaking and the other person

BUILDING COMMUNICATION SKILLS

Praising and Criticizing

Read aloud each of the following statements, first to communicate praise and then to communicate criticism. Identify the paralanguage cues you used to communicate the praise or criticism. Did you also read the statements with different facial expressions, eye movements, and body postures depending on which message you wished to communicate?

1. Now that looks good on you
2. You lost weight
3. You look younger than that
4. You're an expert
5. You're so sensitive; I'm amazed

is doing all or most of the listening), those who talk fast (about 50 percent faster than normal) are more persuasive (MacLachlan, 1979). People agree more with a fast speaker than with a slow speaker and find the fast speaker more intelligent and objective.

When we look at comprehension, rapid speech shows an interesting effect. When the speaking rate is increased by 50 percent, the comprehension level drops by only 5 percent. When the rate is doubled, the comprehension level drops only 10 percent. These 5 and 10 percent losses are more than offset by the increased speed; thus, the faster rates are much more efficient in communicating information. If speeds are more than twice the rate of normal speech, however, comprehension begins to fall dramatically.

Do exercise caution in applying this research to all forms of communication (MacLachlan, 1979). For example, if you increase your rate to increase efficiency, you may create an impression so unnatural that others will focus on your speed instead of your meaning. In addition, be cautious in intercultural situations, as different cultures view speech rate differently. For example, Korean male speakers who spoke rapidly were given unfavorable credibility ratings, in contrast to the results obtained by Americans who spoke rapidly (Lee & Boster, 1992). Researchers have suggested that in individualistic societies a rapid-rate speaker is seen as more competent than a slow-rate speaker, whereas in collectivist cultures a speaker who uses a slower rate is judged more competent.

Silence

Like words and gestures, **silence,** too, communicates important meanings and serves important functions (Johannesen, 1974; Jaworski, 1993). Silence allows the speaker *time to think,* time to formulate and organize his or her verbal communications. Before messages of intense conflict, as well as before those confessing undying love, there's often silence. Again, silence seems to prepare the receiver for the importance of these future messages.

Some people use silence as a *weapon* to hurt others. We often speak of giving someone "the silent treatment." After a conflict, for example, one or both individuals may remain silent as a kind of punishment. Silence used to hurt others may also take the form of refusing to acknowledge the presence of another person, as in disconfirmation (see Unit 7); here silence is a dramatic demonstration of the total indifference one person feels toward the other.

Sometimes silence is used as a *response to personal anxiety,* shyness, or threats. You may feel anxious or shy among new people and prefer to remain silent. By remaining silent you preclude the chance of rejection. Only when you break your silence and make an attempt to communicate with another person do you risk rejection.

Silence may be used to *prevent communication* of certain messages. In conflict situations silence is sometimes used to prevent certain topics from surfacing and to prevent one or both parties from saying

UNDERSTANDING THEORY AND RESEARCH

The Social Clock

Your culture maintains an implicit "schedule" for the right time to do a variety of important things; for example, the right time to start dating, to finish college, to buy your own home, or to have a child. This unspoken timetable provides you with a **social clock,** a schedule that tells you if you're keeping pace with your peers, are ahead of them, or are falling behind (Neugarten, 1979). On the basis of this social clock, which you learned as you grew up, you evaluate your own social and professional development. If you're in synch with the rest of your peers—for example, if you started dating at the "appropriate" age or you're finishing college at the "appropriate" age—then you'll feel well adjusted, competent, and a part of the group. If you're late, you'll probably experience feelings of dissatisfaction. And although in some cultures the social clock is becoming more flexible and more tolerant of deviations from the conventional timetable, it still exerts pressure to keep pace with your peers (Peterson, 1996).

Working with Theories and Research

- *How important is the social clock to you? Have you ever felt out of step with your peers in some area? Did your feeling influence your behavior in any way?*

things they may later regret. In such situations silence often allows us time to cool off before expressing hatred, severe criticism, or personal attacks—which, as we know, are irreversible.

Like the eyes, face, and hands, silence can also be used to *communicate emotional responses* (Ehrenhaus, 1988). Sometimes silence communicates a determination to be uncooperative or defiant; by refusing to engage in verbal communication, you defy the authority or the legitimacy of the other person's position. Silence is often used to communicate annoyance, particularly when accompanied by a pouting expression, arms crossed in front of the chest, and nostrils flared. Silence may express affection or love, especially when coupled with long and longing stares into each other's eyes.

Of course, you may also use silence when you simply have *nothing to say,* when nothing occurs to you, or when you don't want to say anything. James Russell Lowell expressed this best: "Blessed are they who have nothing to say, and who cannot be persuaded to say it." Silence may also be used to avoid responsibility for any wrongdoing (Beach, 1990–91).

Time Communication

The study of **temporal communication**, known technically as **chronemics**, concerns the use of time—how you organize it, react to it, and communicate messages through it (Bruneau, 1985, 1990). Consider, for example, your **psychological time** orientation; the emphasis you place on the past, present, and future. In a past orientation, you have special reverence for the past. You relive old times and regard old methods as the best. You see events as circular and recurring, so the wisdom of yesterday is applicable also to today and tomorrow. In a present orientation, however, you live in the present: for now, not tomorrow. In a future orientation, you look toward and live for the future. You save today, work hard in college, and deny yourself luxuries because you're preparing for the future. Before reading more about time, take the self-test below.

TEST YOURSELF

What Time Do You Have?

For each statement, indicate whether the statement is true (T) or false (F) in relation to your general attitude and behavior. (A few statements are purposely repeated to facilitate scoring and analysis of your responses.)

____ **1.** Meeting tomorrow's deadlines and doing other necessary work comes before tonight's partying.

____ **2.** I meet my obligations to friends and authorities on time.

____ **3.** I complete projects on time by making steady progress.

____ **4.** I am able to resist temptations when I know there is work to be done.

____ **5.** I keep working at a difficult, uninteresting task if it will help me get ahead.

____ **6.** If things don't get done on time, I don't worry about it.

____ **7.** I think that it's useless to plan too far ahead, because things hardly ever come out the way you planned anyway.

____ **8.** I try to live one day at a time.

____ **9.** I live to make better what is rather than to be concerned about what will be.

____ **10.** It seems to me that it doesn't make sense to worry about the future, since fate determines that whatever will be, will be.

____ **11.** I believe that getting together with friends to party is one of life's important pleasures.

____ **12.** I do things impulsively, making decisions on the spur of the moment.

____ **13.** I take risks to put excitement in my life.

____ **14.** I get drunk at parties.

____ **15.** It's fun to gamble.

____ **16.** Thinking about the future is pleasant to me.

____ **17.** When I want to achieve something, I set subgoals and consider specific means for reaching those goals.

____ **18.** It seems to me that my career path is pretty well laid out.

____ **19.** It upsets me to be late for appointments.

____ **20.** I meet my obligations to friends and authorities on time.

____ **21.** I get irritated at people who keep me waiting when we've agreed to meet at a given time.

____ **22.** It makes sense to invest a substantial part of my income in insurance premiums.

____ **23.** I believe that "A stitch in time saves nine."

____ **24.** I believe that "A bird in the hand is worth two in the bush."

____ **25.** I believe it is important to save for a rainy day.

____ **26.** I believe a person's day should be planned each morning.

____ **27.** I make lists of things I must do.

____ **28.** When I want to achieve something, I set subgoals and consider specific means for reaching those goals.

____ **29.** I believe that "A stitch in time saves nine."

HOW DID YOU DO? This time test measures seven different factors. If you selected true (T) for all or most of the statements within any given factor, you are probably high on that factor. If you selected false (F) for all or most of the statements within any given factor, you are probably low on that factor.

The first factor, measured by items 1–5, is a future, work motivation, perseverance orientation. These people have a strong work ethic and are committed to completing a task despite difficulties and temptations. The second factor (items 6–10) is a present, fatalistic, worry-free orientation. High scorers on this factor live one day at a time, not necessarily to enjoy the day but to avoid planning for the next day or anxiety about the future.

The third factor (items 11–15) is a present, pleasure-seeking, partying orientation. These people enjoy the present, take risks, and engage in a variety of impulsive actions. The fourth factor (items 16–18) is a future, goal-seeking, planning orientation. These people derive special pleasure from planning and achieving a variety of goals.

The fifth factor (items 19–21) is a time-sensitivity orientation. People who score high are especially sensitive to time and its role in social obligations. The sixth factor (items 22–25) is a future, practical action orientation. These people do what they have to do—take practical actions—to achieve the future they want.

The seventh factor (items 26–29) is a future, somewhat obsessive daily planning orientation. High scorers on this factor make daily "to do" lists and devote great attention to specific details.

WHAT WILL YOU DO? Now that you have some idea of how you treat time, consider how these attitudes and behaviors work for you. For example, will your time orientations help you achieve your social and professional goals? If not, what might you do about changing these attitudes and behaviors?

Source: From "Time in Perspective" by Alexander Gonzalez and Philip G. Zimbardo in *Psychology Today,* V. 19, pp. 20–26. Reprinted with permission of Sussex Publishers, Inc.

The time orientation you develop depends to a great extent on your socioeconomic class and your personal experiences. Gonzalez and Zimbardo (1985), who developed the time quiz and on whose research the scoring is based, observe: "A child with parents in unskilled and semiskilled occupations is usually socialized in a way that promotes a present-oriented fatalism and hedonism. A child of parents who are managers, teachers, or other professionals learns future-oriented values and strategies designed to promote achievement." Not surprisingly, in the United States income is positively related to future orientation; the more future oriented you are, the greater your income is likely to be.

Different **cultural time** perspectives also account for much intercultural misunderstanding, as different cultures often teach their members drastically different time orientations. For example, members of some Latin cultures would rather be late for an appointment than end a conversation abruptly or before it has come to a natural end. So the Latin may see lateness as a result of politeness. But others may see this as impolite to the person with whom he or she had the appointment (Hall & Hall, 1987).

Smell Communication

Smell communication, or **olfactory communication,** is extremely important in a wide variety of situations and is now big business (Kleinfeld, 1992). For example, there's some evidence (though clearly not very conclusive evidence) that the smell of lemon contributes to a perception of health, the smells of lavender and eucalyptus increase alertness, and the smell of rose oil reduces blood pressure. Findings such as these have contributed to the growth of aromatherapy and to a new profession of aromatherapists (Furlow, 1996). Because humans possess "denser skin concentrations of scent glands than almost any other mammal," it has been argued that it only remains for us to discover how we use scent to communicate a wide variety of messages (Furlow, 1996, p. 41). Research also finds that smells can influence your body's chemistry, which in turn influences your emotional state. For example, the smell of chocolate results in the reduction of theta brain waves, which produces a sense of relaxation and a reduced level of attention (Martin, 1998).

Here are some of the most important messages scent seems to communicate.

- *Attraction messages.* Humans use perfumes, colognes, after-shave lotions, powders, and the like to enhance their attractiveness to others and to themselves. After all, you also smell yourself. When the smells are pleasant, you feel better about yourself. Women, research finds, prefer the scent of men who bear a close genetic similarity to themselves; this finding may account in part for our attraction to people much like ourselves (Ober, Weitkamp, Cox, Dytch, Kostyu, & Elias, 1997; Wade, 2002).

- *Taste messages.* Without smell, taste would be severely impaired. For example, without smell it would be extremely difficult to taste the difference between a raw potato and an apple. Street vendors selling hot dogs, sausages, and similar foods are aided greatly by the smells, which stimulate the appetites of passersby.
- *Memory messages.* Smell is a powerful memory aid; you often recall situations from months and even years ago when you encounter a similar smell.
- *Identification messages.* Smell is often used to create an image or an identity for a product. Advertisers and manufacturers spend millions of dollars each year creating scents for cleaning products and toothpastes, for example, which have nothing to do with their cleaning power. There's also evidence that we can identify specific significant others by smell. For example, young children were able to identify the T-shirts of their brothers and sisters solely on the basis of smell (Porter & Moore, 1981).

Culture and Nonverbal Communication

This chapter has already noted a few cultural and gender differences in nonverbal communication. The importance of culture in certain areas of nonverbal communication, however, has become the focus of sustained research. Here we consider just a sampling of research on the face, color, silence, touch, and time.

ASK THE RESEARCHER

Nonverbal Cues

- *I'm running for office in a class election, and I want to know what I can do nonverbally to make myself more likable and more credible and hence more likely to be elected. Any suggestions?*

In a campaign speech enhance your physical appearance (if female, moderate makeup; if male, shave) and dress slightly better than expected at your school. You should engage in pleasant facial expressions, use a slightly faster speech rate with a good range of inflection, speaking from your diaphragm. Engage in a moderate amount of gestures, but keep them between your neck and waist and spread them away from your body. Engage your audience with a slight forward lean to show interest in them.

In interpersonal contexts where you have already enhanced your physical appearance, close your distance slightly if your partner agrees with you, but increase your distance slightly if s/he disagrees with you. If you have not enhanced your appearance, maintain your initial distance. Allow your natural emotions to flow (provide positive feedback, unless you totally disagree with the point), reduce your range of gestures, and speak with a confident, slightly faster than normal rate, but at a conversational volume.

For further information: Hickson, M. L., Stacks, D. W., & Moore, N. J. (2003). *Nonverbal communication: Studies and applications.* Los Angeles: Roxbury. And Richmond, V. P., & McCroskey, J. C. (2003). *Nonverbal behavior in interpersonal relations.* Boston: Allyn & Bacon.

Don W. Stacks (Ph.D., University of Florida) is professor of advertising and public relations at the University of Miami. He teaches courses in public relations, research methods, nonverbal communication, persuasion, and communication theory and directs the undergraduate and graduate programs in advertising and public relations. In addition, Stacks directs the largest public relations research conference. He is a member of the Commission on Public Relations Measurement and Evaluation and the Commission on Public Relations Education, a board member of the Institute for Public Relations, and a member of the Arthur W. Page Society.

Culture and Facial Expression

The wide variations in facial communication that we observe in different cultures seem to reflect different attitudes about what reactions are permissible in public rather than differences in the way humans show emotions. For example, Japanese and American students watched a film of a surgical operation (Ekman, 1985). The students were videotaped both in an interview situation about the film and alone while watching the film. When alone the students showed very similar reactions; in the interview, however, the American students displayed facial expressions indicating displeasure, whereas the Japanese students did not show any great emotion. Similarly, it's considered "forward" or inappropriate for Japanese women to reveal broad smiles, and so many Japanese women will hide their smile, sometimes with their hands (cf. Ma, 1996). Women in the United States, on the other hand, have no such restrictions and so are more likely to smile openly. Thus, the difference may not be in the way people in different cultures express emotions but rather in the cultural rules for displaying emotions in public (cf. Matsumoto, 1991).

Similarly, people in different cultures may decode the meanings of facial expression differently. For example, American and Japanese students judged the meaning of a smiling and a neutral facial expression. The Americans rated the smiling face as more attractive, more intelligent, and more sociable than the neutral face. In contrast, the Japanese rated the smiling face as more sociable but not as more attractive—and they rated the neutral face as more intelligent (Matsumoto & Kudoh, 1993).

Culture and Colors

Colors vary greatly in their meanings from one culture to another. Some of these cultural differences are summed up in Table 8.3; but before looking at the table think about the meanings given to such colors as red, green, black, white, blue, yellow, and purple in your own culture or cultures.

Table 8.3
Some Cultural Meanings of Color

This table, constructed from research reported by various culture watchers, illustrates only some of the different meanings that colors may communicate, especially in different cultures (Dreyfuss, 1971; Hoft, 1995; Dresser, 1996). As you read this table, consider the meanings you give to these colors and where your meanings came from.

Color	Cultural Meanings and Comments
Red	China, red signifies prosperity and rebirth and is used for festive and joyous occasions; in France and the United Kingdom, masculinity; in many African countries, blasphemy or death; in Japan, anger and danger. Red ink, especially among Korean Buddhists, is used only to write a person's name at the time of death or on the anniversary of the person's death; this creates lots of problems when American teachers use red ink to mark homework.
Green	In the United States, green signifies capitalism, go-ahead, and envy; in Ireland, patriotism; among some Native Americans, femininity; to the Egyptians, fertility and strength; and to the Japanese, youth and energy.
Black	In Thailand, black signifies old age; in parts of Malaysia, courage; and in much of Europe and North America, death.
White	In Thailand, white signifies purity; in many Muslim and Hindu cultures, purity and peace; and in Japan and other Asian countries, death and mourning.
Blue	In Iran, blue signifies something negative; in Egypt, virtue and truth; in Ghana, joy; and among the Cherokee, defeat.
Yellow	In China, yellow signifies wealth and authority; in the United States, caution and cowardice; in Egypt, happiness and prosperity; and in many countries throughout the world, femininity.
Purple	In Latin America, purple signifies death; in Europe, royalty; in Egypt, virtue and faith; in Japan, grace and nobility; and in China, barbarism.

Culture and Touch

The several functions and examples of touching discussed so far have been based on studies in North America; in other cultures these functions are not served in the same way. In some cultures, for example, some task-related touching is viewed negatively and is to be avoided. Among Koreans, it is considered disrespectful for a store owner to touch a customer in, say, handing back change; it is considered too intimate a gesture. Members of other cultures that are used to such touching may consider the Korean's behavior cold and aloof. Muslim children are socialized not to touch members of the opposite sex, a practice which can easily be interpreted as unfriendly by American children who are used to touching each other (Dresser, 1996).

For example, in one study on touch, college students in Japan and in the United States were surveyed (Barnlund, 1989). Students from the United States reported being touched twice as much as did the Japanese students. In Japan there is a strong taboo against touching between strangers, and the Japanese are therefore especially careful to maintain sufficient distance.

Some cultures—including many in southern Europe and the Middle East—are contact cultures; others are noncontact cultures, such as those of northern Europe and Japan. Members of contact cultures maintain close distances, touch one another in conversation, face one another more directly, and maintain longer and more focused eye contact. Members of noncontact cultures maintain greater distance in their interactions, touch one another rarely (if at all), avoid facing one another directly, and maintain much less direct eye contact. As a result, southern Europeans may perceive northern Europeans and Japanese as cold, distant, and uninvolved. Southern Europeans may in turn be perceived as pushy, aggressive, and inappropriately intimate.

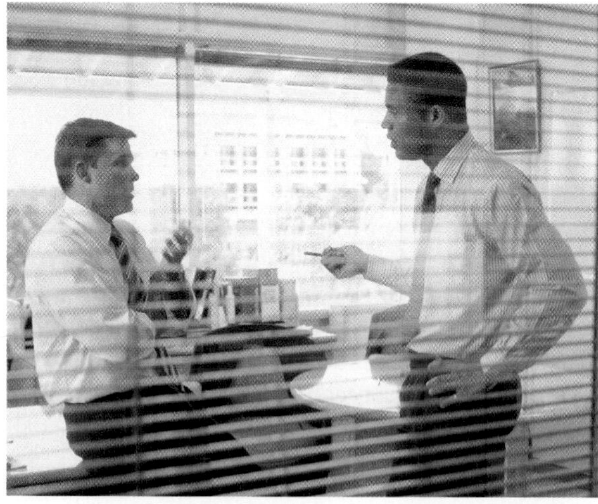

VIEWPOINT

Let's say you're mentoring a student who is about to enter the corporate world. What two, three, or four skills of nonverbal communication would you stress that your protégé be sure to learn and use regularly?

Culture and Silence

Not all cultures view silence in the same way. In the United States, for example, people often interpret silence negatively. At a business meeting or even in an informal social group, the silent member may be seen as not listening, having nothing interesting to add, not understanding the issues, being insensitive, or being too self-absorbed to focus on the messages of others. Other cultures, however, regard silence more positively. In many situations in Japan, for example, silence is a response that is considered more appropriate than speech (Haga, 1988).

In another example, the traditional Apache view silence very differently than European Americans (Basso, 1972). Among the Apache mutual friends do not feel the need to introduce strangers who may be working in the same area or on the same project. The strangers may remain silent for several days. This period enables them to observe and evaluate one another. Once this assessment is made, the individuals talk. When courting, especially during the initial stages, the Apache remain silent for hours; if they do talk, they generally talk very little. Only after a couple has been dating for several months will they have lengthy conversations. These periods of silence are generally attributed to shyness or self-consciousness; but the use of silence is explicitly taught to Apache women, who are especially discouraged from engaging in long discussions with their dates. To many Apache, silence during courtship is a sign of modesty.

Culture and Time

Culture influences people's attitudes toward time in a variety of ways. The Understanding Theory and Research box on page 149 examined one cultural variant, the "social clock." Here we look at two more: formal versus informal time and monochronism versus polychronism.

Formal and Informal Time

In the United States and in most of the world, formal time divisions include seconds, minutes, hours, days,

Table 8.4
Monochronic and Polychronic Time

As you read down this table, based on Hall and Hall (1987), note the potential for miscommunication that these differences might create when M-time and P-time people interact. Have any of these differences ever created interpersonal misunderstandings for you?

The Monochronic-Time Person	The Polychronic-Time Person
does one thing at a time	does several things at once
treats time schedules and plans very seriously; feels they may only be broken for the most serious of reasons	treats time schedules and plans as useful (not sacred); feels they may be broken for a variety of causes
considers the job the most important part of life, ahead of even family	considers the family and interpersonal relationships more important than the job
considers privacy extremely important; seldom borrows or lends to others; works independently	is actively involved with others; works in the presence of and with lots of people at the same time

weeks, months, and years. Some cultures, however, may use phases of the moon or the seasons to delineate their most important time periods. Other formal time units exist, too. For example, in the United States, if your college is on the semester system, your courses are divided into 50- or 75-minute periods that meet two or three times a week for 14-week periods. Eight semesters of 15 or 16 periods per week equal a college education. As these examples illustrate, formal time units are arbitrary. The culture establishes them for convenience.

Informal time terms are more hazy and subject to interpretation—terms such as "forever," "immediately," "soon," "right away," or "as soon as possible." This type of time creates the most communication problems, because the terms have different meanings for different people.

Attitudes toward both formal and informal time vary from one culture to another. One study, for example, measured the accuracy of clocks in six cultures—those of Japan, Indonesia, Italy, England, Taiwan, and the United States. Japan had the most accurate and Indonesia had the least accurate clocks. The researchers also measured the speed at which people in these six cultures walked, and results showed that the Japanese walked the fastest, the Indonesians the slowest (LeVine & Bartlett, 1984).

Monochronism and Polychronism

Another important distinction is that between **monochronic** and **polychronic time orientations** (Hall, 1959, 1976, 1987). Monochronic people or cultures—such as those of the United States, Germany, Scandinavia, and Switzerland—generally schedule one thing at a time. In these cultures time is compartmentalized and there is a time for everything. Polychronic people or cultures, on the other hand—groups such as Latin Americans, Mediterranean people, and Arabs—tend to schedule more than one thing at the same time. Eating, conducting business with several different people, and taking care of family matters may all be conducted simultaneously. No culture is entirely monochronic or polychronic; rather, these are general tendencies that are found across a large part of the culture. Some cultures combine both time orientations; in Japan and in some American groups, for example, both orientations are found. Table 8.4 identifies some of the distinctions between these two time orientations.

Interpersonal Silence

Remaining silent is at times your right, but at other times it may be unlawful.

- You have the right to remain silent so as not to incriminate yourself. You have a right to protect your privacy—to withhold information that has no bearing on the matter at hand. And thus, your previous relationship history, affectional orientation, or religion is usually irrelevant to your ability to function in a job, and thus may be kept private in most job-related situations. On the other hand, these issues may be relevant when, for example, you're about to enter a more intimate phase of a relationship—then there may be an obligation to reveal information about yourself that could have been kept hidden at earlier relationship stages.

- You do not have the right to remain silent and to refuse to reveal information about crimes you've seen others commit. However, psychiatrists, clergy, and lawyers—fortunately or unfortunately—are often exempt from the requirement to reveal information about criminal activities when the information had been gained through privileged communication with clients.

WHAT WOULD YOU DO? On your way to work, you witness a father verbally abusing his three-year-old child. You worry that he might psychologically harm the child, and your first impulse is to speak up and tell this man that verbal abuse can have lasting effects on the child and often leads to physical abuse. At the same time, you don't want to interfere with his right to speak to his child, and you certainly don't want to make him more angry. What is your ethical obligation in this case? What would you do in this situation?

SUMMARY

In this unit we explored nonverbal communication—communication without words—and considered such areas as body movements, facial and eye movements, spatial and territorial communication, artifactual communication, touch communication, paralanguage, silence, and time communication.

1. Nonverbal messages may be integrated with verbal messages to *accent* or emphasize a part of a verbal message; to *complement* or add nuances of meaning not communicated by your verbal message; to *contradict* verbal messages with nonverbal movements—for example, by crossing your fingers or winking to indicate that you're lying; to *regulate*, control, or show your wish to control the flow of verbal messages; to *repeat* or restate the verbal message nonverbally; and to *substitute* for or take the place of verbal messages.
2. Nonverbal researchers have concentrated on the ways in which nonverbal messages serve important relationship functions: forming and managing impressions, forming and defining relationships, structuring conversation and social interaction, influencing others, and expressing emotions.
3. The five categories of body movements are emblems (nonverbal behaviors that directly translate words or phrases), illustrators (nonverbal behaviors that accompany and literally "illustrate" verbal messages), affect displays (nonverbal movements that communicate emotional meaning), regulators (nonverbal movements that coordinate, monitor, maintain, or control the speaking of another individual), and adaptors (nonverbal behaviors that are emitted without conscious awareness and that usually serve some kind of need, as in scratching an itch).
4. Facial movements may communicate a variety of emotions. The most frequently studied are happiness, surprise, fear, anger, sadness, disgust, and contempt. Facial management techniques enable you to control the extent to which you reveal the emotions you feel.
5. The facial feedback hypothesis claims that facial display of an emotion can lead to physiological and psychological changes.
6. Eye contact may seek feedback, signal others to speak, indicate the nature of a relationship, or compensate for increased physical distance. Eye avoidance may help you avoid prying or may signal a lack of interest.
7. Pupil enlargement shows a person's level of interest and positive emotional arousal.
8. Proxemics is the study of the communicative functions of space and spatial relationships. Four major proxemic distances are (1) intimate distance, ranging from actual touching to 18 inches; (2) personal distance, ranging from 18 inches to 4 feet; (3) social distance, ranging from 4 to 12 feet; and (4) public distance, ranging from 12 to more than 25 feet.
9. Your treatment of space is influenced by such factors as status, culture, context, subject matter, gender, age, and positive or negative evaluation of the other person.
10. Territoriality has to do with your possessive reaction to an area of space or to particular objects.
11. Artifactual communication consists of messages that are human-made; for example, communication through color, clothing and body adornment, and space decoration.
12. The study of haptics indicates that touch communication may convey a variety of meanings, the most important being positive affect, playfulness, control, ritual, and task-relatedness. Touch avoidance is the desire to avoid touching and being touched by others.
13. Paralanguage involves the vocal but nonverbal dimensions of speech. It includes rate, pitch, volume, rhythm, and vocal quality as well as pauses and hesitations. Paralanguage helps us make judgments about people, their emotions, and their believability.

14. We use silence to communicate a variety of meanings, from messages aimed at hurting another (the silent treatment) to deep emotional responses.
15. The study of time communication (chronemics) explores the messages communicated by our treatment of time.
16. Smell can communicate messages of attraction, taste, memory, and identification.
17. Among the cultural differences that researchers have focused on are facial expressions and displays, the meanings of color, the uses of silence, the appropriateness and uses of touch, and the ways in which time is treated.

Key Terms

emblems	facial management techniques	artifactual communication
illustrators	civil inattention	haptics
affect displays	pupil dilation	paralanguage
regulators	proxemics	chronemics
adaptors	territoriality	social clock

Thinking Critically About

Nonverbal Messages

1. On a 10-point scale, with 1 indicating "not at all important" and 10 indicating "extremely important," how important is body appearance to your own romantic interest in another person? Do the men and women you know conform to the stereotypes that depict males as more concerned with physical appearance and females as more concerned with personality?
2. One signal of status is an the unwritten "law" granting the right of invasion. Higher-status individuals have more of a right to invade the territory of others than vice versa. The boss, for example, can invade the territory of junior executives by barging into their offices, but the reverse would be unthinkable. Do you notice this "right" of territorial invasion in your workplace?
3. A popular defense tactic in criminal trials for sex crimes against women, gay men, and lesbians is to blame the victim by implying that the way the victim was dressed provoked the attack. Currently, New York and Florida are the only states that prohibit defense attorneys from referring to the way a sex-crime victim was dressed at the time of the attack (*New York Times*, July 30, 1994, p. 22). What do you think of this? If you don't live in New York or Florida, have there been proposals in your state to similarly limit this popular defense tactic?
4. Here are a few findings from research on gender differences in nonverbal expression (Burgoon, Buller, & Woodall 1996; Eakins & Eakins 1978; Pearson, West, & Turner 1995; Arliss 1991; Shannon 1987): (1) Women smile more than men; (2) women stand closer to one another than do men and are generally approached more closely than men; (3) both men and women, when speaking, look at men more than at women; (4) women both touch and are touched more than men; (5) men extend their bodies, taking up greater areas of space, more than women. What problems might these differences create when men and women communicate with each other?
5. Visit the website of a large multinational corporation. Most corporations have Web addresses like this: www.CompanyName.com. What can you learn about nonverbal communication from such elements as the general design, colors, movement, fonts, or spacing used? Can you point out any way that the website could be visually improved?
6. Another type of time is biological time—the different ways your body functions at different times. According to theories of biorhythms, your intellectual, physical, and emotional lives are lived in cycles that influence your effectiveness. You can find detailed explanations and instructions for calculating your own intellectual, physical, and emotional cycles

in DeVito (1989); or, even better, you can visit a website that will compute your biorhythms (www.kfu.com/~nsayer/compat.html).

7. Test your ability to identify emotions on the basis of verbal descriptions. Try to "hear" the following voices and to identify the emotions being communicated (Davitz, 1964). Do you hear affection, anger, boredom, or joy?
   - This voice is soft, with a low pitch, a resonant quality, a slow rate, and a steady and slightly upward inflection. The rhythm is regular, and the enunciation is slurred.
   - This voice is loud, with a high pitch, a moderately blaring quality, a fast rate, an upward inflection, and a regular rhythm.
   - This voice is loud, with a high pitch, a blaring quality, a fast rate, and an irregular up-and-down inflection. The rhythm is irregular, and the enunciation is clipped.
   - This voice is moderate to low in volume, with a moderate-to-low pitch, a moderately resonant quality, a moderately slow rate, and a monotonous or gradually falling inflection. The enunciation is somewhat slurred.

8. What nonverbal cues should you look for in judging whether someone likes you? List cues in the order of their importance, beginning with 1 for the cue that is of most value in making your judgment. Do you really need two lists? One for judging a woman's liking and one for a man's?

UNIT

Interpersonal Communication: Conversation

UNIT CONTENTS

Talking with another person seems so simple and so natural that most people are surprised to learn that the process actually follows a complex set of rules and customs. In this unit we dissect this process and explain how it operates and the kinds of problems that can be created when these rules and customs are broken. In this excursion into conversation, you'll learn

- how the process of conversation works
- how you can become a more satisfying and more effective conversationalist

The Conversation Process

Conversation is the essence of interpersonal communication; in many scholarly views they are equivalent, and among nonscholars the words *conversation* and *interpersonal communication* often mean the same thing (though consider the qualifications noted in Understanding Theory and Research: The Development of Interpersonal Communication). **Conversation** occurs when two or three people exchange

UNDERSTANDING THEORY AND RESEARCH

The Development of Interpersonal Communication

You can view communication as a continuum that has impersonal message at one end and personal or intimate communication at the other. Interpersonal communication occupies a part of the continuum toward the more personal and intimate end and is distinguished from impersonal communication by three factors: psychologically based predictions, explanatory knowledge, and personally established rules (Miller, 1978).

In impersonal encounters you respond to another person on the basis of sociological data—the classes or groups to which the person belongs. For example, a student responds to a particular college professor the way students respond to college professors generally. Similarly, the professor responds to the student the way professors respond to students generally. As the relationship becomes more personal, however, both professor and student begin to respond to each other not just as members of their groups but as individuals. They respond (to some degree) on the basis of *psychological data;* that is, on the basis of the ways the individual differs from the members of his or her group.

In interpersonal interactions, you also base your communications on *explanatory knowledge* of each other. When you know a particular person, you can predict how that person will act in a variety of situations. But as you get to know the person better, you can predict not only how the person will act, but also why the person behaves as he or she does. For example, in an impersonal relationship the professor may be able to predict Pat's behavior and know that Pat will be late to class each Friday. But in an interpersonal situation the professor can also offer explanations for the behavior, giving reasons for Pat's lateness.

Society sets up rules for interaction in impersonal situations. As noted in the example of the student and professor, however, the social rules of interaction set up by the culture lose importance as the relationship becomes more personal. In the place of these social rules, the individuals set up *personal rules.* When individuals establish their own rules for interacting with each other rather than using the rules set down by the society, the situation becomes increasingly interpersonal.

Working with Theories and Research

- *Try applying these three factors to your own interpersonal relationships. Did you experience the kind of progression identified here?*

messages—whether face-to-face, over the telephone, through apartment walls, or on the Internet.

E-mail, originally used primarily as a business convenience, is now a major channel of conversation. In fact, according to one Gallup poll (http://www.gallup.com, July 23, 2001), by 2001 e-mail had become the most common Internet activity. Of those surveyed, 90 percent said they used e-mail at home and 80 percent said they used it at work. Of these, 61 percent of the women and only 44 percent of the men said that e-mail was their main online activity. As a means of communication, e-mail is extremely well liked; 97 percent of those surveyed said that e-mail had made their lives better. Instant messaging, which enables you to communicate with others who are also at their computers in near real time, was used by only 2 percent of computer users polled.

Along with chat groups and mailing lists (which share many characteristics of small groups, and so are discussed in Unit 11) and newsgroups (which are covered in our discussion of public speaking in Unit 14), e-mail is an ever increasingly popular means of conversing. Among college students in the United States e-mail is near universal, and it is becoming standard throughout the world.

Another type of e-mail that is becoming increasingly popular is text messaging, in which you type and send very short messages to another person

COMMUNICATION@WORK

Grapevine Communication

Electronic engineers have yet to devise a better interoffice communication system than the water cooler.

—Leo Ellis

Grapevine messages don't follow any of the formal lines of communication established in an organization; rather, they seem to have a life of their own. They may relate to personal and social matters, or they may concern job-related issues that you want to discuss in a more interpersonal setting. Not surprisingly, the grapevine also grows as the size of the organization increases.

The grapevine is most likely to be used when there are important subjects to be discussed, when formal management communication is lacking, and when the situation is perceived as threatening or insecure (Crampton & Hodge, 1998). In fact, one research study notes that workers spend between 65 and 70 percent of their time on the grapevine during a crisis. And even in non-crisis times, they spend between 10 and 15 percent on the grapevine (Smith, 1996). The grapevine is also surprisingly accurate, with estimates of accuracy ranging from 75 to 95 percent (Davis, 1980; Hellweg, 1992; Smith, 1996).

Here are a few useful suggestions for dealing with the inevitable office grapevine:

- Understand the variety of purposes the grapevine serves. Its speed and general accuracy make it an ideal medium to carry many of the social communications that so effectively bind workers together.
- Treat grapevine information as tentative, as possibly not necessarily true. Although grapevine information is generally accurate, it's often incomplete and may contain crucial distortions.
- Tap into the grapevine. Whether you're a worker or a member of management, it's important to hear grapevine information. It may clue you in to events that will affect your future with the organization, and it will help you network with others in the organization.
- Always assume that what you say in grapevine communication will be repeated to others (Smith, 1996; Hilton, 2000). So be mindful of your organizational communications; the potentially offensive joke that you e-mail a colleague can easily be forwarded to the very people who may take offense.

Communicating@Work

How does the grapevine work at your place of employment? How does it work on campus? What roles do you play in grapevine communication?

GOING ONLINE

Interpersonal Communication

www.abacon.com/commstudies/interpersonal/interpersonal.html

This website is set up and maintained by Allyn & Bacon to complement this textbook's coverage of interpersonal communication. As you can see, it covers a great number of topics discussed in this unit and offers additional points of view and perspectives.

In addition visit the companion website for this text (www.ablongman.com/devito) and take the self-tests that measure how satisfying you find a conversation and how apprehensive you are in conversations. Also try the exercises "Analyzing a Conversation," "Giving and Taking Directions," "Gender and the Topics of Conversation," and "Responding Effectively in Conversation."

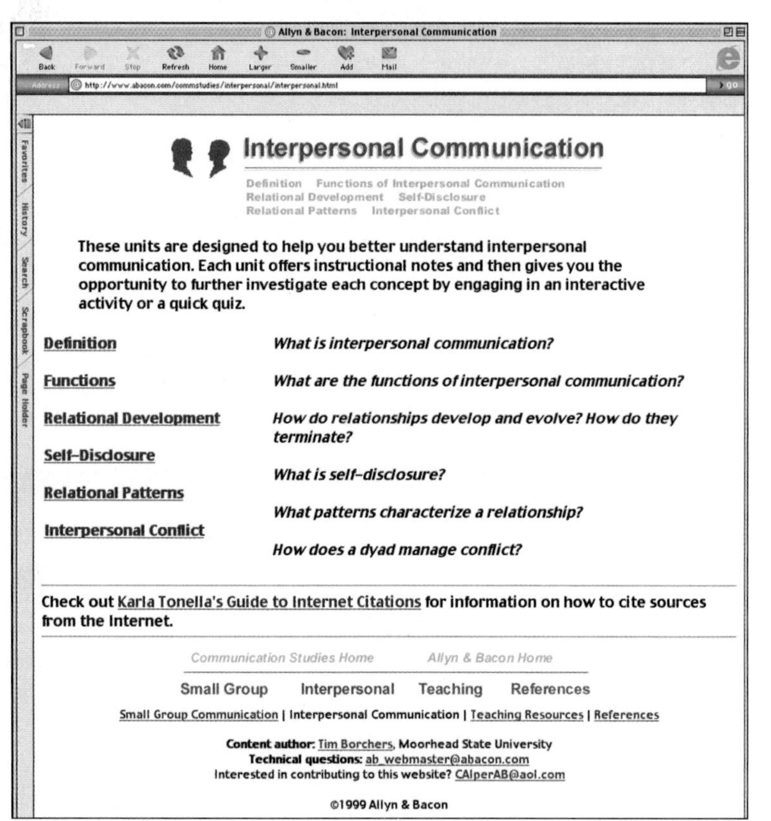

using your pager or cell phone. The New York City Police Department, for example, uses text messaging to check on license plates, and some airlines are using it to notify passengers if their flights will be delayed. Although text messaging lacks the advantages of face-to-face interaction, it has advantages of its own; for example, you can reach lots of people at once at a relatively low cost, and the necessary equipment (the pager or the cell phone) is always with you. Although instant messaging has the advantage of near-real-time interaction, it also has the disadvantage that you can communicate only with those who are at their computers at the same time you are.

Allyn & Bacon: Interpersonal Communication
Interpersonal Communication
Definition Functions of Interpersonal Communication
Relational Development Self-Disclosure
Relational Patterns Interpersonal Conflict
These units are designed to help you better understand interpersonal communication. Each unit offers instructional notes and then gives you the opportunity to further investigate each concept by engaging in an interactive activity or a quick quiz.
Definition
What is interpersonal communication?
Functions
What are the functions of interpersonal communication?
Relational Development
How do relationships develop and evolve? How do they terminate?
Self-Disclosure
What is self-disclosure?
Relational Patterns
What patterns characterize a relationship?
Interpersonal Conflict
How does a dyad manage conflict?
Check out Karla Tonella's Guide to Internet Citations for information on how to cite sources from the Internet.
Communication Studies Home
Allyn & Bacon Home
Small Group Interpersonal Teaching References
Small Group Communication | Interpersonal Communication | Teaching Resources | References
Content author: Tim Borchers, Moorhead State University
Technical questions: ab_webmaster@abacon.com
Interested in contributing to this website? CAlperAB@aol.com
©1999 Allyn & Bacon

In face-to-face interaction the messages exchanged are both verbal and nonverbal. In e-mail today most messages are basically verbal. But with the addition of emoticons and the popularity of digital video cameras and voice software, e-mail messages are increasingly blending the verbal with the nonverbal in much the same way as face-to-face conversation. A website devoted to interpersonal communication, maintained by the publisher of this book, provides additional insights into conversation (see the Going Online box).

When reading about the process of conversation, therefore, keep in mind the wide range of channels through which conversation can take place—face-to-face as well as via the Internet, phones, and other technologies—and the similarities and differences among them.

Similarly, realize that not everyone speaks with the fluency and ease that many textbooks often assume. Speech and language disorders, for example, can seriously disrupt the conversation process if some elementary guidelines aren't followed. Table 9.1 offers suggestions for overcoming such difficulties.

Table 9.1
Communication Tips

Between People with and without Speech and Language Disorders
Speech and language disorders vary widely and include fluency problems such as stuttering; indistinct articulation; and difficulty in finding the right word, or aphasia. Communication between people with and without speech and language disorders can be facilitated by means of a few simple guidelines.

If you're the person without a speech or language disorder:

1. *Avoid finishing the person's sentences.* Although you may think you're helping the person who stutters or has word-finding difficulty, it's not recommended. It may communicate the impression that you're impatient and don't want to spend the extra time necessary to interact effectively.
2. *Avoid giving directions to the person with a speech disorder.* Saying "slow down" or "relax" will often prove insulting and will make further communication more difficult.
3. *Maintain eye contact.* Show interest and at the same time avoid showing any signs of impatience or embarrassment.
4. *Ask for clarification as needed.* If you don't understand what the person said, ask him or her to repeat it. Don't pretend that you understand when you don't.
5. *Don't treat people who have language problems like children.* A person with aphasia, say, who has difficulty with names or nouns generally, is in no way childlike.

If you're the person with a speech or language disorder:

1. *Let the other person know what your special needs are.* For example, if you stutter, you might tell others that you have difficulty with certain sounds and so they need to be patient.
2. *Demonstrate your own comfort.* Show that you have a positive attitude toward the interpersonal situation. If you appear comfortable and positive, others will also.

These suggestions were drawn from a variety of sources: http://www.nsastuter.org, http://www.aphasia.org/NAAcommun.html, and http://www.conniedugan.com/tips.html (all accessed October 23, 2004).

The Conversation Process in Five Stages

Figure 9.1 provides a model of the process of conversation and divides the process into five main stages: (1) opening, (2) feedforward, (3) business, (4) feedback, and (5) closing. Examining each stage will give you an overview of what goes on when two people talk.

The Opening

The first step is to open the conversation, usually with some kind of greeting. Greetings can be verbal or nonverbal and are usually both (Krivonos & Knapp, 1975; Knapp & Vangelisti, 2000). Verbal greetings include, for example, verbal salutes ("Hi," "Hello"), initiation of the topic ("The reason I called . . ."), making reference to the other ("Hey, Joe, what's up?"), and personal inquiries ("What's new?"

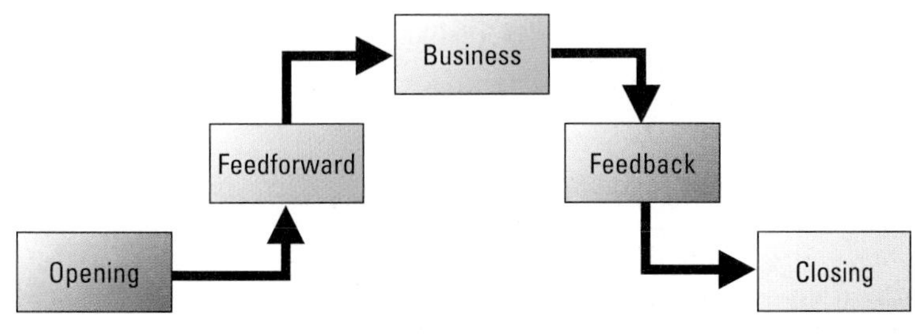

Figure 9.1
The Process of Conversation
This model of the stages of conversation is best seen as a way of looking at conversation and not as defining unvarying stages that all conversations follow. As you read about conversation, consider how accurately you think this model reflects the progression of your last conversation.

"How are you doing?"). Nonverbal greetings include waving, smiling, shaking hands, and winking. Usually you greet another person both verbally and nonverbally: You smile when you say "Hello."

In normal conversation, your greeting is reciprocated with a greeting from the other person that is similar in degree of formality or informality and in intensity. When it isn't—when the other person turns away or responds coldly to your friendly "good morning"—you know that something is wrong. Openings are also generally consistent in tone with the main part of the conversation; a cheery "How ya doing today, big guy?" is not normally followed by news of a family death. This, however, is distinctly cultural; in Finland, for example, the "How are you?" opening is interpreted as a genuine request for information and not simply as a "hello" (Halmari, 1995). In e-mail the opening is the header and the announcement from your ISP of "You got mail" or "Mail truck."

In opening a conversation, consider two general guidelines. First, be positive. Lead off with something positive rather than something negative. Say, for example, "I really enjoy coming here" instead of "Don't you just hate this place?" Second, don't be too revealing; don't self-disclose too early in an interaction. If you do, you risk making the other person feel uncomfortable.

Feedforward

At the second step there's usually some kind of feedforward. Here you give the other person a general idea of what the conversation will focus on: "I've got to tell you about Jack," "Did you hear what happened in class yesterday?" or "We need to talk about our vacation plans." Feedforward also may identify the tone of the conversation ("I'm really depressed and need to talk with you") or the time required ("This will just take a minute") (Frentz, 1976; Reardon, 1987); or you may use it to preface the conversation to ensure that your message will be understood and will not reflect negatively on you (see Unit 1).

In e-mail the title serves as feedforward; it gives the reader some idea of what to expect in the e-mail. Conveniently, this allows for quick deletion of spam and a concentrated focus on e-mail titled "sad news" or "family problem."

UNDERSTANDING THEORY AND RESEARCH

Opening Lines

How do you strike up a conversation with someone you're meeting for the first time? How have people tried to open conversations with you? Researchers investigating this question found three basic types of opening lines (Kleinke, 1986).

- Cute-flippant openers are humorous, indirect, and ambiguous as to whether or not the person opening the conversation really wants an extended encounter. Examples: "Is that really your hair?" "Bet I can outdrink you."
- *Innocuous openers* are highly ambiguous as to whether these are simple comments that might be made to just anyone or whether they're in fact openers designed to initiate an extended encounter. Examples: "What do you think of the band?" "Could you show me how to work this machine?"
- *Direct openers* demonstrate clearly the speaker's interest in meeting the other person. Examples: "I feel a little embarrassed about this, but I'd like to meet you." "Would you like to have a drink after dinner?"

Studies indicate that the opening lines most preferred by both men and women are generally those that are direct or innocuous. Least preferred by both men and women are opening lines that are cute-flippant; women, however, dislike these openers more than men (Kleinke & Dean, 1990).

Working with Theories and Research

- *Do you find support for these conclusions from your own experience? For example, do you find significant gender differences in preferences? What openers do you yourself find most effective? What types do you dislike?*

Business

The third step is the "business," the substance or focus of the conversation. This is obviously the longest part of the conversation and the reason for both the opening and the feedforward. *Business* is a good term to use for this stage, because it emphasizes that most conversations—whether face-to-face, on the phone, or via e-mail—are goal directed. You converse to fulfill one or several of the general purposes of interpersonal communication: to learn, relate, influence, play, or help (Unit 1). The term is also sufficiently general to incorporate all kinds of interactions. In e-mail you can easily supplement your message by attaching hotlinks to websites and to word, sound, and video files, as well as to other e-mails. Although you can also distribute supplementary materials in face-to-face conversation, it's not as common as it is in e-mail communication.

The business is conducted through an exchange of speaker and listener roles. Usually, brief (rather than long) speaking turns characterize the most satisfying conversations. Here you talk about Jack, what happened in class, or your vacation plans. Here is where the similarity between e-mail and face-to-face conversation breaks down a bit. E-mail doesn't have the spontaneity and the frequent interchange of sender–receiver roles—although with voice and video advancements, this distinction between face-to-face and electronic communication will probably blur in coming years.

Another important difference is that in normal face-to-face communication there is no permanent record of the conversation; the record exists only in the memories of those who are present. In e-mail there is a permanent record of the interaction, a record that can easily be sent to third parties. In large organizations employees' e-mails are stored on hard disk or on backup tapes and may be retrieved from archives long thought destroyed. For this reason, using e-mail requires caution. For example, some years ago Dow Chemical fired 24 employees for sending offensive e-mail messages.

Feedback

The fourth step in conversation is the reverse of the second. In feedback (see Unit 1) you reflect back on the conversation to signal that as far as you're concerned, the business is completed: "So, you may want to send Jack a get-well card," "Wasn't that the craziest class you ever heard of?" or "I'll call for reservations while you shop for what we need."

Of course, the other person may not agree that the business is completed and may therefore counter with, for example, "But what hospital is he in?" When this happens, you normally go back a step and continue the business.

Closing

The fifth and last step, the opposite of the first step, is the closing, the good-bye (Knapp, Hart, Friedrich, & Shulman, 1973; Knapp & Vangelisti, 2000). Like the opening, the closing may be verbal or nonverbal but is usually a combination of both. Most obviously, the closing signals the end of accessibility. Just as the opening signaled access, the closing signals the end of access. The closing usually also signals some degree of supportiveness; for example, you express your pleasure in interacting, as in "Well, it was good talking with you." The closing may also summarize the interaction.

In e-mail the closing is similar to that in face-to-face conversation but has the added capability of including a "signature," perhaps along with a favorite quotation or saying or a phone number through which you can be reached.

Closing a conversation is almost as difficult as opening a conversation. It's frequently an awkward and uncomfortable part of interpersonal interaction. Here are a few **leave-taking cues** you might consider for closing a conversation.

- Reflect back on the conversation and briefly summarize it so as to bring it to a close. For example, "I'm glad I ran into you and found out what happened at that union meeting. I'll probably be seeing you at the meetings."
- State the desire to end the conversation directly and to get on with other things. For example, "I'd like to continue talking but I really have to run. I'll see you around."
- Refer to future interaction. For example, "E-mail me when after you've had a chance to read the report," or "Why don't we get together next week sometime and continue this discussion?"
- Ask for closure. For example, "Have I explained what you wanted to know?"
- State that you enjoyed the interaction. For example, "I really enjoyed talking with you."

With any of these closings, it should be clear to the other person that you're attempting to end the conversation. Obviously, you'll have to use more direct methods with those who don't take these subtle hints—those who don't realize that both persons are responsible for bringing the conversation to a satisfying close.

Closing a conversation in e-mail follows the same principles as closing a face-to-face conversation. But exactly when you end an e-mail exchange is often unclear, partly because the absence of nonverbal cues creates ambiguity. For example, if you ask someone a question and the other person answers, do you then e-mail again and say, "Thanks"? If so, should the other person e-mail you back and say "It was my pleasure"? And, if so, should you then e-mail back again and say "I appreciate your willingness to answer my questions"? And, if so, should the other person then respond with something like "No problem"?

On the one hand, you don't want to prolong the interaction more than necessary; on the other hand, you don't want to appear impolite. So how do you signal (politely) that the e-mail exchanges should stop? Here are a few suggestions (Cohen, 2002):

- Include in your e-mail the notation NRN (no reply necessary).
- If you're replying with information the other person requested, end your message with something like "I hope this helps."
- Title or head your message FYI (for your information), indicating that your message is intended merely to keep someone in the loop.
- When you make a request for information, end your message with "Thank you in advance."

Maintaining Conversations

The defining feature of conversation is that the roles of speaker and listener are exchanged throughout the interaction. You accomplish this exchange, or **conversational management,** by using a wide variety of verbal and nonverbal cues to signal **conversational turns**—the changing (or maintaining) of the speaker or listener role during the conversation.

In people with no hearing or vision impairments, turn-taking cues include both audio and visual signals. Among blind speakers the turn taking is governed in larger part by audio signals and often touch. Among deaf speakers turn-taking signals are largely visual and may also involve touch (Coates & Sutton-Spence, 2001).

BUILDING COMMUNICATION SKILLS

Opening and Closing a Conversation

Think about how you might open a conversation with the persons described in each of these situations. What general approaches would meet with a favorable response? What general approaches seem frowned on?

1. On the first day of class, you and another student are the first to come into the classroom and are seated in the room alone.
2. You are a guest at a friend's party. You are one of the first guests to arrive and are now there with several other people to whom you have only just been introduced. Your friend, the host, is busy with other matters.
3. You have just started a new job in a large office where you are one of several computer operators. It seems as if most of the other people know one another.

Now think about how you might go about closing each of the following conversations. What types of closing seem most effective? Which seem least effective?

1. You and a friend have been talking on the phone for the last hour, but at this point not much new is being said. You have a great deal of work to get to and would like to close the conversation. Your friend just doesn't seem to hear your subtle cues.
2. You have had a conference with a supervisor and have learned what you needed to know. This supervisor, however, doesn't seem to know how to end the conversation, seems very ill at ease, and just continues to go over what has already been said. You have to get back to your desk and must close the conversation.
3. You are at a party and notice a person you think you would like to get to know. You initiate a conversation, but after a few minutes you realize that you do not care to spend any more time with this person. You want to close the conversation as soon as possible.

The majority of today's e-mail lacks this frequent exchange of roles between sender and receiver; the exchanges take place with hours, days, or even weeks intervening between the sending and the responding. Such feedback lacks the immediacy that is common in face-to-face conversation—though, again, with video and voice capabilities, this distinction may fade.

Conversational Turns

Combining the insights of a variety of communication researchers (Burgoon, Buller, & Woodall, 1996; Duncan, 1972; Pearson & Spitzberg, 1990), we can look at conversational turns in terms of speaker cues and listener cues.

Speaker Cues

Speakers regulate the conversation through two major types of cues: turn-maintaining cues and turn-yielding cues. Using these cues effectively not only ensures communication efficiency but also increases likability (Place & Becker, 1991; Heap, 1992). The ways of using the conversational turns identified here have been derived largely from studies conducted in the United States. Each culture appears to define the types and appropriateness of turns differently (e.g., Iizuka, 1993). In polychronic cultures, for example, people will often disregard the turn-taking rules used in monochronic cultures. The effect is that to monochronic people—who carefully follow these rules—polychronic people may appear rude as they interrupt and overlap conversations (Lee, 1984; Grossin, 1987). In some cultures (largely individualist) the conversational turn is more often passed to one person; in other cultures (largely collectivist) the turn is more often passed to several individuals (Ng, Loong, He, Liu, & Weatherall, 2000).

Turn-Maintaining Cues. Turn-maintaining cues are designed to enable a person to maintain the role of speaker and can take a variety of forms (Burgoon, Buller, & Woodall, 1996; Duncan, 1972):

- audibly inhaling breath to show that the speaker has more to say
- continuing a gesture or series of gestures to show that the thought is not yet complete
- avoiding eye contact with the listener so as not to indicate that the speaking turn is being passed along
- sustaining the intonation pattern to indicate that more will be said
- vocalizing pauses ("er," "umm") to prevent the listener from speaking and to show that the speaker is still talking

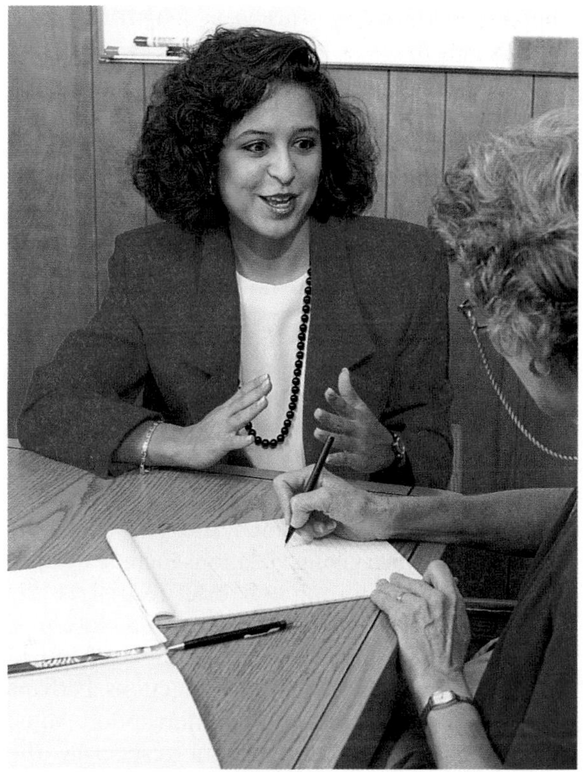

VIEWPOINT
In dialogic interaction between, say, a fluent speaker and a person who has a severe physical or psychological communication problem, the more fluent speaker tries to help the speaker with the problem communicate more effectively, as, say, described in Table 9.1. In fact, some researchers have argued that the more competent communicator has an ethical responsibility to help the other person to better convey his or her meaning (von Tetzchner & Jensen, 1999). Do you consider this an ethical responsibility? Would this provision be a part of your ethical theory of communication?

In most cases we expect the speaker to maintain relatively brief speaking turns and to turn over the speaking role to the listener willingly (when so signaled by the listener). People who don't follow those unwritten rules are likely to be evaluated negatively.

Turn-Yielding Cues. Turn-yielding cues tell the listener that the speaker is finished and wishes to exchange the role of speaker for the role of listener. They tell the listener (and sometimes they're addressed to a specific listener rather than to just any listener) to take over the role of speaker. For example, at the end of a statement you may add some cue such as "okay?" or "right?" which asks one of the listeners to assume the role of speaker. You can also indicate that you've finished speaking by dropping your intonation or by pausing at length (Wennerstrom & Siegel, 2003), by making direct eye contact with a listener, by asking some question, or by nodding in the direction of a particular listener.

In much the same way that we expect a speaker to yield the role of speaker, we also expect the listener to assume the speaking role willingly. Those who don't may be regarded as reticent or as unwilling to involve themselves and take equal responsibility for the conversation. For example, in an analysis of turn-taking violations in the conversations of married couples, the most common violation found was that of no response (DeFrancisco, 1991). Forty-five percent of the 540 violations identified involved a lack of response to an invitation to take on the role of speaker. Of these "no response" violations, 68 percent were committed by men and 32 percent by women. Other turn-taking violations include delayed responses and inappropriately brief responses. DeFrancisco (1991) argues that with these violations, all of which are committed more frequently by men, men silence women in marital interactions. Perhaps the most important violation is interruption. Much research has addressed this issue, especially the question of whether men or women interrupt more. The research that has found a difference indicates that men interrupt more often than women, though much research finds no differences (Stratford, 1998; Crown & Cummins, 1998; Smith-Lovin & Brody, 1989; Donaldson, 1992).

Listener Cues

As a listener you can regulate the conversation by using three types of cues: turn-requesting cues, turn-denying cues, and backchanneling cues.

Turn-Requesting Cues. Turn-requesting cues let the speaker know that you would like to say something and take a turn as speaker. Sometimes you can do this simply by saying, "I'd like to say something," but often it's done more subtly through some vocalized *er* or *um* that tells the speaker that you would now like to speak. The request to speak is also often made with facial and mouth gestures. Frequently a listener will indicate a desire to speak by opening his or her eyes and mouth wide as if to say something, by beginning to gesture with a hand, or by leaning forward.

Turn-Denying Cues. You can use turn-denying cues to indicate your reluctance to assume the role of speaker; for example, by intoning a slurred "I don't know" or by giving some brief grunt that signals you have nothing to say. Often people accomplish turn denying by avoiding eye contact with the speaker (who wishes them now to take on the role of speaker) or by engaging in some behavior that is incompatible with speaking—for example, coughing or blowing their nose.

Backchanneling Cues. People use backchanneling cues to communicate various types of information back to the speaker without assuming the role of the speaker. You can send a variety of messages with backchanneling cues (Burgoon, Buller, & Woodall, 1996; Pearson & Spitzberg, 1990). You can indicate your agreement or disagreement with the speaker through smiles or frowns, gestures of approval or disapproval, brief comments such as "right" or "never," or a vocalization such as *uh-huh*.

You can also indicate your degree of involvement or boredom with the speaker. Attentive posture, forward leaning, and focused eye contact will tell the speaker that you're involved in the conversation—and an inattentive posture, backward leaning, and avoidance of eye contact will communicate your lack of involvement.

Giving the speaker pacing cues helps regulate the speed of speech. You can, for example, ask the speaker to slow down by raising your hand near your ear and leaning forward and to speed up by continuously nodding your head. You can also do this verbally by simply asking the speaker to slow down ("Slow down, I want to make sure I'm getting all this"). Similarly, you can tell the speaker to speed up by saying something like "and—?" or "go on, go on."

A request for clarification is still another function of backchanneling cues. A puzzled facial expression, perhaps coupled with a forward lean, will probably tell most speakers that you want some clarification. Similarly, you can ask for clarification by interjecting some interrogative: "Who?" "When?" "Where?"

Some of these backchanneling cues are actually interruptions. These interruptions, however, are generally confirming rather than disconfirming. They tell the speaker that you are listening and are involved (Kennedy & Camden, 1988).

Figure 9.2 diagrams the various turn-taking cues and shows how they correspond to the conversational wants of speaker and listener.

Reflections on the Model of Conversation

Not all conversations fall neatly into the five-step pattern described earlier. For example, often the opening and the feedforward are combined, as when you see someone on campus and say, "Hey, listen to this," or when in a work situation someone says, "Well, folks, let's get the meeting going." In a

	Conversational Wants	
	To speak	To listen
Speaker	1 Turn-maintaining cues	2 Turn-yielding cues
Listener	3 Turn-requesting cues	4 Turn-denying cues

Figure 9.2
Turn-Taking and Conversational Wants
Quadrant 1 represents the speaker who wants to speak (continue to speak) and uses turn-maintaining cues; quadrant 2, the speaker who wants to listen and uses turn-yielding cues; quadrant 3, the listener who wants to speak and uses turn-requesting cues; and quadrant 4, the listener who wants to listen (continue listening) and uses turn-denying cues. Backchanneling cues would appear in quadrant 4, because they are cues that listeners use while they continue to listen.

similar way, the feedback and the closing may be combined: "Look, I've got to think more about this commitment, okay?"

As already noted, the business is the longest part of the conversation. The opening and the closing are usually about the same length, and the feedforward and feedback are usually about equal in length. When these relative lengths are severely distorted, you may feel that something is wrong. For example, if someone used a long feedforward or a too-short opening, you might suspect that what was to follow was extremely serious.

It's also important to note that effectiveness or competence in conversation and skill in following the appropriate conversational rules will contribute to your own interpersonal attractiveness. For example, researchers studied four conversational skills in 10-year-old girls: making an appropriate request, turn taking, responding without excessive delay when spoken to, and following the logic of the conversation. The girls who demonstrated these skills were liked more and were described in more positive terms than those who lacked these conversational skills (Place & Becker, 1991). Conversational competence is also likely to contribute to the satisfaction or enjoyment you experience when interacting with others.

Of course, each culture will alter the basic conversational steps in different ways. In some cultures the openings are especially short; in others the openings are elaborate, lengthy, and, in some cases, highly ritualized. It's easy in intercultural communication situations to violate another culture's conversational rules. Being overly friendly, too formal, or too forward can easily hinder the remainder of the conversation (Murata, 1994). The reasons such violations can have significant consequences is that people may not be aware of specific conversational rules and hence may see violations not as cultural differences but rather as aggressiveness, stuffiness, or pushiness—and thus may almost immediately dislike the person and put a negative cast on future conversation. Some of the more common conversational problems include:

- Openings that are insensitive; for example, "Wow, you've gained a few pounds!"
- Overly long feedforwards that make you wonder if the other person will ever get to the business.
- Omission of feedforward before a truly shocking message (for example, the death or illness of a friend or relative), which can lead you to see the other person as insensitive or uncaring.
- Introduction of business without the normally expected greeting, as when you go to a doctor who begins the conversation by saying, "Well, what's wrong?"
- Omission of feedback, which leads you to wonder if the other person heard what you said or cared about it.
- Omission of an appropriate closing, which makes you wonder if the other person is disturbed or angry.

How can conversational problems be avoided—or corrected, if they do occur? Many strategies can help. Let's look at one tactic for preventing difficulties (the disclaimer) and one way to repair problems (the excuse).

Preventing Conversational Problems: The Disclaimer

Suppose you fear that your listeners may think that what you're about to say is inappropriate in the present context, or that they may rush to judge you without hearing your full account, or that they may wonder if you're not in full possession of your faculties. In these cases, you may use some form of disclaimer. A **disclaimer** is a statement that aims to ensure that your message will be understood and will not reflect negatively on you.

Think about your own use of disclaimers as you read about these five types (Hewitt & Stokes, 1975; McLaughlin, 1984). *Hedging* helps you to separate yourself from the message so that if your listeners reject your message, they won't reject you (for example, "I may be wrong here, but . . ." or "I didn't read the entire book, but it seems that . . ."). *Credentialing* argues that you should not be disqualified for saying what you're about to say (for example, "Don't get me wrong, I'm not homophobic . . ."). *Sin licenses* ask listeners for permission to deviate in some way from some normally accepted convention (for example, "I know this may not be the place to discuss business, but . . ."). *Cognitive disclaimers* help you make the case that you're in full possession of your faculties (for example, "I know you'll think I'm crazy, but let me explain the logic of the case"). *Appeals for the suspension of judgment* ask listeners to hear you out before making a judgment (for example, "Don't hang up on me until you hear my side of the story").

Disclaimers do work in some situations. For example, disclaimers are generally effective when you think you might offend listeners by telling a joke ("I don't usually like these types of jokes, but . . ."). In one study, 11-year-old children were read a story about someone whose actions created negative effects. Some children heard the story with a disclaimer, and others heard the same story without the disclaimer. When the children were asked to indicate how the person should be punished, those who heard the story with the disclaimer recommended significantly lower punishments (Bennett, 1990).

Disclaimers also can get you into trouble, however. For example, to inappropriately preface remarks with "I'm no liar" may well lead listeners to think that perhaps you are a liar. And if you use too many disclaimers, you may be perceived as someone who doesn't have any strong convictions or who wants to avoid responsibility for just about everything. This seems especially true of hedges.

In responding to statements containing disclaimers, it's often necessary to respond both to the disclaimer and to the statement. By doing so, you let the speaker know that you heard the disclaimer and that

MEDIA WATCH

The Spiral of Silence

The "spiral of silence theory" argues that most people are more likely to voice agreement than disagreement (Noelle-Neumann, 1973, 1980, 1991; Windahl, Signitzer, & Olson, 1992). The theory claims that when a controversial issue arises, you try to estimate public opinion on the issue and figure out which views are popular and which are not, largely by attending to the media (Gonzenbach, King, & Jablonski, 1999; Jeffres, Neuendorf & Atkin, 1999). At the same time, you also judge the likelihood of being punished for expressing minority opinions and the severity of that potential punishment. You then use these estimates to regulate your expression of opinions.

According to this theory, you're more likely to voice your opinions when you agree with the majority than when you disagree. You may avoid expressing minority opinions because you don't want to be isolated from the majority or to confront the unpleasant possibility of being proven wrong. Or you may assume that the majority, because they're a majority, are right.

Not all people seem affected equally by this tendency (Noelle-Neumann, 1991). For example, younger people and men are more likely to express minority opinions than are older people and women. Educated people are more likely to express minority opinions than are those who are less educated. Similarly, the tendency to voice minority opinions will vary from one culture to another (Scheufele & Moy, 2000).

How does the "spiral" effect occur? As people with minority views remain silent, the media position gets stronger, because those who agree with it are the only ones speaking. And as the media's position grows stronger, the silence of the opposition also grows. Thus, the situation becomes an ever-widening spiral.

You and the Media

Do you contribute to this spiral of silence? Do your peers and your family? Does your college provide opportunities for the presentation of minority values, opinions, and beliefs?

you aren't going to view this communication negatively. Appropriate responses might be: "I know you're no sexist, but I don't agree that . . ." or "Well, perhaps we should discuss the money now even if it doesn't seem right."

Repairing Conversational Problems: The Excuse

In Unit 2 we examined the concept of irreversibility—the fact that once something is communicated, it cannot be uncommunicated. In part because of this fact, we need at times to defend or justify messages that may be perceived negatively. Perhaps the most common method for doing so is the excuse (Fraser, 2000). Excuses pervade all forms of communication and behavior. Although this discussion emphasizes their role in conversation, recognize that excuses occur in all forms of communication—interpersonal, group, public, and mass.

You learn early in life that when you do something that will be perceived negatively, an excuse is needed to justify your poor performance. The need for an excuse usually follows from three conditions (Snyder, 1984):

- You say something.
- Your statement is viewed negatively; you desire to disassociate yourself from it.
- Someone hears the message or the results of the message. The "witness" may be an outsider (for example, a boss, a friend, or a colleague) but also could be yourself—you're a witness to your own messages.

More formally, Snyder (1984; Snyder, Higgins, & Stucky, 1983) defines **excuses** as "explanations or actions that lessen the negative implications of an actor's performance, thereby maintaining a positive image for oneself and others."

Excuses seem especially in order when we say or are accused of saying something that runs counter to what is expected, sanctioned, or considered "right" by the people involved or by society in general. The excuse, ideally, lessens the negative impact of the message.

Three kinds of excuses can be identified (Snyder, 1984; Snyder, Higgins, & Stucky, 1983). In the *I didn't do it* type, you claim not to have done the behavior of which you're accused: "I didn't say that." "I wasn't even near the place when it happened." In the *It*

BUILDING COMMUNICATION SKILLS

Formulating Excuses

Although excuses are not always appropriate, they are often helpful in lessening possible negative effects of your mishap. Try formulating an appropriate excuse for any one of the situations listed below, following these five steps (Slade, 1995; Coleman, 2002):

- Demonstrate that you really understand the problem and that your partner's feelings are legitimate and justified.
- Acknowledge your responsibility.
- Acknowledge your own displeasure at what you did.
- Request forgiveness for what you did; be specific.
- Make it clear that this will never happen again.

Situations:

1. Because of some e-mail glitch, other students in your communication class all receive a personal letter you sent to a friend in which you admit to having racist feelings. As you enter class, you hear a group of students discussing your letter. They aren't pleased.
2. Your boss accuses you of making lots of personal long-distance phone calls from work, a practice explicitly forbidden.
3. Your relationship partner catches you in a lie; you weren't at work (as you said you were) but with a former relationship partner.

wasn't so bad type, you claim that the behavior was not really so bad, certainly not as bad as others may at first think: "I only copied one answer." In the *Yes, but* type, you claim that extenuating circumstances accounted for the behavior: "It was the liquor talking." "I really tried to help him; I didn't mean to hurt his feelings."

Some Motives for Excuse Making

The major motive for excuse making seems to be to maintain our self-esteem, to project a positive image to ourselves and to others. Excuses are also offered to reduce the stress that may be created by a bad performance. We feel that if we can offer an excuse—especially a good one that is accepted by those around us—it will lessen the negative reaction and the subsequent stress that accompanies a poor performance.

Anticipatory excuses enable you to take risks and engage in behavior that may be unsuccessful: "My throat's a bit sore, but I'll give the speech a try." The excuse is designed to lessen the criticism should you fail to deliver an acceptable speech.

Excuses also enable us to maintain effective interpersonal relationships even after some negative interaction. For example, after criticizing a friend's behavior and observing the negative reaction to our criticism, we might offer an excuse such as "Please forgive me; I'm really exhausted. I'm just not thinking straight." Excuses enable us to place our messages—even our possible failures—in a more favorable light.

Good and Bad Excuses

To most people the most important question is what makes a good excuse and what makes a bad excuse (Snyder, 1984; Slade, 1995; Schlenker, Pontari, & Christopher, 2001). How can you make good excuses and thus get out of problems, and how can you avoid bad excuses that only make matters worse? Good excuse-makers use excuses in moderation; bad excuse-makers rely on excuses too often. Similarly, unnecessary excuses (which are often disguised attempts to ingratiate yourself) rarely create a positive impression (Levesque, 1995). Good excuse-makers avoid using excuses in the presence of those who know what really happened; bad excuse-makers make excuses even in these inopportune situations. Good excuse-makers avoid blaming others, especially those they work with; bad excuse-makers blame even their work colleagues. In a similar way, good excuse-makers don't attribute their failure to others or to the organization; bad excuse-makers do. Good excuse-makers acknowledge their own responsibility for the failure by noting that they did something wrong; bad excuse-makers refuse to accept any responsibility for their failure.

The best excuses contain five elements (Slade, 1995; Coleman, 2002).

1. You demonstrate that you really understand the problem and that your partner's feelings are legitimate and justified. Avoid minimizing the issue or your partner's feelings ("It was only $100; you're overreacting" or "I was only two hours late").
2. You acknowledge your responsibility. Avoid qualifying your responsibility ("I'm sorry *if* I did anything wrong") or expressing a lack of sincerity ("OK, I'm sorry; it's obviously my fault—*again*").
3. You acknowledge your own displeasure at what you did; make it clear that you're not happy with yourself for having done what you did.
4. You request forgiveness for what you did; be specific.
5. You make it clear that this will never happen again.

Table 9.2 provides examples of how you might incorporate these elements in excuses in romantic and business situations.

The worst excuses are the "I didn't do it" type, because they fail to acknowledge responsibility and offer no assurance that this failure will not happen again.

Conversational Skills

Skill in conversation depends on your ability to make adjustments along a number of dimensions. Recall from Unit 5 that your listening effectiveness depends on your ability to make adjustments between, for example, empathic and objective listening. In a similar way, your effectiveness in conversation depends on your ability to make adjustments along the following specific skill dimensions: openness, empathy, positiveness, immediacy, interaction management, expressiveness, and other orientation. A few general skills, or metaskills, will help you regulate and make the appropriate adjustments in these qualities; let's look first at these.

Metaskills

Four **metaskills** (skills about skills) will prove crucial in helping you adjust and regulate the more specific conversational skills. These general skills are

Table 9.2
Excuses in Romantic and Workplace Relationships

Here are the five intended messages that effective apologies should convey, along with some specific examples. As you read this table, visualize a specific situation in which you recently made an excuse. Can what you said (or should have said) be organized into this five-step structure?

Intended Message	In Romantic Relationships	At Work
1. I see	I should have asked you first; you have a right to be angry.	I understand that we lost the client because of this.
2. I did it	I was totally responsible.	I should have acted differently.
3. I'm sorry	I'm sorry that I didn't ask you first.	I'm sorry I didn't familiarize myself with the client's objections to our last offer.
4. Forgive me	Forgive me?	I'd really like another chance.
5. I'll do better	I'll never lend anyone money without first discussing it with you.	This will never happen again.

mindfulness, flexibility, cultural sensitivity, and metacommunication.

Mindfulness

Mindfulness is a state of awareness in which you're conscious of your reasons for thinking or behaving; its opposite, mindlessness, is a lack of conscious awareness of what or how you're thinking (Langer, 1989). To apply interpersonal skills effectively, become mindful of the unique communication situation you're in, your available communication options, and the reasons why one option is likely to be better than the others (Langer, 1989; Elmes & Gemmill, 1990; Burgoon, Berger, & Waldron, 2000).

Increasing Mindfulness. To increase mindfulness, try the following suggestions (Langer, 1989).

- *Create and recreate categories.* Learn to see objects, events, and especially people as belonging to a wide variety of categories. For example, try to see each person in your life in a variety of roles—as child, parent, employee, neighbor, friend, financial contributor, and so on. Avoid storing in memory an image of any person with only one specific label; if you do, you'll find it difficult to recategorize the person later.
- *Be open to new information and points of view,* even when these contradict your most firmly held beliefs. New information can help you challenge long-held but now inappropriate beliefs and attitudes about, for example, gender, race, or religion. Be willing to see your own and others'

VIEWPOINT

Greetings—whether face-to-face, over the Internet, or on the phone, and whether in speech, gesture, or writing—serve different functions (Knapp & Vangelisti, 2000; Krivonos & Knapp, 1975). For example, greetings may offer access, opening up the channels of communication for more meaningful interaction. Greetings also may reveal important information about a relationship; for example, a big smile and a warm "Hi, it's been a long time" signal that the relationship is still a friendly one. Greetings also may help maintain a relationship. When two workers in an office greet each other as they pass through the office, it assures them that even though they don't stop and talk for an extended period, they still have access to each other. What functions did your last three greetings serve?

ASK THE RESEARCHER

Communicating Support

- *Our 14-year-old son has just told us that he's gay, but he doesn't seem to want to talk about it beyond his recent announcement. We want to help him be whoever he is, comfortably and securely. How can we best accomplish this with our talk? Can you give us any guidelines as to what we might say or what we shouldn't say?*

I applaud you for creating an open environment and nurturing a trusting relationship that allowed him to disclose. Before you offer help, pay attention to your own attitudes and feelings. Homophobic attitudes and beliefs are often deeply buried, and they can be expressed subtly in your tone of voice, facial expressions, posture, questions you ask, assumptions you make. To start a conversation about his recent announcement, I encourage you to acknowledge his disclosure, remind him that he is loved, and explore his feelings by listening actively. You can do this by showing interest, maintaining a feeling of closeness, using positive and encouraging feedback, and avoiding judgments and unsolicited opinions and solutions. Invite him to tell you how you can be most supportive, and let him know that you are open to talk whenever he wishes to do so. Honor his life journey by giving him the time and space to explore his sexuality in his own way.

For further information: Yep, G. A. (2002). From homophobia and heterosexism to heteronormativity: Toward the development of a model of queer interventions in the university classroom. *Journal of Lesbian Studies, 6,* 163–176. And Yep, G. A., Lovaas, K. E., & Elia, J. P. (Eds.). (2003). *Queer theory and communication: From disciplining queers to queering the discipline(s).* New York: Harrington Park Press.

Gust A. Yep (Ph.D., University of Southern California) is professor of speech and communication studies and human sexuality studies at San Francisco State University, where he teaches courses and conducts research in culture, gender, sexuality, and communication. In 1999 Dr. Yep was the San Francisco State University nominee for the Carnegie Foundation "U.S. Professors of the Year" award.

behaviors from the viewpoints of people very different from yourself.

- *Beware of relying too heavily on first impressions* (Chanowitz & Langer, 1981; Langer, 1989). Treat first impressions as tentative, as hypotheses that need further investigation. Be prepared to revise, reject, or accept these initial impressions.

Flexibility

Flexibility is the ability to adjust communication strategies on the basis of the unique situation. One flexibility assessment scale asks you to consider how true you believe certain statements are; for example, "People should be frank and spontaneous in conversation" or "When angry, a person should say nothing rather than say something he or she will be sorry for later." The "preferred" answer to all such questions is "sometimes true," underscoring the importance of flexibility in all interpersonal situations (Hart, Carlson, & Eadie, 1980). For a more extensive test of flexibility, take the self-test below, which will help you learn about your own flexibility.

TEST YOURSELF

How Flexible Are You in Communication?

Here are some situations that illustrate how people sometimes act when communicating with others. The first part of each situation asks you to imagine that you are in the situation; then a course of action is identified, and you are asked to determine how much your own behavior would be like the action described in the scenario. If it is exactly like you, mark a 5; if it is a lot like you, mark a 4; if it is somewhat like you, mark a 3; if it is not much like you, mark a 2; and if it is not at all like you, mark a 1.

Imagine

____ **1.** Last week, as you were discussing your strained finances with your family, family members came up with several possible solutions.

Even though you already decided on one solution, you decided to spend more time considering all the possibilities before making a final decision.

____ **2.** You were invited to a Halloween party, and assuming it was a costume party, you dressed as a pumpkin. When you arrived at the party and found everyone else dressed in formal attire, you laughed and joked about the misunderstanding, and decided to stay and enjoy the party.

____ **3.** You have always enjoyed being with your friend Chris, but do not enjoy Chris's habit of always interrupting you. The last time you met, every time Chris interrupted you, you then interrupted Chris to teach Chris a lesson.

____ **4.** Your daily schedule is very structured and your calendar is full of appointments and commitments. When asked to make a change in your schedule, you replied that changes are impossible before even considering the change.

____ **5.** You went to a party where over 50 people attended. You had a good time, but spent most of the evening talking to one close friend rather than meeting new people.

____ **6.** When discussing a personal problem with a group of friends, you noticed that many different solutions were offered. Although several of the solutions seemed feasible, you already had your opinion and did not listen to any of the alternative solutions.

____ **7.** You and a friend planned a fun evening and you were dressed and ready ahead of time. You found that you are unable to do anything else until your friend arrived.

____ **8.** When you found your seat at the ball game, you realized you did not know anyone sitting nearby. However, you introduced yourself to the people sitting next to you and attempted to strike up a conversation.

____ **9.** You had lunch with your friend Chris, and Chris told you about a too-personal family problem. You quickly finished your lunch and stated that you had to leave because you had a lot to do that afternoon.

____ **10.** You were involved in a discussion about international politics with a group of acquaintances and you assumed that the members of the group were as knowledgeable as you on the topic; but, as the discussion progressed, you learned that most of the group knew little about the subject. Instead of explaining your point of view, you decided to withdraw from the discussion.

____ **11.** You and a group of friends got into a discussion about gun control and, after a while, it became obvious that your opinions differed greatly from the rest of the group. You explained your position once again, but you agreed to respect the group's opinion also.

____ **12.** You were asked to speak to a group you belong to, so you worked hard preparing a 30-minute presentation; but at the meeting, the organizer asked you to lead a question-and-answer session instead of giving your presentation. You agreed, and answered the group's questions as candidly and fully as possible.

____ **13.** You were offered a managerial position where every day you would face new tasks and challenges and a changing day-to-day routine. You decided to accept this position instead of one that has a stable daily routine.

____ **14.** You were asked to give a speech at a Chamber of Commerce breakfast. Because you did not know anyone at the breakfast and would feel uncomfortable not knowing anyone in the audience, you declined the invitation.

HOW DID YOU DO? To compute your score:

1. Reverse the scoring for items 4, 5, 6, 7, 9, 10, and 14. That is, for each of these questions, substitute as follows:
   a. If you answered 5, reverse it to 1.
   b. If you answered 4, reverse it to 2.
   c. If you answered 3, keep it as 3.
   d. If you answered 2, reverse it to 4.
   e. If you answered 1, reverse it to 5.
2. Add the scores for all 14 items. Be sure that you use the reversed scores for items 4, 5, 6, 7, 9, 10, and 14. Use your original scores for items 1, 2, 3, 8, 11, 12, and 13.

   In general, you can interpret your score as follows:
   - 65–70 = much more flexible than average
   - 57–64 = more flexible than average
   - 44–56 = about average
   - 37–43 = less flexible than average
   - 14–36 = much less flexible than average

WHAT WILL YOU DO? Are you satisfied with your level of flexibility? What might you do to cultivate flexibility in general and communication flexibility in particular?

Source: From "Development of a Communication Flexibility Measure" by Matthew M. Martin and Rebecca B. Rubin in *The Southern Communication Journal,* V. 59, Winter 1994, pp. 171–178. Reprinted by permission of the Southern States Communication Association.

Increasing Flexibility. Here are a few ways to cultivate flexibility.

- *Realize that no two situations or people are exactly alike.* Ask yourself what is different about this situation or person, and take differences into consideration as you decide what to say and how to say it.
- *Realize that communication always takes place in a context* (Unit 1); ask yourself what is unique about this specific context and how this uniqueness should influence your messages.
- *Realize that everything is in a state of flux.* The way you communicated last month may have been effective, but that doesn't necessarily mean it will be effective today or tomorrow. Realize, too, that major changes in people's lives (such as the loss of a job or a fatal illness) will influence what are and what are not appropriate messages.
- *Realize that every situation offers you different options* for communicating. Think about these options and try to predict the effects each option might have.

Cultural Sensitivity

Cultural sensitivity, as this book has often emphasized, is an attitude and way of behaving in which you're aware of and acknowledge cultural differences; it's crucial not only on the global level (in efforts for world peace and economic growth) but also for effective interpersonal communication as well as for general personal success (Franklin & Mizell, 1995). Without cultural sensitivity there can be no effective interpersonal communication between people who are different from each other in gender or race or nationality or affective orientation. So be mindful of the cultural differences between yourself and the other person. Remember that the techniques of interpersonal communication that work well with European Americans may not work well with Asian Americans; what proves effective in Japan may not succeed in Mexico. The close physical distance that is normal in Arab cultures may prove too familiar or too intrusive in much of the United States and northern Europe. The empathy that most Americans welcome may be uncomfortable for the average Korean (Yun, 1976).

Increasing Cultural Sensitivity. Here are a few guidelines to follow for achieving greater cultural sensitivity.

- *Prepare yourself.* Read about and listen carefully for culturally influenced behaviors.
- *Recognize and face your own fears* of acting inappropriately with members of different cultures.
- *Recognize differences*: differences between yourself and people of other cultures, among members of the culturally different group, and in meaning (words rarely mean the same thing to members of different cultures).
- *Become conscious of the cultural rules and customs of others.* Resist the temptation to assume that what works in your culture will necessarily work in others.

Metacommunication

Metacommunication, as we saw in Unit 1, is communication that refers to other communications; it's communication about communication. Both verbal and nonverbal messages can be metacommunicational. Verbally, you can say, for example, "Do you understand what I'm trying to say?" Nonverbally, you can hug someone you're consoling.

Interpersonal effectiveness often hinges on the ability to metacommunicate. For example, in conflict situations it's often helpful to talk about the way you fight. In romantic relationships, it's often helpful to talk about what each of you means by "steady" or "really caring." On the job, it's often necessary to talk about the way orders are delegated or the way criticism should be expressed.

Metacommunicating. Here are a few suggestions for increasing your metacommunicational effectiveness.

- *Explain your feelings* along with your thoughts. Often people communicate only the thinking part of their message, with the result that listeners aren't able to appreciate the other parts of their meaning.
- *Give clear feedforward* to help the other person get a general picture of the messages that will follow.
- *Paraphrase.* Paraphrase your own complex messages so as to make your meaning extra clear. Similarly, check on your understanding of another's message by paraphrasing what you think the other person means, then asking if that's what the person meant.
- *Use metacommunication to talk about communication patterns* between yourself and another person. Say, for example, "I'd like to talk about the way you talk about me to our friends" or "I think we should talk about the way we talk about sex."

Specific Skills

The specific skills of conversational effectiveness we'll cover here are are derived from a wide spectrum of ongoing research (Bochner & Kelly, 1974; Wiemann, 1977; Spitzberg & Hecht 1984; Spitzberg & Cupach, 1984, 1989, 2002; Rubin, 1985; Rubin & Graham, 1988; Greene & Burleson, 2003). As you read about these concepts, keep in mind the four general skills or metaskills discussed above.

Openness

Openness has to do with your willingness to self-disclose—to reveal information about yourself that you might normally keep hidden—provided that such disclosure is appropriate (as discussed in Unit 6). Openness also involves your willingness to listen openly and react honestly to the messages of others.

Communicating Openness. Consider these few ideas.

- *Self-disclose when appropriate.* Be mindful about your self-disclosures, remembering that there are both benefits and dangers to this form of intimate communication.
- *Respond to those with whom you're interacting* with spontaneity and with appropriate honesty, but also with an awareness of what you're saying and what the possible outcomes of your messages might be.
- *Own your own feelings and thoughts.* Take responsibility for what you say. Use **I-messages** instead of **you-messages.** Instead of saying, "You make me feel stupid when you don't ask my opinion," own your feelings and say, for example, "I feel stupid when you ask everyone else what they think but don't ask me." When you own your feelings and thoughts—when you use I-messages—you say, in effect, "This is how *I* feel," "This is how *I* see the situation," and "This is what *I* think." When you use I-messages, you make it explicit that your feelings result from the interaction between what is going on outside your skin (what others say, for example) and what is going on inside your skin (your preconceptions, attitudes, and prejudices, for example).

Empathy

Empathy, which we explored in Unit 5, is an ability to feel what another person feels from that person's point of view without losing your own identity. When you empathize, you feel another's feelings in a somewhat similar way; you understand emotionally what another person is experiencing. (To sympathize, in contrast, is to feel *for* the person—to feel sorry or happy for the person, for example.)

Communicating Empathy. Here are a few suggestions to help you communicate empathy effectively (Authier & Gustafson, 1982).

- *Avoid evaluating, judging, or criticizing* the other person's behaviors. Make it clear that you are not evaluating or judging but trying to understand.
- *Focus your concentration.* Maintain eye contact, an attentive posture, and physical closeness. Express your involvement through appropriate facial expressions and gestures.
- *Reflect back to the speaker* the feelings that you think are being expressed so as to check the accuracy of your perceptions and to show your commitment to understanding the speaker. For example, you might make tentative statements such as "You seem really angry with your father" or "I hear some doubt in your voice."
- *When appropriate, use your own self-disclosures* to communicate your understanding. Be careful, however, that you don't get so caught up in your own disclosures that you refocus the discussion on yourself.

Positiveness

Positiveness in interpersonal communication involves the use of positive rather than negative messages. For example, instead of the negative "I wish you wouldn't ignore my opinions," consider the value of the positive alternative: "I feel good when you ask my opinions." Instead of the negative "You look horrible in stripes," consider the value of the positive: "I think you look great in solid colors." Interestingly enough, accumulating research suggests that positiveness in attitude is physically beneficial, making us less susceptible to illness (Goode, 2003).

Communicating Positiveness. Here are just a few suggestions for communicating positiveness. This may be a bit easier for women than for men, because women generally are more apt to express positiveness in their evaluations in both face-to-face and computer-mediated communication (Adrianson, 2001).

- *Look for and compliment the positive* in the person or in the person's work. Compliment specifics; overly general compliments ("Your project was interesting") are rarely as effective as those that are specific and concrete ("Your proposal will mean a great financial saving").
- *Express satisfaction* in interpersonal communication by, for example, using facial expressions,

maintaining a reasonably but appropriately close distance, focusing eye contact, and avoiding glancing away from the other person for long periods of time.

- *Recognize cultural differences* when expressing positiveness (Dresser, 1996; Chen, 1992). For example, in the United States it's considered appropriate for a supervisor to compliment a worker for doing an exceptional job. But in other cultures (collectivist cultures, for example) such praise would be considered inappropriate, because it singles out one individual and separates that person from the group.

Immediacy

Immediacy is a quality of interpersonal effectiveness that creates a sense of togetherness, of oneness between speaker and listener. When you communicate immediacy you show interest and attention; you convey your liking for and attraction to the other person. People respond more favorably to communication that is immediate than to communication that is not. For example, students of instructors who communicated immediacy felt that the instruction was better and the course more valuable than students of instructors who did not communicate immediacy (Moore, Masterson, Christophel, & Shea, 1996; Witt & Wheeless, 2001). Students and teachers liked each other largely on the basis of immediacy (Wilson & Taylor, 2001; Baringer & McCroskey, 2000).

Communicating Immediacy. Here are a few suggestions for communicating immediacy.

- *Express psychological closeness and openness* by, for example, maintaining physical closeness and arranging your body to exclude third parties. Maintain appropriate eye contact, limit looking around at others, smile, and express your interest in the other person.
- *Use the other person's name;* for example, say, "Joe, what do you think?" instead of "What do you think?"
- *Focus on the other person's remarks.* Make the speaker know that you heard and understood what was said, and give the speaker appropriate verbal and nonverbal feedback.
- *Be culturally sensitive when expressing immediacy.* In the United States most people see immediacy behaviors as friendly and appropriate. In other cultures, however, people may view the same immediacy behaviors as overly familiar—as presuming a close relationship when only an acquaintanceship exists (Axtell, 1993).

Interaction Management

Interaction management skills are the techniques and strategies by which you regulate and carry on an interpersonal interaction. Effective interaction management results in an interaction that's satisfying to both parties. Neither person feels ignored or on stage; each contributes to and benefits from the interpersonal exchange.

Managing Communication Interactions. In a sense this entire text is devoted to the effective management of interpersonal interactions. However, here are a few specific suggestions for managing conversations.

- *Maintain conversational turns,* passing the opportunity to speak back and forth through appropriate eye movements, vocal expressions, and body and facial gestures.
- *Keep the conversation fluent*, avoiding long and awkward pauses. For example, it's been found that patients are less satisfied with their interaction with their doctor when the silences between their comments and the doctor's responses are overly long (Rowland-Morin & Carroll, 1990).
- *Communicate with consistent verbal and nonverbal messages*—messages that harmonize and reinforce one another. Avoid sending contradictory signals—for example, a resentful look combined with a verbal expression of thanks.

Expressiveness

Expressiveness is the skill of communicating genuine involvement; it includes abilities such as taking responsibility for your thoughts and feelings, encouraging expressiveness or openness in others, and providing appropriate feedback.

Communicating Expressiveness. Here are a few suggestions for communicating expressiveness.

- *Use appropriate variations* in vocal rate, pitch, volume, and rhythm to convey involvement and interest. Use appropriate variations in verbal language, too; avoid clichés and trite expressions, which can signal a lack of originality and personal involvement.
- *Use appropriate gestures,* especially gestures that focus on the other person rather than yourself. For example, maintain eye contact and lean toward the person; at the same time, avoid making self-touching gestures or directing your eyes to others in the room.
- *Be culturally aware when communicating expressiveness.* Some cultures (Italian and Greek,

for example) encourage expressiveness and teach children to be expressive. Other cultures (Japanese and Thai, for example) encourage a more reserved response style (Matsumoto, 1996). Some cultures (Arab and many Asian cultures, for example) consider expressiveness by women in business settings to be generally inappropriate (Lustig & Koester, 1999; Axtell, 1993; Hall & Hall, 1987).

- *Give verbal and nonverbal feedback* to show that you're listening. Such feedback—called "conversational pitchback" by one researcher—promotes relationship satisfaction (Ross, 1995).

Other-Orientation

Other-orientation is the ability to adapt your messages to the other person. It involves communicating attentiveness and interest in the other person and in what the person says.

Communicating Other-Orientation. You'll recognize the following behaviors in those with whom you enjoy talking.

- *Show consideration and respect*—for example, ask if it's all right to dump your troubles on someone before doing so, or ask if your phone call comes at a good time before launching into your conversation.
- *Acknowledge the other person's feelings as legitimate.* Comments such as "You're right" or "That's interesting" or "I can understand why you're so angry; I would be, too" help focus the interaction on the other person and assure the person that you're listening. At the same time, grant the other person permission to express (or to not express) her or his feelings. A simple statement such as "I know how difficult it is to talk about feelings" opens up the topic of feelings and gives the person permission to pursue such a discussion or to say nothing.
- *Acknowledge the presence and the importance of the other person.* Ask the other person for suggestions and opinions. Similarly, ask for clarification as appropriate. This will ensure that you understand what the other person is saying from that person's point of view.
- *Focus your messages on the other person.* Verbally, use open-ended questions to involve the other person in the interaction (as opposed to questions that merely ask for a yes or no answer) and make statements that directly address the person. Nonverbally, use focused eye contact and appropriate facial expressions; smile, nod, and lean toward the other person.

Gossip

There can be no doubt that we spend a great deal of time gossiping. In fact, **gossip** seems universal among all cultures (Laing, 1993) and among some groups gossip is a commonly accepted ritual (Hall, 1993).

- Gossip involves making social evaluations about a person who is not present during the conversation (Eder & Enke, 1991). Gossip generally occurs when two people talk about a third party.
- People often gossip in order to get some kind of reward; for example, to hear more gossip, gain social status or control, have fun, cement social bonds, or make social comparisons (Rosnow, 1977; Miller & Wilcox, 1986; Leaper & Holliday, 1995).
- Gossiping, however, often leads others to see you more negatively—regardless of whether your gossip is positive or negative or whether you're sharing this gossip with strangers or with friends (Turner, Mazur, Wendel, & Winslow, 2003).

In addition to its negative impact on the gossiper, gossiping often has ethical implications. In many instances gossiping would be considered unethical; for example, when you use it to unfairly hurt another person, when you know it's not true, when no one has the right to such personal information, or when you are breaking a promise of secrecy.

WHAT WOULD YOU DO? Laura and Linda, longtime friends now working in the same company, are competing for the position of sales manager. Laura, Linda knows, has lied on her résumé, claiming that she has had much more experience than she really has—and this claimed experience is likely to land Laura the position over Linda. Laura's lying has not bothered Linda before, but now it's likely to work against her own promotion. Linda wonders if it would be ethical to let it be known, through informal gossip channels, that Laura doesn't really have all the experience she claims to have. If you were Linda, what would you do?

SUMMARY

In this unit we examined the conversation process from opening to closing; the principles of conversational effectiveness; and conversational problems and their prevention and repair.

1. Conversation consists of five general stages: opening, feedforward, business, feedback, and closing.
2. Conversations can be initiated in various ways; for example, with self, other, relational, and context references.
3. The closing of a conversation may be achieved through a variety of methods. For example, you may reflect back on the conversation, as in summarizing; directly state your desire to end the conversation; refer to future interaction; ask for closure; and/or state your pleasure in the interaction.
4. The business of conversation is maintained by the passing of speaking and listening turns; turn-maintaining and turn-yielding cues are used by the speaker, and turn-requesting, turn-denying, and backchanneling cues are used by the listener.
5. One way to avert potential conversational problems is through the disclaimer, a statement that helps ensure that your message will be understood and will not reflect negatively on you.
6. One way to repair a conversational problem is with the excuse, a statement designed to lessen the negative impact of a speaker's messages.
7. The metaskills of conversational effectiveness include mindfulness, flexibility, cultural sensitivity (as appropriate), and metacommunication.
8. Among the skills of conversational effectiveness are openness, empathy, positiveness, immediacy, interaction management, expressiveness, and other-orientation.

KEY TERMS

conversation
leave-taking cues
conversational management
conversational turns
turn-maintaining cues
turn-yielding cues
turn-requesting cues
turn-denying cues
backchanneling cues
disclaimer
excuse
metaskills
mindfulness
flexibility
openness
I-messages
you-messages
positiveness
immediacy
interaction management
expressiveness
other-orientation
gossip

THINKING CRITICALLY ABOUT

Conversation

1. After reviewing the research on the empathic and listening abilities of men and women, Pearson, West, and Turner (1995) conclude: "Men and women do not differ as much as conventional wisdom would have us believe. In many instances, she thinks like a man, and he thinks like a woman because they both think alike." Does your experience support or contradict this observation?
2. Animal researchers have argued that some animals show empathy. For example, consider the male gorilla who watched a female try in vain to get water that had collected in an automobile tire and who then secured the tire and brought it to the female. This gorilla, it has been argued, demonstrated empathy; he felt the other gorilla's thirst (Angier, 1995b). Similarly, the animal that cringes when another of its species gets hurt seems also to be showing empathy. What evidence would you demand before believing that animals possess empathic abilities? What evidence would you want before believing that a relationship partner or a friend feels empathy for you?
3. Although empathy is almost universally considered positive, there is some evidence to show that it has a negative side. For example, people are most empathic with those who are similar—racially and ethnically as well as in appearance and social status. The more empathy we feel toward our own group, the less empathy—possibly even the more hostil-

ity—we feel toward other groups. The same empathy that increases our understanding of our own group decreases our understanding of other groups. So while empathy may encourage group cohesiveness and identification, it can also create dividing lines between "us" and "them" (Angier, 1995b). Have you ever witnessed these negative effects of empathy?

4. Try collecting and analyzing examples of disclaimers from your interpersonal interactions as well as from the media. For example, what type of disclaimer is being used? Why is it being used? Is the disclaimer appropriate? What other kinds of disclaimers could have been used more effectively?

5. If you have access, visit Research Navigator (www.researchnavigator.com) and search the communication, sociological, and psychological databases for an article dealing with some aspect of conversation. What can you learn about conversation and interpersonal communication from this article?

6. Visit one of the many chat groups and lurk for 5 to 10 minutes. What characterizes the conversation on the channel you observe? What is the topic of conversation? What is the most obvious purpose of the group? If possible, try comparing your reactions with those of others who have visited other channels.

7. Another way of looking at conversational rule violations is as breaches of etiquette. When you fail to follow the rules of etiquette, you're often breaking a conversational rule. A variety of websites focus on etiquette in different communication situations. For the etiquette of online conversation, see http://www.internetiquette.org/; for Web etiquette see http://www.w3.org/Provider/Style/Etiquette.html; and for cell phone etiquette see http://www.cell-phone-etiquette.com/index.htm. Visit one or more of these websites and record any rules you find particularly applicable to interpersonal communication and conversation.

8. Research shows that hedging reflects negatively on both men and women when it indicates a lack of certainty or conviction resulting from some inadequacy on the part of the speaker. On the other hand, hedging will be more positively received if listeners feel it reflects the speaker's belief that tentative statements are the only kinds anyone can reasonably make (Wright & Hosman, 1983; Hosman, 1989; Pearson, West, & Turner, 1995). From your experience in using and listening to hedges, do you find this to be true?

9. Review the characteristics of effective conversation and consider each in terms of its role in successful dating. What qualities are especially important? Are there any qualities that don't matter at all?

10. On the basis of your own experience, do you find that people who demonstrate the qualities of effectiveness identified here are also well liked and that people who don't demonstrate these qualities are less well liked? How would you describe the relationship between effective use of interpersonal skills and interpersonal popularity?

11. You've been invited to a colleague's house for dinner. Around two hours before you're scheduled to leave for the dinner, it begins to snow, and your colleague calls to say that you shouldn't feel you have to come to dinner in the snow; the roads may get dangerous. The snow is only a light dusting, and your SUV would have no trouble getting there. You wonder what your colleague was really saying—whether it's "I'd like to cancel the dinner and I'm using the snow as an excuse" or "I'm concerned about your safety and I don't want you to travel in potentially dangerous weather just because of this dinner; the dinner is no big deal." What do you say?

12. For 6,000 yen a month (about $70) a Japanese cable radio network provides listeners with several "excuse" stations. These stations broadcast background noise such as the sound of a train station, coffee shop, or telephone booth. Thus, when you want to have someone believe you're at a train station, you can play the radio while you're on the phone to say that you can't be home on time (*New York Times Magazine,* July 16, 1995, p. 8). What do you think of this service? Would you subscribe to it? Would you invest money in it? Would it be more popular with one sex than the other? Would it be more popular in some cultures than in others?

13. Not surprisingly, each culture has its own conversational taboos—topics that should be avoided, especially by visitors from other cultures. A few examples: In Norway avoid talk of salaries and social status; in Spain avoid discussing family, religion, or jobs, and don't make negative comments on bullfighting; in Egypt avoid talk of Middle Eastern politics; in Japan avoid talking about World War II; in the Philippines avoid talk of politics, religion, corruption, and foreign aid; in Mexico avoid talking about the Mexican-American war and illegal aliens; in the Caribbean avoid discussing race, local politics, and religion (Axtell, 1993). Do you consider some topics taboo? In particular, are there topics that you do not want members of other cultures to talk about? Why?

14. In an analysis of 43 published studies on interruptions and gender differences, men interrupted significantly more than women (Anderson, 1998). Among the reasons offered to explain why men interrupt more is men's desire to shift the focus to areas of their competence (and away from areas of incompetence) and to maintain power and control. Do you find that your own experience supports these findings on gender differences in interrupting? Based on your experiences, how would you explain the reasons for interrupting?

15. What other suggestions could you offer for improving communication between people who do and do not have speech and language disorders?

UNIT

10

Interpersonal Relationships

UNIT CONTENTS

Much of your life is focused on relationships; friendships, romantic relationships, and family relationships occupy an enormous part of your day-to-day thoughts and experiences. In this unit you'll learn

- how relationships can develop, be maintained, deteriorate, and be repaired
- how you can make your relationships more satisfying and more productive

Interpersonal relationships come in a variety of forms. Although the romantic relationship perhaps comes to mind most quickly, interpersonal relationships exist between friends, between mentors and protégés, between family members, and between work team colleagues, to mention a few examples. The quality that makes a relationship interpersonal is interdependency: The actions of one person have consequences for the other person. The actions of a stranger (for example, working overtime or flirting with a coworker) will have no impact on you; you and the stranger are independent, and your actions have no impact on each other. If, however, you were in an interpersonal relationship and your partner worked overtime or flirted with a coworker, it would have an effect on you and on the relationship in some way. For additional insight into what defines a relationship as interpersonal, see the Understanding Theory and Research box on page 160).

You establish your interpersonal relationships in stages. You don't become intimate friends with someone immediately upon meeting. Rather, you grow into an intimate relationship gradually, through a series of steps—from the initial contact, through intimacy, and perhaps on to dissolution. And the same is probably true with most other relationships as well.

In all, six major stages are identifiable (see Figure 10.1): (1) contact, (2) involvement, (3) intimacy, (4) deterioration, (5) repair, and (6) dissolution. Each stage can be divided into an early and a late phase, as noted in the diagram. For each specific relationship, you might wish to modify and revise the basic model in various ways. As a general description of relationship development, however, the stages seem fairly standard. These stages occur in all interpersonal relationships—whether developed and maintained through face-to-face interaction or through Internet hookups.

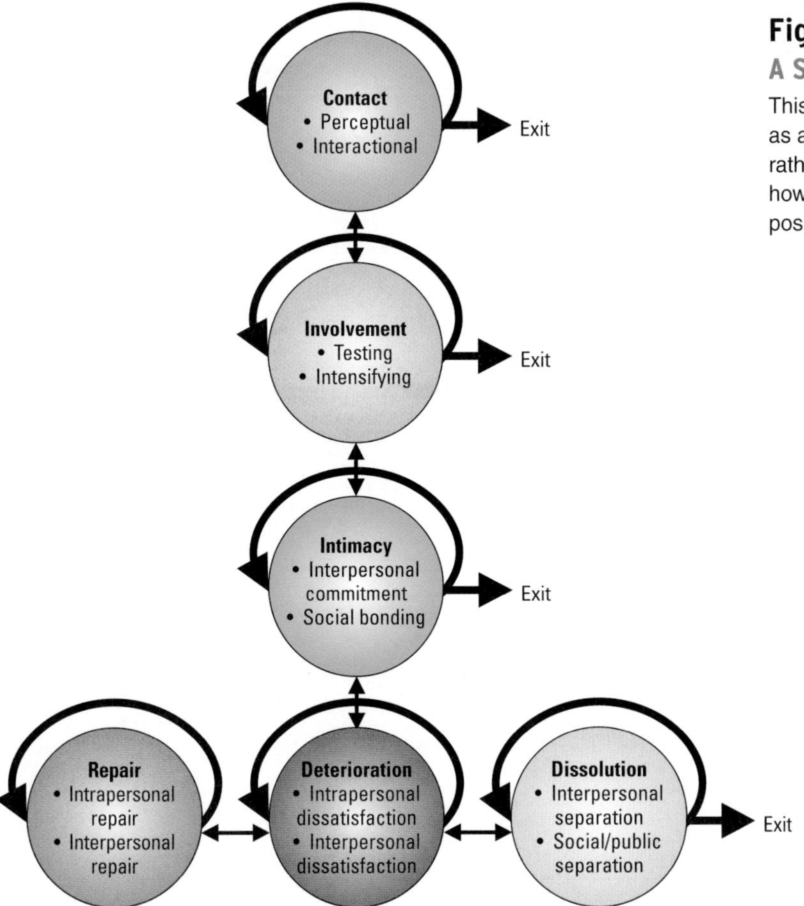

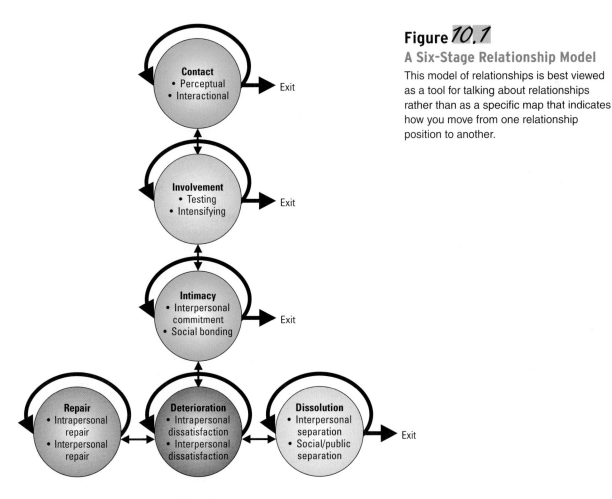

Figure 10.1
A Six-Stage Relationship Model
This model of relationships is best viewed as a tool for talking about relationships rather than as a specific map that indicates how you move from one relationship position to another.

Movement is depicted in Figure 10.1 by the different types of arrows. The exit arrows show that each stage offers the opportunity to exit the relationship. After saying "hello" you can say "goodbye" and exit. The vertical movement arrows going to the next stage and back again represent the fact that you can move to another stage, either one that is more intense (say, from involvement to intimacy) or one that is less intense (say, from intimacy to deterioration). The self-reflexive arrows—the arrows that return to the beginning of the same level or stage—signify that any relationship may become stabilized at any point. You may, for example, continue to maintain a relationship at the intimate level without its deteriorating or going back to a less intense stage of involvement. Or you might remain at the "Hello, how are you?" stage—the contact stage—without getting any further involved.

Movement to a stage that you prefer to the stage you're at now will depend largely on your communication skills—your abilities to initiate relationships, to present yourself as likable, to express affection, to

GOING *ONLINE*

Interpersonal Relationships

http://novaonline.nvcc.edu/eli/spd110td/interper/index.html

This useful website offers additional online information about interpersonal communication and specifically about interpersonal relationships.

In addition, visit the companion website for this text (www.ablongman.com/devito). It contains a variety of materials relevant to this unit, including four self-tests on beliefs about relationships, the type of relationship you prefer, romanticism, and relationship commitment as well as several exercises and discussions: "Making Relationship Predictions," "Repairing Relationships," "Relationship Theories and Relationship Movement," "The Needs Friendships Serve," "Stages and Communication in Friendship Development," "Culture, Gender, and Friendship," "Culture, Gender, and Love," "Other Views of Love," "Family Rules," "Family Communication Patterns," "A POSITIVE Communication Approach to Relationship Effectiveness," "Analyzing Stage Talk," "Til This Do Us Part," "Interpersonal Relationships in Songs and Cards," "Relationship Repair from Advice Columnists," "Getting Someone to Like You," "Mate Preferences," and "The Television Relationship."

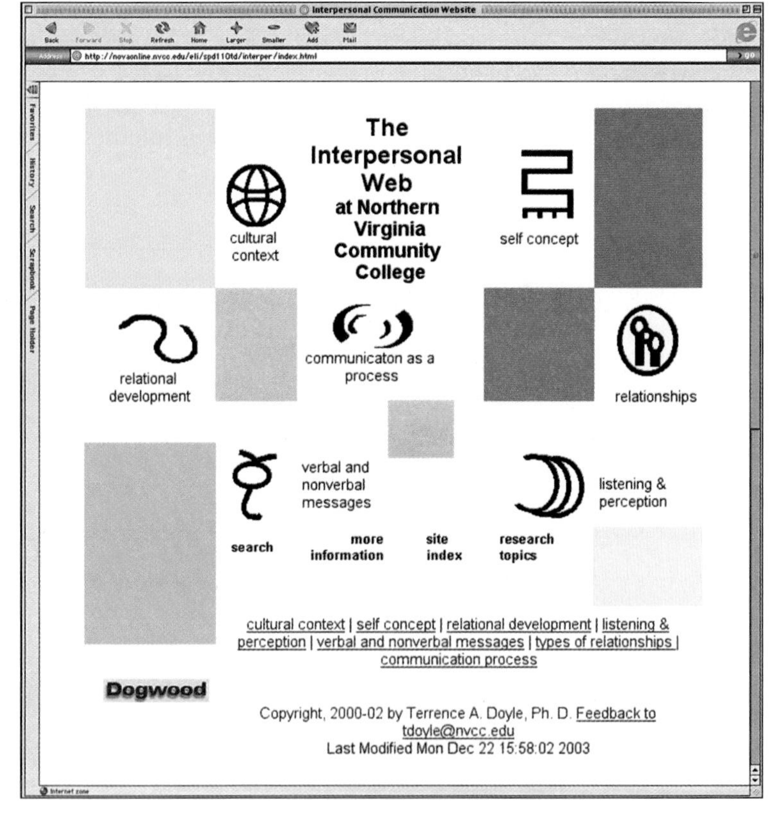

self-disclose appropriately, and in fact all the communication skills you've been acquiring throughout this course (cf. Dindia & Timmerman, 2003).

Relationship Processes

Relationships are living things; they're forever changing, sometimes for the good and sometimes not. In this section we look at the major processes involved in interpersonal relationships:

- development—the contact, involvement, and intimacy stages shown in the six-stage model in Figure 10.1
- maintenance, in which you stay at or maintain a certain level of involvement, neither advancing toward more intimacy nor moving toward deterioration
- deterioration, in which the bonds holding you together begin to wear thin and dissatisfaction sets in and which may progress to dissolution and the end of the relationship
- repair, in which you attempt to change (correct, improve) the relationship as well as to nurture yourself

Relationship Development

There's probably nothing as important to most people as contact with others. So important is this contact that when it's absent for prolonged periods, depression sets in, self-doubt surfaces, and people find it difficult to conduct even the basics of daily living. **Relationship development** includes the initial contact stage as well as increasing **involvement** and **intimacy.**

Reasons for Relationship Development

Each person pursues a relationship for unique reasons, of course. Yet there are also some general reasons for developing relationships: to lessen loneliness, to secure stimulation, to acquire self-knowledge, and to maximize pleasures and minimize pain.

Think about the development of your own relationships as you read on. Are the reasons described here adequate to explain why you've developed the relationships you did? Are there other reasons that motivated your relationships that are not noted here?

One reason we enter relationships is that contact with another human being helps lessen loneliness. It doesn't always, of course. At times, for example, you may experience loneliness even though you're with other people. And at other times you don't feel lonely even when physically alone (Perlman & Peplau, 1981). Yet generally, contact with other people helps lessen the uncomfortable feelings of loneliness (Peplau & Perlman, 1982; Rubenstein & Shaver, 1982).

Human beings need stimulation, and interpersonal relationships provide one of the best ways to get this stimulation. Because you are in part an intellectual creature and need intellectual stimulation, you talk about ideas, attend classes, and argue about different interpretations of a film or novel. Because you're also a physical creature and need physical stimulation, you touch and are touched, hold and are held. Because you're an emotional creature and need emotional stimulation, you laugh and cry, feel hope and surprise, and experience warmth and affection. Such stimulation comes most easily within an interpersonal relationship—a friendship, love, or family relationship.

It's largely through contact with other human beings that you gain self-knowledge. As noted in the discussion of self-awareness (Unit 6), you see yourself in part through the eyes of others. And those with the best eyesight are usually your friends, lovers, or family members.

The most general reason to establish relationships, and one that could include all the others, is that we seek human contact to maximize our pleasures and minimize our pains. Most people want to share with others both their good fortune and their emotional or physical pain. Our first impulse, when something extreme happens (positive or negative), is often to talk about it to a relationship partner.

Initiating Relationships: The First Encounter

Perhaps the hardest and yet the most important aspect of relationship development is the beginning. Meeting the person, presenting yourself, and somehow moving to another stage is a difficult process. Three major phases can be identified in the first encounter: examining the qualifiers, determining clearance, and communicating your desire for contact.

Your first step is to examine the *qualifiers,* those qualities that make the individual you wish to meet an appropriate choice (Davis, 1973). Some qualifiers are obvious, such as beauty, style of clothes, jewelry, and the like. Others are hidden, such as personality, health, wealth, talent, and intelligence. These qualifiers tell you something about who the person is and help you to decide if you wish to pursue this initial encounter.

Your second step is to determine *clearance*—to see if the person is available for the type of meeting you're interested in (Davis, 1973). If you're hoping for a date, then you might look to see if the person is wearing a wedding ring. Does the person seem to be waiting for someone else?

The next stage is to make *contact*. You need to open the encounter nonverbally and verbally. Nonverbally you might signal this desire for contact in a variety of ways. Here are just a few things you might do:

- Establish eye contact. The eyes communicate awareness of and interest in the other person.
- While maintaining eye contact, smile and further signal your interest in and positive response to the other person.
- Concentrate your focus. Nonverbally shut off from your awareness the rest of the room. Be careful, however, that you don't focus so directly that you make the person uncomfortable.
- Establish physical closeness, or at least lessen the physical distance between the two of you. Approach the other person, though not to the point of discomfort, so your interest in making contact is obvious.
- Maintain an open posture. Throughout the encounter, maintain a posture that communicates a willingness to enter into interaction with the other person. Hands crossed over the chest or clutched around your stomach communicate a closedness, an unwillingness to let others enter your space.
- Reinforce the positive behaviors of the other person so as to signal continued interest and a further willingness to make contact. Again, nod, smile, or somehow communicate your favorable reaction.

Although nonverbal contact is signaled first, much of the subsequent nonverbal contact takes place at the same time that you're communicating verbally. Here are some methods for making verbal contact:

- Introduce yourself. Try to avoid trite opening lines such as "Haven't I seen you here before?" It's best simply to say, "Hi, my name is Pat."
- Focus the conversation on the other person. Get the other person talking about himself or herself. No one enjoys talking about any topic more than this one. Also, you'll gain an opportunity to learn something about the person you want to get to know. For example, hidden qualifiers or disqualifiers, such as intelligence or the lack of it, will begin to emerge.
- Exchange favors and rewards. Compliment the other person. If you can't find anything to compliment, then you might want to reassess your interest in this person.
- Stress the positives. Positiveness contributes to a good first impression, simply because people are more attracted to positive than to negative people.
- Avoid self-disclosures that are negative or too intimate. Enter a relationship gradually and gracefully. Disclosures should come slowly and should be reciprocal (see Unit 6). Anything too intimate or too negative, when revealed too early in the relationship, will create a negative image. If you can't resist self-disclosing, try to stick to the positives and to issues that are not overly intimate.
- Establish commonalities. Seek to discover in your interaction those things you have in common with the other person—attitudes, interests, personal qualities, third parties, places—anything that will stress a connection.

Relationship Maintenance

Relationship maintenance consists of the relationship processes in which you act to keep the relationship

- *intact*—to retain the semblance of a relationship, to prevent completely dissolving the relationship
- *at its present stage*—to prevent it from moving too far toward either less or more intimacy
- *satisfying*—to maintain a favorable balance between rewards and penalties

Some people, after entering a relationship, assume that the relationship will continue unless something catastrophic happens. And so, although they may seek to prevent any major mishaps, they're unlikely to engage in much maintenance behavior. Others will be ever on the lookout for something wrong and will seek to patch up any difficulties as quickly and as effectively as possible. In between lie most people, who will engage in maintenance behaviors when things are going wrong and when there's the possibility that the relationship can be improved. Behaviors directed at improving badly damaged or even broken relationships are considered under the topic of "repair," later in this unit.

Reasons for Maintaining a Relationship

The most obvious reason for maintaining a relationship is that the individuals have an emotional attachment; they like or love each other and want to preserve their relationship. They don't see potential alternative partnerships as inviting or as potentially enjoyable—the individuals' needs are being satisfied, so the relationship is maintained.

Often a relationship involves neither great love nor great need satisfaction but is maintained for rea-

UNDERSTANDING *THEORY* AND *RESEARCH*

Relationship Commitment

An important factor influencing the course of relationship deterioration (as well as relationship maintenance) is the degree of *commitment* the individuals have toward each other and toward the relationship. Three types of commitment are often distinguished and can be identified from your answers to the following questions (Johnson, 1973, 1982, 1991; Knapp & Taylor, 1995; Kurdek, 1995):

- Do I *want* to stay in this relationship? Do I have a desire to keep this relationship going?
- Do I have a moral *obligation* to stay in this relationship?
- Do I have to stay in this relationship? Is it a *necessity* for me to stay in this relationship?

All relationships are held together, in part, by want, obligation, or necessity or by some combination of these elements. The strength of the relationship, including its resistance to possible deterioration, is related to the degree of commitment. When a relationship shows signs of deterioration and yet there's a strong commitment to preserving it, the individuals may well surmount the obstacles and reverse the process. In contrast, when commitment is weak and the individuals doubt that there are good reasons for staying together, the relationship deteriorates faster and more intensely.

Working with Theories and Research

- *Has commitment or the lack of it (from either or both of you) ever influenced the progression of one of your relationships? What happened?*

sons of convenience. Perhaps the partners may jointly own a business or may have mutual friends who are important to them. In these cases it may be more convenient to stay together than to break up and go through the difficulties involved in finding another person to live with or another business partner or another social escort. Another factor is children; relationships are often maintained, rightly or wrongly, because children are involved.

Fear motivates many couples to stay together. The individuals may fear the outside world; they may fear being alone and facing others as "singles." As a result they may elect to preserve their current relationship as the better alternative. Sometimes the fear concerns the consequences of violating some religious or parental tenet that tells you to stay together, no matter what happens.

Financial advantages motivate many couples to stick it out. Divorces and separations are expensive both emotionally and financially. Some people fear a breakup that may cost them half their wealth or even more. And, depending on where the individuals live and their preferred lifestyle, being single can be expensive.

A major reason for the preservation of many relationships is inertia. In physics inertia is defined as the tendency for a body at rest to remain at rest and for a body in motion to remain in motion. In terms of relationships, many people simply go along with the program, and it hardly occurs to them to consider changing their status; change seems too much trouble. Inertia is greatly aided by the media and the Internet. That is, it's easier for many individuals to remain in their present relationship and to seek vicarious satisfactions from television dramas or chat room interactions than to act to change their circumstances.

Maintenance Strategies

Among the most significant **maintenance strategies** used in relationships are those of **relational communication.** The kind of relational communication that effectively helps maintain a relationship is the same as that described for effective conversation in Unit 9: It is open, empathic, positive, immediate, managed effectively, expressive, and other-oriented, and it is performed mindfully, flexibly, and with cultural sensitivity. Add to these qualities the skills of appropriate self-disclosure, active listening, and confirmation—and in fact all the skills considered throughout this text—and you have a pretty comprehensive list of potentially useful communication tools for maintaining a relationship.

Other maintenance strategies include the following (Ayres, 1983; Canary & Stafford, 1994a, 1994b;

Dindia & Baxter, 1987; Canary, Stafford, Hause, & Wallace, 1993; Dainton & Stafford, 1993; Guerrero, Eloy, & Wabnik, 1993):

- *Prosocial behaviors:* Being polite, cheerful, and friendly; avoiding criticism; and compromising even when it involves self-sacrifice. Prosocial behaviors also include talking about a shared future; for example, talking about planning a future vacation or buying a house together.
- *Ceremonial behaviors:* Celebrating birthdays and anniversaries, discussing past pleasurable times, and eating at a favorite restaurant.
- *Communication behaviors:* Calling just to say, "How are you?," talking about the honesty and openness in the relationship, and talking about shared feelings. Responding constructively in a conflict (even when your partner may act in ways harmful to the relationship) is another type of communicative maintenance strategy (Rusbult & Buunk, 1993).
- *Togetherness behaviors:* Spending time together visiting mutual friends, doing specific things as a couple, and sometimes just being together with no concern for what is done. Controlling extra-relational activities constitutes another type of togetherness behavior (Rusbult & Buunk, 1993).
- *Assurance behaviors:* Assuring the other of the significance of the relationship; for example, comforting each other, putting the partner first, and expressing love for the person.
- *Sharing joint activities:* Spending time with the other; for example, playing ball together, going to events together, simply talking, or even cleaning the house together.
- *Using social networks:* Relying on friends and relatives for support and help with various problems.

Researchers have also identified such strategies as openness (engaging in direct discussion); humor (making jokes or teasing the other); talk (engaging in small talk and establishing specific times for talking); affection, including sexual intimacy (acting affectionately and romantically); and focus on self (making oneself look good) (Canary, Stafford, Hause, & Wallace, 1993; Dainton & Stafford, 1993).

Relationship Deterioration

The opposite end of relationship development is **deterioration** and possible dissolution. Relational deterioration, the weakening of the bonds that hold people together, may be gradual or sudden, slight or extreme. Murray Davis (1973), in his book *Intimate Relations,* uses the terms "passing away" to designate gradual deterioration and "sudden death" to designate abrupt deterioration. An example of passing away occurs when one of the parties develops close ties with a new intimate and this new relationship gradually pushes out the old. An example of sudden death occurs when one or both of the parties break a rule that was essential to the relationship (for example, the rule of fidelity). As a result, both realize that the relationship must be terminated immediately.

Although you may be accustomed to thinking of relationship breakup as negative, this is not necessarily so. If a relationship is unproductive for one or both parties, a breakup may be the best thing that could happen. The end of a relationship may provide an opportunity for the individuals to regain their independence and self-reliance. Some relationships are so absorbing that there's little time for the partners to reflect about themselves, others, and the relationship itself. In these cases, distance often helps. For the most part, it's up to you to draw from any decaying relationship some positive characteristics and some learning that can be used later on.

Causes of Relationship Deterioration

The causes of **relationship deterioration** are as numerous as the individuals involved. All these causes also may be seen as effects of relational deterioration. For example, when things start to go sour, the individuals may remove themselves physically from each other in response to the deterioration. This physical separation may in turn cause further deterioration by driving the individuals farther apart emotionally and psychologically. Or it may encourage them to seek other partners. Gossip and news items frequently note what might be called "relationship addiction": a tendency among some people to move rapidly from one relationship to another to another. Exactly how widespread this is hasn't been documented. But some researchers have argued that anonymity, convenience, and ease of escape (ACE) make these fleeting relationships especially easy to enter, and that such encounters can take up a significant part of a person's relationship life (Young et al., 2000).

When the reasons you developed the relationship change drastically, your relationship may deteriorate. For example, when loneliness is no longer lessened, the relationship may be on the road to decay. When the stimulation is weak, one or both may begin to look elsewhere. If self-knowledge and self-growth prove insufficient, you may become dissatisfied with yourself, your partner, and your relationship. When the pains (costs) begin to exceed the pleasures (rewards), you begin to look for ways to exit the relationship—or, in some cases, for ways to improve or repair it.

Relational changes in one or both parties may encourage relational deterioration. Psychological changes such as the development of different intellectual interests or incompatible attitudes may create relational problems. Behavioral changes such as preoccupation with business or schooling may strain the relationship and create problems. Status changes also may create difficulties for a couple.

Sometimes one or both parties have unrealistic expectations. This often occurs early in a relationship—when, for example, many individuals think that they will want to spend all their time together. When they discover that both of them need more "space," each may resent this "lessening" of feeling in the other. The resolution of such conflicts lies not so much in meeting these unrealistic expectations as in discovering why they were unrealistic and substituting more attainable expectations.

Few sexual relationships are free of sexual difficulties. In fact, sexual problems rank among the top three problems in almost all studies of newlyweds (Blumstein & Schwartz, 1983). Although sexual frequency is not related to relational breakdown, sexual satisfaction is. It's the quality and not the quantity of a sexual relationship that is crucial. When the quality is poor, the partners may seek sexual satisfaction outside the primary relationship. Extrarelational affairs contribute significantly to breakups for all couples, whether married or cohabiting, whether heterosexual or homosexual. Even "open relationships"—ones that are based on sexual freedom outside the primary relationship—experience these problems and are more likely to break up than the traditional "closed" relationship.

Unhappiness with work often leads to difficulties in relationships. Most people can't separate problems with work from their relationships (Blumstein & Schwartz, 1983). This is true for all types of couples. With heterosexual couples (both married and cohabiting), if the man is disturbed over the woman's job—for example, if she earns a great deal more than he does or devotes a great deal of time to the job—the relationship is in for considerable trouble. And this is true whether the relationship is in its early stages or is well established. One research study, for example, found that husbands whose wives worked were less satisfied with their own jobs and their own lives than were men whose wives did not work (Staines, Pottick, & Fudge, 1986). Often the man expects the woman to work but does not reduce his expectations concerning her household responsibilities. The man may become resentful if the woman does not fulfill these expectations, and the woman may become resentful if she takes on both outside work and full household duties.

In surveys of problems among couples, financial difficulties loom large. Money is seldom discussed by couples beginning a relationship—yet it proves to be one of the major problems faced by all couples as they settle into their relationship. Dissatisfaction with money usually leads to dissatisfaction with the relationship. This is true for married and cohabiting heterosexual couples and gay male couples. It's not true for lesbian couples, who seem to care a great deal less about financial matters. This difference has led some researchers to speculate that tendencies to equate money with power and relational satisfaction represent largely male attitudes (Blumstein & Schwartz, 1983).

Money also creates problems in heterosexual relationships because men and women view it differently. To many men, money is power. To women, it more often means security and independence. Such different perceptions can easily precipitate conflicts over how a couple's money is to be spent or invested (Blumstein & Schwartz, 1983).

Communication in Relationship Deterioration

Like relational development, relational deterioration involves unique and specialized communication. These communication patterns are in part a response to the deterioration itself. However, these patterns are also causative; that is, the way you communicate influences the course of a relationship. Such patterns include nonverbal and verbal withdrawal, a decline in self-disclosure, increased deception, increases in negativity and conflict, and declines in exchanges of favors and compliments.

Nonverbally, **withdrawal** is seen in the greater space each person seems to require and the ease with which tempers are aroused when that space is encroached on. When people are close emotionally, they can comfortably occupy close physical quarters; when they're growing apart, they need wider spaces. Withdrawal of another kind may be seen in a decrease in similarities in clothing and in a decline in the display of "intimate trophies" such as bracelets, photographs, and rings (Knapp & Vangelisti, 2000). Other nonverbal signs include failure to engage in eye contact, to look at each other generally, or to touch each other (Miller & Parks, 1982).

Verbally, withdrawal is seen in many different forms. Where once there was a great desire to talk and listen, there's now less desire—perhaps none. At times people engage in small talk as an end in itself. Whereas small talk is usually a preliminary to serious conversation, here it's used as an alternative to or a means of forestalling serious talk. Thus people in the throes of dissolution may talk a great deal about insignificant events—the weather, a movie on television, a neighbor down the hall. This way they avoid confronting serious issues.

Self-disclosure declines significantly when a relationship deteriorates. Self-disclosure may not be thought worth the effort if the relationship is dying. Or people also may limit self-disclosures because they feel that their partner will not be supportive or may use the disclosures against them. Probably the most general reason is that people no longer have a desire to share intimate thoughts and feelings with someone for whom their positive feelings are decreasing.

Deception generally increases as relationships break down. Lies may be seen as a way to avoid arguments—such as quarrels over staying out all night, not calling, or being seen in the wrong place with the wrong person. At other times people use lies because of some feeling of shame. Perhaps you want to save the relationship and don't want to add another obstacle or to appear to be the cause of any further problems, so you lie. Sometimes deception takes the form of avoidance—the lie of omission. You talk about everything except the crux of the difficulty. Whether by omission or commission, deception has a way of escalating and creating a climate of distrust and disbelief.

Relational deterioration often brings an increase in negative evaluations and a decrease in positive evaluations. Where once you praised the other's behaviors, talents, or ideas, you now criticize them. Often the behaviors have not changed significantly. What has changed is your way of looking at them. Negative evaluation frequently leads to outright fighting and conflict. And although conflict is not necessarily bad (see Unit 13), in relationships that are deteriorating, unresolved conflict (often coupled with withdrawal) frequently adds to the partners' problems.

Finally, during relational deterioration there's little favor exchange. Compliments, once given frequently and sincerely, are now rare. Positive stroking is minimal. Positive nonverbal behaviors such as eye contact, smiling, touching, caressing, and holding each other occur less frequently.

Relationship Repair

When a relationship begins to deteriorate, you may wish to try to save it by repairing the problems and differences. Sometimes, too, you'll suffer emotional damage from relationships and may need to repair yourself. Each of these types of **relationship repair** is considered here.

Interpersonal Repair

If you wish to salvage a relationship, you may try to do so by changing your communication patterns and, in effect, putting into practice the insights and skills learned in this course. You can look at the strategies for interpersonal repair in terms of the following six suggestions, which conveniently spell out the word REPAIR:

- Recognize the problem
- Engage in productive conflict resolution
- Propose possible solutions
- Affirm each other
- Integrate solutions into normal behavior
- Risk

Your first step is to *recognize the problem* both intellectually and emotionally. Specify what is wrong with your present relationship (in concrete, specific terms) and what changes would be needed to make it better (again, in specific terms). Without this first step there's little hope for improving any interpersonal relationship. It sometimes helps to create a picture of your relationship as you would want it to be and to compare that picture to the way the relationship looks now. You can then specify the changes that would have to take place to transform the present picture into the idealized picture.

Engage in productive conflict resolution. Interpersonal conflict is an inevitable part of relationship life. It's not so much the conflict that causes relationship difficulties but rather the way in which the conflict is pursued. If the partners confront a conflict by means of productive strategies, the conflict may be resolved and the relationship may actually emerge stronger and healthier. If, on the other hand, the partners use unproductive and destructive strategies, the relationship may well deteriorate further. Because this topic is so crucial, Unit 13 is devoted exclusively to the process of conflict and especially to the ways people can engage in productive interpersonal conflict.

After the problem is identified, *propose possible solutions* to identify ways to lessen or eliminate the difficulty. Look for solutions that will enable both of you to win. Try to avoid "solutions" whereby one person wins and the other person loses; in such circumstances resentment and hostility are likely to fester. The suggestions offered in Unit 11's discussion of problem-solving groups are especially applicable to this phase of relationship repair.

It should come as no surprise that happily married couples *affirm each other.* That is, they engage in greater positive behavior exchange—they communicate more agreement, approval, and positive affect—

than do unhappily married couples (Dindia & Fitzpatrick, 1985). Clearly, these behaviors result from the positive feelings these spouses have for each other. But it can also be argued that these expressions help to increase the positive regard that each person has for his or her partner. Other affirming messages include the exchange of favors, compliments, positive stroking, and all the nonverbals that say "I care."

Often solutions that are reached after an argument are followed for only a very short time; then the couple goes back to its previous unproductive behavior patterns. Instead, ***integrate solutions into your normal behavior*** so that the solutions become integral to your everyday relationship interactions. Favors, compliments, and cherishing behaviors need to become a part of everyday communication.

Risk. Take risks in trying to improve your relationship. Risk giving favors without any certainty of reciprocity. Risk rejection; make the first move to make up or say you're sorry. Be willing to change, to adapt, and to take on new tasks and responsibilities. And, of course, be willing to try new and different communication strategies.

Self-Repair

Of course, some relationships end. Sometimes there's simply not enough to hold the couple together or there are problems that can't be resolved. Sometimes the costs are too high and the rewards too few, or the relationship is recognized as destructive and escape seems the only alternative. Given the inevitability that some relationships will end in **dissolution,** *self-repair* is an important concept—because the end of a relationship (whether between friends or lovers or through death, separation, or relationship breakup) often brings significant

BUILDING COMMUNICATION SKILLS

Repairing Relationships

Whether expert or novice, each of us tries to repair relationships—not only our own but also those of others. Here are three situations that call for repair. Can you use what you've read about here (as well as your own experiences, readings, observations, and so on) to come up with some reasonable repair advice? What specific suggestions would you offer to each of the people in these situations?

1. *Friends and colleagues:* Mike and Jim, friends for 20 years, have had a falling out over the fact that Mike supported another person for promotion over Jim. Jim is resentful and feels that Mike should have helped him; Mike's support would have ensured Jim's getting the promotion and a good raise, which Jim and his large family could surely use. Mike feels that his first obligation was to the company and that he chose the person he believed would do the best job. Mike feels that if Jim resents him and can't understand or appreciate his motives, then he no longer cares to be friends. Assuming that both Mike and Jim want the friendship to continue or will at some later time, what do you suggest that Mike do? What do you suggest that Jim do?
2. *Coming out:* Tom, a junior in college, recently came out as gay to his family. Contrary to his every expectation, they went ballistic. His parents want him out of the house, and his two brothers refuse to talk with him. In fact, Tom's family now refer to him only in the third person, and when they do speak of him it is with derogatory hate speech. Assuming that all parties will be sorry at some later time if the relationship is not repaired, what would you suggest that Tom's mother and father do? What do you suggest that Tom's brothers do? What do you suggest that Tom do?
3. *Betraying a confidence:* Pat and Chris have been best friends since elementary school. Even now, in their twenties, they speak every day and rely on each other for emotional and sometimes financial support. Recently Pat betrayed a confidence and told several mutual friends that Chris had been having emotional problems and had been considering suicide. Chris found out and no longer wants to maintain the friendship; in fact, Chris refuses even to talk with Pat. Assuming that the friendship is more good than bad and that both parties will regret it if they don't patch up the friendship, what do you suggest that Pat do? What do you suggest that Chris do?

emotional problems and may actually create as much pain as can physical injuries (Eisenberger, Lieberman, & Williams, 2003). Here are some suggestions for self-repair.

Break the loneliness-depression cycle. Loneliness and depression, the two feelings experienced most after the end of a relationship, are serious. Depression, for example, may lead to physical illness. Ulcers, high blood pressure, insomnia, stomach pains, and sexual difficulties frequently accompany or are seriously aggravated by depression. In most cases loneliness and depression are temporary. Your task then is to eliminate or lessen these uncomfortable and potentially dangerous feelings by changing the situation. When depression does last or proves particularly upsetting, it's time to seek professional help.

Take time out. Take time out for yourself. Renew your relationship with yourself. If you were in a long-term relationship, you probably saw yourself as part of a team, as part of a couple. Now get to know yourself as a unique individual, standing alone now but fully capable of entering a meaningful relationship in the near future.

Bolster your self-esteem. When relationships fail, self-esteem often falls. You may feel guilty for having been the cause of the breakup or inadequate for not holding on to a permanent relationship. You may feel unwanted and unloved. All of these feelings contribute to a lowering of self-esteem. Your task here is to regain the positive self-image you need to function effectively as an individual and as a member of another relationship. Take positive action to raise your self-esteem (see Unit 6).

Avoid repeating negative patterns. Many people enter second and third relationships with the same blinders, faulty preconceptions, and unrealistic expectations with which they entered their earlier relationships. It is possible, however, to learn from failed relationships and not repeat the same patterns. Ask yourself at the start of a new involvement if you're entering a relationship modeled on the previous one. If the answer is yes, be especially careful not to fall into old behavior patterns. At the same time, don't become a prophet of doom. Don't see in every new relationship vestiges of the old. Treat the new relationship as the unique relationship it is and don't evaluate it through past experiences. Past relationships and experiences should be guides, not filters.

Relationship Types

Each relationship, whether friendship, love, or a primary relationship, is unique. Yet there are general types that research has identified—and these categories offer unusual insight into interpersonal relationships.

Types of Friendships

One theory of **friendship** identifies three major types: friendships of reciprocity, receptivity, and association (Reisman, 1979, 1981). The *friendship of reciprocity,* the ideal type, is characterized by loy-

VIEWPOINT
It has been argued that you don't actually experience an attraction toward those who are similar to you but rather feel repulsed by those who are dissimilar (Rosenbaum, 1986). For example, you may be repulsed by those who disagree with you and therefore exclude them from people with whom you might develop a relationship. You're therefore left with a pool of possible partners who have attitudes similar to yours. What do you think of this repulsion hypothesis?

ASK THE RESEARCHER

Topic Avoidance

- *Just recently I've started dating seriously, and I want to know if there are certain topics that are best avoided in romantic relationships. And while I'm at it, are there topics friends should avoid? Any suggestions?*

Your concern about damaging the relationship is a common fear that often motivates avoidance. However, those fears are sometimes exaggerated. It does seem that avoidance of certain topics (for example, past relational partners, future of the relationship) can sometimes help relationships. On the other hand, most research shows that the strongest relationships are those in which there is relatively limited avoidance. That's also the case in friendships. A lot of friendships, especially ones with potential for romance, never develop into closer relationships because of people's tendency to avoid talking about the most important issue—the relationship. So, as a general rule, less avoidance is better, but it serves little purpose to bring up issues that you know will incite conflict. Of course, avoiding disclosure of issues that would clearly be of interest to your partner (for example, infidelity) or your friend (for example, theft) is a different ball game and almost never advised.

For further information: Petronio, S. (Ed). (2000). *Balancing the secrets of private disclosures*. Mahwah, NJ: Erlbaum. And Greene, K., Derlega, V. J., Yep, G. A., & Petronio, S. (2003). *Privacy and disclosure of HIV in interpersonal relationships: A sourcebook for researchers and practitioners*. Mahwah, NJ: Erlbaum. And Afifi, W. A., & Guerrero, L. K. (2000). Motivations underlying topic avoidance in close relationships. In S. Petronio (Ed.), *Balancing the secrets of private disclosures* (pp. 165–180). Mahwah, NJ: Erlbaum.

Walid A. Afifi (Ph.D., University of Arizona) is an associate professor at Pennsylvania State University, where he teaches courses in interpersonal and relational communication and conducts research in information seeking, topic avoidance, and health communication (w-afifi@psu.edu).

alty, self-sacrifice, mutual affection, and generosity. A friendship of reciprocity is based on equality: Each individual shares equally in giving and receiving the benefits and rewards of the relationship.

In the *friendship of receptivity,* in contrast, there is an imbalance in giving and receiving; one person is the primary giver and the other the primary receiver. This is a positive imbalance, however, because each person gains something from the relationship. The different needs of both the person who receives affection and the person who gives it are satisfied. This is the friendship that may develop between a teacher and a student or between a doctor and a patient. In fact, a difference in status is essential for the friendship of receptivity to develop.

The *friendship of association* is transitory; it might be described as a friendly relationship rather than a true friendship. Associative friendships are the kind we often have with classmates, neighbors, or coworkers. There is no great loyalty, no great trust, no great giving or receiving. The association is cordial but not intense.

Types of Lovers

Like friends, lovers come in different styles as well. Before reading about these styles, take the following self-test to identify your own love style.

TEST YOURSELF

What Kind of Lover Are You?

Respond to each of the following statements with T for "true" (if you believe the statement to be a generally accurate representation of your attitudes about love) or F for "false" (if you believe the statement does not adequately represent your attitudes about love).

____ **1.** My lover and I have the right physical "chemistry" between us.

TEST YOURSELF, continued

____ **2.** I feel that my lover and I were meant for each other.

____ **3.** My lover and I really understand each other.

____ **4.** I believe that what my lover doesn't know about me won't hurt him/her.

____ **5.** My lover would get upset if he/she knew of some of the things I've done with other people.

____ **6.** When my lover gets too dependent on me, I want to back off a little.

____ **7.** I expect to always be friends with my lover.

____ **8.** Our love is really a deep friendship, not a mysterious, mystical emotion.

____ **9.** Our love relationship is the most satisfying because it developed from a good friendship.

____ **10.** In choosing my lover, I believed it was best to love someone with a similar background.

____ **11.** An important factor in choosing a partner is whether or not he/she would be a good parent.

____ **12.** One consideration in choosing my lover was how he/she would reflect on my career.

____ **13.** Sometimes I get so excited about being in love with my lover that I can't sleep.

____ **14.** When my lover doesn't pay attention to me, I feel sick all over.

____ **15.** I cannot relax if I suspect that my lover is with someone else.

____ **16.** I would rather suffer myself than let my lover suffer.

____ **17.** When my lover gets angry with me, I still love him/her fully and unconditionally.

____ **18.** I would endure all things for the sake of my lover.

HOW DID YOU DO? This scale, from Hendrick and Hendrick (1990), is based on the work of Lee (1976), as is the discussion of the six types of love that follows. This scale is designed to enable you to identify your own beliefs about love. The statements refer to the six types of love that we discuss below: eros, ludus, storge, pragma, mania, and agape. Statements 1–3 are characteristic of the eros lover. If you answered "true" to these statements, you have a strong eros component to your love style. If you answered "false," you have a weak eros component. Statements 4–6 refer to ludus love, 7–9 to storge love, 10–12 to pragma love, 13–15 to manic love, and 16–18 to agapic love.

WHAT WILL YOU DO? Are there things you can do to become more aware of the different love styles and to become a more well-rounded lover? Incorporating the qualities of effective interpersonal communication—for example, being more flexible, more polite, and more other-oriented—will go a long way toward making you a more responsive love partner.

Source: From "A Relationship-Specific Version of the Love Attitudes Scale" by C. Hendrick and S. Hendrick (1990), *Journal of Social Behavior and Personality 5,* 1990. Used by permission of Select Press.

Eros love seeks beauty and sensuality and focuses on physical attractiveness, sometimes to the exclusion of qualities we might consider more important and more lasting. The erotic lover has an idealized image of beauty that is unattainable in reality. Consequently, the erotic lover often feels unfulfilled.

Ludic love seeks entertainment and excitement and sees love as fun, a game. To the ludic lover, love is not to be taken too seriously; emotions are to be held in check lest they get out of hand and make trouble. The ludic lover retains a partner only so long as the partner is interesting and amusing. When the partner is no longer interesting enough, it's time to change.

Storge love is a peaceful and tranquil love. Like ludus, storge lacks passion and intensity. Storgic lovers set out not to find a lover but to establish a companionlike relationship with someone they know and with whom they can share interests and activities. Storgic love is a gradual process of unfolding thoughts and feelings and is sometimes difficult to separate from friendship.

Pragma love is practical and traditional and seeks compatibility and a relationship in which important needs and desires will be satisfied. The pragma lover is concerned with the social qualifications of a potential mate even more than with personal qualities; family and background are extremely important to the pragma lover, who relies not so much on feelings as on logic.

Manic love is an obsessive love that needs to give and receive constant attention and affection. When this is not given or received, or when an expression of increased commitment is not returned, reactions such as depression, jealousy, and self-doubt are often experienced and can lead to the extreme lows characteristic of the manic lover.

Agapic love is compassionate and selfless. The agapic lover loves both the stranger on the road and the annoying neighbor. Jesus, Buddha, and Gandhi practiced and preached this unqualified spiritual love—a love that is offered without concern for personal reward or gain and without any expectation that the love will be returned or reciprocated.

Intimacy and Risk

Some people perceive relational intimacy as extremely risky. To others, intimacy connotes only low risk. Consider your own view of relationship risk by responding to the following questions.

- Is it dangerous to get really close to people?
- Are you afraid to get really close to someone because you might get hurt?
- Do you find it difficult to trust other people?
- Do you believe that the most important thing to consider in a relationship is whether you might get hurt?

People who answer yes to these and similar questions see intimacy as involving considerable risk (Pilkington & Richardson, 1988). Such people have fewer close friends, are less likely to have a romantic relationship, have less trust in others, have a low level of dating assertiveness, have lower self-esteem, are more possessive and jealous in their love, and are generally less sociable and extroverted than those who see intimacy as involving little risk (Pilkington & Woods, 1999). And by the way, not surprisingly, comfort with risk taking has been found to be common to people who make midlife career changes (Ingram, 1998).

Types of Primary Relationships

Primary relationships are central to family life. We should note, however, that the American **family** comes in many configurations and has undergone some profound changes in recent decades. Table 10.1 on page 197 provides a few statistics on the U. S. family in 1970 and in 2000. One obvious example of change is the rise in one-parent families. There are now almost 12

COMMUNICATION@WORK

Romance in the Workplace

Love is a gross exaggeration of the difference between one person and everyone else.

—George Bernard Shaw

Opinions vary widely concerning workplace romances. On the positive side, the work environment seems a perfect place to meet a potential partner. By virtue of the fact that you're working in the same office, you're probably both interested in the same field, have similar training and ambitions, and spend considerable time together—all factors that foster the development of a successful interpersonal relationship.

If you're romantically attracted to another worker, it can make going to work, working together, and even working added hours more enjoyable. If the relationship is mutually satisfying, you're likely to develop empathy for each other and to act in ways that are supportive, cooperative, friendly, and beneficial to the organization.

On the negative side, even if a workplace relationship is good for the lovers themselves, it may not necessarily be good for other workers. They may see the lovers as a team that has to be confronted as a pair and may feel that they can't criticize one partner without incurring the wrath of the other. Such relationships may also cause problems for management—for example, when a promotion is to be made or when relocation decisions are necessary.

Of course, if an office romance goes bad or if it's one-sided, it can be stressful for the individuals involved to see each other regularly and perhaps to work together. Also, other workers may feel they have to take sides, being supportive of one partner and critical of the other. This can easily cause friction throughout the organization.

Communicating@Work

Management is necessarily concerned with the potential that office romances gone bad can lead to charges of sexual harassment. This concern has prompted some organizations to consider "love contracts" (Pierce & Aguinis, 2001; Schaefer & Tudor, 2001). If you were management, what would you seek to include in such a love contract to protect your organization from charges of sexual harassment?

MEDIA WATCH

Parasocial Relationships

Parasocial relationships are relationships that viewers perceive themselves to have with media personalities (Rubin & McHugh, 1987; Giles, 2001). Some viewers develop these relationships with real media personalities—Katie Curic, Regis Philbin, Oprah Winfrey, or Dr. Phil, for example. As a result they may watch these people faithfully and communicate with the individual in their own imaginations. In other cases the relationship is with a fictional character—an investigator on *CSI*, a lawyer on *Law and Order*, or a doctor on a soap opera. In fact, actors who portray doctors frequently get mail asking for medical advice. And soap opera stars who are about to be "killed" frequently get warning letters from their parasocial relationship fans. Obviously, most people don't go quite this far.

The chat sessions that celebrities hold on the Internet help to foster the illusion of a real interpersonal relationship. And the screen savers of television performers make it difficult not to think of them in relationship terms when they face you every time you leave your computer idle for a few minutes.

Parasocial relationships develop from an initial attraction based on the character's social and task roles, then progress to a perceived relationship and finally to a sense that this relationship is important (Rubin & McHugh, 1987). The more you can predict the behavior of a character, the more likely you are to develop a parasocial relationship with that character (Perse & Rubin, 1989). As can be expected, these parasocial relationships are most important to those who spend a great deal of time with the media, who have few interpersonal relationships, and who are generally anxious (Rubin, Perse, & Powell, 1985; Cole & Leets, 1999).

You and the Media

Some research indicates that parasocial relationships actually facilitate interpersonal interaction (May, 1999). How might parasocial relationships function in this way? Can you think of how parasocial relationships might hinder interpersonal interaction?

million single-family households in the United States. In 1998 about 28 percent of children under 18 lived with just one parent (about 23 percent with their mother and about 4 percent with their father), according to the *World Almanac and Book of Facts, 2002*.

Another obvious example is the increasing number of people living together in an exclusive relationship who are not married. For the most part these cohabitants live as if they were married: There is an exclusive sexual commitment; there may be children; there are shared financial responsibilities, shared time, and shared space. These relationships mirror traditional marriages, except that in marriage the union is recognized by a religious body, the state, or both, whereas in a relationship of cohabitants it generally is not.

Some families are headed by gay male or lesbian couples who live together as domestic partners or, in some cases spouses. Many of these couples have children from previous heterosexual unions, through artificial insemination, or by adoption. Although accurate statistics are difficult to secure, primary relationships among gays and lesbians seem more common than the popular media might lead us to believe. Research some decades ago (Blumstein & Schwartz, 1983) estimated the number of gay and lesbian couples to be 70 percent to more than 80 percent of the gay population (itself estimated variously at between 4 percent and 16 percent of the total population, depending on the definitions used and the studies cited).

The communication principles that apply to the traditional nuclear family (the mother–father–child family) also apply to these relationships. In the following discussion, the term *primary relationship* denotes the relationship between the two principal parties—the husband and wife, the lovers, or the domestic partners, for example—just as the term *family* now may denote a broader constellation that includes children, relatives, and assorted significant others.

A **primary relationship** is a relationship between two people that the partners see as their most important interpersonal relationship. An interesting typology of primary relationships (based on

Table 10.1
The Changing Face of the Family

Here are a few statistics on the nature of the American family for 1970 and 2000 as reported by the *New York Times Almanac* (2004), together with some trends these figures may indicate. What other trends do you see occurring in the family?

Family Characteristic	1970	2000	Trends
Number of members in average family	3.58	3.17	Tendency toward smaller families
Families without children	44.1%	52.9%	Growing number of families opting not to have children
Families headed by married couples	86.9%	76.8%	Growing trends for heterosexual couples to live as a family without marriage, for singles to have children, and for same-sex couples to form families
Females as heads of households	10.7%	17.6%	Growing number of women having children without marriage and increase in divorce and separation
Unmarried couples living together	523,000	4.7 million	Growing trends for couples to form families without being married
Unmarried couples living together with children under 15	196,000	1.675 million	Growing trends for couples to form families and have children without marriage

more than 1,000 couples' responses to questions concerning their degree of sharing, their space needs, their conflicts, and the time they spend together) identifies three basic types: traditionals, independents, and separates (Fitzpatrick, 1983, 1988, 1991; Noller & Fitzpatrick, 1993).

Traditional couples share a basic belief system and philosophy of life. They see themselves as a blending of two persons into a single couple rather than as two separate individuals. They're interdependent and believe that each individual's independence must be sacrificed for the good of the relationship. Traditionals believe in mutual sharing and do little separately. This couple holds to the traditional sex roles, and there are seldom any role conflicts. There are few power struggles and few conflicts, because each person knows and adheres to a specified role within the relationship. In their communications traditionals are highly responsive to each other. Traditionals lean toward each other, smile, talk a lot, interrupt each other, and finish each other's sentences.

Independents stress their individuality. The relationship is important but never more important than each person's individual identity. Although independents spend a great deal of time together, they don't ritualize it, for example, with schedules. Each individual spends time with outside friends. Independents see themselves as relatively androgynous—as individuals who combine traditionally feminine and traditionally masculine roles and qualities. The communication between independents is responsive. They engage in conflict openly and without fear. Their disclosures are quite extensive and include high-risk and negative disclosures that are typically absent among traditionals.

Separates live together but view their relationship more as a matter of convenience than a result of their mutual love or closeness. They seem to have little desire to be together and, in fact, usually are together only at ritual occasions such as mealtime or holiday get-togethers. It's important to these separates that each has his or her own physical as well as psychological space. Separates share little; each seems to prefer to go his or her own way. Separates hold relatively traditional values and beliefs about sex roles, and each person tries to follow the behaviors normally assigned to each role. What best characterizes this type, however, is that each person sees himself or herself as a separate individual and not as a part of a "we."

In addition to these three pure types, there are also combinations. For example, in the separate-traditional couple one individual is a separate and one a traditional. Another common pattern is the traditional-independent, in which one individual believes in the traditional view of relationships and one in autonomy and independence.

Relationship Theories

Several theories offer insight into why and how we develop and dissolve our relationships. Here we'll examine five such theories: attraction, relationship rules, social penetration, social exchange, and equity.

Attraction Theory

Attraction theory holds that people form relationships on the basis of **attraction.** You are no doubt drawn, or attracted, to some people and not attracted to others. In a similar way, some people are attracted to you and some are not. If you're like most people, then you're attracted to others on the basis of four major factors:

- *Similarity.* If you could construct your mate, according to the **similarity** principle, it's likely that your mate would look, act, and think very much like you (Burleson, Samter, & Luccetti, 1992; Burleson, Kunkel, & Birch, 1994). Generally, people like those who are similar to them in nationality, race, abilities, physical characteristics, intelligence, and attitudes. (Pornpitakpan, 2003). Research also finds that you're more likely to help someone who is similar in race, attitude, and general appearance. Even the same first name is significant. For example, when an e-mail (asking receivers to fill out surveys of their food habits) identified the sender as having the same name as the receiver, there was a greater willingness to comply with the request (Gueguen, 2003). Sometimes people are attracted to their opposites in a pattern called **complementarity;** for example, a dominant person might be attracted to someone who is more submissive. Generally, however, people prefer those who are similar.
- *Proximity.* If you look around at people you find attractive, you will probably find that they are the people who live or work close to you. People who become friends are the people who have the greatest opportunity to interact with each other. **Proximity,** or physical closeness, is most important in the early stages of interaction—for example, during the first days of school (in class or in dormitories). It decreases, though always remaining significant, as the opportunity to interact with more distant others increases.
- *Reinforcement.* Not surprisingly, **reinforcement theory** points out that you're attracted to people who give rewards or reinforcements, which can range from a simple compliment to an expensive cruise. You're also attracted to people you reward (Jecker & Landy, 1969; Aronson, Wilson, & Akert, 1999). That is, you come to like people for whom you do favors; for example, you've probably increased your liking for persons after buying them an expensive present or going out of your way to do them a special favor. In these situations you justify your behavior by believing that the person was worth your efforts; otherwise, you'd have to admit to spending effort on people who don't deserve it.
- *Physical attractiveness and personality.* It's easily appreciated that people like physically attractive people more than they like physically unattractive people. What isn't so obvious is that we also feel a greater sense of familiarity with more attractive people than with less attractive people; that is, we're more likely to think we've met a person before if that person is attractive (Monin, 2003). Also, although culture influences what people think is physical attractiveness and what isn't, some research indicates that there are certain facial features that seem to be thought attractive in all cultures—a kind of universal attractiveness (Brody, 1994). Additionally, you probably tend to like people who have a pleasant rather than an unpleasant personality (although people will differ on what is and what is not an attractive personality).

VIEWPOINT

It has been argued that you don't actually develop an attraction to those who are similar to you but rather that you develop a repulsion for those who are dissimilar (Rosenbaum, 1986). How would you apply this repulsion hypothesis to the way people respond to those who are homeless or who are alcoholics or addicted to drugs?

Relationship Rules Approach

You can gain an interesting perspective on interpersonal relationships by looking at them in terms of the rules that govern them (Shimanoff, 1980). The general assumption of **rules theory** is that relationships—friendship and love in particular—are held together by adherence to certain rules. When those rules are broken, the relationship may deteriorate and even dissolve.

Relationship rules theory helps us clarify several aspects of relationships. First, these rules help identify successful versus destructive relationship behavior. In addition, these rules help pinpoint more specifically why relationships break up and how they may be repaired. Further, if we know what the rules are, we will be better able to master the social skills involved in relationship development and maintenance. And because these rules vary from one culture to another, it is important to identify those unique to each culture so that intercultural relationships may be more effectively developed and maintained.

Friendship Rules

One approach to friendship argues that friendships are maintained by rules (Argyle & Henderson, 1984; Argyle, 1986). When these rules are followed, the friendship is strong and mutually satisfying. When these rules are broken, the friendship suffers and may die. For example, the rules for keeping a friendship include such behaviors as these: standing up for your friend in his or her absence, sharing information and feelings about successes, demonstrating emotional support for your friend, trusting and offering to help your friend when in need, and trying to make your friend happy when you're together. On the other hand, a friendship is likely to be in trouble when one or both friends are intolerant of the other's friends, discuss confidences with third parties, fail to demonstrate positive support, nag, and/or fail to trust or confide in the other. The strategy for maintaining a friendship then depends on your knowing the rules and having the ability to apply the appropriate interpersonal skills (Trower, 1981; Blieszner & Adams, 1992).

Romantic Rules

Other research has identified the rules that romantic relationships establish and follow. These rules, of course, will vary considerably from one culture to another. For example, the different attitudes toward permissiveness and sexual relations with which Chinese and American college students view dating influence the romantic rules each group will establish and live by (Tang & Zuo, 2000). Leslie Baxter (1986) has identified eight major romantic rules. Baxter argues that these rules keep the relationship together—or, when broken, lead to deterioration and eventually dissolution. The general form for each rule, as Baxter phrases it, is, "If parties are in a close relationship, they should . . .":

1. acknowledge each other's individual identities and lives beyond the relationship
2. express similar attitudes, beliefs, values, and interests
3. enhance each other's self-worth and self-esteem
4. be open, genuine, and authentic with each other
5. remain loyal and faithful to each other
6. have substantial shared time together
7. reap rewards commensurate with their investments relative to the other party
8. experience a mysterious and inexplicable "magic" in each other's presence

Social Penetration Theory

Social penetration theory is a theory not of why relationships develop but of what happens when they do develop; it describes relationships in terms of the number of topics that people talk about and their degree of "personalness" (Altman & Taylor, 1973). The **breadth** of a relationship has to do with the number of topics you and your partner talk about. The **depth** of a relationship involves the degree to which you penetrate the inner personality—the core—of the other individual. We can represent an individual as a circle and divide that circle into various parts. These parts represent the topics or areas of interpersonal communication, or breadth. Further, visualize the circle and its parts as consisting of concentric inner circles, rather like an onion. These represent the different levels of communication, or the depth.

When a relationship begins to deteriorate, the breadth and depth will, in many ways, reverse themselves, in a process called **depenetration.** For example, while ending a relationship, you might cut out certain topics from your interpersonal communications. At the same time you might discuss the remaining topics in less depth. In some instances of relational deterioration, however, both the breadth and the depth of interaction increase. For example, when a couple breaks up and each is finally free from an oppressive relationship, they may—after some time—begin to discuss problems and feelings they would never have discussed when they were together. In fact, they may become extremely close

UNDERSTANDING *THEORY* AND *RESEARCH*

Relationship Dialectics

Relationship dialectics theory argues that people in a relationship experience dynamic tensions between pairs of opposing motives or desires. Research generally finds three such pairs of opposites (Baxter, 1988, 1990; Baxter & Simon, 1993; Rawlins, 1989, 1992):

- The tension between *closedness and openness* has to do with the conflict between the desire to be in a closed, exclusive relationship and the wish to be in a relationship that is open to different people.
- The tension between *autonomy and connection* involves the desire to remain an autonomous, independent individual but also to connect intimately to another person and to a relationship. This tension, by the way, is a popular theme in women's magazines, which teach readers to want both autonomy and connection (Prusank, Duran, & DeLillo, 1993).
- The tension between *novelty and predictability* centers on the competing desires for newness, different experiences, and adventure on the one hand and for sameness, stability, and predictability on the other.

The closedness-openness tension occurs most during the early stages of relationship development, whereas both the autonomy-connection and the novelty-predictability tensions occur more often as the relationship progresses.

Each individual in a relationship will experience a somewhat different set of desires. For example, one person may want exclusivity above all, whereas that person's partner may want some degree of openness. Sometimes a happy combination can be negotiated; at other times these differences are irreconcilable, with the result that the couple becomes dissatisfied with their relationship or dissolves it.

Perhaps the major implication of relationship dialectics theory is that these tensions will influence a wide variety of behaviors. For example, the person who finds the primary relationship excessively predictable may seek novelty elsewhere, perhaps with a vacation to exotic places, perhaps with a different partner. The person who finds the primary relationship too connected (even suffocating) may need physical and psychological space to meet his or her autonomy needs. Meeting your partner's needs—while also meeting your own needs—is one of the major challenges in maintaining a relationship.

Working with Theories and Research

- *How would you describe your own needs for closedness versus openness, autonomy versus connection, and novelty versus predictability? How do these needs influence your relationship behavior?*

friends and come to like each other more than when they were together. In these cases the breadth and depth of their relationship may increase rather than decrease (Baxter, 1983).

Social Exchange Theory

Social exchange theory claims that you develop relationships that will enable you to maximize your profits (Chadwick-Jones, 1976; Gergen, Greenberg, & Willis, 1980; Thibaut & Kelley, 1986)—a theory based on an economic model of profits and losses. The theory begins with the following equation: Profits = Rewards − Costs. Rewards are anything that you would incur costs to obtain. Research has identified six types of rewards in a love relationship: money, status, love, information, goods, and services (Baron & Byrne, 1984). For example, to get the reward of money, you might have to work rather than play. To earn the status of an A in an interpersonal communication course, you might have to write a term paper or study more than you want to.

Costs are things that you normally try to avoid, that you consider unpleasant or difficult. Examples might include working overtime; washing dishes and ironing clothes; watching your partner's favorite television show, which you find boring; or doing favors for those you dislike.

Using this basic economic model, social exchange theory claims that you seek to develop the friendships and romantic relationships that will give you the greatest profits; that is, relationships in which the rewards are greater than the costs. The most preferred relationships, according to this theory, are those that give you the greatest rewards with the least costs.

When you enter a relationship you have in mind a *comparison level*—a general idea of the kinds of rewards and profits that you feel you ought to get out of such a relationship. This comparison level consists of your realistic expectations concerning what you feel you deserve from this relationship. For example, a study of married couples found that most people expect high levels of trust, mutual respect, love, and commitment. Couples' expectations are significantly lower for time spent together, privacy, sexual activity, and communication (Sabatelli & Pearce, 1986). When the rewards that you get equal or surpass your comparison level, you feel satisfied with your relationship.

However, you also have a *comparison level for alternatives*. That is, you compare the profits that you get from your current relationship with the profits you think you could get from alternative relationships. Thus, if you see that the profits from your present relationship are below the profits that you could get from an alternative relationship, you may decide to leave your current relationship and enter a new, more profitable relationship.

Equity Theory

Equity theory uses the ideas of social exchange but goes a step farther and claims that you develop and maintain relationships in which the ratio of your rewards relative to your costs is approximately equal to your partner's (Walster, Walster, & Berscheid, 1978; Messick & Cook, 1983). For example, if you and a friend start a business and you put up two-thirds of the money and your friend puts up one-third, equity would demand that you get two-thirds of the profits and your friend get one-third. An equitable relationship, then, is simply one in which each party derives rewards that are proportional to their costs. If you contribute more toward the relationship than your partner, then equity requires that you should get greater rewards. If you both work equally hard, then equity demands that you should both get approximately equal rewards. Conversely, inequity will exist in a relationship if you pay more of the costs (for

BUILDING COMMUNICATION SKILLS

Talking Cherishing

The concept of **cherishing behaviors,** especially insightful ways to affirm another person and to increase favor exchange, comes from the work of William Lederer (1984). Cherishing behaviors are those small gestures you enjoy receiving from your partner (a smile, a wink, a phone call, a kiss).

Prepare a list of 10 cherishing behaviors that you would like to receive from your real or imagined relationship partner. Identify cherishing behaviors that are

1. specific and positive—nothing overly general or negative
2. focused on the present and future rather than related to issues about which the partners have argued in the past
3. capable of being performed daily
4. easily executed—nothing you really have to go out of your way to accomplish

In an actual relationship each partner would prepare a list; then the partners would exchange lists. Ideally, each partner would then perform the cherishing behaviors the other had chosen. At first these behaviors might seem self-conscious and awkward. In time, however, they'd become a normal part of your interaction, which is exactly what you would hope to achieve. If you have a relationship partner, you may want to try out this idea.

example, if you do more of the unpleasant tasks) but your partner enjoys more of the rewards. Inequity will also exist if you and your partner work equally hard but one of you gets more of the rewards.

Much research supports this idea that people want equity in their interpersonal relationships (Ueleke et al., 1983). The general idea behind the theory is that if you are underbenefited (you get less than you put in), you'll be angry and dissatisfied. If, on the other hand, you are overbenefited (you get more than you put in), you'll feel guilty. Some research, however, has questioned this rather neat but intuitively unsatisfying assumption and finds that the overbenefited person is often quite happy and contented; guilt from getting more than you deserve seems easily forgotten (Noller & Fitzpatrick, 1993).

Equity theory puts into clear focus the sources of relational dissatisfaction seen every day. For example, in a relationship both partners may have full-time jobs, but one partner may also be expected to do the major share of the household chores. Thus, although both may be deriving equal rewards—they have equally good cars, they live in the same three-bedroom house, and so on—one partner is paying more of the costs. According to equity theory, this partner will be dissatisfied because of this lack of equity.

Equity theory claims that you will develop, maintain, and be satisfied with relationships that are equitable. You will not develop, will terminate, and will be dissatisfied with relationships that are inequitable. The greater the inequity, the greater the dissatisfaction and the greater the likelihood that the relationship will end.

Relationships, Culture, and Technology

Although this unit has mentioned cultural and technological factors in relationships from time to time, it's helpful to bring these topics together now that we've covered a major part of our relationship discussion. The research and theory discussed here derive in great part from research conducted in the United States and on heterosexual couples. This research and the corresponding theory reflect the way most heterosexual relationships are viewed in the United States.

Relationships and Culture

In U.S. society it is assumed in discussions of relationship development—such as the model presented in this text—that you voluntarily choose your relationship partners. You consciously choose to pursue certain relationships and not others. In some cultures, however, your romantic partner is chosen for you by your parents. In some cases your husband or wife is chosen to unite two families or to bring some financial advantage to your family or village. An arrangement such as this may have been entered into by your parents when you were an infant or even before you were born. In most cultures, of course, there's pressure to marry "the right" person and to be friends with certain people and not others.

Similarly, U.S. researchers study and textbook authors write about dissolving relationships and how to survive relationship breakups. It's assumed that you have the right to exit an undesirable relationship. But in some cultures you cannot simply dissolve a relationship once it's formed or once there are children. In the practice of Roman Catholicism, once people are validly married, they're always married and cannot dissolve that relationship. More important in such cultures may be such issues as "How do you maintain a relationship that has problems?" "What can you do to survive in this unpleasant relationship?" or "How can you repair a troubled relationship?" (Moghaddam, Taylor, & Wright, 1993).

Further, the culture will influence the difficulty that you go through when relationships do break up. For example, married persons whose religion forbids divorce and remarriage will experience religious disapproval and condemnation as well as the same economic and social difficulties everyone else goes through. In the United States child custody almost invariably goes to the woman, and this presents an added emotional burden for the man. In Iran child custody goes to the man, which presents added emotional burdens for the woman. In India women experience greater difficulty than men in divorce because of their economic dependence on men, the cultural beliefs about women, and the patriarchal order of the family (Amato, 1994). And it was only as recently as 2002 that the first wife in Jordan was granted a divorce. Prior to this, only men had been granted divorces (*New York Times,* May 15, 2002, p. A6).

In most of the United States, interpersonal friendships are drawn from a relatively large pool. Out of all the people you come into regular contact with, you choose relatively few of these as friends. With computer chat groups, the number of friends you can have has increased enormously, as has the range from which these friends can be chosen. In rural areas and in small villages throughout the world, however, you would have very few choices. The two or three other children your age would become your friends; there would be no real choice, because these would be the only possible friends you could make.

Most cultures assume that relationships should be permanent or at least long lasting. Consequently, it's assumed that people want to keep relationships together and will expend considerable energy to maintain relationships. Because of this bias, there is little research that has studied how to move effortlessly from one intimate relationship to another or that advises you how to do this more effectively and efficiently.

Culture influences heterosexual relationships by assigning different roles to men and women. In the United States men and women are supposed to be equal—at least that is the stated ideal. As a result, both men and women can initiate relationships and both can dissolve them. Both men and women are expected to derive satisfaction from their interpersonal relationships; and when that satisfaction isn't present, either person may seek to exit the relationship. In Iran, on the other hand, only the man has the right to dissolve a marriage without giving reasons.

Gay and lesbian relationships are accepted in some cultures and condemned in others. In some areas of the United States "domestic partnerships" may be registered, and these grant gay men, lesbians, and (in some cases) unmarried heterosexuals rights that were formerly reserved only for married couples, such as health insurance benefits and the right to make decisions when one member is incapacitated. In Norway, Sweden, Belgium, the Netherlands, and Denmark, same-sex relationship partners have the same rights as married partners. As of this writing, only one U.S. state, Massachusetts, has issued marriage licenses to same-sex couples. In many countries same-sex couples would be considered criminals and could face severe punishment—in some cultures death.

Relationships and Technology

Perhaps even more obvious than culture is the influence of technology on interpersonal relationships. Clearly, online interpersonal relationships are on the increase. The number of Internet users is rapidly increasing, and commercial websites devoted to helping people meet other people are proliferating, making it especially easy to develop online relationships. The daytime television talk shows frequently focus on computer relationships, especially bringing together individuals who have established a relationship online but who have never met. Clearly, many people are turning to the Internet to find a friend or romantic partner. In MOOs (online role-playing games), 93.6 percent of the users formed ongoing friendship and romantic relationships (Parks & Roberts, 1998). Some people use the Internet as their only means of interaction; others use it as a way of beginning a relationship and intend to supplement computer talk later with photographs, phone calls, and face-to-face meetings. Intrestingly, a *New York Times* survey found that by 2003 online dating was losing its earlier stigma as a last resort for losers (June 29, 2003, p. A1).

Other research on Internet use found that almost two-thirds of newsgroup users had formed new acquaintances, friendships, or other personal relationships with someone they met on the Net. Almost one-third said that they communicated with their partner at least three or four times a week; more than half communicated on a weekly basis (Parks & Floyd, 1996).

Women, it seems, are more likely to form relationships on the Internet than men. About 72 percent of women and 55 percent of men had formed personal relationships online (Parks & Floyd, 1996). Not surprisingly, those who communicated more frequently formed more relationships.

As relationships develop on the Internet, network convergence occurs; that is, as a relationship between two people develops, they begin to share their network of other communicators with each other (Parks, 1995; Parks & Floyd, 1996). This, of course, is similar to relationships formed through face-to-face contact. Online work groups are also on the increase and have been found to be more task oriented and more efficient than face-to-face groups (Lantz, 2001). Online groups also provide a sense of belonging that may once have been thought possible only through face-to-face interactions (Silverman, 2001).

There are lots of advantages to establishing relationships online. For example, online relationships are safe in terms of avoiding the potential for physical violence or sexually transmitted diseases. Unlike relationships established in face-to-face encounters, in which physical appearance tends to outweigh personality, Internet communication reveals your inner qualities first. Rapport and mutual self-disclosure become more important than physical attractiveness in promoting intimacy (Cooper & Sportolari, 1997). And contrary to some popular opinions, online relationships rely just as heavily on the ideals of trust, honesty, and commitment as do face-to-face relationships (Whitty & Gavin, 2001). Friendship and romantic interaction on the Internet are a natural boon to shut-ins and extremely shy people, for whom traditional ways of meeting someone are often difficult. Computer talk is empowering for those with "physical disabilities or disfigurements," for whom face-to-face interactions are often superficial and often end with withdrawal (Lea & Spears, 1995; Bull & Rumsey, 1988). By eliminating the physical cues, computer talk equalizes the interaction and doesn't put the disfigured person, for example, at an immediate disadvantage in a society where physical attractiveness is so highly valued. On the Internet you're free to reveal as much or as little about your physical self as you wish, when you wish.

Another obvious advantage is that the number of people you can reach is so vast that it's relatively easy to find someone who matches what you're looking for. The situation is like finding a book that covers just what you need from a library of millions of volumes rather than from a collection holding only several thousand.

Of course, there are also disadvantages. For one thing, you can't see the person. Unless you exchange photos or meet face-to-face, you won't know what the person looks like. Even if photos are exchanged, how certain can you be that the photos are of the person or that they were taken recently? In addition, you can't hear the person's voice, and this too hinders you as you seek to develop a total picture of the other person. Of course, you can always add an occasional phone call to give you this added information.

Online, people can present a false self with little chance of detection. For example, minors may present themselves as adults, and adults may present themselves as children in order to conduct illicit and illegal sexual communications and, perhaps, meetings. Similarly, people can present themselves as poor when they're rich, as mature when they're immature, as serious and committed when they're just enjoying the online experience. Although people can also misrepresent themselves in face-to-face relationships, the fact that it's easier to do online probably accounts for greater frequency of misrepresentation in computer relationships (Cornwell & Lundgren, 2001).

Another potential disadvantage—though some might argue it is actually an advantage—is that computer interactions may become all consuming and may substitute for face-to-face interpersonal relationships.

REFLECTIONS ON ETHICS

Relationship Ethics

The ethical issues and guidelines that operate within a friendship, romantic, family, or workplace relationship can be reviewed with the acronym ETHICS—empathy (Cheney & Tompkins, 1987), talk rather than force, honesty (Krebs, 1990), interaction management, confidentiality, and supportiveness (Johannesen, 2001).

- *Empathy:* People in a relationship have an ethical obligation to try to understand what others are feeling and thinking from their point of view. This is especially important when relationship members from different cultures communicate.
- *Talk:* Decisions in a relationship should be arrived at by talk, not by force—by persuasion rather than coercion.
- *Honesty:* Relationship communication should be honest and truthful.
- *Interaction management:* Relationship communication should be satisfying and comfortable and is the responsibility of all individuals.
- *Confidentiality:* People in a relationship have a right to expect that what they say in confidence will not be made public or even whispered about.
- *Supportiveness:* A supportive and cooperative climate should characterize interpersonal interactions in a relationship.

WHAT WOULD YOU DO? You're managing a work team of three colleagues charged with redesigning the company website. The problem is that Jack doesn't do any work and misses most of the meetings. You spoke with him about it, and he confided that he's going through a divorce and can't concentrate on the project. You feel sorry for Jack and have been carrying him for the last few months but now realize that you'll never be able to bring the project in on time if you don't replace Jack. In addition, you really don't want to get a negative appraisal because of Jack; in fact, you were counting on the raise that this project was going to get you. What would you do in this situation?

SUMMARY

In this unit we looked at interpersonal relationships; at their nature, stages, and types; at the theories that try to explain what happens in an interpersonal relationship; and at cultural and technological factors in interpersonal relationships.

1. People enter into relationships for a variety of reasons; some of the most important are to lessen loneliness, secure stimulation, gain self-knowledge, and maximize pleasures and minimize pain.
2. Relationships tend to develop in stages. Recognize at least these: contact, involvement, intimacy, deterioration, repair, and dissolution.
3. Three main phases in initiating relationships are examining qualifiers, determining clearance, and communicating a desire for contact.
4. In initiating relationships, the following nonverbal behaviors are useful: establish eye contact, signal posi-

tive response, concentrate your focus, establish proximity, maintain an open posture, respond visibly, and use positive behaviors. The following verbal behaviors are helpful: introduce yourself, focus the conversation on the other person, exchange favors and rewards, stress the positives, avoid negative or too-intimate self-disclosures, and establish commonalities.

5. Relationship maintenance consists of behaviors designed to continue the relationship, to keep it intact, to keep it at its present stage, or to keep it from deteriorating.
6. Relationships may stay together because of emotional attachments, convenience, children, fear, financial considerations, and/or inertia. Effective communication patterns also tend to sustain ongoing relationships.
7. Relationship deterioration—the weakening of the bonds holding people together—may be gradual or sudden and may have positive as well as negative effects.
8. Among the causes for relationship deterioration are diminution of the reasons for establishing the relationship, relational changes, unrealistic expectations, sex conflicts, work problems, financial difficulties, and the inequitable distribution of rewards and costs.
9. Among the communication changes that take place during relationship deterioration are general withdrawal, a decrease in self-disclosure, an increase in deception, a decrease in positive and an increase in negative evaluative responses, and a decrease in the exchange of favors.
10. A useful approach to relationship repair is to recognize the problem, engage in productive conflict resolution, pose possible solutions, affirm each other, integrate solutions into relationship behaviors, and take risks.
11. If the relationship does end, engage in self-repair. Break the loneliness–depression cycle, take time out, bolster self-esteem, seek emotional support, and avoid repeating negative patterns.
12. Friendships may be classified as those of reciprocity, receptivity, and association.
13. Six primary love styles have been identified: eros, ludus, storge, mania, pragma, and agape. Intimacy in general seems risky to some people but less threatening to others.
14. Although family structures vary, couples in primary relationships may be classified into traditionals, independents, and separates.
15. Attraction, relationship rules, social penetration, social exchange, and equity theories are five explanations of what happens when you develop, maintain, and dissolve interpersonal relationships.
16. Attraction depends on four factors: attractiveness (physical and personality), similarity (especially attitudinal), proximity (physical closeness), and reinforcement.
17. The relationship rules approach views relationships as held together by adherence to an agreed-upon set of rules.
18. Social penetration theory describes relationships in terms of breadth and depth: respectively, the number of topics we talk about, and the degree of personalness with which we pursue topics.
19. Social exchange theory holds that we develop relationships that yield the greatest profits. We seek relationships in which the rewards exceed the costs and are more likely to dissolve relationships when the costs exceed the rewards.
20. Equity theory claims that we develop and maintain relationships in which rewards are distributed in proportion to costs. When our share of the rewards is less than would be demanded by equity, we are likely to experience dissatisfaction and exit the relationship.
21. Both cultural and technological factors have major impacts on interpersonal relationships around the world.

Key Terms

relationship development
contact
involvement
intimacy
relationship maintenance
maintenance strategies
relational communication
relationship deterioration
relationship repair
dissolution
friendship
primary relationship
parasocial relationships
family
attraction theory
similarity
complementarity
proximity
reinforcement
relationship dialectics theory
rules theory
social penetration theory
breadth
depth
depenetration
social exchange theory
cherishing behaviors
equity theory

Thinking Critically About

Interpersonal Relationships

1. It was only as recently as 1967—after nine years of trials and appeals—that the U.S. Supreme Court forbade any state laws against interracial marriage (Crohn, 1995). How would you describe the state of interracial romantic relationships today? What obstacles do such relationships face? What advantages do they offer?
2. One way to improve communication during difficult times is to ask your partner for positive behaviors rather than to stop negative behaviors. How might you use this suggestion to replace the following statements? (1) "I hate it when you ignore me at business functions." (2) "I can't stand going to these cheap restaurants; when are you going to start spending a few bucks?" (3) "Stop being so negative; you criticize everything and everyone."
3. The "matching hypothesis" claims that people date and mate people who are very similar to themselves in physical attractiveness (Walster & Walster, 1978). When this does not happen—when a very attractive person dates someone of average attractiveness—there may be "compensating factors," factors that the less attractive person possesses that compensate or make up for being less physically attractive. What evidence can you find to support or contract this theory? How would you go about testing this theory?
4. Test out the predictions of the five relationship theories on your own interpersonal relationships. For example:
   - Are you attracted to people who are physically attractive, have a pleasing personality, are near to you, are similar to you, and reinforce you?
   - Do you maintain relationships when rules are followed and break up when rules are broken?
   - Do you talk about more topics and in greater depth in close relationships than in mere acquaintanceships?
   - Do you pursue and maintain relationships that give you profits (that is, in which rewards are greater than costs)? Were the relationships that you did not pursue or that you ended unprofitable? That is, were their costs greater than their rewards?
   - Are you more satisfied with equitable relationships than with inequitable ones?
5. Research finds that relationship dissolution is a significant factor in suicide by men but not in suicide by women (Kposowa, 2000). Can you identify any reasons for this finding?
6. Research generally finds that the relationships of heterosexuals, gay men, and lesbians are similar (Spiers, 1998). Do you find that the media generally reflect the research in their depiction of these relationships?
7. At least one research study shows that romanticism seems to increase on the basis of the amount of choice you have in selecting a partner. In countries where there is much choice, as in the United States and Europe, romanticism is high; in countries where there is less choice, as in India and parts of Africa, romanticism is lower (Medora, Larson, Hortacsu, & Dave, 2002). Internet dating provides greater choice than do face-to-face interactions, so does it follow that romanticism will be higher in Internet interactions?
8. Some theories of gender differences in relationships, particularly social Darwinism, hold that men focus on youth and attractiveness as they seek a partner with whom to have children, whereas women seek men who have wealth and power and so can offer protection and security. Recent research seems to cast some doubt on this theory and suggests that both men and women who see themselves as especially attractive will seek partners who are also attractive. Similarly, those who are wealthy will seek others who have similar wealth (Angier, 2003).
9. How would you respond to each of these interpersonal communication situations?
   - Your friend asks you for a loan of $150 to pay off some bills. But this person has never paid back your loans in the past, and you simply don't want to lend money now. Yet you don't want to lose this friend. Aside from a chronic inability to manage money, this is a really wonderful person. What do you say?
   - You lied to a friend about being out of town so you wouldn't have to attend her retirement party, but you were found out. This has soured your friendship; a person who was once a best friend is now "barely an acquaintance." Several months have gone, by, and you want to repair this relationship. What do you say?
   - Your dating partner communicates as if you're at the intimacy stage, whereas you see the relationship in much less intimate (even casual) terms. You want to correct this misinterpretation. What do you say?
10. Some cultures consider sexual relationships to be undesirable outside of marriage; others consider sex a normal part of intimacy and see chastity as undesirable. Intercultural researchers Hatfield and Rapson (1996, p. 36) recall a meeting at which colleagues from Sweden and the United States were discussing ways of preventing AIDS. When members from the United States suggested teaching abstinence, Swedish members asked, "How will

teenagers ever learn to become loving, considerate sexual partners if they don't practice?" "The silence that greeted the question," note the researchers, "was the sound of two cultures clashing." How have your cultural beliefs and values influenced what you consider appropriate relationship behavior?

11. Throughout the life of a relationship, there exist "turning points"—jumps or leaps that project you from one relationship level to another. Do men and women see turning points in the same way? For example, what turning points are most important to women? Which are most important to men?

12. How would you feel if you were in a relationship in which you and your partner contributed an equal share of the costs (that is, you each worked equally hard) but your partner derived significantly greater rewards? How would you feel if you and your partner contributed an equal share of the costs but you derived significantly greater rewards?

13. Even though women are now firmly in the workplace, they are still the primary caregivers and perform the bulk of household duties. In fact, Switzerland has initiated a "fair play at home" campaign to get men to take on more of the household chores. If you were in charge of such a campaign in the United States, what would you say to men? What would you say to women?

14. When researchers asked college students to identify the features that characterize romantic love, the five qualities most frequently noted were trust, sexual attraction, acceptance and tolerance, spending time together, and sharing thoughts and secrets (Regan, Kocan, & Whitlock, 1998). How would you characterize love? Would men and women characterize love similarly? Would heterosexuals and homosexuals characterize love similarly?

UNIT

Small Group Communication

UNIT CONTENTS

A great deal of your social and professional life will revolve around your participation in groups—groups for developing ideas, increasing self-awareness, learning, and solving problems. Understanding the nature and function of small groups and how you can use these groups effectively and efficiently will help you throughout your social and professional career. In this unit you'll learn

- how small groups operate and the rules the various types of groups follow
- how you can use groups to achieve a variety of personal, social, and professional goals

Small Groups

A **group** is a collection of individuals who are connected to one another by some common purpose and have some degree of organization among them. For *small groups* in particular, each of these characteristics needs to be explained a bit further.

A small group is, first, a collection of individuals few enough in number so that all members may communicate with relative ease as both senders and receivers. Generally, a small group consists of approximately 5 to 12 people. The important point to keep in mind is that each member should be able to function as both source and receiver with relative ease. If the group gets much larger than 12, this becomes difficult.

Second, the members of a group must be connected to one another through some common purpose. People on a bus normally do not constitute a group, because they're not working at some common purpose. If the bus gets stuck in a ditch, the riders may quickly become a group and work together to get the bus back on the road. In a small group the behavior of one member is significant for all other members. This does not mean that all members must have exactly the same purpose in being part of the group. But generally there must be some similarity in the individuals' reasons for interacting.

Third, the members must be connected by some organizing rules or structure. At times the structure is rigid—as in groups operating under parliamentary procedure, in which each comment must follow prescribed rules. At other times, as in a social gathering, the structure is very loose. Yet in both instances there's some organization and some structure: Two people don't speak at the same time, comments or questions by one member are responded to by others rather than ignored, and so on. A website devoted to small group communication, maintained by the publisher of this book, provides a wealth of additional insights (see the Going Online box on page 210).

Basic Types of Groups

A good way to begin the study of small group communication is to look at the various types of groups in which we all participate: relationship and task groups and reference and membership groups.

Relationship and Task Groups

You can look at groups as serving two broad and overlapping purposes: social or relationship purposes on the one hand and work or task purposes on the other. Social or relationship groups are what sociologists call *primary groups*. These are the groups in which we participate early in life and include, for example, our immediate family, our group of friends at school, and perhaps our neighbors. Usually these groups serve our relationship needs for affiliation, affirmation, and affection. Some of these groups, like family, are extremely long lasting; some, like friends at college, may last only a year or two. It is largely through participating in primary groups and through our strong identification with other group members that we develop our self-concept.

Task groups (sociologists call these *secondary groups*) are groups formed to accomplish something. Some task groups are put together to solve a specific problem; for example, a committee of college professors might be formed to hire a new faculty member, select a textbook, or serve on a graduate student's dissertation committee. Once the specific task is accomplished, the group is dissolved. Other task groups have more long-range concerns; for example, a committee to oversee diversity in the workplace, to monitor fairness in advertising, or to rate feature films may be an ongoing, permanent group. Unlike relationship groups, which are informal and in which the reward of participation consists simply of being together, task groups are more formal, and the reward of participation comes from accomplishing the specific task.

Another interesting difference between relationship and task groups is that in relationship groups each member is irreplaceable and unique. In task groups, in contrast, each member plays a role but can be replaced by a similarly competent individual. For example, in a group formed to develop a core curriculum for undergraduates, the professor representing the sciences could easily be replaced by another science professor and the group would remain essentially the same.

Relationship and task functions often overlap. In fact, it would be difficult to find a group in which these two functions were not combined in some way at some times. The coworkers who bowl together or the two chemistry professors who begin dating are clear examples of how functions can overlap. Not surprisingly, when groups normally devoted to one function

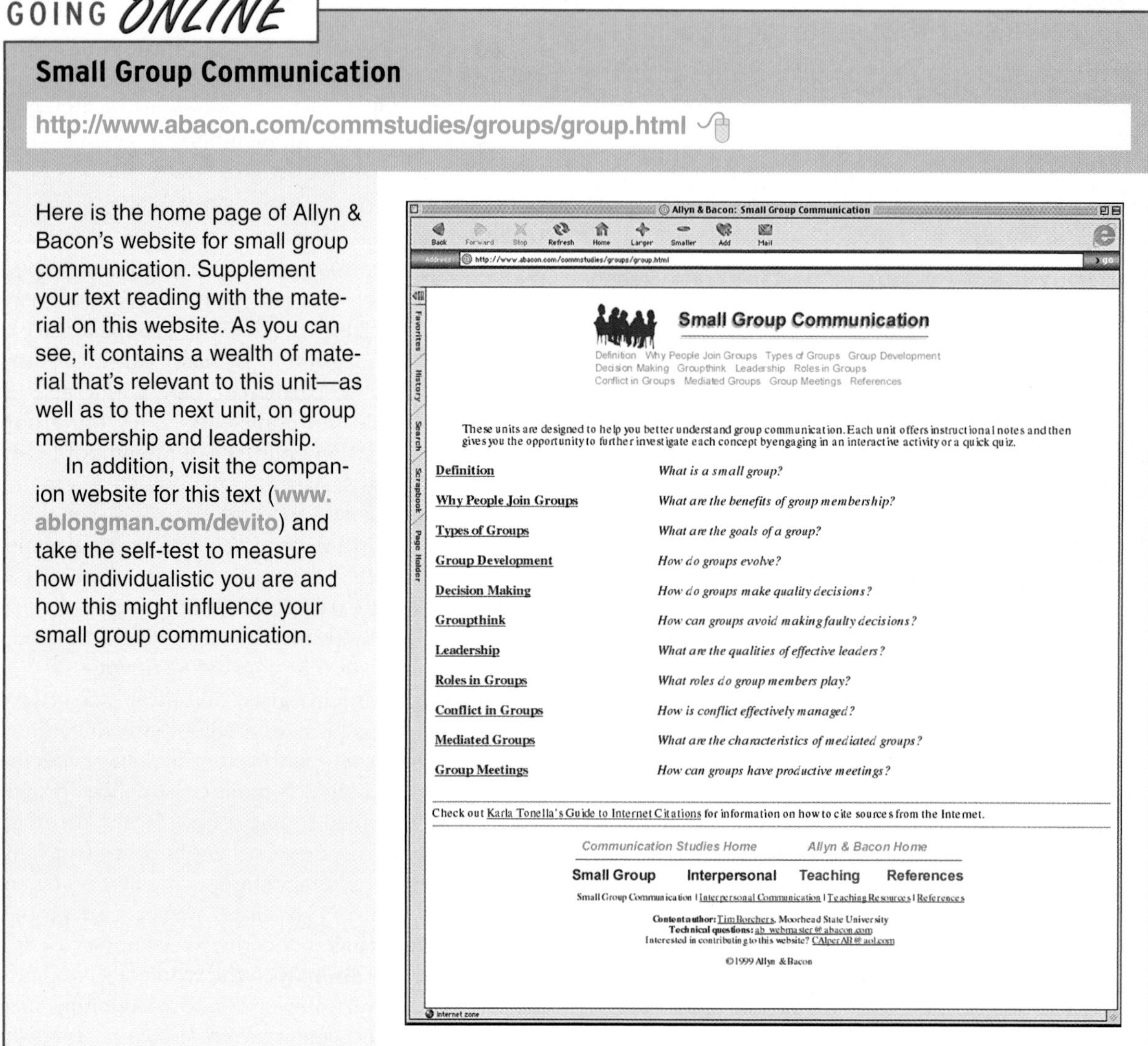

GOING *ONLINE*

Small Group Communication

http://www.abacon.com/commstudies/groups/group.html

Here is the home page of Allyn & Bacon's website for small group communication. Supplement your text reading with the material on this website. As you can see, it contains a wealth of material that's relevant to this unit—as well as to the next unit, on group membership and leadership.

In addition, visit the companion website for this text (www.ablongman.com/devito) and take the self-test to measure how individualistic you are and how this might influence your small group communication.

start serving another function, they often encounter difficulties. For example, the much-in-love couple who are effective at home may find their relationship under stress when they open a business together.

Reference and Membership Groups

A *reference group* is a group from which you derive your values and norms of behavior. It is a group you use as a standard and against which you compare yourself; in other words, you judge your successes and failures in comparison with the outcomes of other members of reference groups. Reference groups may be primary or secondary. For example, early in life you may compare yourself with and measure your successes against those of your siblings or cousins (primary groups); later you may look to classmates or coworkers (generally secondary groups) as reference groups.

A *membership group* is a group you participate in but do not use as a guide or to measure yourself. Reference and membership groups are often the same. For the most part you participate in the groups whose values you share, and, at the same time, you acquire the values of the groups in which you participate. In some cases, however, reference and membership groups may differ. For example, while studying to be a doctor and not yet a member of the doctor group, you may nevertheless have learned the norms and values of this group, may take this as your reference group, and may come to emulate doctors as you journey toward your MD.

Small Group Stages

The small group develops in much the same way that a conversation develops. As in conversation,

COMMUNICATION@WORK

Networking

If I have seen further, it is by standing on the shoulders of giants.

—Sir Isaac Newton

Networking is more than a technique for securing a job; it's a broad process of enlisting the aid of other people to help you solve a problem or offer insights that bear on your problem—for example, on how to publish your manuscript, where to go for low-cost auto insurance, how to find an apartment, or how to empty your e-mail cache (Heenehan, 1997).

Start your networking with people you already know. You'll probably discover that you know a great number of people with specialized knowledge who can be of assistance (Rector & Neiva, 1996). You can also network with people who know the people you know. Thus, you may contact a friend's friend to find out if the firm where he or she works is hiring. Or you may contact people with whom you have no connection. Perhaps you've read something the person wrote or heard the person's name raised in connection with an area in which you're interested, and you want to get more information. With e-mail addresses so readily available, it's now quite common to e-mail individuals who have particular expertise and ask your questions. Newsgroups and chat rooms are other obvious networking avenues.

Try to establish relationships that are mutually beneficial. If you can provide others with helpful information, it's more likely that they'll provide helpful information for you. In this way you establish a mutually satisfying and productive network.

Create folders, files, and directories of potentially useful sources that you can contact. For example, if you're a freelance artist, you might develop a list of persons in positions to offer you work or who may lead you to others who could offer work, such as authors, editors, art directors, administrative assistants, or people in advertising.

Be proactive; initiate contacts rather than waiting for them to come to you. If you're also willing to help others, there's nothing wrong in asking these same people to help you. If you're respectful of your contacts' time and expertise, it's likely that they will respond favorably to your networking attempts. Following up your requests with thank-you notes will help you establish networks that can be ongoing relationships.

Communicating@Work

Have you ever networked to enlist the aid of someone who had information you needed? Have others ever enlisted your aid? How did these interactions work? Were they mutually productive?

there are five stages: (1) opening, (2) feedforward, (3) business, (4) feedback, and (5) closing.

The *opening stage* is usually a getting-acquainted time in which members introduce themselves and engage in social small talk, or **phatic communication.** After this preliminary get-together, there's usually *a feedforward stage* in which members make some attempt to identify what needs to be done, who will do it, and so on. In formal business groups the meeting agenda (which is a perfect example of feedforward) may be reviewed and the tasks of the group identified. In informal social groups the feedforward may consist simply of introducing a topic of conversation or talking about what the group's members should do.

The *business stage* is the actual work on the tasks—the problem solving, the sharing of information, or whatever else the group needs to do. At the *feedback stage*, the group may reflect on what it has done and perhaps on what remains to be done. Some groups may even evaluate their performance at this stage. At the *closing stage*, the group members again return to their focus on individuals and will perhaps exchange closing comments—"Good seeing you again," and the like.

These stages are rarely separate from one another. Rather, they blend into one another. For example, the opening stage is not completely finished before the feedforward begins. Rather, as the opening comments are completed, the group begins to introduce feedforward; as the feedforward begins to end, the business starts.

Small Group Formats

Small groups serve their functions in a variety of formats. Among the most popular small group formats for relatively formal functions are the round table, the panel, the symposium, and the symposium–forum (Figure 11.1).

The Round Table

In the **round table** format, group members arrange themselves in a circular or semicircular pattern. They share the information or solve the problem without any set pattern of who speaks when. Group interaction is informal, and members contribute as they see fit. A leader or moderator may be present; he or she may, for example, try to keep the discussion on the topic or encourage more reticent members to speak up.

The Panel

In the **panel,** group members are "experts" but participate informally and without any set pattern of who speaks when, as in a round table. The difference is that there's an audience whose members may interject comments or ask questions. Many talk shows, such as the Jerry Springer and Oprah Winfrey shows, use this format.

A variation is the two-panel format, with an expert panel and a lay panel. The lay panel discusses the topic but may turn to the expert panel members when in need of technical information, additional data, or direction.

The Symposium

In the **symposium,** each member delivers a prepared presentation much like a public speech. All speeches are addressed to different aspects of a single topic. A symposium leader introduces the speakers, provides transitions from one speaker to another, and may provide periodic summaries.

The Symposium–Forum

The symposium–forum consists of two parts: a symposium, with prepared speeches, and a **forum,** with questions from the audience and responses by the speakers. The leader introduces the speakers and moderates the question-and-answer session.

Small Groups Online

Small groups use a wide variety of channels. Often, of course, they take place face-to-face; this is the channel that probably comes to mind when you think of group interaction. But today much small group interaction also takes place online and serves both relationship or social purposes on the one hand and business and professional purposes on the other.

Two major types of online groups may be noted here: the mailing list group and the chat group. In conjunction with the following discussions, take a look at the "Credo for Free and Responsible Use of Electronic Communication Networks" at www.natcom.org. It's one attempt by a national communication association to articulate some of the ethical issues in electronic group communication.

Figure 11.1
Small Group Formats
These four formats are general patterns that may describe a wide variety of groups. Within each type there will naturally be considerable variation. For example, in the symposium–forum there's no set pattern for how much time will be spent on the symposium part and how much time will be spent on the forum part. Similarly, combinations may be used. Thus, for example, group members may each present a position paper (basically a symposium) and then participate in a round table discussion.

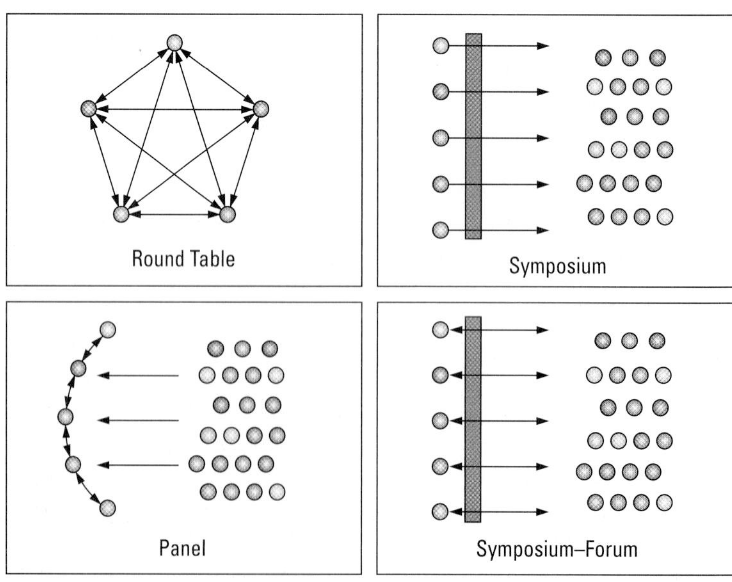

VIEWPOINT

Research on chat groups finds that people are more likely to comment on a participant's message when that message is negative than when it is positive (Rollman, Krug, & Parente, 2000). Why do you think this occurs? Do you find that this occurs in face-to-face conversations as well?

Mailing List Groups

Mailing list groups are groups of people interested in particular topics who communicate with one another through e-mail. Generally, you subscribe to a list and communicate with all other members by addressing your mail to the group e-mail address. Any message you send to this address will be sent to all members who subscribe to the list at the same time; there are no asides to the person sitting next to you (as in face-to-face groups). A huge number of mailing lists are available at www.liszt.com. A list of frequently asked questions and mailing list addresses can be found at http://www.intuitive.com/social-faq.html. Of course you could also go to one of the search engines and search for mailing lists. To locate a mailing list on your next speech topic, you might e-mail your request to listserv@listserv.net. Send the message: "list public-speaking-topic"; for example, "list United Nations."

Communication through mailing lists does not take place in real time. It's like regular e-mail; you may send your message today, but it may not be read until next week and you may not get an answer for another week. Much of the spontaneity created by real-time communication is lost. For example, you may be very enthusiastic about a topic when you send your e-mail but may practically forget about it by the time someone responds.

Chat Groups

Chat groups have proliferated across the Internet. These groups enable members to communicate with one another in real time in discussion groups called channels. At any one time there may be perhaps 4,000 channels and 20,000 users online, so your chances of finding a topic you're interested in are fairly high. If you need help with chat group communication, take a look at the website for this text. If you want help with chat groups or Internet Relay Chat groups, check http://www.mirc.com/ircintro.html, or http://www.irchelp.org/.

Unlike mailing lists, chat group communication takes place in real time; you see and in many cases hear a member's message as it's being sent, with virtually no delay. As in mailing lists and face-to-face conversation, the purposes of chat groups vary from communication that simply maintains connection with others (what many would call "idle chatter" or phatic communication) to extremely significant interchanges of ideas.

Communication in a chat group resembles the conversation you would observe at a large party. The total number of guests divide up into small groups varying from two on up, and members of each subgroup discuss their own topic or their own aspect of a general topic. For example, in a group about food, 10 people may be discussing food calories, 8 people may be discussing restaurant food preparation, and 2 people may be discussing the basic food groups, all on this one channel. So although you may be communicating in one primary group (say, dealing with restaurant food), you also have your eye trained to pick up something particularly interesting in another group, much as you do at a party. Chat groups also notify you when someone new comes into the group and when someone leaves the group. Like mailing lists, chat groups have the great advantage that they enable you to communicate with people you would never meet or interact with otherwise. Because such groups are international, they provide excellent exposure to other cultures, other ideas, and other ways of communicating.

In face-to-face group communication, you're expected to contribute to the ongoing discussion. In chat groups you can simply observe; in fact, you're encouraged to lurk—to observe the group's interaction before you say anything yourself. In this way you'll be able to learn the customs of the group and not violate any of its rules or norms.

Small Group Culture

Many groups, especially those of long standing like work groups, develop small cultures with their own norms. **Group norms** are rules or standards of behavior identifying which behaviors are considered appropriate (for example, being willing to take on added tasks or directing conflict toward issues rather than toward people) and which are considered inappropriate (for example, coming in late or not contributing actively). Sometimes these rules for appropriate behavior are explicitly stated in a company contract or policy, such as "All members must attend department meetings." Sometimes the rules are implicit: "Members should be well groomed." Regardless of whether norms are spelled out or not, they're powerful regulators of members' behaviors.

Small group norms may apply to individual members as well as to the group as a whole and, of course, will differ from one society to another (Axtell, 1993). For example, in the United States men and women in business are expected to interact when making business decisions as well as when socializing. In Muslim and Buddhist societies, however, there are religious restrictions that prevent mixed-gender groups. In groups in some societies, including those of the United States, Bangladesh, Australia, Germany, Finland, and Hong Kong, punctuality for business meetings is very important. But in Morocco, Italy, Brazil, Zambia, Ireland, and Panama, time is less

ASK THE RESEARCHER

Team Problems

- *My professor placed us in teams to work on a project for the whole semester. Our group is having problems with several members' dominating the team, especially when we need to make a "team decision." These people just assume we all accept their decisions because we don't say anything different. We want to say something, but if we are going to work with them all semester, we don't want to get them mad at us or hurt their feelings. What can we do to survive this team experience and still get our voices heard?*

Teams and small groups all have their own personalities. Your team is made up of individuals! It is common for some members to dominate or talk all the time—perhaps even argue for arguing's sake. You can use idea-generating techniques to enable all members to have a voice in the decisions being made by your team. Your team needs to try out the nominal group technique described in this unit. It enables all members to participate by writing and presenting their ideas one at a time in a round-robin fashion. The technique even has a rank-ordering procedure to let the team members understand how important each suggestion was to the majority of its members. Try it! I think it will work for your team. Sometimes talking can be hazardous to a team's health. The technique will enable all members to participate whether they like to talk or not. It also takes the personality out of decision suggestions.

For further information: Moore, C. M. (1994). *Group techniques for idea building* (2nd ed.). Thousand Oaks, CA: Sage.

Carole A. Barbato (Ph.D., Kent State University) is an associate professor of communication studies and graduate faculty member at Kent State. She teaches classes in public speaking, small group, and interpersonal communication. Her research interests include small group communication, communication motives, and communication and aging. Carole (cbarbato@kent.edu) has provided team training to numerous organizations and small businesses. She is coauthor with W. I. Gorden, E. L. Nagel, and S. A. Myers of the 1996 book, *The Team Trainer: Winning Tools and Tactics for Successful Workouts*, published by Irwin. This book contains helpful suggestions for working in teams along with team-building exercises.

highly regarded; being late is no great insult and is even expected. In the United States and in much of Asia and Europe, meetings are typically held between two parties at a time. In many Persian Gulf states, however, the business executive is likely to conduct meetings with several different people—sometimes dealing with totally different issues—at the same time. In this situation you have to expect to share what in the United States would be "your time" with these other parties. In the United States very little interpersonal touching goes on during business meetings; in Arab countries, however, touching (for example, hand holding) is common and is a gesture of friendship.

Norms that regulate a particular group member's behavior, called **role** expectations, identify what each person in an organization is expected to do; for example, Pat is great at formatting and editing and so should play the role of secretary.

You're more likely to accept the norms of your group's culture when you feel your group membership is important and want to continue your membership in the group. You're also more likely to accept these norms when your group is cohesive. **Cohesiveness** means that you and the other members are closely connected, are attracted to one another, and depend on one another to meet your needs. Lastly, you're more apt to accept these norms if you'd be punished by negative reactions or exclusion from the group for violating them (Napier & Gershenfeld, 1992).

Power in the Small Group

Power permeates all small groups and in fact all relationships. It influences what you do, when, and with whom. It influences the employment you seek and the employment you get. It influences the friends you choose and don't choose and those who choose you and those who don't. It influences your romantic and family relationships—their success, failure, and level of satisfaction or dissatisfaction.

Power is what enables one person (the one with power) to control the behaviors of others. Thus, if A has power over B and C, then A, by virtue of this power and through the exercise of this power (or the threat of exercising it), can control the behaviors of B and C. Differences in individuals' amounts and types of power influence who makes important decisions, who will prevail in an argument, and who will control the finances.

Although all relationships involve power, they differ in the types of power that the people use and to which they respond. The following self-test will help you identify the six major types of power.

TEST YOURSELF

How Powerful Are You?

For each statement, indicate which of the following descriptions is most appropriate, using the following scale: 1 = true of 20 percent or fewer of the people I know; 2 = true of about 21 to 40 percent of the people I know; 3 = true of about 41 to 60 percent of the people I know; 4 = true of about 61 to 80 percent of the people I know; and 5 = true of 81 percent or more of the people I know.

____ **1.** My position is such that I often have to tell others what to do. For example, a mother's position demands that she tell her children what to do, a manager's position demands that he or she tell employees what to do, and so on.

____ **2.** People wish to be like me or identified with me. For example, high school football players may admire the former professional football player who is now their coach and want to be like him.

____ **3.** People see me as having the ability to give them what they want. For example, employers have the ability to give their employees increased pay, longer vacations, or improved working conditions.

____ **4.** People see me as having the ability to administer punishment or to withhold things they want. For example, employers have the ability to reduce voluntary overtime, shorten vacation time, or fail to improve working conditions.

____ **5.** Other people realize that I have expertise in certain areas of knowledge. For example, a doctor has expertise in medicine and so others turn to the doctor to tell them what to do. Someone knowledgeable about computers similarly possesses expertise.

____ **6.** Other people realize that I possess the communication ability to present an argument logically and persuasively.

HOW DID YOU DO? These statements refer to the six major types of power, as described in the text following this self-test. Low scores (1s and 2s) indicate your belief that you possess little of these particular types of power, and high scores (4s and 5s) indicate your belief that you possess a great deal of these particular types of power.

WHAT WILL YOU DO? How satisfied are you with your level of power? If you're not satisfied, what might you do about it? A good starting place, of course, is to learn the skills of communication—interpersonal, small group, and public speaking—discussed in this text. Consider

TEST YOURSELF, continued

the kinds of communication patterns that would help you communicate power and exert influence in group situations.

The six types of power covered in the self-test are (1) legitimate, (2) referent, (3) reward, (4) coercive, (5) expert, and (6) information or persuasion power (French & Raven, 1968; Raven, Centers, & Rodrigues, 1975). You have **legitimate power** (self-test statement 1) over another when this person believes you have a right by virtue of your position (for example, you're the appointed group leader) to influence or control his or her behavior. Legitimate power usually comes from the leadership roles people occupy. Teachers are often seen to have legitimate power, and this is doubly true for religious teachers. Parents are seen as having legitimate power over their children. Employers, judges, managers, doctors, and police officers are others who may hold legitimate power.

You have **referent power** (statement 2) over another person when that person wishes to be like you or identified with you. For example, an older brother may have referent power over a younger brother because the younger sibling wants to be like his older brother. Your referent power over another person increases when you're well liked and well respected, when you're seen as attractive and prestigious, when you're of the same gender, and when you have attitudes and experiences similar to those of the other person. This is why role models are so important: By definition, role models (sports figures are probably the best examples) possess referent power and exert great influence on those looking up to them.

You have **reward power** (statement 3) over a person if you have the ability to give that person rewards—either material (money, promotions, jewelry) or social (love, friendship, respect). Reward power increases attractiveness; we like those who have the power to reward us and who do in fact give us rewards.

Conversely, you have **coercive power** (statement 4) if you have the ability to remove rewards or to administer **punishments.** Usually, the two kinds of power go hand in hand; if you have reward power, you also have coercive power. For example, parents may grant as well as deny privileges to their children.

You possess **expert power** (statement 5) if group members regard you as having expertise or

UNDERSTANDING THEORY AND RESEARCH

Group Power

Recall (from Unit 3) that high-power-distance cultures are those in which power is concentrated in the hands of a few and there's a great difference in the power held by these people and by the ordinary citizen; in contrast, in low-power-distance cultures power is more evenly distributed throughout the citizenry (Hofstede, 1997). Groups also may be viewed in terms of high and low power distance. In high-power-distance groups the leader is far more powerful than the members. In low-power-distance groups leaders and members differ much less in their power.

Of the groups in which you'll participate—as a member or a leader—some will be high in power distance and others will be low. The skill is to recognize which is which, to follow the rules generally, and to break them only after you've thought through the consequences. For example, in low-power-distance groups, you're expected to confront a group leader (or friend or supervisor) assertively; acting assertively denotes a general feeling of equality (Borden, 1991). In high-power-distance groups, direct confrontation and assertiveness toward the leader (or any person in authority, such as a teacher or doctor) may be viewed negatively (Westwood, Tang, & Kirkbride, 1992; also see Bochner & Hesketh, 1994).

Working with Theories and Research

- *If you have access, visit Research Navigator (*www.researchnavigator.com*) and search the communication and sociology databases for "power." What types of questions engage the attention of researchers?*

knowledge—whether or not you truly possess such expertise. Expert power increases when you are seen as being unbiased and having nothing to gain personally from influencing others. It decreases if you are seen as biased and as having something to gain from securing the compliance of others.

You have **information power**, or persuasion power (statement 6), if you're seen as someone who can communicate logically and persuasively. Generally, persuasion power is attributed to people who are seen as having significant information and the ability to use that information in presenting a well-reasoned argument.

Idea-Generation Groups

Idea-generation groups are small groups that exist solely to generate ideas and often follow a formula called brainstorming (Osborn, 1957; Beebe & Masterson, 2000; DeVito, 1996). **Brainstorming** is a technique for bombarding a problem and generating as many ideas as possible. This technique involves two stages. The first is the brainstorming period proper; the second is the evaluation period.

The procedures are simple. A problem is selected that is amenable to many possible solutions or ideas. Group members are informed of the problem to be brainstormed before the actual session so that they can think about the topic. When the group meets, each person contributes as many ideas as he or she can think of. All ideas are recorded either in writing or on tape. During this idea-generating session, four general rules are followed.

Brainstorm Rule 1: Don't Criticize. In a brainstorming session all ideas are recorded. They're not evaluated, nor are they even discussed. Any negative criticism—whether verbal or nonverbal—is itself criticized by the leader or the members. This is a good general rule to follow in all creative thinking: Allow your idea time to develop before you look for problems with it. At the same time, don't praise the ideas either. All evaluations should be suspended during the brainstorming session.

Brainstorm Rule 2: Strive for Quantity. Linus Pauling, Nobel Prize winner for chemistry in 1954 and for peace in 1962, once said, "The best way to have a good idea is to have lots of ideas." This second rule of brainstorming embodies this concept. If you need an idea, you're more likely to find it in a group of many than in a group of few. Thus, in brainstorming, the more ideas the better.

Brainstorm Rule 3: Combine and Extend Ideas. Although you may not criticize a particular idea, you may extend it or combine it in some way. The value of a particular idea may be the way it stimulates someone to combine or extend it. Even if your modification seems minor or obvious, say it. Don't censor yourself.

Brainstorm Rule 4: Develop the Wildest Ideas Possible. The wilder the idea, the better. It's easier to tone an idea down than to build it up. A wild idea can easily be tempered, but it's not so easy to elaborate on a simple or conservative idea.

Sometimes a brainstorming session may break down, with members failing to contribute new ideas.

BUILDING COMMUNICATION SKILLS

Combating Idea Killers

Think about how you can be on guard against negative criticism and how you can respond to "idea killers" or "killer messages." Some expressions, such as those listed below, aim to stop an idea from being developed—to kill it in its tracks before it can even get off the ground. As you read down the list of these commonly heard killer messages, formulate at least one response you might give if someone used one of these on you or if you yourself used it to censor your own creative thinking.

1. It'll never work.
2. No one would vote for it.
3. It's too complex.
4. It's too simple.
5. It would take too long.
6. It's too expensive.
7. It's not logical.
8. What we have is good enough.
9. It just doesn't fit us.
10. It's impossible.

At this point the moderator may prod the members with statements such as the following:

- Let's try to get a few more ideas before we close this session.
- Can we piggyback any other ideas or add extensions on the suggestion to. . . .
- Here's what we have so far. As I read the list of contributed suggestions, additional ideas may come to mind.
- Here's an aspect we haven't focused on. Does this stimulate any ideas?

After all the ideas are generated—a period lasting no longer than 15 or 20 minutes—the group evaluates the entire list of ideas, using the critical thinking skills developed throughout this text. The ideas that are unworkable are thrown out; those that show promise are retained and evaluated. During this stage negative criticism is allowed.

Personal Growth Groups

Some *personal growth groups*, sometimes referred to as support groups, aim to help members cope with particular difficulties—such as drug addiction, having an alcoholic parent, being an ex-convict, or having a hyperactive child or a promiscuous spouse. Other groups are more clearly therapeutic and are designed to change significant aspects of an individual's personality or behavior.

Popular Personal Growth Groups

There are many varieties of support or personal growth groups. The *encounter group*, for example, tries to facilitate personal growth and the ability to deal effectively with other people (Rogers, 1970). One of its assumptions is that the members will be more effective psychologically and socially if they get to know and like themselves better. Consequently, the atmosphere of the encounter group is one of acceptance and support. Freedom to express one's inner thoughts, fears, and doubts is stressed.

The *assertiveness training group* aims to increase the willingness of its members to stand up for their rights and to act more assertively in a wide variety of situations (Adler, 1977).

The *consciousness-raising group* aims to help people cope with the problems society confronts them with. The members of a consciousness-raising group all have one characteristic in common (for example, they may all be women, unwed mothers, gay fathers, or recently unemployed executives). It's this commonality that leads the members to join together and help one another. In the consciousness-raising group the assumption is that similar people are best equipped to assist one another's personal growth. Structurally, the consciousness-raising group is leaderless. All members (usually numbering from 6 to 12) are equal in their control of the group and in their presumed knowledge.

Although all personal growth groups function somewhat differently, we can illustrate at least one possible pattern by looking at the steps and procedures that a sample consciousness-raising group might follow. These procedures are generally much more flexible than those followed in a problem-solving group, for example.

Some Rules and Procedures

Each group is likely to develop its own unique rules and procedures, yet you can get some idea of how such groups operate by looking at a fairly typical consciousness-raising group. The group may start each meeting by selecting a topic, usually by majority vote of the group. This topic may be drawn from a prepared list or suggested by one of the group members. But regardless of what topic is selected, it's always discussed from the point of view of the larger topic that brings these particular people together—let's say, sexual harassment. Whether the topic is men, employment, or family, it's pursued in light of the issues and problems of sexual harassment.

After a topic is selected, the first speaker is selected through some random procedure. That member speaks for about 10 minutes on his or her feelings, experiences, and thoughts. The focus is always on the individual. No interruptions are allowed. After the member has finished, the other group members may ask questions of clarification. The feedback from other members is to be totally supportive.

After questions of clarification have been answered, the next member speaks. The same procedure is followed until all members have spoken. After the last member has spoken, a general discussion follows. During this time members may relate different aspects of their experience to what the others have said. Or they may tell the group how they feel about some of the issues raised by others.

This procedure helps raise members' consciousness by giving them an opportunity to formulate and verbalize their thoughts on a particular topic, hear how others feel and think about the same topic, and formulate and answer questions of clarification.

BUILDING COMMUNICATION SKILLS

Listening to New Ideas

A useful skill for listening to new ideas is PIP'N, a technique that derives from Carl Rogers's (1970) emphasis on paraphrasing as a means for ensuring understanding and Edward deBono's (1976) PMI (plus, minus, and interesting) technique. PIP'N involves four steps:

P = *Paraphrase*. State in your own words what you think the other person is saying. This will ensure that you and the person proposing the idea are talking about the same thing. Your paraphrase also will provide the other person with the opportunity to elaborate or clarify his or her ideas.

I = *Interesting*. State something interesting that you find in the idea. Say why you think this idea might be interesting to you, to others, to the organization.

P = *Positive*. Say something positive about the idea. What is good about it? How might it solve a problem or make a situation better?

N = *Negative*. State any negatives that you think the idea might entail. Might it prove expensive? Difficult to implement? Is it directed at insignificant issues?

Try using PIP'N the next time you hear about a new idea; say, in conversation or in a small group. For practice, try PIP'N on the PIP'N technique itself: (1) Paraphrase the PIP'N technique; (2) say why the technique is interesting; (3) say something positive about it; and (4) say something negative about it.

Information-Sharing Groups

The purpose of information-sharing groups is to enable members to acquire new information or skills through a sharing of knowledge. In most information-sharing groups, all members have something to teach and something to learn. In some, however, the interaction takes place because some members have information and some don't.

Educational or Learning Groups

In *educational or learning groups,* the members pool their knowledge to the benefit of all, as in the popular law and medical student learning groups. Members may follow a variety of discussion patterns. For example, a historical topic might be developed chronologically, with the discussion progressing from the past into the present and perhaps predicting the future. Issues in developmental psychology, such as physical maturity or language development in the child, also might be discussed chronologically. Some topics lend themselves to spatial development. For example, study of the development of the United States might take either a spatial pattern, going from east to west, or a chronological pattern, going from 1776 to the present. Other suitable patterns, depending on the nature of the topic and the needs of the discussants, might be developed in terms of causes and effects, problems and solutions, or structures and functions.

Perhaps the most popular is the topical pattern. A group might discuss the challenges of raising a hyperactive child by itemizing and discussing each of the major problems. The structure of a corporation might also be considered in terms of its major divisions. As can be appreciated, topical approaches may be further systematized; for instance, a learning group might rank the problems of hyperactivity in terms of their importance or complexity or might order the major structures of the corporation in terms of decision-making power.

Focus Groups

A different type of learning group is the **focus group,** a small group assembled for a kind of in-depth interview. The aim here is to discover what people think about an issue or product; for example, what do men between 18 and 25 think of the new aftershave lotion and its packaging? What do young executives earning more than $100,000 think about buying a foreign luxury car?

In the focus group a leader tries to discover the beliefs, attitudes, thoughts, and feelings that members have so as to help an organization make decisions on changing the scent or redesigning the packaging or constructing advertisements for luxury cars. It is the leader's task to prod members to analyze their thoughts and feelings on a deeper level and to use the thoughts of one member to stimulate the thoughts of others.

Generally, approximately 12 people are assembled. The leader explains the process, the time limits, and the general goal of the group—let's say, for example, to discover why these 12 individuals requested information on the XYZ health plan but purchased a plan from another company. The idea, of course, is that these 12 people are standing in for or representing a wider population. In this example, the leader, who is usually a professional focus group facilitator rather than a member of the client organization itself, would ask a variety of questions such as: How did you hear about the XYZ health plan? What other health plans did you consider before making your actual purchase? What influenced you to buy the plan you eventually bought? Were any other people influential in helping you make your decision? Through the exploration of these and similar questions, the facilitator and the relevant members of the client organization (who may be seated behind a one-way mirror, watching the discussion) may put together a more effective health plan or more effective advertising strategies.

Problem-Solving Groups

A **problem-solving group** is a collection of individuals who meet to solve a problem or to reach a decision. In one sense this is the most exacting kind of group to participate in. It requires not only a knowledge of small group communication techniques but also a thorough knowledge of the particular problem. And it usually demands faithful adherence to a somewhat rigid set of rules. We'll look at this group first in terms of the classic and still popular problem-solving approach whereby we identify the steps to go through in solving a problem. In the context of this sequence, we'll consider the major decision-making methods. Finally, we'll survey some types of groups that are popular in organizations today: the nominal group, the Delphi method, quality circles and improvement groups.

The Problem-Solving Sequence

The approach developed by philosopher John Dewey (1910), the **problem-solving sequence,** is probably the one used most often. The six steps of the sequence (see Figure 11.2) are designed to make problem solving more efficient and effective: (1) De-

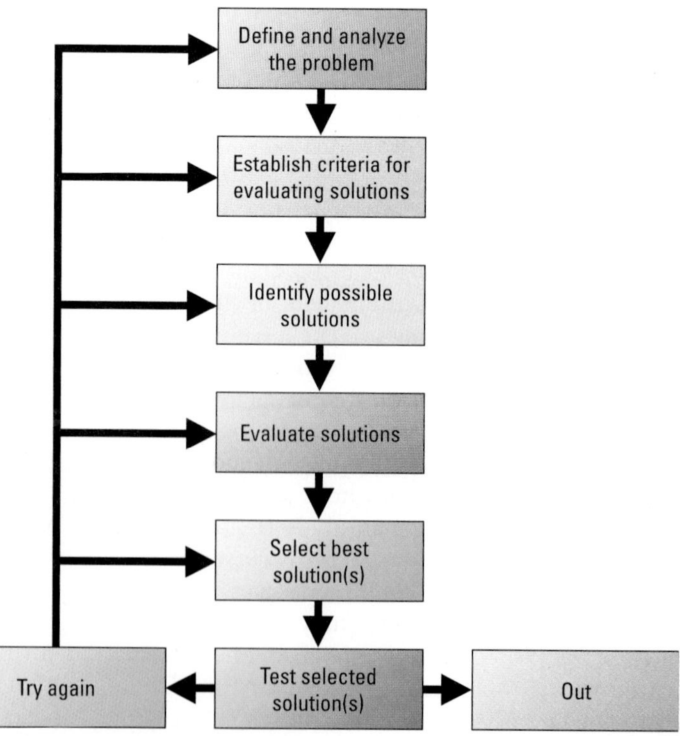

Figure 11.2
Steps in Problem-Solving Discussion
Although most small group theorists would advise you to follow the problem-solving pattern as presented here, others would alter it somewhat. For example, the pattern here advises you first to define the problem and then to establish criteria for identifying possible solutions. You would then keep these criteria in mind as you generated possible solutions (step 3). Another school of thought, however, would advise you to generate solutions first and to consider how they will be evaluated only after these solutions are proposed (Brilhart & Galanes, 1992). The advantage of this second approach is that you may generate more creative solutions if you're not restricted by standards of evaluation. The disadvantage is that you may spend a great deal of time generating very impractical solutions that would never meet the standards you'll eventually propose.

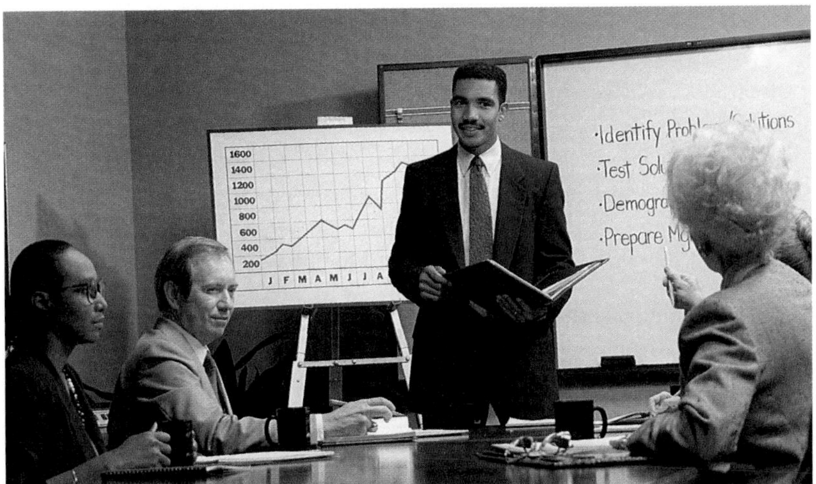

VIEWPOINT

What one principle of small group interaction do you find is violated most often? How would the groups you participate in be different if this principle were followed instead of violated?

fine and analyze the problem, (2) establish criteria, (3) identify possible solutions, (4) evaluate solutions, (5) select the best solution(s), and (6) test the selected solution(s).

Define and Analyze the Problem

In many instances the nature of the problem is clearly specified. For example, a group of designers might discuss how to package a new soap product. In other instances, however, the problem may be vague, and it may remain for the group to define it in concrete terms. Thus, for example, the general problem may be poor campus communications. But such a vague and general topic is difficult to tackle in a problem-solving discussion, so it's helpful to specify the problem clearly.

Limit the problem so that it identifies a manageable area for discussion. A question such as "How can we improve our company?" is too broad and general. The group might limit the question by, for example, identifying one issue within the company on which to focus. You might, for example, choose among issues such as the company website, internal memos, management-worker relationships, qualifications for bonuses, flexible time schedules, and office furniture.

Define the problem as an open-ended question ("How can we improve the company website?") rather than as a statement ("The company website needs to be improved") or a yes/no question ("Does the website need improvement?"). The open-ended question allows for greater freedom of exploration. It doesn't restrict the ways in which the group may approach the problem.

Appropriate questions for most problems revolve around the following issues: (1) Duration: How long has the problem existed? Is it likely to continue in the future? What is the predicted course of the problem? For example, will it grow or lessen in impact? (2) Causes: What are the major causes of the problem? How certain can we be that these are the actual causes? (3) Effects: What are the effects of the problem? How significant are they? Who is affected by this problem? How significantly are they affected? Is this problem causing other problems? How important are these other problems?

Establish Criteria for Evaluating Solutions

Before any solutions are proposed, you need to decide how to evaluate them. At this stage you identify the standards or criteria that you'll use in evaluating solutions or in selecting one solution over another. Generally, two types of criteria need to be considered. First, there are the practical criteria. For example, you might decide that solutions to the website problem must not increase the budget, must lead to a higher volume of business, must be constructed inhouse, must load almost immediately, and so on. Second, there are the value criteria. These are more difficult to identify. These might include, for example, requirements that the website reflect the culture of the company or that it represent the company's commitment to multiculturalism.

Identify Possible Solutions

At this stage identify as many solutions as possible. Focus on quantity rather than quality. Brainstorming may be particularly useful at this point (see the earlier discussion of idea-generation groups). Solutions to the website problem might include incorporating reviews of publications by company members, reviews of restaurants in the area, recruitment guidelines, and new employment opportunities within the company.

Evaluate Solutions

After all the solutions have been proposed, you go back and evaluate each according to the criteria you have established. For example, to what extent does incorporating reviews of area restaurants meet the evaluation criteria? Will it increase the budget? Each potential solution should be matched against the criteria.

An especially insightful technique for evaluating solutions (or gaining a different perspective on a problem) was offered by **critical thinking** pioneer Edward deBono (1987). DeBono's **critical thinking hats technique** involves thinking with six different "hats" and, in doing so, subjecting an issue to a six-part analysis.

- The *fact hat* focuses attention on the data—the facts and figures that bear on the problem. For example: What are the relevant data on the website? How can you get more information on the website's history? How much does it cost to establish and maintain a website? How much advertising revenue can you get?
- The *feeling hat* focuses attention on your feelings, emotions, and intuitions concerning the problem. How do you feel about the website and about making major changes?
- The *negative argument hat* asks that you become the devil's advocate. Why might this proposed solution fail? What is the worst-case scenario?
- The *positive benefits hat* asks that you look at the upside. What opportunities will a new format open up? What benefits will this website provide for employees? What would be the best thing that could happen?
- The *creative new idea hat* focuses attention on new ways of looking at the problem and can be easily combined with the techniques of brainstorming discussed earlier in this unit. What other ways can you look at this problem? What other functions can a website serve that have not been thought of? Can the website provide a service to the community as well?
- The *control of thinking hat* helps you analyze what you have done and are doing. It asks that you reflect on your own thinking processes and synthesize the results of your thinking. Have you adequately defined the problem? Are you focusing

MEDIA WATCH

The Third-Person Effect

The *third-person effect* concept is a theory of media influence claiming that people routinely believe they are influenced less by the media than their peers are. So, according to this theory, you tend to believe that your friends, neighbors, and coworkers are influenced more by the media than you are; you believe yourself to be the most resistant to influence. A variety of studies conducted on college students have supported this idea (Davison, 1983). Whether the topic was political advertising, rap music, or pornography, students felt they were less susceptible to media influence than were their peers (Hoffner et al., 2001). This belief, research finds, is especially strong when the media message is a negative or socially unacceptable one; for example, people think that messages of violence, racism, or sexism influence them *much* less than their peers. The effect is weakened but still present when the message is a more acceptable one (for example, public service announcements).

You and the Media

If you have access and want to learn more about this interesting theory, log on to Research Navigator (www.researchnavigator.com) and search the communication and psychology databases for "third-person effect." What can you add to the brief discussion presented here? You also might wish to try testing out this theory. For example, survey 10 or 20 people and ask them how influenced they feel they are by, say, media violence or racism. Then ask them if their friends and relatives are influenced by such media messages more than they are. Then conduct the same type of two-step survey with a more socially acceptable message, such as a media campaign on the value of education or the importance of proper diet. Do you find a third-person effect this time?

too much on insignificant issues? Have you given enough attention to possible negative effects?

Select the Best Solution(s)

At this stage the best solution or solutions are selected and put into operation. For instance, in the company website example, if "reviews of area restaurants" and "listings of new positions" best met the evaluation criteria, the group might then incorporate these two new items in the redesign of the website.

Groups may use different decision-making methods in deciding, for example, which criteria to use or which solutions to accept. Generally, groups use one of three methods: decision by authority, majority rule, or consensus.

Decision by Authority. In decision by authority members voice their feelings and opinions but the leader, boss, or CEO makes the final decision. This is surely an efficient method; it gets things done quickly, and the amount of discussion can be limited as desired. Another advantage is that experienced and informed members (for example, those who have been with the company longest) will probably exert a greater influence on the final decision. The great disadvantage is that group members may not feel the need to contribute their insights and may become distanced from the power within the group or organization. Another disadvantage is that this method may lead members to tell the decision maker what they feel she or he wants to hear, a condition that can easily lead to groupthink (Unit 12).

Majority Rule. With this method the group members agree to abide by the majority decision and may vote on various issues as the group works toward solving its problem. Majority rule is efficient, as there's usually the option of calling for a vote when the majority is in agreement. This is a useful method for issues that are relatively unimportant (What company should service the water cooler?) and when member satisfaction and commitment are not essential. One disadvantage is that it can lead to factioning, in which various minorities align against the majority. The method may also lead to limiting discussion once a majority has agreed and a vote is called.

Consensus. In some situations *consensus* means unanimous agreement; for example, a criminal jury must reach a unanimous decision to convict or acquit a defendant. In most business groups, however, consensus means that members agree that they can live with the solution; they agree that they can do whatever the solution requires (Kelly, 1994). Consensus is especially important when the group wants each member to be satisfied with and committed to

UNDERSTANDING THEORY AND RESEARCH

Group Polarization

Groups frequently make more extreme decisions than individuals—a tendency known as *group polarization* (Brauer, Judd, & Gliner, 1995; Friedkin, 1999; Bullock, McCluskey, Stamm, Tanaka, Torres, & Scott, 2003). For example, a group will take greater risks if the members are already willing to take risks, or will become more cautious if the members are already cautious. What seems to happen is that as a group member you estimate how others in the group feel about risk taking. If you judge the group as one of high risk takers, you're likely to become more willing to take risks than you were before the group interaction. When the group supports risky decisions, the polarization is referred to as the *risky-shift phenomenon*. Similarly, if you judge the group members as cautious and as low risk takers, you'll become even more cautious than you were before the interaction. In other words—and not surprisingly—your own attitudes toward risk will be heavily influenced by the attitudes you think the group possesses, and you'll change your attitudes to more closely match those of the group.

Working with Theories and Research

- *Have you ever observed group polarization? What happened? What implications does this theory have for, say, gang members, professors joining a new faculty, or investment analysts?*

the decision and the decision-making process as a whole (DeStephen & Hirokawa, 1988; Beebe & Masterson, 2000). The consensus method obviously takes the longest, and it can lead to a great deal of wasted time if members wish to prolong the discussion process needlessly or selfishly. This method may also put great pressure on the person who honestly disagrees but who doesn't want to prevent the group from making a decision.

Test Selected Solution(s)

After solutions are put into operation, test their effectiveness. The group might, for example, poll employees about the website changes or examine the number of hits. Or you might analyze the advertising revenue.

If the solutions you have adopted prove ineffective, you will need to go back to one of the previous stages and repeat part of the process. Often this takes the form of selecting other solutions to test. But it may also involve going farther back—to, for example, a reanalysis of the problem, an identification of other solutions, or a restatement of evaluation criteria.

Problem-Solving Groups at Work

The problem-solving sequence discussed here is used widely in business in a variety of different types of groups. Let's examine three group approaches popular in business that rely largely on the problem-solving techniques just discussed: the nominal group technique, the Delphi method, and quality circles.

The Nominal Group Technique

The **nominal group** technique is a method of problem solving that uses limited discussion and confidential voting to obtain a group decision. It's especially helpful when some members may be reluctant to voice their opinions in a regular problem-solving group or when the issue is controversial or sensitive. With this technique, each member contributes equally and each contribution is treated equally. Another advantage of the nominal group process is that it can be accomplished in a relatively short period of time. The nominal group approach can be divided into seven steps (Kelly, 1994):

1. The problem is defined and clarified for all members.
2. Each member writes down (without discussion or consultation with others) his or her ideas on or possible solutions to the problem.
3. Each member—in sequence—states one idea from his or her list, which is recorded on a board or flip chart so everyone can see it. This process is repeated until all suggestions are stated and recorded. Duplicates are then eliminated. Group agreement is secured before overlapping ideas are combined.
4. Each suggestion is clarified (without debate). Ideally, each suggestion is given equal time.
5. Each member rank orders the suggestions in writing.
6. The rankings of the members are combined to get a group ranking, which is then written on the board.
7. Clarification, discussion, and possible reordering may follow.
8. The highest-ranking solution may then be selected to be tested, or perhaps several high-ranking solutions may be put into operation.

The Delphi Method

In the **Delphi method** a group of "experts" is established, but there's no interaction among them; instead, they communicate by repeatedly responding to questionnaires (Tersine & Riggs, 1980; Kelly, 1994). The Delphi method is especially useful when you want to involve people who are geographically distant from one another, when you want all members to become part of the solution and to uphold it, or when you want to minimize the effects of dominant members or even of peer pressure. The method is best explained as a series of steps (Kelly, 1994):

1. The problem is defined (for example, "We need to improve intradepartmental communication"). What each member is expected to do is specified (for example, each member should contribute five ideas on this specific question).
2. Each member then anonymously contributes five ideas in writing. This step used to be completed through questionnaires sent through traditional mail but now is more frequently done through e-mail, which greatly increases the speed with which this entire process can be accomplished.
3. The ideas of all members are combined, written up, and distributed to all members.
4. Members then select the three or four best ideas from this composite list and submit these.
5. From these responses another list is produced and distributed to all members.
6. Members then select the one or two best ideas from the new list and submit these.
7. From these responses another list is produced and distributed to all members. The process may be repeated any number of times, but usually three rounds are sufficient for achieving a fair degree of agreement.

8. The "final" solutions are identified and are communicated to all members.

Quality Circles

A **quality circle** is a group of workers (usually about 6 to 12) whose task it is to investigate and make recommendations for improving the quality of some organizational function. The members are drawn from the workers whose area is being studied. Thus, for example, if the problem were to improve advertising on the Internet, then the quality circle membership would be drawn from the advertising and technology departments. Generally, the motivation for establishing quality circles is economic; the company's aim is to improve quality and profitability. Another related goal is to improve worker morale; because quality circles involve workers in decision making, workers may feel empowered and see themselves as more essential to the organization (Gorden & Nevins, 1993).

The basic idea is that people who work on similar tasks will be better able to improve their departments or jobs by pooling their insights and working through problems they share. The quality circle style of problem solving is often considered one of the major reasons for the success of many Japanese businesses, which use it extensively. Hundreds of U.S. organizations also use quality circles, but generally with less success than those in Japan (Gorden & Nevins, 1993).

Quality circle members investigate problems using any method they feel might be helpful; for example, they may form face-to-face problem-solving groups or use nominal groups or Delphi methods. The group then reports its findings and its suggestions to those who can do something about it. In some cases the quality circle members may implement their solutions without approval from upper management levels.

A somewhat similar type of group is the improvement or *kaizen* group, named for a Japanese term meaning "continual improvement" (Beebe & Masterson, 2000). Kaizen groups are based on the assumption that every process or product in any organization can be improved. Such groups may be set up for a certain amount of time or may be permanent.

Telling Secrets

In groups of close friends, among family members, or in standing workplace committees, people often exchange secrets with the implied assumption that they will not be revealed to outsiders. Revealing or not revealing such secrets often has ethical implications. In *Secrets* (1983), ethicist Sissela Bok identifies three types of situations in which she argues it would be unethical to reveal the secrets of another person. These conditions aren't always easy to identify in any given instance, but they do provide excellent starting points for asking whether or not it's ethical to reveal what we know about another person. And, of course, for any situation, there may be legitimate exceptions.

- It's unethical to reveal information that you have promised to keep secret. When you promise to keep information hidden, you take on an ethical responsibility.
- It's unethical to say things about another person when you know the information to be false. When you try to deceive listeners by telling falsehoods about another, your communication is unethical.
- It's unethical to invade the privacy to which everyone has a right—to reveal information that no one else has a right to know. This is especially unethical when such disclosures can hurt the individual involved.

There may be situations when you have an obligation to reveal a secret. For example, Bok (1983) argues that you have an obligation to reveal a secret when keeping the information hidden will do more harm than good—a situation that often is not easy to determine.

WHAT WOULD YOU DO? How would you handle the following situations? (1) An instructor who supervises your study group confides that she is a confirmed racist and proud of it. (2) A 16-year-old member of the wilderness group you're leading confides that she's having unprotected sex with her supervisor at work, a married man. (3) A community religious leader confides that he's skimming a portion of the members' contributions to fund his retirement. (4) An 18-year-old student whose internship you're supervising confides to you that he intends to commit suicide (an example offered by Bok).

SUMMARY

This unit introduced the nature of the small group and discussed four major types of groups and their functions.

1. A small group is a collection of individuals that is small enough for all members to communicate with relative ease as both senders and receivers. The members are connected to one another by some common purpose and have some degree of organization or structure among them.

2. Relationship groups (primary groups) generally serve relationship needs for affiliation, affirmation, and affection and include family and friendship networks. Task groups (secondary groups) are formed to accomplish something, often work related, and may then be disbanded.
3. Reference groups are groups from which you derive your values and norms of behavior; membership groups are groups in which you participate but whose values you don't necessarily adopt.
4. Small groups make use of four major formats: the round table, the panel, the symposium, and the symposium–forum.
5. Most small groups develop norms or rules that operate much like a culture's norms, identifying what is considered appropriate behavior for the group members.
6. Power operates in all groups. Six types of power may be identified: legitimate, referent, reward, coercive, expert, and information or persuasion.
7. The idea-generation or brainstorming group attempts to generate as many ideas as possible.
8. The personal growth group helps members to deal with personal problems and to function more effectively. Popular types of personal growth groups are the encounter group, the assertiveness training group, and the consciousness-raising group.
9. The educational or learning group attempts to acquire new information or skill through a mutual sharing of knowledge or insight.
10. The focus group aims to discover what people think about an issue or product through a kind of in-depth group interview.
11. The problem-solving group attempts to solve a particular problem, or at least to reach a decision that may cause the problem to solve itself.
12. The six steps in the problem-solving sequence are: Define and analyze the problem; establish criteria for evaluating solutions; identify possible solutions; evaluate solutions; select best solution(s); and test solution(s).
13. The six hats technique is especially useful in analyzing problems and consists of focusing on different aspects of the problem: facts, feelings, negative arguments, positive benefits, creative or new ways of viewing problems, and control of thinking processes.
14. Decision-making methods include authority, majority rule, and consensus.
15. Small groups that are widely used in business today include the nominal group, the Delphi method, and quality circles.

KEY TERMS

group
small group stages
phatic communication
small group formats
round table
panel
symposium
symposium–forum
mailing list group
chat groups
group norms
role
cohesiveness
power
legitimate power
referent power
reward power
coercive power
expert power
information power
idea-generation group
brainstorming
personal growth groups
information-sharing groups
focus group
problem-solving group
problem-solving sequence
critical thinking
critical thinking hats technique
nominal group
Delphi method
quality circles

THINKING CRITICALLY ABOUT

Small Group Communication

1. Studies find that persons high in communication apprehension are generally less effective in idea-generation groups than are those low in apprehension (Jablin, 1981; Comadena, 1984; Cragan & Wright, 1990). Why do you think this is so?
2. What norms govern your class in human communication? What norms govern your family? Your place of work? Do you have any difficulty with these norms?
3. In research on chat groups, it was found that people were more likely to comment on a participant's message when that message was negative than when it was positive (Rollman, Krug, & Parente, 2000). Do you find this to be true? If so, why do you think this occurs?
4. Is the problem-solving sequence described in this unit also appropriate for resolving interpersonal conflicts? Can you trace an example through this sequence?
5. What type of criteria would an advertising agency use in evaluating a campaign to sell soap? A university in evaluating a new multicultural curriculum? Parents in evaluating a preschool for their children?
6. Visit the Creativity Web at http://members/optusnet.com.au/~charles57/creative/index2.html for a wealth of links to all aspects of creativity—quotations, affirmations, humor, discussions of the brain and the creative process, and more. What can you find here that might be of value to brainstorming and to idea generation generally?

UNIT 12

Members and Leaders

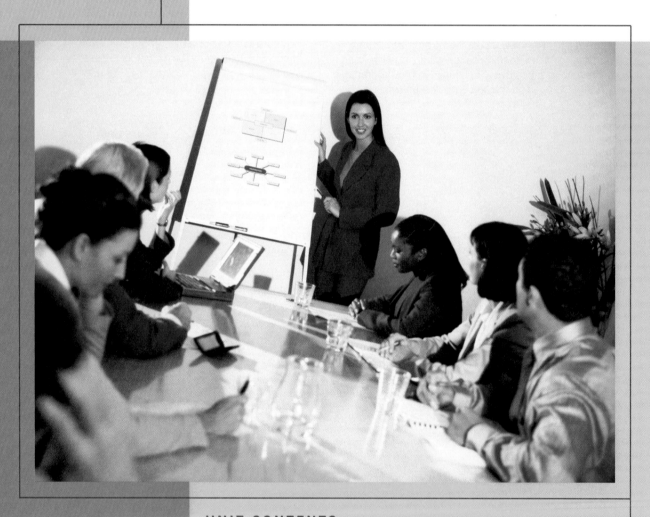

UNIT CONTENTS

Throughout your life you'll participate in a wide variety of groups—as a member of a work group, as a part of a social or neighborhood group, or as a player on a team. Probably you'll also lead some of these social or work groups, and your leadership responsibilities are likely to increase as you rise in the group hierarchy. In this unit you'll learn

- how membership and leadership work in groups
- how you can become a more effective member and a more responsive and influential leader

Members in Small Group Communication

You can view membership in small group communication situations from a variety of perspectives—in terms of the roles that members serve, the types of contributions they make, and the principles for more effective participation.

Member Roles

Group member roles fall into three general classes—group task roles, group building and maintenance roles, and individual roles—a classification introduced in early research (Benne & Sheats, 1948) and still widely used today (Lumsden & Lumsden, 1996; Beebe & Masterson, 2000). These roles are, of course, frequently served by leaders as well.

Think about your own behavior, your own membership style, as you read down the lists in the role descriptions that follow. Which of these do you regularly serve? Are there productive roles that you never or rarely serve? Are there destructive roles that you often serve?

Group Task Roles

Group task roles are those that help the group focus more specifically on achieving its goals. In serving any of these roles, you act not as an isolated individual but rather as a part of the larger whole. The needs and goals of the group dictate the task roles you serve. As an effective group member you would serve several of these functions.

Some people, however, lock into a few specific roles. For example, one person may almost always seek the opinions of others; another may concentrate on elaborating details; still another, on evaluating suggestions. Usually this kind of single focus is counterproductive. It's usually better for group task roles to be spread more evenly so that each member may serve many roles. The 12 specific group task roles are these:

- The *initiator-contributor* presents new ideas or new perspectives on old ideas, suggests new goals, or proposes new procedures or organizational strategies.
- The *information seeker* asks for facts and opinions and seeks clarification of the issues being discussed.
- The *opinion seeker* tries to discover the values underlying the group's task.
- The *information giver* presents facts and opinions to the group members.
- The *opinion giver* presents values and opinions and tries to spell out what the values of the group should be.
- The *elaborator* gives examples and tries to work out possible solutions, trying to build on what others have said.
- The *coordinator* spells out relationships among ideas and suggested solutions and coordinates the activities of the different members.
- The *orienter* summarizes what has been said and addresses the direction the group is taking.
- The *evaluator-critic* evaluates the group's decisions, questions the logic or practicality of the suggestions, and thus provides the group with both positive and negative feedback.
- The *energizer* stimulates the group to greater activity.
- The *procedural technician* takes care of various mechanical duties such as distributing group materials and arranging seating.
- The *recorder* writes down the group's activities, suggestions, and decisions; he or she serves as the memory of the group.

Group Building and Maintenance Roles

Most groups focus not only on the task to be performed but on interpersonal relationships among members. If the group is to function effectively, and if members are to be both satisfied and productive, these relationships must be nourished. When these needs are not met, group members may become irritable when the group process gets bogged down, may engage in frequent conflicts, or may find the small group process as a whole unsatisfying. The group and its members need the same kind of support that individuals need. The *group building and maintenance roles* serve this general function. Group building and maintenance functions are broken down into seven specific roles:

- The *encourager* supplies members with positive reinforcement in the form of social approval or praise for their ideas.

- The *harmonizer* mediates differences among group members.
- The *compromiser* offers compromises as a way to resolve conflicts between his or her ideas and those of others.
- The *gatekeeper-expediter* keeps the channels of communication open by reinforcing the efforts of others.
- The *standard setter* proposes standards for the functioning of the group or for its solutions.
- The *group observer and commentator* keeps a record of the proceedings and uses this in the group's evaluation of itself.
- The *follower* goes along with the members of the group, passively accepts the ideas of others, and functions more as an audience than as an active member.

Individual Roles

The group task and group building and maintenance roles just considered are productive roles; they aid the group in achieving its goals. *Individual roles,* on the other hand, are counterproductive; they hinder the group's productivity and member satisfaction, largely because they focus on serving individual rather than group needs. Eight specific types are identified:

- The *aggressor* expresses negative evaluation of the actions or feelings of the group members; he or she attacks the group or the problem being considered.
- The *blocker* provides negative feedback, is disagreeable, and opposes other members or suggestions regardless of their merit.
- The *recognition seeker* tries to focus attention on himself or herself rather than on the task at hand, boasting about his or her own accomplishments.
- The *self-confessor* expresses his or her own feelings and personal perspectives rather than focusing on the group.
- The *playboy/playgirl* jokes around without any regard for the group process.
- The *dominator* tries to run the group or the group members by pulling rank, flattering members of the group, or acting the role of the boss.
- The *help seeker* expresses insecurity or confusion or deprecates himself or herself and thus tries to gain sympathy from the other members.
- The *special interest pleader* disregards the goals of the group and pleads the case of some special group.

As you might expect, your tendency to play group versus individual roles will be influenced by your culture—and especially by your individualist or collectivist orientation, as discussed in Unit 3.

Interaction Process Analysis

Another way of looking at the contributions group members make is through **interaction process analysis** (IPA), developed by Robert Bales (1950). In this system you analyze the contributions of members under four general categories: (1) social-emotional positive contributions, (2) social-emotional negative contributions, (3) attempted answers, and (4) questions. Each of these four areas contains three subdivisions, yielding a total of 12 categories into which you can classify group members' contributions (Table 12.1). Note that the categories under social-emotional positive are the natural opposites of those under social-emotional negative, and those under attempted answers are the natural opposites of those under questions. You may want to try out Bales's IPA system by listening to a small group discussion or a televised situation comedy or drama and recording the interactions using Table 12.1.

Both the three-part member role classification and the IPA categories are useful for analyzing the contributions members make in small group situations. When you look at member contributions through these systems, you can see, for example, if one member is locked into a particular role or if the group process is breaking down because too many people are serving individual rather than group goals or because social-emotional negative comments dominate the discussion. You should also be in a better position to offer improvement suggestions for individual members based on this analysis.

Member Participation

For another perspective on group membership, let's consider the recommendations for effective participation in small group communication. Look at these suggestions as an elaboration and extension of the characteristics of effective conversation enumerated in Unit 9.

Be Group or Team Oriented

In the small group you're a member of a team, a larger whole. As a group your task is to pool your talents, knowledge, and insights so as to arrive at a better solution than any one person could have developed. This call for group orientation is not to be taken as a suggestion that members abandon their individuality or give up their personal values or be-

Table 12.1
Interaction Process Analysis Form

The names of participants appear in the top spaces, as shown by the examples here. In the column under each participant's name, you place a slash mark for each contribution in each of the 12 categories.

		Joe	Judy	Liz	Mike	Peg
Social–Emotional Positive Contributions	Shows solidarity					
	Shows tension release					
	Shows agreement					
Social–Emotional Negative Contributions	Shows disagreement					
	Shows tension					
	Shows antagonism					
Attempted Answers	Gives suggestions					
	Gives opinions					
	Gives information					
Questions	Asks for suggestions					
	Asks for opinions					
	Asks for information					

liefs for the sake of the group, however. Individuality with a group orientation is what is advocated here.

Center Conflict on Issues

It's particularly important in the small group to center conflict on issues rather than on personalities. When you disagree, make it clear that your disagreement is with the solution suggested or with the ideas expressed, not with the person who expressed them. Similarly, when someone disagrees with what you say, don't take it as a personal attack. Instead, view this as an opportunity to discuss issues from an alternative point of view.

Be Critically Open-Minded

Because the most effective and creative solutions often emerge from a combination of ideas, approach small group situations with flexibility; come to the group with ideas and information but without firmly formulated conclusions. Advance any solutions or conclusions tentatively rather than with certainty. Be willing to alter your suggestions and revise them in light of the discussion.

Ensure Understanding

Make sure that your ideas are understood by all participants. If something is worth saying, it's worth saying clearly. When in doubt, ask: "Is that clear?" "Did I explain that clearly?" Make sure, too, that you understand fully the contributions of other members, especially before you take issue with them. In fact, as explained in Unit 11, it's often wise to preface any extended disagreement with some kind of paraphrase to give the other person the opportunity to clarify, deny, or otherwise alter what was said. For example, you might say "As I understand it, you want to exclude freshmen from playing on the football team. Is that correct? I disagree with that idea and I'd like to explain why I think that would be a mistake."

Beware of Groupthink

Groupthink is a way of thinking that people use when agreement among members has become excessively important. Overemphasis on agreement among members tends to shut out realistic and logical analysis of a problem or of possible alternatives (Janis, 1983; Mullen, Tara, Salas, & Driskell, 1994). The term *groupthink* itself is meant to signal a "deterioration of mental efficiency, reality testing, and moral judgment that results from in-group pressures" (Janis, 1983, p. 9).

The following symptoms should help you recognize groupthink in groups you observe or participate in (Janis, 1983; Schafer & Crichlow, 1996):

- Group members think the group and its members are invulnerable.
- Members create rationalizations to avoid dealing with warnings or threats.
- Members believe their group is moral.
- Those opposed to the group are perceived in simplistic, stereotyped ways.
- Group pressure is applied to any member who expresses doubts or questions the group's arguments or proposals.
- Members censor their own doubts.
- Group members believe all are in unanimous agreement, whether this is stated or not.
- Group members emerge whose function it is to guard the information that gets to other members, especially when it may create diversity of opinion.

Here are three suggestions for combating groupthink.

1. When too-simple solutions are offered to problems, try to illustrate (with specific examples, if possible) for the group members how the complexity of the problem is not going to yield to the solutions offered.
2. When you feel that members are not expressing their doubts about the group or its decisions, encourage members to voice disagreement. Ask members to play devil's advocate, to test the adequacy of the solution. Or, if members resist, do it yourself. Similarly, if you feel there is unexpressed disagreement, ask specifically if anyone disagrees. If you still get no response, it may be helpful to ask everyone to write his or her comments anonymously, then read them aloud to the group.
3. To combat the group pressure toward agreement, reward members who do voice disagreement or doubt. Say, for example, "That's a good argument; we need to hear more about the potential problems of this proposal. Does anyone else see any problems?"

Leaders in Small Group Communication

A leader influences the thoughts and behaviors of others and establishes the direction that others follow. In many small groups one person serves as leader. In other groups leadership may be shared by several persons.

In some groups a person may be appointed the leader or may serve as leader because of her or his position within the company or hierarchy. In other groups the leader may emerge as the group proceeds in fulfilling its functions or may be elected leader by the group members. Two significant factors exert considerable influence on who emerges as group leader. One is the extent of active participation: The person who talks the most is more likely to emerge as leader (Mullen, Salas, & Driskell, 1989; Shaw & Gouran, 1990). The second factor is effective listening: Members who listen effectively will emerge as leaders more often than those who don't (Johnson & Bechler, 1998; Bechler & Johnson, 1995).

The emergent leader performs the duties of leadership, though not asked or expected to, and gradually becomes recognized by the members as the group's leader. And because this person has now proved herself or himself an effective leader, it's not surprising that this emergent leader often becomes the designated leader for future groups. Generally, the emergent leader serves as leader as long as the group members are satisfied. When they're not, they may encourage another member to emerge as leader. But as long as the emergent leader serves effectively, the group will probably not look to others.

In any case the role of the leader or leaders is vital to the well-being and effectiveness of the group. Even in leaderless groups in which all members are equal, leadership functions must still be served.

Approaches to Leadership

Not surprisingly, **leadership** has been the focus of considerable attention from theorists and researchers, who have used numerous approaches to understand this particular communication behavior. Before reading about these approaches, you may wish to take the self-test below to examine yourself as a leader.

TEST YOURSELF

Are You Leader Material?

This self-test is designed to stimulate you to think about yourself in the role of leader. Respond to the following statements in terms of how you perceive yourself and how you think others perceive you, using a 10-point scale ranging from 10 (extremely true) to 1 (extremely false).

Others see me as		I see myself as		Perceptions
____	1.	____	1.	Generally popular with group members

ASK THE RESEARCHER

Becoming a Leader

■ *I'm going to start a new job—a great position at a large investment firm. I'm very focused on rising in the organization (yes, I want status and money), and I want to know what I can do to establish myself as someone who has leadership potential. Are there any communication skills that are absolutely essential and that I should concentrate on?*

There are a number of things you can do to establish yourself as having leadership potential. First and foremost, demonstrate task-relevant expertise. Don't be a know-it-all, but do share accurate information and insightful interpretations of complex data when you have the opportunity to do so. If you don't know the answer to a question, say so, but show initiative by offering to find the answer for the person who posed the question. Then be sure to follow up with a correct, detailed response in a timely way.

Second, demonstrate relational competence. Always be civil and pleasant to your colleagues, regardless of the circumstances. Don't engage in political squabbles with your peers, but do work to maintain productive lines of communication between conflicted persons or groups.

Finally, let your word be your bond. Credibility is your most precious possession. Always be authentic in your dealings with others. If you want to be a leader, your colleagues must trust you.

For further information: Frey, L. R., & Barge, J. K. (1997). *Managing group life: Communicating in decision-making groups.* Boston: Houghton Mifflin. And Hawkins, K. W., & Fillion, B. (1999). Perceived communication skill needs for work groups. *Communication Research Reports, 16,* 167–174.

Katherine Hawkins (Ph.D., University of Texas) is professor of communication studies at Clemson University. She teaches courses in communication theory and research methods. She also serves as department chair and is a past president of the Southern States Communication Association.

____ 2. ____ 2. Knowledgeable about the topics and subjects discussed

____ 3. ____ 3. Dependable

____ 4. ____ 4. Effective in establishing group goals

____ 5. ____ 5. Competent in giving directions

____ 6. ____ 6. Capable of energizing group members

____ 7. ____ 7. Charismatic (dynamic, engaging, powerful)

____ 8. ____ 8. Empowering of group members

____ 9. ____ 9. Moral and honest

____ 10. ____ 10. Skilled in balancing the concerns of getting the task done and satisfying the group members' personal needs

____ 11. ____ 11. Flexible in adjusting leadership style on the basis of the unique situation

____ 12. ____ 12. Able to delegate responsibility

HOW DID YOU DO? This test was designed to encourage you to look at yourself in terms of the four approaches to leadership that will be discussed in the following text. Phrases 1–3 refer to the traits approach to leadership, which defines a leader as a person who possesses certain qualities. Phrases 4–6 refer to the functional approach, which defines a leader as a person who performs certain functions. Phrases 7–9 refer to the transformational approach, which defines a leader as a person who inspires the group members to become the best they can be. Phrases 10–12 refer to the situational approach, which defines a leader as someone who can adjust his or her style to balance the needs of the specific situation.

To compute your scores:

TEST YOURSELF, continued

1. Add your scores for statements 1–3: ________. This will give you an idea of how you and others see you in terms of the leadership qualities identified by the *traits approach.*
2. Add your scores for statements 4–6: ________. This will give you an idea of how you and others see you in relation to the varied leadership functions considered in the *functional approach.*
3. Add your scores for statements 7–9: ________. This will give you an idea of how you and others see you as a *transformational leader.*
4. Add your scores for statements 10–12: ________. This will give you an idea of how you and others see you as a *situational leader.*

WHAT WILL YOU DO? As you read the remainder of this unit and the rest of the book, try to identify specific skills and competencies you might learn that would enable you to increase your scores on all four approaches to leadership. Also, try searching the Web for information on "leadership" as well as, say, "business leadership" and "political leaders."

The *traits approach to leadership* argues that leaders must possess certain qualities if they're to function effectively. Some of the traits found to be associated with leadership are intelligence, dominance, honesty, foresight, altruism, popularity, sociability, cooperativeness, knowledge, and dependability (Hackman & Johnson, 1991). The problem with the traits approach is that the specific qualities called for will vary with the situation, with the members, and with the culture in which the leader functions. Thus, for example, the leader's knowledge and personality are generally significant factors; but for

COMMUNICATION@WORK

Mentoring as Leadership

True leadership must be for the benefit of the followers, not the enrichment of the leaders.

—Robert Townsend

In a mentoring relationship, an experienced individual (mentor) helps to train a less experienced person (mentee or protégé). An accomplished teacher, for example, might mentor a newly arrived or novice teacher. The mentor guides the new person through the ropes, teaches the strategies and techniques for success, and otherwise communicates his or her knowledge and experience to the newcomer.

Mentoring usually involves a one-on-one relationship between an expert and a novice—a relationship that is supportive and trusting. There's a mutual and open sharing of information and thoughts about the job. The relationship enables the novice to try out new skills under the guidance of an expert, to ask questions, and to obtain the feedback so necessary in learning complex skills.

In a study of middle-level managers, those who had mentors and participated in mentoring relationships were found to earn more frequent promotions and higher salaries than those who didn't (Scandura, 1992). And the mentoring relationship is one of the three primary paths to career achievement among African American men and women (Bridges, 1996). It's also interesting to note that similarity in race or gender between mentor and protégé doesn't seem to influence the mentoring experience (Barr, 2000).

At the same time that a mentor helps a novice, the mentor benefits from clarifying his or her thoughts, from seeing the job from the perspective of a newcomer, and from considering and formulating answers to a variety of questions. Much the way a teacher learns from teaching and from students, a mentor learns from mentoring and from protégés.

Communicating@Work

Although mentoring is generally a positive experience, mentoring relationships can be dysfunctional (O'Neill & Sankowsky, 2001). What kinds of mentoring would you consider dysfunctional?

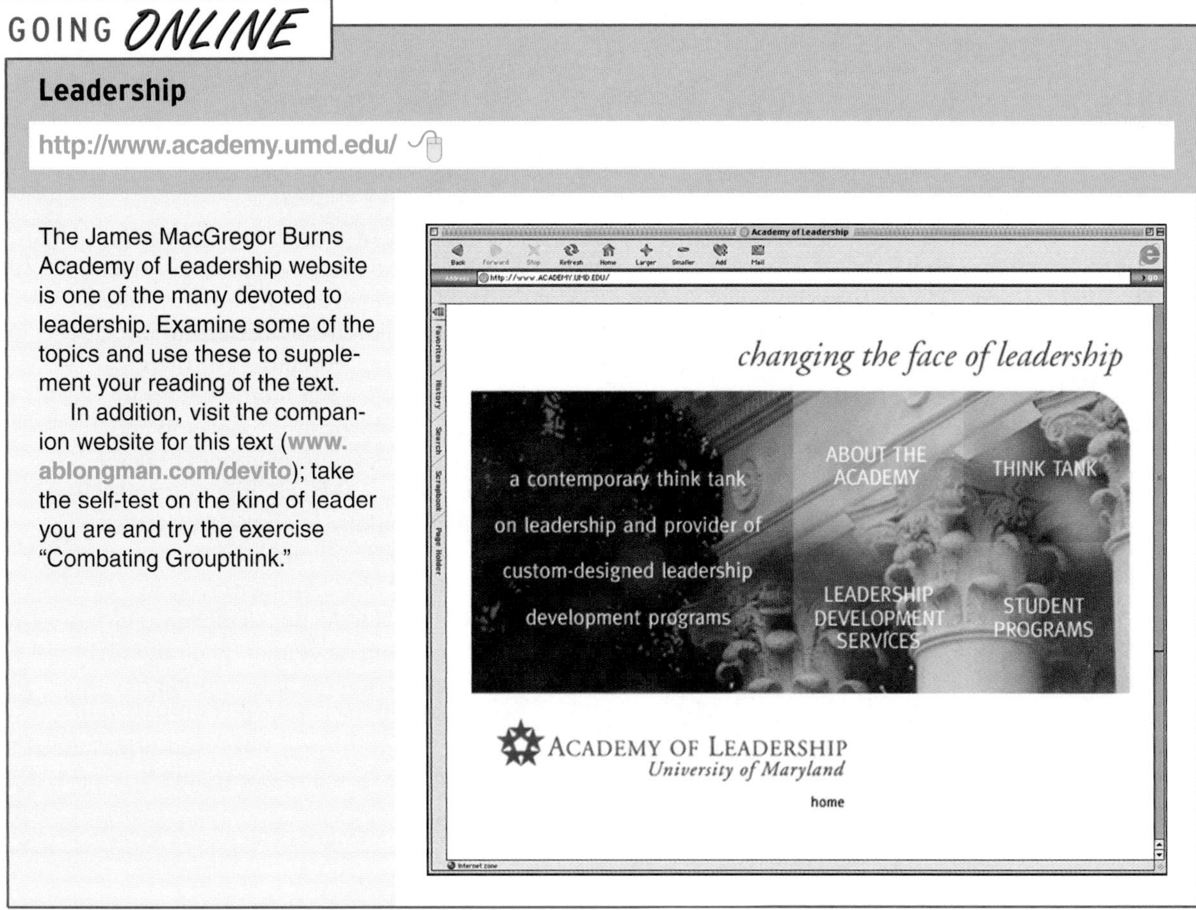
GOING ONLINE
Leadership
http://www.academy.umd.edu/
The James MacGregor Burns Academy of Leadership website is one of the many devoted to leadership. Examine some of the topics and use these to supplement your reading of the text.
In addition, visit the companion website for this text (www.ablongman.com/devito); take the self-test on the kind of leader you are and try the exercise "Combating Groupthink."
changing the face of leadership
a contemporary think tank on leadership and provider of custom-designed leadership development programs
ABOUT THE ACADEMY
THINK TANK
LEADERSHIP DEVELOPMENT SERVICES
STUDENT PROGRAMS
ACADEMY OF LEADERSHIP
University of Maryland
home

some groups a knowledge of financial issues and a serious personality might be effective, whereas for other groups a knowledge of design and a more humorous personality might be effective.

The *functional approach to leadership* focuses on what the leader should do in a given situation. We have already considered some of these functions in the discussion of group membership, which identified group roles. Other functions found to be associated with leadership are setting group goals, giving direction to group members, and summarizing the group's progress (Schultz, 1996). Still other functions are identified in the section entitled "Functions of Leadership," later in this unit.

In the *transformational approach to leadership* the leader elevates the group's members, enabling them not only to accomplish the group task but to also emerge as more empowered individuals (Li & Shi, 2003). At the center of the transformational approach is the concept of charisma, that quality of an individual that makes us believe in or want to follow him or her. Gandhi, Martin Luther King Jr., and John F. Kennedy may be cited as examples of transformational leaders. These leaders were seen as role models of what they asked of their members, were perceived as extremely competent and able leaders, and articulated moral goals (Northouse, 1997). We'll return to this concept of charisma in the discussion of credibility in Unit 18.

The *situational approach to leadership* focuses on the two major responsibilities of the leader—accomplishing the task at hand and ensuring the satisfaction of the members—and recognizes that the leader's style must vary on the basis of the specific situation. Just as you adjust your interpersonal style in conversation or your motivational appeals in public speaking on the basis of the particular situation, so you must adjust your leadership style. Leadership effectiveness, then, depends on combining the concerns for task and people according to the specifics of the situation. Some situations will call for high concentration on task issues but will need

UNDERSTANDING THEORY AND RESEARCH

Styles of Leadership

Small group communication researchers distinguish three basic types of group leaders: laissez-faire, democratic, and authoritarian (Bennis & Nanus, 1985; Hackman & Johnson, 1991).

The **laissez-faire leader** takes no initiative in directing or suggesting alternative courses of action. Rather, this leader allows the group to develop and progress on its own, even allowing it to make its own mistakes. The laissez-faire leader answers questions and provides information only when specifically asked. During the group interaction, this leader neither compliments nor criticizes the group's members or their progress. Generally, this type of leadership results in a satisfied but inefficient group.

The **democratic leader** provides direction but allows the group to develop and progress the way its members wish. This leader encourages group members to determine their own goals and procedures and works to stimulate the self-direction and self-actualization of group members. Unlike the laissez-faire leader, the democratic leader does contribute suggestions and does comment on member and group performance. Generally, this form of leadership results in both satisfaction and efficiency.

The **authoritarian leader,** the opposite of the laissez-faire leader, determines group policies and makes decisions without consulting or securing agreement from the members. This leader discourages member-to-member communication but encourages communication from member to leader. The authoritarian leader is concerned with getting the group to accept his or her decisions rather than making its own. If the authoritarian leader is competent, the group may be highly efficient, but its members are likely to be less personally satisfied.

Working with Theories and Research

- *Which leadership style—say, in a work situation with colleagues—are you likely to feel most comfortable using? Most comfortable working with as a group member?*

little in the way of people encouragement. For example, a group of scientists working on AIDS research would probably need a leader primarily to provide them with the needed information to accomplish their task. They would be self-motivating and would probably need little in the way of social and emotional encouragement. On the other hand, a group of recovering alcoholics might require leadership that stressed the social and emotional needs of the members.

An interesting extension of the situational approach portrays four basic leadership styles, as illustrated in Figure 12.1 (Hersey, Blanchard, & Johnson, 2001). This theory claims that groups differ in their task and relationship maturity. A group high in task maturity has members who are knowledgeable about and experienced with the topic, task, and group process. Because of this maturity, group members are able to set realistic and attainable goals and are willing to take responsibility for their decisions. A group high in relationship maturity has members who are motivated to accomplish the task and are confident in their abilities to accomplish it. Maturity varies with the task; an individual may, for example, be highly mature when dealing with discussions of food and exercise but very immature when dealing with discussions of finances.

Effective leadership, then, depends on the leader's assessment of the group's task and relationship maturity. And, to complicate matters just a bit, the maturity of the group will change as the group develops—so the style of leadership will have to change in response to the changes in the group. The model identifies four different styles:

- The *telling style,* most appropriate for the group lacking both task and relationship maturity, is highly directive; the leader, who is significantly more knowledgeable or more powerful than the members, tells the group what has to be done

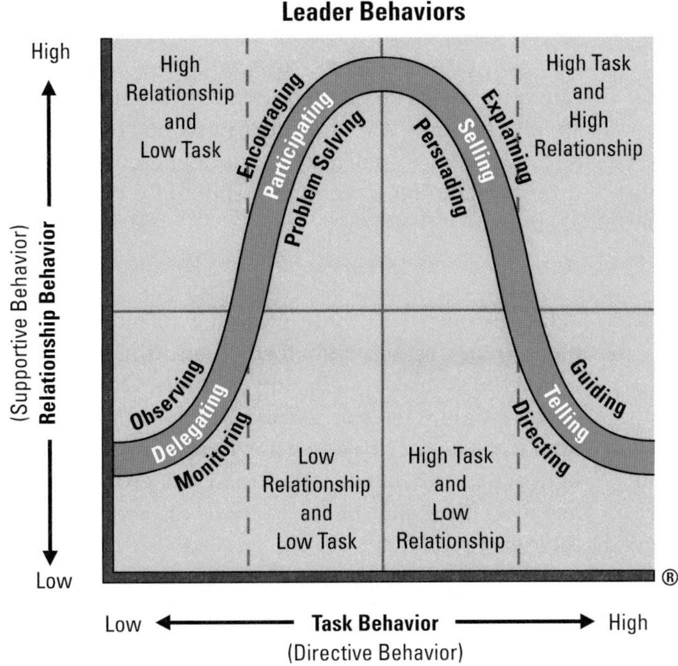

Figure 12.1

A Model of Situational Leadership

This figure depicts four different styles of leadership that differ in the degree to which they are supportive (relationship oriented) or directive (task oriented). Are there any leadership styles with which you're uncomfortable? What skills can you acquire to help you feel more comfortable and competent with these styles?

Source: "Model of Situational Leadership" by Paul Hersey and Kenneth Blanchard in *Management of Organizational Behavior,* p. 277. Used by permission of Situational Services, Inc. Donald A. Brown.

and what they have to do to accomplish it. The experienced surgeon might use this style in leading a group of young interns through the required surgical procedures.

- The *selling style* is both directive and supportive. The leader using this style, sometimes called *coaching,* tries to sell the members on the task to be accomplished much the way a coach would energize and motivate the team before a big game.
- The *participating style* is nondirective and highly supportive; the leader's focus is almost entirely on member satisfaction and member relationships. A leader supervising a group of volunteers working for a political candidate might use this style; the group is already committed to the task but may need supportive leadership to continue their volunteering.
- The *delegating style,* often used with mature and knowledgeable groups, is low in both direction and support. This leader allows the group to set its own goals, to define the problem as they see fit, and to progress through the problem-solving process with little leader interference.

As you can tell from these descriptions, the leader exerts more control with immature groups (telling and selling) and less control with mature groups (participating and delegating). As groups become more mature, members assume greater responsibility and control and leaders' control diminishes.

Functions of Leadership

In relatively formal small group situations, as when politicians plan a strategy, advertisers discuss a campaign, or teachers consider educational methods, the leader has several specific functions. These functions—a mixture of task and people functions—are not the exclusive property of the leader. Nevertheless, when there's a specific leader, he or she is expected to perform them.

As you read these functions, keep in mind that an effective leader needs not only knowledge of the topic of the discussion but also communication competence—the ability to effectively use the group process as well as to use mindfulness, flexibility, and cultural sensitivity plus the more specific skills of openness, empathy, positiveness, immediacy, interaction management, expressiveness, and other-orientation that we discussed in Unit 9.

Still another skill the leader needs is the ability to manage any group conflict that might arise. Unit 13 will examine group conflict along with interpersonal and relationship conflict.

Prediscussion Functions

It often falls to the leader to provide members with necessary materials prior to the meeting. Prediscussion functions may include, for example, arranging a convenient meeting time and place; informing members of the purposes and goals of the meeting; providing them with materials they should read or view; and recommending that they come to the meeting with, for example, general ideas or specific proposals.

Similarly, groups form gradually and need to be eased into meaningful discussion. Diverse members should not be expected to sit down and discuss a problem without becoming familiar with one another. Put more generally, the leader is responsible for any preparations and preliminaries necessary to ensure an orderly and productive group experience.

Activating the Group Agenda

Most groups have an agenda. An **agenda** is simply a list of the tasks the group wishes to complete. It's an itemized listing of what the group should devote its attention to. In some cases the supervisor or consultant or CEO prepares the agenda and simply presents it to the group; the group is then expected to follow the agenda item by item. In other cases the group will develop its own agenda, usually as its first or second order of business.

Generally, the more formal the group, the more important the agenda becomes. In informal groups the agenda may simply consist of general ideas in the minds of the members (for example, "We'll review the class assignment and then make plans for the weekend"). In formal business groups the agenda will be much more detailed and explicit. Some agendas specify not only the items that must be covered but also the order in which they should be covered and even the amount of time that should be devoted to each item.

Activating Group Interaction

Many groups need some prodding to interact. Perhaps the group is newly formed and the members feel a bit uneasy with one another. One of the leader's functions is to stimulate the members to interact. A leader also serves this function when members act as individuals rather than as a group. In this instance the leader needs to focus the members on their group task.

Maintaining Effective Interaction

Suppose that you are leading a group and have successfully stimulated group interaction, but now the discussion begins to drag. Your job is to prod the group to maintain effective interaction: "Do we have

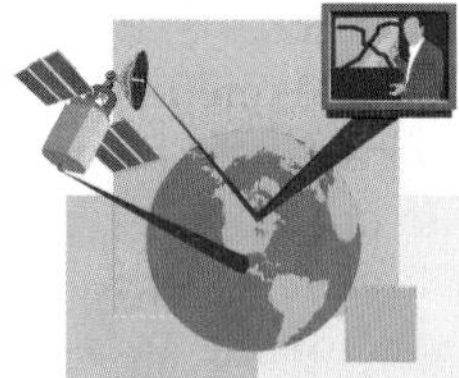

MEDIA WATCH

Agenda-Setting Theory

In much the same way that a group leader sets an agenda, so do the media. In fact, researches on **agenda setting** argue that the media establish your agenda by focusing attention on certain people and events. The media tell you—by virtue of what they cover—who is important and what events are significant (McCombs & Shaw, 1972, 1993). Rather than telling you what to think, the media tell you what to think *about* (Edelstein, 1993; McCombs, Lopez-Escobar, & Llamas, 2000).

Two characteristics of media coverage influence the media's ability to establish your agenda: salience and obtrusiveness (Folkerts & Lacy, 2001).

- *Salience* is the importance of an issue to you. For example, if you live in a high-crime city, then news of crime, crime deterrents, and crime statistics are probably important to you. If the media cover such salient issues, then their ability to establish your agenda is enhanced. If they fail to cover such issues, then you're less likely to set your agenda on the basis of what the media say.
- *Obtrusiveness* has to do with your experience with an issue. If you have direct experience with an issue, then it's obtrusive; if you don't have direct experience, then it's unobtrusive. For example, if tuition costs go up, then the issue is obtrusive, because you (presumably) have direct experience with it. But if a volcano erupts on some unknown island, it's unobtrusive. The media's agenda-setting influence is likely to be greater for unobtrusive issues: You have no direct experience with these matters and hence have to rely on what the media tell you is or isn't important.

You and the Media

How do the media establish your agenda? Can you identify specific examples?

any additional comments on the proposal to eliminate required courses?" "What do those of you who are members of the college curriculum committee think about the English Department's proposal to restructure required courses?" "Does anyone want to make any additional comments on eliminating the minor area of concentration?" As the leader you must strive to ensure that all members have an opportunity to express themselves.

Empowering Group Members

An important function in at least some leadership styles (though not limited to leadership) is to empower others—to help other group members (but also your relational partner, coworkers, employees, other students, or siblings) to gain increased power over themselves and their environment. Some ways to empower others include the following:

- Raise the person's self-esteem. Compliment, reinforce. Resist faultfinding; it doesn't benefit anyone and in fact disempowers.
- Share skills as well as decision-making power and authority.
- Be constructively critical. Be willing to offer your perspective, to lend an ear to a first-try singing effort, to listen to a new poem. Be willing to react honestly to suggestions from all group members and not just those in high positions.
- Encourage growth in all forms: academic, relational, and professional, among others. The growth and empowerment of the other person enhances your own growth and power.

Keeping Members on Track

Many individuals are egocentric and will pursue only their own interests and concerns, even in a group setting. Your task as the leader is to keep all members reasonably on track. Here are a few ways you might accomplish this:

- Ask questions that focus on the specific topic at hand, especially of those who seem to be wandering off in other directions.
- Interject internal summaries in which you briefly identify what has been accomplished and what the group needs to move on to next.
- Consider setting a formal agenda and sticking to it.

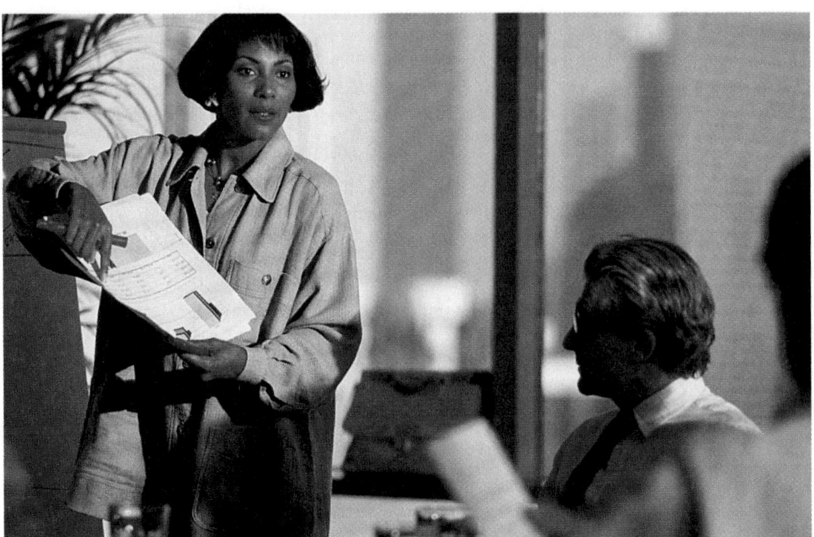

VIEWPOINT

Research finds that most people will be influenced more by speakers using task cues (maintaining eye contact, sitting at the head of the table, using a relatively rapid speech rate, speaking fluently, and gesturing appropriately) than by speakers using dominance cues (speaking in a loud and angry voice, pointing fingers, maintaining rigid posture, using forceful gestures, and lowering the eyebrows) (Driskell, Olmstead, & Salas, 1993). People also tend to see speakers who use task cues as more competent and more likable; they perceive persons who use dominance cues as less competent, less influential, less likable, and more self-oriented. However, can you suggest situations in which dominance cues would be more effective than task cues in gaining compliance from group members?

BUILDING COMMUNICATION SKILLS

Empowering Others

For each situation below, indicate what you might say to help empower the other person, using such strategies as *(a)* raising the other person's self-esteem; *(b)* listening actively and supportively; *(c)* being open, positive, and empathic; and *(d)* avoiding verbal aggressiveness or any unfair conflict strategies.

1. Your partner is having lots of difficulties—recently he lost his job, received poor grades in a night class, and started gaining a lot of weight. At the same time, you're doing extremely well. You want to give your partner back his confidence. What do you say?
2. You're managing four college interns who are redesigning your company's website, three men and one woman. The men are extremely supportive of one another and regularly contribute ideas. Although equally competent, the woman doesn't contribute; she seems to lack confidence. But the objective of this redesign is to increase the number of female visitors, so you really need her input and want to empower her. What do you say?
3. You're a third-grade teacher. Most of the students are from the same ethnic–religious group; three, however, are from a very different group. The problem is that these three have not been included in the social groupings of the students; they're considered outsiders. As a result these children stumble when they have to read in front of the class and make a lot of mistakes at the chalkboard (though they consistently do well in private). You want to empower these students. What do you say?

- Focus your own attention on the topics at hand; your example will influence the behavior of the other members.

Ensuring Member Satisfaction

Group members have different psychological needs and wants; in fact, many people enter groups primarily to satisfy these personal concerns. Even though a group may, for example, deal with political issues, the members may have come together for reasons that are more psychological than political. If a group is to be effective, it must meet not only the surface purposes of the group but also the underlying or interpersonal purposes that motivated many of the members to come together in the first place.

Depending on the specific people involved, special adjustments may have to be made to accommodate group members with disabilities. You can easily adapt to group situations the principles identified in the special tables in Units 1, 3, 5, and 9 that deal with communication between people with and without disabilities.

Encouraging Ongoing Evaluation and Improvement

Most groups encounter obstacles as they try to solve a problem, reach a decision, or generate ideas. Therefore, most could use some improvement. If the group is to improve, it must focus on itself. Along with trying to accomplish some objective task, it must try to solve its own internal problems as well; issues such as personal conflicts, the failure of members to meet on time, or the tendency of some members to come unprepared. As the leader, try to identify any such difficulties and to encourage and help the group to analyze and resolve them.

Postdiscussion Functions

Just as the leader is responsible for prediscussion functions, the leader also is responsible for postdiscussion functions. Such functions might include summarizing the group's discussion, organizing future meetings, or presenting the group's decisions to some other group. All in all, the leader is responsible for doing whatever needs to be done to ensure that the group's experience is productive.

Membership, Leadership, and Culture

Most research on and theories about small group communication, membership, and leadership have

BUILDING COMMUNICATION SKILLS

Dealing with Small Group Complaints

Assume that you're the leader of a work team consisting of members from each of the major departments in your company. For any one of the complaints listed below, explain what you would say and the objectives you'd hope to achieve.

In framing your responses follow these guidelines: *(a)* Let the person know that you're open to complaints and that you do view them as essential sources of information; *(b)* show that you're following the suggestions for effective listening discussed in Unit 5, such as listening supportively and with empathy; *(c)* show that you understand both the thoughts and the feelings that go with the complaint; and *(d)* ask the other person what he or she would like you to do about the complaint.

1. You're calling these meetings much too often and much too early to suit us. We'd like fewer meetings scheduled for later in the day.
2. That's not fair. Why do I always have to take the minutes of these meetings? Can't we have a real secretary here?
3. There's a good reason why I don't contribute to the discussion. I don't contribute because no one listens to what I say.

emerged from universities in the United States and reflect U.S. culture. For example, in the United States—and in individualist cultures generally—the individual group member is extremely important. But in collectivist cultures the individual is less important; it's the group that is the significant entity. In

UNDERSTANDING THEORY AND RESEARCH

Attila's Theory of Leadership

From a totally different perspective, consider these leadership qualities, paraphrased from Wes Roberts's *Leadership Secrets of Attila the Hun* (1987).

- *Empathy:* Leaders must develop an appreciation for and an understanding of other cultures and the values of their members.
- *Courage:* Leaders should be fearless and have the courage to complete their assignments; they must not complain about obstacles or be discouraged by adversity.
- *Accountability:* Leaders must hold themselves responsible for their own actions and for those of their members.
- *Dependability:* Leaders must be dependable in carrying out their responsibilities; leaders must also be willing to depend on their members to accomplish matters they themselves can't oversee.
- *Credibility:* Leaders must be seen as believable by both friends and enemies; they must possess the integrity and intelligence needed to secure and communicate accurate information.
- *Stewardship:* Leaders must be caretakers of their members' interests and well-being; they must guide and reward subordinates.

Working with Theories and Research

- *Of these six qualities, which would be most important to you in your personal and social life? In your business and professional life?*

Japan, for example, group researchers find that "individual fulfillment of self is attained through finding and maintaining one's place within the group" (Cathcart & Cathcart, 1985, p. 191). In the United States, in contrast, individual fulfillment of self is attained by the individual and through his or her own efforts, not by the group.

It's often thought that because group membership and group identity are so important in collectivist cultures, it's the group that makes important decisions. Actually, this does not seem to be the case. In fact, a study of 48 (highly collectivist) Japanese organizations found that participating in decision-making groups did not give the members decision-making power. Group members were encouraged to contribute ideas, but the decision-making power was reserved for the CEO or for managers higher up the organizational ladder (Brennan, 1991).

The discussion of member roles earlier in this unit devoted an entire category to individual roles: roles adopted by individuals to satisfy individual rather than group goals. In other cultures (notably collectivist cultures) these roles probably would not even be mentioned—simply because they wouldn't be acted out often enough to deserve such extended discussion. For example, in many collectivist cultures the group orientation is too pervasive for individuals to violate it by acting as the blocker, the recognition seeker, or the dominator.

One obvious consequence of this cultural difference can be seen when a group member commits a serious error. For example, let's say a team member submits the wrong advertising copy to the media. In a group governed by individualistic norms, that member is likely to be singled out, reprimanded, and perhaps fired. Further, the leader or supervisor is likely to distance himself or herself from this member for fear that blame for the error will "rub off." In a more collectivist culture, the error is more likely to be seen as a group mistake. The individual is unlikely to be singled out—especially not in public—and the leader is likely to shoulder part of the blame. The same is true when one member comes up with a great idea. In individualistic cultures that person is likely to be rewarded, and the person's work group benefits only indirectly. In a collectivist culture it is the group that gets recognized and rewarded for the idea.

In a similar way, each culture's belief system influences group members' behavior. For example, members of many Asian cultures, influenced by Confucian principles, believe that "the protruding nail gets pounded down" and are therefore not likely to voice disagreement with the majority of the group. Americans, on the other hand, influenced by the belief that "the squeaky wheel gets the grease," are more likely to voice disagreement or to act differently from other group members in order to get what they want.

Also, each culture has its own rules of preferred and expected leadership style. In the United States the general and expected style for a group leader is democratic. Our political leaders are elected by a democratic process; similarly, boards of directors are elected by the shareholders of a corporation. In other situations, of course, leaders are chosen by those in authority. The directors choose the president of a company, and the president will normally decide who will supervise and who will be supervised within the organization. Even in this situation, however, we expect the supervisor to behave democratically—to listen to the ideas of employees, to

VIEWPOINT

One leadership theorist argues that critical leadership depends on five main principles and the behaviors that stem from them: self-confidence and self-awareness, integrity, enthusiasm and drive, empathy, and social skills (for example, skill in establishing rapport and building relationships) (Roebuck, 1999). How do you rate yourself on these qualities and behaviors?

take their views into consideration when decisions are to be made, to keep them informed of corporate developments, and generally to respect their interests. Also, we expect that leaders will be changed fairly regularly. We elect a president every four years, and company directors' elections are normally held each year.

In some other cultures, in contrast, leaders are chosen by right of birth. They're not elected, nor are they expected to behave democratically. Similarly, their tenure as leaders is usually extremely long; they may hold their position their entire lives and then pass it on to their children. In other cases, leaders in a wide variety of roles may be named by a military dictator.

The important point to realize is that your membership and leadership styles are influenced by the culture in which you were raised. Consequently, when in a group with members of different cultures, consider the differences in both membership and leadership styles that individuals bring with them. For example, a member who plays individual roles may be tolerated in many groups in the United States and in some cases may even be thought amusing and different. That same member playing the same roles in a group with a more collectivist orientation is likely to be evaluated much more negatively. Multicultural groups may find it helpful to discuss members' views of group membership and leadership and what constitutes comfortable interaction for them.

REFLECTIONS ON ETHICS

The Leader's Ethical Responsibilities

Ethical qualities often figure prominently in the traits approach to leadership. For example, an effective leader should possess the following traits:

- *Honesty:* Leaders should be honest with the group members by, for example, revealing any hidden agendas and presenting information fairly.
- *Accountability:* Leaders should take responsibility for their actions and decisions.
- *Concern for the welfare of their members:* Leaders who are more concerned with their own personal interests, rather than with the group task or the interpersonal needs of the members, would clearly be acting unethically.

WHAT WOULD YOU DO? You are leading a discussion among a group of high school freshmen whom you're mentoring. The topic turns to marijuana, and the students ask you directly if you smoke pot. The truth is that on occasion you do—but it's a very controlled use, and you feel that it would only destroy your credibility and lead the students to experiment with or continue smoking pot if they knew you did (something you definitely do not want to do). At the same time, you wonder if you can ethically lie to them and tell them that you do not smoke. What would you do in this situation?

SUMMARY

This unit examined the roles of members and leaders and the principles that govern effective group interaction.

1. A popular classification of small group member roles divides them into group task roles, group building and maintenance roles, and individual roles.
2. Twelve group task roles are: initiator–contributor, information seeker, opinion seeker, information giver, opinion giver, elaborator, coordinator, orienter, evaluator–critic, energizer, procedural technician, and recorder.
3. Seven group building and maintenance roles are: encourager, harmonizer, compromiser, gatekeeper–expediter, standard setter, group observer and commentator, and follower.
4. Eight individual roles are: aggressor, blocker, recognition seeker, self-confessor, playboy/playgirl, dominator, help seeker, and special interest pleader.
5. Interaction process analysis categorizes group members' contributions into four areas: social–emotional positive contributions, social–emotional negative contributions, attempted answers, and questions.
6. Member participation should be group-oriented, should center conflict on issues, should be critically open-minded, and should ensure understanding.
7. Groupthink is a way of thinking that develops when concurrence seeking in a cohesive group overrides realistic appraisal of alternative courses of action.
8. The traits approach to leadership focuses on personal characteristics that contribute to leadership; the functional approach centers on what the leader does (the functions the leader serves); and the transformational approach focuses on the leader's empowerment of the group members.
9. In the situational theory of leadership, leadership is seen as concerned with both accomplishing the

task and serving the interpersonal needs of the members. The degree to which either concern is emphasized should depend on the specific group and the unique situation.

10. An extension of this situational approach to leadership identifies four major leadership styles: the telling style, the selling style, the participating style, and the delegating style. The appropriate style to use depends on the group's level of task and relationship maturity.

11. Three major leadership styles are: laissez-faire, democratic, and authoritarian. The laissez-faire leader avoids directing or suggesting what members should do. The democratic leader provides direction but allows members to do as they wish. The authoritarian leader makes the decisions for the group.

12. Among the leader's functions are to activate the group agenda, activate group interaction, maintain effective interaction, empower group members, keep members on track, ensure member satisfaction, encourage ongoing evaluating and improvement, and wrap up the discussion (with summaries or notices of future meetings, for example). In addition, the leader is responsible for appropriate pre- and post-discussion functions.

13. The culture in which people are raised will greatly influence the ways in which members and leaders interact in small groups.

Key Terms

interaction process analysis
groupthink
leadership
laissez-faire leader
democratic leader
authoritarian leader
agenda
agenda setting

Thinking Critically About

Members and Leaders in Group Communication

1. Can you identify roles that you habitually serve in certain groups? Do you serve these roles in your friendship, love, and family relationships as well?
2. Have you ever been in a group when groupthink was operating? If so, what were its symptoms? What effect did groupthink have on the process and conclusions of the group?
3. How would you characterize the leadership style of one of your local politicians, religious leaders, college instructors, or talk show hosts? How would you characterize your own leadership style? For example, are you usually more concerned with people or with tasks? Are you more likely to be a laissez-faire, democratic, or authoritarian leader?
4. It's been found that the group member with the highest rate of participation is the person most likely to be chosen leader (Mullen, Salas, & Driskell, 1989). Do you find this to be true of the groups in which you have participated? Why do you suppose this relationship exists?
5. In a social group at a friend's house, any leadership style other than laissez-faire would be difficult to tolerate. When all members are about equal in their knowledge of the topic or are very concerned with their individual rights, the democratic leader seems the most appropriate. When time and efficiency are critical, or when group members continue to lack motivation despite repeated democratic efforts, authoritarian leadership may be the most effective. In what other situations would a laissez-faire, democratic, or authoritarian leadership style be appropriate? Does serving individual functions in a group make a member unpopular with other group members?
6. Think about the groups that you're a member of and describe them in terms of task and relationship maturity. What implications does the level of maturity have for the leadership of these groups?
7. Do you find that women and men respond similarly to the different leadership styles? Do women and men exercise the different leadership styles with equal facility?

UNIT 13

Interpersonal and Small Group Conflict

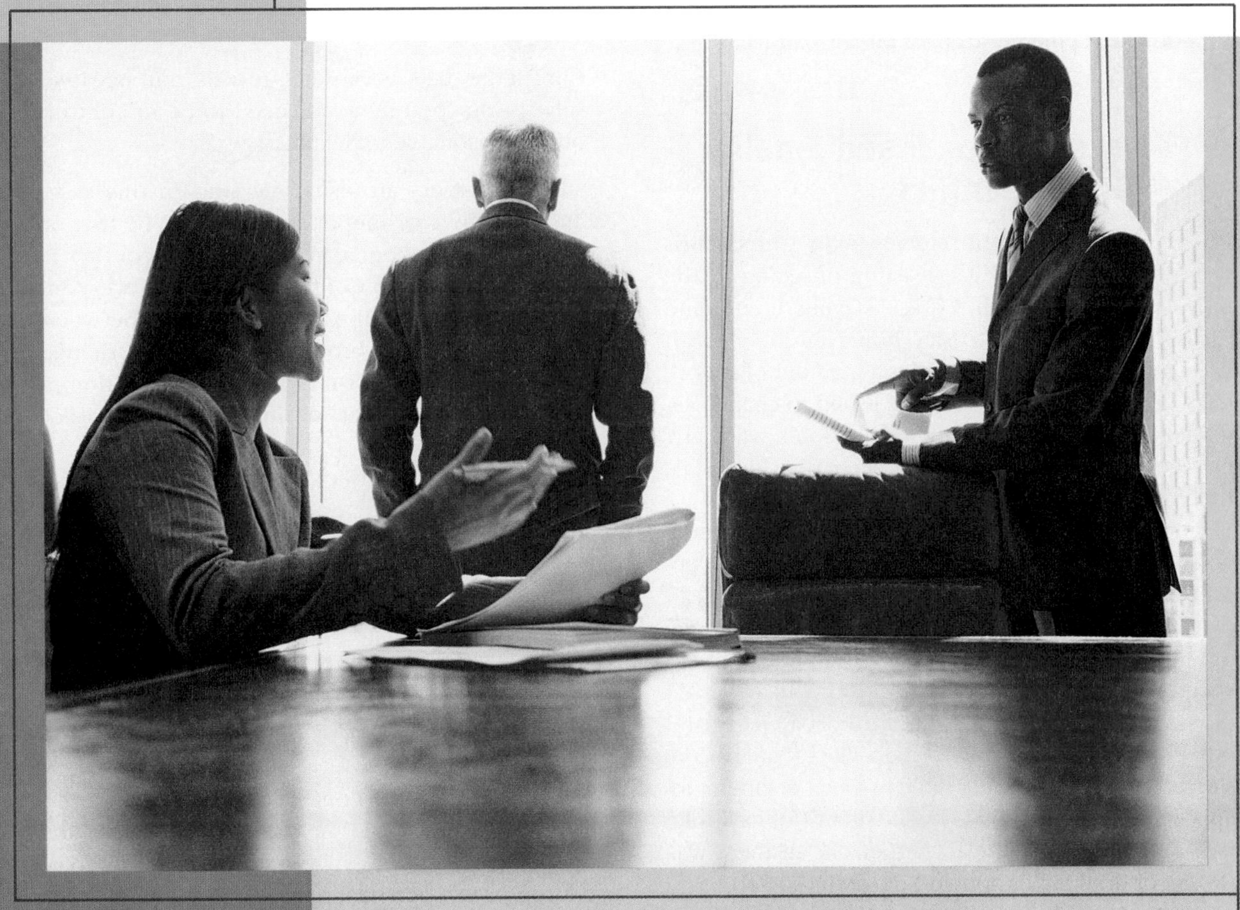

UNIT CONTENTS

No matter how effective a communicator you are, you'll still experience conflict and disagreements in interpersonal relationships and in the social and work groups of which you are a part. At some point in your personal, social, and work relationships you'll find yourself in conflict with another person or even with an entire group. Because conflict is an inevitable part of interpersonal and group life, it's essential to learn how it works, how it can go wrong, and what you can do to resolve conflicts effectively. In this unit you'll learn

- what conflict is and how it operates
- how you can engage in conflict so that differences can be resolved and your relationships and your groups can emerge stronger rather than weaker

Interpersonal and Small Group Conflict

Pat wants to go to the movies with Chris; Chris wants to stay home. Pat's insisting on going to the movies interferes with Chris's staying home, and Chris's determination to stay home interferes with Pat's going to the movies. Carl is a member of a work team and wants to convince the group to change advertising agencies; other members don't want any change. Each person in these scenarios has goals that interfere with someone else's desired goals.

Interpersonal and small group conflicts may concern goals to be pursued (for example, parents get upset that their child wants to become an actor instead of a doctor); the allocation of resources such as money or time (for example, group members differ on how to spend the advertising dollar); decisions to be made (for example, some people want a holiday party and others want a cash bonus); or behaviors that are considered appropriate or desirable by one person but inappropriate or undesirable by the other (for example, two people disagree over whether one of them was flirting or drinking or not working at full speed).

As these examples illustrate, interpersonal and small group **conflict** occurs when people:

- are interdependent; what one person does has an effect on the other person.
- perceive their goals to be incompatible; if one person's goal is achieved, the other's cannot be (for example, if one person wants to buy a new car and the other person wants to save the money for a house).
- see each other as interfering with the attainment of their own goals (Hocker & Wilmot, 1985; Folger, Poole, & Stutman, 1997).

Myths about Conflict

One of the problems many people have in dealing with conflict is that they may be operating on the basis of false assumptions about what conflict is and what it means. Think about your own assumptions about interpersonal and small group conflict, which were probably derived from the communications you witnessed in your family and in your social interactions. For example, do you think the following are true or false?

- If two people are in a relationship conflict, it means they have a bad relationship.
- Conflict damages an interpersonal relationship or small group.
- Conflict is bad because it reveals our negative selves—our pettiness, our need to be in control, our unreasonable expectations.

Simple answers are usually wrong. In this case, each of the three assumptions above may be true or may be false. It depends. In and of itself, conflict is neither good nor bad. Conflict is a part of every interpersonal relationship—of relationships between parents and children, brothers and sisters, friends, lovers, coworkers. If it isn't, then the interaction is probably dull, irrelevant, or insignificant. Conflict seems inevitable.

It's not so much conflict that creates problems as the way in which you approach and deal with the conflict. Some ways of approaching conflict can resolve difficulties and actually improve a relationship. Other ways can hurt the relationship; they can destroy self-esteem, create bitterness, and foster suspicion. Your task, therefore, is not to try to create relationships or groups that will be free of conflict but rather to learn appropriate and productive ways of managing conflict.

Similarly, it's not the conflict (the disagreement itself) that will reveal your negative side but the fight strategies you use. Thus, if you attack other people, use force, or use personal rejection or manipulation, you will reveal your negative side. But in fighting you can also reveal your positive self—your willingness to listen to opposing points of view, your readiness to change unpleasant behaviors, your willingness to accept imperfection in others.

The Context of Conflict

Conflict, like any form of communication, takes place in a context that is physical, sociopsychological, temporal, and—perhaps most important—cultural.

UNDERSTANDING *THEORY* AND *RESEARCH*

Conflict Issues

Think about your own interpersonal conflicts, and particularly about the issues you fight over. What exactly do you fight about?

Here are the results of two studies that investigated what couples fight about. One study focused on heterosexual couples and identified the four conditions that most often led up to a couple's "first big fight" (Siegert & Stamp, 1994): uncertainty over commitment, jealousy, violation of expectations, and personality differences.

Another study asked what heterosexual, gay, and lesbian couples argued about most and found that all three types of couples were amazingly similar in their conflict issues. All three types argued primarily about these six issues (Kurdek, 1994):

- *Intimacy* issues such as affection and sex
- *Power* issues such as excessive demands or possessiveness, lack of equality in the relationship, friends, and leisure time
- *Personal flaws* issues such as drinking or smoking, personal grooming, and driving style
- *Personal distance* issues such as frequently being absent and school or job commitments
- *Social* issues such as politics, friendships, parents, and personal values
- *Distrust* issues such as previous lovers and lying

Working with Theories and Research

- *If you have access, log on to Research Navigator (*www.researchnavigator.com*) and search the* New York Times *archives for recent articles dealing with world conflict. How much of the conflict in the world can be interpreted in communication terms?*

The Physical, Sociopsychological, and Temporal Contexts

The *physical context*—for example, whether you engage in conflict privately or publicly, alone or in front of children or relatives—will influence the way the conflict is conducted as well as the effects that this conflict will have.

The *sociopsychological context* also will influence the conflict. If the atmosphere is one of equality, for example, the conflict is likely to progress very differently than it would in an atmosphere of inequality. A friendly or a hostile context will exert different influences on the conflict.

The *temporal context* will likewise prove important to understand. A conflict that follows a series of similar conflicts will be seen differently than a conflict that follows a series of enjoyable experiences and an absence of conflict. A conflict immediately after a hard day of work will engender feelings different from a conflict after an enjoyable dinner.

The Cultural Context

The *cultural context* will exert considerable influence on the issues people fight about as well as on how they engage in conflict. A particularly clear example occurs frequently in many large cities throughout the country; it's seen in the conflict between African American customers, who prefer a personal involvement with the people with whom they do business, and Korean storekeepers, who prefer to maintain considerable distance between themselves and their customers. To the African American customer, the Korean storeowner seems to be disconfirming and unwilling to provide courteous service. To the Korean, the African American's personal approach is seen as disrespectful (Bailey, 1997).

There are numerous other examples of the importance of culture in conflict. To mention just a few: Eighteen-year-olds are more likely to experience conflict with their parents about their living style if they live in the United States than if they live in Sweden, where cohabitation is much more accepted. Similarly, male infidelity is more likely to cause conflict in American couples than in southern European couples. Students from the United States are more likely to engage in conflict with another U.S. student than with someone from another culture; Chinese students, on the other hand, are more likely to engage in a conflict with a non-Chinese student than with another Chinese (Leung 1988). In a comparison of German and Indonesian adolescents, German students preferred a more confrontational style, whereas Indonesian students preferred a more submissive response style (Haar & Krahe, 1999). Vietnamese are more likely to avoid conflict than are people from the United States (Dsilva & Whyte, 1998).

In other research, when Americans and Chinese students were asked to analyze a conflict episode, say between a mother and her daughter, they saw it quite differently (Goode, 2000). American students, for example, were more likely to decide in favor of the mother or the daughter—they tended to see one side as right and the other as wrong. The Chinese students, however, were more likely to see the validity of both sides; both mother and daughter were right but both were also wrong. This finding is consistent with the Chinese preference for proverbs that contain a contradiction (for example, "Too modest is half boastful"), which Americans often see as "irritating."

Another example of the cultural influence on conflict is the tendency of people in collectivist cultures to avoid conflict more than members of individualist cultures (Dsilva & Whyte, 1998; Haar & Krahe, 1999; Cai & Fink, 2002). Further, Americans and Japanese differ in their view of the aim or purpose of conflict. Most Japanese see conflicts and their resolution in terms of compromise; Americans, on the other hand, generally see conflict in terms of winning (Gelfand, Nishii, Holcombe, Dyer, Ohbuchi, & Fukuno, 2001).

The ways in which members of different cultures express conflict also differ. In Japan, for example, it's especially important that you not embarrass the person with whom you are in conflict, especially if that conflict occurs in a small group or in public. This face-saving principle prohibits the use of such strategies as personal rejection or verbal aggressiveness. In the United States both men and women (ideally at least) are expected to express their desires and complaints openly and directly, but many Middle Eastern and Pacific rim cultures would discourage women from such expressions and would expect a more agreeable and permissive posture. Even within a given general culture, more specific subcultures differ from one another in their methods of conflict management. African American men and women and European American men and women, for example, engage in conflict in very different ways (Kochman, 1981). The issues that cause and aggravate conflict, the conflict strategies that are expected and accepted, and the entire attitude toward conflict vary from one group to the other. For example, according to one study, African American men prefer to manage conflict with clear arguments and a focus on problem solving; African American women, however, deal with conflict through being assertive and respectful (Collier, 1991). Another study found that African American females used more direct controlling strategies (for example, assuming control over the conflict and arguing persistently for their point of view) than did European American females. European American females, on the other hand, used more problem-solution-oriented conflict management styles than did African American women. Interestingly, African American and European American men were very similar in their interpersonal conflict management strategies: Both tended to avoid or withdraw from relationship conflict. They preferred to keep quiet about their differences or downplay their significance (Ting-Toomey, 1986).

Among Mexican Americans, researchers found that men sought to achieve mutual understanding by discussing the reasons for the conflict, whereas women focused on being supportive of the relationship. Among Anglo Americans, men tended to prefer direct and rational argument, whereas women often preferred flexibility. Similarly, people in Mexico (a collectivist culture) preferred conflict styles that emphasized concern for the others involved more than did people in the United States (an individualist culture) (Gabrielides, Stephan, Ybarra, Pearson, & Villareal, 1997).

The Negatives and Positives of Conflict

The kind of conflict we are considering here is conflict among or between "connected" individuals, whether in a primary relationship or in a small group. Such conflict occurs frequently between lovers, best friends, siblings, and parent and child; it also occurs within the extended family as well as in workplaces or on sports teams. Such conflict is all the more difficult because, unlike many other conflict situations, interpersonal and small group disagreements often involve people you care for, like, even love. At the very least these are people with whom you're going to have to interact—so even if there were no other reason, you might as well make conflict as pleasant and productive as you can. There are both negative and positive aspects or dimensions to conflict; and let's look at each of these.

Some Negatives of Conflict

Conflict often leads to increased negative regard for the opponent; when this opponent is someone you

UNDERSTANDING THEORY AND RESEARCH

Conflict and Gender

Not surprisingly, there are significant gender differences in interpersonal conflict. For example, men are more apt to withdraw from a conflict situation than are women. It's been argued that this may be due to the fact that men become more psychologically and physiologically aroused during conflict (and retain this heightened level of arousal much longer) than do women and so may try to distance themselves and withdraw from the conflict to prevent further arousal (Gottman & Carrere, 1994; Canary, Cupach, & Messman, 1995; Goleman, 1995). Women, on the other hand, want to get closer to the conflict; they want to talk about it and resolve it. Even adolescents reveal these differences; in a study of boys and girls aged 11 to 17, boys withdrew more than girls (Lindeman, Harakka, & Keltikangas-Jarvinen, 1997; Heasley, Babbitt, & Burbach, 1995).

Other research has found that women are more emotional and men are more logical when they argue (Schaap, Buunk, & Kerkstra, 1988; Canary, Cupach, & Messman, 1995). Women have been defined as conflict "feelers" and men as conflict "thinkers" (Sorenson, Hawkins, & Sorenson, 1995). Another difference is that women are more apt to reveal their negative feelings than are men (Schaap, Buunk, & Kerkstra, 1988; Canary, Cupach, & Messman, 1995).

It should be noted that much research fails to support the supposed gender differences in conflict style that cartoons, situation comedies, and films portray so readily and so clearly. For example, numerous studies of both college students and men and women in business found no significant differences in the ways men and women engage in conflict (Wilkins & Andersen, 1991; Canary & Hause, 1993; Gottman & Levenson, 1999).

Working with Theories and Research.

- *If you have access, log on to Research Navigator (www.researchnavigator.com) and search the communication, psychology, and sociology databases for research on gender and conflict. What can you add to the discussion presented here?*

love or work with on a daily basis, it can create serious problems for the relationship. One reason is that many conflicts involve unfair fighting methods that aim largely to hurt the other person. When one person hurts the other, increased negative feelings are inevitable; even the strongest relationship has limits.

Conflict frequently leads to a depletion of energy better spent on other areas. This is especially true in the small group context; days and even weeks of 10 or 12 people's time can be wasted on conflicts instead of being devoted to solving the problem at hand.

At times conflict leads you to close yourself off from the other people involved. In an intimate relationship, for example, you may hide your true self on the theory that it would not be to your advantage to reveal your weaknesses to your "enemy." But at the same time, closing yourself off may also prevent meaningful communication from taking place. One possible consequence is that one or both parties may seek intimacy elsewhere. This often leads to further conflict, mutual hurt, and resentment—all of which can add heavily to the costs carried by the relationship. As these costs increase, exchanging rewards may become difficult, perhaps impossible. The result is a situation in which the costs increase and the rewards decrease—a situation that often results in relationship deterioration and eventual dissolution.

Some Positives of Conflict

The major value of interpersonal and small group conflict is that it forces you to examine a problem and work toward a potential solution. If people use productive conflict strategies, the relationship or group may well emerge from the encounter stronger, healthier, and more satisfying than before.

Conflict enables each of you to state what you want and—if the conflict is resolved effectively—perhaps to get it. In fact, a better understanding of each other's feelings has been found to be one of the main results of the "first big fight" (Siegert & Stamp, 1994).

Conflict also prevents hostilities and resentments from festering. Suppose you're annoyed at your partner for e-mailing colleagues from work for two hours instead of giving that time to you. If you say nothing, your annoyance and resentment are likely to grow. Further, by saying nothing you implicitly approve of the e-mailing and so make it more likely that such behavior will be repeated. In contrast, through conflict and its resolution you can stop resentment from increasing. In the process you each can let your own needs be known—for example, that you need lots of attention when you come home from work and that your partner needs to review and get closure on the day's work. If you both can appreciate the legitimacy of each other's needs, then solutions may be easily identified. Perhaps the e-mailing can be done after your attention needs are met, or perhaps you can delay your need for attention until your partner gets closure about work. Or perhaps you can learn to provide for your partner's closure needs—and in doing so also get the attention you need.

Consider, too, that when you try to resolve conflict within an interpersonal or small group situation, you're saying in effect that the relationship or group is worth the effort; otherwise you'd walk away from such a conflict. Although there may be exceptions—as when you engage in conflict to save face or to gratify some ego need—usually confronting a conflict indicates concern, commitment, and a desire to improve the relationship or group.

Types of Conflict

Conflict can occur in many situations and may be of varied types. Especially important to understand are the differences between (1) content and relationship conflicts, (2) online and workplace conflicts, and (3) the various conflict styles that individuals have.

Content and Relationship Conflicts

Using concepts developed in Unit 2, we may distinguish between content conflict and relationship conflict. *Content conflicts* center on objects, events, and persons in the world that are usually, but not always, external to the parties involved in the conflict. These include the millions of issues that you argue and fight about every day—the value of a particular movie, what to watch on television, the fairness of the last examination or job promotion, the way to spend your savings.

Relationship conflicts are equally numerous and include such conflict situations as a younger brother who does not obey his older brother, group members who all want the final say in what the group decides, and the mother and daughter who each want to have the final word concerning the daughter's lifestyle. Here the conflicts are concerned not so much with some external object as with the relationships between the individuals—with such issues as who is in charge, how equal the partners in a primary relationship are, the importance of each group member, or who has the right to set down rules of behavior.

Content conflicts are usually manifest; they're clearly observable and identifiable. Relationship conflicts are often latent; they tend to be hidden and much more difficult to identify. Thus, a conflict over where you should vacation may on the surface, or manifest, level center on the advantages and disadvantages of Mexico versus Hawaii. On a relationship and often latent level, however, the conflict may be about who has the greater right to select the place to vacation, who should win the argument, who is the decision maker in the relationship, and so on.

Online and Workplace Conflicts

Two special conflict situations should be noted. The first is online conflict: Just as you can experience disagreement in face-to-face communication, you can experience conflict online. But there are a few conflict situations that are unique to online communication, and we'll look at them here. The second is conflict in the workplace or formal group—in any group that consists of a leader and various members of the organization.

Online Conflicts

Sending commercial messages to those who didn't request them often creates conflict. Junk mail is junk mail; but on the Internet, junk mail slows down the entire Internet system as well as the individual who has to sit through the downloading of unwanted messages. In many cases (when you access your e-mail from an Internet café, for example) you have to pay for the time it takes to download junk mail.

Spamming often causes conflict. Spamming is sending someone unsolicited mail, repeatedly sending the same mail, or posting the same message on lots of bulletin boards, even when the message is irrelevant to the focus of the group. One of the very practical reasons spamming is frowned upon is that it generally costs people money. And even if the e-mail is free, it takes up valuable time and energy to read something you didn't want in the first place.

Another reason, of course, is that spam clogs the system, slowing it down for everyone.

Flaming, especially common in newsgroups, is sending messages that personally attack another user. Flaming frequently leads to flame wars in which everyone in the group gets into the act and attacks other users. Generally, flaming and flame wars prevent us from achieving our goals and so are counterproductive.

Workplace and Formal Group Conflicts

Unlike conflicts that might occur in an informal group of friends or in a family, which are more similar to interpersonal encounters disagreements in the workplace group present a specific set of issues.

In formal groups it's often the leader's responsibility to manage conflict. Small group communication researchers distinguish between procedural and people conflicts and offer a wide variety of conflict management strategies (Patton, Giffin, & Patton, 1989; Folger, Poole, & Stutman, 1997; Kindler, 1996).

Procedural conflicts involve disagreements over who is in charge (who is the leader or who should be the leader), what the agenda or task of the group should be, and how the group should conduct its business. The best way to deal with procedural problems is to prevent them from occurring in the first place by establishing early in the group's interaction who is to serve as leader and what the agenda should be. If procedural problems arise after these agreements are reached, the leader or members can refer the conflicting participants to the group's earlier decisions. When members oppose or become dissatisfied with these early decisions, however, they may become negative or antagonistic and cease to participate in the discussion. If this happens (or if members want to change procedures), a brief discussion on the procedures can be held. The important point is to deal with procedural conflicts as procedural conflicts and not allow them to escalate into something else.

People conflicts can occur when one member dominates the group, when several members battle for control, or when some members refuse to participate. The leader should try to secure the commitment of all members and to convince them that the progress of the group depends on everyone's contributions. At times it may be necessary to concentrate on people needs—on the importance of satisfying members' needs for group approval, for periodic rewards, or for encouragement. People conflicts also can develop in the course of debate if members attack people rather than ideas. The leader needs to ensure that attacks and disagreements are clearly focused on ideas, not people. If a personal attack does get started, the leader should step in to refocus the discussion to the idea and away from the person.

The conflict management strategies presented later in this unit are applicable to the workplace or formal group situation. In addition, here are four principles that have special relevance to conflict in this type of group (Kindler, 1996):

- *Preserve the dignity and respect of all members.* Assume, for example, that each person's disagreement is legitimate and stems from a genuine concern for the good of the group. Therefore, treat disagreements kindly; even if someone attacks you personally, it's generally wise not to respond in kind but to redirect the criticism to the issue at hand.
- *Listen empathically.* See the perspectives of the other members; try to feel what they're feeling without making any critical judgments. Try to ask yourself why others see the situation differently from the way you see it.
- *Seek out and emphasize common ground.* Even in the midst of disagreement, there are areas of common interest, common beliefs, and common aims. Find these and build on them.
- *Value diversity and differences.* Creative solutions often emerge from conflicting perspectives. So don't gloss over differences; instead, explore them for the valuable information they can give you.

Conflict Styles

Figure 13.1 on page 252 illustrates an approach to conflict that identifies five basic styles or ways of engaging in conflict and is especially helpful in relation to interpersonal and small group conflicts (Blake & Mouton, 1984). The five-styles model, plotted along the dimensions of "concern for oneself" and "concern for the other person," provides considerable insight into the ways people engage in conflict and some of the advantages and disadvantages of each approach. As you read through these styles, try to identify the conflict style you generally use as well as the styles of those with whom you have close relationships.

- *Competing:* The competitive style reflects great concern for your own needs and desires and little for those of others. As long as your needs are met, the conflict has been dealt with successfully. In conflict motivated by competitiveness, you'd be likely to be verbally aggressive while blaming the other person. This style represents an *I win, you lose* philosophy.
- *Avoiding:* The avoider fails to address his or her own or the other's needs or desires. This person

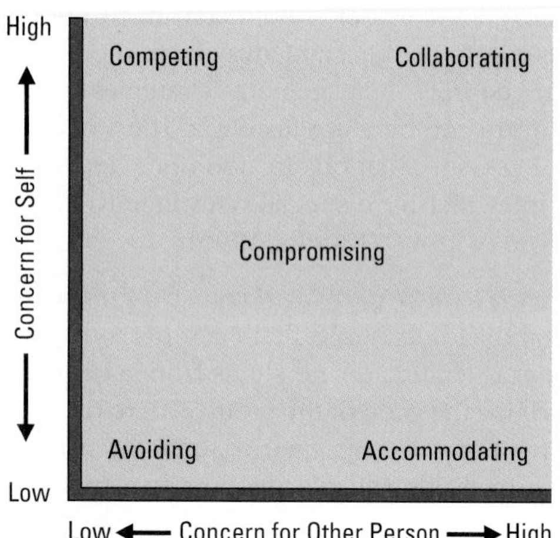

Figure 13.1
Five Conflict Styles
This figure is adapted from Blake and Mouton's (1984) approach to managerial leadership and conflict. Try to locate your usual conflict style on this grid. How well does this style work for you?

avoids any real communication about the problem, changes the topic when the problem comes up, and generally withdraws from the scene both psychologically and physically. As you can appreciate, this style does little to resolve any conflicts and may be viewed as an *I lose, you lose* philosophy.

- *Accommodating:* In accommodating you sacrifice your own needs for the needs of the other person. Your major purpose is to maintain harmony and peace in the relationship or group. This style may help you achieve the immediate goal of maintaining peace and perhaps may satisfy the other person; but it does little to meet your own needs, which are unlikely to go away. This style represents an *I lose, you win* philosophy.
- *Collaborating:* In collaborating you focus on both your own and the other person's needs. This style, often considered the ideal, takes time and a willingness to communicate, and especially a readiness to listen to the perspectives and needs of the other person. Ideally, this style of conflict resolution results in each person's needs being satisfied, an *I win, you win* situation.
- *Compromising:* The compromising style is in the middle; there is some concern for your own needs and some concern for the other's needs. It's the kind of strategy you might refer to as "meeting each other halfway," "horse trading," or "give and take." Compromising is likely to help you maintain peace but to involve some dissatisfaction over the inevitable losses that have to be endured. It results in an *I win and lose and you win and lose* outcome.

Conflict Management Skills

In managing conflict you can choose from a variety of strategies, which this section will describe. Realize, however, that the strategies you choose will be influenced by several different factors, including (1) the goals to be achieved, (2) your emotional state, (3) your cognitive assessment of the situation, (4) your personality and communication competence, and (5) your culture and gender. Understanding these factors may help you select more appropriate and more effective strategies. And recent research finds that using productive conflict strategies can have lots of beneficial effects—whereas using inappropriate strategies may be linked to poorer psychological health (Weitzman & Weitzman, 2000; Weitzman, 2001; Neff & Harter, 2002).

The *goals* (short-term and long-term) you wish to achieve will influence what strategies seem appropriate to you. If all you want is to salvage today's date, you may want to simply give in and ignore the difficulty. In contrast, if you want to build a long-term relationship, you may want to analyze the cause of the problem and look for strategies that will enable both parties to win.

Your *emotional state* will influence your strategies. You're unlikely to select the same strategies when you're sad as when you're angry. You'll turn to different strategies if you're seeking to apologize than you would use if you were looking for revenge.

Your *cognitive assessment* of the situation will exert powerful influence. For example, your attitudes and beliefs about what is fair and equitable will affect your readiness to acknowledge the fairness in the other person's position. Your own assessment of who (if anyone) is the cause of the problem also will influence your conflict style. You may also assess the likely effects of potential strategies. For example, what do you risk if you fight with your boss by using blame or personal rejection? Do you risk alienating your teenager if you use force?

Your *personality and level of communication competence* will influence the way you engage in conflict. For example, if you're shy and unassertive, you may be more likely to want to avoid a conflict than to fight actively. If you're extroverted and have a strong desire to state your position, then you may be more likely to fight actively and to argue forcefully.

Your *culture and gender* also will influence your strategies. As noted earlier, many Asian cultures em-

GOING *ONLINE*

Interpersonal and Small Group Conflict

http://humanservices.ucdavis.edu/CustomTraining/Interpersonal/Index.asp

This website, maintained by the University of California at Davis, is a particularly good resource for learning more about conflict, how it can be resolved, and how violence can be prevented.

In addition, visit the companion website for this text (www.ablongman.com/devito) and take the self-tests to measure your own argumentativeness and assertiveness. Try also working with the exercises and reading the additional discussions: "Managing Power Plays," "Assertiveness," "The Influence of Culture on Conflict: An Example," "Analyzing a Conflict Episode," and "How Do you Fight? Like a Man? Like a Woman?"

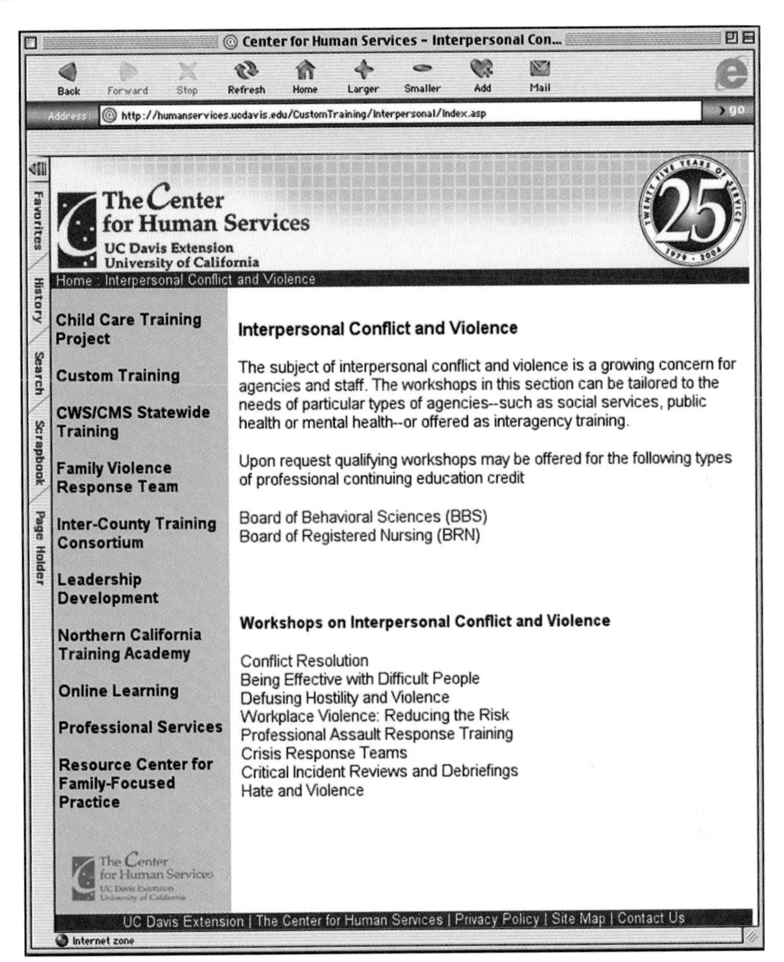

phasize the importance of saving face; consequently, Asians are less likely to use conflict strategies such as blame and personal rejection, as these are likely to result in a loss of face. People from cultures that look favorably on open conflict may be more apt to use argumentativeness and to fight actively. Students from collectivist cultures prefer mediation and bargaining as conflict resolution strategies, whereas students from individualist cultures prefer a more adversarial and confrontational conflict style (Leung, 1987; Berry, Poortinga, Segall, & Dasen, 1992). Asian women are expected to be exceptionally polite, especially when in public conflict with men (Tannen, 1994a, 1994b). In the United States, although conflict equality may be verbalized, many people expect women to be more polite and to pursue conflict is a nonargumentative way, whereas men are expected to argue forcefully and logically.

Win-Lose and Win-Win Strategies

If you look at interpersonal and small group conflict in terms of winning and losing, you'll see that there are four potential outcomes: (1) A wins, B loses; (2) A loses, B wins; (3) A loses, B loses; and (4) A wins, B wins.

In managing conflict you have a choice and can seek to achieve any one of those combinations of winning and losing. You can look for solutions in which one person or one side wins (usually you or your side) and the other person or other side loses: *win-lose solutions.* Or you can look for solutions in

COMMUNICATION@WORK

Sexual Harassment

All human beings are born free and equal in dignity and rights.

—United Nations Declaration of Human Rights, Article 1

No discussion of communication in the workplace could omit a discussion of **sexual harassment,** one of organizations' major problems today. Sexual harassment violates Title VII of the Civil Rights Act of 1964 as amended by the Civil Rights Act of 1991 (http://www.eeoc.gov/laws/vii.html, last modified January 15, 1997, accessed May 4, 2002). There are two general categories of sexual harassment: quid pro quo (a Latin term that literally means "something for something") and the creation of a hostile environment.

In quid pro quo harassment, employment opportunities (as in hiring and promotion) may be made dependent on the granting of sexual favors. Quid pro quo harassment also can include threats of reprisals and various negative consequences that would result from the failure to grant such sexual favors.

Hostile environment harassment is much broader and includes all sexual behaviors (verbal and nonverbal) that make a worker uncomfortable. For example, putting sexually explicit pictures on the office bulletin board, using sexually explicit screen savers, telling sexual jokes and stories, and using sexual and demeaning language or gestures all would constitute sexual harassment.

- *How can you avoid sexual harassment behaviors?* You can avoid conveying messages that might be considered sexual harassment by following these suggestions (Bravo & Cassedy, 1992). First, begin with the assumption that others at work are not interested in your sexual advances, sexual stories and jokes, or sexual gestures. Second, listen and watch for negative reactions to any sex related discussion. Use the suggestions and techniques discussed throughout this book (such as perception checking and critical listening) to become aware of such reactions. When in doubt, find out; ask questions, for example. Third, avoid saying or doing anything you think your parent, partner, or child would find offensive in the behavior of someone with whom she or he worked.
- *What can you do about sexual harassment?* If you think you're being sexually harassed, consider these suggestions (Petrocelli & Repa, 1992; Bravo & Cassedy, 1992; Rubenstein, 1993):
  1. Talk to the harasser. Tell this person, assertively, that you do not welcome the behavior and that you find it offensive. If this doesn't solve the problem, then consider the next suggestion.
  2. Collect evidence—perhaps get corroboration from others who have experienced similar harassment and/or keep a log of the offensive behaviors.
  3. Use the channels established by the organization to deal with such grievances. If this doesn't stop the harassment, consider going farther.
  4. File a complaint with an organization or governmental agency, or perhaps take legal action.
  5. Don't blame yourself. Like many who are abused, you may tend to blame yourself, feeling that you are responsible for being harassed. You aren't; however, you may need to secure emotional support from friends or perhaps from trained professionals.

Communicating@Work

If you have access, log on to Research Navigator (www.researchnavigator.com) and search the New York Times *database for "sexual harassment." What types of harassment occur most often?*

which both you and the other person or side win: *win-win solutions.*

Obviously, win-win solutions are the most desirable. Perhaps the most important reason is that win-win solutions lead to mutual satisfaction and prevent the resentment that win-lose solutions often engender. Looking for and developing win-win solutions makes the next conflict less unpleasant; the

BUILDING COMMUNICATION SKILLS

Finding Win-Win Solutions

As this section explains, win-win conflict/strategies are preferable to win-lose approaches, at least when the conflict is interpersonal. Often, however, people fail even to consider what possible win-win solutions might exist. To get into the habit of looking for these types of solutions, try generating as many win-win solutions as possible (that you feel the individuals could reasonably accept) for the following scenarios. Give yourself two minutes for each case. If possible, share your win-win solutions with other individuals or groups; also, consider ways in which you might incorporate win-win strategies into your own conflict management behavior.

1. Pat and Chris plan to take a two-week vacation in August. Pat wants to go to the shore and relax by the water. Chris wants to go the mountains and go hiking and camping.
2. Pat recently got a totally unexpected $3,000 bonus. Pat wants to buy a new computer and printer for the home office; Chris wants to take a much-needed vacation.
3. Philip has recently come out as gay to his parents. He wants them to accept him and his life (which includes a committed relationship with another man). His parents want him to seek religious counseling for help in changing his orientation.

participants can more easily view conflict as "solving a problem" rather than as "fighting." Still another advantage is that win-win solutions promote mutual face-saving: Both parties can feel good about themselves. Also, people are more likely to abide by the decisions reached in a win-win conflict than they are in win-lose or lose-lose situations. For all these reasons, win-win solutions are worth seeking whenever possible.

Take an interpersonal example: Let's say that I want to spend our money on a new car (my old one is unreliable) and you want to spend it on a vacation (you're exhausted and feel the need for a rest). Through our conflict and its resolution, ideally we learn what each of us really wants. We may then be able to figure out a way for each of us to get what we want. I might accept a good used car and you might accept a less expensive vacation. Or we might buy a used car and take an inexpensive road trip. Each of these win-win solutions will satisfy both of us; each of us wins, each of us gets what we wanted.

Avoidance and Active Fighting

One nonproductive conflict strategy is **avoidance.** Avoidance may involve actual physical flight: You may leave the scene (walk out of the apartment or meeting room). Or you may simply psychologically tune out all incoming arguments or problems. In the United States men are more likely to use avoidance than women (Markman, Silvern, Clements, & Kraft-Hanak, 1993; Oggins, Veroff, & Leber, 1993), often additionally denying that anything is wrong (Haferkamp, 1991-92).

Nonnegotiation is a special type of avoidance. Here you refuse to discuss the conflict or to listen to the other person's argument. At times nonnegotiation takes the form of hammering away at your own point of view until the other person gives in, a method referred to as steamrolling.

Instead of avoiding the issues, take an active role in your conflicts. Don't close your ears (or mind) or walk out during an argument. This does not mean that taking time out to cool off is not a useful first strategy. Sometimes it is. In an e-mail conflict, for example, a cooling-off period is an easy-to-use and often effective strategy. By delaying your response until you've had time to think things out more logically and calmly, you'll be better able to respond constructively and to address possible ways to resolve the conflict and get the relationship back to a less hostile stage.

To take an active role, involve yourself on both sides of the communication exchange. That is, participate actively as a speaker-listener; voice your own feelings and listen carefully to the voicing of your opponent's feelings. Be willing to communicate as both sender and receiver—to say what is on your mind and to listen to what the other person is saying.

Another part of active fighting involves taking responsibility for your thoughts and feelings. For example, when you disagree with your partner or with other group members, say, "I disagree with . . ." or "I don't like it when you . . . . " Avoid statements that

MEDIA WATCH

Violence and the Media

Most research on media violence has focused on television and to a lesser extent on films. But increasingly researchers are examining video games, music, and Internet entertainment for their violent content and potential influence on children. For example, a study of Nintendo and Sega Genesis video games showed that approximately 80 percent of the games included aggression or violence as an essential part of the strategy (Dietz, 1998).

Generally, research finds that media violence can contribute to a variety of effects (Rodman, 2001; Bok, 1998):

- The viewing of violence can teach young people how to be violent; it can teach them the techniques of violence.
- Media violence often gives people (and children especially) role models to emulate (Derne, 1999).
- Because media violence is so prevalent, it can desensitize people to real-life violence around them, which often is not as extreme as they regularly see on television and in the movies.
- Media violence can make viewers afraid of becoming victims of violence.

The extent to which watching media violence contributes to actual viewer violence, however, has not been determined. In its latest study, unfortunately already more than 20 years old, the National Institute of Mental Health (1982) reported that heavy viewing of violence is related to aggressive behavior and that the greater the viewing of violence, the more likely the person is to be aggressive. But there are probably other factors that lead some people to watch violent films, and these factors may well contribute—in large or small part—to aggressive behavior. Family and social factors, developmental and affective disorders, substance abuse, experience with crime, and the motivation to watch violence, for example, interact with exposure to media violence to produce violent behavior (Withecomb, 1997; Haridakis & Rubin, 2003).

You and the Media

How do you feel about violence in the media? If you're unhappy with the current state of media violence, what would you like to see changed? How might you go about effecting these changes?

deny your responsibility, as in, "Everybody thinks you're wrong about . . ." or "Even the photography department thinks we shouldn't . . . ."

Force and Talk

When confronted with conflict, many people prefer not to deal with the issues but rather to force their position on the other person. **Force** may be emotional or physical. In either case, it is an unproductive strategy: The issues are avoided and the person who "wins" is merely the combatant who exerts the most force. This is the technique used by warring nations, children, and even some normally sensible and mature adults. It seems also to be the technique of some persons who are dissatisfied with the power they perceive themselves to have in a relationship, as research shows that perpetrators of violence against both men and women often are motivated to gain control or to defend their own image (Ronfeldt, Kimerling, & Arias, 1998; Felson, 2002).

The use of force is surely one of the most serious problems confronting relationships today, although many approach it as if it were a minor—or even humorous—issue. Researchers found that more than 50 percent of both single and married couples reported that they had experienced physical violence in their relationship. If we add symbolic violence (for example, threatening to hit the other person or throwing something), the percentages are above 60 percent for singles and above 70 percent for marrieds (Marshall & Rose, 1987). In a study of divorced couples, 70 percent reported at least one episode of violence in their premarital, marital, or postmarital relationship. Violence during marriage was higher than for pre- or postmarital relationships (Olday & Wesley, 1990). In another study, 47 percent of a sample of 410 college students reported some experience with violence in a dating relationship (Deal & Wampler, 1986). In most cases the violence was reciprocal—each person in the relationship used violence. In cases in which only one person was violent, the research results are conflicting. For example, in cases in which only one partner was violent, the aggressor was significantly more often the female partner (Deal & Wampler, 1986). Earlier research found similar gender differences (for example, Cate et al., 1982). Other research, however, has tended to confirm the widespread view that men are more likely to use force than women (DeTurck, 1987). Still other research shows that both men and women are likely to use violence but that women are more likely to be injured (Frieze, 2000).

Findings such as these point to problems well beyond the prevalence of unproductive conflict strategies that we want to identify and avoid. They demonstrate the existence of underlying pathologies that we are discovering are a lot more common than were thought previously, when issues like these were never mentioned in college textbooks or lectures. Awareness, of course, is only a first step in understanding and eventually combating such problems.

The only real alternative to force is talk. Instead of using force, you need to talk and listen. The qualities of empathy, openness, and positiveness (see Unit 9), for example, are suitable starting points.

VIEWPOINT

One of the most puzzling findings on violence is that many victims interpret it as a sign of love. For some reason they see being beaten or verbally abused as a sign that their partner is fully in love with them. Also, many victims blame themselves for the violence instead of blaming their partners (Gelles & Cornell, 1985). Why do you think this is so?

Blame and Empathy

Conflict is rarely caused by a single, clearly identifiable problem or by only one of the parties. Usually conflict occurs because of a wide variety of factors, and all concerned play a role. Any attempt to single out one person for **blame** is sure to be unproductive. Even so, a frequently used fight strategy is to blame another person. Consider, for example, the couple who fight over their child's getting into trouble with the police. Instead of dealing with the conflict itself, the parents may blame each other for the child's troubles. Such blaming, of course, does nothing to resolve the problem or to help the child.

Often when you blame someone you attribute motives to the person, a process often referred to as "mind reading." Thus, if the person forgot your birthday and this disturbs you, tackle the actual behavior—the forgetting of the birthday. Try not to presuppose motives: "Well, it's obvious you just don't care about me. If you really cared, you could never have forgotten my birthday!"

Empathy is an excellent alternative to blame. Try to feel what the other person is feeling and to see the situation as the other person does. Try to see the situation as punctuated by the other person, and think about how this differs from your own punctuation.

Demonstrate empathic understanding. Once you have empathically understood the feelings of the other person or group members, validate those feelings as appropriate. If your partner is hurt or angry and you feel that such feelings are legitimate and justified (from the other person's point of view), say so; say, "You have a right to be angry; I shouldn't have said what I did. I'm sorry. But I still don't want to go on vacation with your college roommate." In expressing validation you're not necessarily expressing agreement on the point at issue; you're merely stating that your partner's feelings are legitimate and that you recognize them as such.

Gunnysacking and Present Focus

A gunnysack is a large bag, usually made of burlap. The unproductive conflict strategy known as **gunnysacking** is the practice of storing up grievances so as to unload them at another time (Bach & Wyden, 1968). The occasion for unloading may be relatively minor (or so it might seem at first); for example, you come home late without calling, or you fail to fulfill your assigned task before a meeting at work. Instead of addressing the immediate problem, the gunnysacker unloads all past grievances. The birthday you forgot, the times you were absent from meetings, the hotel reservations you forgot to make. As you probably know from experience, gunnysacking begets gunnysacking. When one person gunnysacks, the other person gunnysacks. The result is that both sides dump their stored-up grievances on each other. Frequently the trigger problem never gets addressed. Instead, resentment and hostility escalate.

Focus your conflict on the here and now rather than on issues that occurred two months ago. Similarly, focus your conflict on the person with whom you're fighting, not on the person's mother, child, or friends.

Manipulation and Spontaneity

Manipulation involves an avoidance of open conflict. The manipulative individual tries to divert conflict by being especially charming (disarming, actually). The manipulator gets the other individual into a receptive and noncombative frame of mind, then presents his or her demands to a weakened opponent. The manipulator relies on our tendency to give in to people who are especially nice to us.

Instead of manipulating, try expressing your feelings with **spontaneity** and honesty. Remember that in conflict situations there's no need to plan a strategy to win a war. The objective is not to win but to increase mutual understanding and to reach a decision that both parties can accept.

Personal Rejection and Acceptance

A person practicing **personal rejection** withholds approval and affection from his or her opponent in conflict, seeking to win the argument by getting the other person to break down in the face of this withdrawal. The individual acts cold and uncaring in an effort to demoralize the other person. In a group situation a person might practice rejection by not listening, not giving any positive feedback, or perhaps even giving negative feedback, making you think everything you're saying is gibberish. In withdrawing positive messages, the rejecting individual hopes to make the other person question his or her own self-worth. Once the other is demoralized and feels less than worthy, it's relatively easy for "rejectors" to get their way. They hold out the renewal of approval and affection as a reward for a resolution in their own favor.

Instead of rejection, express positive feelings for the other person and for the relationship or group. Throughout any conflict, harsh words will probably be exchanged, later to be regretted. The words cannot be unsaid or uncommunicated, but they can be partially offset by the expression of positive statements.

Fighting below and above the Belt

Much like boxers in a ring, each of us has a "belt line." When you hit someone below the emotional belt line, a tactic called **beltlining,** you can inflict serious injury. When you hit above the belt, however, the person is able to absorb the blow. With most interpersonal relationships, especially those of long standing, we know where the belt line is. You know, for example, that to hit Pat with the inability to have children is to hit below the belt. You know that to hit Chris with the failure to get a permanent job is to hit below the belt. You know that to stress the number of years your colleague has been in the same position without a promotion is to hit below the belt. Hitting below the belt line causes everyone involved added problems. Keep blows to areas your opponent can absorb and handle.

Remember that the aim of interpersonal and small group conflict is not to win and have your opponent lose. Rather, it's to resolve a problem and strengthen the relationship or group. Keep this ultimate goal always in clear focus, especially when you're angry or hurt.

Face-Detracting and Face-Enhancing Strategies

Another dimension of conflict strategies is that of *face orientation*. Face-detracting or face-attacking strategies involve treating the other person as incompetent or untrustworthy, as unable or bad (Donohue & Kolt, 1992). Such attacks can vary from mildly embarrassing to severely damaging to the other person's ego or reputation (Imahori & Cupach, 1994). When such attacks become extreme they may be similar to verbal aggressiveness—another unproductive tactic that we'll consider shortly. Protecting our image (or face), especially in the midst of conflict, is important to everyone, but especially important to members of the collectivist cultures of Asia (Zane & Yeh, 2002).

Face-enhancing techniques, in contrast, help the other person maintain a positive image—an image as competent and trustworthy, able and good. There's some evidence to show that even when, say, you get what you want in a bargaining situation, it is wise to help the other person retain positive face. This makes it less likely that future conflicts will arise (Donohue & Kolt, 1992).

Not surprisingly, people are more likely to make a greater effort to support their opponent's "face" if they like the opponent than if they don't (Meyer, 1994). So be especially careful to avoid "fighting words"—words that are sure to escalate the conflict rather than to help resolve it. Words like *stupid, liar*, and *bitch,* as well as words like *always* and *never* (as in "you always" or "you never"), invariably create additional problems. In contrast, confirming the other person's definition of self, avoiding attack and blame, and using excuses and apologies as appropriate are some generally useful face-positive strategies.

Nonassertive and Assertive Strategies

Nonassertiveness can be unproductive because it involves the failure to express your thoughts and feelings in certain or all communication situations. Nonassertive people often fail to assert their rights. In many instances these people do what others tell them to do—parents, employers, and the like—without questioning. They operate with a "you win, I lose" philosophy, giving others what they want without concern for themselves (Lloyd, 2001). Nonassertive people often ask permission from others to do what is their perfect right. They are often anxious in social situations and their self-esteem is likely to be low.

Assertiveness means acting in your own best interests *without* denying or infringing on the rights of others. Not surprisingly, assertiveness can be especially helpful in conflict situations (Fodor & Collier, 2001). Assertive people operate with an "I win, you win" philosophy; they assume that both parties can gain something from conflict. Assertive people speak their minds and welcome others' doing likewise. Assertive people also tend to be more positive and generally score higher on measures of hopefulness than nonassertive individuals (Velting, 1999).

There are wide cultural differences in assertiveness. For example, individualist cultures are more likely to value assertiveness than are collectivist cultures. That is, cultures that stress competition, individual success, and independence also will admire assertiveness; cultures that stress cooperation, group success, and the interdependence of all members will value assertiveness much less. American students, for example, are found to be significantly more assertive than Japanese or Korean students (Thompson, Klopf, & Ishii, 1991; Thompson & Klopf, 1991). Thus, in conflict situations assertiveness may prove an effective strategy in one culture but may create problems in another culture.

Here are a few suggestions to help you communicate more assertively:

- *Describe the problem; don't evaluate or judge it:* "We both want what's right for the kids, but we haven't gotten together to discuss the problems." Be sure to use I-messages and to avoid messages that accuse or blame the other person.
- *State how this problem affects you:* "I'm worrying about this during the day and it's affecting my job."
- *Propose solutions that are workable and that allow the person to save face:* "Let's make some time tomorrow to discuss how we want to handle things."
- *Confirm understanding:* "Would that be okay? Say, about eight?"

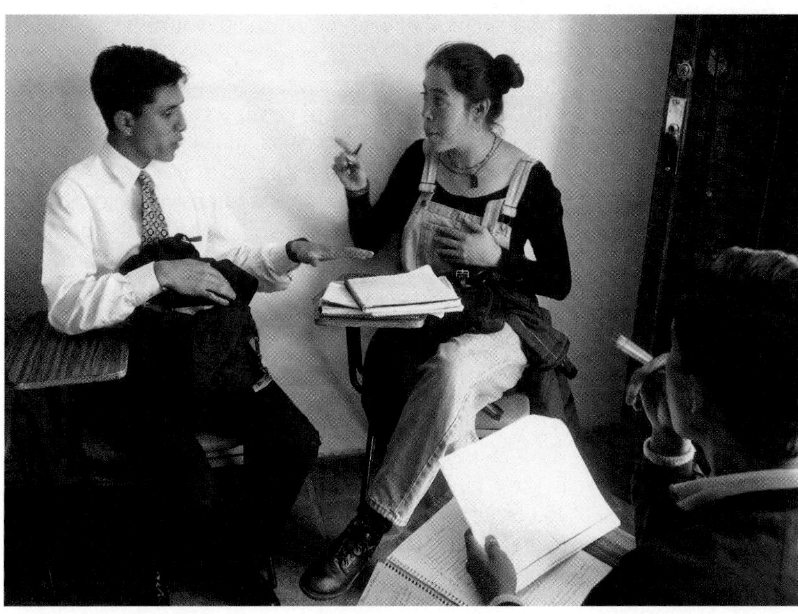

VIEWPOINT

Take a good look at your own conflict behaviors. What changes would you make? What conflict skills and strategies would you seek to integrate into your own interpersonal and small group conflict resolution behavior?

Aggressiveness and Argumentativeness

An especially interesting perspective on conflict has emerged from researchers' work on verbal aggressiveness and argumentativeness (Infante, 1988; Rancer, 1998; Wigley, 1998). Understanding these two concepts will help you understand some of the reasons why things go wrong and some of the ways in which you can use conflict to actually improve your relationships.

Verbal Aggressiveness

Verbal aggressiveness is an unproductive conflict strategy in which one person tries to win an argument by inflicting psychological pain, by attacking the other person's self-concept. The technique relies on many of the other unproductive conflict strategies we've already considered. It's a type of disconfirmation in that it seeks to discredit the individual's view of self (see Unit 7). To explore this tendency further, take the following self-test of verbal aggressiveness.

TEST YOURSELF

How Verbally Aggressive Are You?

This scale is designed to measure how people try to obtain compliance from others. For each statement, indicate the extent to which you feel it's true for you in your attempts to influence others. Use the following scale: 1 = almost never true; 2 = rarely true; 3 = occasionally true; 4 = often true; and 5 = almost always true.

1. I am extremely careful to avoid attacking individuals' intelligence when I attack their ideas.
2. When individuals are very stubborn, I use insults to soften the stubbornness.
3. I try very hard to avoid having other people feel bad about themselves when I try to influence them.
4. When people refuse to do a task I know is important, without good reason, I tell them they are unreasonable.
5. When others do things I regard as stupid, I try to be extremely gentle with them.
6. If individuals I am trying to influence really deserve it, I attack their character.
7. When people behave in ways that are really in very poor taste, I insult them in order to shock them into proper behavior.
8. I try to make people feel good about themselves even when their ideas are stupid.
9. When people simply will not budge on a matter of importance, I lose my temper and say rather strong things to them.
10. When people criticize my shortcomings, I take it in good humor and do not try to get back at them.
11. When individuals insult me, I get a lot of pleasure out of really telling them off.
12. When I dislike individuals greatly, I try not to show it in what I say or how I say it.
13. I like poking fun at people who do things which are very stupid in order to stimulate their intelligence.
14. When I attack a person's ideas, I try not to damage their self-concepts.
15. When I try to influence people, I make a great effort not to offend them.
16. When people do things which are mean or cruel, I attack their character in order to help correct their behavior.
17. I refuse to participate in arguments when they involve personal attacks.
18. When nothing seems to work in trying to influence others, I yell and scream in order to get some movement from them.
19. When I am not able to refute others' positions, I try to make them feel defensive in order to weaken their positions.
20. When an argument shifts to personal attacks, I try very hard to change the subject.

HOW DID YOU DO? In order to compute your verbal aggressiveness score, follow these steps:

1. Add your scores on items 2, 4, 6, 7, 9, 11, 13, 16, 18, 19.
2. Add your scores on items 1, 3, 5, 8, 10, 12, 14, 15, 17, 20.
3. Subtract the sum obtained in step 2 from 60.
4. To compute your verbal aggressiveness score, add the total obtained in step 1 to the result obtained in step 3.

If you scored between 59 and 100, you're high in verbal aggressiveness; if you scored between 39 and 58, you're moderate in verbal aggressiveness; and if you scored between 20 and 38, you're low in verbal aggressiveness. In looking over your responses, make special note of the characteristics identified in the 20 statements that refer to the tendency to act verbally aggressive. Note those inappropriate behaviors that you're especially prone to commit. High agreement (4s or 5s) with statements 2, 4, 6, 7, 9, 11, 13, 16, 18, and 19 and low agreement (1s or 2s) with statements 1, 3, 5, 8, 10, 12, 14, 15, 17, and 20 will help you highlight any significant verbal aggressiveness you might have.

WHAT WILL YOU DO? Because verbal aggressiveness is likely to seriously hamper interpersonal effectiveness, you probably want to reduce your tendencies to respond aggressively. Review the times when you acted verbally aggressive. What effect did such actions have on your subsequent interaction? What effect did they have on your relationship with the other person? What alternative ways of getting your point across might you have used? Might these have proved more effective? Perhaps the most general suggestion for reducing verbal aggressiveness is to increase your argumentativeness; as we'll discuss next.

Source: From "Verbal Aggressiveness" by Dominic Infante and C. J. Wigley, *Communication Monographs,* V. 53, 1986, pp. 61–69. Used by permission of the National Communication Association and Authors.

Argumentativeness

Contrary to popular belief, argumentativeness is a quality to be cultivated rather than avoided. The term **argumentativeness** in this context refers to your willingness to argue for a point of view, your tendency to speak your mind on significant issues. It's the mode of dealing with disagreements that is the preferred alternative to verbal aggressiveness (Infante & Rancer, 1995).

Generally, people who are high in argumentativeness have a strong tendency to state their position on controversial issues and to argue against the positions of others. A highly argumentative individual sees debate as exciting and intellectually challenging—as an opportunity to win a kind of contest.

The person who is low in argumentativeness tries to prevent arguments. This person experiences satisfaction not from arguing but from avoiding arguments. The low argumentative sees arguing as unpleasant and unsatisfying. Not surprisingly, this person has little confidence in his or her ability to argue effectively.

Men generally score higher in argumentativeness (and in verbal aggressiveness) than women. Men are also more apt to be perceived (by both men and women) as more argumentative and more verbally aggressive than women (Nicotera & Rancer, 1994). High and low argumentatives also differ in the way in which they view the uses of argument (Rancer, Kosberg, & Baukus, 1992). High argumentatives not only see arguing as enjoyable but also view its outcomes as pragmatic. They see arguing as having a

ASK THE RESEARCHER

Verbal Aggressiveness

- *My boyfriend is really sweet, and I know he really loves me. But at times he's verbally aggressive. Sometimes he gets really angry (like when I do something wrong) and says really hurtful things. He's asked me to move in with him, and I'm not sure what to do. Any ideas?*

Can a sweet guy be hurtful? Some people attack so often, they become less sensitive to the hurtful nature of their remarks. Let him know how you feel, and offer a few comments of his that made you feel badly. If he were more aware of his unfriendly language, maybe he'd curtail it.

When you "do something wrong," he gets angry. Is his behavior justified by your "mistakes"? Most people believe justified aggression is okay (like shooting back!) but that aggression without justification is bad. Is verbal aggression ever justified? Here's a simple test: Would he react to your "mistake" the same way if it were done by someone like his boss (who could fire him)? I'll bet he wouldn't! There are many positive alternatives to aggression, such as assertiveness and constructive arguing.

Remember, words can't hurt you, only people can hurt you. Should you move in with him? Harry Connick sings, never "build a house in a hurricane."

For more information: Venable, K.V., & Martin, M. M. (1997). Argumentativeness and verbal aggressiveness in dating relationships. *Journal of Social Behavior and Personality, 12* (4), 955–964.

Charles J. Wigley III (Ph.D., Kent State University; J.D., University of Akron) is professor of communication at Canisius College and teaches research methods and organizational communication (wigley@canisius.edu). An experienced defense attorney, he studies the role of communication in jury selection. He once tried to build a house in a hurricane!

positive impact on their self-concept, offering functional outcomes, and being highly ego involving. Low argumentatives, on the other hand, believe that arguing has a negative impact on their self-concept, that it has dysfunctional outcomes, and that it's not very ego involving. They see arguing as providing little in the way of either enjoyment or pragmatic outcomes.

The researchers who developed the self-test above note that both high and low argumentatives may experience communication difficulties (Infante & Rancer, 1982). The high argumentative, for example, may argue needlessly, too often, and too forcefully. The low argumentative may avoid taking a stand even when it seems necessary.

Persons scoring somewhere in the middle on the argumentativeness scale are probably the most interpersonally skilled and adaptable, arguing when it's necessary but avoiding arguments that are needless and repetitive.

Here are some suggestions for cultivating argumentativeness and for preventing it from degenerating into aggressiveness (Infante, 1988):

- Treat disagreements as objectively as possible; avoid assuming that because someone takes issue with your position or your interpretation, they're attacking you as a person.
- Avoid attacking a person rather than a person's arguments. Even if this would give you a short-term tactical advantage, it will probably backfire at some later time and make your relationship or group participation more difficult. Center your arguments on issues, not personalities.
- Reaffirm the other person's sense of competence; compliment the other person as appropriate.
- Avoid interrupting; allow the other person to state her or his position fully before you respond.
- Stress equality, and stress the similarities that you have with the other person or persons; stress your areas of agreement before attacking the disagreements.
- Express interest in the other person's position, attitude, and point of view.
- Avoid presenting your arguments too emotionally; using an overly loud voice or interjecting vulgar expressions will prove offensive and eventually ineffective.
- Allow people to save face; never humiliate another person.

Before and after the Conflict

If you want to make conflict truly productive, consider a few suggestions for preparing for the conflict and for using the conflict as a method for relational or group growth.

Before the Conflict

Try to fight in private—within the relationship or within the group. When you air your conflicts in front of others, you create a wide variety of other problems. You may not be willing to be totally honest when third parties are present; you may feel you have to save face and therefore must win the fight at all costs. This may lead you to use strategies to win the

BUILDING COMMUNICATION SKILLS

Engaging in Conflict

Think about the major productive and unproductive conflict strategies discussed in this section as they might apply to the specific situations described below. Assume that each of the following statements is made by someone close to you. Try developing an unproductive approach and an alternative productive strategy for any one or two of these situations.

1. You're late again. You're always late. Your lateness is so inconsiderate of my time and my interests. What is wrong with you?
2. I just can't bear another weekend of sitting home watching television. You never want to do anything. I'm just not going to do that again and that's final.
3. Why don't you stay out of the neighbors' business? You're always butting in and telling people what to do. Why don't you mind your own business and take care of your own family instead of trying to run everybody else's?

argument rather than strategies to resolve the conflict. Also, of course, you run the risk of embarrassing others, which will incur resentment and hostility.

Be sure everyone is ready to fight. Although conflicts arise at the most inopportune times, you can choose the time when you will try to resolve them. The moment when your partner comes home after a hard day of work may not be the right time for a confrontation. When a group is completing the company's most important project on a deadline, it may not be the wisest time to raise minor conflict issues. In general, make sure that all individuals are relatively free of other problems and ready to deal with the conflict at hand.

Know what you're fighting about. Sometimes people in a relationship or in a close-knit group become so hurt and angry that they lash out at the other person just to vent their own frustration. The "content" of the conflict is merely an excuse to express anger. Any attempt at resolving such a "problem" will of course be doomed to failure, because the problem addressed is not what really gave rise to the conflict. Instead, it may be underlying hostility, anger, and frustration that need to be dealt with.

At other times, people argue about general and abstract issues that are poorly specified; for example, a friend's or collegue's lack of consideration or failure to accept responsibility. Only when you define your differences in specific terms can you begin to understand them and thus resolve them.

Fight about problems that can be solved. Fighting about past behaviors or about family members or situations over which you have no control solves nothing; instead, it creates additional difficulties. Any attempt at resolution is doomed, because by their nature such problems can't be solved. Often such conflicts are concealed attempts at expressing frustration or dissatisfaction.

Consider what beliefs you hold that may need to be reexamined. Unrealistic beliefs are often at the heart of interpersonal and group conflicts. Such beliefs include ideas like "If my partner really cared, he or she would do what I ask," "If people really cared about the success of the group, they'd devote 100 percent of their time to the project," or "People don't listen to what I have to say."

After the Conflict

After the conflict is resolved, there's still work to be done. Often after one conflict is supposedly settled, another conflict will emerge—because, for example, one person may feel harmed and may feel the need to retaliate and take revenge in order to restore self-worth (Kim & Smith, 1993). So it's especially important that the conflict be resolved in such a way that it does not generate other, perhaps more significant, conflicts.

Learn from the conflict and from the process you went through in trying to resolve it. For example, can you identify the fight strategies that aggravated the situation? Do some people need a cooling-off period? Do you need extra space when upset? Can you identify when minor issues are going to escalate into major arguments? Does avoidance make matters worse? What issues are particularly disturbing and likely to cause difficulties? Can these be avoided?

Keep the conflict in perspective. Be careful not to blow it out of proportion—to define your relationship or your social or work group in terms of the conflict. Also, avoid the tendency to see disagreement as inevitably leading to major blowups. Conflicts in most interpersonal and group situations actually occupy a very small percentage of real time, even though in recollection they often loom extremely large.

Negative feelings frequently arise after a conflict, most often because unfair fight strategies were used—strategies such as personal rejection, manipulation, or force. Resolve surely to avoid such unfair tactics in the future, but at the same time let go of guilt and blame for yourself and others. If you think it would help, discuss these feelings with your partner, your group members, or even a therapist.

Increase the exchange of rewards and cherishing behaviors to demonstrate your positive feelings and to show that you're over the conflict. It's a good way of saying you want the relationship or the group to survive and to flourish.

Ethical Fighting

This unit has emphasized the differences between effective and ineffective conflict strategies. But all communication strategies also have an ethical dimension, so we need to look at the ethical implications of conflict resolution strategies. For example:

- Does conflict avoidance have an ethical dimension? For example, is it unethical for one person to refuse to discuss issues of disagreement?
- Is it ever ethical to force someone to accept your position? Can physical force be ethical? Can you identify a situation in which it would be appropriate for someone with greater physical strength to overpower another person to enforce his or her point of view?
- Is it ever ethical to use face-detracting strategies? In other words, are face-detracting strategies inherently unethical, or might it be appropriate to use them in certain situations? Can you identify such situations?

- What are the ethical implications of verbal aggressiveness?

WHAT WOULD YOU DO? At your high-powered and highly stressful job you sometimes use coke with your colleagues. This happens several times a month. You don't use drugs of any kind at any other times. Your partner—who you know hates drugs and despises people who use any recreational drug—asks you if you take drugs. Because your use is so limited, but mostly because you know that admitting it will cause a huge conflict in a relationship that's already having difficulties, you wonder: Can you ethically lie about this?

SUMMARY

In this unit we explored interpersonal and small group conflict, the types of conflicts that occur, the don'ts and dos of conflict management, and what to do before and after the conflict.

1. Relationship and small group conflict occurs among people who are connected but who have opposing goals that interfere with others' desired goals. Conflicts may occur face-to-face or on the Internet, through e-mail, in newsgroups, and in other contexts.
2. Content conflicts center on objects, events, and persons in the world that are usually, though not always, external to the parties involved.
3. Relationship conflicts are concerned not so much with some external object as with relationships between individuals—with such issues as who is in charge, how equal the partners are in a primary relationship, or who has the right to set down rules of behavior.
4. Unproductive and productive conflict strategies include: win–lose and win–win approaches, avoidance and fighting actively, force and talk, blame and empathy, gunnysacking and present focus, manipulation and spontaneity, personal rejection and acceptance, fighting below and above the belt, face-detracting and face-enhancing tactics, nonassertive and assertive approaches, and fighting aggressively and argumentatively.
5. To cultivate constructive argumentativeness, treat disagreements objectively and avoid attacking the other person, reaffirm the other's sense of competence, avoid interrupting, stress equality and similarities, express interest in the other's position, avoid presenting your arguments too emotionally, and allow the other to save face.
6. In preparation for conflict, try to fight in private and when all are ready to fight. Have a clear idea of what you want to fight about and be specific, fight about things that can be solved, and reexamine beliefs that may be unrealistic.
7. After the conflict, assess what you've learned, keep the conflict in perspective, let go of negative feelings, and increase positiveness.

KEY TERMS

interpersonal and small group conflict
content conflict
relationship conflict
win–lose strategies
win–win strategies
avoidance
nonnegotiation
force
blame
gunnysacking
manipulation
spontaneity
personal rejection
beltlining
verbal aggressiveness
argumentativeness

THINKING CRITICALLY ABOUT

Interpersonal and Small Group Conflict

1. Why do you think men are more likely to withdraw from conflict than women? For example, what arguments can you present for or against any of these reasons (Noller, 1993): Because men have difficulty dealing with conflict? Because the culture has taught men to avoid it? Because withdrawal is an expression of power?
2. If you have access, log on to Research Navigator (www.researchnavigator.com) and locate an article dealing with interpersonal or group conflict. What can you learn about conflict and communication from this article?
3. Visit some game websites and examine the rules of the games. What kinds of conflict strategies do these game rules embody? Do you think such games influence people's interpersonal conflict strategies?
4. What does your own culture teach about conflict and its management? What strategies does it prohibit? Are some strategies prohibited in conflict with certain people (say, your parents) but not with others (say, your friends)? Does your culture prescribe certain ways of dealing with conflict? Does it have different expectations for men and for women? To what degree have you internalized these teachings? What effect do these teachings have on your actual conflict behaviors?
5. How would you describe your conflict style in your own close relationships in terms of competing, avoiding, accommodating, collaborating, and compromising?
6. In your experience, what topics cause the most conflict among your friends? Your family? Your romantic partners? Your work colleagues? What can you learn from this topic analysis?

Part 3 Public Speaking

UNIT

Public Speaking Topics, Audiences, and Research

UNIT CONTENTS

As you move up the hierarchy in your business and professional lives, you'll find an ever greater need for public speaking. In this unit you'll learn

- what public speaking is and the nature of the normal nervousness that most people feel
- how to control your anxiety and accomplish the first few steps in preparing a public speech—selecting and limiting your topic, analyzing your specific audience, and researching your topic

Introducing Public Speaking

Fair questions to ask of a book or a course are "What will I get out of this?" and "How will the effort and time I put into this subject benefit me?" Let's answer these questions in relation to public speaking.

The Benefits of Public Speaking

Here are just a few of the benefits you'll derive from this book's units on public speaking.

- *Personal and social competencies:* In the pages that follow you'll learn such skills as self-awareness, self-confidence, and ways to deal with the fear of communicating—skills that you'll apply in public speaking but that also will prove valuable in all of your social interactions.
- *Academic and career skills:* Among skills you'll learn are the ability to conduct research; explain complex concepts; support an argument with logical, emotional, and ethical appeals; organize a variety of messages; and evaluate the validity of persuasive appeals.
- *General communication abilities:* As you acquire the skills of public speaking, you'll also develop and refine your general communication abilities; you'll develop a more effective communication style, learn to give and respond appropriately to criticism, improve your listening skills, and refine your delivery skills.
- *Public speaking competencies:* And, of course, you'll become a more effective public speaker. Through instruction, exposure to different speeches, feedback, and individual learning experiences, you'll acquire the competencies, the skills, of public speaking.

Beliefs about Public Speaking

A good way to begin your study of public speaking is to examine your own beliefs about public speaking and public speakers. Compare some common beliefs with the research and theory that bear on these beliefs:

Belief: Good public speakers are born, not made.

Research finds that effective public speaking is actually a learned skill. Although some people are born brighter or more extroverted—which will certainly help in public speaking—all people can improve their abilities and become more effective public speakers.

Belief: The more speeches you give, the better you'll become at it.

Research finds that this is true only if you practice effective skills. If you practice bad habits, you're more likely to grow less effective than to become more effective; consequently, it's important to learn and follow the principles of effectiveness.

Belief: You'll never be a good public speaker if you're nervous giving speeches.

Research finds that most speakers are nervous; managing, not eliminating, the fear will enable you to become effective regardless of your current level of anxiety. In fact, your fear may actually encourage you to prepare more thoroughly and to practice more often, which will contribute to more effective speaking.

Belief: It's best to memorize your speech, especially if you're fearful.

Research finds that acting on this belief is likely to be detrimental. Memorizing your speech is one of the worst things you can do; there are easier ways to deal with fear.

Belief: The skills of public speaking are similar throughout the world.

Research finds that they are not; the techniques of public speaking are culture specific. In other words, what proves effective with an Asian audience may not work with audiences in the United States or in Latin America, and vice versa.

A Definition of Public Speaking

In **public speaking** a speaker presents a relatively continuous message to a relatively large audience in a unique context (see Figure 14.1 on page 268). Like all forms of communication, public speaking is transactional (Watzlawick, Beavin, & Jackson 1967; Watzlawick 1978): Each element in the public speaking process depends on and interacts with all other elements. For example, the way in which you organize a speech will

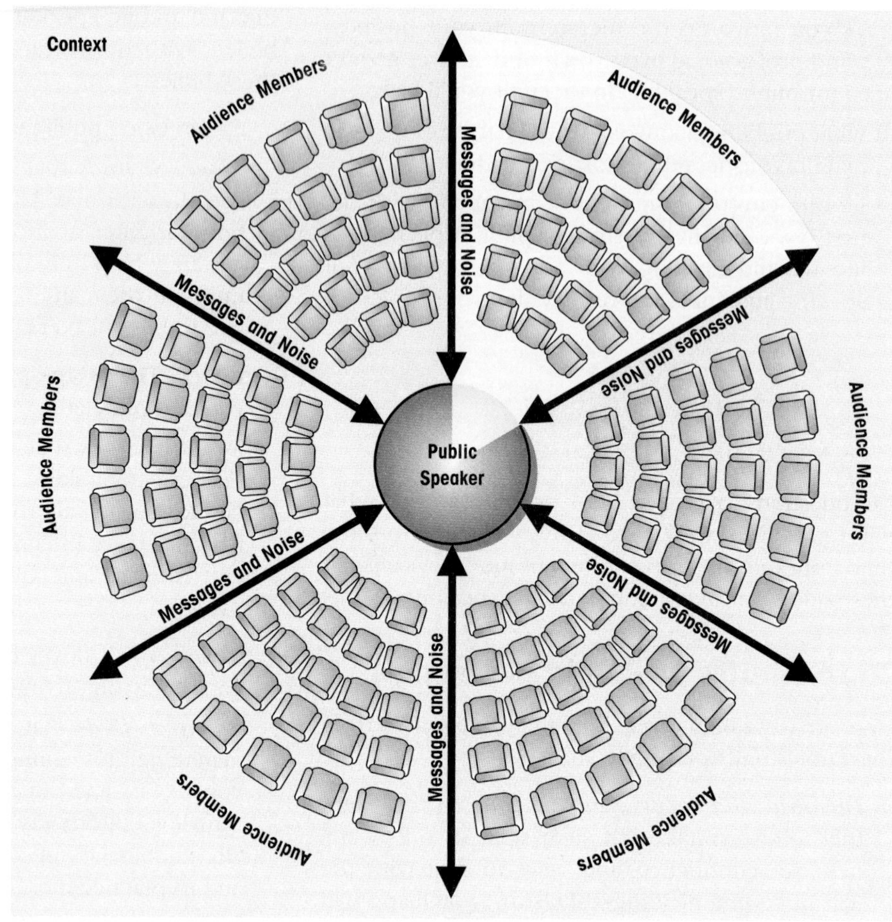

Figure 14.1
The Process and Elements of Public Speaking
This diagram illustrates the essential elements in the public speaking process. The physical setup that you'll face in most of your public speaking will probably resemble the shaded area of the diagram, but this figure emphasizes (1) that the speaker is the center of the public speaking process, and (2) that the audience for a public speech does not consist merely of the listeners in front of you. How would you diagram the process of public speaking?

depend on such factors as the speech topic, the specific audience, the purpose you hope to achieve, and a host of other variables—all of which are explained in the remainder of this unit and in the units to follow.

Especially important is the mutual interaction and influence between speaker and listeners. True, when you give a speech, you do most of the speaking and the listeners do most of the listening. However, the listeners also send messages in the form of feedback—for example, applause, bored looks, nods of agreement or disagreement, and attentive glances. The audience also influences how you'll prepare and present your speech. It influences your arguments, your language, your method of organization, and, in fact, every choice you make. You would not, for example, present the same speech on saving money to high school students as you would to senior citizens.

Apprehension in Public Speaking

Being fearful of giving a public speech is perfectly normal. Everyone experiences some degree of fear in the relatively formal public speaking situation. After all, in public speaking you're the sole focus of attention and are usually being evaluated for your performance. So experiencing fear or anxiety isn't strange or unique.

And although you may at first view apprehension as harmful, it's not necessarily so. In fact, apprehension can work for you. Fear can energize you. It may motivate you to work a little harder to produce a speech that will be better than it might have been. Further, the audience cannot see the apprehension that you may be experiencing. Even though you may think that the audience can hear your heart beat faster and faster, they can't. They can't see your knees tremble. They can't sense your dry throat—at least not most of the time.

Before beginning the actual speech preparation process, let's look first at fear of public speaking, or what is now called **communication apprehension.** People experience apprehension in all forms of communication (as illustrated throughout this text), but public speaking apprehension is the most common (Richmond & McCroskey, 1998; Daly, McCroskey, Ayres, Hopf, & Ayres, 1997). Take the fol-

ASK THE RESEARCHER

Nervousness

- *I'm nervous giving speeches, and I feel this comes through to the audience and I'm not as effective as I'd like to be. What can I do to help reduce and manage my apprehension? Is there anything I can do to hide the symptoms of nervousness from the audience?*

Feeling anxious and nervous prior to a presentation is normal. Try these ideas before a presentation:

1. Know your subject matter better than the audience.
2. Dress and look like a competent communicator.
3. Spend time in the room in which you are to give the presentation and practice.
4. Relax and reassure yourself that you have the knowledge and skills to give a presentation.
5. Review videos of previous students who have given presentations.
6. Think positive thoughts, not negative ones, and attempt to relax.

During the presentation, look at a positive person first. Looking at this one positive person can lower your nervousness. Next, look at other members of the audience. Scan the audience on a regular basis, avoiding negative persons (e.g., the person who is asleep or yawning). Practice your nonverbal immediacy skills. Remember that immediacy behaviors on your part will generate a positive audience response and can generate an easy rapport with your audience.

For more information: Richmond, V. P., & McCroskey, J. C. (1998), *Communication: Apprehension, avoidance, and effectiveness* (5th ed.). Boston: Allyn & Bacon. And Mottet, T., Richmond, V. P., & McCroskey, J. C. (2005). *Instructional communication: Rhetorical and relational perspectives.* Boston: Allyn & Bacon. Or go to www.virginiapeckrichmondphd.com or www.jamescmccroskey.com.

Virginia P. Richmond (Ph.D., University of Nebraska) is professor of communication studies at West Virginia University, where she teaches and conducts research in the areas of instructional communication, nonverbal communication, and organizational communication.

lowing apprehension test to measure your own fear of speaking in public.

TEST YOURSELF

How Apprehensive Are You in Public Speaking?

This questionnaire consists of six statements concerning your feelings about public speaking. Indicate the degree to which each statement applies to you, using the following scale: 1 = strongly agree; 2 = agree; 3 = are undecided; 4 = disagree; 5 = strongly disagree. There are no right or wrong answers. Don't be concerned that some of the statements are similar to others. Work quickly; just record your immediate response.

1. I have no fear of giving a speech.
2. Certain parts of my body feel very tense and rigid while giving a speech.
3. I feel relaxed while giving a speech.
4. My thoughts become confused and jumbled when I am giving a speech.
5. I face the prospect of giving a speech with confidence.
6. While giving a speech, I get so nervous that I forget facts I really know.

HOW DID YOU DO? To obtain your public speaking apprehension score, begin with the number 18 (selected so that you won't wind up with negative numbers) and add to it the scores for items 1, 3, and 5. Then, from this total,

TEST YOURSELF, continued

subtract the scores from items 2, 4, and 6. A score above 18 shows some degree of apprehension. Most people score above 18, so if you scored relatively high, you're among the vast majority of people.

WHAT WILL YOU DO? As you read the suggestions for reducing apprehension in the text that follows, consider what you can do to incorporate these into your own public speaking experiences. Consider too how these suggestions might be useful in reducing apprehension more generally; for example, in social situations and in small groups and meetings.

Source: From James C. McCroskey, *An Introduction to Rhetorical Communication*, 7th edition. Copyright © 1997. Reprinted by permission of Allyn & Bacon.

Reducing Your Apprehension

The following suggestions will help you overcome communication apprehension in public speaking as well as in small group and interpersonal communication situations (Beatty, 1988; Richmond & McCroskey, 1998).

- *Gain experience:* New and different situations such as public speaking are likely to make you anxious, so try to reduce their newness and differentness. The best way to do this is to get as much public speaking experience as you can. With experience your initial fears and anxieties will give way to feelings of control, comfort, and pleasure. Experience will show you that the feelings of accomplishment in public speaking are rewarding and will outweigh any initial anxiety. Try

GOING ONLINE

Public Speaking Website

http://www.ablongman.com/pubspeak/

Visit Allyn & Bacon's website for public speaking. It contains information on assessing your speech-making situation, analyzing your audience, researching your topic, organizing and writing your speech, and delivering your presentation.

In addition, visit the companion website for this text (www.ablongman.com/devito). For this unit it contains two self-tests on satisfaction with public speaking and knowledge of research; discussions entitled "Historical Roots of Public Speaking," "Growth and Development of Public Speaking," "Apprehension," "Developing Confidence in Public Speaking," and "The Dictionary of Topics" (suitable for your classroom speeches); and the exercises "Analyzing and Adapting to Your Audience during the Speech," "Seeking Audience Information," and "Fishbone Diagram for Limiting Topics."

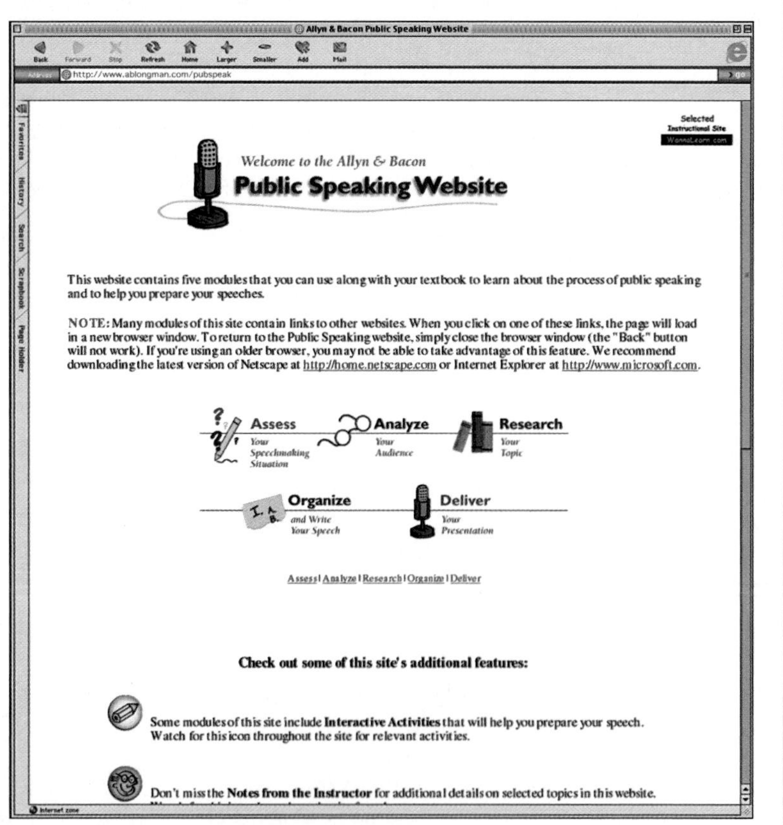

UNDERSTANDING THEORY AND RESEARCH

Systematic Desensitization

The theory of **systematic desensitization** holds that you can reduce fear through a process of gradually adapting to lesser and then successively greater versions of the thing you fear. This technique has been used to deal with many kinds of fear, including public speaking fears (Wolpe 1957; Goss, Thompson, & Olds, 1978; Richmond & McCroskey, 1998). In the case of public speaking, the general idea of systematic desensitization is to create a hierarchy of behaviors leading up to the desired but feared behavior. One specific hierarchy might look like this:

5. Giving a speech in class
4. Introducing another speaker to the class
3. Speaking in a group in front of the class
2. Answering a question in class
1. Asking a question in class

You begin at the bottom of this hierarchy and rehearse this behavior mentally over a period of days until you can clearly visualize asking a question in class without any uncomfortable anxiety. Once you can accomplish this, move to the second level. Here you visualize a somewhat more threatening behavior, say, answering a question. Once you can do this, move to the third level, and so on until you get to the desired behavior.

Working with Theories and Research

- *Create a hierarchy for dealing with communication apprehension. Use small steps to help you get from one step to the next more easily.*

also to familiarize yourself with the public speaking context. For example, try to rehearse in the room in which you will give your speech.

- *Think positively:* When you see yourself as inferior—when, for example, you feel that others are better speakers or that they know more than you do—anxiety increases. Therefore, think positive thoughts and build your confidence through especially thorough preparation. At the same time, maintain realistic expectations for yourself. Fear increases when you feel that you can't meet your own or your audience's expectations (Ayres, 1986). Your second speech does not have to be better than that of the previous speaker, but it should be better than your own first one.
- *See public speaking as conversation:* When you are the center of attention, as you are in public speaking, you feel especially conspicuous, and this often increases anxiety. It may help, therefore, to think of public speaking as another type of conversation (some theorists call it "enlarged conversation"). Or, if you're comfortable talking in small groups, visualize your audience as an enlarged small group; it may dispel some of the anxiety you feel.
- *Stress similarity:* When you feel similar to (rather than different from) your audience, your anxiety should lessen. Therefore, try to emphasize the likenesses between yourself and your audience, especially when your audience consists of people from cultures different from your own (Stephan & Stephan, 1992). When cultural differences exist, you're likely to feel less similarity with your listeners and therefore experience greater anxiety (Gudykunst & Nishida, 1984; Gudykunst, Yang, & Nishida, 1985). So with all audiences, but especially with multicultural listeners, stress commonalities in attitudes, values, and beliefs, for example; it will make you feel more at one with your listeners.
- *Prepare and practice thoroughly:* Much of the fear you experience is a fear of failure. Adequate and even extra preparation will lessen the possibility of failure and the accompanying apprehension. Because apprehension is greatest at the beginning of the speech, try memorizing the first

UNDERSTANDING *THEORY* AND *RESEARCH*

Performance Visualization

The theory of *performance visualization* argues that you can reduce the outward signs of apprehension and the negative thinking that often creates anxiety through a few simple techniques (Ayres & Hopf, 1992, 1993; Ayres, Hopf, & Ayres, 1994).

First, develop a positive attitude and a positive self-perception. Visualize yourself in the role of the effective public speaker. Visualize yourself walking to the front of the room—fully and totally confident, fully in control of the situation. The audience pays rapt attention to your talk and bursts into wild applause as you finish. Throughout this visualization, avoid all negative thoughts. As you visualize yourself as this effective speaker, take note of how you walk, look at your listeners, handle your notes, and respond to questions; especially, think about how you feel about the public speaking experience.

Second, model your performance on that of an especially effective speaker. View a particularly competent public speaker on video, for example, and make a mental "movie" of it. As you review the actual video and mental movie, shift yourself into the role of speaker; become this speaker.

Working with Theories and Research

- *Try performance visualization as you rehearse for your next speech. Did it help reduce your apprehension?*

few sentences of your speech. If there are complicated facts or figures, be sure to write these out; plan to read them and so remove the worry of forgetting them.

- *Move about and breathe deeply:* Physical activity—gross bodily movements as well as small movements of the hands, face, and head—lessens apprehension. Using a visual aid, for example, will temporarily divert attention from you and will allow you to get rid of your excess energy. Also, try breathing deeply a few times before getting up to speak. You'll sense your body relax, and this will help you overcome your initial fear of walking to the front of the room.
- *Avoid chemicals as tension relievers:* Unless prescribed by a physician, chemical means for reducing apprehension are not a good idea. Tranquilizers, marijuana, or artificial stimulants are likely to create problems rather than reduce them. They're likely to impair your ability to remember the parts of your speech, to accurately read audience feedback, and to regulate the timing of your speech. And, of course, alcohol does nothing to reduce public speaking apprehension (Himle, Abelson, & Haghightgou, 1999).

With the nature of public speaking and its benefits in mind and with an understanding of communication apprehension and some ways for managing it, we can look at the essential steps for preparing an effective public speech (Figure 14.2): (1) Select the topic and purpose; (2) analyze the audience; (3) research the topic; (4) develop the thesis and main points; (5) support the main points; (6) organize the speech materials; (7) construct the conclusion, introduction, and transitions; (8) outline the speech; (9) word the speech; and (10) rehearse and deliver the speech. The first three of these steps are discussed in this unit; the remaining seven are discussed in the next two units.

Step 1: Select Your Topic and Purpose

Your first step in preparing to give a speech is to select your topic and purpose (see Figure 14.2).

Your Topic

A suitable speech topic should be (1) worthwhile, dealing with matters of substance; (2) appropriate to you and your audience; (3) limited in scope; and (4) sensitive and appropriate to the culture in which the speech takes place. Let's consider each briefly.

First, the topic should be *worthwhile;* it should address an issue that has significant implications for

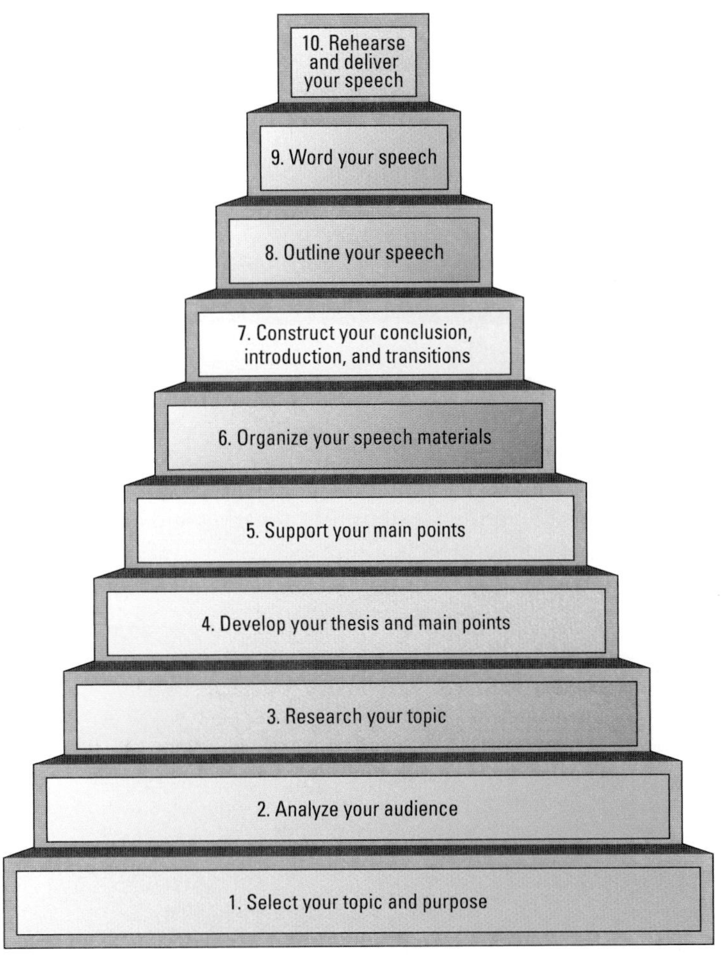

Figure 14.2

The Steps in Public Speaking Preparation and Delivery

Speakers differ in the order in which they follow these steps. Some speakers, for example, prefer to begin with audience analysis; they ask themselves what the audience is interested in and then select the topic and purpose. Some speakers prefer to identify their main points before conducting extensive research, whereas others prefer to allow the points to emerge from the research. The order presented here will prove useful to most speakers for most situations, but you can vary the order to serve your purposes. As long as you cover all steps, you should be in good shape.

the audience. Topics that are worthwhile have consequences—social, educational, political, and so on. The topic must be important enough to merit the time and attention of a group of intelligent and educated persons.

Second, a suitable topic is *appropriate* to you as the speaker, to the audience you'll address, and to the occasion. When you select a topic you're interested in, you'll enjoy thinking and reading about it, and your interest and enjoyment will come through in your speech. Also look at your topic in terms of its appropriateness to the audience. What are they interested in? What would they like to learn more about? What topics will make them feel that the time listening to your speech was well spent? It's a lot easier to please an audience when the topic interests them.

The topic also should be appropriate for the occasion. Some occasions call for humorous subjects or speeches of personal experience that would be out of place in other contexts. Similarly, time limitations will force you to exclude certain topics because they're too complex to cover in the time you have available.

Third, topics must be *limited in scope*. Probably the most common mistake made by beginning speakers is to attempt to cover a huge topic in five minutes. The history of Egypt, why our tax structure should be changed, or the sociology of film—such topics try to cover too much. With too broad a topic, all the speaker succeeds in doing is telling the audience what it already knows.

Finally, topics need to be *culturally sensitive*. In many Arab, Asian, and African cultures, discussing sex in an audience of both men and women would be considered offensive. In other cultures (that of Scandinavia is a good example), sex is expected to be discussed openly and without embarrassment or discomfort. Each culture has its own **taboo** topics—subjects that should be avoided, especially by visitors from other cultures. For example, Roger Axtell in *Do's and Taboos around the World* (1993) recommends that visitors from the United States avoid discussing politics, language differences between

THE PUBLIC SPEAKING SAMPLE ASSISTANT

Throughout these five public speaking units, you'll find a total of eight Public Speaking Sample Assistant boxes. These boxes present complete speeches or outlines with annotations; they will help you to see the public speech as a whole and to ask critical questions about structure, support, language, and numerous other public speaking factors we consider in these units.

A Speech of Introduction

One of the first speeches you may be called upon to make is the speech in which you introduce yourself or (as illustrated in this particular speech) some other person. This speech also will let you see a public speech as a whole and will give you reference points for examining each of the 10 steps for preparing and delivering a public speech.

Introduction

It's a real pleasure to introduce Joe Robinson to you. I want to tell you a little about Joe's background, his present situation, and his plans for the future.

In this introduction, the speaker accomplishes several interrelated purposes: to place the speech in a positive context, to explain the purpose of the speech and orient the audience, to tell them what the speech will cover and that it will follow a time pattern—beginning with the past, moving to the present, and then ending with the proposed future. What other types of opening statements might be appropriate? In what other ways might you organize a speech of introduction?

Transition

Let's look first at Joe's past.

This transitional statement alerts listeners that the speaker is moving from the introduction to the first major part of what is called the "body" of the speech.

Body, first main point (the past)

Joe comes to us from Arizona where he lived and worked on a small ranch with his father and grandparents—mostly working with dairy cows. Working on a farm gave Joe a deep love and appreciation for animals that he carries with him today and into his future plans.

Joe's mother died when he was three years old, and so he lived with his father most of his life. When his father, an air force lieutenant, was transferred to Stewart Air Force Base here in the Hudson Valley, Joe thought it would be a great opportunity to join his father and continue his education.

The speaker here gives us information about Joe's past that makes us see him as a unique individual. We also learn something pretty significant about Joe, namely that his mother died when he was very young. The speaker continues here to answer one of the questions that audience members probably have, namely, why this somewhat older person is in this class and in this college. If this were a longer speech, what else might the speaker cover here? What else would you want to know about Joe's past?

Joe also wanted to stay with his father to make sure he eats right, doesn't get involved with the wrong crowd, and meets the right woman to settle down with.

Here the speaker shows that Joe has a sense of humor in his identifying why he wanted to stay with his father, the very same things that a father would say about a son. Can you make this more humorous?

Transition

So Joe and his father journeyed from the dairy farm of Arizona to the Hudson Valley.

Here's simple transition, alerting the audience that the speaker is moving from the first main point (the past) to the second (the present). In what other ways might you state such a transition?

Second main point (the present)

Right now, with the money he saved while working on the ranch and with the help of a part-time job, Joe's here with us at Hudson Valley Community College.

Like many of us, Joe is a little apprehensive about college and worries that it's going to be a difficult and very different experience, especially at 28. Although an avid reader—mysteries and biographies are his favorites—Joe hasn't really studied, taken an exam, or written a term paper since high school, some 10 years ago. So he's a bit anxious, but at the same time he's looking forward to the changes and the challenges of college life.

And, again, like many of us, Joe's a bit apprehensive about taking a public speaking course.

Joe is currently working for a local animal shelter. He was especially drawn to this particular shelter because of their no-kill policy; lots of shelters will kill the animals they can't find adopted homes for, but this one sticks by its firm no-kill policy.

Here the speaker shifts to the present and gives Joe a very human dimension by identifying his fears and concerns about being in college and taking this course and his concern for animals. The speaker also explains some commonalities between Joe and the rest of the audience (for example, being apprehensive in a public speaking class is something shared by nearly everyone). Some textbook writers would suggest that telling an audience that a speaker has apprehension about speaking is a bad idea. What do you think of its disclosure here?

Transition

But it's not the past or the present that Joe focuses on, it's the future.

This transition tells listeners that the speaker has finished talking about the past and present and is now moving on to the future.

Third main point (the future)

Joe is planning to complete his AB degree here at Hudson Valley Community and then move on to the State University of New Paltz, where he intends to major in communication with a focus on public relations.

His ideal job would be to work for an animal rights organization. He wants to help make people aware of the ways in which they can advance animal rights and stop so much of the cruelty to animals common throughout the world.

From the present, the speaker moves to the future and identifies Joe's educational plans. This is the one thing that everyone has in common and something that most in the class would want to know. The speaker also covers Joe's career plans: again, something the audience is likely to be interested in. In this the speaker also reveals important aspects of Joe's interests and belief system—his concern for animals and his dedication to building his career around this abiding interest. What kinds of information might this speech of introduction give you about the attitudes and beliefs of its listeners?

Transition, internal summary

Joe's traveled an interesting road from a dairy farm in Arizona to the Hudson Valley, and the path to New Paltz and public relations should be just as interesting.

This transition (a kind of internal summary) tells you that the speaker has completed the three-part discussion (past, present, and future) and offers a basic summary of what has been discussed.

Conclusion

Having talked with him for the last few days, I'm sure he'll do well—he has lots of ideas, is determined to succeed, is open to new experiences, and enjoys interacting with people. I'd say that gives this interesting dairy farmer from Arizona a pretty good start as a student in this class, as a student at Hudson Valley Community, and as a soon-to-be public relations specialist.

In this concluding comment the speaker appropriately expresses a positive attitude toward Joe and summarizes some of Joe's positive qualities. These qualities are then tied to the past-present-future organization of the speech. Although the speaker doesn't say "thank you"—which can get trite when 20 speakers in succession say this—it's clear that this is the end of the speech from the last sentence, which brings Joe into his future profession. How effective do you think this conclusion is? What other types of conclusions might the speaker have used?

French and Flemish, and religion in Belgium; family, religion, jobs, and negative comments on bullfighting in Spain; World War II in Japan; politics, religion, corruption, and foreign aid in the Philippines; and race, local politics, and religion in the Caribbean.

Finding Topics

Having difficulty finding a topic is not uncommon; many, if not most, students of public speaking feel the same way. But do not despair. The objective of making classroom speeches is to learn not only the skills of public speaking but also the technique of finding topics—and there are literally thousands of subjects to talk about. Searching for speech topics is actually a relatively easy process. Here are four ways to find topics: topic lists, surveys, news items, and brainstorming.

VIEWPOINT

Your college or communication classroom very likely has its own cultural norms governing what would be seen as an appropriate topic. Consider, for example, whether the following speeches would be considered "appropriate" by members of your public speaking class or by the general college community: (1) a speech seeking to convert listeners to a specific religious cult, (2) a speech supporting neo-Nazi values, (3) a speech supporting racial segregation, or (4) a speech giving listeners tips on how to cheat on their income tax.

Topic Lists. Most public speaking textbooks contain suggestions for topics suitable for public speeches (DeVito, 2000; Osborn & Osborn, 2000; Verderber, 2000), as do books for writers (e.g., Lamm & Lamm, 1999). *The Speech Writer's Workshop Guide CD-ROM, Version 2.0* (2000; see the preface to this book) contains a computerized list of hundreds of topics.

Surveys. Survey data are easier than ever to get now that many of the larger poll results are available on the Internet. For example, the Gallup organization website at http://www.gallup.com includes national and international surveys on political, social, consumer, and other issues speakers often talk about. The Polling Report website (www.pollingreport.com) also will prove useful; it provides a wealth of polling data on issues in political science, business, journalism, health, and social science. Another way is to go to the search directories such as Hotbot or Yahoo! and examine the major directory topics and any subdivisions of those you'd care to pursue—a process that's explained later in this unit. Many search engines and browsers provide lists of "hot topics," which are often useful starting points. These lists pinpoint the subjects people are talking about and therefore often provide excellent speech topics.

Or you can conduct a survey yourself. Roam through the nonfiction section of your bookstore—online, if you prefer (for example, at Amazon, www.amazon.com; Barnes & Noble, www.bn.com; or Borders, www.borders.com)—and you'll quickly develop a list of the topics book buyers consider important. A glance at your newspaper's nonfiction best-seller list will give you an even quicker overview.

News Items. Another useful starting point is a good newspaper or magazine. Here you'll find the important international and domestic issues, the financial issues, and the social issues all conveniently packaged in one place. The editorial page and the letters to the editor also help indicate what people are concerned about. Newsmagazines like *Time* and *Newsweek* and financial magazines such as *Forbes, Money,* and *Fortune* will provide a wealth of suggestions. Just about all major newspapers and newsmagazines now maintain websites that you can access without charge. Generally the newspaper or magazine will follow the pattern www.nameofpaper.com; for example, www.washingtonpost.com. The fastest-growing news sources are the news websites; for example, http://www.cnn.com/, http://www.sfgate.com/, http://www.usatoday.com/, or www.nytimes.com. If you want news on technology, there are lots of available websites. Take a look at Mercury Center (www.mercurycenter.com), CNETNews (www.news.com), Tech Web: The IT Network (www.techweb.com), and ZDNet (www.zdnet.com). Similarly, news shows like *20/20, 60 Minutes, Meet the Press*, and even the ubiquitous talk shows often identify the very issues that people are concerned with and on which there are conflicting points of view.

Brainstorming. Another useful method is brainstorming, a technique discussed in Unit 11. Using brainstorming to generate topics is simple. You begin with your "problem," which in this case is "What will I talk about?" You then record any idea that occurs to you. Allow your mind to free-associate. Don't censor yourself; instead, allow your ideas to flow as freely as possible. Record all your thoughts, regardless of how silly or inappropriate they may seem. Write them down or record them on tape. Try to generate as many ideas as possible. The more ideas you think of, the more chance there is that a suitable topic may emerge from the pile. After you've generated a sizable list—it should take no longer than five minutes—read over the list or replay the tape. Do any of the topics suggest other topics? If so, write these down as well. Can you combine or extend your ideas? Which ideas seem workable?

Limiting Topics

As we've seen, to be suitable for a public speech—or for any type of communication—a topic must be limited in scope; it must be narrowed down to fit the time constraints. Narrowing your topic also will help you focus your collection of research materials. If your topic is too broad, you'll be forced to review a lot more research material than you're going to need. Here are three methods for narrowing and limiting your topic.

Topoi: The System of Topics. In the topoi technique, which comes to us from the classical rhetorics of ancient Greece and Rome, you ask a series of questions about your general subject. The process helps you see divisions or aspects of your general topic on which you might want to focus. For example, by asking the typical reporter's questions (Who? What? Why? When? Where?) and a series of subquestions, you'll see different aspects of a topic. Let's say you want to give a speech on homelessness. Applying the system of topoi, you would ask such questions as:

- Who are the homeless?
- What does homelessness do to the people themselves and to society in general?
- Why are there so many homeless people?
- Where is homelessness most prevalent?
- How does someone become homeless?
- How can we help the homeless and prevent others from becoming homeless?
- Why must we be concerned with homelessness?

Tree Diagrams. The construction of tree diagrams (actually, they resemble upside-down trees) can also help you narrow your topic. Let's say, for example, that you want to do a speech on mass communication. You might develop a tree diagram with branches for the various divisions, as shown in Figure 14.3. Thus, you can divide mass communication into film,

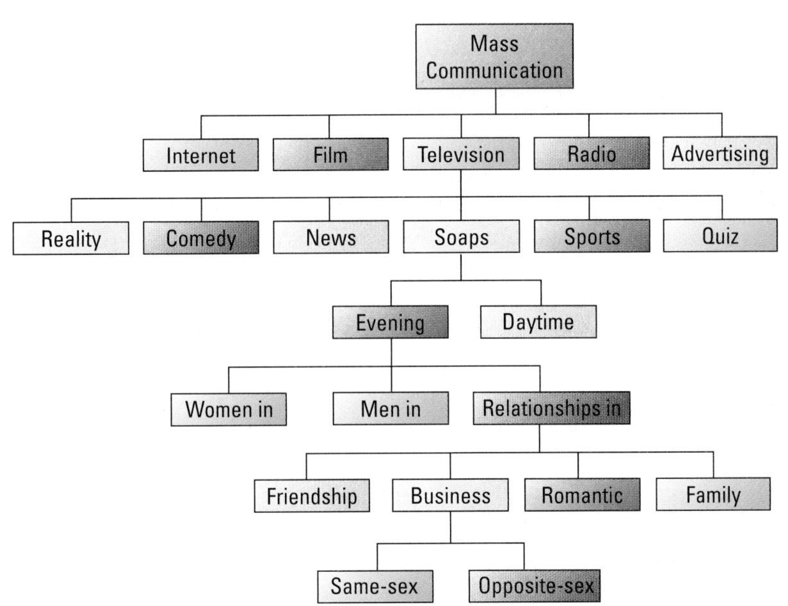

Figure 14.3
A Tree Diagram for Limiting Speech Topics
How would you draw a tree diagram for limiting topics beginning with such general subjects as immigration, education, sports, transportation, or politics?

BUILDING COMMUNICATION SKILLS

Limiting a Topic

Here are some overly general speech topics. Limit each of these topics to a subtopic that would be reasonable for a 5- to 10-minute speech.

1. Dangerous sports
2. Race relationships
3. Parole
4. Censorship on the Internet
5. Ecological problems
6. Problems faced by college students
7. Morality
8. Health and fitness
9. Ethical issues in politics
10. Urban violence

television, radio, newspapers, and magazines. If television interested you most, then you'd develop branches from television; for example, reality, comedy, news, soaps, sports, and quiz shows. Now let's say that it's the soaps that most interest you. In this case you'd create categories of soaps, perhaps prime-time and daytime. Keep dividing the topic until you get something that's significant, appropriate to you and your audience, and capable of being covered in some depth in the allotted time.

Search Directories. A more technologically sophisticated way of both selecting and limiting your topic is to let a search directory, for example, do some of the work for you. A search directory is simply a nested list of topics. You go from the general to the increasingly more specific by selecting a topic, and then a subdivision of that topic, and then a subdivision of that subdivision. Search directories are discussed in more detail under "Step 3" later in this unit.

Your Purpose

The purpose of your speech is the goal you hope to achieve by making your speech. It identifies the effect that you want your speech to have on your audience. In constructing your speech, identify first your general and second your specific purpose.

General Purposes

The two general purposes of public speeches are to inform and to persuade. In the *informative speech* you seek to create understanding: to clarify, enlighten, correct misunderstandings, demonstrate how to do something, describe how something works, or define a concept. In this type of speech you rely most heavily on materials that support—examples, illustrations, definitions, testimony, audiovisual aids, and the like. In the *persuasive speech* you try to influence attitudes or behaviors; you seek to strengthen or change existing attitudes or to prompt the audience to take some action. In this type of speech you rely heavily on materials that offer proof—on evidence, argument, and psychological appeals, for example.

Any persuasive speech is in part an informative speech and as such contains materials that amplify, illustrate, define, and so on. In its focus on strengthening or changing attitudes and behaviors, however, the persuasive speech must go beyond simply providing information. Logical, motivational, and credibility appeals (discussed in Unit 18) are essential.

Another type of speech—part informative and part persuasive—is the *special occasion speech,* a category that includes speeches of presentation and acceptance, toasts, eulogies, apologies, and speeches designed to secure goodwill. A complete unit on "Developing the Special Occasion Speech" is available on CD-ROM.

Specific Purposes

After you have established your general purpose, identify your specific purpose, which states more precisely what you aim to accomplish. For example, in an informative speech, your specific speech purpose will identify the information you want to convey to your audience, such as "to inform my audience about recent progress in AIDS research" or "to inform my audience about the currently used tests for HIV infection."

In a persuasive speech, your specific purpose identifies what you want your speech to lead your audience to believe, think, or perhaps do; for example, "to persuade my audience to get tested for HIV infection" or "to persuade my audience to learn more about how AIDS can be transmitted."

In formulating your specific purpose, be sure to limit it to what you can reasonably develop in the allotted time. For instance, a purpose "to inform my audience about clothing design" is too broad; a more limited and appropriate one would be "to inform my audience of the importance of color in clothing design."

Use an infinitive phrase. Begin the statement of your specific purpose with the word "to," as in "to persuade my audience to contribute a book to the library fund-raiser."

Step 2: Analyze Your Audience

The characteristic that seems best to define an audience is common purpose: A public speaking audience is a group of individuals gathered together to hear a speech. If you're to be a successful speaker, then you must know your audience. This knowledge will help you in selecting your topic; phrasing your purpose; establishing a relationship between yourself and your audience; and choosing examples, illustrations, and logical and emotional appeals.

Your first step in audience analysis is to construct an audience profile in which you analyze audience members' sociological or demographic characteristics. These characteristics help you estimate the attitudes, beliefs, and values of your audience. If you want to effect changes in these attitudes, beliefs, and values, you have to know what they are.

Attitudes, Beliefs, and Values

An **attitude** is a tendency to act for or against a person, object, or position. If you have a positive

COMMUNICATION@WORK

Workplace Analysis

If you're going to play the game properly, you'd better know every rule.

—Barbara Jordan

Much as you would analyze an audience so as to tailor your messages to them, you can analyze a workplace to reduce your uncertainty (Berger & Bradac, 1982). In this way you'll be better able to fit your messages to the organization, the hierarchy, and your coworkers. Here are five kinds of information you might focus on in your workplace analysis:

- *Cultural norms:* All organizations have rules for interacting, beliefs about their mission, and values that they seek to cultivate. Discover what these are.
- *Communication pathways:* Organizations have specific pathways that they expect communication to follow; for example, interns do not send messages directly to the CEO of a large corporation but might address them to other interns or to those who are supervising the internship program.
- *Grapevine:* In most organizations, grapevines flourish; tap into the grapevine to learn about your workplace. The grapevine will often cue you in to what is going on in the organization and will provide the very information that you need to interact effectively with a wide variety of individuals.
- *Power:* All organizations exercise power over those who work for them. Seek to understand who has power and what types of power are used. Ultimately, you'll want to learn how to acquire such power yourself.
- *Reward system:* All organizations exercise control through a system of rewards (for example, promotions, raises, bonuses, choice offices, and the like) and punishments (termination, no bonuses, undesirable offices, and the like). Seek to discover the behaviors that are rewarded and those that are punished as well as who controls the reward system.

Communicating@Work

How would you characterize some or all of the factors listed here in reference to an organization you've recently been a part of?

attitude toward the death penalty, you're likely to argue or act in favor of the death penalty (for example, vote for a candidate who supports the death penalty). If you have a negative attitude toward the death penalty, then you're likely to argue or act against it. Attitudes toward the death penalty will influence how favorably or unfavorably listeners will respond to a speaker who supports or denounces capital punishment.

A **belief** is the confidence or conviction you have in the truth of some proposition. For example, you may believe that there is an afterlife, that education is the best way to rise from poverty, that democracy is the best form of government, or that all people are born equal. If your listeners believe that the death penalty is a deterrent to crime, for example, then they will be more likely to favor arguments for (and speakers who support) the death penalty than will listeners who don't believe in the connection between the death penalty and deterrence.

The term **value** refers to your perception of the worth or goodness (or worthlessness or badness) of some concept or idea. For example, you probably attribute positive values to financial success, education, and contributing to the common welfare. At the same time, you probably place negative values on chemical weapons, corrupt politicians, and selling drugs to children. Because the values an audience holds will influence how it responds to ideas related to those values, it's essential that you learn the values of your specific audience. For example, if the people in your audience place a high positive value on child welfare, then they are likely to vote for legislation that protects children or allocates money for breakfasts and lunches in school—and they might consider signing a petition, volunteering their time, or donating their money to advance the welfare of children. If you find that your audience places a negative value on big business, you may want to reconsider using the testimony of corporate leaders or the statistics compiled by corporations.

Analyzing the Sociology of the Audience

In analyzing an audience be careful not to assume that people covered by the same label are necessarily all alike. As soon as you begin to think about a sociological characteristic in terms of an expressed or implied "all," consider the possibility that you may be stereotyping. Don't assume that all women or all older people or all highly educated people think or believe the same things. They don't.

Nevertheless, there are characteristics that seem to be more common among one group than another, and it is these characteristics that you want to explore in your sociological analysis of your audience. Let's look at four major sociological or demographic variables: (1) cultural factors, (2) age, (3) gender, and (4) religion and religiousness.

Cultural Factors

Cultural factors such as nationality, race, and cultural identity are crucial in audience analysis. Largely because of different training and experiences, the interests, values, and goals of various cultural groups will differ. Further, cultural factors will influence each of the remaining sociological factors; for example, attitudes toward age and gender will differ greatly from one culture to another. Perhaps the primary question to ask is "Are the cultural beliefs and values of the audience relevant to your topic and purpose?" That is, might the cultural background(s) of your audience members influence the way they see your topic? If so, find out what these beliefs and values are and take these into consideration as you build your speech.

Age

Different age groups have different attitudes and beliefs, largely because they have had different experiences in different contexts. Take these differences into consideration in preparing your speeches. For example, let's say that you're an investment counselor and you want to persuade your listeners to invest their money to increase their earnings. Your speech to an audience of retired people (say in their 60s) would be very different from an address to an audience of young executives (say in their 30s). In considering the age of your audience, ask yourself if the age groups differ in goals, interests, and day-to-day concerns that may be related to your topic and purpose. Graduating from college, achieving corporate success, raising a family, and saving for retirement are concerns that differ greatly from one age group to another. Ask too if the groups differ in their ability to absorb and process information. Will they differ in their responses to visual cues? With a young audience, it may be best to keep up a steady, even swift pace. With older persons, you may wish to maintain a more moderate, measured pace.

Gender

Gender is one of the most difficult audience variables to analyze. In recent decades rapid social changes have made it difficult to pin down the effects of gender. As you analyze your audience in terms of gender, ask yourself if men and women differ in the values they consider important insofar as these values are related to your topic and purpose.

For example, traditionally, men have been found to place greater importance on theoretical, economic, and political values. Traditionally, women have been found to place greater importance on aesthetic, social, and religious values. In framing appeals and in selecting examples, take into account the values your audience members consider most important.

Ask too if your topic will be seen as more interesting by one gender or the other. Will men and women have different attitudes toward the topic? Men and women do not, for example, respond in the same way to such topics as abortion, rape, and equal pay for equal work. Select your topics and supporting materials in light of the gender of your audience members. When your audience is mixed, make a special effort to relate "women's" topics to men and "men's" topics to women.

Religion and Religiousness

The religion and religiousness of your audience often will influence their responses to your speech. Religion permeates all topics and all issues. On a most obvious level, we know that such issues as attitudes toward birth control, abortion, and divorce are often connected to religion. Similarly, people's views on premarital sex, marriage, child rearing, money, cohabitation, responsibilities toward parents, and thousands of other issues are frequently influenced by religion. Religion is also important, however, in areas where its connection is not so obvious. For example, religion influences many people's ideas concerning such topics as obedience to authority; responsibility to government; and the usefulness of such qualities as honesty, guilt, and happiness.

Ask yourself if your topic or purpose might be seen as an attack on the religious beliefs of any segment of your audience. If so, then you might want to make adjustments—not necessarily to abandon your purpose, but to rephrase your arguments or incorporate different evidence. When arguing against any religious beliefs, recognize that you're going to meet stiff opposition. Proceed slowly and inductively; in other words, carefully present your evidence before expressing your argument.

Analyzing the Psychology of the Audience

In addition to looking at the sociological characteristics of audience members, it's often useful to consider their psychological characteristics—particularly their willingness to listen to you, their favorableness to your purpose, and their background knowledge.

UNDERSTANDING *THEORY* AND *RESEARCH*

Secular and Sacred Cultures

In analyzing the cultural composition of your audience, consider whether members identify themselves as being a part of a secular or a sacred culture. Secular cultures are those in which religion does not dominate the attitudes and views of the people or greatly influence political or educational decisions (Hofstede, 1997; Dodd, 1995). Liberal Protestant cultures such as those of the Scandinavian countries would be clearly secular. Sacred cultures, on the other hand, are those in which religion and religious beliefs and values dominate everything a person does and influence politics, education, and just about every topic or issue imaginable. Islamic cultures would be traditional examples of sacred cultures. Technically, the United States would be a secular culture (the Constitution, for example, expressly separates church and state); but in some areas of the country, religion exerts a powerful influence on schools (from prayers to condom distribution to sex education) and in politics (from the selection of political leaders to concern for social welfare to gay rights legislation).

Working with Theories and Research

- *How would you describe your communication class in terms of secular and sacred? Can you identify topics, purposes, or theses that would be effective and others that would be ineffective, given the secular/sacred cultures of your class members?*

How Willing Is Your Audience?

Your immediate concern in a public speaking class, of course, is with audience willingness on the part of your fellow students. Do they come to hear your speech because they have to, or do they come because they're interested in what you'll say? If they're a willing group, then you have few problems. And even if they're an unwilling group, all is not lost; you just have to work a little harder in preparing your speech. The unwilling audience demands special and delicate handling. Here are a few suggestions to help change your listeners from unwilling to willing:

- Secure their interest and attention as early in your speech as possible, and reinforce their interest throughout the speech by using little-known facts, quotations, startling statistics, examples, narratives, audiovisual aids, and the like.
- Reward the audience for their attendance and attention. Let the audience know you're aware they're making a sacrifice in coming to hear you speak. Tell them you appreciate it.
- Relate your topic and supporting materials directly to your audience's needs and wants. Show the audience how they can—for example—save time, make money, solve important problems, or become more popular. If you fail to do this, then your audience has good reason for not listening.

How Favorable Is Your Audience?

Audiences vary in the degree to which their ideas and attitudes will be favorable or unfavorable toward you, your topic, or your point of view. You may wish to examine your ability to predict audience favor toward various topics or beliefs by taking the self-test below.

TEST YOURSELF

How Well Do You Know Your Audience?

Here are some statements of beliefs that members of your class may agree or disagree with—and which you might want to use as basic theses (propositions) in your in-class speeches. Try predicting how favorable or unfavorable you think your class members would be to each of these beliefs. Use a 10-point scale ranging from 1 (extremely unfavorable) through 5 (relatively neutral) to 10 (extremely favorable).

____ **1.** The welfare of the family must come first, even before your own.

____ **2.** Sex outside of marriage is wrong and sinful.

____ **3.** In a heterosexual relationship, a wife should submit graciously to the leadership of her husband.

____ **4.** Individual states should be allowed to fly the Confederate flag if they wish.

____ **5.** Intercultural relationships are OK in business but should be discouraged when it comes to intimate or romantic relationships; generally, the races should be kept "pure."

____ **6.** Money is good; the quest for financial success is a perfectly respectable (even noble) one.

____ **7.** Immigration into the United States should be curtailed, at least until current immigrants are assimilated.

____ **8.** Parents who prevent their children from receiving the latest scientific cures because of a belief in faith healing should be prosecuted.

____ **9.** Same-sex marriage should be legalized.

____ **10.** Medicinal marijuana should be readily available.

____ **11.** Physician-assisted suicide should be legalized.

____ **12.** Male and female prostitution should be legalized and taxed like any other job that produces income.

HOW DID YOU DO? After you've indicated your predictions, discuss these with the class as a whole. How accurate were you in guessing your audience's beliefs?

WHAT WILL YOU DO? Practice adapting a thesis to both the favorable and the unfavorable audience. Select a thesis (one of those listed in this self-test or one of your own) toward which your audience would be highly favorable, and indicate how you'd adapt your speech to them. Then try the more difficult task: Select a thesis toward which your audience would be highly unfavorable, and indicate how you'd adapt to them.

If, on analyzing the question, you conclude that your audience will be unfavorable to your chosen topic or viewpoint, the following suggestions should help.

- Clear up any possible misapprehensions that may be generating disagreement. For example, if the audience is hostile to your proposed team approach for a certain project because they wrongly think it will cause a reduction in their autonomy, then tell them very directly that it won't, and perhaps explain why it won't.
- Build on commonalities; stress what you and the audience share as people, as interested citizens, as fellow students. When an audience sees similarity or common ground between itself and you,

it becomes more favorable to both you and your speech.

- Organize your speech inductively. Try to build your speech from areas of agreement, through areas of slight disagreement, up to the major differences between the audience's attitudes and your position. Once areas of agreement are established, it's easier to bring up differences.
- Strive for small gains. Don't try, in a five-minute speech, to convince a pro-life group to contribute money for a new abortion clinic or to persuade a pro-choice group to vote against liberalizing abortion laws. Be content to get the audience to listen fairly and to see some validity in your position.
- Acknowledge the differences explicitly. If it is clear to the audience that they and you are at opposite ends of an issue, it may be helpful to acknowledge this directly. Show the audience that you understand and respect their position but that you'd like them to consider a different way of looking at things.

How Knowledgeable Is Your Audience?

Listeners differ greatly in the knowledge they have. Some listeners will be quite knowledgeable about a given topic; others will be almost totally ignorant. Mixed audiences are the most difficult to address. Treat audiences that lack knowledge of your topic very carefully. Never confuse a lack of audience knowledge with a lack of ability to understand.

- Don't talk down to your audience. No one wants to listen to a speaker putting them down.
- Don't confuse a lack of knowledge with a lack of intelligence. An audience may have no knowledge of your topic but be quite capable of following a clearly presented, logically developed argument. Try especially hard to use concrete examples, audiovisual aids, and simple language. Fill in background details as required. Avoid jargon and other specialized terminology that may not be clear to someone new to the subject. In short, never underestimate your audience's intelligence, but never overestimate their knowledge. Conversely, audiences with much knowledge also require special handling—because their response may well be "Why should I listen to this? I already know about this topic."
- Let the audience know that you're aware of their knowledge and expertise. Try to do this as early in the speech as possible. Emphasize that what you have to say will not be redundant. Tell them that you'll be presenting recent developments or new approaches. In short, let them know that they will not be wasting their time listening to your speech.
- Emphasize your credibility, especially your competence in this general subject area.

Analyzing and Adapting during the Speech

In addition to analyzing your audience and making adaptations in your speech *before* delivering your speech, devote attention to analysis and adaptation *during* the speech. Although this during-the-speech analysis is especially important when you know little of your audience or find yourself facing a very different audience than you expected, it is always crucial to public speaking success. Here are a few suggestions:

Focus on Listeners as Message Senders

As you're speaking, look at your listeners. Remember that just as you're sending messages to your audience, they're also sending messages to you. Pay attention to these messages; and on the basis of what they tell you, make whatever adjustments are necessary.

You can make a wide variety of adjustments to each type of audience response. For example, if your audience shows signs of boredom, increase your volume, move closer to them, or tell them that what you're going to say will be of value to them. If your audience shows signs of disagreement or hostility, stress a similarity you have with them. If your audience looks puzzled or confused, pause a moment and rephrase your ideas, provide necessary definitions, or insert an internal summary. If your audience seems impatient, say, for example, "my last argument . . ." instead of your originally planned "my third argument . . . ."

Ask "What If" Questions

This process of asking "what if" questions is really handled throughout your speech preparation but comes into play most clearly during the speech, and so it's included here. As you prepare your speech it's helpful to ask "what if" questions. These will help you make any necessary on-the-spot adjustments and adaptations. For example, let's say you have been told that you're to explain the opportunities available to the nontraditional student at your college. You've been told that your audience will consist mainly of working women in their 30s and 40s who are just beginning college. As you prepare your speech with this audience in mind, ask yourself "what if" questions. For example:

- What if the audience has a large number of men?
- What if the audience consists of women much older than 40?

- What if the audience members also come with their spouses or their children?

Keeping such questions in mind will force you to consider alternatives as you prepare your speech. Then you'll have ideas readily available if you face a new or different audience.

Address Audience Responses Directly

Another way of dealing with audience responses is to confront them directly. To those who are giving disagreement feedback, for example, you could say something like:

> You may disagree with this position, but all I ask is that you hear me out and see if this new way of doing things will not simplify your accounting procedures.

Or, to those who seem puzzled, you might say:

> I know this plan may seem confusing, but bear with me; it will become clear in a moment.

Or, to those who seem impatient, you might respond:

> I know this has been a long day, but give me just a few more minutes and you'll be able to save hours recording your accounts.

By responding to your listeners' reactions and feedback, you acknowledge your audience's priorities. You let them know that you hear them, that you're with them, and that you're responding to their very real needs.

VIEWPOINT

George and Iris want to give their speeches on opposite sides of Megan's Law—the law requiring that residents of an area be notified if a convicted sex offender is living in close proximity. George is against the law and Iris is for it. If George and Iris were giving their speeches to your class, what would you advise each of them to do concerning the statement of their theses?

Step 3: Research Your Topic

Throughout the process of preparing your public speeches, you'll need to find information to use as source material in your speech. This means doing research. Through research you'll find examples, illustrations, and definitions to help you inform your listeners; testimony, statistics, and arguments to support your major ideas; personal anecdotes, quotations, and stories to help you bring your topics to life.

Research, however, also serves another important function: It helps you persuade your listeners because it makes you appear more believable. For example, if your listeners feel you've examined lots of research, they'll be more apt to see you as competent and knowledgeable and therefore more apt to believe what you say. And of course, presenting the research is itself convincing. When you present research to your listeners, you give them the very reasons they need to draw conclusions or decide on a course of action.

General Research Principles

Here are a few principles to help you research your speeches more effectively and more efficiently.

Examine What You Know. Begin your search by examining what you already know. For example, write down relevant books, articles, or websites that you're familiar with or people who might know something about the topic. Also consider what you know from your own personal experiences and observations. In this way you can attack the problem systematically and not waste effort and time.

Begin with a General Overview. Continue your search by getting an authoritative but general overview of the topic. An encyclopedia article, book chapter, or magazine article in print or online will serve this purpose well. This general overview will help you see the topic as a whole and understand how its various parts fit together.

Consult Increasingly Specific Sources. Follow up the general overview with increasingly more detailed and specialized sources. Fortunately, many of the general articles contain references or links to di-

BUILDING COMMUNICATION SKILLS

Using Cultural Beliefs as Assumptions

Evaluate each of the cultural beliefs listed below in terms of how effective each would be if used as a basic assumption by a speaker addressing your public speaking class. Use the following scale:

A = The audience would accept this assumption and would welcome a speaker with this point of view.
B = Some members would listen receptively and others wouldn't.
C = The audience would reject this assumption and would not welcome a speaker with this point of view.

____ 1. A return to religious values is the best hope for the world.

____ 2. The welfare of our country must come first, even before your own.

____ 3. Sex outside of marriage is wrong and sinful.

____ 4. Winning is all important; it's not how you play the game, it's whether or not you win that matters.

____ 5. Keeping our country militarily superior is the best way to preserve world peace.

rect this next stage of your search for more specific information.

Research Notes

The more accurate your research notes are, the less time you'll waste going back to sources to check on a date or a spelling. Accurate records also will prevent you from going to sources you've already consulted but may have forgotten about. The following suggestions may prove helpful to you as you take notes during the research process.

Create Folders. If you want to collect your material on paper, loose-leaf notebooks or simple manila folders work well to keep everything relating to a speech or article in the same place. If you want to file your material electronically, create a general folder and subfolders as you need them. This will work especially well if you can scan into your folder material you find in print. In this notebook or folder, you can consolidate the sources consulted, quotations, ideas, arguments, suggested references, preliminary outlines, and material you've printed or downloaded.

Key Your Notes. Notes are most effective when they're keyed to specific topics. For example, let's say that your speech is to be on animal experimentation. Your notebook or major folder might be titled *Animal Experimentation.* The notebook divisions or subfolders might then be labeled "Basic Information" (statistics on animal experimentation, people to contact, organizations involved in this issue), "Arguments for Animal Experimentation," and "Arguments against Animal Experimentation." Taking notes with reference to your preliminary outline will help focus your research and will remind you of those topics for which you need more information. It will also help you keep the information logically organized.

Take Complete Notes. Make sure your notes are complete (and legible). If you have to err, then err on the side of too much detail. You can always cut the quotation or select one example out of the three at a later time. As you take notes, be sure to identify the source of the material—so that you can find that reference again should you need it, and so that you can reference it in your speech outline. When you use material from a Web source, be sure to print out or save to folder the web page, noting the URL and the date you accessed this site. This way you'll be able to cite a source even if the Web page disappears, a not unlikely possibility.

Sources of Information

The resources available to you today are rich and varied. A brief survey follows.

Libraries

Libraries are the major depositories of stored information and have evolved from a traditional emphasis on print sources to today's sophisticated use of computerized databases. Increasingly you'll want to go to a virtual or online library to access other virtual libraries or databases maintained by local and national governments, cultural institutions, and various corporations and organizations. Of course, you'll also go to a brick-and-mortar library because you will want materials that are not on the Net or may wish to access items in print. Because each library functions somewhat differently, your best bet in learning about a specific library (such as your own college library) is to talk with your librarian about what the library has available, what kinds of training or tours it offers, and how its materials are most easily accessed.

Here are a few online libraries that you'll find especially helpful.

- To locate a list of library catalogs to help you find the location of the material you need, try www.lights.com/webcats. Click on "library-type index" to get a list of categories of libraries; for example, "government" or "medical" or "religious."
- The largest library in the United States is the Library of Congress, which houses millions of books, maps, multimedia, and manuscripts. Time spent at this library (begin with www.loc.gov) will be well invested. The home page will guide you to a wealth of information.
- Maintained by the National Archives and Records Administration, the presidential libraries may be accessed at www.nara.gov/nara/present/address.html.
- The Virtual Library is a collection of links to 14 subject areas; for example, the realms of agriculture, business and economics, computing, communication and media, and education. Visit this at www.vlib.org.
- If you're not satisfied with your own college library, visit the libraries of some of the large universities such as the University of Pennsylvania (www.library.upenn.edu/resources/reference/reference.html) or the University of Illinois (http://gateway.library.uiuc.edu).
- The Internet Public Library (www.ipl.org) is actually not a library; it's a collection of links to a wide variety of materials. But it will function much like the reference desk at any of the world's best libraries.
- Quick Study, the University of Minnesota's Library Research Guide (http://tutorial.lib.umn.edu), will help you learn how to find the materials you need and will answer lots of questions you probably have about research.

General Reference Works

Begin researching your topic with general reference works, one of the best of which is the standard encyclopedia. A good encyclopedia will give you a general overview of the subject and suggestions for additional reading. The most comprehensive and the most prestigious is the *Encyclopaedia Britannica,* which is available in print (32 volumes), on CD-ROM, and online. A variety of other encyclopedias are also available on CD-ROM or online; for example, *Compton's Multimedia Encyclopedia, Grolier's, Collier's,* and *Encarta*. CD-ROM and online encyclopedias have great advantages; for example, they allow you to locate articles, maps, diagrams, and even definitions of difficult terms more easily and efficiently than hard-copy volumes. Video illustrations and audio capabilities enable you to see the volcano exploding and the heart pumping blood and to hear the pronunciation of foreign terms and the music of particular instruments. Hypertext capabilities enable you to get additional information on any term or phrase that is highlighted in the video display. Simply select the highlighted phrase and you'll get this other article on screen. Most of the CD-ROM encyclopedias have accompanying websites that provide periodic updates of the articles and additional materials, thus ensuring both recency and completeness.

A useful place to start is with www.internetoracle.com/encyclop.htm, which provides hotlinks to a wide variety of online encyclopedias, both general and specific. Another especially useful source is Freeality.com (www.freeality.com), a guide to all sorts of reference and research materials.

Should you want information on the world's languages, household income levels, presidential elections, the countries of the world, national defense, sports, noted personalities, economics and employment, the environment, awards and prizes, science and technology, health and medicine, maps, world travel information, or postal rates, an almanac will prove extremely useful. Numerous inexpensive versions published annually are among the most up-to-date sources of information on many topics. The most popular are *The World Almanac and Book of Facts* (also available on CD-ROM), *The Universal Almanac,* and *The Canadian Almanac and Directory*. The *Information Please Almanac*'s website provides access to a wide variety of almanacs (www.infoplease.com/almanacs.html). Another useful source is the Internet Public Library's list of almanac resources at www.ipl.org/ref/RR/static/ref05.00.00.html.

Specialized Reference Works

There are also many specialized encyclopedias. Those devoted to religion include the *New Catholic Encyclopedia* (15 volumes), which contains articles on such topics as philosophy, science, and art as these have been influenced by and have influenced the Catholic Church; *Encyclopaedia Judaica* (16 volumes plus yearbooks), which emphasizes Jewish life and includes biographies and detailed coverage of Jewish contributions to world culture; and *Encyclopedia of Islam* and *Encyclopaedia of Buddhism,* which cover the development, beliefs, institutions, and personalities of Islam and Buddhism, respectively. Supplement these with appropriate websites devoted to specific religions; for example, http://www.utm.edu/martinarea/fbc/bfm.html (Southern Baptist Convention), http://www.catholic.org/index.html (Catholicism), http://www.geocities.com/RodeaDrive/1415/indexd.html (Hinduism), http://www.utexas.edu/students/amso (Islam), and http://jewishnet.net (Judaism).

For the physical, applied, and natural sciences there's the 20-volume *McGraw-Hill Encyclopedia of Science and Technology*. This is complemented by annual supplements. *Our Living World of Nature* is a 14-volume popular encyclopedia, dealing with natural history from an ecological point of view (the online version is by subscription). *The International Encyclopedia of the Social Sciences* concentrates on the theory and methods of the social sciences in 17 well-researched volumes. Other widely used specialized encyclopedias include the *Encyclopedia of Bioethics* (4 volumes), the *Encyclopedia of Religion* (16 volumes), and the *Encyclopedia of Philosophy* (4 volumes). Also check *The Internet Encyclopedia of Philosophy* at www.utm.edu/research/iep.

E-mail and Listservs

E-mail may prove useful in public speaking in several ways. For example, you can write to specific people who may be experts in the topic you're researching. Internet services now make it quite easy to locate a person's e-mail address. Try, for example, Yahoo's directory (http://www.yahoo.com/search/people/) and its links to numerous other directories and the White Pages (http://www.whitepages.com/). Also try the sites that specialize in e-mail addresses, such as WhoWhere? (http://www.whowhere.com) and Switchboard (www.switchboard.com).

Of course, e-mail (and instant messaging) also is useful for communicating with your instructor, with other students, or with those who share your topic interests to secure needed information and helpful feedback.

You also can join a mailing list or listserv that focuses on the topic you're researching and learn from the collective insights of other members. In joining a listserv remember to lurk before contributing; get a feel for the group and for the types of messages they send. Read the FAQs to avoid asking questions that have already been answered.

Some classes have their own listservs, chat rooms, or message boards so that you can communicate with everyone else through e-mail. With such a setup you'd be able, for example, to distribute an audience analysis questionnaire to see what your audience knows about your topic or what their attitudes are about a variety of issues. You'd also be able to set up a critique group with a few others from your class to give one another feedback and moral support on speeches or outlines. Such a group would be helpful for people who want to ask questions or try out an idea before presenting it in the actual speech.

Newsgroups and Chat Groups

Newsgroups are discussion forums for the exchange of ideas on a wide variety of topics. There are thousands of newsgroups on the Internet; you can post your messages, read the messages of others, and respond to the messages you read. Newsgroups are much like listservs, in that they bring together a group of people interested in communicating about a common topic. Some newsgroups also include messages from news services such as the Associated Press or Reuters.

Newsgroups are useful to the public speaker for a variety of reasons. The most obvious reason is that newsgroups are sources of information; they contain news items, letters, and papers on just about any topic you can think of. Also, you can save to your own file the news items you're particularly interested in. An especially useful search engine for discussion groups is Google (http://groups.google.com/); although you can use any search engine to search for groups in which you might be interested. Google will search the available newsgroups for the topics you request. You simply submit key words that best describe your research topic, and the program will search its database of newsgroups and provide you with a list of article titles and authors along with the date on which they were written and the relevance score for each article. You then click on the titles that seem most closely related to what you're looking for.

Newsgroups offer lots of additional advantages. For example, on newsgroups that get news feeds the information is extremely current and often more detailed than you'd find in newspapers, which have to cut copy to fit space limitations. You're also more likely to find a greater diversity of viewpoints than you'd find in, say, most newspapers or newsmagazines. Another advantage is that through newsgroups you can ask questions and get the opinions of others for your next speech. Newsgroups also provide an easily available and generally receptive audience to whom you can communicate your thoughts and feelings.

Chat groups such as you'll find on the commercial internet service providers (ISPs) enable you to communicate with others in real time. (This is called *synchronous conversation*—as opposed to *asynchronous conversation,* in which there's a delay between message sending and message receiving.) Real-time communication obviously has its advantages; you can ask questions, respond to feedback, and otherwise adjust your message to the specific receivers. One great disadvantage, however, is that you may not find anyone you want to talk with when you log on. Unlike e-mail, chat groups don't enable you to leave a message. Chat groups, like listservs and newsgroups, are subject specific; and because there are so many of them (they number in the thousands) you're likely to find some dealing with the topics you're researching.

Searching the Web

In most cases searching the Web efficiently requires the use of search engines and subject directories, plus some knowledge of how these tools operate. A *search engine* is a program that searches a database or index of Internet sites for the specific words you submit. These search engines are easily accessed through your Internet browser, and both Netscape and Internet Explorer have search functions as a part of their own home pages; they also provide convenient links to the most popular online search engines and directories.

A *directory* is a list of subjects or categories of web links. Especially useful directories are www.looksmart.com, www.pointcom.com, www.beaucoup.com, and www.lycos.com. In these directories you select the category you're most interested in, then a subcategory of that, then a subcategory of that until you reach your specific topic. A directory doesn't cover everything; rather, the documents that it groups under its various categories are selected by the directory's staff members from those they deem to be especially worthwhile. Many search engines also provide directories, so you can use the method you prefer.

Some search engines are metasearch engines; these search the databases of a variety of search engines at the same time. These programs are especially useful if you want a broad search and you have the time to sift through lots of websites. Some of the more popular include Ask Jeeves at www.ask.com, Google at www.google.com, Dog Pile at www.dogpile.com, and Vivisimo at www.vivisimo.com. Other useful search engines (some of which also contain directories) include Yahoo! (www.yahoo.com), AltaVista (http://altavista.com), and Go (http://www.go.com).

In using search engines (and in searching many CD-ROM databases), it's often helpful to limit your search with "operators"—words and symbols that define relationships among the terms for which you're searching. Perhaps the most common are the capitalized words AND, OR, and NOT. Searching for *drugs AND violence* will limit your search to only those documents that contain both words—in any order. Searching for *drugs OR violence* will expand your search to all documents containing either word. And searching for *violence AND schools NOT elementary* will yield documents containing both *violence* and *schools* except those that contain the word *elementary*. Each search engine uses a somewhat different system for limiting searches, so you'll have to learn the specific system used by your favorite search engines.

News Sources

Often you'll want to read reports on accidents, political speeches, congressional actions, obituaries, financial news, international developments, United Nations actions, or any of a host of other topics. Or you may wish to locate the time of a particular event and learn something about what else was going on in the world at that particular time. For this type of information, you may want to consult a reliable newspaper. Especially relevant are newspaper indexes, newspaper databases, newspaper and magazine websites, news wire services, and news networks online.

Newspaper Indexes. One way to start a newspaper search is to consult one of the newspaper indexes. For example, the *National Newspaper Index* covers 27 newspapers, including the *Christian Science Monitor,* the *Wall Street Journal,* the *Los Angeles Times,* and the *Washington Post.* Each of these newspapers also has its own index. The *New York Times* is available through Research Navigator.

Electronic Newspaper Databases. Many newspapers can be accessed online or through CD-ROM databases to which your college library probably subscribes. The *New York Times* database, for example, contains complete editorial content of the paper, one of the world's most comprehensive newspapers. All aspects of news, sports, editorials, columns, obituaries, New York and regional news, and the *New York Times Book Review* and *Magazine* are included.

Newspaper and Newsmagazine Websites. Most newspapers now maintain their own websites, from which you can access current and past issues. Here are a few to get you started: www.latimes.com/ (*Los Angeles Times*), www.usatoday.com/ (*USA Today*), www.wsj.com/ (*Wall Street Journal*), and www.nytimes.com (*New York Times*). The *Washington Post* (www.washingtonpost.com) maintains an especially extensive website. Two particularly useful websites are http://www.newslink.org/menu.html, which provides access to a variety of online newspapers and magazines, and Hotlinks to Newspapers Online, which provides links to more than 1,000 daily, more than 400 weekly, and more than 100 international newspapers (http://www.newspaperlinks.com).

News Wire Services. Three wire services should prove helpful. The Associated Press can be accessed at http://www1.trib.com/NEWS/Apwire.html, Reuters at http://www.reuters.com/, and PR Newswire at http://www.prnewswire.com/. The advantage of getting your information from a news wire service is that it's more complete than you'd find in a newspaper; also, in some cases newspapers may put a politically or socially motivated spin on the news.

News Networks Online. All of the television news stations maintain extremely useful websites. Here are some of the most useful: Access CNN at http://www.cnn.com/, ESPN at http://espn.sportszone.com/, ABC News at http://www.abcnews.com/newsflash, CBS News at http://www.cbs.com/news/, and MSNBC News at http://www.msnbc.com/news.

Biographical Material

As a speaker you'll often need information about particular individuals. For example, you may want to look up authors of books or articles to find out something about their education and training or their other writings. Or you may wish to discover if there have been any critical evaluations of their work in, say, book reviews or articles about them or their writings. Knowing something about your sources enables you to more effectively evaluate their competence, present their credibility to the audience, and answer audience questions about your sources.

First, consult the *Biography and Genealogy Master Index* in print, on CD-ROM, or online; it indexes several hundred biographical indexes. This index will send you to numerous specialized works—among them *The Dictionary of American Biography* (DAB), which contains articles on famous deceased Americans from all areas of accomplishment; *Current Biography,* which is the best single source for living individuals and includes both favorable and unfavorable comments on the individual; and *Who's Who in America,* which also covers living individuals.

In addition, there are a host of other more specialized works whose titles indicate their scope: *The Dictionary of Canadian Biography, The Dictionary of National Biography* (British), *Directory of American Scholars, International Who's Who, Who Was Who in America, Who's Who* (primarily British), *American Men and Women of Science, Great Lives from History, Notable American Women, Who's Who in the Arab World, Who's Who in Finance and Industry, Who's Who in American Politics, Who's Who Among Black Americans, Who's Who of American Women, Who's Who Among Hispanic Americans,* and the *Biographical Directory of the American Congress.*

Not surprisingly there are lots of Internet sources for biographical information. For example, http://www.nobel.se/search/all_laureates_c.html provides links to biographical information on all Nobel Prize winners. If you want information on members of the House of Representatives, try http://www.house.gov. And http://www.biography.com/ will provide you with brief biographies of some 25,000 famous people, living and dead. Other excellent sources include Lives, the Biography Resource at http://amillionlives.com and the Biographical Dictionary at http://s9.com/biography, which covers more than 28,000 men and women.

Academic Research Articles

Academic research forms the core of what we know about people and the world; it is the most valid and the most reliable source of information you're likely to find. Research articles are reports of studies conducted by academicians around the world. For the most part these articles are conducted by unbiased researchers using the best research methods available. Further, before publication this research is subjected to careful critical review by experts in the specific field of the research.

Each college library subscribes to a somewhat different package of CD-ROM and online databases. These databases contain information on the nature and scope of the database and user-friendly directions for searching, displaying, printing, and saving the retrieved information to disk. In addition you may have access to Research Navigator, which Unit 1 introduced and which you may have been using throughout the course. Research Navigator makes searching for these articles extremely easy.

MEDIA WATCH

The Diffusion of Innovations

Mass media audiences are even more diverse and varied than public speaking audiences. One of the most interesting theories related to this diversity is the theory of the *diffusion of innovations.* This theory focuses on the way in which mass communications influence people to adopt something new or different. The term *diffusion* refers to the passage of new information, innovations, or processes through society. The innovation may be of any type—soft contact lenses, laptop computers, PDAs, PowerPoint public speaking software. *Adoption* refers to people's positive reactions to and use of the innovation. Obviously, not all people adopt or reject any given innovation at the same time. Research in the area of information diffusion distinguishes five types of adopters (see Figure 14.4):

- The *innovators* (approximately 3 percent of the population) are the first to adopt the innovation. They are not necessarily the originators of the new idea, but they're the ones who introduce it on a reasonably broad scale.
- The *early adopters* (approximately 14 percent), sometimes called "the influentials," legitimize the idea and make it acceptable to people in general.
- The *early majority* (approximately 34 percent) follows the influentials and further legitimizes the innovation.
- The *late majority* (approximately 34 percent) adopts the innovation after about half the population has adopted it.
- The *laggards* (approximately 14 percent) are the last group to adopt the innovation and may take the lead from any of the preceding groups.

One last group, the *diehards,* never adopts the innovation. These include, for example, accountants who continue to do tax returns without the aid of computer software; teachers who never use multimedia in their classes; and lawyers and doctors who do their research solely through books, never availing themselves of computerized databases.

Not surprisingly, the innovators and usually the early adopters are usually younger than the late majority and the laggards and are of a higher socioeconomic status. They are more oriented toward change and make more use of available information.

You and the Media

Where would you position yourself on this diffusion of innovation curve when it comes to technology? Are you generally pleased with this positioning? If not, what might you do about it?

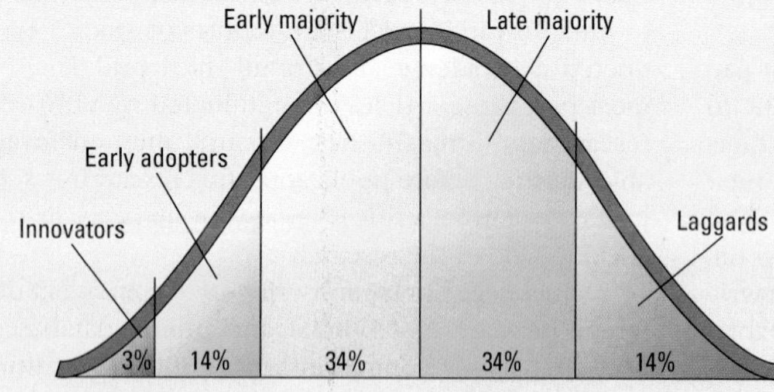

Figure 14.4

The Five Types of Adopters

Source: Reprinted with permission of The Free Press, a Division of Simon & Schuster, Inc., from *The Diffusion of Inventions,* Fourth Edition, by Everett M. Rogers. Copyright © 1995 by Everett M. Rogers, Copyright © 1962, 1971, 1983 by The Free Press.

General Research and Opinion Posts

In preparing a special occasion speech—or any speech—you'll find magazines a useful source. Articles in magazines differ greatly from those in professional journals. For example, they're most often written by professional writers rather than by researchers.

Magazine articles may be summaries of research by others or may be largely in the nature of opinion. Often they're simplified accounts of rather complex issues written for the general public rather than an audience of professional researchers. Further, they seldom undergo the rigorous review process that accompanies publication in a professional academic journal. As a result, articles appearing in popular magazines are much less reliable than those appearing in such professional research journals as, say, *Communication Monographs, Journal of Experimental Psychology,* or *The New England Journal of Medicine*. Nevertheless, magazine articles and general posts are often very helpful for speakers. Here are a few suggestions for finding the information you want.

Indexes. The *Readers' Guide to Periodical Literature,* available in print and electronic formats, covers magazine articles for the period from 1900 to the present. This guide indexes by subject and by author (in one convenient alphabetical index) articles published in about 180 different magazines. The *Readers' Guide* is valuable for its broad coverage, but it's limited in that it covers mostly general publications and only a few of the more specialized ones. The *Alternative Press Index* (also available on CD-ROM, to which your library may subscribe) indexes approximately 250 "alternative, radical, and left publications." This index is valuable for speakers dealing with such issues as the Third World, minority rights, socialism, and the like. The National Institutes of Health maintain the National Library of Medicine at www.nlm.nih.gov/, an essential site for any topic dealing with health and medicine. A similar general index for legal issues is available from FindLaw at www.findlaw.com, and an index for financial issues from Goinvest at www.financialfind.com.

Listservs, Usenet Groups, and the World Wide Web. Listservs, newsgroups, and the World Wide Web contain a wide variety of articles, many more than you could possibly use in any one or even many speeches. Explore relevant listservs through Topica (www.topica.com), newsgroups through Google (http://groups.google.com/), and the vast array of World Wide Web documents with the help of your favorite search engines.

Book Sources

Books will provide you with especially detailed information.

Each library catalogs its books, journals, and government documents in a slightly different way, depending on its size and the needs of its users. All, however, make use of some form of computerized catalog. These are uniformly easy and efficient to use. The catalog is the best place to find out what books are in your college library or in other libraries whose books you can secure on interlibrary loan.

Generally, you access material by looking up your major subject heading(s). A good way to do this is to make a list of the five or six major concepts that appear in your speech and look each of these up in the library catalog. Create a reasonably complete bibliography of available sources and examine each one. Sometimes you may want to locate works by or about a particular person; in this case you'd look up the author's name much as you would a concept.

Browsing through any large brick-and-mortar bookstore, too, is almost sure to give you insights into your topic. If you're talking about something that people are interested in today, there's likely to be a book dealing with it available in bookstores. And visit online bookstores as well; for example, Amazon (www.amazon.com), Barnes and Noble (www.bn.com), or Borders (www.borders.com). Other useful sites include http://aaupnt.org (Association of American University Presses) and http://www.cs.cmu.edu/Web/People/spok/banned-books.html (contains links to texts of books that have been banned in the United States and elsewhere). Some online bookstores now enable you to search some of the books for specific topics and read a paragraph or so on each topic reference.

U.S. Government Publications

The U.S. Government Printing Office (GPO) is the largest publisher in the world. Its publications originate in the various divisions of the federal government's 13 departments, each of which is a prolific publisher. The Departments of Agriculture, Commerce, Defense, Education, Energy, Health and Human Services, Housing and Urban Development, Interior, Justice, Labor, State, Treasury, and Transportation each issue reports, pamphlets, books, and assorted documents dealing with their various concerns. Because of the wealth of published material, it would be best first to consult one of the guides to government publications. A few of the more useful ones that should be in your college library include *Government Reference Books* (1968 to date), *A Bibliography of United States Government Bibliographies*, and *U. S. Government Books: Recent Releases* (published quarterly). The *Congressional Record* (1873 to date) is issued daily when Congress is in session.

Museum Collections and Exhibits

Not too long ago, museums weren't even included in research discussions; good museums were so far away from most people that any one person's chances of visiting any given museum were remote. Now, however, you have the world of museums literally at your fingertips. Every museum amasses information pertaining to the institution's major focus; for example, to natural history, science, or art. Visits to a few museum websites will be time well spent. Here are a few especially good ones: Franklin Institute Science Museum at http://sln.fi.edu/, the Metropolitan Museum of Art at www.metmuseum.org/home.asp, London's Museum of Natural History at http://www.mhm.ac.uk, and the Smithsonian Institution at http://www.si.edu/. An especially good site if you don't know what museum you'd like to visit is http://www.comlab.ox.ac.uk/archive/other/museums/usa.html, which contains links to museums, archives, and galleries throughout the United States.

Evaluating Research

In evaluating research (1) distinguish between primary and secondary sources, (2) investigate reliability, and (3) check to make sure that your research is current, fair, and sufficient.

Primary and Secondary Sources

Both as researcher and as a listener, distinguish between primary and secondary source material. Primary sources include, for example, an original research study as reported in an academic journal, a corporation's annual report, or an eyewitness report of an accident. In primary sources there is nothing (or very little) standing between the event (say, an accident) and the reporting of it (the eyewitness testimony). Secondary sources include, for example, a summary of research in a popular magazine, a television news report on a corporation's earnings, or a report by someone who talked to someone who witnessed an accident. With secondary sources someone stands between the actual event and the report, as when a science reporter reads the scientist's monograph (primary source) and then writes up a summary for the popular press (secondary source).

As a speaker and as a listener, you'll use and hear both types of source material. Yet there are important differences that you should keep in mind. Secondary source material is less reliable than primary source material, because it is a step removed from the actual facts or events. The writer of the material may have forgotten important parts, may be biased and so may have slanted the reporting, or may have distorted the material because he or she misunderstood the data. On the other hand, the writer may have been able to express complicated data in simple language—often making it easier for a nonspecialist to understand than the original report. When using or listening to secondary sources, examine the information for any particular spin the writer may be giving the material. If possible, check with the primary source material to see what might have been left out, or if the conclusions drawn are really warranted on the basis of the primary evidence.

Reliability

Reliable research findings or conclusions are those you can count on, those that are trustworthy and dependable. In estimating how reliable a source's conclusions are, ask yourself if the conclusions have been arrived at logically rather than, say, emotionally. Does the author offer clear evidence and sound arguments rather than, say, anecdotes or testimonials to support conclusions?

Another way to estimate reliability is to look at the publisher of the material. Major textbook and trade book publishers go to enormous effort to ensure the accuracy of what appears in print or on their websites, so the information they offer is generally reliable. But some publishers are arms of special interest groups with specific corporate, religious, political, or social agendas. If this is the case with one of the sources you have selected, try to balance this source's perspective with information that represents the other sides of the issue.

On the other hand, if an article appears in a scholarly journal such as the publications sponsored by the American Psychological Association or the National Communication Association, for example, you can be pretty sure that experts in the field have carefully reviewed the article before publication. If an article appears in a well-respected major publication like the *New York Times,* the *Washington Post,* the *Wall Street Journal,* or in any of the major newsmagazines or network news programs (or online on their websites), again, you can be pretty sure that the information is reliable.

Do realize that these claims of accuracy are generalizations. On occasion both academic journals and newspapers have printed erroneous or fraudulent articles; for example, in September 2003 the *New York Times*—one of the world's greatest newspapers—experienced a significant credibility gap for printing as fact articles that turned out to be no more than fiction. So inaccuracies do creep into even the most respected sources.

Currency, Fairness, and Sufficiency

Finally, when you hear research reported by a speaker or when you collect research yourself, listen to it critically for currency, fairness, and sufficiency.

Currency. Generally, the more recent the material, the more useful it will be. With some topics, such as unemployment statistics, developments in AIDS research, or tuition costs, the currency of the information is crucial to its usefulness. To ensure currency, check important figures in a recent almanac (for example, the *Information Please Almanac*, available online in full text at www.infoplease.com); in a newspaper (most major newspapers have free online access, generally following the format www.nameofpaper.com; or at a frequently updated Internet source such as Federal Statistics at www.fedstats.gov.

Fairness. Does the author present the information objectively, or is there a bias favoring one position? Reviewing the research in the area will help you see how other experts view the issue. It also will enable you to see if this author's view of the situation takes into consideration all sides of the issue and represents these sides fairly and accurately.

Sufficiency. Is the collected information sufficient to prove the case? The opinion of one dietitian is insufficient to support the usefulness of a particular diet; the statistics on tuition increases from five private colleges are insufficient to illustrate national trends in rising tuition costs.

Integrating Research into Your Speech

By integrating and acknowledging your sources of information in the speech, you'll give fair credit to those whose ideas and statements you're using, and at the same time you'll help establish your own reputation as a responsible researcher. You will also lessen the risk that anything you say can be interpreted as plagiarism (a subject we'll consider shortly). Here are a few suggestions for integrating your research into your speech.

Mention the sources in your speech by citing (at least) the author and, if helpful, the publication and the date. Check out some of the speeches presented in the Public Speaking Sample Assistant boxes in this book and note especially how the speakers integrate their sources in their speeches. In your written outline, give the complete bibliographical reference.

Here's an example of how to cite a source and establish its credibility at the same time:

> Don't expect an extremely effective drug to treat most cases of hepatitis C within the next two years. Dr. Howard J. Worman of New York Presbyterian Hospital, one of the leading scientists in the field of liver disease, the author of more than 70 medical and scientific papers and of *The Liver Disorders Sourcebook*, and the creator of the Diseases of the Liver website, expressed this opinion in his article "Hepatitis C: An epidemic ignored," published on the healthology.com website, which I accessed this week.

Here's another example:

> My discussion of the symptoms of arrhythmia is based on the insights of Dr. Anthony R. Magnano (2001), a clinical fellow in cardiology at Columbia University College of Physicians and Surgeons. Magnano is an active researcher on arrhythmia and has written widely on the topic. In an article on arrhythmias on the healthology.com website, which I accessed on January 21, Magnano identifies three symptoms he sees most often in his patients: heart palpitations, lightheadedness, and fainting spells.

In the reference list accompanying the written outline, this speaker would identify the author, the date and title of the article, the URL address, and the speaker's date of accessing the site. The reference would look like this:

> Magnano, A. R. (2001). Arrhythmias: An introduction. Retrieved January 21, 2005, from http://earthlink2.healthology.com/focus_article.asp?f=xmlpressfeed&c=arrhythmias/

Although it's possible to overdo the oral citation—giving more information than the listeners really need—there are even greater dangers in leaving out potentially useful source information. Because your speeches in this course are learning experiences, it will be better to err on the side of being more rather than less complete.

Avoid useless expressions such as, "I have a quote here," or "I want to quote an example." Let the audience know that you're quoting by pausing before the quote, taking a step forward, or referring to your notes to read the extended quotation. If you want to state more directly that this is a quotation, you might do it this way:

> Recently, Mary Kay Ash put this in perspective, saying, "A woman can no more duplicate the male style of leadership than an American businessman can exactly reproduce the Japanese style."

Citing Research Sources

In citing references, first find out what style manual is used in your class or at your school. Generally, it will be one of the style manuals developed by the American Psychological Association (APA), the

Modern Language Association (MLA), or the University of Chicago (in their *Chicago Manual of Style*). Different schools and different departments within a given college often rely on different formats for citing research; these diverse policies, quite frankly, make a tedious process even worse.

Fortunately, there are a variety of websites that provide guides to the information you'll need to cite any reference in your speech. For example, Purdue University offers an excellent site that covers APA and MLA style formats and provides examples for citing books, articles, newspaper articles, websites, e-mail, online posting, electronic databases, and more (http://owl.english.purdue.edu/handouts/research). This site also provides extremely useful advice for searching the Web and evaluating website information. Another excellent website is Capital Community College's Guide for Writing Research Papers (http://webster.commnet.edu). Like the Purdue website, this one also provides useful guides to research and to writing research papers. Guidelines for using the *Chicago Manual of Style* may be found at Ohio State's website http://www.lib.ohio-state.edu/. This site provides guidance for citing all types of print and electronic sources. Another valuable source is the Columbia Guide to Online Style (http://www.columbia.edu/cu/cup/cgos/idx_basic.html). This site provides detailed instructions and examples for citing MOOs, MUDs, and IRCs, e-mail, listservs, newsgroup communications, and even software programs and video games. Another useful guide is the International Federation of Library Associations and Institutions website (http://www.ifla.org/I/training/citation/citing.html), which provides guidelines for citing electronic sources and links to a variety of useful websites concerned with citing research. After reviewing these websites, print out the one or two that you find most useful so you can have them in easy reach.

Plagiarism

The word **plagiarism** refers to the process of passing off the work (ideas, words, illustrations) of others as our own. It is *not* the act of using another's ideas—we all do that. Plagiarism is using another's ideas without acknowledging that they are the ideas of this other person; it is passing off the ideas as if they were ours.

Plagiarism exists on a continuum, ranging from appropriating an entire term paper or speech written by someone else to using a quotation or research finding without citing the author.

Plagiarism also includes situations in which, for example, a student gets help from a friend without acknowledging this assistance. In some cultures—especially in collectivist cultures (cultures that emphasize the group and mutual cooperation) such as those of Korea, Japan, and China—teamwork is strongly encouraged. Students are taught to help other students with their work. But in the United States and in many other individualist cultures (cultures that emphasize individuality and competitiveness), teamwork without acknowledgment is considered plagiarism.

In U.S. institutions of higher education, plagiarism is a serious violation of the rules of academic honesty and carries serious penalties, sometimes even expulsion. And it's interesting to note that instructors are mobilizing and educating themselves in the techniques for detecting plagiarism (Finn & Bates, 2003). Further, as with all crimes, ignorance of the law is not an acceptable defense against charges of plagiarism. This last point is especially important because a good deal of plagiarism is committed through a lack of information as to what does and what does not constitute plagiarism. Here are just a few reasons why plagiarism is wrong.

Why Plagiarism Is Unacceptable

Plagiarism is unacceptable for a variety of reasons:

- Plagiarism is a violation of another's intellectual property rights. Much as it would be wrong to take another person's watch without permission, it's wrong to take another person's ideas without acknowledging that you did it.
- You're in college to develop your own ideas and ways of expressing them; plagiarism defeats this fundamental purpose.
- Evaluations (everything from grades in school to promotions in the workplace) assume that what you present as your work is in fact your work.

Avoiding Plagiarism

Let's start with the easy part. You do not have to—and should not—cite sources for common knowledge: information that is readily available in numerous sources and is not likely to be disputed. For example, the population of Thailand, the amendments to the U.S. Constitution, the actions of the United Nations, or the way the heart pumps blood are all common knowledge, and you would not cite an almanac or political science text from which you got this information. On the other hand, if you were talking about the attitudes of people from Thailand or the reasons constitutional amendments were adopted, then you'd need to cite your sources, because this information is not common knowledge and may well be disputed.

For information that is not common knowledge, you need to acknowledge your source. Here are a few simple rules that will help you avoid even the suggestion of plagiarism:

1. *Acknowledge the source of any ideas you present that are not your own.* If you learned of an idea in your history course, then cite the history instructor or history textbook. If you read an idea in an article, then cite the article.
2. *Acknowledge the words of another.* It's obvious what to do when you're quoting another person exactly; you need to cite the person you're quoting. You should also cite others even when you paraphrase their words, because you are still using others' ideas; but when paraphrases need to be credited may not always be so clear. To help with this question, some of the plagiarism websites established by different universities include exercises and extended examples; see, for example, Indiana University's site at www.indiana.edu/~uts/wts/plagiarism.html or Purdue University's at http://owl.english.purdue.edu/handouts/print/reseach/r-plagiar.html. The same is true when you use the organizational structure of another person; just say, for example, "I'm following the line of reasoning proposed by Andrew Rancer in his comparison of aggression and argument."
3. *Acknowledge help from others.* If your roommate gave you examples or ideas or helped you style your speech, acknowledge the help.

REFLECTIONS ON ETHICS

Plagiarizing

This unit has looked at plagiarism, explaining what it is, why it's unacceptable, and how to avoid it. Consider, here, the following situations.

WHAT WOULD YOU DO? You're really pressed to come up with a persuasive speech on a contemporary social issue and just don't have the time to research it. Fortunately, you can easily adapt a friend's term paper to this assignment. You figure that it's similar to using research you'd find yourself; and besides, you're writing the outline and delivering the speech. Would you use your friend's paper? If so, how would you acknowledge your sources?

WHAT WOULD YOU DO? While listening to an impressive speech in your class, you recognize that you've read this exact same material in an obscure online magazine. You're annoyed that this student has not done the work that everyone else has done and yet will probably earn a high grade. However, you wonder if you want to or should take on being the ethical conscience of your class. What would you do?

SUMMARY

This unit introduced the nature of public speaking and covered selecting and limiting the topic and purpose, analyzing and adapting to your audience, and researching your speech.

1. Public speaking also provides training to improve your personal and social competencies, academic and career skills, and general communication abilities.
2. Apprehension in public speaking is normal and can be managed by reversing the factors that cause anxiety, practicing performance visualization, and systematically desensitizing yourself.
3. The preparation of a public speech involves 10 steps: (1) select the topic and purpose; (2) analyze the audience; (3) research the topic; (4) formulate the thesis and identify the main points; (5) support the main points; (6) organize the speech materials; (7) construct the conclusion, introduction, and transitions; (8) outline the speech; (9) word the speech; and (10) rehearse and deliver the speech. The first three of these steps were discussed in this unit; the remaining seven are discussed in the next two units.
4. Speech topics should deal with significant issues that interest the audience. Subjects and purposes should be limited in scope.
5. In analyzing an audience, consider their attitudes, beliefs, and values.
6. In analyzing the audience, also consider age, gender, cultural factors, religion and religiousness, the occasion, and the specific context.
7. Also analyze and adapt to your audience's willingness to hear your speech, how favorable the audience is to your point of view, and the knowledge that your audience has of your topic.
8. Research the topic, beginning with general sources and gradually exploring more specific and specialized sources.
9. Useful sources of information include libraries, reference works, electronic sources, news media, scholarly articles, popular publications, government publications, museum collections, and more.
10. Critically evaluate your research by asking if the research is current, if it is fair and unbiased, and if the evidence is reliable and the reasoning logical.

11. Integrate research into your speech by mentioning the sources, providing smooth transitions, and avoiding useless expressions such as "I have a quote."

12. Avoid plagiarism by clearly acknowledging the source of any words or ideas you use that are not your own.

Key Terms

public speaking
communication apprehension
performance visualization
systematic desensitization
topic
taboo
topoi
tree diagrams
search directories
general purpose
specific purpose
informative speech
persuasive speech
special occasion speech
audience
audience analysis
attitude
belief
value
sociological analysis
audience willingness
audience favor
audience knowledge
e-mail
newsgroups
World Wide Web
search engine
directory
database
primary and secondary source material
plagiarism

Thinking Critically About

Public Speaking Topics, Audiences, and Research

1. If you have access, visit Research Navigator (www.researchnavigator.com) and search for key terms and concepts discussed in this unit; for example, attitude, value, belief, and audience psychology. On the basis of this search, what might you add to this unit's discussion?

2. Using Liszt (www.liszt.com), explore the listservs that deal with topics related to your next speech. How many can you find? Using Google (http://groups.google.com/), investigate the available newsgroups dealing with topics related to your next speech. Try to find at least three.

3. One of the common beliefs about religious people is that they're more honest, more charitable, and more likely to reach out to those in need than are nonreligious people. A review of research, however, finds that this seemingly logical connection does not exist (Kohn, 1989). For example, in a study of cheating among college students, religious beliefs bore little relationship to honesty; in fact, atheists were less likely to cheat than those who identified themselves as religious. Other studies have found that religious people were not any more likely than others to help those in need—for example, to give time to work with retarded children or to comfort someone lying in the street. What assumptions about people's behavior can you make from knowing only that they are very religious?

4. Jack is scheduled to give a speech on careers in computer technology to a group of high school students who have been forced to go to a Saturday "career day" and to attend at least three of the speeches. The audience is definitely an unwilling group. What advice can you give Jack to help him deal with this type of audience?

5. Jill wants to give a speech on television talk shows and wants to include biographical information on some of the talk show hosts. What sources might Jill go to in order to get authoritative and current information on these hosts? What sources might she go to in order to get "fan" type information? What advice would you give Jill for distinguishing the two types of sources and information?

6. Prepare and deliver a two-minute speech in which you do one of the following:
   - evaluate the topics of recent talk shows against the criteria for a worthwhile and appropriate topic
   - explain the cultural factors operating in this class that need to be taken into consideration by the speaker selecting a topic and purpose
   - explain a particularly strong belief that you hold
   - describe members of your class in terms of how willing, favorable, and knowledgeable you believe them to be about any specific topic or speaker
   - describe the audience of a popular magazine or television show or movie
   - explain the value of one reference book, website, database, listserv, or newsgroup for research in public speaking

UNIT

15

Supporting and Organizing Your Speech

UNIT CONTENTS

Here the discussion of public speaking continues. In this unit you'll learn

- about speech theses and main points, supporting materials, and organizational patterns and strategies
- how to develop your thesis and main points; support and organize them; and introduce, conclude, and tie the pieces of your speech together

Step 4: Formulate Your Thesis and Main Points

Your **thesis** is your main assertion; it's what you want the audience to absorb from your speech. The thesis of the *Rocky* movies was that the underdog can win; the thesis of the Martin Luther King Jr. "I Have a Dream" speech was that true equality must be granted to African Americans and to all people. From your thesis you'll be able to derive your main points, the major ideas that you will explore in order to prove or support your thesis.

Your Thesis

In an informative speech the thesis statement focuses on what you want your audience to learn. For example, a thesis for an informative speech on jealousy might be: "There are two main theories of jealousy." In a persuasive speech your thesis is what you want your audience to believe as a result of your speech. For example, a thesis for a persuasive speech against using animals for experimentation might be: "Animal experimentation should be banned." Notice that in informative speeches the thesis is relatively neutral and objective. In persuasive speeches, however, the thesis statement puts forth a point of view, an opinion; it's an arguable, debatable proposition.

Be sure to limit the thesis statement to one central idea. A statement such as "Animal experimentation should be banned, and companies engaging in it should be prosecuted" contains not one but two basic ideas.

Word your thesis as a simple declarative sentence: "Animal experimentation must be banned." This will

UNDERSTANDING *THEORY* AND *RESEARCH*

Primacy and Recency

Let's say that you have three points that you intend to arrange in topical order. How will you determine which to put first? The theory and research on primacy and recency offer help. The rule of primacy tells you that what an audience hears first will be remembered best and will have the greatest effect. The rule of recency tells you that what the audience hears last (or most recently) will be remembered best and will have the greatest effect. Research findings on these seemingly incompatible "rules" offer a few useful general suggestions.

- The middle is remembered least and has the least general effect. Thus, if you have a speech with three points, put the weakest one in the middle.
- If your listeners are favorable or neutral, lead with your strongest point. In this way you'll strengthen the conviction of those who are already favorable and you'll get the neutrals on your side early.
- If your audience is hostile or holds very different views than you, put your most powerful argument last and work up to it gradually—assuming, that is, that you can count on the listeners' staying with you until the end.

Research on memory tells us that the audience will remember very little of what you say in a speech. Therefore, repeat your main assertions—whether you put them first or last in your speech—in your conclusion.

Working with Theories and Research

- *Examine your previous speech or the speech you're currently working on in terms of the order of the main points. What insights does primacy-recency theory give you for ordering your main points?*

COMMUNICATION@WORK

Team Presentations

The achievements of an organization are the result of the combined efforts of each individual.

—Vince Lombardi

Team presentations are extremely popular in business settings. Generally, they follow the same rules and principles as do other public speeches. There are some differences, however.

Team presentations are given by two, three, four, or even more people to an audience. Each person on the team delivers a part of the speech. For example, in a presentation on the design of the new office space, one person may speak on the architectural layout, another on the furnishings, and still another on the temporary inconvenience that the change will necessitate. In a presentation on employee health plans, representatives from the health plans might each speak on their specific plan, identifying its provisions and its advantages, and handling audience questions. In an advertising company's presentation to a client, one team member might present the creative idea; another the media analysis, the cost, and the audience they hope to address; and a third the anticipated sales projections.

In using a team presentation, be sure that you allow time for the planning needed to coordinate the presentations, so that each person knows exactly what the other person is going to talk about (so as not to repeat or contradict). Give special attention to the introduction and conclusion. The introduction should provide the audience with a clear unifying statement that helps the speeches blend into one unified presentation. And the conclusion should wrap up the entire presentation, not just the last speech. Between the speeches, use transitions so that the audience members know how the speech they just heard is connected to the speech they're going to hear. For example, a speaker who has just spoken on the proposed advertising campaign's creative concept might say: "Now that the creative concept is clear, Margaret is going to explain what audience this campaign is intended to reach and the media we intend to use." Your overriding goal should be to have the audience see these speeches, although delivered by different people, as parts of one unified, coordinated presentation.

Communicating@Work

What other advantages do you see to team presentations as compared with single-speaker presentations? What are some disadvantages?

help you focus your thinking, your collection of materials, and your organizational tasks.

Use the thesis statement to help you generate your main points. Each thesis contains within it an essential question, and it is this question that allows you to explore and subdivide the thesis. Your objective is to find this question and ask it of your thesis. For example, let's say your thesis is: "The Hart bill provides needed services for senior citizens." Stated in this form, the thesis suggests the obvious question "What are they?" The answers to this question suggest the main points of your speech; for example, health care, food, shelter, and recreational services. These four areas then become the four main points of your speech.

Use the thesis to help focus the audience's attention on your central idea. In some cases you may wish to state your thesis early in your speech. In other cases, such as situations in which your audience may be hostile to your thesis, it may be wise to give your evidence first and gradually move the audience into a more positive frame of mind before stating your thesis. Here are a few guidelines to help you make the right decision about when to introduce your thesis:

- In an informative speech, state your thesis early and state it clearly and directly.
- In a persuasive speech before a neutral or positive audience, state your thesis explicitly and early in your speech.
- In a persuasive speech before an audience that is hostile to your position, delay revealing your thesis until you've moved your listeners closer to your point of view.

- Recognize that there are cultural differences in the way a thesis should be stated. In some Asian cultures, for example, making a point too directly or asking directly for audience compliance may be considered rude or insulting.

Main Points

If your speech were a play, the main points would be its acts. Let's look at how you can select and word your main points and how you can logically arrange them.

As we discussed earlier, you can develop your main points by asking strategic questions. To see how this works in detail, imagine that you are giving a speech on the values of a college education to a group of high school students. Your thesis is: "A college education is valuable." You then ask, "Why is it valuable?" From this question you generate your main points. Your first step might be to brainstorm this question and generate as many answers as possible without evaluating them. You might come up with answers such as the following:

1. It helps you get a good job.
2. It increases your earning potential.
3. It gives you greater job mobility.
4. It helps you secure more creative work.
5. It helps you to appreciate the arts more fully.
6. It helps you to understand an extremely complex world.
7. It helps you understand different cultures.
8. It allows you to avoid taking a regular job for a few years.
9. It helps you meet lots of people and make new friends.
10. It helps you increase your personal effectiveness.

There are, of course, many other possibilities—but for purposes of illustration, these 10 possible main points will suffice. But not all 10 are equally valuable or relevant to your audience, so you should look over the list to see how to make it shorter and more meaningful. Try these suggestions:

- Eliminate those points that seem least important to your thesis. On this basis you might want to eliminate number 8, as this seems least consistent with your intended emphasis on the positive values of college.
- Combine those points that have a common focus. Notice, for example, that the first four points all center on the value of college in terms of jobs. You might, therefore, consider grouping these four items into one proposition: A college education helps you get a good job. This main point and its elaboration might look like this in your speech outline:

    I. A college education helps you get a good job.
        A. College graduates earn higher salaries.
        B. College graduates enter more creative jobs.
        C. College graduates have greater job mobility.

    Note that A, B, and C all relate to aspects or subdivisions of a "good job."
- Select the points that are most relevant or interesting to your audience. You might decide that high school students would be interested in increasing personal effectiveness, so you might

BUILDING COMMUNICATION SKILLS

Generating Main Points

Try generating two or three main points (suitable for an informative or persuasive speech) from any one of the following thesis statements by asking strategic questions of each. Try following the general format illustrated in the text in the example of the values of a college education.

1. Property owned by religious organizations should be taxed.
2. Adoption agencies should be required to reveal the names of birth parents to all children when they reach 18 years of age.
3. The growing of tobacco should be declared illegal.
4. Medicinal marijuana should be legalized.
5. Gay men and lesbians should be granted full equality in the military.

select point 10 for inclusion as a second main point.

- In general, limit the number of main points. For your class speeches, which will generally range from 5 to 15 minutes, use two, three, or four major ideas. Too many main points will result in a speech that is confusing, contains too much information and too little amplification, and proves difficult to remember.
- Word each of your main points in the same (parallel) style. When outlining, phrase points labeled with Roman numerals in a similar (parallel) style. Likewise, phrase points labeled with capital letters and subordinate to the same Roman numeral (for example, A, B, and C under point I or A, B, and C under point II) in a similar style. In item 2 above, parallel style was used in the example on college education and getting a good job. This parallel styling helps the audience follow and remember your speech.
- Develop your main points so they are separate and discrete; don't allow them to overlap one another. Each section labeled with a Roman numeral should be a separate entity.

Step 5: Support Your Main Points

Now that you've identified your main points—and having learned in Unit 14 how to search for information—you can devote attention to your next step: supporting your main points. Supporting materials (such as examples, statistics, and presentation aids) are essential to the public speaker: They give life to the main points; they help maintain attention; and they contribute to your purpose, whether that is to inform or to persuade. Presenting examples of homelessness, for instance, helps you show your listeners what homelessness is, how it happens, and how it affects people. Presenting statistics on the new health insurance plans helps your listeners understand why they should make certain decisions and not make others. Showing slides of your main points will help your listeners remember the most important parts of your speech.

Among the most important sources of support are examples, narratives, testimony, statistics, and presentation aids, all of which this section will cover in depth. But first, let's look more briefly at some of the many other forms of support that you can use:

- *Quotations,* the exact words of another person, are useful for adding spice and wit as well as authority to your speeches. Make sure they're relatively short, easily understood, directly related to your point, and properly attributed.
- *Definitions,* statements of the meanings of terms, are helpful when you introduce complex terms or when you wish to provide a unique perspective on a subject. Don't overdo definitions; if too many definitions are needed, then your subject may be too complex for a short speech.
- *Comparisons and contrasts* are useful for highlighting similarities and differences between concepts; say, between two health care plans or between two cultures. A few major points of comparison and contrast may work better than an exhaustive list of similarities and differences, which listeners won't be able to remember.
- *Facts or series of facts*—verifiable truths—are useful to help you support a main idea. Don't allow individual facts to cloud your major propositions; make sure the facts are clearly linked to the point they support.
- *Repetition* means repeating your idea in the same words at strategic places throughout your speech; *restatement* means repeating your idea in different words. Both tactics are helpful for emphasizing a particular point, and both may be especially helpful when you are addressing listeners who learned your language as a second language and may not easily understand idioms and figures of speech. Repetition and restatement can be overdone and get boring, however; limit yourself to what is reasonable for increasing audience comprehension.

Examples

Examples are specific instances that are explained in varying degrees of detail. Examples are useful when you wish to make an abstract concept or idea concrete. It's easier for an audience to understand what you mean by, say, "love" or "friendship" if you provide a specific example along with your definition.

In using examples, keep in mind that their function is to make your ideas vivid and easily understood. Examples are useful for explaining a concept; they're not ends in themselves. Make them only as long as necessary to ensure that your purpose is achieved.

Also, use only enough examples to make your point. Make sure that the examples are sufficient to re-create your meaning in the minds of your listeners, but be careful not to use so many that the audience loses the very point you are making.

Make the relationship between your assertion and your example explicit. Show the audience exactly how your example relates to the assertion or concept you are explaining. Here, for example, former New York mayor Rudolph Giuliani, in his address to the United Nations after the World Trade Center attack of September 11, 2001, gave relevant examples to support his point that we are a land of immigrants and must continue to be so (www.ci.nyc.ny.us/html/om/html/96/united.html):

> New York City was built by immigrants and it will remain the greatest city in the world as long as we continue to renew ourselves with and benefit from the energizing spirit from new people coming here to create a better future for themselves and their families. Come to Flushing, Queens, where immigrants from many lands have created a vibrant, vital commercial and residential community. Their children challenge and astonish us in our public school classrooms every day. Similarly, you can see growing and dynamic immigrant communities in every borough of our city: Russians in Brighton Beach, West Indians in Crown Heights, Dominicans in Washington Heights, the new wave of Irish in the Bronx, and Koreans in Willow Brook on Staten Island.

Narratives

Narratives, or stories, are often useful as supporting materials in a speech. Narratives give the audience what it wants: a good story. They help you maintain your audience's attention, because listeners automatically perk up when a story is told. The main value of narratives is that they allow you to bring an abstract concept down to specifics. Narratives may be of different types, and each serves a somewhat different purpose. Following Clella Jaffe (1998), we can distinguish three types of narrative: explanatory, exemplary, and persuasive.

- *Explanatory narratives* explain the way things are. The biblical book of Genesis, for example, explains the development of the world from a particular religious viewpoint. An eyewitness report might explain the events leading up to an accident.
- *Exemplary narratives* provide examples of excellence (or its opposite)—examples to follow or admire (or to avoid following). The stories of the lives of saints and martyrs are exemplary narratives, as are the Horatio Alger success stories. Similarly, many motivational speakers often include exemplary narratives in their speeches and will tell stories of what they were like when they were out of shape or on drugs or deep in debt.
- *Persuasive narratives* try to strengthen or change beliefs and attitudes. When Sally Struthers tells us of the plight of starving children, she's using a persuasive narrative. The parables in religious writings are persuasive in urging listeners to lead life in a particular way.

Keep your narratives relatively short and few in number. In most cases, one or possibly two narratives should be sufficient in a short 5- to 15-minute speech. Make explicit the connection between your story and the point you are making. If the people in the audience don't get this connection, you lose not only the effectiveness of the story but also their attention (as they try to figure out why you told that story).

Testimony

The term *testimony* refers to the opinions of experts or the accounts of witnesses. Testimony helps to amplify your speech by adding a note of authority to your arguments. For example, you might want to use the testimony of a noted economist to support your predictions about inflation, or the testimony of someone who spent two years in a maximum-security prison to discourage young people from committing crimes.

When you cite testimony, stress first the competence of the person, whether that person is an expert or a witness. For example, citing the predictions of a world-famous economist of whom your audience has never heard will mean little unless you first explain the person's competence. You might say something like "This prediction comes from the world's leading economist, who has successfully predicted all major financial trends over the past 20 years." Now the audience will be prepared to lend credence to what this person says.

Second, stress the unbiased nature of the testimony. If the audience perceives the testimony to be biased—whether or not it really is—it will have little effect. You want to check out any possible biases in a witness so that you can present accurate information. But you also want to make the audience see that the testimony is in fact unbiased.

Third, stress the recency of the testimony. If an audience has no way of knowing when the statement was made, it has no way of knowing how true this statement is today.

Statistics

Let's say you want to show that significant numbers of people are now getting their news from the Internet, that the cost of filmmaking has skyrocketed over the last 20 years, or that women buy signifi-

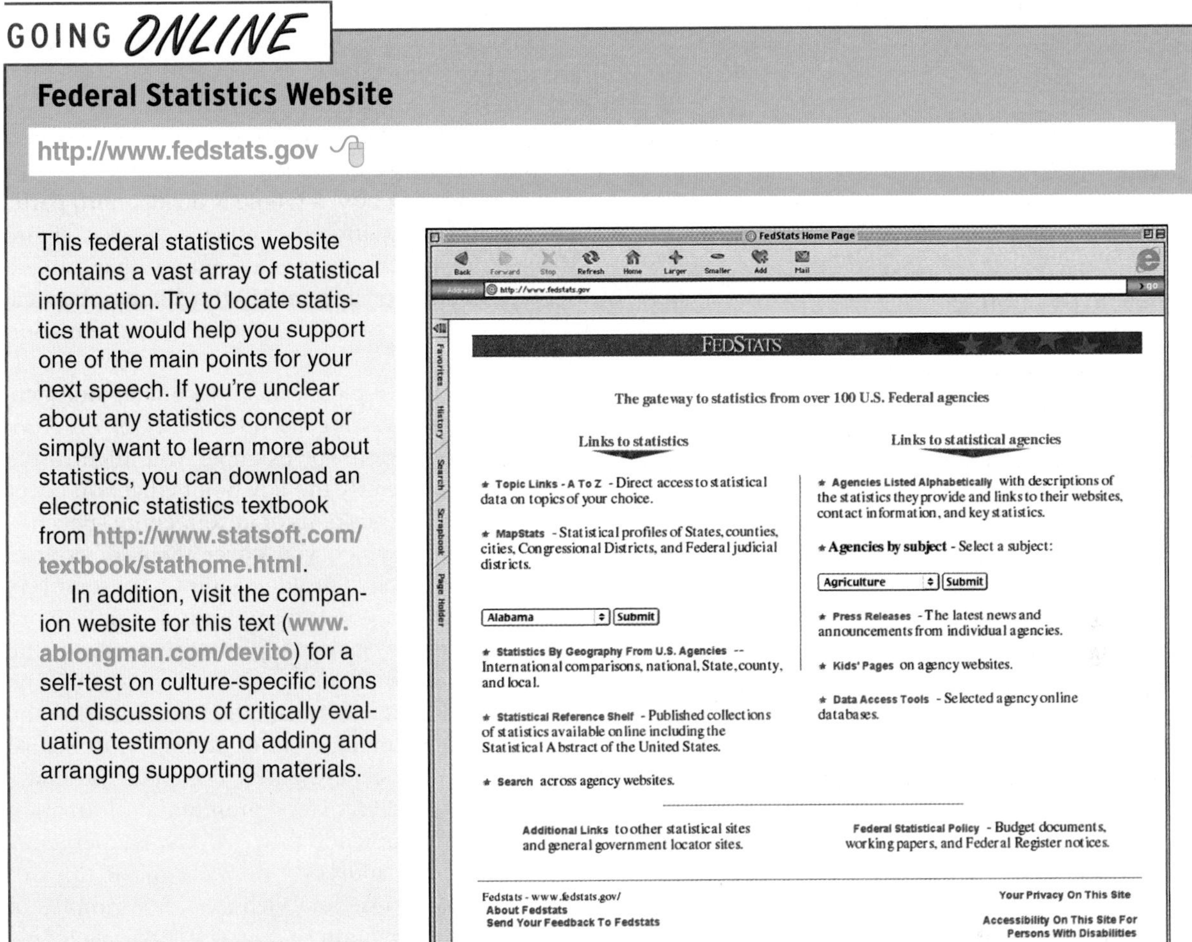

GOING ONLINE

Federal Statistics Website

http://www.fedstats.gov

This federal statistics website contains a vast array of statistical information. Try to locate statistics that would help you support one of the main points for your next speech. If you're unclear about any statistics concept or simply want to learn more about statistics, you can download an electronic statistics textbook from http://www.statsoft.com/textbook/stathome.html.

In addition, visit the companion website for this text (www.ablongman.com/devito) for a self-test on culture-specific icons and discussions of critically evaluating testimony and adding and arranging supporting materials.

cantly more books and magazines than men. To communicate these types of information, you'd use *statistics*—summary numbers that help you communicate the important characteristics of an otherwise complex set of numbers. Statistics help the audience see, for example, the percentage of people getting their news from the Internet, the average cost of films in 2002 versus previous years, or the difference between male and female book and magazine purchases. For a wealth of statistics see Going Online.

- *Make the statistics clear to your audience.* Remember, they'll hear the figures only once. Round off figures so they are easy to understand and retain.
- *Make the statistics meaningful.* When you are using statistics, it's often helpful to remind the audience of what the statistic itself means. For example, if you say, "The median price of a co-op apartment in San Francisco is $875,000," remind the audience that this means the middle price—that half the prices are above $875,000 and half are below. Also, present numbers so that the audience can appreciate the meaning you want to convey. To say, for example, that the Sears Tower in Chicago is 1,559 feet tall doesn't help your hearers visualize its height. So consider saying something like "The Sears Tower is 1,559 feet tall. Just how tall is 1,559 feet? Well, it's as tall as the length of more than five football fields. It's as tall as 260 six-foot people standing on each other's heads."
- *Connect the statistics with your point.* Make explicit the connection between the statistics and what they show. A statement, for example, that college professors make an average of $85,000 per year needs to be related specifically to the proposition that teachers' salaries should be raised—or lowered, depending on your point of view.

- *Use statistics in moderation.* Most listeners' capacity for numerical data presented in a speech is limited, so in most cases statistics should be used sparingly.
- *Visually (and verbally) reinforce the statistics.* Numbers are difficult to grasp and remember when they are presented without some kind of visual reinforcement, so it's often helpful to complement your oral presentation of statistics with some type of presentation aid—perhaps a graph or a chart.

Presentation Aids

When you're planning a speech, consider using some kind of presentation aid—a visual or auditory means for clarifying ideas. Ask yourself how you can represent visually (or via audio) what you want your audience to remember. How can you reinforce your ideas with additional media? If you want your audience to grasp increases in the sales tax, consider showing them a chart of rising sales taxes over the last 10 years. If you want them to see that Brand A is superior to Brand X, consider showing them a comparison chart identifying the superior qualities of Brand A.

Types of Presentation Aids

Among the presentation aids you have available are the actual object, models of the object, graphs, word charts, maps, people, photographs and illustrations, and tapes and CDs.

As a general rule (to which there are many exceptions), the best presentation aid is the object itself; bring it with you if you can. Notice that infomercials sell their product not only by talking about it but also by showing it to potential buyers. You see what George Foreman's Lean Mean Grilling Machine looks like and how it works. You see the jewelry, the clothing, and the new mop from a wide variety of angles and in varied settings. If you want to explain some tangible thing and you can show it to your audience, do so.

Models—replicas of actual objects—are useful for a variety of purposes. For example, if you wanted to explain complex structures such as the hearing or vocal mechanism, the brain, or the structure of DNA, you would almost have to use a model. You may remember from science classes that these models (and the pictures of them in the textbooks) make a lot more sense than verbal explanations alone. Models help to clarify relative size and position and how each part interacts with each other part. Large models can be used to help listeners visualize objects that are too small (or unavailable) to appreciate otherwise. In other cases, small models of large objects—objects that are too large to bring to your speech—are helpful. For example, in a speech on stretching exercises, one student used a 14-inch wooden artist's model.

Graphs are useful for showing differences over time, for showing how a whole is divided into parts, and for showing different amounts or sizes. Figure 15.1 shows different types of graphs that can be drawn freehand or generated with the graphics capabilities of any word-processing or presentation software.

Word charts (which can also contain numbers and even graphics) are useful for lots of different types of information. For example, you might use a word chart to identify the key points that you cover in one of your propositions or in your entire speech—in the order in which you cover them, of course. Slide 5 in the Public Speaking Sample Assistant box on page 311 is a good example of a simple word chart listing the major topics discussed in the speech. Or you could use word charts to identify the steps in a process; for example, to summarize the steps in programming a VCR, dealing with sexual harassment, or installing a new computer program. Another use of charts is for presenting information you want your audience to write down. Emergency phone numbers, addresses to write to, or titles of recommended books and websites are examples of the type of information that listeners will welcome in written form.

Maps are useful for illustrating a wide variety of concepts. If you want to show the locations of cities, lakes, rivers, or mountain ranges, maps will obviously prove useful as presentation aids. One speaker, for example, used a map to show the sizes and locations of rain forests. Maps are also helpful for illustrating population densities, immigration patterns, varied economic conditions, the spread of diseases, and hundreds of other issues you may wish to develop in your speeches. For example, in a talk on natural resources, one speaker used maps to illustrate the locations of large reserves of oil, gas, and precious metals. Another speaker used maps to illustrate concentrations of wealth; still another used maps to show worldwide differences in mortality rates.

You also can use maps to illustrate numerical differences. For example, you might use a map to show the wide variation in literacy rates throughout the world. You could color the countries with 90 to 100 percent literacy red, the countries with 80 to 89 percent literacy green, and so on. When you use maps in this way, it's often helpful to complement them with charts or graphs that, for example, give the specific literacy rates for the specific countries on which you

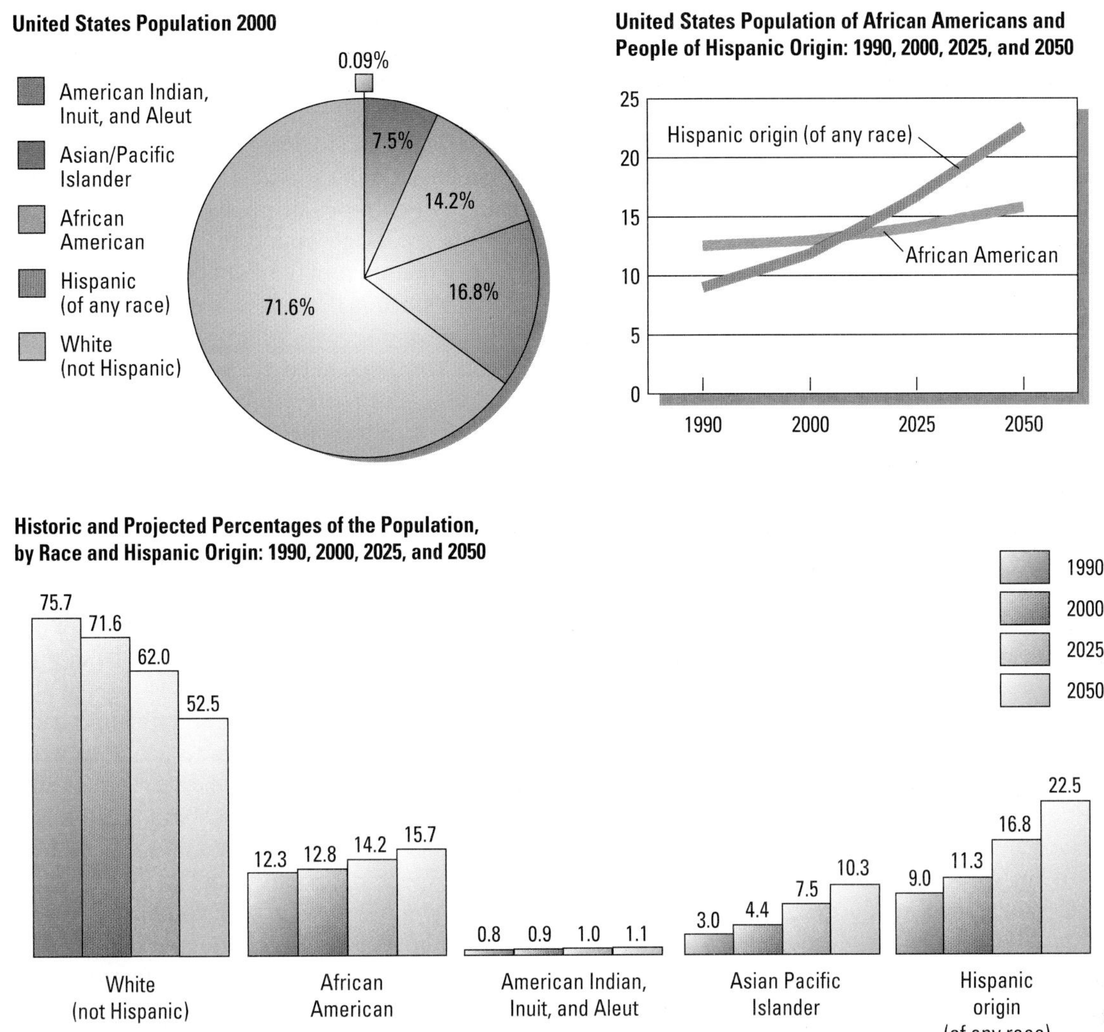

Figure 15.1

Assorted Graphs

Notice that each of the graphs serves a somewhat different purpose. The *pie chart* is especially useful if you want to show how some whole is divided into its parts and the relative sizes of the parts. From the pie chart you can easily see the relative percentages of the different groups in the U.S. population. Pie charts are especially helpful when you have three to five values to illustrate; any more than five creates a pie that is difficult to read at a glance. The *bar graph,* used in Unit 3 to illustrate demographic changes, presents the same information as the pie chart but for four different time periods. You might have used four pie charts—with each pie representing a different year—but comparisons would not have been as easy for an audience to make. The *line graph* shows how comparisons can be visualized with a very simple illustration. Notice that the graph is especially clear because it focuses on only 2 groups. Had it focused on 8 or 10 groups, it would have been difficult for an audience to understand.

want to concentrate. Although maps may seem complex to construct, computer programs now make the creation of such maps relatively simple. Further, a wide variety of maps may be downloaded from the Internet and then shown as slides or transparencies. Chances are you'll find a map on the Internet for exactly the purpose you need.

Oddly enough, *people* can function effectively as "presentation aids." For example, if you wanted to demonstrate the muscles of the body, you might use a bodybuilder. If you wanted to discuss different voice patterns, skin complexions, or hairstyles, you might use people as your aids. Aside from the obvious assistance they provide in demonstrating their muscles or voice qualities, people help to secure and maintain the attention and interest of the audience.

And don't overlook yourself as a (kind of) presentation aid. For example, if you are giving a speech on boxing strategies, exercise techniques, or sitting and standing postures that can lead to backaches, consider demonstrating them yourself. As an added plus, going through these demonstrations is likely to reduce your apprehension and make you more relaxed.

Photographs and illustrations are useful aids for a variety of purposes. Speeches on types of trees, styles of art or architecture, or types of exercise machines would profit greatly from a few well-chosen photographs or illustrations. If you want to show these but don't have the opportunity to put them onto slides, you may try simply holding them up as you refer to them. There are many hazards involved in using this type of aid, however, so pictures are recommended only with reservations. If the image is large enough for all members of the audience to see clearly (say, poster size); if it clearly illustrates what you want to illustrate; and if it's mounted on cardboard, then use it. Otherwise, don't. Fortunately, it's relatively easy to have photos enlarged or put onto slides.

Do not pass pictures around the room. This only draws attention away from what you are saying: Listeners will look for the pictures before the pictures circulate to them, will wonder what the pictures contain, and meanwhile will miss a great deal of your speech.

Tapes and CDs can be useful for many types of speeches as well. For a speech on advertising, for example, actual samples of commercials as played on radio or television would go a long way in helping the audience see exactly what you are talking about. These aids also provide variety by breaking up the oral presentation.

The Media of Presentation Aids

Once you've decided on the type of presentation aid you'll use, you need to decide on the medium you'll use to present it. Some of these media are low tech—for example, chalkboards, transparencies, and flip charts. These media are generally more effective in smaller, more informal situations, and especially for presentations that arise without prior notice, for which you simply don't have the time to prepare high-tech resources. Low-tech devices are also useful for highly interactive sessions; for example, the flip chart is still one of the best ways to record group members' contributions. More high-tech media such as slides and videotapes are generally more effective with larger, more formal groups, in which you do most of the talking and the audience does most of the listening. High-tech materials also may be your only choice if the material you have to communicate is extremely complex or if the norms of your organization simply require that you use high-tech presentation formats.

The best strategy is to learn how to use both low- and high-tech resources. The decisions you make concerning which types of media to use should be based on the message you want to communicate and on the audience to whom you'll be speaking.

The *chalkboard* is the easiest to use, but not necessarily the most effective. All classrooms have such boards, and you have seen them used by teachers with greater or lesser effect; in some way, you've had "experience" with them. The chalkboard may be used effectively to present key terms or important definitions or even to outline the general structure of your speech. But don't use it if you can present the same information with a prepared chart or model. It takes too long to write out anything substantial. If you do write on the board, be careful not to turn your back to the audience. In this brief time you can easily lose their attention.

Chartboards (large pieces of semiflexible cardboard that can be held up for an audience to read, placed on an easel or bulletin board, or taped to a chalkboard) are useful when you have just one or two relatively simple charts that you want to display during your speech. If you want to display your charts for several minutes, be sure you have a way of holding them up. For example, bring masking tape if you intend to secure them to the chalkboard, or enlist the aid of an audience member to hold them up. Use a light-colored board; white generally works best. Write in black; it provides the best contrast and is the easiest for people to read.

Flip charts, charts on large pads of paper (usually about 24 by 24 inches) mounted on a stand, can be used to record many types of information, which you reveal by flipping the pages as you deliver your speech. For example, if you were to discuss the various departments in an organization, you might have the key points relating to each department on a separate page of your flip chart. As you discussed the advertising department, you would show the advertising department chart. When you moved on to discuss the personnel department, you would flip to the chart dealing with personnel. You may find this device useful if you have a large number of word charts that you want to have easy control over. Make sure that the flip chart is positioned so that everyone in the audience can see it clearly and that the folding legs are positioned securely so it doesn't collapse when you flip the first page. Make sure you write large enough so that the people in the back can read your material without straining their eyes.

Flip charts also are especially useful for recording ideas at small group meetings. Unlike the chalkboard, the flip chart enables you to retain a written record of the meeting; should you need to, you can easily review the group's contributions.

Slides and transparency projections are helpful for showing a series of visuals that may be of very different types; for example, photographs, illustrations, charts, or tables. The slides can easily be created with many popular computer programs (see "Computer-Assisted Presentations" on page 308). To produce actual 35mm slides, you'll need considerable lead time; be sure to build this into your preparation time.

If you don't have access to a slide projector or don't have the lead time needed to construct slides, consider somewhat less sophisticated transparencies. You can create your visual in any of the word-processing or spreadsheet programs you normally use and probably can find a printer that will enable you to print transparencies. Another alternative is to use a copier that will produce transparencies.

When using any presentation aid, but especially with slides and transparencies, make sure that you have the proper equipment; for example, a projector, a table, a working outlet nearby, control over the lighting in the room, and whatever else you'll need to have the audience see your projections clearly.

An advantage of transparencies is that you can write on the transparencies (and on slides in computer presentations, as we discuss later) while you're speaking. You can circle important items, underline key terms, and draw lines connecting different terms.

Videotapes may serve a variety of purposes in public speaking. Basically, you have two options with videotapes. First, you can tape a scene from a film or television show with your VCR and show it at the appropriate time in your speech. Thus, for example, you might videotape examples of sexism in television sitcoms, violence on television talk shows, or types of transitions used in feature films and show these excerpts during your speech. As you can see, however, this type of video takes a great deal of time and preparation, so if you are going to use such excerpts you must plan well in advance. As a teacher, I use a variety of films and film excerpts to illustrate breakdowns in interpersonal communication, studies in which experimenters teach animals to communicate, aspects of nonverbal communication, and various other topics.

Second, you can create your own video with a simple camcorder. One student created a video of ethnic store signs to illustrate the "interculturalization" of the city. With the help (and agreement to be videotaped) of a few friends, another student created a three-minute video of religious holidays as celebrated by members of different religions and carefully coordinated each segment with her discussion of the relevant holiday.

In using videotapes do make sure that they don't occupy too much of your speaking time; after all, your main objective is to learn the principles of public speaking.

Handouts, or printed materials that you distribute to members of the audience, are especially helpful in explaining complex material and also in providing listeners with a permanent record of some aspect of your speech. Handouts are also useful for presenting information that you want your audience to refer to throughout the speech. Handouts encourage listeners to take notes, especially if you leave enough white space or even provide a specific place for notes—and this keeps them actively involved in your presentation. Handouts also reward the audience by giving them something for their attendance and attention. A variety of handouts can be easily prepared with many of the computer presentation packages that we'll consider in the last section of this unit.

You can distribute handouts at the beginning of, during, or after your speech; but realize that whichever system you use has both pros and cons. If you distribute materials before or during your speech, you run the risk of your listeners' reading the handout and not concentrating on your speech. On the other hand, if the listeners are getting the information you want to communicate—even if primarily from the handout—that isn't too bad. And, in a way, handouts allow listeners to process the information at their own pace.

You can encourage your audience to listen to you when you want them to and to look at the handout when you want them to by simply telling them: "Look at the graph on the top of page two of the handout; it summarizes recent census figures on immigration" or "We'll get back to the handout in a minute; now, however, I want to direct your attention to this next slide [or the second argument]."

If you distribute your handouts at the end of the speech, they will obviously not interfere with your presentation—but they may not be read at all. After all, listeners might reason, they heard the speech; why bother going through the handout? To counteract this very natural tendency, you might include additional material in the handout and mention this to your audience, saying something like "This handout contains all the slides shown here and three additional slides that provide economic data for Thailand, Cambodia, and Vietnam, which I didn't have time to cover. When you look at the data, you'll see that they mirror exactly the data provided in my talk on the other countries." When you provide additional information on your handout, it's more likely that it will get looked at and thus provide the reinforcement you want.

Preparing Presentation Aids

In preparing presentation aids make sure that they add clarity to your speech, that they're appealing to the listeners, and that they're culturally sensitive. *Clarity* is the most important consideration, and you can achieve it by following these simple guidelines:

1. Use colors that will make your message instantly clear; light colors on dark backgrounds or dark colors on light backgrounds provide the best contrast and seem to work best for most purposes. Be cautious about using yellow, which is often difficult to see, especially if there's glare from the sun.
2. Use direct phrases (not complete sentences); use bullets to highlight your points or your support (see the slides in the Public Speaking Sample Assistant box on pages 311–312). Just as you phrase your main points in parallel style whenever possible, try to phrase your bullets in parallel style, usually by using the same part of speech (for example, all nouns or all infinitive phrases). And make sure that the meaning or relevance of any graphic is immediately clear. If it isn't, explain it.
3. Use the aid to highlight a few essential points; don't clutter it with too much information. Four bullets on a slide or chart, for example, are as much information as you should include.
4. Use typefaces that can be read easily from all parts of the room. (For a chart of typefaces available with most word-processing programs and suggestions for their use, see Table 15.1.
5. Give the slide or chart or transparency a title—a general heading—to further guide your listeners' attention and focus.

Create presentation aids so that they're *appealing* to your audience. Presentation aids should be attractive enough to engage the attention of the audience, but not so attractive that they're distracting. An almost nude body draped across a car may be effective in selling underwear but will probably detract if your objective is to explain the profit-and-loss statement of General Motors.

Make sure your presentation aids are *culturally sensitive* and can be easily interpreted by people from other cultures. Just as your words will be interpreted within a cultural framework, so too will the symbols and colors you use in your aids. For example, when speaking to international audiences, you need to use universal symbols or explain those that are not universal. Be careful that your icons don't reveal an ethnocentric bias: Using the American dollar sign to symbolize "wealth" might be quite logical in your public speaking class but could be interpreted as ethnocentric if used with an audience of international visitors.

Using Presentation Aids

Keep the following guidelines clearly in mind when using presentation aids.

- Know your aids intimately. Be sure you know in what order they are to be presented and how you plan to introduce them. Know exactly what goes where and when.
- Test the aids before using them. When testing the presentation aids ahead of time, be certain that they can be seen easily from all parts of the room.
- Rehearse your speech with the presentation aids incorporated into the presentation. Practice your actual movements with the aids you'll use. If you're going to use a chart, how will you use it? Will it stand by itself? Can you tape it somewhere? Do you have tape with you?
- Integrate your aids seamlessly into your speech. Just as a verbal example should flow naturally into the text and seem an integral part of the speech, so should the presentation aid. It should appear not as an afterthought but as an essential part of the speech.
- Don't talk to your aid. Both you and the aid should be focused on the audience. Know your aids so well that you can point to what you want without breaking eye contact with your audience. Or, at most, break audience eye contact for only a few seconds at a time.
- Use the aid when it's relevant: Show it when you want the audience to concentrate on it, then remove it. If you don't remove it, the audience's attention may remain focused on the visual when you want them to focus on your next point.

Computer-Assisted Presentations

There are a variety of presentation software packages available: PowerPoint, Corel Presentations, and Lotus Freelance are among the most popular and are very similar in what they do and how they do it. The Public Speaking Sample Assistant box on pages 311–312 illustrates what a set of slides might look like; the slides are built around a speech outline that

Table 15.1
Some Typefaces

You have an enormous number of typefaces to choose from. Generally, select typefaces that are easy to read and that are consistent in tone with the message of your speech.

Typeface	Comments
Palatino Century Schoolbook Garamond Times	Serif typefaces retain some of the cursive strokes found in handwriting. The cursive stroke is illustrated especially in the *m* and *n,* which begin with a slight upsweep. Serif styles are easy to read and useful for blocks of text.
Helvetica Bauhaus Avant Garde Futura	Sans-serif typefaces (a style that is more bold and doesn't include the serif or upsweep) are useful for titles and headings but make reading long text difficult.
Serif Gothic Black **STENCIL** **Gill Sans Ultra Bold**	These extremely bold typefaces are tempting to use; but, as you can see, they're not easy to read. They're most appropriate for short titles.
Akzidenz Grotesk BETON COMPRESSED BOLD Franklin Gothic	These compressed typefaces are useful when you have to fit a lot of text into a small space. They are, however, difficult to read and so should generally be avoided (or at least used sparingly) in slides. It would be better to use an easier-to-read typeface and spread out the text over additional slides.
CASTELLAR ROSEWOOD JAZZ ASHLEY INLINE Linotext	Decorative styles like these, although difficult to read for extended text, make great headings or titles. Be careful, however, that the originality of your typefaces doesn't steal attention away from your message.
Mistral *Brush Script* *Freestyle Script* *Pepita*	Script typefaces are interesting and will give your presentation a personal look, as if you wrote it longhand. But they'll be difficult to read. If you're going to read the slides aloud word for word, then typefaces that are a bit more difficult to read may still be used with considerable effect.

we'll discuss in Unit 16 and were constructed in PowerPoint, though a similar slide show could be produced with most presentation software programs. Also, realize that you can easily import photographs and have slides of these inserted into your slide show; or you can add video clips. As you review the speech in the Public Speaking Sample Assistant box, try to visualize how you would use a slide show in presenting your next speech.

Ways of Using Presentation Package Software. Computer presentation software enables you to produce a variety of aids; the software will produce what you want. For example, you can construct slides on your computer, save them on a disk, and then have 35mm slides developed from the disk. To do this you need access to a slide printer—or you can send your files out (you can do this via modem) to a lab specializing in converting electronic files into 35mm slides. There may be a slide printer at your school, so check there first. Similarly, your local office supply store or copy shop, such as Staples, OfficeMax, or Kinko, may have exactly the services you need.

Or you can create your slides and then show them on your computer screen. If you are speaking to a very small group, it may be possible to have your listeners gather around your computer as you speak. With larger audiences, however, you'll need a computer projector or an LCD projection panel. Assuming that you have a properly equipped computer in the classroom, you can copy your entire presentation to a floppy disk and bring it with you on the day of the speech.

Computer presentation software also enables you to print out a variety of handouts:

- the slides shown during your speech, as well as additional slides that you may not have time to include in the speech but that you nevertheless want your listeners to look at when they read your handout
- the slides plus speaker's notes, the key points that you made as you showed each of the slides (the function that was used to produce the Public Speaking Sample Assistant box)
- the slides plus places for listeners to write notes next to each of them
- an outline of your talk
- any combination of the above

Overhead transparencies also can be created from your computer slides. To make overheads on many printers and most copiers, simply substitute transparency paper for computer or copy paper. If you create your slides with a computer presentation package, you'll be able to produce professional-looking transparencies.

Suggestions for Using Presentation Software. The templates and the suggestions of the program "wizards" will parallel the suggestions offered here. Nevertheless, it's important to understand the qualities of effective slides in case you want to make changes in the suggested formats or even want to start from scratch.

In developing your slides, strive for clarity and consistency. For example, choose typeface styles, sizes, and colors that clearly distinguish the major propositions from the supporting materials. At the same time, use a consistent combination of fonts, colors, backgrounds, and graphics throughout your slides to give your presentation unity.

Use color (of type and background) and graphics sparingly. Remember that clarity is your goal; you want your audience to remember your ideas and not just the fact that all your slides were red, white, and blue. Likewise, too many graphics will distract your audience's attention from your verbal message. Also, be sure to choose graphics that support your tone. If your speech is on a serious topic, then the graphics (and photographs or illustrations) should contribute to this tone. Also, try to use graphics that are consistent with one another; generally it's better to use all shadow figures or all stick figures or all Victorian images than to mix them.

Generally, put one complete thought on a slide. Don't try to put too many words on one slide; use a few words on each slide, and expand on these during your speech. Try not to use more than two levels of thought in a slide—a major statement and two to four subordinate phrases (bulleted) are about all you can put on one slide. Avoid using subheads of subheads of subheads. Generally, use a sans-serif type (more attention-getting) for headings and a serif type (easier to read) for text (see Table 15.1).

A good guideline to follow in designing your slides is to give all items in your outline that have the same level heads (for example, all the Roman numeral heads) the same typeface, size, and color throughout your presentation. Similarly, use the same font for all the A, B, C subheads, and so on. This will help your listeners follow the organization of your speech. Notice that this principle is followed for the most part in the slides in the Public Speaking Sample Assistant box. The rule is broken in one case, however: The introduction and conclusion are set apart by being in a color and typeface different from the rest of the slides.

Consider using graphs, charts, and tables; you have a tremendous variety of graph and chart types (for example, pie and bar graphs and cumulative charts) and tables to choose from. If you are using presentation software that's part of a suite, then you'll find it especially easy to import files from your word processor or spreadsheet.

If there's a question-and-answer period following your speech, consider preparing a few extra slides to support responses to questions you anticipate being asked. Then, when someone asks you a predicted question, you can say: "I anticipated that someone might ask that question; it raises an important issue. The data I've been able to find are presented in this chart." You then show the slide and explain it more fully. This is surely going the extra mile, but it can easily make your speech a real standout.

Use transitions wisely. Just as verbal transitions help you move from one part of your speech to another, presentational transitions help you move from one slide to the next with the desired effect—for example, blinds folding from left or right or top or bottom, or a quick fade.

THE *PUBLIC SPEAKING* SAMPLE ASSISTANT

A Slide Show Speech

As explained in the text, this speech on culture shock is designed to illustrate the general structure of a PowerPoint speech. The speech follows the sample outline discussed in Unit 16 on pages 329–331. The annotations point out specific features and some dos and don'ts.

Slide 1

Speech title

Have You Ever Been Culture Shocked?

This first slide introduces the topic with the title of the speech. Follow the general rules for titling your speech: Keep it short, provocative, and focused on your audience. If you put a graphic on this page, make sure that it doesn't detract from your title. What other graphics might work well here?

Slide 2

The thesis of the speech

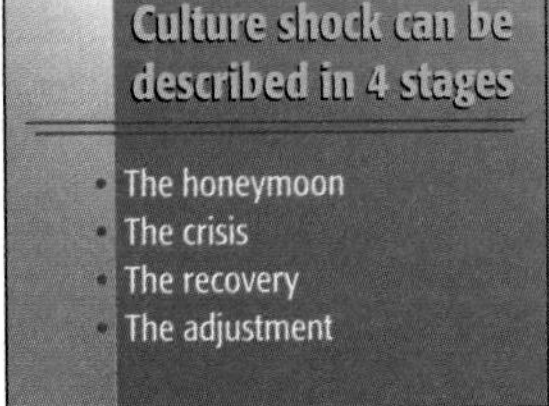

You may or may not want to identify your thesis directly right at the beginning of your speech. Consider the arguments for and against identifying your thesis—both cultural and strategic—and the suggestions for when and how to state the thesis on pages 299–300. As a listener, do you prefer it when speakers state their thesis right at the beginning? Or do you prefer it when the thesis is only implied and left for you to figure out?

Slide 3

Attention-getting device; corresponds to the Introduction's "I A"

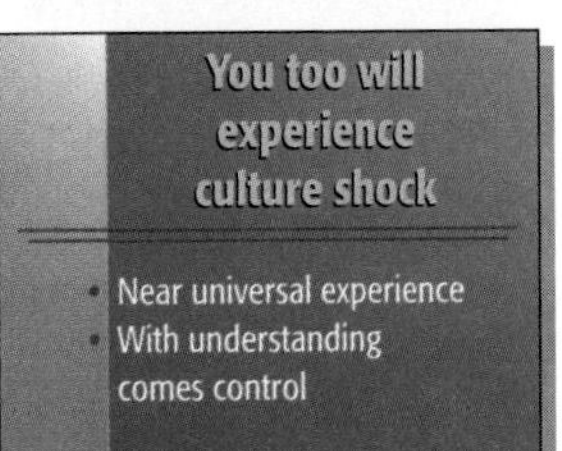

This slide gains attention by relating the topic directly to the audience; it answers the listener's obvious question, "Why should I listen to this speech?"

Slide 4

S-A-T connection; corresponds to the Introduction's "II A–B"

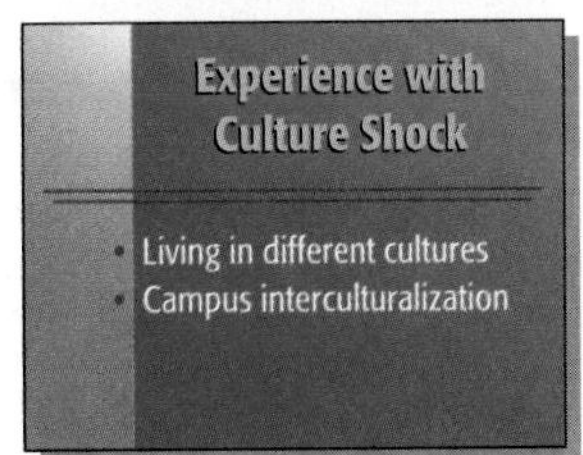

This slide connects the speaker, the audience, and the topic. Because you talk about yourself in this part of your speech, some speakers may prefer to eliminate a verbal slide and use a graphic or a photo. Another alternative is to include your S-A-T connection with the previous attention-getting slide.

Slide 5

Orientation; corresponds to the Introduction's "III A–D"

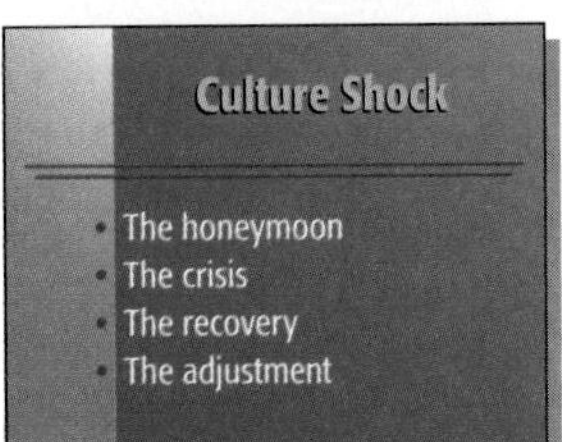

In this slide you give your orientation by identifying your main points. These four bullets will become your four main points.

Slide 6
First main point; corresponds to the Body's "I A"

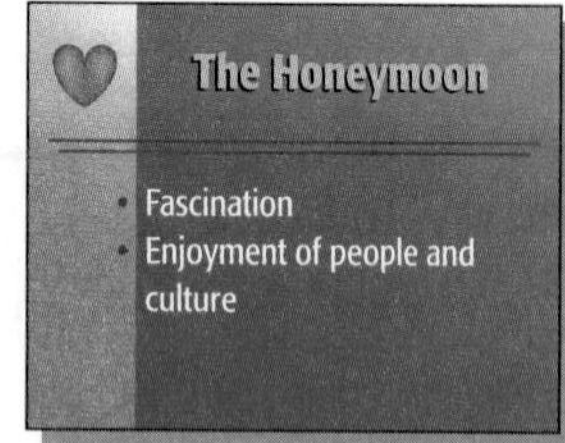

This is your first main point. You'd introduce it, perhaps, by saying, "The honeymoon occurs first." If you wanted your audience to keep track of the stage number, you could use numbers in your slide; for example, "1. The Honeymoon" or "Stage 1: The Honeymoon." The graphic of the heart is meant to associate culture shock with good times and a romancelike experience. As a listener, would you prefer that the speaker explain this graphic or say nothing about it?

Slide 7
Second main point; corresponds to the Body's "II A–B"

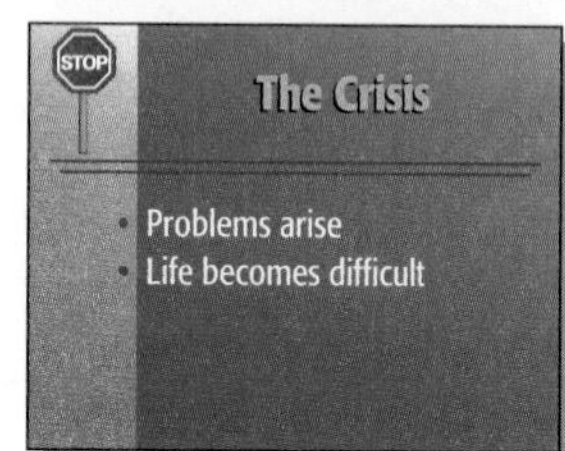

This is your second main point and follows the previous slide in format. Again, a graphic is used. Can you think of a better graphic?

Slide 8
Third main point; corresponds to the Body's "III A–B"

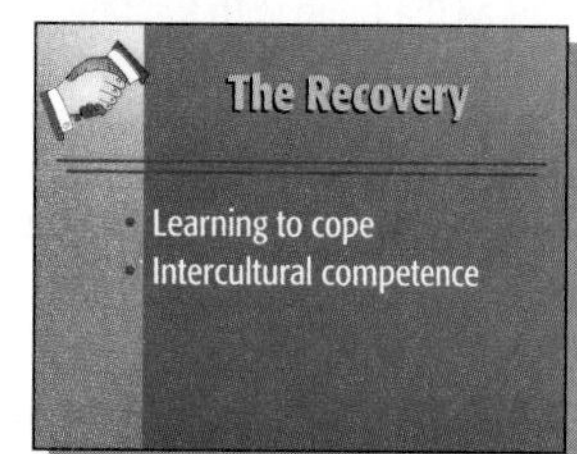

This is your third main point and again follows the format of the previous two slides.

Slide 9
Fourth main point; corresponds to the Body's "IV A–B"

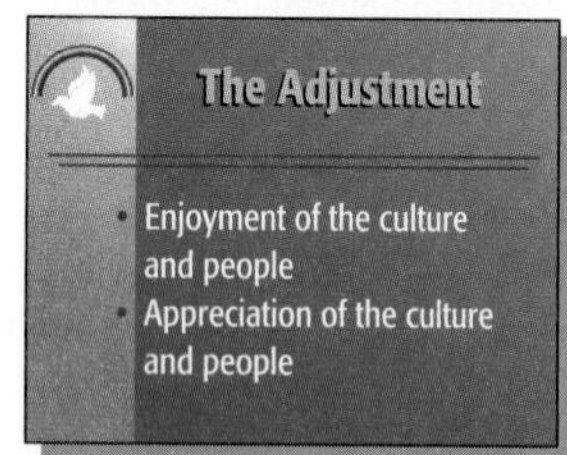

This is your fourth main point. As noted in the text, the sound of applause is programmed to come on with this slide, reinforcing the idea that we do adjust to this shock. Examine the sound effects you have available; what other sound effects would you use in this speech?

Slide 10
Summary; corresponds to the Conclusion's "I A–D"

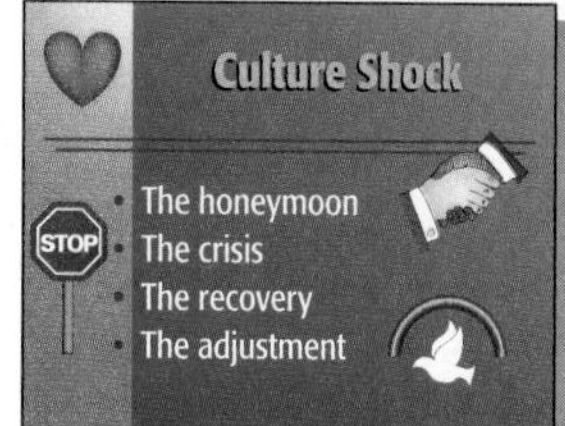

This is your summary of your four main points; notice that it's the same as your orientation (Slide 5). This slide violates the general rule to use graphics in moderation. What do you think of the repetition of graphics? Do you think they add reinforcement? Do they detract from the verbal message?

Slide 11
Motivation; corresponds to the Conclusion's "II A–B"

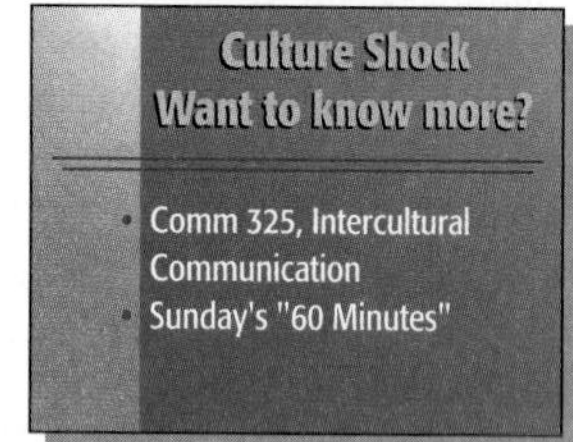

This part of the summary ideally motivates your listeners to pursue the topic in more detail.

Slide 12
Closure; corresponds to the Conclusion's "III"

This slide is intended to wrap up the speech—it contains the title and two graphics that will support the speaker's concluding statement: "By knowing about culture shock you'll be in a better position to deal with it at school and on the job." Notice that the conclusion is tied to the introduction by a similarity in font and text color; it helps signal that this is the last slide and the end of the speech.

Generally, consistency works best. Don't try to use too many different transitions in the same talk; it will detract attention from what you are saying. Generally, use the same transitions for all the slides in a single presentation. You might vary this a bit by, say, having the last slide introduced by a somewhat different transition; but any more variation is likely to work against the listeners' focusing on your message. In choosing transitions select one that's consistent with your speech purpose; don't use a frivolous black-and-yellow checkerboard transition in a speech on child abuse, for example.

Consider using sound effects with your transitions; but again, go easy. Overdoing it is sure to make your speech seem carelessly put together. In the slides in the Public Speaking Sample Assistant box, I programmed "applause" (one of the readily available sound effects) to come on as Slide 9—"The Adjustment"—comes on. As you read through the slides, you may find additional places where sound could be used effectively.

Build effects with bulleted items to focus your listeners' attention. For example, you can have each bulleted phrase fly from the top of the screen into its position; with the next mouse click, the second bullet flies into position. Or you can have your bullets slide in from right to left or from left to right, and so on.

In listing four or five bulleted items, consider the value of hiding or dimming the previous bullet as you introduce the next one. Making the previous bullet disappear or fade into a lighter color when the next bullet appears further enables you to focus your listeners' attention on exactly the point you're discussing. Do be careful that you allow the audience time to read each bullet; otherwise they'll be frustrated when it disappears.

Use the spell-checker. You don't want to show professional-looking slides with misspellings; it can ruin your credibility and seriously damage the impact of your speech.

Step 6: Organize Your Speech

When you organize your ideas, you derive a variety of benefits. First, organization will help you prepare the speech. For example, as you organize your speech you'll be able to see if you have adequately and fairly supported each of your main points and if you are devoting approximately equal time to each main idea. Organization also makes your speech easy to understand and remember. When you organize perhaps 30 pieces of specific information (such as statistics, statement of thesis, examples, illustrations, testimonials, transitions) into, say, three or four or five chunks, you're making it much easier for the audience to remember what you want them to remember. An added bonus here is that organization will also help you remember your speech. You'll be less likely to forget a carefully organized speech than you would a disorganized one. Organization will also contribute to your credibility. The audience is more likely to see the well-organized speaker as more competent, more knowledgeable, and more in control of the information in the speech.

Once you've identified the main points you wish to include in your speech, you need to devote attention to how you'll arrange these points in the body of your speech. When you follow a clearly identified organizational pattern, your listeners will be able to see your speech as a whole and will be able to grasp the connections and relationships among your various pieces of information. Should they have a momentary lapse in attention—as they surely will at some point in just about every speech—you will be able to refocus their attention.

Consider each of the following organizational patterns in terms of the topics to which it's most applicable and the ways in which you can arrange your main points and supporting materials. The introduction, conclusion, and transitions are considered in depth under Step 7 in this unit. The mechanical aspects of outlining and additional guidance in preparing the outline are presented in Unit 16. Additional help on organization may be found at the publisher's website for public speaking, whose home page appears on page 270, and in the Speaker's Workshop CD-ROM, available with this text.

Temporal Pattern

Organization on the basis of some temporal (time) relationship is a pattern listeners will find easy to follow. Generally, when you use a *temporal pattern*, you organize your speech into two, three, or four major parts, beginning with the past and working up to the present or the future—or beginning with the present or the future and working back to the past.

The temporal (sometimes called "chronological") pattern is especially appropriate for informative speeches in which you wish to describe events or processes that occur over time. It's also useful when you wish to tell a story, demonstrate how something works, or examine the steps involved in some process. The events leading up to the Civil War, the steps toward a college education, or the history of writing would all be appropriate for temporal patterning. A speech on the development of language in the child might be organized in a temporal pattern and could be broken down something like this:

I. Babbling occurs around the 5th month.
II. Lallation occurs around the 6th month.
III. Echolalia occurs around the 9th month.
IV. "Communication" occurs around the 12th month.

Spatial Pattern

You can also organize your main points on the basis of space. The *spatial pattern* is especially useful when you wish to describe objects or places. Like the temporal pattern, it's an organizational pattern that listeners will find easy to follow as you progress—from top to bottom, from left to right, from inside to outside, or from east to west, for example. The structure of a place, an object, or even an animal is easily placed into a spatial pattern. You might describe the layout of a hospital, a school, or a skyscraper, or perhaps even the structure of a dinosaur, with a spatial pattern of organization. Here's an example of an outline describing the structure of the traditional textbook and using a spatial pattern:

I. The front matter contains the preface and the table of contents.
II. The text proper contains the chapters or units.
III. The back matter contains the glossary, bibliography, and index.

Topical Pattern

When your topic conveniently divides itself into subdivisions, each of which is clear and approximately equal in importance, the *topical pattern* is most useful. A speech on important cities of the world might be organized into a topical pattern, as might be speeches on problems facing the college graduate, great works of literature, the world's major religions, and the like. The topical pattern would be an obvious one for organizing a speech on the powers of the government. The topic itself divides into three parts: legislative, executive, and judicial. A sample outline might look like this:

I. The legislative branch is controlled by Congress.
II. The executive branch is controlled by the president.
III. The judicial branch is controlled by the courts.

Problem-Solution Pattern

The *problem-solution pattern* is especially useful in persuasive speeches in which you want to convince the audience that a problem exists and that your solution would solve or lessen the problem. Let's say that you believe that jury awards for damages have gotten out of hand. You may want to persuade your audience, then, that jury awards for damages should be limited. A problem-solution pattern might be appropriate here. In the first part of your speech, you'd identify the problem(s) created by these large awards; in the second part, you'd propose the solution. A sample outline for such a speech might look something like this:

I. Jury awards for damages are out of control. [the general problem]
   A. These awards increase insurance rates. [a specific problem]
   B. These awards increase medical costs. [a second specific problem]
   C. These awards place unfair burdens on business. [a third specific problem]

II. Jury awards need to be limited. [the general solution]
   A. Greater evidence should be required before a case can be brought to trial. [a specific solution]
   B. Part of the award should be turned over to the state. [a second specific solution]
   C. Realistic estimates of financial damage must be used. [a third specific solution]

Cause-Effect/Effect-Cause Pattern

Similar to the problem-solution pattern is the cause-effect or effect-cause pattern. This pattern is useful in persuasive speeches in which you want to convince your audience of the causal connection existing between two events or elements. In the *cause-effect pattern* you divide the speech into two major sections: causes and effects. For example, a speech on the reasons for highway accidents or birth defects might lend itself to a cause-effect pattern. Here you might first consider, say, the causes of highway accidents or birth defects, then turn to some of the effects; for example, the number of deaths, the number of accidents, and so on.

Or suppose you wanted to demonstrate the causes for the increase in AIDS in your state. In this case you might use an effect-cause pattern that might look something like this:

I. AIDS is increasing. [general effect]
   A. AIDS is increasing among teenagers. [a specific effect]
   B. AIDS is increasing among IV drug users. [a second specific effect]
   C. AIDS is increasing among women. [a third specific effect]

II. Three factors contribute to this increase. [general causal statement]
   A. Teenagers are ignorant about how the HIV virus is transmitted. [a specific cause]
   B. IV drug users exchange contaminated needles. [a second specific cause]
   C. Women are not practicing safe sex. [a third specific cause]

As you can see from this example, this type of speech is often combined with the problem-solution type. For example, after identifying the causes, the speaker might then treat the causes as problems and offer solutions for each problem/cause (for example: education for teens, free needle exchange programs, and education for men and women).

The Motivated Sequence

The *motivated sequence* is an organizational pattern in which you arrange your information so as to motivate your audience to respond positively to your purpose (McKerrow, Gronbeck, Ehninger, & Monroe, 2000). In contrast to the previous organizational patterns, which provided ways of organizing the main ideas in the body of the speech, the motivated sequence is a pattern for organizing the entire speech. Here the speech (introduction, body, and conclusion) is divided into five parts or steps: (1) attention, (2) need, (3) satisfaction, (4) visualization, and (5) action.

1. The attention step makes the audience give you their undivided *attention*. If you execute this step effectively, your audience should be ready and eager to hear what you have to say.

ASK THE RESEARCHER

The Motivated Sequence

- *What's so special about the motivated sequence, and how can I use it in preparing to speak on the job?*

Alan Monroe originally adapted it from 1920s sales workshops he'd attended, when motivational psychology was all the rage. Since then, it's been thought about more as a convenient organizational form, but one that still makes motivational appeals central to persuasion: Unless I can make you *want* to act, you won't. Since the '20s, motivational psychology, thanks particularly to Professor David McClelland, has gotten more sophisticated, for he groups motivational appeals into three clusters: (1) affiliation (appeals to positive relationships with others), (2) achievement (appeals to individual success), and (3) power (appeals to dominance or defense). McClelland's work guides your selection of specific appeals for specific audiences, while the motivated sequences provides an easy-to-use organizational pattern for any speech. Get decision-makers' attention, convince them it's in their self-interest to listen, make your pitch, depict the results vividly, and clinch the deal—that's it! It works!

For further information: www.ablongman.com/german15e. On motivational psychology, see Hoyenga, K. B., & Hoyenga, H. (1984). *Motivational explanations of behavior: Psychological and cognitive ideas.* Monterey, CA: Brooks/Cole.

Bruce E. Gronbeck (Ph.D., University of Iowa) is A. Craig Baird Distinguished Professor of Public Address. As director of the University of Iowa Center for Media Studies and Political Culture, he studies the impact of television and the Internet on political public address. Every four years, he becomes one of the national experts on the Iowa caucuses, doing newspaper, radio, and television interviews on presidential candidates' performances (bruce-gronbeck@uiowa.edu).

UNDERSTANDING *THEORY* AND *RESEARCH*

Culture and Speech Organization

Members of low-context cultures (see Unit 3) are usually direct in their messages and appreciate directness in others. But directness may be unnecessary or even insulting to the high-context cultural member. Conversely, the indirectness of the high-context member may appear vague or even dishonest to a low-context member.

High-context cultures prefer indirectness. Speakers in Japan, to take one well-researched example, need to be careful lest they make their point too obvious or too direct and insult the audience. Speakers in Japan are expected to lead their listeners to the conclusion through example, illustration, and various other indirect means (Lustig & Koester, 2003). In contrast, in the United States (a low-context culture) speakers are encouraged to be explicit and direct—to tell the listeners, for example, exactly what the speaker wants them to do.

Another cultural difference influences how focused the speech ought to be. For example, in the United States, each main point of a speech or written composition should be developed by itself. Only when one point is fully developed and finalized does the speaker or writer move on to the next. Hindi culture, however, is less rigid and allows for many ideas' being considered in the same paragraph of an essay or in the same part of a speech (Lustig & Koester, 2003).

Working with Theories and Research

- *As a listener, what type of organization do you prefer? For example, do you prefer a speaker who is direct or indirect? Do you prefer speakers who clearly separate the main points or who consider several points together?*

You can gain audience attention through a variety of means; examples include, asking a question (rhetorical or actual) or making reference to audience members. These methods are presented in the "Introduction" discussion in the Step 7 section of this unit.

2. In the second part of your speech, you establish that a *need* exists for some kind of change. The audience should feel that something has to be learned or something has to be done because of this demonstrated need.
3. You satisfy the need by presenting the answer or the solution to the need you demonstrated in step 2 of the motivated sequence. On the basis of this *satisfaction* step, the audience should now believe that what you are informing them about or persuading them to do will satisfy the need.
4. *Visualization* intensifies the audience's feelings or beliefs. In this step you take the people in the audience beyond the present time and place and enable them to imagine the situation as it would be if the need were satisfied as you suggested in step 3. You might, for example, demonstrate the benefits that people would receive if your ideas were put into operation—or perhaps demonstrate the negative effects that people would suffer if your plan were not put into operation.
5. Tell the audience what *action* they should take to ensure that the need (step 2) is satisfied (step 3) as visualized (step 4). Here you want to move the audience in a particular direction—for example, to contribute free time to read to the blind. You can accomplish this step by stating what the audience members should do, using a variety of supporting materials and logical, emotional, and ethical appeals.

Unit 18 will discuss the use of the motivated sequence in persuasive speeches and Table 18.1 (pages 392–393) offers a useful summary of the essential characteristics of this important organizational strategy.

Additional Organizational Patterns

The six patterns just considered are the most common and the most useful for organizing most public

VIEWPOINT

You're to give a speech to your coworkers on the need to establish a day care center at work for parents who have no means to hire people to take care of their children while they work. You want to use the motivated sequence. How would you gain attention? Establish the need? Satisfy the need? Visualize the problem solved? Ask for action?

speeches. But there are other patterns that might be appropriate for different topics:

Structure-Function. The *structure-function pattern* is well suited to informative speeches in which you want to discuss how something is constructed (its structural aspects) and what it does (its functional aspects). This pattern might be useful, for example, in a speech to explain what an organization is and what it does, the parts of a university and how they operate, or the sensory systems of the body and their various functions. This pattern also might be useful in a discussion of the nature of a living organism: its anatomy (that is, its structures) and its physiology (that is, its functions).

Comparison and Contrast. Arranging your material in a *comparison-and-contrast pattern* is useful in informative speeches in which you want to analyze, for example, two different theories, proposals, departments, or products in terms of their similarities and differences. In this type of speech you would be concerned not only with explaining each theory or proposal but also with clarifying how they're similar and how they're different.

Pro and Con, Advantages and Disadvantages. The *pro-and-con pattern,* sometimes called the advantages-disadvantages pattern, works well in informative speeches in which you want to explain objectively the advantages (pros) and the disadvantages (cons) of, say, a plan, method, or product.

Claim and Proof. The *claim-and-proof pattern* is especially appropriate in a persuasive speech in which you want to prove the truth or usefulness of a particular proposition. It's the pattern that you see frequently in trials: The prosecution claims that the defendant is guilty and that the proof is the varied evidence—for example, evidence that the defendant had a motive, the defendant had the opportunity, and the defendant had no alibi. In this pattern your speech would consist of two major parts. In the first part you'd explain your claim (tuition must not be raised, library hours must be expanded, courses in Caribbean studies must be instituted). In the second part you'd offer your evidence or proof as to why, for example, tuition must not be raised.

Multiple Definition. The *multiple-definition pattern* is often helpful for explaining specific concepts: What is a born-again Christian? What is a scholar? What is multiculturalism? In this pattern each major heading consists of a different type of definition or way of looking at the concept. A variety of definition types are discussed in Unit 17.

Who? What? Why? Where? When? The *5W pattern* is the pattern of the journalist and is useful when you wish to report or explain an event such as a robbery, political coup, war, ceremony, or trial. In this pattern you'd have five major parts to the body of your speech, each dealing with the answers to one of these five questions.

Step 7: Construct Your Introduction, Conclusion, and Transitions

Now that you have the body of your speech organized, devote your attention to the introduction, conclusion, and transitions that will hold the parts of your speech together.

Introduction

Begin collecting suitable material for your *introduction* as you prepare the entire speech, but wait until all the other parts are completed before you put the introduction together. In this way you'll be better able to determine which elements should be included and which should be eliminated.

Together with your general appearance and your nonverbal messages, the introduction gives your audience its first impression of you and your speech. Your introduction sets the tone for the rest of the speech; it tells your listeners what kind of a speech they'll hear.

Your introduction should serve three functions: It should (1) gain attention, (2) establish a speaker-audience-topic connection, and (3) orient the audience as to what is to follow. Let's look at each of these functions and at the ways you can serve these functions.

Gain Attention

In your introduction, gain the attention of your audience and focus it on your speech topic. (Then, of course, maintain that attention throughout your speech.) You can secure attention in numerous ways; here are just a few of them.

- Ask a question. Questions are effective because they are a change from declarative statements and call for an active response from listeners.
- Refer to audience members. Talking about the audience makes them perk up and pay attention, because you are involving them directly in your talk.
- Refer to recent happenings. Citing a previous speech, recent event, or prominent person currently making news helps you gain attention, because the audience is familiar with this current event and will pay attention to see how you are going to connect it to your speech topic.
- Use humor. A clever (and appropriate) anecdote is often useful in holding attention.
- Use an illustration or dramatic story. Much as we are drawn to soap operas, so are we drawn to illustrations and stories about people.
- Stress the importance of the topic. People pay attention to what they feel is important to them and ignore what seems unimportant or irrelevant. If your topic focuses on the interests of the audience, you might begin by referring directly to the audience.
- Use a presentation aid. Presentation aids are valuable because they are new and different. They engage our senses and thus our attention.
- Tell the audience to pay attention. A simple, "I want you to listen to this frightening statistic," or "I want you to pay particularly close attention to . . . ," used once or twice in a speech, will help gain audience attention.
- Use a quotation. Quotations are useful because the audience is likely to pay attention to the brief and clever remarks of someone they've heard of or read about. Do make sure, however, that the quotation relates directly to your topic.
- Cite a little-known fact or statistic. Little-known facts or statistics will help perk up an audience's attention. For example, headlines on unemployment statistics, crime in the schools, and political corruption sell newspapers because they gain attention.

Establish a Speaker-Audience-Topic Relationship

In addition to gaining attention, your introduction should establish connections among yourself as the speaker, the audience members, and your topic. Try to answer your listeners' inevitable question: Why should we listen to you speak on this topic? You can establish an effective speaker-audience-topic or S-A-T relationship in many different ways.

- Refer to others present. Not only will this help you to gain attention; it will also help you to establish a bond with the audience.
- Refer to the occasion. Often your speech will be connected directly with the occasion. By referring to the reason the audience has gathered, you can establish a connection between yourself, the audience, and the topic.
- Express your pleasure or interest in speaking.
- Establish your competence in the subject. Show the audience that you are really interested in and knowledgeable about the topic.
- Compliment the audience. Pay the people in the audience an honest and sincere compliment, and they will not only give you their attention but will also feel a part of your speech. In some cultures—those of Japan and Korea are good examples—the speaker is expected to compliment the

MEDIA WATCH

Public Relations Strategies

The field of public relations—communications designed to establish positive relationships between a corporation, agency, or similar group and the public—is very similar to advertising. Like advertising, public relations has two major purposes: informing and persuading, with a clear emphasis on the latter (Folkerts & Lacy, 2001; Rodman 2001). To accomplish these two purposes, public relations practitioners engage in a wide variety of activities:

- *Lobbying* to influence government officials or agencies to fund proposals, support nominees, or vote for or against upcoming bills.
- *Raising funds* for colleges, political candidates, charities, or public broadcasting stations.
- *Controlling crises* in an effort to repair potentially damaged images in cases of defective or problematic products—whether cars, dietary supplements, drugs, or an organization's financial problems.
- *Influencing public opinion* about, for example, political candidates or initiatives or current issues—abortion, campaign financing, gay rights, or any of a host of other issues that are in the news every day.
- *Establishing good relationships* between, say, a community and a company that wants to erect a mall in the neighborhood, between a community and its police department, or between a company and the general public. Microsoft's donations to public education and to health organizations and the numerous companies that support AIDS and cancer research, literacy programs, college scholarships, and safe driving are good examples.

To get a better view of public relations, take a look at a variety of websites dealing with this area. Try, for example, www.prsa.org (the Public Relations Society of America, a professional accrediting agency), www.prwatch.org (the Center for Media and Democracy, an organization that monitors public relations efforts), and www.bm.com (Burson-Marsteller, currently the largest public relations firm in the United States). What can you learn about public relations from these websites?

You and the Media

Visualize yourself as a public relations professional whose job it is to raise funds for your college. What kinds of supporting materials would you use in, say, letters that you send to alumni? Or suppose you are in PR and your job is to reduce mistrust between a community and its police department. What kinds of supporting materials would you use in a speech to new police recruits? In a speech to community leaders?

audience. It's one of the essential parts of the introduction. Visitors from the United States who are speaking in a foreign country are often advised to compliment the country itself, its beauty, its culture.

- Express similarities with the audience. By stressing your own similarity with members of the audience, you create a relationship with them and become an "insider" instead of an "outsider."

Orient the Audience

The introduction should orient the audience in some way as to what is to follow in the body of the speech. Preview for the audience what you are going to say, as in "Tonight I'm going to discuss nuclear waste"; give a detailed preview, perhaps outlining your major propositions; or identify your goal by, for example, stating your thesis.

Conclusion

Your conclusion is especially important, because it's often the part of the speech that the audience remembers most clearly. It's your conclusion that in many cases determines what image of you is left in the minds of the audience. Devote special attention to this brief but crucial part of your speech. Let your conclusion serve three major functions: to (1) summarize, (2) motivate, and (3) provide closure.

Summarize

The *summary* function is particularly important in an informative speech, less so in persuasive speeches or in speeches to entertain. You may summarize your speech in a variety of ways:

- Restate your thesis or purpose. In this type of brief summary, you restate the essential thrust of your speech, repeating your thesis or perhaps the goals you hoped to achieve.
- Restate the importance of the topic. Tell the audience again why your topic or thesis is so important.
- Restate your main points. That is, restate both your thesis and the major points you used to support it.

Motivate

A second function of the conclusion—most appropriate in persuasive speeches—is to motivate the people in the audience to do what you want them to do. In your conclusion you have the opportunity to give the audience one final push in the direction you wish them to take. Whether it's to buy stock, vote a particular way, or change an attitude, you can use the conclusion for a final *motivation,* a final appeal. Here are two excellent ways to motivate:

- Ask for a specific response. Specify what you want the audience to do after listening to your speech.
- Provide directions for future action. Spell out, most often in general terms, the direction you wish the audience to take.

Close

The third function of your conclusion is to provide *closure*. Often your summary will accomplish this, but in some instances it will prove insufficient. End your speech with a conclusion that is crisp and definite. Make the audience know that you have definitely and clearly ended. Some kind of wrap-up, some sort of final statement, is helpful in providing this feeling of closure. You may achieve closure through a variety of methods:

- Use a quotation. A quotation is often an effective means of providing closure.
- Refer to subsequent events. You may also achieve closure by referring to future events—events taking place either that day or soon afterwards.
- Refer back to the introduction. It's sometimes useful to connect your conclusion with your introduction.
- Pose a challenge or question. You may close your speech by leaving the audience with a provocative question to ponder or a challenge to consider. Or, you can pose a question and answer it by recapping your thesis and perhaps some of your major arguments or propositions.
- Thank the audience. Speakers frequently conclude their speeches by thanking the audience for their attention or for their invitation to address them.

Transitions

Transitions are words, phrases, or sentences that connect the various parts of your speech. They provide

BUILDING COMMUNICATION SKILLS

Constructing Conclusions and Introductions

Prepare a conclusion and an introduction to a hypothetical speech on one of the topics listed below, making sure that in your conclusion you (a) review the speech's main points and (b) provide closure and that in your introduction you (a) gain attention and (b) orient the audience. Be prepared to explain the methods you used to accomplish each of these functions.

1. Proficiency in a foreign language should be required of all college graduates.
2. All killing of wild animals should be declared illegal.
3. Suicide and its assistance by qualified medical personnel should be legalized.
4. Gambling should be legalized by all states.
5. Maximum sentences should be imposed for hate crimes.
6. Alcoholic beverages should be banned from campus.

the audience with guideposts that help them follow the development of your thoughts and arguments. Use transitions in at least the following places:

- between the introduction and the body of the speech
- between the body and the conclusion
- between the main points in the body of the speech

Here are the major transitional functions and some stylistic devices that you might use to serve these functions.

To announce the start of a major proposition or piece of evidence: First, . . . , A second argument . . . , A closely related problem . . . , If you want further evidence, look at . . . , Next . . . , Consider also . . . , An even more compelling argument . . . , My next point . . . .

To signal that you're drawing a conclusion from previously given evidence and argument: Thus, . . . , Therefore, . . . , So, as you can see . . . , It follows, then, that . . . .

To alert the audience to your introduction of a qualification or exception: But, . . . , However, also consider . . . .

To remind listeners of what has just been said and of its connection with another issue that will now be considered: In contrast to . . . ; Consider also . . . ; Not only . . . but also . . . ; In addition to . . . we also need to look at . . . ; Not only should we . . . , we should also . . . .

To signal the part of your speech you're approaching: By way of introduction . . . ; In conclusion . . . ; Now, let's discuss why we're here today . . . ; So, what's the solution? What should we do?

To signal your organizational structure: I'll first explain the problems with jury awards and then propose a workable solution.

To summarize what you've already discussed. Consider using a special kind of transition: the internal summary. It's a statement that usually summarizes some major subdivision of your speech. Incorporate several internal summaries into your speech—perhaps working them into the transitions connecting, say, the major parts of your speech. An internal summary that also serves as a transition might look something like this:

> Inadequate recreational facilities, poor schooling, and a lack of adequate role models seem to be the major problems facing our youngsters. Each of these, however, can be remedied and even eliminated. Here's what we can do.

This brief passage reminds listeners of what they've just heard and previews what they'll hear next. The clear connection in their minds will fill in any gaps that may have been created through inattention, noise, and the like.

You can enhance your transitions by pausing between your transition and the next part of your speech. This will help the audience realize that a new part of your speech is coming. You might also take a step forward or to the side after saying your transition. This will also help to reinforce the movement from one part of your speech to another.

Mistakes in Introductions, Conclusions, and Transitions

In addition to understanding the principles of effective pubic speaking, it often helps to become aware of common mistakes. Here, then, are some of the common mistakes you'll want to avoid.

In your introduction:

- Don't apologize (generally). In the United States and western Europe, an apology may be seen as an excuse and so is to be avoided. In certain other cultures (those of Japan, China, and Korea are good examples), however, speakers are expected

VIEWPOINT

What do you think is the single most important principle for preparing and delivering a public speech? What is the mistake people make most frequently in public speaking?

to begin with an apology. It's a way of complimenting the audience.

- Avoid promising something you won't deliver. The speaker who promises to tell you how to make a fortune in the stock market or how to be the most popular person on campus (and fails to deliver such insight) quickly loses credibility.
- Avoid gimmicks that gain attention but are irrelevant to the speech or inconsistent with your treatment of the topic. For example, slamming a book on the desk or telling a joke that bears no relation to your speech may accomplish the limited goal of gaining attention, but quickly the audience will see that they've been fooled, and they'll resent it.
- Don't introduce your speech with ineffective statements such as "I'm really nervous, but here goes" or "Before I begin my talk, I want to say . . . ." These statements will make your audience uncomfortable and will encourage them to focus on your delivery rather than on your message.

In your conclusion:

- Don't introduce new material. Instead, use your conclusion to reinforce what you've already said and to summarize.
- Don't dilute your position. Avoid being critical of your own material or your presentation. Saying, for example, "The information I presented is probably dated, but it was all I could find" or "I hope I wasn't too nervous" will detract from the credibility you've tried to establish.
- Don't drag out your conclusion. End crisply.

In your transitions:

- Avoid too many or too few transitions. Either extreme can cause problems. Use transitions to help your listeners, who will hear the speech only once, to understand the structure of your speech.
- Avoid transitions that are out of proportion to the speech parts they connect. If you want to connect the two main points of your speech, you need something more than just "and" or "the next point." In contrast, if you want to connect two brief examples, then a simple "another example occurs when . . ." will do.

ON ETHICS

Communicating in Cyberspace

Because of the explosion in computer communication, nethics (the ethics of Internet communication) has become an important part of ethical communication. Of course, the same principles that govern ethical public speaking should also prevail when you communicate on the Internet. Here, however, are a few ethical principles with special relevance to computer communication. It is unethical to:

- Invade the privacy of others. Reading the files of another person or breaking into files that you're not authorized to read is unethical.
- Harm others or their property. Creating computer viruses; publishing instructions for making bombs; and creating websites that promote sexism, racism, ageism, or heterosexism are some examples of unethical computer use.
- Spread falsehoods. Lying on the Internet—about other people, the powers of medical or herbal treatment, or yourself—is just as unethical as it is in other forms of communication.
- Plagiarize. Appropriating the work of another as your own—whether the original work appeared on the Internet or in a book or journal—is unethical.
- Steal passwords, PINs, or authorization codes that belong to others.
- Copy software programs that you haven't paid for.

WHAT WOULD YOU DO? As an experiment, you develop a computer virus that can destroy websites. Recently you've come across a variety of websites that market child pornography. You wonder if you can ethically destroy these websites. Indeed, you wonder if not destroying them is actually more unethical than using your newly developed virus. What do you decide to do?

SUMMARY

This unit covered ways of supporting and organizing your main thoughts and introducing and concluding your speech.

1. Formulate the thesis of the speech. Develop your major propositions by asking relevant questions about this thesis.
2. Reinforce your main points with a variety of materials that support them. Suitable supporting materials include examples, narratives, testimony, statistics, and presentation aids as well as such devices as quotations, definitions, comparisons, statements of facts, and repetition and restatement.

3. Among the presentation aids you might consider are the actual object, models of the object, graphs, word charts, maps, people, photographs and illustrations, and tapes and CDs. These can be presented with a variety of media; for example, the chalkboard, chartboards, flip charts, slides and transparency projections, videotapes, and handouts. Presentation aids work best when they add clarity to your speech, are appealing to listeners, and are culturally sensitive.
4. Computer-assisted presentations such as PowerPoint, which have become extremely popular, allow you to communicate lots of information in an interesting format, to print handouts to coordinate with your speech, and to create an outline and speaker's notes for your speech.
5. Organize the speech materials into a clear, easily identifiable thought pattern. Suitable organizing principles include temporal, spatial, topical, problem–solution, cause–effect/effect–cause, motivated sequence, structure–function, comparison-and-contrast, pro-and-con, claim-and-proof, multiple-definition, and who-what-why-where-when (5W) patterns.
6. Introductions should gain attention, establish a speaker–audience–topic (S-A-T) connection, and orient the audience as to what is to follow.
7. Conclusions should summarize the main ideas, provide a final motivation, and provide a crisp closing to the speech.
8. Transitions and internal summaries help connect and integrate the parts of the speech; they also help the listeners to better remember the speech.

KEY TERMS

thesis
proposition
example
narrative
testimony
statistics
presentation aid
temporal pattern
spatial pattern
topical pattern
problem–solution pattern
cause–effect pattern
motivated sequence
structure–function pattern
pro-and-con pattern
claim-and-proof pattern
comparison-and-contrast pattern
multiple-definition pattern
5W pattern
attention
speaker–audience–topic connection
orientation
summary
motivation
closure
transitions

THINKING CRITICALLY ABOUT

Supporting and Organizing a Public Speech

1. What strategies of arrangement would you use if you were giving a pro-choice speech to a pro-life audience? What strategies would you use if you were giving a speech in favor of domestic partnership insurance to the assembled leaders of various gay rights organizations?
2. Jamie, a student at a community college in Texas, wants to give a speech on the cruelty of cockfighting. Most people in the predominantly Hispanic audience come from Mexico, where cockfighting is a legal and popular sport. Among the visuals Jamie is considering are extremely vivid photographs of cocks literally torn to shreds by their opponents, which have razor blades strapped to their feet. Would you advise Jamie to use these photographs if the listeners were, say, moderately in favor of cockfighting? What if they were moderately against cockfighting? What general principle underlies your recommendations?
3. Visit one of the websites for quotations, for example, try: www.bartleby.com or http://us.imdb.com/ (a database of quotations from films). Select a quotation suitable for use with the slide show of the speech on culture shock in the Public Speaking Sample Assistant box on pages 311–312, and explain how you would use this on a new slide or on one of the 12 presented in the box.
4. Shana wants to illustrate the rise and fall in the prices of 12 stocks over the last 10 years. She wants to show that her investment club (an audience of 16 members who are active participants in

the club's investments) should sell 3 of the stocks and keep the other 9. This is the first time Shana will be using visual aids and she needs advice on what types of aids might best serve her purpose. What suggestions do you have for Shana?

5. Dave wants to set up a system of folders so he can conveniently store all the information he collects for his next three speeches, all of which will be built around the general topic of suicide. The first speech will deal with cultural views of suicide, the second will examine the current laws governing doctor-assisted suicides, and the third will be a persuasive speech on doctor-assisted suicides. Dave wants to store all his outlines, research, speech critique forms, and anything else in a series of folders, which he's heard about but doesn't really know how to use. What advice can you give Dave to help him organize his speech folders? (The assumption here is that these are computer "folders," but physical folders also would work, though not as efficiently.)

6. Prepare and deliver a two-minute speech in which you do any one of the following:

   - explain how you'd outline a speech on the geography of the United States, the structure of a table lamp, the need for improved sex education on campus, or why class members should contribute to UNICEF
   - tell a personal story to illustrate a specific point, being sure to follow the suggestions offered in this unit
   - explain a print ad that relies on statistics and show how the advertiser uses statistics to make a point
   - select an advertisement and analyze it in terms of the motivated sequence
   - describe the events portrayed in a recently seen television program, using a temporal pattern
   - discuss a recent newspaper editorial or op-ed letter, using a problem–solution or cause–effect pattern
   - explain how television commercials get your attention
   - describe the introductions and conclusions used on television talk shows or on news programs
   - explain a print ad that contains a visual and explain how the visual and the text complement each other

UNIT

16

Style and Delivery in Public Speaking

UNIT CONTENTS

Here the last three steps in public speaking are discussed. In this unit you'll learn

- the principles of outlining, style, and rehearsal and delivery
- how you can outline your speech so that an audience can easily follow it and remember it, word it for clarity and persuasiveness, and rehearse and deliver it for maximum impact

Step 8: Outline Your Speech

The *outline* is a blueprint for your speech; it lays out the elements of the speech and their relationship to one another. With this blueprint in front of you, you can see at a glance all the elements of organization—the functions of the introduction and conclusion, the transitions, the main points and their relationship to the thesis and purpose, and the adequacy of the supporting materials. And, like a blueprint for a building, the outline enables you to spot weaknesses that might otherwise go undetected.

Begin outlining when you first begin constructing your speech. In this way you'll take the best advantage of one of the major functions of an outline—to tell you where change is needed. Change and alter the outline as necessary at every stage of the speech construction process.

Outlines may be extremely detailed or extremely general. But because you're now in a learning environment whose objective is to make you a more proficient public speaker, a detailed full-sentence outline will serve best. The more detail you put into the outline, the easier it will be for you to examine the parts of the speech for all the qualities and characteristics that make a speech effective.

Constructing the Outline

After you've completed your research and mapped out an organizational plan for your speech, put this plan (this blueprint) on paper. Construct a "preparation outline" of your speech, using the following guidelines.

Preface the Outline with Identifying Data. Before you begin the outline proper, identify the general and specific purposes as well as your thesis. This prefatory material should look something like this:

Title: What Media Do

General Purpose: To inform.

Specific Purpose: To inform my audience of four major functions of the mass media.

Thesis: The mass media serve four major functions.

These identifying notes are not part of your speech proper. They're not, for example, mentioned in your oral presentation. Rather, they're guides to the preparation of the speech and the outline. They're like road signs to keep you going in the right direction and to signal when you've gone off course. One additional bit of identifying data should preface the preface: the title of your speech.

Outline the Introduction, Body, and Conclusion as Separate Units. The introduction, body, and conclusion of the speech, although intimately connected, should be labeled separately and should be kept distinct in your outline. Like the preliminary identifying data, these labels are not spoken to the audience but are further guides to your preparation.

By keeping the introduction, body, and conclusion separate, you'll be able to see at a glance if they do in fact serve the functions you want them to serve. You'll be able to see where further amplification and support are needed. In short, you'll be able to see where there are problems and where repair is necessary.

At the same time, do make sure that you examine and see the speech as a whole—how the introduction leads to the body and the conclusion summarizes your propositions and brings your speech to a close.

Insert Transitions. Insert [using square brackets, like these] transitions between the introduction and the body, the body and the conclusion, the main points of the body, and wherever else you think they might be useful.

Append a List of References. Some instructors require that you append a list of references to your speeches. If this is requested, then do so at the end of the outline or on a separate page. Some instructors require that only sources cited in the speech be included in the list of references, whereas others require that the full list of sources consulted be provided (those mentioned in the speech as well as those not mentioned).

Your research and references will prove most effective with your audience if you carefully integrate them into the speech. It will count for little if you consulted the latest works by the greatest authorities but never mention this to your audience. So, when appropriate, weave into your speech the source

GOING *ONLINE*

The Douglass Website

http://douglassarchives.org

Visit the Douglass website, a great collection of speeches. For a variety of speeches and speaker resources visit http://speeches.com/index.shtml. You can also listen to (and read) selected speeches of U.S. presidents at www.ipl.org/ref/POTUS. What resources do these websites contain that might be of value to you in learning public speaking?

In addition, visit the companion website for this text (www.ablongman.com/devito). It contains 13 skeletal outlines to help you organize a wide variety of speeches, and there are extended discussions of "Oral and Written Style," "Making Your Speech Easy to Remember," "Humor in Public Speaking," and "Using Visual Aspects to Reflect Your Organization." Exercises include "Organizing a Scrambled Outline," "Rephrasing Clichés," "Making Concepts Specific," "Undertaking a Long-Term Delivery Improvement Program," and "Communicating Vocally but Nonverbally."

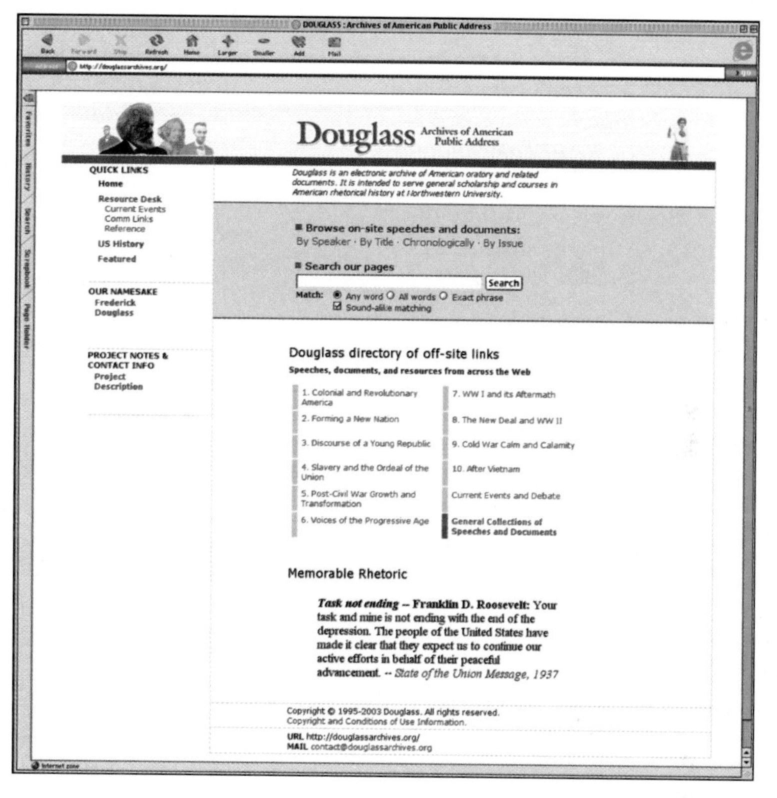

material you've consulted. In your outline, refer to the source material by author's name, date, and page in parentheses and then provide the complete citation in your list of references.

In your actual speech a source citation might be phrased something like this:

> According to John Naisbitt, author of the nationwide best-seller *Megatrends,* the bellwether states are California, Florida, Washington, Colorado, and Connecticut.

Regardless of what specific sourcing system is required (find out before you prepare your outline), make certain to include all sources of information, not just written materials. Personal interviews, information derived from course lectures, and data learned from television should all be included in your list of references.

Use a Consistent Set of Symbols. The following is the standard, accepted sequence of symbols for outlining:

I.
  A.
    1.
      a.
        (1)
          (a)

Begin the introduction, the body, and the conclusion with Roman numeral I. Treat each of the three major parts as a complete unit.

Use Visual Aspects to Reflect the Organizational Pattern. Use proper and clear indentation. The outlining function of word-processing programs has many of these suggestions built into them.

Not this:

I. Television caters to the lowest possible intelligence.
II. Talk shows illustrate this.
III. *General Hospital*

This:

Television caters to the lowest possible intelligence.
 A. Talk shows illustrate this.
  1. *Montel*
  2. *The Ricki Lake Show*
  3. *The Jerry Springer Show*
 B. Soap operas illustrate this.
  1. *As the World Turns*
  2. *General Hospital*
  3. *The Young and the Restless*

Use One Discrete Idea per Symbol. If your outline is to reflect the organizational pattern structuring the various items of information, use just one discrete idea per symbol. Compound sentences are sure giveaways that you have not limited each item to a single idea. Also, be sure that each item is discrete; that is, that it does not overlap with any other item. Instead of the overlapping "Education might be improved if teachers were better trained and if students were better motivated," break this statement into two propositions: "I. Education would be improved if teachers were better trained" and "II. Education would be improved if students were better motivated."

Use Complete Declarative Sentences. Phrase your ideas in the outline in complete declarative sentences rather than as questions or as phrases. This will further assist you in examining the essential relationships. It's much easier, for example, to see if one item of information supports another if both are phrased in the declarative mode. If one is a question and one is a statement, this will be more difficult.

Sample Outlines

Now that the principles of outlining are clear, let's look at some specific examples to illustrate how those principles are put into operation in specific outlines. We'll look first at preparation outlines with two different organizational patterns; then at a skeletal outline, a kind of template for a speech outline; and finally at a delivery outline, the type of outline you might take with you when you deliver your speech.

The Preparation Outline

Two *preparation outlines* are presented in the Public Speaking Sample Assistant boxes on pages 329–333. One uses a topical organizational pattern, perhaps the most common pattern among public speeches; the other uses the motivated sequence, an extremely popular pattern both for informative talks (see Unit 17) and for persuasive speeches (see Unit 18).

These full-sentence outlines are similar to the written materials you might prepare in constructing your own speeches. The side notes in the boxes are designed to clarify both the content and the format of full-sentence outlines.

The Skeletal Outline

Here's a *skeletal outline*—a kind of template for structuring a speech. This particular outline would be appropriate for a speech using a temporal, spatial, or topical organization pattern. Note that in this skeletal outline there are three main points (I, II, and III in the body). These correspond to the III A, B, and C in the introduction (where you'd orient the audience) and to the I A, B, and C in the conclusion (where you'd summarize your main points. Once again, the transitions are signaled by square brackets. As you review this outline, the phrases printed in light ink will remind you of the functions of each outline item.

Title: ______.

General Purpose: your general aim (to inform, to persuade, to entertain) ______.

Specific Purpose: what you hope to achieve from this speech ______.

Thesis: your main assertion; the core of your speech ______.

Introduction

I. gain attention ______.

II. establish S-A-T connection ______.

III. orient audience ______.

 A. first main point; same as I in body ______.

 B. second main point; same as II in body ______.

 C. third main point; same as III in body ______.

[Transition: connect the introduction to the body]

(outline continues on page 331)

THE *PUBLIC SPEAKING* SAMPLE ASSISTANT

A Preparation Outline (Topical Organization)

This sample illustrates how an outline using a topical organizational pattern might look. This is the preparation outline from which the PowerPoint slides shown in the Public Speaking Sample Assistant box in Unit 15 (pages 311–312) were developed.

Have You Ever Been Culture Shocked?

General Purpose: To inform.

Specific Purpose: To inform my audience of the four phases of culture shock.

Thesis: Culture shock can be described in four stages.

Note the general format for the outline; note that the headings are clearly labeled and that the indenting helps you to see clearly the relationship that one item bears to the other. For example, in Introduction II, the outline format helps you to see that A and B are explanations (amplification, support) for II.

Generally the title, general and specific purposes, and thesis of the speech are prefaced to the outline. When the outline is an assignment that is to be handed in, additional information may be requested.

Introduction

Note that the introduction, body, and conclusion are clearly labeled and separated visually.

I. Many of you have experienced or will experience culture shock.
   A. Many people experience culture shock, that reaction to being in a culture very different from what you were used to.
   B. By understanding culture shock, you'll be in a better position to deal with it if and when it comes.

The speaker assumes that the audience knows the general nature of culture shock and so does not go into detail as to its definition. But, just in case some audience members don't know and to refresh the memory of others, the speaker includes a brief definition.

II. I've always been interested in the way in which people adapt to different cultures.
   A. I've lived in four different cultures myself.
   B. With our own campus becoming more culturally diverse every semester, the process of culture shock becomes important for us all.

Here the speaker attempts to connect the speaker, audience, and topic by stressing intercultural experiences and an abiding interest in the topic. Also, the speaker makes the topic important to the audience by referring to their everyday surroundings.

III. Culture shock occurs in four stages (Oberg, 1960).
   A. The Honeymoon occurs first.
   B. The Crisis occurs second.
   C. The Recovery occurs third.
   D. The Adjustment occurs fourth.

Note that references are integrated throughout the outline just as they would be in a term paper. In the actual speech, the speaker might say: "Anthropologist Kalervo Oberg, who coined the term *culture shock,* said it occurs in four stages."

The introduction serves the three functions noted: It gains attention (by involving the audience and by stressing the importance of the topic to the audience's desire to gain self-understanding); it connects the speaker, audience, and topic in a way that establishes the credibility of the speaker; and it orients the audience as to what is to follow. This particular orientation identifies both the number of stages and their names. If this speech were a much longer and more complex one, the orientation might also have included brief definitions of each stage.

[Let's follow the order in which these four stages occur and begin with the first stage, the Honeymoon.]

This transition cues the audience into a four-part presentation. Also, the numbers repeated throughout the outline will further aid the audience in keeping track of where you are in the speech. Most important, it tells the audience that the speech will follow a temporal thought pattern.

Body

I. The Honeymoon occurs first.
   A. The honeymoon is the period of fascination with the new people and culture.
   B. You enjoy the people and the culture.
      1. You love the people.
         a. For example, the people in Zaire spend their time very differently from the way New Yorkers do.
         b. For example, my first 18 years living on a farm was very different from life in a college dorm.
      2. You love the culture.
         a. The great number of different religions in India fascinated me.
         b. Eating was an especially great experience.

Notice the parallel structure throughout the outline. For example, note that I, II, III, and IV in the body are all phrased in exactly the same way. Although this may seem unnecessarily redundant, it will help your audience follow your speech more closely and will also help you in logically structuring your thoughts.

Notice that there are lots of examples throughout this speech. These examples are identified only briefly in the outline and would naturally be elaborated on in the speech.

Notice too the internal organization of each major point. Each main assertion in the body contains a definition of the stage (IA, IIA, IIIA, and IVA) and examples (IB, IIB, IIIB, and IVB) to illustrate the stage.

[But, like many relationships, life is not all honeymoon; soon there comes a crisis.]

II. The Crisis occurs second.
   A. The crisis is the period when you begin to experience problems.
      1. One-third of American workers abroad fail because of culture shock (Samovar & Porter, 1995, p. 232).
      2. The personal difficulties also are great.
   B. Life becomes difficult in the new culture.
      1. Communication is difficult.
      2. It's easy to offend people without realizing it.

Because this is a specific fact, some style manuals require that the page number be included in the reference citation.

[As you gain control over the crises, you begin to recover.]

III. The Recovery occurs third.
   A. The recovery is the period in which you learn how to cope.
   B. You begin to learn intercultural competence (Lustig & Koester, 2003).
      1. You learn how to communicate.
         a. Being able to go to the market and make my wants known was a great day for me.
         b. I was able to ask for a date.
      2. You learn the rules of the culture.
         a. The different religious ceremonies each have their own rules.
         b. Eating is a ritual experience in lots of places throughout Africa.

Note that each statement in the outline is a complete sentence. You can easily convert this outline into a phrase or keyword outline for use in delivery. In the preparation outline, however, full sentences will help you see more clearly the relationships among items.

[Your recovery leads naturally into the next and final stage, the adjustment.]

IV. The Adjustment occurs fourth.
   A. The adjustment is the period when you come to enjoy the new culture.
   B. You come to appreciate the people and the culture.

[Let me summarize the stages you go through in experiencing culture shock.]

The transitions are inserted between all major parts of the speech. Although they may seem too numerous in this abbreviated outline, they will be appreciated by your audience, because the transitions will help them follow your speech.

Conclusion

I. Culture shock can be described in four stages.
   A. The Honeymoon is first.
   B. The Crisis is second.
   C. The Recovery is third.
   D. The Adjustment is fourth.

Notice that these four points correspond to I, II, III, and IV of the body and to III A, B, C, and D of the introduction. Notice how the similar wording adds clarity.

II. Culture shock is a fascinating process; you may want to explore it more fully.
   A. Lots of books on culture shock are on reserve for Communication 325: Culture and Communication.
   B. Sunday's *60 Minutes* is going to have a piece on culture shock.

This step, in which the speaker motivates the listeners to continue learning about culture shock, is optional in informative speeches.

III. By knowing the four stages, you can better understand the culture shock you may now be experiencing on the job, at school, or in your private life.

This step provides closure; it makes it clear that the speech is finished. It also serves to encourage reflection on the part of the audience as to their own experiences of culture shock.

References

This reference list includes just those sources that appear in the completed speech.

Lustig, Myron W., & Koester, Jolene. (2003). *Intercultural competence: Interpersonal communication across cultures,* (4th ed.). Boston: Allyn & Bacon.

Oberg, Kalervo. (1960). Culture shock: Adjustment to new cultural environments. *Practical Anthropology, 7,* 177–182.

Samovar, Larry A., & Porter, Richard E. (1995). *Communication between cultures*, (2nd ed.). Belmont, CA: Wadsworth.

Body

I. first main point ______.

   A. support of I (the first main point) ______.

   B. further support for I ______.

[Transition: connect the first main point to the second ______]

II. second main point ______.

   A. support for II (the second main point) ______.

   B. further support for II ______.

[Transition: connect the second main point to the third ______]

III. third main point ______.

(outline continues on page 333)

THE *PUBLIC SPEAKING* SAMPLE ASSISTANT

A Preparation Outline (Motivated Sequence Organization)

This outline illustrates how you might construct an outline and a speech using the motivated sequence. This outline focuses on the establishment of a youth center as a means of combating juvenile crime. In a longer speech, if you wanted to persuade an audience to establish a youth center, you might include two or three issues and not limit yourself to the single issue of reducing juvenile crime.

As you will see, in the motivated sequence outline, the five steps identified in Unit 15 (attention, need, satisfaction, visualization, and action) take the place of the Introduction, Body, and Conclusion structure of many outlines discussed earlier and of the topical organization in the Public Speaking Sample Assistant box on pages 329–331.

The Youth Center

Thesis: A youth center will reduce juvenile crime.

General Purpose: To persuade.

Specific Purpose: To persuade my listeners to vote in favor of Proposition 14, which would establish a community youth center.

I. If you could reduce juvenile crime by some 20 percent by just flipping a lever, would you do it?
   A. Thom's drugstore was broken into by teenagers.
   B. Loraine's video store windows were broken by teenagers.

Step 1: Attention
The speaker asks a question to gain attention and follows it with specific examples of juvenile crime that audience members have experienced. The question and the specific examples focus on one single issue: the need to reduce juvenile crime. If the speech were a broader and longer one and included other reasons for the youth center, then it would have been appropriate to preview them here as well.

II. Juvenile crime is on the rise.
   A. The overall number of crimes has increased.
      1. In 2000 there were 32 juvenile crimes.
      2. In 2002 there were 47 such crimes.
      3. In 2004 there were 63 such crimes.
   B. The number of serious crimes also has increased.
      1. In 2000 there were 30 misdemeanors and 2 felonies.
      2. In 2004 there were 35 misdemeanors and 28 felonies.

Step 2: Need
The speaker states directly and clearly the need and shows that a problem exists. The speaker then demonstrates that the rise in crime is significant both in absolute numbers and in the severity of the crimes. To help the listeners understand these figures, the speaker could display these figures on a chalkboard, on a prepared chart, or on PowerPoint slides. In a longer speech, other needs might also be identified in this step; for example, teenagers' needs for vocational and social skills.

III. A youth center will help reduce juvenile crime.

Step 3: Satisfaction
In this step, the speaker shows the listeners that the proposal to establish a youth center offers great benefits and no significant drawbacks.

A. Three of our neighboring towns reduced juvenile crime after establishing a youth center.
   1. In Marlboro there was a 20 percent decline in overall juvenile crime.
   2. In both Highland and Ellenville the number of serious crimes declined 25 percent.

B. The youth center will not increase our tax burden.
   1. New York State grants will pay for most of the expenses.
   2. Local merchants have agreed to pay any remaining expenses.

The speaker argues that the youth center will satisfy the need to reduce juvenile crime by showing statistics from neighboring towns. The speaker also preemptively answers any objections about increased taxes. If the speaker had reason to believe that listeners had other possible objections, these concerns too should be addressed in this step.

IV. Juvenile crime will decrease as a result of the youth center.
   A. If we follow the example of our neighbors, our juvenile crime rates are likely to decrease by 20 to 25 percent.
   B. Thom's store would not have been broken into.
   C. Loraine's windows would not have been broken.

Step 4: Visualization
Here the speaker visualizes what the town would be like if the youth center were established, using both the statistics developed earlier and the personal examples introduced in the beginning of the speech.

V. Vote yes on Proposition 14.
   A. In next week's election you'll be asked to vote on Proposition 14, establishing a youth center.
   B. Vote yes if you want to help reduce juvenile crime.
   C. Urge your family members, your friends, and your work colleagues also to vote yes.

Step 5: Action
In this step the speaker asks the audience for a specific action—to vote in favor of the youth center—and urges listeners to influence others to do the same. The speaker also reiterates the main theme of the speech; namely, that the youth center will help reduce juvenile crime.

A. support for III (the third main point).

B. further support for III.

[Transition: connect the third main point (or all main points) to the conclusion]

Conclusion

I. summary.
   A. first main point; same as I in body.
   B. second main point; same as II in body.
   C. third main point; same as III in body.

II. motivation.

III. closure.

References

Alphabetical list of sources cited

The Delivery Outline

Now that you've constructed a preparation outline, you need to construct a delivery outline. Resist the temptation to use your preparation outline to deliver the speech. If you use your preparation outline, you'll tend to read from the outline instead of presenting a seemingly extemporaneous speech in which you attend to and respond to audience feedback. Instead, construct a brief *delivery outline:* an outline that will assist rather than hinder your delivery of the speech. Here are some guidelines to follow in preparing this delivery outline.

- Be brief. Try to limit yourself to one side of one sheet of paper.
- Be clear. Be sure that you can see the outline while you're speaking. Use different colored inks,

underlining, or whatever system will help you communicate your ideas.

- Be delivery minded. Include any guides to delivery that will help while you're speaking. Note in the outline when you'll use your presentation aid and when you'll remove it. A simple "show PA" or "remove PA" should suffice. You might also wish to note some speaking cues, such as "slow down" when reading a poetry excerpt, or perhaps a place where an extended pause might help.
- Rehearse with the delivery outline. In your rehearsals, use the delivery outline only. Remember, the objective is to make rehearsals as close to the real thing as possible.

The following is a sample delivery outline constructed from the preparation outline on culture shock (on pages 329-331). Note that the outline is brief enough so that you'll be able to use it effectively without losing eye contact with the audience. It uses abbreviations (for example, CS for culture shock) and phrases rather than complete sentences. And yet it's detailed enough to include all essential parts of your speech, including transitions. It contains delivery notes specifically tailored to your own needs, such as pause suggestions and guides to using visual aids. Note also that it's clearly divided into introduction, body, and conclusion and uses the same numbering system as the preparation outline.

PAUSE!

LOOK OVER THE AUDIENCE!

I. Many experience CS
  A. CS: the reaction to being in a culture very different from your own
  B. By understanding CS, you'll be better able to deal with it

PAUSE SCAN AUDIENCE

II. I've experienced CS
III. CS occurs in 4 stages (WRITE ON BOARD)
  A. Honeymoon
  B. Crisis
  C. Recovery
  D. Adjustment

[Let's examine these stages of CS]

PAUSE/STEP FORWARD

I. Honeymoon
  A. Fascination with people and culture
  B. Enjoyment of people and culture
    1. love the people (Zaire, dorm examples)
    2. love the culture (India, eating examples)

[But, life is not all honeymoon—the crisis]

II. Crisis
  A. problems arise
    1. 1/3 Am workers fail abroad
    2. personal difficulties
  B. life becomes difficult
    1. communication
    2. offend others

[As you gain control over the crises, you learn how to cope]

PAUSE

III. Recovery
  A. period of learning to cope
  B. you learn intercultural competence
    1. communication becomes easier
    2. you learn the culture's rules

[As you recover you adjust]

IV. Adjustment
  A. learn to enjoy (again) the new culture
  B. appreciate people and culture

[These then are the four stages; let me summarize]

PAUSE BEFORE STARTING CONCLUSION

I. CS occurs in 4 stages: honeymoon, crisis, recovery, & adjustment
II. You can learn more about CS: books, *60 minutes*
III. By knowing the 4 stages, you can better understand the culture shock you may now be experiencing on the job, at school, or in your private life.

PAUSE

ANY QUESTIONS?

Step 9: Word Your Speech

You're a successful public speaker when your listeners create in their minds the meanings you want them to create. You're successful when your listeners adopt the attitudes and behaviors you want them to adopt. The language choices you make—the words you select and the sentences you form—will greatly influence the meanings your listeners receive and, thus, how successful you are.

Oral Style

Oral style is the quality of spoken language that differentiates it from written language. You do not speak as you write (Akinnaso, 1982). The words and sentences you use differ. The major reason for this difference is that you compose speech instantly. You select your words and construct your sentences as

UNDERSTANDING *THEORY* AND *RESEARCH*

One-Sided versus Two-Sided Messages

When you're presenting persuasive arguments, should you devote all your time to your side of the case—or should you also mention the other side and show why that side is not acceptable? Originally studied during the 1940s this question continues to engage the attention of researchers. Early studies found that one-sided presentations were more effective with less-educated audiences, whereas two-sided presentations were more effective with more-educated listeners. One-sided presentations also were more effective with people who were already in favor of the speaker's point of view, whereas two-sided presentations were more persuasive with those who were initially opposed to the speaker's position.

Whether you choose to use a one-sided or a two-sided persuasive approach will depend on your topic (are there two competing positions?), the time you have available (limited time may prevent you from covering both sides), your audience's existing attitude (if they already reject the other position, there may not be a need to include it), and perhaps other factors as well.

If you do decide to present both sides, here are a few points to consider:

1. Using a two-sided presentation generally helps establish your credibility; by mentioning the other side, you demonstrate your knowledge of the entire area and by implication tell the audience that you understand both positions.
2. In a two-sided presentation be sure to demonstrate the superiority of your position and the reasons why the other position is not as good as yours (O'Keefe, 1999). If you merely mention the other position without pointing out its flaws, then you risk creating doubt in minds of your listeners about the superiority of your position.
3. If your audience is aware of an alternative position, then you need to demonstrate that you too are aware of it but that it's not as good as your position.
4. Demonstrate that you have analyzed the alternative position as carefully and thoroughly as the position you're supporting.

Working with Theories and Research

- *Take a look at print, television, or Internet ads and identify a few ads that use a two-sided approach (Brand A is better than Brand X). What makes a two-sided advertisement effective?*

you think your thoughts. There's very little time between the thought and the utterance. When you write, however, you compose your thoughts after considerable reflection. Even then you probably often rewrite and edit as you go along. Because of this, written language has a more formal tone. Spoken language is more informal, more colloquial.

Generally, spoken language consists of shorter, simpler, and more familiar words than does written language. Also, there's more qualification in speech than in writing. For example, when speaking you probably make greater use of such expressions as *although, however, perhaps,* and the like. When writing, you probably edit these out.

Spoken language has a greater number of self-reference terms (terms that refer to the speaker herself or himself): *I, me, our, us,* and *you*. Spoken language also has a greater number of "allness" terms such as *all, none, every, always*, and *never*. When you write, you're probably more careful to edit out such allness terms, realizing that such terms often are not very descriptive of reality.

Spoken language has more pseudo-quantifying terms (for example, *many, much, very, lots*) and terms that include the speaker as part of the observation (for example, *It seems to me that* or *As I see it*). Further, speech contains more verbs and adverbs; writing contains more nouns and adjectives.

ASK THE RESEARCHER

Making Myself Clear

- *I notice that some people are very good at getting their ideas across clearly, while others are quite confusing. I'd like to know some things the clear speakers are doing that confusing speakers often fail to do.*

It's important to recognize that your listeners view your topic differently than you do. Your picture is clear, while theirs is blurry. So first, give listeners a general sense or overview of your topic. Tell them in general terms what you'll be discussing. Second, condense your topic to three or four main points—too many main points will only confuse an audience, especially if the topic is new to them. Then, to truly make your topic clear and vivid to listeners, give examples, tell stories as illustrations, and use analogies, for example. Audiences like this, and it will enhance clarity, as long as listeners can see how these supporting materials relate to your topic. Third, begin with terms that are familiar to your audience before introducing terms or concepts that are new or unique to your topic. By the end of the speech, your audience's blurry sense of the topic will become clearer.

For further information: Chesebro, J. L. (2002). Teaching clearly. In J. L. Chesebro & J. C. McCroskey (Eds.), *Communication for teachers*. (Boston: Allyn & Bacon. And Civikly, J. M. (1992). Clarity: Teachers and students making sense of instruction. *Communication Education, 41,* 138–152. And Rowan, K. E. (2003). Informing and explaining skills: Theory and research on informative communication. In J. Green & B. Burleson (Eds.), *Handbook of communication and social interaction skills* (pp. 403–438). Mahwah, NJ: Erlbaum.

Joseph Chesebro (Ed.D., West Virginia University) is an assistant professor of communication at the State University of New York at Brockport. He teaches courses in interpersonal and organizational communication and conducts research on clear teaching and conversational sensitivity as an aspect of listening. He also plays drums.

Spoken and written language not only *do* differ, they *should* differ. The main reason why spoken and written language should differ is that the listener hears speech only once; therefore, speech must be instantly intelligible. The reader can reread an essay or look up an unfamiliar word; the reader can spend as much time as he or she wishes with the written page. The listener, in contrast, must move at the pace set by the speaker. The reader may reread a sentence or paragraph if there's a temporary attention lapse. The listener doesn't have this option.

For the most part, it's wise to use "oral style" in your public speeches. The public speech is composed much like a written essay, however. There's considerable thought and deliberation and much editing and restyling. Because of this, you'll need to devote special effort to retaining and polishing your oral style. In the rest of this section I'll present specific suggestions for achieving this goal.

Choosing Words

Choose carefully the words you use in your public speeches. Choose words to achieve clarity, vividness, appropriateness, a personal style, and forcefulness.

Clarity

Clarity in speaking style should be your primary goal. Here are some guidelines to help you make your speech clear.

Be Economical. Don't waste words. Notice the wasted words in such expressions as "at nine A.M. *in the morning*," "we *first* began the discussion," "I *myself personally*," and "*blue in color*." By withholding the italicized terms you eliminate unnecessary words and move closer to a more economical and clearer style.

Use Specific Terms and Numbers. As we get more and more specific, we get a clearer and more detailed picture. Be specific. Don't say "dog" when you want your listeners to picture a St. Bernard. Don't say "car" when you want them to picture a limousine. The same is true of numbers. Don't say "earned a good salary" if you mean "earned $90,000 a year." Don't say "taxes will go up" when you mean "taxes will increase 7 percent."

Use Guide Phrases. Use guide phrases to help listeners see that you're moving from one idea to another—phrases such as "now that we have seen how . . . , let us consider how . . . ," and "my next argument . . . ." Terms such as *first, second, and also, although*, and *however* will help your audience follow your line of thinking.

Use Short, Familiar Terms. Generally, favor the short word over the long one. Favor the familiar word over the unfamiliar word. Favor the more commonly used term over the rarely used term.

Here are a few examples:

Poor Choices	Better Choices
innocuous	*harmless*
elucidate	*clarify*
utilize	*use*
ascertain	*find out*
erstwhile	*former*
eschew	*avoid*
expenditure	*cost* or *expense*

Carefully Assess Idioms. Idioms are expressions that are unique to a specific language and whose meaning cannot be deduced from the individual words used. Expressions such as "kick the bucket," or "doesn't have a leg to stand on" are idioms: Either you know the meaning of the expression or you don't; you can't figure it out from only a knowledge of the individual words.

The positive side of idioms is that they give your speech a casual and informal air; they make your speech sound like a speech and not like a written essay. The negative side of idioms is that they create problems for listeners who are not native speakers of your language. Many non-native speakers will simply not understand the meaning of your idioms. This problem is especially important because audiences are becoming increasingly intercultural and because the number of idioms we use is extremely high.

Distinguish between Commonly Confused Words. Many words, because they sound alike or are used in similar situations, are commonly confused. Try the self-test below, which covers 10 of the most frequently confused words.

Can You Distinguish between Commonly Confused Words?

Underline the word in parentheses that you would use in each sentence.

1. She (accepted, excepted) the award and thanked everyone (accept, except) the producer.
2. The teacher (affected, effected) his students greatly and will now (affect, effect) an entirely new curriculum.
3. Are you deciding (between, among) red and green or (between, among) red, green, and blue?
4. I've scaled higher mountains than this, so I'm sure I (can, may) scale this one; I and a few others know the hidden path, but I (can, may) not reveal this.
5. The table was (cheap, inexpensive) but has great style; the chairs cost a fortune but look (cheap, inexpensive).
6. We (discover, invent) uncharted lands but (discover, invent) computer programs.
7. He was direct and (explicit, implicit) in his denial of the crime but was vague and only (explicit, implicit) concerning his whereabouts.
8. She (implied, inferred) that she'd seek a divorce; we can only (imply, infer) her reasons.
9. The wedding was (tasteful, tasty) and the food (tasteful, tasty).
10. The student seemed (disinterested, uninterested) in the lecture. The teacher was (disinterested, uninterested) in who received what grades.

HOW DID YOU DO? Here are the principles that govern correct usage: (1) Use *accept* to mean "receive" and *except* to mean with "the exclusion of." (2) Use *to affect* to mean "to have an effect on or to influence," and *to effect* to mean "to produce a result." (3) Use *between* when referring to two items and *among* when referring to more than two items. (4) Use *can* to refer to ability and *may* to refer to permission. (5) Use *cheap* to refer to something that is inferior and *inexpensive* to something that costs little. (6) Use *discover* to refer to the act of finding something out or learning something previously unknown, but use *invent* to refer to the act of originating something new. (7) Use *explicit* to mean "directly stated" and *implicit* to indicate the act of expressing something without actually stating it. (8) Use *imply* to mean "state

TEST YOURSELF, continued

indirectly" and *infer* to mean "draw a conclusion." (9) Use *tasteful* to refer to good taste, but use *tasty* to refer to something that tastes good. (10) Use *uninterested* to indicate a lack of interest and use *disinterested* to mean "objective" or "unbiased."

WHAT WILL YOU DO? Your use of language can greatly enhance (or detract from) your persuasiveness. A word used incorrectly can lessen your credibility and general persuasiveness. Review your English handbook and identify other commonly confused words. Get into the habit of referring to a good dictionary whenever you have doubts about which word is preferred.

Vividness

Select words to make your ideas vivid and to help your arguments come alive in the minds of your listeners: Use active verbs, strong verbs, figures of speech, and imagery.

Use Active Verbs. Favor verbs that communicate activity rather than passivity. The verb to be, in all its forms—*is, are, was, were, will be*—is relatively inactive. Try using verbs of action instead. Rather than saying "The teacher was in the middle of the crowd," say "The teacher stood in the middle of the crowd." Instead of saying "The report was on the president's desk for three days," try "The report rested [or slept] on the president's desk for three days." Instead of saying "Management will be here tomorrow," consider "Management will descend on us tomorrow" or "Management jets in tomorrow."

Use Strong Verbs. The verb is the strongest part of your sentence. Choose verbs carefully, and choose them so they accomplish a lot. Instead of saying "He walked through the forest," consider such terms as wandered, prowled, rambled, or roamed. Consider whether one of these might not better suit your intended meaning. Consult a thesaurus for any verb you suspect might be weak.

Use Figures of Speech. Figures of speech help achieve vividness, in addition to making your speech more memorable and giving it a polished, well-crafted tone. Figures of speech are stylistic devices that have been a part of rhetoric since ancient times. Here are some of the major figures of speech; you may wish to incorporate a few of these into your next speech.

- *Alliteration* is the repetition of the same initial sound in two or more words, as in "fifty famous flavors" or the "cool, calculating leader."
- *Hyperbole* is the use of extreme exaggeration, as in "He cried like a faucet" or "I'm so hungry I could eat a whale."
- *Irony* is the use of a word or sentence whose literal meaning is the opposite of the message actually conveyed; for example, a teacher handing back failing examinations might say, "So pleased to see how many of you studied so hard."
- *Metaphor* compares two unlike things by stating that one thing "is" the other, as in "She's a lion when she wakes up" or "He's a real bulldozer."
- *Synecdoche* is the use of a part of an object to stand for the whole object, as in "All hands were on deck" (where "hands" stands for "sailor" or "crew member") or "green thumb" for "expert gardener."
- *Metonymy* is the substitution of a name for a title with which it's closely associated, as in "City Hall issued the following news release," in which "City Hall" stands for "the mayor" or "the city council."
- *Antithesis* is the presentation of contrary ideas in parallel form, as in "My loves are many, my enemies are few." Charles Dickens's opening words in *A Tale of Two Cities* are a famous antithesis: "It was the best of times; it was the worst of times."
- *Simile,* like metaphor, compares two unlike objects; but simile explicitly uses the words *like* or *as*; for example, "The manager is as gentle as an ox."
- *Personification* is the attribution of human characteristics to inanimate objects, as in "This room cries for activity" or "My car is tired and wants a drink."
- *Rhetorical questions* are questions used to make a statement or to produce a desired effect rather than to secure an answer, as in "Do you want to be popular?" "Do you want to get well?"

Use Imagery. Appeal to the senses, especially our visual, auditory, and tactile senses. Make your audience see, hear, and feel what you're talking about.

In describing people or objects, create word "pictures" or *visual imagery*. When appropriate, describe such visual qualities as height, weight, color, size, shape, length, and contour. Let your audience see the sweat pouring down the faces of the coal miners; let them see the short, overweight, cigar-smoking executive in his pin-striped suit.

Use *auditory imagery* to describe sounds; let your listeners hear the car's tires screeching, the

COMMUNICATION@WORK

Talking Up and Down

To me, the most important element in management is the human being. So the first essential is to treat people with consideration.

—Yoshiki Yamasaki

Talking up and talking down are two forms of communication that present problems in a workplace setting—at least in the United States, where a kind of communication equality generally prevails.

When you talk up, you talk as a subordinate, as someone who is inferior to the person you're addressing. To be sure, it's important to demonstrate respect for others and to acknowledge that in some situations others know more than you do; but it's also important to show that you have power and information. Statements that put yourself down ("I'm really bad at writing reports"), that are unnecessarily and overly complimentary ("If I only had your finesse"), or that are overly polite may give the impression that you may not be up to the job at hand. Others may interpret your talking up as an indication that you are in fact inferior to others.

Talking down is probably the more common mistake. Here, you present yourself as all-knowing. Examples include the doctor who speaks in medicalese to a sick patient—or who meets a new patient and says, "Hello Pat, I'm Dr. Gonzalez"—or the lawyer who uses legal terminology without any explanation and assumes that you understand what he or she is saying. People also talk down when they tell others how they should act or feel: "You really shouldn't have said that" or "Don't be shy, speak your mind." Comments like these tell others that you know the right way to do things and that what they've been doing is wrong. So be especially careful of statements containing "should" and "ought"; they're often signals that you're talking down.

Communicating@Work

Can you provide examples of talking up or talking down that you've witnessed or been a party to recently? What effect did such messages have?

wind whistling, the bells chiming, the angry professor roaring.

Use terms referring to temperature, texture, and touch to create *tactile imagery*. Let your listeners feel the cool water running over their bodies or the punch of the prizefighter; let them feel the smooth skin of the newborn baby.

Appropriateness

Use language that is appropriate to you as the speaker—and that is appropriate to your audience, the occasion, and the speech topic. Here are some general guidelines to help you achieve this quality.

Speak on the Appropriate Level of Formality. The most effective public speaking style is less formal than the written essay but more formal than conversation. One way to achieve an informal style is to use contractions. Say *don't* instead of *do not, I'll* instead of *I shall*, and *wouldn't* instead of *would not*. Contractions give a public speech the sound and rhythm of conversation, a quality that most listeners react to favorably. Also, use personal pronouns rather than impersonal expressions. Say "I found" instead of "It has been found," or "I will present three arguments" instead of "Three arguments will be presented."

Avoid Unfamiliar Terms. Avoid using terms the audience doesn't know. Avoid foreign and technical terms unless you're certain the audience is familiar with them. Similarly, avoid jargon (the technical vocabulary of a specialized field) unless you're sure the meanings are clear to your listeners. Some acronyms (such as NATO, UN, NOW, and CORE) are probably familiar to most audiences; many, however, are not. When you wish to use any specialized terms or abbreviations, explain their meaning fully to the audience.

Avoid Slang. **Slang** is language that is used by special groups but is generally considered impolite or not quite proper. *Webster's New World College*

Dictionary defines *slang* as "highly informal speech that is outside conventional or standard usage and consists both of coined words and phrases and of new or extended meanings attached to established terms." Generally, it's best to avoid slang, which may offend or embarrass your audience. Although your listeners may use slang interpersonally, they probably don't want to hear it in a relatively formal situation such as public speaking. If you're in doubt about whether a word is considered slang, consult a dictionary; usually, dictionaries identify slang terms as "informal."

Avoid Ethnic Expressions (Generally). Unit 7 discussed the dangers of using sexist, racist, heterosexist, or ageist terms; these can only insult the audience members themselves or people they know and care about. So avoid these terms at all costs. In addition, however, avoid ethnic expressions, at least generally. Ethnic expressions are words and phrases that are peculiar to a particular ethnic group. At times these expressions are known only by members of the ethnic group; at other times they may be known more widely but still recognized as ethnic expressions.

When you are speaking to a multicultural audience, it's generally best to avoid ethnic expressions unless they're integral to your speech and you explain them. Such expressions are often interpreted as exclusionist; they highlight the connection between the speaker and the members of that particular ethnic group and the lack of connection between the speaker and all others who are not members of that ethnic group. And, of course, ethnic expressions should never be used if you're not a member of the ethnic group.

If, on the other hand, you're speaking to people who all belong to one ethnic group and if you're also a member, then such expressions are fine. In fact, they may well prove effective; being part of the common language of speaker and audience, they can help you stress your own similarities with the audience.

Personal Style

Audiences favor speakers who speak in a personal rather than an impersonal style, who speak with them rather than at them. You can achieve a more personal style by using personal pronouns, asking questions, and creating immediacy.

Use Personal Pronouns. Say *I, me, he, she,* and *you*. Avoid impersonal expressions such as one (as in "One is led to believe . . ."), *this speaker*, or *you, the listeners*. These expressions distance the audience and create barriers rather than bridges.

Use Questions. Ask the audience questions to involve them. In a small audience, you might even briefly entertain responses. In larger audiences, you might ask the question, pause to allow the audience time to consider their responses, and then move on. When you direct questions to your listeners, they feel a part of the public speaking transaction.

Create Immediacy. Immediacy, as discussed in Unit 9, is a connectedness, a relatedness with one's listeners. Immediacy is the opposite of disconnectedness and separation. Here are some suggestions for creating immediacy through language:

- Use personal examples.
- Use terms that include both you and the audience; for example, *we* and *our*.
- Address the audience directly; say *you* rather than *students;* say "You'll enjoy reading" instead of "Everyone will enjoy reading"; say "I want you to see" instead of "I want people to see."
- Use specific names of audience members when appropriate.
- Express concern for the audience members.
- Reinforce or compliment the audience.
- Refer directly to commonalities between you and the audience; for example, "We are all children of immigrants" or "We all want to see our team in the playoffs."
- Refer to shared experiences and goals; for example, "We all want, we all need a more responsive PTA."
- Recognize audience feedback and refer to it in your speech. Say, for example, "I can see from your expressions that we're all anxious to get to our immediate problem."

Forcefulness/Power

Forceful or powerful language will help you achieve your purpose, whether it be informative or persuasive. Forceful language enables you to direct the audience's attention, thoughts, and feelings. To make your speech more forceful, eliminate weakeners, vary intensity, and avoid overused expressions.

Eliminate Weakeners. Delete phrases that weaken your sentences. Among the major weakeners are uncertainty expressions and weak modifiers. Uncertainty expressions such as "I'm not sure of this, but"; "Perhaps it might"; or "Maybe it works this way" communicate a lack of commitment and conviction and will make your audience wonder if you're worth listening to. Weak modifiers such as "It works pretty well," "It's kind of like," or "It may be the one we want" make you seem unsure and indefinite about what you're saying.

Cut out any unnecessary verbiage that reduces the impact of your meaning. Instead of saying "There are lots of things we can do to help," say "We can do lots of things to help." Instead of saying "I'm sorry to be so graphic, but Senator Bingsley's proposal . . . ," say "We need to be graphic. Senator Bingsley's proposal . . . ." Instead of saying "It should be observed in this connection that, all things considered, money is not productive of happiness," say "Money doesn't bring happiness."

Here are a few additional suggestions—which, of course, are not limited in application to public speaking but relate as well to interpersonal and small group communication.

MEDIA WATCH

Advertising Purposes

Like public speeches, advertisements serve two major functions: to inform and to persuade. Advertising informs you in a variety of ways:

- Advertising makes you aware of a particular product or service, a function that's especially important with new products. Advertising also informs you about the product and perhaps its ingredients or its uses. Cereal commercials on television, for example, proudly tell you the fiber content (though seldom the sugar content). Aluminum foil ads tell you of foil's many uses, perhaps including some you hadn't thought of previously.
- Advertising tells you where to buy the product and perhaps how much it costs. Infomercials regularly give this information—the exact price of the product, the shipping and handling charges, and the phone number you need to call to get the bargain price.
- Advertising may correct erroneous claims made in previous ads. Thus, for example, Listerine was required to advertise that it doesn't kill germs that cause colds—as had been previously advertised.

Of course, advertising's real business is persuasion.

- Advertising seeks to establish an image of a product—to make you think a certain way about the product or associate a particular feeling with it. Beer and soft drink advertisers regularly associate friendship and fun with their products; the idea is that when you see their products, you'll have positive feelings and ultimately buy the beverages. Advertising also may work in the opposite direction and try to associate a product with negative feelings. The American Cancer Society's advertisements against smoking regularly attack the glamour image that cigarette manufacturers communicate, showing pictures of wrinkled and sick smokers.
- Advertisers may aim to convince you of the superiority of their product and the inferiority of the competition. This comparative advertising pits one detergent against another ("Ours has twice the cleaning power") or one car against another ("Ours is $2,000 less expensive and gives you greater mileage").
- Advertising often aims to get you to buy a product. Whether it's eyeglasses, furniture, perfume, or appliances, the advertiser wants to get you to go the store, make the phone call, or type in your credit card number and buy the product or service.

You and the Media

Television commercials help to sell products; but, in the scenarios they use, they also communicate about relationships—about what is desirable and what is not desirable in a relationship, about what a family kitchen should look like, about how children and parents should talk to each other, and so on. Watch a variety of television commercials for just about any product and keep a log of all the relationship messages they communicate. Or, if you are a sci-fi enthusiast, consider what an alien who sees only American television commercials would think of interpersonal relationships in the United States.

- Avoid hesitations ("I, er, want to say that, ah, this one is, er, the best, you know"); they make you sound unprepared and uncertain.
- Avoid using too many intensifiers ("Really, this was the greatest; it was truly phenomenal"); audiences will begin to doubt the speaker who goes overboard with the superlatives.
- Avoid tag questions ("I'll review the report now, okay?" "That is a great proposal, don't you think?"); they signal your need for approval and your own uncertainty and lack of conviction.
- Avoid self-critical statements ("I'm not very good at this," "This is my first speech"); they signal a lack of confidence and make public your sense of inadequacy.
- Avoid slang and vulgar expressions; they may signal low social class and hence little power.

Vary Intensity as Appropriate. Just as you can vary your voice in intensity, you can also phrase your ideas with different degrees of stylistic intensity. You can, for example, refer to an action as "failing to support our position" or as "stabbing us in the back"; you can say that a new proposal will "endanger our goals" or will "destroy us completely"; you can refer to a child's behavior as "playful," "creative," or "destructive." Vary your language to express different degrees of intensity—from mild through neutral to extremely intense.

Avoid Bromides and Clichés. Bromides are trite sayings that are worn out because of constant usage. A few examples:

- Honesty is the best policy.
- If I can't do it well, I won't do it at all.
- I don't understand modern art, but I know what I like.

When we hear these hackneyed statements, we recognize them as unoriginal and uninspired.

Clichés are phrases that have lost their novelty and part of their meaning through overuse. Clichés call attention to themselves because of their overuse. Here are some examples of clichés to avoid:

- in this day and age
- tell it like it is
- free as a bird
- in the pink
- no sooner said than done
- it goes without saying
- few and far between
- over the hill
- no news is good news
- the life of the party
- keep your shirt on

Phrasing Sentences

Give the same careful consideration that you give to words to the sentences of your speech as well. Some guidelines follow.

Use Short Sentences

Short sentences are more forceful and economical. They are also easier for your audience to comprehend and remember. Listeners don't have the time or the inclination to unravel long and complex sentences. Help them to listen more efficiently. Use short rather than long sentences.

Use Direct Sentences

Direct sentences are easier to understand. They are also more forceful. Instead of saying "I want to tell you of the three main reasons why we should not adopt Program A," say "We should not adopt Program A. There are three main reasons."

Use Active Sentences

Active sentences—that is, sentences whose verbs are in the active voice—are easier to understand than passive ones. They also make your speech seem livelier and more vivid. Instead of saying "The lower court's decision was reversed by the Supreme Court," say "The Supreme Court reversed the lower court's decision." Instead of saying "The proposal was favored by management," say "Management favored the proposal."

Use Positive Sentences

Sentences phrased positively are easier to comprehend and remember than sentences phrased negatively. Notice how sentences *a* and *c* are easier to understand than sentences *b* and *d*:

a. The committee rejected the proposal.
b. The committee did not accept the proposal.
c. This committee works outside the normal company hierarchy.
d. This committee does not work within the normal company hierarchy.

Vary the Types of Sentences

The preceding advice to use short, direct, active, positive sentences is valid most of the time. Yet too many sentences of the same type or length will make your speech sound boring. So follow (generally) the preceding advice, but add variations as well.

Step 10: Rehearse and Deliver Your Speech

Your last step is to rehearse and deliver your speech. Let's look first at rehearsal.

Rehearsal

Use your rehearsal time effectively and efficiently for the following purposes:

- To develop a delivery that will help you achieve the objectives of your speech.
- To time your speech; if you time your rehearsals, you'll be able to see if you can add material or if you have to delete something.
- To see how the speech will flow as a whole and to make any changes and improvements you think necessary.
- To test the presentation aids, and to detect and resolve any technical problems.
- To learn the speech thoroughly.
- To reduce any feelings of apprehension and gain confidence.

The following procedures should assist you in achieving these goals.

Rehearse the Speech as a Whole

Rehearse the speech from beginning to end, not in parts. Rehearse it from getting out of your seat through the introduction, body, and conclusion, to returning to your seat. Be sure to rehearse the speech with all the examples and illustrations (and any audiovisual aids) included. This will enable you to connect the parts of the speech and see how they interact.

Time the Speech

Time the speech during each rehearsal. Make the necessary adjustments on the basis of this timing. If you're using computer presentation software, you'll be able to time your speech very precisely. Also time the individual parts of your speech so you can achieve the balance you want—for example, you might want to spend twice as much time on the solutions as on the problems, or you might want to balance the introduction and conclusion so that each portion constitutes about 10 percent of your speech.

BUILDING COMMUNICATION SKILLS

Speaking Impromptu

The following experience may prove useful as an exercise in delivery. Each student should take three index cards and write an impromptu speech topic on each card. The topics should be familiar but not clichés; they should be worthwhile and substantive, not trivial; and they should be neither too simplistic nor too complex. The cards should be collected and placed face down on a table. Each speaker, chosen through some random process, should then select two cards, read the topics, choose one of them, and take approximately one or two minutes to prepare a two- to three-minute impromptu speech. A few guidelines:

1. Don't apologize. Everyone will have difficulty with this assignment, so there is no need to emphasize any problems you may have.
2. Don't express verbally or nonverbally any displeasure or any negative responses to the experience, the topic, the audience, or even yourself. Approach the entire task with a positive attitude and a positive appearance. It will help make the experience more enjoyable for both you and your audience.
3. When you select your topic, jot down two or three subtopics that you will cover and perhaps two or three bits of supporting material that you will use in amplifying these two or three subtopics.
4. Develop your conclusion. It is probably best to use a simple summary conclusion in which you restate your main topic and the subordinate topics that you discussed.
5. Develop an introduction. Here it is probably best simply to identify your topic and orient the audience by telling them the two or three subtopics that you will cover.

Approximate the Actual Speech Situation

Rehearse the speech under conditions as close as possible to those under which you'll deliver it. If possible, rehearse the speech in the same room in which you'll present it. If this is impossible, try to simulate the actual conditions as closely as you can—even in your living room or bathroom. If possible, rehearse the speech in front of a few supportive listeners. It's always helpful (and especially for your beginning speeches) that your listeners be supportive rather than too critical. Merely having listeners present during your rehearsal will further simulate the conditions under which you'll eventually speak. Get together with two or three other students in an empty classroom where you can take turns as speakers and listeners.

See Yourself as a Speaker

Rehearse the speech in front of a full-length mirror. This will enable you to see yourself and see how you'll appear to the audience. This may be extremely difficult at first, and you may have to force yourself to watch. After a few attempts, however, you'll begin to see the value of this experience. Practice your eye contact, your movements, and your gestures in front of the mirror.

Incorporate Changes and Make Delivery Notes

Make any needed changes in the speech between rehearsals. Do not interrupt your rehearsal to make notes or changes; if you do, you may never experience the entire speech from beginning to end. While making these changes note any words whose pronunciation you wish to check. Also, insert pause notations, "slow down" warnings, and other delivery suggestions into your outline.

If possible, record your speech (ideally, on videotape) so you can hear exactly what your listeners will hear: your volume, rate, pitch, pronunciation, and pauses. You'll thus be in a better position to improve these qualities.

Rehearse Often

Rehearse the speech as often as seems necessary. Two useful guides are: (1) Rehearse the speech at least three or four times; less rehearsal than this is sure to be too little. (2) Rehearse the speech as long as your rehearsals continue to result in improvements in the speech or in your delivery. Some suggestions for a long-term delivery improvement program are presented next.

Undertake a Long-Term Delivery Improvement Program

To become a truly effective speaker, you may need to undertake a long-term delivery improvement program. Approach this project with a positive attitude: Tell yourself that you can do it and that you will do it.

1. First, seek feedback from someone whose opinion and insight you respect. Your public speaking instructor may be a logical choice, but someone majoring in communication or working in a communication field might also be appropriate. Get an honest and thorough appraisal of both your voice and your bodily action.
2. Learn to hear, see, and feel the differences between effective and ineffective patterns. For example, is your pitch too high or your volume too loud? A tape recorder will be very helpful. Learn to feel your rigid posture or your lack of arm and hand gestures. Once you've perceived these voice and/or body patterns, concentrate on learning more effective habits. Practice a few minutes each day. Avoid becoming too conscious of any source of ineffectiveness. Just try to increase your awareness and work on one problem at a time. Do not try to change all your patterns at once.
3. Seek additional feedback on the changes. Make certain that listeners agree that the new patterns you're practicing really are more effective. Remember that you hear yourself through bone conduction as well as through air transmission. Others hear you only through air transmission. So what you hear and what others hear will be different.
4. For voice improvement, consult a book on voice and diction for practice exercises and for additional information on the nature of volume, rate, pitch, and quality.
5. If difficulties persist, see a professional. For voice problems, see a speech clinician. Most campuses have a speech clinic, and you can easily avail yourself of its services. For bodily action difficulties, talk with your public speaking instructor.
6. Seek professional help if you're psychologically uncomfortable with any aspect of your voice or bodily action. It may be that all you have to do is to hear yourself or see yourself on a videotape—as others hear and see you—to convince yourself that you sound and look just fine. Regardless of what is causing this discomfort, however, if you're uncomfortable, do

something about it. In a college community there's more assistance available to you at no cost than you'll ever be offered again. Make use of it.

Delivery

If you're like my own students, delivery creates more anxiety for you than any other aspect of public speaking. Few speakers worry about organization or audience analysis or style. Many worry about delivery, so you have lots of company. In this section we'll examine general methods and principles of effectiveness in presentation that you can adapt to your own personality.

Methods of Delivery

Speakers vary widely in their methods of delivery: Some speak off-the-cuff, with no apparent preparation; others read their speeches from manuscript. Some memorize their speeches word for word; others construct a detailed outline, rehearse often, then speak extemporaneously.

VIEWPOINT
In what ways are the delivery skills used in public speaking similar to and different from the delivery skills used in interpersonal and small group communication?

Speaking Impromptu. In an **impromptu speech** you talk without any specific preparation. You and the topic meet for the first time and immediately the speech begins. On some occasions you will not be able to avoid speaking impromptu. For example, in a classroom, after someone has spoken, you might give a brief impromptu speech of evaluation. In asking or answering questions in an interview situation you're giving impromptu speeches, albeit extremely short ones. At a meeting you may find yourself explaining a proposal or defending a plan of action; these too are impromptu speeches. Of course, impromptu speeches don't permit attention to the details of public speaking such as audience adaptation, research, and style.

Speaking from Manuscript. In a **manuscript speech** you read aloud the entire speech, which you've written out word for word. The manuscript speech allows you to control the timing precisely—a particularly important benefit when you are delivering a speech that will be recorded (on television, for example). Also, there's no risk of forgetting, no danger of being unable to find the right word. Another feature of the manuscript method is that it allows you to use the exact wording that you (or a team of speechwriters) want. In the political arena this is often crucial. And, of course, because the speech is already written out, you can distribute copies and are therefore less likely to be misquoted.

Many audiences, however, don't like speakers to read their speeches, except perhaps with TelePrompTers on television. In face-to-face situations, audiences generally prefer speakers who interact with them. Reading a manuscript makes it difficult to respond to listener feedback. You cannot easily make adjustments on the basis of feedback. And with the manuscript on a stationary lectern, as it most often is, it's impossible for you to move around.

Speaking from Memory. In **memorized delivery** you write out the speech word for word (as in the manuscript method); but instead of reading it, you then commit the speech to memory and recite it or "act it out." Speaking from memory allows you freedom to move about and otherwise concentrate on delivery. It doesn't, however, allow easy adjusting to feedback, and you thus lose one of the main advantages of face-to-face contact.

One potential problem with this method is the risk of forgetting your speech. In a memorized speech each sentence cues the recall of the following sentence. Thus, when you forget one sentence, you may forget the rest of the speech. This danger, along with the natural nervousness that speakers feel, makes the memorizing method a poor choice in most situations.

Speaking Extemporaneously. An **extemporaneous speech** involves thorough preparation but no commitment to the exact wording to be used during the speech. It often involves memorizing your opening lines (perhaps the first few sentences), your closing lines (perhaps the last few sentences), and your main points and the order in which you'll present them. You can also, if you wish, memorize selected phrases, sentences, or quotations. Memorizing the opening and closing lines will help you to focus your complete attention on the audience and will also put you more at ease. Once you know exactly what you'll say in opening and closing the speech, you'll feel more in control.

The extemporaneous method is useful in most speaking situations. Good college lecturers use the extemporaneous method. They prepare thoroughly and know what they want to say and in what order they want to say it, but they've made no commitment to exact wording. This method allows you to respond easily to feedback. Should a point need clarification, you can elaborate on it at the moment when it will be most effective. This method makes it easy to be natural, too, because you're being yourself. It's the method that comes closest to conversation. With the extemporaneous method, you can move about and interact with the audience.

Making Delivery More Effective

Strive for delivery that is natural, reinforces the message, is varied, and has a conversational tone.

Be Natural. Listeners will enjoy and believe you more if you speak naturally, as if you were conversing with a small group of people. Don't allow your delivery to call attention to itself. Your ultimate aim should be to deliver the speech so naturally that the audience won't even notice your delivery. This will take some practice, but you can do it. When voice or bodily action is so prominent that it's distracting, the audience concentrates on the delivery and will fail to attend to your speech.

Use Delivery to Reinforce Your Message. Effective delivery should aid instant intelligibility. Your main objective is to make your ideas understandable to an audience. A voice that listeners have to strain to hear, a decrease in volume at the ends of sentences, or slurred diction will obviously hinder comprehension.

Dress Appropriately. When you give a public speech, everything about you communicates. You cannot prevent yourself from sending messages to others. The way in which you dress is no exception. In fact, your attire will figure significantly in the way your audience assesses your credibility and even the extent to which they give you attention. In short, the way you present yourself physically will influence your effectiveness in all forms of persuasive and informative speaking. Unfortunately, there are no rules that will apply to all situations for all speakers. Thus, only general guidelines are offered here. Modify and tailor these for yourself and for each unique situation.

- Avoid extremes: Don't allow your clothes, hairstyle, and so on to detract attention from what you're saying.
- Dress comfortably: Be both physically and psychologically comfortable with your appearance so that you can concentrate your energies on what you're saying.
- Dress appropriately: Your appearance should be consistent with the specific public speaking occasion.

Vary Your Delivery. Listening to a speech is hard work for the audience. Flexible and varied delivery eases the listeners' task. Be especially careful to avoid monotonous patterns and predictable patterns.

Speakers who are monotonous keep their voices at the same pitch, volume, and rate throughout the speech. The monotonous speaker maintains a uniform level from the introduction to the conclusion. Like the drone of a motor, this easily puts the audience to sleep. Vary your pitch levels, your volume, and your rate of speaking. In a similar way, avoid monotony in bodily action. Avoid standing in exactly the same position throughout the speech. Use your body to express your ideas, to communicate to the audience what is going on in your head.

A predictable vocal pattern is a pattern in which, for example, the volume levels vary but always in the same sequence. Through repetition, the sequence soon becomes predictable. For example, each sentence may begin loud and then decline to a barely audible volume. In bodily action, the predictable speaker repeatedly uses the same movements or gestures. For example, a speaker may scan the audience from left to right to left to right throughout the entire speech. If the audience can predict the pattern of your voice or your bodily action, your speech will almost surely be ineffective. A patterned and predictable delivery will draw the audience's attention away from what you're saying.

Be Conversational. Although more formal than conversation, delivery in public speaking should have some of the most important features of conversation. These qualities include immediacy, eye contact, expressiveness, and responsiveness to feedback.

Just as you can create a sense of immediacy through language, as discussed earlier, you can also create it with delivery. Make your listeners feel that you're talking directly and individually to each of them. You can communicate immediacy through delivery in a number of ways:

- Maintain appropriate eye contact with the audience members.
- Maintain a physical closeness that reinforces a psychological closeness; don't stand behind a desk or lectern.
- Smile.
- Move around a bit; avoid the appearance of being too scared to move.
- Stand with a direct and open body posture.
- Talk directly to your audience, not to your notes or to your visual aids.

When you maintain eye contact, you make the public speaking interaction more conversational (in addition to communicating immediacy). Look directly into your listeners' eyes. Lock eyes with different audience members for short periods.

When you're expressive, you communicate genuine involvement in the public speaking situation. You can communicate this quality of expressiveness, of involvement, in several ways:

- Express responsibility for your own thoughts and feelings.
- Vary your vocal rate, pitch, volume, and rhythm to communicate involvement and interest in the audience and in the topic.
- Allow your facial muscles and your entire body to reflect and echo this inner involvement.
- Use gestures appropriately; too few gestures may signal lack of interest, but too many can communicate uneasiness, awkwardness, or anxiety.

Read carefully the feedback signals sent by your audience. Then respond to these signals with verbal, vocal, and bodily adjustments. For example, respond to audience feedback signals communicating lack of comprehension or inability to hear with added explanation or increased volume.

Avoid Common Mistakes. Be sure to avoid the frequently made mistakes that detract from the power of your speech. Here are a few:

- Don't start your speech immediately. Instead, survey your audience; make eye contact and engage their attention. Stand in front of the audience with a sense of control. Pause briefly, then begin speaking.
- Don't display any discomfort or displeasure. When you walk to the speaker's stand, display enthusiasm and your desire to speak. People much prefer listening to a speaker who seems to enjoy speaking to them.
- Don't race away from the speaker's stand. After your last statement, pause, maintain audience eye contact, and then walk (don't run) to your seat. Show no signs of relief; focus your attention on whatever activity is taking place, glance over the audience, and sit down. If a question period follows your speech and you're in charge of this, pause after completing your conclusion. Ask audience members in a direct manner if they have any questions. If there's a chairperson who will ask for questions, pause after your conclusion, then nonverbally signal to the chairperson that you're ready.

Use Notes Appropriately. For many speeches it may be helpful to use notes. A few simple guidelines may help you avoid some of the common errors made in using notes.

1. Keep notes to a minimum. The fewer notes you take with you, the better off you will be. The reason so many speakers bring notes with them is that they want to avoid the face-to-face interaction required. With experience, however, you should find this face-to-face interaction the best part of the public speaking experience.
2. Resist the normal temptation to bring with you the entire speech outline. You may rely on it too heavily and lose the direct contact with the audience. Instead, compose a delivery outline, as discussed earlier in this unit, using only key words. Bring this to the lectern with you—one side of an index card or at most an $8\frac{1}{2}$-by-11-inch sheet should be sufficient. This will relieve any anxiety over the possibility of forgetting your speech but will not be extensive enough to interfere with direct contact with your audience.
3. Don't make your notes more obvious than necessary, but at the same time don't try to hide them. For example, don't gesture with your notes—but don't turn away from the audience to steal glances at them, either. Use them openly and honestly but gracefully, with "open subtlety." To do this effectively, you'll have to

know your notes intimately. Rehearse with the same notes that you will take with you to the speaker's stand.

4. When referring to your notes, pause to examine them; then regain eye contact with the audience and continue your speech. Don't read from your notes, just take cues from them. The one exception to this guideline is an extensive quotation or complex set of statistics that you have to read; immediately after reading, however, resume direct eye contact with the audience.

Voice

Three dimensions of voice are significant to the public speaker: volume, rate, and pitch. Your manipulation of these elements will enable you to control your voice to maximum advantage.

Vocal Volume. *Vocal volume* is the relative intensity of the voice. (Loudness, on the other hand, refers to hearers' perception of that relative intensity.) In an adequately controlled voice, volume will vary according to several factors. For example, the distance between speaker and listener, the competing noise, and the emphasis the speaker wishes to give an idea will all influence volume.

Problems with volume are easy to identify in others, though difficult to recognize in ourselves. One obvious problem is a voice that is too soft. When speech is so soft that listeners have to strain to hear, they will soon tire of expending so much energy. A voice that is too loud can also prove disturbing, because it intrudes on our psychological space. However, it's interesting to note that a voice louder than normal communicates assertiveness (Page & Balloun, 1978) and will lead people to pay greater attention to you (Robinson & McArthur, 1982). On the other hand, it can also communicate aggressiveness and give others the impression that you'd be difficult to get along with.

The most common problem is too little volume variation. Also, as mentioned earlier, a related problem is a volume pattern that, although varied, varies in an easily predictable pattern. If the audience can predict the pattern of volume changes, they will focus on that pattern and not on what you're saying.

A speaker who tends to fade away at the end of sentences is particularly disturbing to the audience. Here the speaker uses a volume that is largely appropriate but speaks the last few words of sentences at an extremely low volume. Be particularly careful when finishing sentences; make sure the audience is able to hear you without difficulty.

If you're using a microphone, test it first. Whether it's the kind that clips around your neck, the kind you hold in your hand, or the kind that is stationed at the podium, try it out first. Some speakers—talk show host Montel Williams is a good example—use the hand microphone as a prop and flip it in the air or from hand to hand as they emphasize a particular point. For your beginning speeches, it's probably best to avoid such techniques and to use the microphone as unobtrusively as you can.

Vocal Rate. Your *vocal rate* is the speed at which you speak. About 150 words per minute seems average for speaking as well as for reading aloud. Rate problems include speaking too fast, too slow, with too little variation, or with too predictable a pattern. If you talk too fast, you deprive your listeners of time they need to understand and digest what you're saying. If the rate is extreme, the listeners will simply not be willing to expend the energy needed to understand your speech.

VIEWPOINT

Television commercials frequently play at a higher volume than the regular programming. In your next speech how might you use—without abusing—the theory that volume change gains attention?

UNDERSTANDING *THEORY* AND *RESEARCH*

Speech Rate

You've probably noticed that advertisers and salespeople generally talk at a rate faster than normal speech. But is this effective? Are people who speak faster more persuasive? The answer is: It depends (Smith & Shaffer, 1991, 1995). The rapid speaker who speaks *against* your existing attitudes is generally more effective than the speaker who speaks at a normal rate. But the rapid speaker who speaks *in favor of* your existing attitudes (say, in an attempt to strengthen them) is actually less effective than the speaker who speaks at a normal rate. The reason for this is quite logical. In the case of the speaker speaking against your existing attitudes, rapid speech doesn't give you the time you need to think of counterarguments to rebut the speaker's position. So you're more likely to be persuaded, because you don't have time to consider why the speaker may be incorrect. In the case of the speaker speaking in favor of your existing attitudes, rapid speech doesn't give you time to mentally elaborate on the speaker's arguments; consequently, they don't carry as much persuasive force as they would if you had the time to add the speaker's arguments to those you already have.

Working with Theories and Research

- *With specific reference to your next speech, how might you apply this research to increase your own persuasiveness?*

If your rate is too slow, it will encourage your listeners' thoughts to wander to matters unrelated to your speech. Be careful, therefore, neither to bore the audience by presenting information at too slow a rate, nor to set a pace that is too rapid for listeners to absorb. Strike a happy medium. Speak at a pace that engages the listeners and allows them time for reflection but without boring them.

As with volume, rate variations may be underused or totally absent. If you speak at the same rate throughout the entire speech, you're not making use of this important speech asset. Use variations in rate to call attention to certain points and to add variety. For example, if you describe the dull routine of an assembly line worker in a rapid and varied pace or evoke the wonder of a circus in a pace with absolutely no variation, you're surely misusing this important vocal dimension. Again, if you're interested in and conscious of what you're saying, your rate variations should flow naturally and effectively. Too predictable a pattern of rate variations is sometimes as bad as no variation at all. If the audience can predict—consciously or unconsciously—your rate pattern, you're in a vocal rut. You're not communicating ideas but reciting words you've memorized.

Vocal Pitch. *Vocal pitch* is the relative highness or lowness of your voice as perceived by your listener. More technically, pitch results from the rate at which your vocal folds vibrate. If they vibrate rapidly, listeners will perceive your voice as having a high pitch. If they vibrate slowly, listeners will perceive your voice as having a low pitch.

Pitch changes often signal changes in the meanings of sentences. The most obvious is the difference between a statement and a question. Thus, vocal inflection or pitch makes the difference between the declarative sentence "So this is the proposal you want me to support" and the question "So this is the proposal you want me to support?"

The obvious problems that arise in relation to pitch are levels that are too high, too low, and too patterned. Neither of the first two problems is common in speakers with otherwise normal voices, and with practice you can correct a pitch pattern that is too predictable or monotonous. With increased speaking experience, pitch changes will come naturally from the sense of what you're saying. After all, each sentence is somewhat different from every other sentence, so there should be a normal variation—a variation that results not from some conscious or predetermined pattern but rather from the meanings you wish to convey to the audience.

Pauses

Pauses come in two basic types: filled and unfilled. Filled pauses are pauses in the stream of speech that we fill with vocalizations such as *er, um, ah,* and the like. Even expressions such as *well* and *you know,* when used to fill up silence, are called filled pauses. These pauses are ineffective and weaken the strength of your message. They will make you appear hesitant, unprepared, and unsure of yourself.

Unfilled pauses, in contrast, are silences interjected into the normally fluent stream of speech. Unfilled pauses can be extremely effective if used correctly. Here are just a few examples of places where unfilled pauses—silences of a few seconds—should prove effective.

- Pause at transitional points. This will signal that you're moving from one part of the speech to another or from one idea to another. It will help the listeners separate the main issues you're discussing.
- Pause at the end of an important assertion. This will allow the audience time to think about the significance of what you're saying.
- Pause after asking a rhetorical question. This will give your listeners time to think about how they would answer the question.
- Pause before an important idea. This will help signal that what comes next is especially significant.

In addition, pauses are helpful both before you begin to speak and after you've concluded. Don't start speaking as soon as you get to the front of the room; rather, pause to scan the audience and gather your thoughts. Also, don't leave the podium as you speak your last word: Pause to allow your speech to sink in—and to avoid giving the audience the impression that you're anxious to leave them.

Bodily Action

Your body is a powerful instrument in your speech. You speak with your body as well as with your mouth. The total effect of the speech depends not only on what you say but also on the way you present it. It depends on your movements, gestures, and facial expressions as well as your words.

Six aspects of bodily action are especially important in public speaking: eye contact, facial expression, posture, gestures, movement, and proxemics.

Eye Contact. As I've emphasized so often before, the most important single aspect of bodily communication is eye contact. The two major problems with eye contact in public speaking are not enough eye contact and eye contact that does not cover the audience fairly. Speakers who do not maintain enough eye contact appear distant and unconcerned and may be seen as less trustworthy than speakers who look directly at their audience. And, of course, without eye contact, you will not be able to secure that all-important audience feedback.

Maintain eye contact with the entire audience. Involve all listeners in the public speaking transaction. Communicate equally with the members on the left and on the right, in both the back and the front.

Use eye contact to secure audience feedback. Are they interested? Bored? Puzzled? In agreement? In disagreement? Use your eyes to communicate your commitment to and interest in what you're saying. Communicate your confidence and commitment by making direct eye contact; avoid staring blankly through your audience or gazing over their heads, down at the floor, or out the window.

Facial Expression. Facial expressions are especially important in communicating **emotions**—your anger or fear, boredom or excitement, doubt or surprise. If you feel committed to and believe in your thesis, you'll probably display your emotional messages appropriately and effectively.

Nervousness and anxiety, however, can sometimes prevent you from relaxing enough so that your emotions come through. Fortunately, time and practice will allow you to relax, and the emotions you feel will reveal themselves appropriately and automatically.

Generally, members of one culture will be able to recognize the emotions displayed facially by members of other cultures. But there are differences in what each culture considers appropriate to display. Each culture has its own "display rules" (Ekman, Friesen, & Ellsworth, 1972). For example, Japanese Americans watching a stress-inducing film spontaneously displayed the same facial emotions as did other Americans when they thought they were unobserved. But when an observer was present, the Japanese Americans masked (tried to hide) their emotional expressions more than did the other Americans (Gudykunst & Kim, 1992).

Posture. When delivering your speech, stand straight but not stiff. Try to communicate command of the situation without communicating the discomfort that is actually quite common for beginning speakers.

Avoid the common posture mistakes: putting your hands in your pockets, or leaning on the desk, the podium, or the chalkboard. With practice you'll come to feel more at ease and will communicate this by the way you stand before the audience.

Gestures. Gestures in public speaking help illustrate your verbal messages. We do this regularly in conversation. For example, when saying "Come here," you probably move your head, hands, arms, and perhaps your entire body to motion the listener in your direction. Your body and your verbal message say "Come here."

Avoid using your hands to preen; for example, restrain yourself from fixing your hair or adjusting your clothing. Avoid fidgeting with your watch, ring, or jewelry. Also avoid keeping your hands in your pockets or clasped in front of you or behind your back.

Effective gestures help you as the speaker, your relationship with the audience, and the subject matter of your speech seem spontaneous and natural. If gestures look planned or rehearsed, they'll appear phony and insincere. As a general rule, don't do anything with your hands that doesn't feel right for you; the audience will recognize it as unnatural. If you feel relaxed and comfortable with yourself and your audience, you'll generate natural bodily action without conscious or studied attention.

Movement. By *movement* here I am referring to your large bodily movements. It helps to move around a bit. It keeps both the audience and you more alert. Even when speaking behind a lectern, you can give the illusion of movement. You can step back or forward or flex your upper body so you appear to be moving more than you are.

Avoid three potential problems of movement: too little, too much, and too patterned. Speakers who move too little often appear strapped to the podium, afraid of the audience, or too detached to involve themselves fully. At the other extreme, when there's too much movement, the audience begins to concentrate on the movement itself, wondering where the speaker will wind up next. With movement that is too patterned, the audience may become bored—too steady and predictable a rhythm quickly becomes tiring. The audience will often view the speaker as nonspontaneous and uninvolved.

Use gross movements to emphasize transitions or to emphasize the introduction of a new and important assertion. Thus, when making a transition, you might take a step forward to signal that something new is coming. Similarly, this type of movement might signal the introduction of an important assumption, a key piece of evidence, or a closely reasoned argument.

If you're using a lectern, you may wish to signal transitions by stepping to the side or in front of it and then behind it again as you move from one point to another. As always, it's best to avoid the extremes; too much movement around the lectern and no movement from the lectern are both to be avoided. You may wish to lean over the lectern when, say, posing a question to your listeners or advancing a particularly important argument. But never lean on the lectern; never use it as support.

Proxemics. Proxemics, as discussed in Unit 8, is the study of how you use space in communication. In public speaking the space between you and your listeners and among the listeners themselves is often a crucial factor. If you stand too close to the people in the audience, they may feel uncomfortable, as if their personal space is being violated. If you stand too far away from your audience, you may be perceived as uninvolved, uninterested, and uncomfortable. Watch where your instructor and other speakers stand, and adjust your own position accordingly.

Answering Questions

In many public speaking situations a question-and-answer period will follow the speech. So be prepared to answer questions. Here are a few suggestions for making this Q&A session more effective.

- If you wish to encourage questions, preface the question period with some kind of encouraging statement; for example, "I know you've lots of questions—especially on how the new health program will work and how we'll finance it. I'll be happy to respond to your questions. Anyone?"
- Maintain eye contact with the audience. Let the audience know that you're still speaking with them.
- After you hear the question, pause to think about the question and about your answer. If you suspect that some members of the audience didn't hear the question, repeat it; then begin your answer.
- Control defensiveness. Don't assume that a question is a personal attack. Assume, instead, that the question is an attempt to secure more information or perhaps to challenge a position you've taken.
- If appropriate, thank the questioner or note that it's a good question. This will encourage others also to ask questions.
- Don't bluff. If you're asked a question and you don't know the answer, say so.
- Consider the usefulness of a persuasive answer. Question-and-answer sessions often give you opportunities to further advance your purpose by connecting the question and its answer with one or more of your major points: "I'm glad you asked about child care, because that's exactly the difference between the two proposals we're here to vote on. The plan I'm proposing . . . ."

All of these suggestions are based on the assumption that you want to encourage questions and dialogue. And generally speakers want audience questions, because the dialogue gives them an opportunity

BUILDING COMMUNICATION SKILLS

Responding Strategically and Ethically

Consider the following situations that might arise in a public speaking situation. How would you respond to achieve your purpose and yet not violate any of your own ethical standards?

1. You've just given a speech to a racially diverse high school class on why they should attend your college. One audience member asks how racially diverse your faculty and students are. Your faculty is 94 percent European American, 4 percent Asian American, and 2 percent African American. You do know that the administration aims to recruit a more diverse faculty, but so far no action has been taken. Your student population is approximately 40 percent European American, 40 percent African American, 10 percent Hispanic, and 10 percent Asian American. What do you say?
2. You've just given a speech advocating banning alcohol on campus. In the speech you claimed that more than 70 percent of the students favor banning alcohol. At the end of the speech, you realize that you made a mistake and that only 30 percent favor banning alcohol; you were nervous and mixed up the figures. There's a question-and-answer period, but no one asks about the figures. What do you say?
3. You represent the college newspaper and are asking the student government to increase the paper's funding. The student government objects to giving extra money, because the paper has taken up lots of unpopular causes. You feel that it's essential for the paper to give visibility to minority views and fully expect to continue to do exactly as you have in the past. But if you say this, you won't get the added funding—and the paper won't be able to survive without increased funds. You will get the funding if you say you'll give primary coverage to majority positions. What do you say?

to talk more about something they're interested in. In some cases, too, there seems an ethical obligation for the speaker to entertain questions; after all, if the audience sat through what the speaker wanted to say, the speaker should listen to what they want to say.

There are situations, however, when you may want to discourage questions. Perhaps you want your audience to think about the material for a while, or you don't want to go into a matter in detail before sufficient data are available, or you know that there are people in the audience who want to use the question-and-answer period as an opportunity to push their own ideas. If you want to discourage questions, then, obviously, reverse many of the suggestions I've given.

REFLECTIONS ON ETHICS

Criticizing Ethically

Just as speakers and listeners have ethical obligations, so do critics. To be an ethical critic, keep in mind these guidelines:

- Separate personal feelings about the speaker from your evaluations. Liking the speaker should not lead you to evaluate a speech positively, nor should disliking the speaker lead you to evaluate a speech negatively.
- Separate personal feelings about the issues from your evaluation of the validity of the arguments. Recognize the validity of an argument even if it contradicts a deeply held belief; by the same token, recognize the fallaciousness of an argument even if it supports a deeply held belief.
- Demonstrate cultural sensitivity and be conscious of your own ethnocentrism. Beware of evaluating customs and forms of speech negatively simply because they differ from your own. Conversely, be careful not to evaluate a speech positively just because it supports your own cultural beliefs and values. Avoid any inclination to discriminate for or against speakers simply because they're of a particular gender, race, nationality, religion, age group, or affectional orientation.

WHAT WOULD YOU DO? You and your best friend are taking this course together. Your friend just gave a pretty terrible speech, and unfortunately, the instructor has asked you to offer a critique. The wrinkle here is that the instructor's grades for speeches seem to be heavily influenced by what student critics say. So in effect your critique will largely determine your friend's grade. You'd like to give your friend a positive critique so he can earn a good grade—which he badly needs—and you figure you can always tell him the truth later and even help him to improve. What would you do? Would you do anything differently, if *you* were to receive a grade for the critique based on how perceptive and accurate it was?

SUMMARY

This unit focused on outlining, style, rehearsal, and delivery and offered suggestions for using preparation, skeletal, and delivery outlines; choosing words and phrasing sentences; and rehearsing and delivering your speech.

1. An outline is a blueprint that helps you organize and evaluate your speech. The preparation outline is extremely detailed and includes all of your main points, supporting materials, introduction, conclusion, transition, and references. The skeletal outline is a kind of template that can help you see where certain material can be placed. The delivery outline is a brief version of your preparation outline that you use as a guide when delivering your speech.
2. Compared with written style, oral style contains shorter, simpler, and more familiar words; greater qualification; and more self-referential terms.
3. Effective public speaking style is clear (be economical and specific; use guide phrases; and stick to short, familiar, and commonly used terms), vivid (use active verbs, strong verbs, figures of speech, and imagery), appropriate to your audience (speak on a suitable level of formality; avoid jargon and technical expressions; avoid slang, vulgarity, and offensive terms), personal (use personal pronouns, ask questions, and create immediacy), and forceful (eliminate weakeners, vary intensity, and avoid trite expressions).
4. In constructing sentences for public speeches, favor short, direct, active, and positively phrased sentences. Vary the type and length.
5. Use rehearsal to time your speech; perfect your volume, rate, and pitch; incorporate pauses and other delivery notes; and perfect your bodily action.
6. There are four basic methods of delivering a public speech. The impromptu method involves speaking without any specific preparation. The manuscript method involves writing out the entire speech and reading it to the audience. Memorized delivery involves writing out the speech, memorizing it, and reciting it. The extemporaneous method involves thorough preparation and memorizing of the main ideas and their order of appearance but no commitment to exact wording.
7. Effective delivery is natural, reinforces the message, is varied, and has a conversational quality. When you deliver your speech, regulate your voice for greatest effectiveness. Adjust your vocal volume, rate, and pitch as appropriate.
8. Use unfilled pauses to signal a transition between the major parts of the speech, to allow the audience time to think, to allow the audience to ponder a rhetorical question, or to signal the approach of a particularly important idea. Avoid filled pauses; they weaken your message.
9. Effective body action involves maintaining eye contact with your entire audience, allowing your facial expressions to convey your feelings, using your posture to communicate command of the public speaking interaction, gesturing naturally, and moving around a bit.
10. In answering sessions after the speech: encourage questions, maintain eye contact, repeat the question if necessary, avoid any signs of defensiveness, express thanks for the question (if appropriate), don't bluff, and consider the usefulness of a persuasive answer.

KEY TERMS

outline
preparation outline
skeletal outline
delivery outline
oral style
clarity
vividness
figures of speech
jargon
slang
personal style
immediacy
weakeners
clichés
impromptu speech

manuscript speech
memorized delivery
extemporaneous speech
monotonous patterns
predictable patterns
vocal volume
vocal rate
vocal pitch
pauses
emotions

Thinking Critically About

Style and Delivery

1. As part of her second employment interview, Shandra is asked to give a speech to a group of analysts she'll supervise if she gets the job (as well as to the management that will make the hiring decision). Shandra knows very little about the corporate culture; people working there describe it as "conservative," "professional but friendly," and "hardworking." What advice would you give Shandra concerning her speaking style? For example, should she strive for a personal style or an impersonal one? A powerful style? Should she strive for immediacy or should she signal distance? Would your advice differ if Shandra were significantly older than the group she'd be supervising? Would your advice differ if Shandra were significantly younger than the group? Would you give different advice if the audience were all male? All female? Mixed?
2. Francisco is scheduled to give two speeches, one to a predominantly female audience of health professionals and one to a predominantly male audience of small business owners. His topic for both groups is the same: neighborhood violence. What advice—if any—would you give Francisco for tailoring his speech to the two different audiences? If you would not offer advice, why not?
3. John has this great joke that is only tangentially related to his speech topic. But the joke is so great that it will immediately get the audience actively involved in his speech; this, John thinks, outweighs the fact that the joke isn't integrally related to the speech. John asks your advice; what do you suggest?
4. Michael has a very formal type of personality; he's very restrained in everything he does. But he wants to try to project a different image—a much more personable, friendly, informal quality—in his speeches. What advice would you give Michael?
5. Whether or not you speak English as a second language, visit a website devoted to ESL (for example, http://www.lang.uiuc.edu/r-li5/esl/). What do you learn from this website that could supplement what was covered in this unit?
6. Try rephrasing each of these clichés or idioms so that they are clear, vivid, appropriate, personal, and forceful.
    - It's a blessing in disguise.
    - You have to take the bitter with the sweet.
    - He meant well, but he drove everyone up the wall.
    - He just has to get his act together.
    - She has a heart of gold.
    - I talked and talked, but it was in one ear and out the other.
    - He let it slip through his fingers.
    - Well, it's easy being a Monday-morning quarterback.
    - Don't put all your eggs in one basket.
    - They gave the detective a real snow job.
    - It was fun, but it wasn't what it was cracked up to be.
    - Wow, you're touchy. You get up on the wrong side of the bed?
7. Mary comes from a background very different from that of the other students in her class—Mary's family dressed for dinner, women were encouraged to be accepting rather than assertive, and politeness was emphasized above all else. If Mary communicates this image of herself, she thinks that the class will see her as an outsider, not only as a speaker but also as a person. She wonders if there's anything she can do in her speeches to present herself in a light that others will respond to positively. What advice would you give Mary?
8. This unit's text offered ideas for using imagery to make your speech more vivid than, say, normal conversation. However, some evidence suggests that overly vivid images may actually make your speech less memorable and less persuasive than it would be otherwise (Frey & Eagly, 1993). When images are too vivid, they divert the brain from following a logically presented series of thoughts or arguments. Thus, if listeners focus on extremely vivid images, they may lose track of your sequence of points. The advice, therefore, is to use vividness when it adds clarity to your ideas. When there's the possibility that your listeners may concentrate on the imagery rather than the idea, tone down the imagery. What would make imagery too vivid for a speech in your class? Can you find examples of imagery that you consider too vivid in advertisements or in public speeches?
9. Prepare and deliver a two-minute speech in which you do one of the following:

- describe the language of a noted personality (television, politics, arts, etc.)
- describe the delivery of a speaker you consider effective and the delivery of one you consider ineffective
- describe the delivery style of a prominent comedian, or compare the delivery styles of any two comedians
- introduce an excerpt from literature and read the excerpt as you might a manuscript speech
- analyze an advertisement in terms of one or two of the characteristics of effective style: clarity, vividness, appropriateness, personal style, or forcefulness
- describe an object in the room using visual, auditory, and tactile imagery

UNIT

The Informative Speech

UNIT CONTENTS

Many of the speeches you'll deliver will be informative speeches, in which you'll explain to an audience how something works or how to do something. In this unit you'll learn

- the principles of informing listeners
- how you can develop speeches that describe objects, people, and events; define terms and theories; and demonstrate how something works or how to do something

Guidelines for Informative Speaking

When you communicate "information," you tell your listeners something new, something they don't know. You may tell them about a new way of looking at old things or an old way of looking at new things. You may discuss a theory not previously heard of or a familiar theory not fully understood. You may discuss

ASK THE RESEARCHER

Communicating and Teaching

- *I'm planning to become a high school history teacher, and I'm wondering if there's anything I can start doing now to become a really successful instructor. Are there particular communication skills I should focus on or emphasize?*

Effective teachers are also effective informative speakers. Three informative speech-making skills that will enhance your ability to teach are learning how to create relevant and clear messages, and learning how to adapt to your audience.

- *Make messages relevant.* Show students how history will benefit their personal development and professional work lives. Relate history to your audience members' experiences and interests. Be prepared and ready to share yourself with your audience. Explain why you find history so fascinating.
- *Make messages clear.* Use language and examples that your audience will understand and find interesting. Teaching history is storytelling. Explain and illustrate in a vivid manner the historical context, the setting, the characters, and then pull your students through the story.
- *Adapt to your audience.* Carefully interpret your students' nonverbal behavior. Are they following you? Anticipate confusion and be prepared to offer multiple examples to illustrate your content. Be prepared to make abstract terms and concepts more concrete.

For further information: Chesebro, J. L., & McCroskey, J. C. (Eds.). (2002). *Communication for teachers*. Boston: Allyn & Bacon. See specifically Mottet, T. P., & Richmond, V. P., "Student nonverbal communication and its influence on teachers and teaching" (pp. 47–61) in the Chesebro and McCroskey book.

Timothy P. Mottet (Ed.D., West Virginia) is associate professor in the Department of Communication Studies at Texas State University, San Marcos, where he teaches courses in instructional communication, communication assessment, and communication research methods and theory. His current program of research examines the effects of student communication behaviors on teachers and their teaching in traditional and distance education classroom contexts. Dr. Mottet (tm15@txstate.edu) is also director of the basic communication course at Texas State and is responsible for training and developing graduate teaching assistants.

events that the audience may be unaware of or may have misconceptions about. Regardless of what type of informative speech you intend to give, the following guidelines should help.

In addition, the Public Speaking Sample Assistant boxes illustrate some of the pitfalls you'll want to avoid in a poorly constructed informative speech (see pages 363–364) and some of the principles you'll want to follow in an excellent informative speech (see pages 370–373).

Limit the Amount of Information

Resist the temptation to overload your listeners with information. Limit the breadth of information you communicate; instead, expand its depth. Limiting the amount of information lets you present a few items of information and explain these with examples, illustrations, and descriptions rather than presenting a wide array of items without this needed amplification. The speaker who attempts to discuss the physiological, psychological, social, and linguistic differences between men and women, for example, is clearly trying to cover too much and is going to be forced to cover these areas only superficially, with the result that little new information will be communicated. Even covering one of these areas is likely to prove too broad. Instead, select one subdivision of one area—say, language development or differences in language problems—and develop that in depth.

Adjust the Level of Complexity

As you know from attending college classes, information can be presented in a very simplified form or in an extremely complex form. Adjusting the level of complexity on which you communicate is key and should be guided by a wide variety of factors we have already considered: the level of knowledge your audience has, the time you have available, the pur-

COMMUNICATION@WORK

Information Overload

Everybody gets so much information all day long that they lose their common sense.

—Gertrude Stein

Information overload is one of the greatest barriers to efficiency in business and has even been linked to health problems in more than one-third of managers (Lee, 2000). Information is now generated at such a rapid rate that it's impossible to keep up with all that's relevant to your job. Invariably, you must select only certain information to attend to. The junk mail and spam that seems to grow every day is a perfect example. Today the American worker is exposed to more information in one year than a person living in 1900 was in his or her entire life.

One of the problems information overload creates is that it absorbs an enormous amount of time for workers at all levels of an organization. The more messages you have to deal with, the less time you have for those messages or tasks that are central to your functions. Similarly, errors become more likely under conditions of information overload, simply because you cannot devote the needed time to any one item.

Several suggestions should help you deal with information overload (Uris, 1986):

- Think before passing on messages. Not all messages must be passed on; not everyone needs to know everything.
- Use the messages as they come to you; record the relevant information and then throw them out. Similarly, throw out materials that contain information that can be easily located elsewhere.
- Organize your messages. Create folders to help you store and retrieve the information you need quickly.
- Get rid of extra copies. When you receive multiple copies of an item, get rid of all but the one (if any) that you need.

Communicating@Work

How do you cope with information overload? What might you do to deal more effectively with this inevitable overload?

UNDERSTANDING *THEORY* AND *RESEARCH*

Information Theory

In the 1940s, engineers working at Bell Telephone Laboratories developed the mathematical theory of communication—which became known as information theory (Shannon & Weaver, 1949). This theory defined **information** as that which reduces uncertainty. For example, if I tell you my name and you already know it, then I haven't communicated information—because my message (my name) didn't reduce uncertainty; you already knew my name and so had no uncertainty in this connection. If, on the other hand, I tell you my salary or my educational background or my fears and dreams, that constitutes information, because these are things you presumably didn't know. Although this theory doesn't explain many of the complexities of human communication very well (see Unit 1), it is helpful when you are thinking about the purpose of the informative speech: to communicate information, to tell the members of the audience something they didn't already know, or to send messages that reduce the uncertainty of your listeners about your speech topic. If you don't communicate enough information, the audience will be bored (they'll already know what you're saying). But if you communicate too much information, they'll be overwhelmed. The art of the effective speaker is to strike an appropriate balance.

Working with Theories and Research

- *Review the speech you're working on now. How much is information? How much does the audience already know? Is this the appropriate balance, or do you need to make adjustments?*

pose you hope to achieve, the topic on which you're speaking, and so on. If you simplify a topic too much, you risk boring or, even worse, insulting your audience. If your talk is too complex, you risk confusing your audience and failing to communicate the desired information.

Generally, however, beginning speakers err on the side of being too complex and do not realize that a 5- or 10-minute speech does not allow much time to introduce sophisticated concepts or make an audience understand how a complicated process works. At least in your beginning speeches, try to keep it simple rather than complex. For example, make sure the words you use are familiar to your audience—or, if they're not, explain and define the terms as you use them. Remember too that jargon and technical vocabulary of specialized fields often will need translation. Always see your topic from the point of view of the members of the audience; ask yourself how much they know about your topic and its unique language.

Stress Relevance and Usefulness

Listeners will remember your information best when they see it as useful and relevant to their own needs or goals. Notice that as a listener you regularly follow the principle of stressing relevance and usefulness. For example, in class you may attend to and remember the stages in the development of language in children simply because you know you'll be tested on the information and you want to earn a high grade. Or you may attend to the information because it will help you make a better impression in your job interview, make you a better parent, or enable you to deal with relationship problems.

Like you, listeners attend to information that will prove useful to them. So if you want the audience to listen to your speech, relate your information to their needs, wants, or goals (Frymier & Shulman, 1995). Throughout your speech, but especially in the beginning, make sure your audience knows that the information you're presenting is relevant and useful to them now—or will be in the immediate future. For example, you might say something like:

> We all want financial security. We all want to be able to buy those luxuries we read so much about in magazines and see every evening on television. Wouldn't it be nice to be able to buy a car without worrying about where you're going to get the down payment or how you'll be able to make the monthly payments? Actually, that is not an unrealistic goal, as I'll demonstrate in this speech. In fact, I will show you several methods for investing

VIEWPOINT

A useful way to make sure you'll stress usefulness is to assume, as you're preparing and refining your speech, that each person in the audience is going to be asking, "What's in this for me?" "How will this benefit me?" "Why should I be here listening to this speech?" With your next speech topic in mind, how would you answer these audience questions?

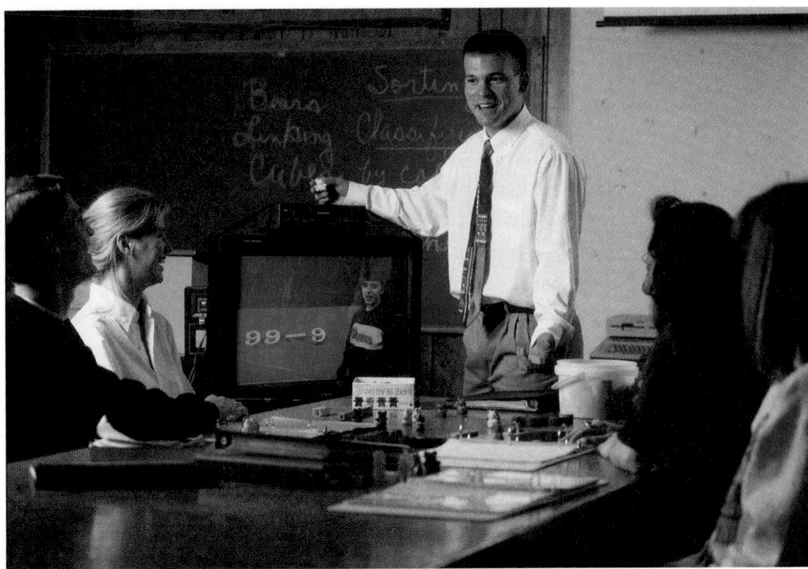

your money that will enable you to increase your income by at least 20 percent.

Relate New Information to Old

Listeners will learn information more easily and retain it longer when you relate it to what they already know. In relating new information to old, link the unfamiliar to the familiar, the unseen to the seen, the untasted to the tasted. Here, for example, Teresa Jacob, a student at Ohio State University (Schnoor, 1997, p. 97), relates the problems of drug interactions (the new) to mixing chemicals in the school lab (the old or familiar):

> During our high school years, most of us learned in a chemistry class the danger of mixing harmless chemicals in lab. Add one drop of the wrong compound and suddenly you've created a stink bomb, or worse, an explosion. Millions of Americans run the same risk inside their bodies each day by combining drugs that are supposed to help restore or maintain good health.

Vary the Levels of Abstraction

You can talk about freedom of the press in **abstractions**—for example, by talking about the importance of getting information to the public, by referring to the Bill of Rights, and by relating a free press to the preservation of democracy. That is, you can talk about the topic on a relatively high **level of abstraction.** But you can also talk about freedom of the press by citing specific examples: how a local newspaper was prevented from running a story critical of the town council or how Lucy Rinaldo was fired from the *Accord Sentinel* after she wrote a story critical of the mayor. In other words, you can talk about the topic on a relatively low level of abstraction, a level that is specific and concrete.

Varying the levels of abstraction—combining the abstract and the specific—seems to work best. Too many high abstractions without specifics or too many specifics without high abstractions will generally prove less effective than a combination of the two approaches.

Here, for example, is an excerpt from a speech on the issue of homelessness. Note that in the first paragraph we have a relatively abstract description of homelessness. In the second paragraph, we get into specifics. In the last paragraph the abstract and the concrete are connected.

> Homelessness is a serious problem for all metropolitan areas throughout the country. It's currently estimated that there are more than 200,000 homeless people in New York City alone. But what is this really about? Let me tell you what it's about.
>
> It's about a young man. He must be about 25 or 30, although he looks a lot older. He lives in a cardboard box on the side of my apartment house. We call him Tom, although we really don't know his name. All his possessions are stored in this huge box. I think it was a box from a refrigerator. Actually, he doesn't have very much, and what he has easily fits in this box. There's a blanket my neighbor threw out, some plastic bottles he puts water in, and some Styrofoam containers he picked up from the garbage from Burger King. He uses these to store whatever food he finds.
>
> What is homelessness about? It's about Tom and 200,000 other "Toms" in New York and thousands of others throughout the rest of the country. And not all of them even have boxes to live in.

BUILDING COMMUNICATION SKILLS

Using the Abstraction Ladder

The "abstraction ladder" is a device that illustrates the different levels of abstraction on which different terms exist. For example, as you go from "animal" to "dog" to "poodle" to "pampered white toy poodle," you're going down the ladder in terms of abstraction; you're getting less abstract and more concrete and specific. As you get more specific, you more clearly and easily direct the listener's attention to what you wish. For each of the terms listed below, indicate at least four possible terms (or phrases) that indicate increasing specificity. The first example is done for you.

Level 1	**Level 2** *(more specific than 1)*	**Level 3** *(more specific than 2)*	**Level 4** *(more specific than 3)*	**Level 5** *(more specific than 4)*
house	mansion	brick mansion	large brick mansion	the governor's mansion
desire				
car				
toy				
magazine				
sports				

Now that we've considered these guidelines for informative speaking, let's look at the kinds of informative speeches that you may be called upon to present. This unit will examine three types: speeches of (1) description, (2) definition, and (3) demonstration. But these three categories are just one way of grouping informative speech types. Here are some additional classifications of information speeches offered by other writers on public speaking; taken together, these interesting approaches further define the range of informative speaking.

Stephen Lucas (2004) uses a four-part classification:

- speeches about objects, persons, places, or things; for example, the contributions of a noted scientist or philosopher
- speeches about processes or a series of actions; for example, how to do something
- speeches about events or happenings; for example, your first date
- speeches about concepts, beliefs, or ideas; for example, theories of economics

George Rodman and Ron Adler (1997) offer a different four-part classification for classroom speeches:

- introductions—of yourself as well as of objects, events, and concepts
- instructions on how to do something; for example, how to use a scanner
- demonstrations to show how something works; for example, how CPR works
- explanations of why something works; for example, why cocaine has the effects it does

George Grice and John Skinner (2004) offer an eight-part system:

- speeches about people (Cesar Chavez, Margaret Mead)
- speeches about objects (electric cars, the Great Wall of China)
- speeches about places (Ellis Island, the Nile)
- speeches about events (sinking of the Titanic, Woodstock festivals)
- speeches about processes (cartooning, waterproofing)
- speeches about concepts (liberty, nihilism)
- speeches about conditions (McCarthyism, the civil rights movement)
- speeches about issues (use of polygraph, fetal tissue research)

We'll now turn to the first of this book's three categories of informative speech: the speech of description.

The Speech of Description

When you prepare a speech of description, you're concerned with explaining an object, person, event, or process. Here are a few examples:

Describing an Object or Person

- the structure of the brain
- the inventions of Thomas Edison
- the parts of a telephone
- the layout of the Alamo
- the hierarchy of a corporation
- the human body
- the components of a computer system

Describing an Event or Process

- the attack on the World Trade Center
- the events leading to World War II
- how to organize a body-building contest
- the breakdown of Russian communism
- how a newspaper is printed
- the process of buying a house
- purchasing stock online
- how a child acquires language
- how to read a textbook

Strategies for Describing

Here are some suggestions for describing objects, people, events, and processes.

Select an Appropriate Organizational Pattern

Choose the organizational pattern (see Unit 15) that best suits your topic. Consider using a spatial or a topical organization when describing objects and people, a temporal pattern for events and processes. For example, if you were to describe the layout of Philadelphia, you might start from the north and work down to the south (using a spatial pattern). If you were to describe the inventions of Thomas Edison, you might select the three or four major projects and discuss each of these equally (using a topical pattern).

If you were describing the events leading up to World War II, you might use a temporal pattern, starting with the earliest and working up to the latest. A temporal pattern would also be appropriate for describing how a hurricane develops or how a parade is put together.

Use a Variety of Descriptive Categories

Describe the object or event with lots of descriptive categories. For example, for physical categories ask yourself questions such as these:

- What color is it?
- How big is it?
- What is it shaped like?
- How high is it?
- How much does it weigh?
- How long or short is it?
- What is its volume?
- How attractive/unattractive is it?

Also consider social, psychological, and economic categories, among others. In describing a person, for example, consider such categories as friendly/unfriendly, warm/cold, rich/poor, aggressive/meek, and pleasant/unpleasant.

Consider Using Presentation Aids

Presentation aids such as those described in Unit 15 will help you describe almost anything. Use them if you possibly can. In describing an object or person, show your listeners a picture of, for example, the brain, the inside of a telephone, or the human skeleton. In describing an event or process, show them a diagram or flowchart to illustrate the stages or steps; for example, show the steps involved in buying stock, publishing a newspaper, or putting a parade together.

Consider Who, What, Where, When, and Why

The 5W categories (Unit 15) are especially useful when you want to describe an event or process. For example, if you're going to describe how to purchase a house, you might want to consider the people involved (who?), the steps you have to go through (what?), the places you'll have to go (where?), the time or sequence in which each of the steps has to take place (when?), and the advantages and disadvantages of buying the house (why?).

Developing the Speech of Description

Here are two sample outlines showing how you might go about constructing a speech of description. Each example includes both the thesis and the question asked of the thesis (which helps identify the main points of the speech). In this first example, the speaker describes four suggestions for increasing assertiveness (following a temporal sequence).

THE *PUBLIC SPEAKING* SAMPLE ASSISTANT

A Poorly Constructed Informative Speech

This poorly constructed informative speech was written by the author to demonstrate some of the faults that beginning speakers sometimes make and that you'll want to avoid.

Three Jobs

Three Jobs

In general, don't use your title as your opening words. This title seems adequate, though it's not terribly exciting. After reading the speech, try to come up with a more appealing title.

Well, I mean, hello. Er . . . I'm new at public speaking, so I'm a little nervous. I've always been shy. So don't watch my knees shake.

The speaker's nervous opening remarks reveal an anxiety that's understandable but is probably best not shared with the listeners. After all, you don't want the audience to be uncomfortable for you.

Ehm, let me see my notes here. [Mumbles to self while shuffling notes: "One, two, three, four, five—oh, they're all here."] Okay, here goes.

Going through your notes makes the audience feel that you didn't prepare adequately and may be wasting their time.

Three Jobs. That's my title and I'm going to talk about three jobs.

This is the speaker's orientation. Is this sufficient? What else might the speaker have done in the introduction?

The Health Care Field. This is the fastest-growing job in the country, one of the fastest, I guess I mean. I know that you're not interested in this topic and that you're all studying accounting. But there are a lot of new jobs in the health care field. The *Star* had an article on health care and said that health care will be needed more in the future than it is now. And now, you know, like they need a lot of health care people. In the hospital where I work—on the west side, uptown—they never have enough health aides and they always tell me to become a health aide, like, you know, to enter the health care field. To become a nurse. Or maybe a dental technician. But I hate going to the dentist. Maybe I will.

Such expressions of uncertainty make us question the speaker's competence.

And we begin to wonder, why is the speaker talking about this to us?

Stories in the *Star* may be entertaining, but they don't necessarily constitute evidence. What does this tabloid reference do to the credibility you ascribe to the speaker?

Everything in the speech must have a definite purpose. Asides such as comments about not liking to go to the dentist are probably best omitted.

I don't know what's going to happen with the president's health plan, but whatever happens, it won't change the need for health aides. I mean, people will still get sick; so it really doesn't matter what happens with health care.

Here the speaker had an opportunity to connect the topic with important current political events but failed to say anything that was not obvious.

The Robotics Field. This includes things like artificial intelligence. I don't really know what that is but its like growing real fast. They use this in making automobiles and planes and I think in computers. Japan is a leading country in this field. A lot of people in India go into this field, but I'm not sure why.

Introducing each topic this way is clear but probably not very interesting. How might the speaker have introduced each of the three main points more effectively?

Notice how vague the speaker is—"includes things like," "and I think in computers," "I'm not sure why." Such statements communicate very little information to listeners and leave them with little confidence that the speaker knows what he or she is talking about.

The Computer Graphics Field. This field has a lot to do with designing and making lots of different products, like CAD and CAM. This field also includes computer-aided imagery—CAI. And in movies, I think. Like *Star Wars* and *Terminator 2*. I saw *Terminator 2* four times. I didn't see *Star Wars* but I'm gonna rent the video. I don't know if you have to know a lot about computers or if you can just like be a designer and someone else will tell the computer what to do.	Again, this part of the speech offers little specific information. CAD and CAM are not defined, and CAI is explained merely as "computer-aided imagery." Unless we already knew what these were, we would have no idea even after hearing the speaker. And again the speaker inserts personal notes (for example, seeing *Terminator 2* four times) that have no meaningful connection to the topic.
I got my information from a book that Carol Kleiman wrote, *The 100 Best Jobs for the 1990s and Beyond*. It was summarized on the Internet somewhere.	The speaker uses only one source and, to make matters worse, doesn't even go to the original source but relies on a summary "somewhere" on the Internet. Especially with a topic like this, listeners are likely to want a variety of viewpoints and additional reliable sources.
	Note too that the speech lacked any statistics. This is a subject where statistics are essential. Listeners will want to know how many jobs will be available in these fields, what these fields will look like in 5 or 10 years, how much these fields pay, and so on.
My Conclusion. These are three of the fastest-growing fields in the U.S. And in the world, I think—not in Third World countries, I don't think. China and India and Africa. More like Europe and Germany. And the U.S.—the U.S. is the big one. I hope you enjoyed my speech. Thank you.	Using the word *conclusion* to signal that you're concluding is not a bad idea, but work it into the text instead of using it as if it were a heading in a book chapter.
	Once more, this lack of certainty makes us question the speaker's competence and preparation.
I wasn't as nervous as I thought I'd be. Are there any questions?	Again, personal comments are best left out.

Notice that the steps follow the order a person would follow in becoming more assertive.

General Purpose: To inform.
Specific Purpose: To describe how we can become more assertive.
Thesis: Assertiveness can be increased. (How can assertiveness be increased?)

I. Analyze assertive behaviors.
II. Record your own assertive behaviors.
III. Rehearse assertive behaviors.
IV. Act assertively.

In this second example, the speaker describes the way in which fear works in intercultural communication.

General purpose: To inform.
Specific purpose: To describe the way fear works in intercultural communication.
Thesis: Fear influences intercultural communication. (How does fear influence intercultural communication?)

I. We fear disapproval.
II. We fear embarrassing ourselves.
III. We fear being harmed.

In delivering such a speech, the speaker might begin by saying:

> There are three major fears that interfere with intercultural communication. First, there's the fear of disapproval—from members of our own group as well as from members of the other person's group. Second, we fear embarrassing ourselves, even making fools of ourselves, by saying the wrong thing or appearing insensitive. And third, we may fear being harmed—our stereotypes of the other group may lead us to see its members as dangerous or potentially harmful to us.
>
> Let's look at each of these fears in more detail so as to see how they influence our own intercultural communication behavior.
>
> Consider, first, the fear of disapproval . . . .

The Speech of Definition

What is leadership? What is a born-again Christian? What is the difference between sociology and psychology? What is a cultural anthropologist? What is safe sex? These are all topics for informative speeches of definition.

A *definition* is a statement of the meaning or significance of a concept or term. Use a speech of definition when you wish to explain a difficult or unfamiliar concept or when you wish to make a concept more vivid or forceful. You might wish to complement this discussion with a visit to one or more of the online dictionaries; start with Your Dictionary at www.yourdictionary.com/ for a wide variety of word books and materials.

In defining a particular term or in giving an entire speech of definition, you may focus on defining a term, elucidating a system or theory, or pinpointing the similarities and/or differences among terms or systems. It may be a subject new to the audience or one familiar to them but presented in a new and different way. Here are some examples of topics for speeches of definition:

Defining a Term

- What is multiculturalism?
- What is terrorism?
- What is a smart card?
- What is machismo?
- What is creativity?
- What is affirmative action?
- What is date rape?
- What is classism?
- What is political correctness?
- What is inflation?

Defining a System or Theory

- What is the classical theory of public speaking?
- What are the parts of a generative grammar?
- What are the major beliefs of Confucianism?
- What is expressionism?
- What is futurism?
- What is the "play theory" of mass communication?

Defining Similar and Dissimilar Terms or Systems

- Football and soccer: What's the difference?
- Communism and socialism: What are the similarities and differences?
- What do Christians and Muslims have in common?
- Oedipus and Electra: How do they differ?

UNDERSTANDING *THEORY* AND *RESEARCH*

Signal-to-Noise Ratio

A useful way of looking at information is in terms of its **signal-to-noise ratio.** *Signal* in this context refers to information that is useful to you, information that you want. *Noise,* on the other hand, is what you find useless; it's what you do not want. So, for example, if a mailing list or newsgroup contained lots of useful information, it would be high on signal and low on noise; if it contained lots of useless information, it would be high on noise and low on signal. Spam is high on noise and low on signal, as is static that interferes with radio, television, or telephone transmission.

From the public speaker's point of view, noise is anything that diverts audience attention away from the speech (the signal)—pictures on the walls, writing on the chalkboard, people talking in the hallways, the rustle of newspapers, and so on. The speaker's task is to keep the audience's focus on the speech instead of the noise.

Working with Theories and Research

- *Look around the classroom in which you give your speeches. What sources of potential noise can you identify? What can you do to prevent the audience from focusing on the noise instead of your speech?*

MEDIA WATCH

The Knowledge Gap

The term *knowledge gap* refers to the difference in knowledge between one group and another; it's the division between those who have a great deal of knowledge and those who have significantly less. Researchers who have focused on the influence of the media in widening this knowledge gap have generated what is known as the *knowledge gap hypothesis* (Tichenor, Donohue, & Olien, 1970; Severin & Tankard, 1988; Viswanath & Finnegan, 1995).

Information is valuable; it gives power and it can bring wealth. It gives you the means you need to get a high-paid job, to live a healthy life, to plan for retirement, or to accomplish just about any task you set for yourself (Mastin, 1998).

But information is also expensive, and not everyone has equal access to it. This is especially true as we live more of our lives in cyberspace. The new communication technologies—computers, CD-ROMS, high-speed Internet connections, and satellite and cable television, for example—are major means for gaining information. The knowledge gap hypothesis says that better-educated people have the money to own and the skills to master the new technologies and thus acquire more information. Less-educated people don't have the money to own or the skills to master the new technologies and thus cannot acquire much of the information that is out there. But the educated have the means for becoming even better educated, so the gap widens.

You also see the knowledge gap when you compare different cultures. Developed countries, for example, have the new technologies in their schools and offices, and many people can afford to buy their own computers and satellite systems. Access to the new technologies helps these countries develop even further. Developing countries, with little or no access to such technologies, cannot experience the same gains in knowledge and information as those with more technological access.

Even the language of a culture may influence the extent of the knowledge gap. For example, English dominates the Internet, so the Internet is more easily accessible to people in English-speaking countries—as well as to English-speaking people in non-English-speaking countries—than it is to groups who do not speak English.

You and the Media

Do you see the knowledge gap operating in your community or school? Can you see it in different cultures with which you're familiar?

- How do genetics and heredity relate to each other?
- What do ballet and square dancing have in common?
- What are the differences between critical and creative thinking?
- What do animal and human rights have in common?
- What are keyword and directory searches?
- How do freshwater and saltwater fishing differ?

Strategies for Defining

There are several approaches to defining your topic. Here are some suggestions.

Use a Variety of Definitions

When explaining a concept, it's helpful to define it in a few different ways. Here are some of the most important ways to define a term.

Define by Etymology. The etymology or history of the development of a term can help clarify its meaning. If you look up the word *communication*, you may note that it comes from the Latin *communis*, meaning "common"; in communicating you seek to establish a commonness, a sameness, a similarity with another individual. And *woman* comes from the Anglo-Saxon *wifman*, which meant literally a "wife man," where the word *man* was applied to both sexes. Through phonetic change *wifman* became *woman*. Most larger dictionaries and, of course, etymological dictionaries will help you find useful etymological definitions.

Define by Authority. The words of expert authorities also can help with definition. You might, for example, define lateral thinking by authority and say that Edward deBono, who developed his conceptualization of lateral thinking in 1966, stated that "lateral thinking involves moving sideways to look at things in a different way. Instead of fixing on one particular approach and then working forward from that, the lateral thinker tries to find other approaches."

Or you might define love and friendship by turning to the authority of cynic and satirist Ambrose Bierce, who defined love as nothing but "a temporary insanity curable by marriage" and friendship as "a ship big enough to carry two in fair weather, but only one in foul."

Define by Negation. You also might define a term by negation—by noting what the term is not. "A wife," you might say, "is not a cook, a cleaning person, a baby-sitter, a seamstress, a sex partner. A wife is . . . ." Or "A teacher is not someone who tells you what you should know but rather one who . . . ." Here Michael Marien (1992, p. 340) defines futurists first negatively and then positively:

> Futurists do not use crystal balls. Indeed, they're generally loath to make firm predictions of what will happen. Rather, they make forecasts of what is probable, sketch scenarios of what is possible, and/or point to desirable futures—what is preferable and what strategies we should pursue to get there.

Define by Direct Symbolization. You also might define a term by direct symbolization—by showing the actual thing or a picture or model of it. For example, a sales representative explaining a new computer keyboard would obviously use an actual keyboard in the speech. Similarly, a speech on magazine layout or on types of fabrics could include actual layout pages or fabric samples.

Use Definitions to Add Clarity

If the purpose of the definition is to clarify, then it must do just that. This might seem too obvious to mention—but in reality many speakers, perhaps for want of something to say, define terms that don't need extended definitions. Some speakers even use definitions that don't clarify but that actually complicate already complex concepts. Make sure your definitions define only what needs defining.

VIEWPOINT

Look over the principles of informative speaking with special reference to the stand-up comic's routine. In what ways are the principles of informative speaking applicable to successful stand-up? In what ways do the principles not fit stand-up?

Use Credible Sources

When you quote an authority to define a term, make sure the person is in fact an authority. Tell the audience who the authority is and the basis for the individual's expertise. In the following excerpt, note how Russell Peterson (1985, p. 549) uses the expertise of Robert McNamara in his definition:

> When Robert McNamara was president of the World Bank, he coined the term "absolute poverty" to characterize a condition of life so degraded by malnutrition, illiteracy, violence, disease and squalor, to be beneath any reasonable definition of human decency. In 1980, the World Bank estimated that 780 million persons in the developing countries lived in absolute poverty. That's about three times as many people as live in the entire United States.

Proceed from the Known to the Unknown

Start with what your audience knows and work up to what is new or unfamiliar. Let's say you want to explain the concept of phonemics, a topic with which your audience is totally unfamiliar. The specific idea you wish to get across is that each phoneme stands for a unique sound. You might proceed from the known to the unknown and begin your definition with something like this:

> We all know that in our written language each letter of the alphabet stands for a unit of the written language. Each letter is different from every other letter. A *t* is different from a *g* and a *g* is different from a *b* and so on. Each letter is called a grapheme. In English we know we have 26 such letters.
>
> We can look at the spoken language in much the same way. Each sound is different from every other sound. A *t* sound is different from a *d* and a *d* is different from a *k* and so on. Each individual sound is called a phoneme.
>
> Now, let me explain in a little more detail what I mean by a phoneme.

Developing the Speech of Definition

Here are two examples of how you might go about constructing a speech of definition. In this first example, the speaker explains the symptoms of Alzheimer's disease, using a topical order to treat all symptoms equally.

General Purpose: To inform.
Specific Purpose: To define the major symptoms of Alzheimer's disease.
Thesis: There are four major symptoms of Alzheimer's. (What are these four symptoms?)

I. Alzheimer's patients may experience memory impairment.
II. Alzheimer's patients may experience speech difficulties.
III. Alzheimer's patients may experience a loss in abstract thinking.
IV. Alzheimer's patients may experience personality changes.

In this second example, the speaker selects three major types of lying for discussion and arranges these in a topical pattern.

General Purpose: To inform.
Specific Purpose: To define lying by explaining the major types of lying.
Thesis: There are three major kinds of lying. (What are the three major kinds of lying?)

I. Concealment is the process of hiding the truth.
II. Falsification is the process of presenting false information as if it were true.
III. Misdirection is the process of acknowledging a thought or feeling but misidentifying its cause.

In delivering such a speech, a speaker might begin the speech by saying:

> A lie is a lie is a lie. True? Well, not exactly. Actually, there are three different ways we can lie. We can lie by concealing the truth. We can lie by falsification, by presenting false information as if it were true. And we can lie by misdirection, by acknowledging a thought or feeling but misidentifying its cause. Let's look at the first type of lie—the lie of concealment.
>
> Most lies are lies of concealment. Most of the time when we lie we simply conceal the truth. We don't actually make any false statements. Rather, we simply don't reveal the truth. Let me give you some examples I overheard recently . . . .

BUILDING COMMUNICATION SKILLS

Defining a Term

Get some practice in defining terms—an essential skill in all forms of communication—by selecting one of the following terms and defining it, using at least three different types of definitions (etymology, authority, negative, or direct symbolism): *communication, love, friendship, conflict, leadership, audience*. If you have the opportunity, compare your definitions with those of others. You'll find it helpful to visit a few online dictionaries or thesauruses; try http://www.m-w.com/netdict.htm, http://humanities.uchicago.edu/forms_unrest/ROGET.html, www.dictionary.com, or www.thesaurus.com.

GOING ONLINE

Gifts of Speech

http://gos.sbc.edu/

Visit Sweet Briar College's Gifts of Speech website, a site devoted to women speakers, and read one of the speeches. In what way does the speaker follow or not follow the suggestions for communicating information discussed in this unit?

In addition, take a look at the CD-ROM that is available with this text. It contains two additional units on public speaking: "Criticism in the Classroom," which expands on ways to give and receive criticism, and "Developing Special Occasion Speeches," which covers a variety of ceremonial speeches such as speeches of introduction, presentation and acceptance speeches, commencement speeches, eulogies, toasts, and others.

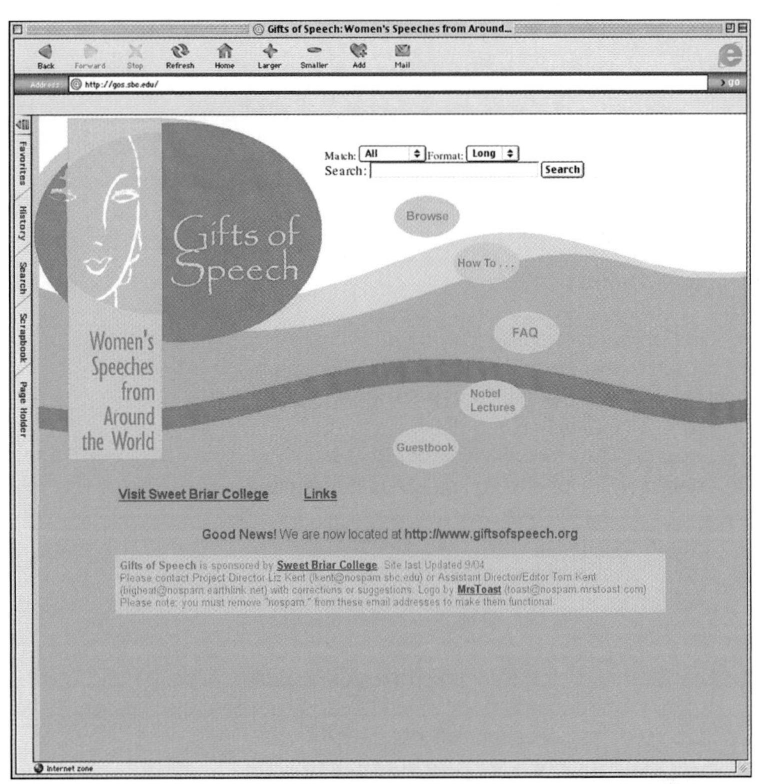

The Speech of Demonstration

In using demonstration (or in a speech devoted entirely to demonstration), you would explain how to do something or how something operates. Here are some examples of topics well adapted to the speech of demonstration:

Demonstrating How to Do Something

- how to give mouth-to-mouth resuscitation
- how to use PowerPoint
- how to balance a checkbook
- how to pilot a plane
- how to drive defensively
- how to mix colors
- how to say no
- how to prevent burnout
- how to ask for a raise
- how to burglarproof your house
- how to develop your body

Demonstrating How Something Operates

- how the body maintains homeostasis
- how a thermostat operates
- how perception works
- how the Internet works
- how divorce laws work
- how e-mail works
- how probate works
- how a hurricane develops
- how a heart bypass operation is performed

Strategies for Demonstrating

In demonstrating how to do something or how something operates, consider the following guidelines.

THE PUBLIC SPEAKING SAMPLE ASSISTANT

An Excellent Informative Speech

This is an excellent informative speech given by Stephen Zammit of Cornell University. It defines what the electric heart is and describes how it works. A reading of the speech along with the annotations will help clarify and make specific many of the principles of effective informative speaking.

The Electric Heart

Steve Zammit

On February 21, 2000, David Letterman returned to the *Late Show* after his quadruple bypass with a list of the Top 10 Things You Don't Want to Hear When You Wake Up from Surgery." They include: Number 2—"Hello Mr. Letterman . . . or should I say Miss Letterman?" and Number 1—"We did what we could, Mr. Letterman, but this is Jiffy Lube." But after the gags, Dave brought his doctors on stage and choked up as he thanked them for "saving my life."

How effective was the introduction? What purposes did it accomplish? Would you have sought to accomplish any other purpose(s)? If so, what would you have said?

One year later, the *New York Times* of February 1, 2001, announced conditional FDA approval for a medical device that will bring similar results to millions of heart patients. But rather than bypass a clogged artery, this revolutionary device bypasses the heart itself, thus fulfilling the life vision of 55-year-old scientist and heart surgeon, Dr. David Lederman. Dr. David Lederman is the inventor of the (VA) Electric Heart.

How would you describe the level of complexity in this speech?

Note that the speaker incorporates parenthetical (VA) (visual aid) notes as presentation guides.

The Electric Heart is a safe, battery operated, permanent replacement that is directly implanted into the body. The February 12, 2001, *Telegram and Gazette* predicts that within one generation more than 10 million Americans will be living with terminal heart disease. For them, and for the 100,000 transplant candidates who pray for a new heart when only 2,000 are annually available, hope has been fleeting . . . until now.

So to learn why UCLA transplant surgeon Dr. Steven Marelli calls it the "Holy Grail of Heart Surgery," let's first plug into the heart's development and see how it works. Next, flesh out its current status. So that finally we can see how the device's future impact will be heart stopping.

What did you think of the way the speaker phrased the orientation to the major propositions of the speech? Did it add clarity? Did it add humor? Did the speaker's informal sentence fragments work for you?

In early 1982, Washington dentist Barney Clark's heart was stopping—literally. The world watched as Dr. Robert Jarvik implanted Clark with the first ever artificial heart. After 112 days marked by kidney failure, respiratory problems, and severe mental confusion, the heart stopped. It didn't take a rocket scientist to see that, as the *New York Times* of May 16, 1988, declared, artificial heart research was medical technology's version of Dracula. Basically, it sucked. Getting Dracula out of his coffin would require a little thinking outside the box. Enter Dr. David Lederman, who, in a happy coincidence, reported *Forbes* of April 17, 2000, is an actual rocket scientist. In fact, Lederman changed his career path in the early 1970s when he heard a lecture by a physicist who insisted artificial hearts would rise or fall based on fluid mechanics.

What functions did the Dracula example serve? Do you feel this was too flippant for a speech on such a serious topic. Or do you feel it added the right note of levity?

Lederman's design can be likened to space flight in that the concept is easy, but the tiniest problems can prevent a launch or cause an explosion. *What separates the Electric Heart from Jarvik's earlier model is the development and implementation of space age technology.* In particular, the *Pittsburgh Post-Gazette* of January 28, 2001, explains that an artificial heart must simultaneously weigh two pounds, be flexible enough to expand and contract, and tough enough to absorb 40 million beats a year. The solution is a proprietary titanium compound called Angioflex, the first manmade material on earth that fits the mold.

Does the speaker stress relevance and usefulness to maintain your attention? How would you have stressed relevance and usefulness?

A typical heart pumps blood through constant muscular contractions regulated by the nervous system. (VA) But Lederman's model propels blood using an internal motor regulated by a microprocessor imbedded inside the abdomen. A small external belt transmits energy through the skin to a copper coil, allowing the entire system to be continuously stimulated.

Although you can't see the visual aids the speaker used, you can imagine what they were and you can see where they were used. If you had been listening to this speech, what would you have liked to see in these visuals?

When he returned last February, David Letterman was stimulated by a hospital gown clad Robin Williams, who performed a zany striptease . . . I'll spare you the VA. But to see if Dr. Lederman is himself a tease, we must now evaluate his project's current status as well as the obstacles it faces.

Can you identify transitions the speaker used to connect the speech parts?

The *Houston Chronicle* of January 31, 2001, reveals that FDA approval of the electric heart was based on its wild success when implanted in animals. More than 100 cows have been recipients of the heart, and in Dr. Lederman's words, three hours after surgery, "I have seen the animals standing in their stalls munching hay, with their original hearts in a jar nearby." Sometime in early June, surgical teams will

As you read the speech, do you feel that the speaker successfully involves you in the speech? If not, what might the speaker have done to make you feel he was talking about you to you?

swap an electric heart for the failing one in five critically ill human patients, for what Dr. Lederman calls "the most public clinical trials in history." For those skeptics who argue it's a little early to break out the bubbly, Dr. Lederman adamantly agrees. He told the February 5, 2001, *Glasgow Herald*, "At first, you had the Wright brothers. Today, you can easily cross the Atlantic. Our heart is the equivalent of making the flight from Boston to New York." But the trip across the Atlantic is only a matter of time.

Despite the optimism, the beat will not go on until Dr. Lederman convincingly addresses two concerns about practicality. As the *British Medical Journal* of March 17, 2001, explains, organ transplant recipients must take expensive nauseating drugs to prevent clotting and rejection. Fortunately, Angioflex's producer, Abiomed, revealed in a 2000 Securities and Exchange Commission filing that the material is perfectly seamless and can withstand over 20 years of abuse without cracking. No cracks, no place for clots to form. And since the electric heart is made of inert materials, UCLA transplant surgeon Dr. Steven Marelli told the February 7, 2001, *University Wire,* the body will not reject it, an observation confirmed by animal trials. Essentially, Electric Heart recipients will come back without expensive drug therapy.

How effectively did the speaker integrate research into the speech?

Does the speaker limit the amount of information he communicates so that there is significant depth? Would you have done things differently?

Speaking of comebacks, just as David Letterman's return culminated in an Emmy nomination, Dr. Lederman will soon be picking up some awards of his own, due to the Electric Heart's impact on individuals and society. As transplant pioneer Robert Jarvik once said, "the artificial heart must not only be dependable, but truly forgettable." But during periods of increased energy demand—including making love—Jarvik's model required a user to be tethered to a power unit in the wall. Lederman's model, in the words of the February 2001 *GQ*, is "The Love Machine." As *GQ* observes, the internal battery can allow "unassisted" exercise for 30 minutes—every man's dream. But the *Boston Globe* of February 1, 2001, reveals advances in battery technology eventually will allow a sleeping user to be charged for a full day—allowing recipients to emulate the Energizer Bunny in more ways than one.

Has the speaker followed the principle stating that an informative speech should relate new information to old?

Of all the research sources cited in the speech, which did you think was the most effective? Which was the least effective? Why?

But by normalizing life for individuals, the Electric Heart will be revolutionizing medicine in society. The March 26, 2001, *Los Angeles Times* notes that 400,000 Americans are diagnosed with heart failure each year. Add the number of other failing internal organs, as well as a glut of

Did the speaker vary the levels of abstraction effectively, or would you have wished for more high-level or more low level abstractions?

aging baby boomers, and we are a generation away from a crisis. To cope, some researchers have famously approached organ shortages by genetically engineering them to grow in a lab, a process that will still take years. But the Electric Heart is both more immediate, and carries none of the ethical entanglements of manipulating the human genome. As Dr. Ed Berger, vice president of Abiomed, explained in an April 2, 2001, telephone interview, Angioflex is so versatile, it could eventually be used to construct artificial kidneys and lungs.

What influence did the research and its integration into the speech have on your image of the speaker's credibility?

How effective do you think the speech title, "The Electric Heart," was? What other titles might have worked?

Unfortunately, the *American Journal of Medicine* of February 1, 2001, reports that heart disease disproportionately strikes those in lower socioeconomic brackets, a group that often lacks access to advanced technology. But the April 19, 2001, *Boston Herald* predicts the procedure will eventually retail for about $25,000, the same as a traditional heart bypass. Coupled with the cost savings on drug treatment, the procedure should be affordably covered by most insurance companies, including Medicare. So whether rich or poor, young or old, resting or energized, the Electric Heart will be an equal opportunity lifesaver.

What one thing will you remember most from this speech? Why will you remember this? That is, what did the speaker say that made this one thing most memorable?

Although you can never mend a broken heart, Dr. Lederman has done the next best thing. By reviewing the Electric Heart's unusual development and current testing, we have seen its future impact on viewers around the world. On the night of his comeback, David Letterman put a human face on heart disease. But for thousands who find themselves in the comedian's shoes, laughter—and everything else—are insufficient medicine. But soon, Dr. David Lederman will reach audiences with a message of hope. For them, the Electric Heart will not just make the Top 10 List. It will be number one.

How effective was the speaker's conclusion? What function did the conclusion serve? What other functions might it have served?

Now that you've finished reading this speech (don't look back), what were the main points of the speech? What did you learn from the speech?

Use Temporal Organization

In most cases a temporal pattern will work best in speeches of demonstration. Demonstrate each step in the order in which it's performed. In this way you'll avoid one of the major difficulties in demonstrating a process, backtracking. Don't skip steps, even if you think they're familiar to the audience; they may not be.

Connect each step to the next with appropriate transitions. For example, in explaining the Heimlich maneuver, you might say:

> Now that you have your arms around the choking victim's chest, your next step is to . . . ."

Assist your listeners by labeling the steps clearly; for example, say "the first step," "the second step," and so on.

Begin with an Overview

It's often helpful when demonstrating to give a broad general picture and then present each step in turn. For example, let's say you are talking about how to prepare a wall for painting. You might begin with a general overview:

> In preparing the wall for painting, you want to make sure that the wall is smoothly sanded, free of dust, and dry. Sanding a wall is not like sanding a block of wood. So let's look at the proper way to sand a wall.

In this way, your listeners will have a general idea of how you'll go about demonstrating the process.

Consider the Value of Presentation Aids

Presentation aids are especially helpful in showing the sequential steps of a process. To appreciate how aids can work, think about the signs in restaurants showing the Heimlich maneuver. These signs depict the steps with pictures as well as words. The combination of verbal and graphic information makes it easy to understand this lifesaving process. In a speech on the Heimlich maneuver, however, the best aid would be the pictures alone—so that the written words would not distract your audience from your oral explanation. Or, perhaps even better, you might enlist the aid of another person and demonstrate the actual movements.

Developing the Speech of Demonstration

Here are two examples of the speech of demonstration. In this first example, the speaker explains the proper way to argue by identifying the ways we should not argue. As you can see, these unproductive fight strategies are all about equal in value and are arranged in a topical order.

General Purpose: To inform.
Specific Purpose: To demonstrate how to fight fairly by identifying and demonstrating four unfair conflict strategies.
Thesis: Conflict can be made more productive. (How can conflict be made more productive?)

I. Blame the other person.
II. Unload all your previous grievances.
III. Make light of the other person's displeasure.
IV. Hit the other person with issues he or she cannot handle effectively.

In the next example, the speaker identifies and demonstrates how to listen actively.

General Purpose: To inform.
Specific Purpose: To demonstrate three techniques of active listening.
Thesis: We can learn active listening. (How can we learn active listening?)

I. Paraphrase the speaker's meaning.
II. Express understanding of the speaker's feelings.
III. Ask questions.

In delivering the active listening speech, the speaker might begin by saying:

> Active listening is a special kind of listening. It's listening with total involvement, with a concern for the speaker. It's probably the most important type of listening you can engage in. Active listening consists of three steps: paraphrasing the speaker's meaning, expressing understanding of the speaker's feelings, and asking questions.
>
> Your first step in active listening is to paraphrase the speaker's meaning. What is a paraphrase? A paraphrase is a restatement in your own words of the speaker's meaning. That is, you express in your own words what you think the speaker meant. For example, let's say that the speaker said . . . .

REFLECTIONS ON ETHICS

Speaking Ethically

One interesting approach to ethics that has particular relevance to public speaking identifies four key rules for speakers (Wallace, 1955; Johannesen, 2001). As an ethical speaker, you should be guided by the following principles:

- Have a thorough knowledge of the topic, an ability to answer relevant questions, and an awareness of the significant facts and opinions bearing on the issues you discuss.
- Present both facts and opinions fairly, without bending or spinning them to personal advantage. You must allow listeners to make the final judgment.
- Reveal the sources of these facts and opinions, and help listeners evaluate any biases and prejudices in the sources.
- Acknowledge and respect opposing arguments and evidence; advocate a tolerance for diversity.

WHAT WOULD YOU DO? You're giving a persuasive speech arguing for condom machines in rest rooms on campus. You know, however, that the money to install these machines will have to come from an increase in student fees. You wonder if you can ethically give the speech without mentioning that student fees will have to be increased. After all, you don't have time to include all the arguments and evidence—even points that support your position. You also figure that it's the listeners' responsibility to ask where the money is coming from, not your job to tell them. What do you do?

SUMMARY

This unit focused on the informative speech, examining the guidelines to follow in informing others and the various types of informative speeches.

1. Informative speeches are more likely to be effective when they adhere to the following principles of informative speaking: Limit the amount of information you communicate, adjust the level of complexity, stress the relevance and the usefulness of the information to your audience, relate new information to old, and vary the levels of abstraction.
2. Speeches of description describe a process or procedure, an event, an object, or a person.
3. Speeches of definition define a term, system, or theory or explain similarities and/or differences among terms.
4. Speeches of demonstration show how to do something or how something operates.

KEY TERMS

informative speech
limiting the amount of information
information overload
adjusting the level of complexity
stressing relevance and usefulness
relating new information to old
varying the levels of abstraction
abstractions
speech of description
speech of definition
speech of demonstration

THINKING CRITICALLY ABOUT

Informative Speeches

1. You want to give an informative speech on virtual reality simulation, but most of your audience members have never experienced it. How would you communicate this concept and this experience to your audience?
2. You're planning to give an informative speech on the history of doctor-assisted suicide and are considering the strategies that you might use. What organizational pattern would be appropriate? What types of presentation aids might you use? How would you define "doctor-assisted suicide"? How would you introduce your speech?
3. You're scheduled to be the third speaker in a series of six presentations today. Unfortunately, the first speaker presented a really excellent speech on the same topic you're speaking on—how the Internet works. What should you do?
4. Select an advertisement (television or print) and examine how closely it follows the principles of informative speaking identified here. In what ways does an advertisement differ from a speech?
5. Visit the website of the Society for Technical Communication at http://www.stc-va.org/ for guides for writing and speaking on technical matters.
6. Prepare a two-minute informative speech on one of the following:
    - Explain a card game: Explain the way a card game such as solitaire, poker, gin rummy, bridge, canasta, or pinochle is played.
    - Explain a board game: Explain the way a board game such as chess, backgammon, Chinese checkers, Go, Othello, Scrabble, Yahtzee, or Monopoly is played.
    - Explain food preparation: Explain how to make a pie, a soup, a western omelet, a pizza, roast beef, a dip, or a casserole (any kind you'd like).
    - Explain a sport: Explain the way a sport such as football, baseball, basketball, hockey, soccer, tennis, or golf is played.

7. Prepare and deliver a two-minute speech in which you do one of the following:
   - describe some common object in the classroom
   - define one of the following terms, using at least two different types of definitions: *love, friendship, power, pride, jealousy, truth, freedom, honesty*, or *faithfulness*
   - demonstrate—without the aid of the object—how to tie a shoelace, use a food processor, make a phone call, sew on a button, open a door with a credit card, move a block of text on a computer, print out a computer file, or use a template
   - explain one of the principles of informative speaking, using a variety of examples
   - explain how one or more of the principles of informative speaking are used or violated in one of your textbooks

UNIT

18

The Persuasive Speech

UNIT CONTENTS

In addition to informing others, you'll also be called upon to deliver speeches of persuasion—speeches that aim to influence the attitudes and beliefs and sometimes the behaviors of your listeners. In this unit you'll learn

- the guidelines to follow in your persuasive speaking
- how you can develop a wide variety of persuasive speeches

Most of the speeches you hear are persuasive. The speeches of politicians, advertisers, and religious leaders are clear examples. In many of your own speeches, you too will aim at **persuasion;** that is, you'll try to change your listeners' attitudes and beliefs or perhaps get them to do something. In school you might try to persuade others to (or not to) expand the core curriculum, use a plus-minus or a pass-fail grading system, disband the basketball team, allocate increased student funds for the school newspaper, establish competitive majors, or eliminate fraternity initiation rituals. On your job you may be called upon to speak in favor of (or against) a union, a wage increase proposal, a health benefit package, or the election of a new shop steward.

Recall from the discussion of the audience in Unit 14 that the attitudes, beliefs, and values of your listeners are important in persuasion—because people's behavior, which is what you ultimately want to influence, depends on their attitudes, beliefs, and values. So if you can change your listeners' beliefs about, say, abortion, you may get them to vote one way or another or to contribute to a group advocating a particular abortion position. If you can change the values that people place on animals and animal experimentation, you may get them to boycott (or not boycott) cosmetics companies that use animals in their testing.

Further, the audience members' attitudes, beliefs, and values will influence how they respond to your thesis, your main points, your arguments, your evidence, and just about everything else in your speech. For example, if you were going to give a speech defending doctor-assisted suicide, it would be crucial for you to know the attitudes, beliefs, and values held by your audience before you framed and supported your various points. You would have to prepare very different speeches for an audience that saw suicide of any kind as morally wrong as opposed to an audience whose concern centered on how doctor-assisted suicides should be monitored to prevent violations of the patients' wishes.

So, in constructing your persuasive speeches and in following the guidelines for persuasive speaking presented below, be sure to take into consideration the attitudes, beliefs, and values of the audience as these relate to anything you'll say in your speech—but particularly to your thesis, main points, and main supports.

In this unit, we'll look first at general guidelines for persuasive speaking, then at three broad categories of persuasive speeches—speeches on questions of fact, of value, and of policy. Two Public Speaking Sample Assistant boxes will offer bad (pages 389–390) and good (pages 398–401) examples of persuasive speeches accompanied by critical commentary.

Guidelines for Persuasive Speaking

To succeed in strengthening or changing attitudes or beliefs and in moving your listeners to action, follow these guidelines for persuasive speaking.

Anticipate Selective Exposure

Listeners follow the "law of selective exposure." As Unit 4 explained, this principle has two parts: (1) Listeners actively seek out information that supports their opinions, beliefs, values, decisions, and behaviors; and (2) listeners actively avoid information that contradicts their existing opinions, beliefs, attitudes, values, decisions, and behaviors.

Of course, if people are very sure that their opinions and attitudes are logical and valid, then they may not bother to seek out supporting information or to avoid contradictory messages. People exercise selective exposure most often when their confidence in their opinions and beliefs is weak.

So if you want to persuade an audience that holds attitudes different from your own, anticipate selective exposure operating and proceed inductively; that is, hold back on your thesis until you've given them your evidence and argument. Only then relate this evidence and argument to your initially contrary thesis.

If you were to present your listeners with your thesis first, they might tune you out without giving your position a fair hearing. So become thoroughly familiar with the attitudes of your audience if you want to succeed in making these necessary adjustments and adaptations.

Let's say you're giving a speech on the need to reduce spending on college athletic programs. If your audience is composed of listeners who agree with you and want to cut athletic spending, you might lead with your thesis. Your introduction might go something like this:

UNDERSTANDING *THEORY* AND *RESEARCH*

Balance Theories

An especially interesting group of theories of persuasion go under the general term *balance theories.* The general assumption of balance theories is that people strive to maintain consistency between their beliefs and their behaviors. For example, if you believe that people should exercise regularly (because you believe it's the healthy thing to do) but you don't exercise (because you feel exercise is difficult and boring), then you'll be in a state of imbalance or dissonance. According to balance theory, you will then strive either to change your beliefs about exercise (to make them consistent with your behavior) or to change your behavior (to make it consistent with your beliefs).

Applied to persuasion, balance theories claim that people look for information that will maintain or restore balance or consonance. For example, if you as a speaker demonstrate that you offer an easy and enjoyable (not difficult and boring) exercise plan, you stand a good chance of influencing the audience—because they are looking for the very means to restore balance that you are now providing. Conversely, of course, you might assert that exercise is unhealthy; the belief that exercise is unhealthy would be consistent with their no-exercise behavior and also would restore balance.

Working with Theories and Research

- *How might you use the insights of balance theories in preparing a speech on why the audience should start investing, give up junk food, or quit smoking?*

> Our college athletic program is absorbing money that we can more profitably use for the library, science labs, and language labs. Let me explain how the money now going to unnecessary athletic programs could be better spent in these other areas.

On the other hand, suppose you're addressing alumni who strongly favor the existing athletic programs. In this case, you may want to lead with your evidence and hold off stating your thesis until the end of your speech.

Ask for Reasonable Amounts of Change

The greater and more important the change you want to encourage in your audience, the more difficult your task will be. The reason is simple: We normally demand a greater number of reasons and a lot more evidence before we make important decisions such as, say, changing careers, moving to another state, or investing in stocks. On the other hand, we may be more easily persuaded (and demand less evidence) on relatively minor issues—whether to take "Small Group Communication" rather than "Persuasion" or whether to give to the United Heart Fund instead of the American Heart Fund.

Generally, people change gradually, in small degrees over a long period of time. Persuasion, therefore, is most effective when it strives for small changes and works over a period of time. For example, a persuasive speech stands a better chance when it tries to get the alcoholic to attend just one AA meeting rather than asking the drinker to give up alcohol for life. If you try to convince your audience to change their attitudes radically or to engage in behaviors to which they're initially opposed, your attempts may backfire. In this type of situation, the audience may tune you out, closing its ears to even the best and most logical arguments.

In your classroom speeches set reasonable goals for what you want the audience to do. Remember that you have only perhaps 10 minutes; in that time you cannot move the proverbial mountain. So ask your listeners for small, easily performed behaviors—signing a petition, voting in the next election, donating a small amount of money.

When you're addressing an audience that is opposed to your position and trying to change their attitudes and beliefs, be especially careful to seek change in small increments. Let's say, for example, that your ultimate goal is to get an antiabortion group to favor abortion on demand. Obviously, this goal is too great to achieve in one speech. Therefore, strive for small changes. For example, in the following excerpt the speaker attempts to get an audience that opposes legalized abortion to agree that at least some abortions should be legalized. The speaker begins:

> One of the great lessons I learned in college was that most extreme positions are wrong. Most of the important truths lie somewhere between the extreme opposites. And today I want to talk with you about one of these truths. I want to talk with you about rape and the problems faced by the mother carrying a child conceived in this most violent of all violent crimes we can imagine.

Notice that the speaker does not state a totally pro-choice position but instead focuses on one area of the abortion issue and attempts to get the audience to ask themselves, "What if my daughter was raped and abortion was unavailable?" and perhaps ultimately to agree that in some cases the possibility of abortion should be available.

When you have the opportunity to persuade your audience on several occasions (rather than simply delivering one speech), two strategies will prove helpful: the foot-in-the-door and door-in-the-face techniques.

Foot-in-the-Door Technique

As its name implies, the foot-in-the-door technique involves requesting something small, something that your audience will easily agree to. Once they agree to this small request, you then make your real request (Cialdini, 1984; Dejong, 1979; Freedman & Fraser, 1966; Pratkanis & Aronson, 1991). People are more apt to comply with a large request after they have complied with a similar but much smaller request. For example, in one study the objective was to get people to put a "Drive Carefully" sign on their lawn (a large request). When this (large) request was made first, only about 17 percent of the people were willing to agree. However, when this request was preceded by a much smaller request (to sign a petition), between 50 and 76 percent granted permission to install the sign. Agreement with the smaller request paves the way for the larger request and puts the audience into an agreeable mood.

Door-in-the-Face Technique

With this technique, the opposite of foot-in-the-door, you first make a large request that you know will be refused and then follow it with a more moderate request. For example, your large request might be "We're asking people to donate $100 for new school computers." When this is refused, you make a more moderate request, the one you really want your listeners to comply with (for example, "Might you be willing to contribute $10?"). In changing from the large to the more moderate request, you demonstrate your willingness to compromise and your sensitivity to your listeners. The general idea here is that your listeners will feel that since you've made concessions, they should also make concessions and at least contribute something. Listeners will probably also feel that $10 is actually quite a small amount considering the initial request and are more likely to donate the $10 (Cialdini, 1984; Cialdini & Ascani, 1976).

Identify with Your Audience

If you can show your audience that you and they share important attitudes, beliefs, and values you'll clearly advance your persuasive goal. Other similarities are also important. For example, in some cases similarity of cultural, educational, or social background may help you identify yourself with your audience. Be aware, however, that insincere or dishonest identification is likely to backfire and create problems for the speaker. So avoid even implying similarities between yourself and your audience that don't exist.

Similarly, as a general rule, never ask the audience to do what you have not done yourself. So demonstrate your own willingness to do what you want the audience to do. If you don't, the audience will rightfully ask, "Why haven't *you* done it?" In addition to making it clear that you have done what you want your listeners to do, show them that you're happy about it. Tell them of the satisfaction you have derived from, for example, donating blood or reading to blind students.

Use Logical Appeals

Logical, emotional, and credibility appeals are all effective tools in persuasion, and we will examine all three. However, it is persuasion from logical argument that proves to be the most effective. When the speaker persuades listeners with **logic,** the listeners are more likely to remain persuaded over time and are more likely to resist counterarguments that may come up in the future (Petty & Wegener, 1998). Let's look at three kinds of reasoning that you can use in logical appeals.

Reasoning from Specific Instances and Generalizations

In **reasoning from specific instances** (or examples), you examine several specific instances and then arrive at a generalization about the whole. This form of reasoning, known as induction, is useful when you want to develop a general principle or conclu-

COMMUNICATION@WORK

Reward and Coercive Power

The perks of power work best in the corporate world when they're rewards for a job well done.

—John O. Whitney and Tina Packer

As explained in Unit 11 (page 216), you have *reward power* over a person if you have the ability to give that person rewards—material (money, promotion, jewelry) or social (love, friendship, respect). Conversely, you have *coercive power* if you have the ability to remove rewards from a person or to administer punishments. Usually, if you have reward power you also have coercive power. A manager can shower an employee with praise for work well done and can offer a nice year-end bonus (reward power), but also can criticize and deny a promotion to that same employee (coercive power).

Reward power increases attractiveness; we like those who have the power to reward us and who do in fact give us rewards. Coercive power, on the other hand, decreases attractiveness; we dislike those who have the power to punish us and who threaten us with punishment, whether they actually follow through or not. Thus, as a manager, a teacher, or a group leader, you'll be better liked, more persuasive, and more powerful if you reward people for their desirable behaviors instead of punishing them for undesirable behaviors.

Communicating@Work

How do you respond to the reward and coercive power of others? How do you wield reward and coercive power over others? How might you exercise your power more effectively?

sion but cannot examine the whole. For example, you sample a few communication courses and conclude something about communication courses in general; you visit several Scandinavian cities and conclude something about the whole of Scandinavia. Critically analyze reasoning from specific instances by asking the following questions.

Were enough specific instances examined? Two general guidelines may help you decide how many instances are enough. First, the larger the group you wish covered by your conclusion, the greater the number of specific instances you should examine. If you wished to draw conclusions about members of an entire country or culture, you'd have to examine a considerable number of people before drawing even tentative conclusions. On the other hand, if you were attempting to draw a conclusion about a bushel of apples, sampling a few apples probably would be sufficient.

Second, the greater the diversity of items in the class, the more specific instances you will have to examine. Some classes or groups of items are relatively homogeneous, whereas others are more heterogeneous; this will influence how many specific instances constitute a sufficient number. Pieces of spaghetti in boiling water are all about the same; thus, sampling one usually tells you something about all the others. On the other hand, communication courses probably differ widely, so valid conclusions about communication courses as a group will require a much larger sample.

Are there significant exceptions? When you examine specific instances and attempt to draw a conclusion about the whole, take into consideration the exceptions. Thus, if you examine the GPA of computer science majors and discover that 70 percent have GPAs above 3.5, you may be tempted to draw the conclusion that computer science majors are especially bright. But what about the 30 percent who have lower GPAs? How much lower are these scores? This may be a significant exception that you'll need to take into account and may require you to qualify your conclusion in significant ways. Exactly how many exceptions will constitute "significant exceptions" will depend on the unique situation.

Reasoning from Causes and Effects

In **reasoning from causes and effects,** you may go in either of two directions. You may reason from cause to effect (from observed cause to unobserved effect) or from effect to cause (from observed effect to unobserved cause). In testing reasoning from cause to effect or from effect to cause, ask yourself the following questions.

Might other causes be producing the observed effect? If you observe a particular effect (say, high crime or student apathy), you need to ask if causes other than the one you're postulating might be producing these effects. For example, you might postulate that poverty leads to high crime, but there might be other factors actually causing the high crime rate. Or poverty might be one cause, but it might not be the most important cause. Therefore, explore the possibility of other causes' producing the observed effects.

Is the causation in the direction postulated? If two things occur together, it's often difficult to determine which is the cause and which is the effect. For example, a lack of interpersonal intimacy and a lack of self-confidence are often seen in the same person. The person who lacks self-confidence seldom has intimate relationships with others. But which is the cause and which is the effect? It might be that the lack of intimacy "causes" low self-confidence; it might also be, however, that low self-confidence "causes" a lack of intimacy. Of course, it might also be that some other cause (a history of negative criticism, for example) might be producing both the lack of intimacy and the low self-confidence.

Reasoning from Sign

Reasoning from sign involves drawing a conclusion on the basis of the presence of signs because they frequently occur together. Medical diagnosis is a good example of reasoning by sign. The general procedure is simple. If a sign and an object, event, or condition are frequently paired, the presence of the sign is taken as proof of the presence of the object, event, or condition. For example, fatigue, extreme thirst, and overeating are signs of hyperthyroidism, because they frequently accompany the condition. In reasoning from sign, ask yourself these questions.

Do the signs necessitate the conclusion drawn? Given fatigue, extreme thirst, and overeating, how certain can you be of the "hyperthyroid" conclusion? With most medical and legal matters we can never be absolutely certain, but we can be certain beyond a reasonable doubt.

Are there other signs that point to the same conclusion? In the thyroid example, the extreme thirst could have been brought on by any number of factors. Similarly, the fatigue and the overeating could have been attributed to other causes. Yet, taken together they seemed to point to only one reasonable diagnosis. Generally, the more signs that point toward the conclusion, the more confidence you can have that it's valid.

Are there contradictory signs? Are there signs pointing toward contradictory conclusions? For example, if the butler had a motive and a history of violence (signs supporting the conclusion that the butler was the murderer), but also had an alibi (a sign pointing to the conclusion of innocence), then the conclusion of guilt would have to be reconsidered or discarded.

Fallacies in Reasoning

Another useful way to approach logical appeals is to become aware of various fallacies you'll want to avoid in your own reasoning and will want to identify in the speeches you hear. Here are 10 such fallacies along with some examples (Lee & Lee 1972, 1995; Pratkanis & Aronson, 1991; Herrick, 2004). As you read these, try to think of examples you've heard or read recently.

- *Anecdotal evidence:* Often you'll hear people use anecdotes to "prove" a point: "Women are like that; I have three sisters" or "That's the way Japanese managers are; I've seen plenty of them." One reason this type of "evidence" is inadequate is that it relies on too few observations; it's usually a clear case of overgeneralizing on the basis of too little evidence. A second reason is that one person's observations may be unduly clouded by his or her own attitudes and beliefs; your attitudes toward women or the Japanese, for example, may influence your perception of their behaviors.
- *Straw man:* A straw man argument (like a man made of straw) is an argument that's set up merely to be knocked down. In this fallacy a speaker creates an easy-to-destroy oversimplification or distortion of the opposing position (that is, a "straw man") and then proceeds to demolish it. But, of course, if the opposing case were presented fairly and without bias, it wouldn't be so easy to destroy.
- *Appeal to tradition:* Speakers often argue against change by appealing to tradition—that is, by claiming that something is wrong or some change should not be adopted because it was never done before. But, of course, not all tradition is good; in addition, the fact that something has not been done before says nothing about its value or whether it should be done now.
- *Bandwagon:* **Bandwagon** appeals, often referred to as appeals *ad populum* (appeals to the people), attempt to persuade the audience to accept or reject an idea or proposal because "everybody's doing it" or because the "right" people support it. The speaker tries to suggest that you should jump on this large and popular bandwagon—or be left out by yourself. This is a popular technique in political elections, in which cam-

paigns use results of polls to get undecided voters to jump on candidates' bandwagons. After all, you don't want to vote for a loser. Fortunately, mindfulness, discussed in Unit 9, is a good defense against bandwagon appeals (Fiol & O'Connor, 2003).

- *Testimonial:* The **testimonial** technique involves using the image associated with some person to gain your approval (if you respect the person) or your rejection (if you don't respect the person). This is the technique of advertisers who use people dressed up to look like doctors or plumbers or chefs to sell their products. Sometimes testimonial appeals cite only vague and general "authorities," as in "Experts agree," "Scientists say," "Good cooks know," or "Dentists advise."
- *Transfer:* In **transfer** appeals the speaker associates her or his idea with something you respect (to gain your approval) or with something you detest (to gain your rejection). For example, a speaker might characterize a proposal for condom distribution in schools as "saving our children from AIDS" (to encourage acceptance) or as "promoting sexual promiscuity" (to encourage disapproval). Sports car manufacturers try to get you to buy their cars by associating them with high status and sex appeal; exercise clubs and diet plans suggest associations with health, self-confidence, and interpersonal appeal.
- *Plain folks:* Using the **plain folks** approach, the speaker identifies himself or herself with the audience. The speaker is good—the "reasoning" goes—because he or she is one of the people, just "plain folks" like everyone else. Of course, the speaker who presents himself or herself as one of the plain folks is often not. And even if he or she is one of the plain folks, it has nothing to do with the issue under discussion.
- *Card stacking:* In **card stacking** the speaker selects only the evidence and arguments that support his or her case and may even falsify evidence or distort facts to better fit the case. Despite these misrepresentations, the speaker presents the supporting materials as "fair" and "impartial."
- *Thin entering wedge:* In another type of pseudo-argument, a speaker argues against a position on the grounds that it is a thin entering wedge that will open the floodgates to all sorts of catastrophes (Chase, 1956). People have used this argument throughout history to argue against change—contending, for example, that school integration and interracial marriage are just the start of the collapse of American education and society, same-sex marriage will destroy the family, computers will lead to mass unemployment, and banning smoking in public places will lead to the collapse of the restaurant industry.
- *Agenda setting:* In agenda setting, as we saw in Unit 12, a speaker indicates that X is the issue and that all others are unimportant and insignificant. This kind of fallacious appeal is heard frequently: "Balancing the budget is the key to the city's survival," or "There's only one issue confronting elementary education in our largest cities, and that is violence." In almost all situations, however, there are many issues and many sides to each issue. Often the person proclaiming that X is the issue really means, "I'll be able to persuade you if you focus solely on X and ignore the other issues."

Use Emotional Appeals

Appeals to emotions, needs, desires, and wants can be powerful means of persuasion (Wood, 2000). When you use motivational appeals, you appeal to those forces that energize, move, or motivate people to develop, change, or strengthen their attitudes or ways of behaving. For example, one motive might be the desire for status. This desire might motivate you to enter a high-status occupation or to dress a certain way.

Developed more than 30 years ago, one of the most useful analyses of motives remains Abraham Maslow's fivefold hierarchy of needs, reproduced in Figure 18.1 on page 384 (Bailey & Pownell, 1998; Kiel, 1999; Maslow, 1970). The theory proposes that you seek to fulfill the needs at the lowest level first and that only when those needs are satisfied do the needs at the next level begin to exert influence on your behavior. For example, you would not concern yourself with the need for security or freedom from fear if you were starving (if your need for food had not been met). Similarly, you would not be concerned with friendship if your need for protection and security had not been fulfilled. The implication for you as a speaker is that you have to know what needs of your audience are unsatisfied. These are the needs you can appeal to in motivating them. Let's look in detail at Maslow's model.

Physiological Needs

In many parts of the world, and even in parts of the United States, the physiological needs of the people are not fully met and thus, as you can appreciate, are powerful motivating forces. Lech Walesa, former leader of the Polish Solidarity Party, recognized this when he wrote: "He who gives food to the people will win." In many of the poorest countries of the

Figure 18.1

Maslow's "Hierarchy of Needs"

Abraham Maslow's model of lower-order and higher-order needs has long influenced theories of persuasion. As you read about these needs, consider which would work best with your specific class members. Are there some that would not work, at least generally?

Source: Maslow & Frager (1987). *Motivation and Personality,* 3rd ed. Adapted by permission of Pearson Education, Inc. Upper Saddle River, New Jersey.

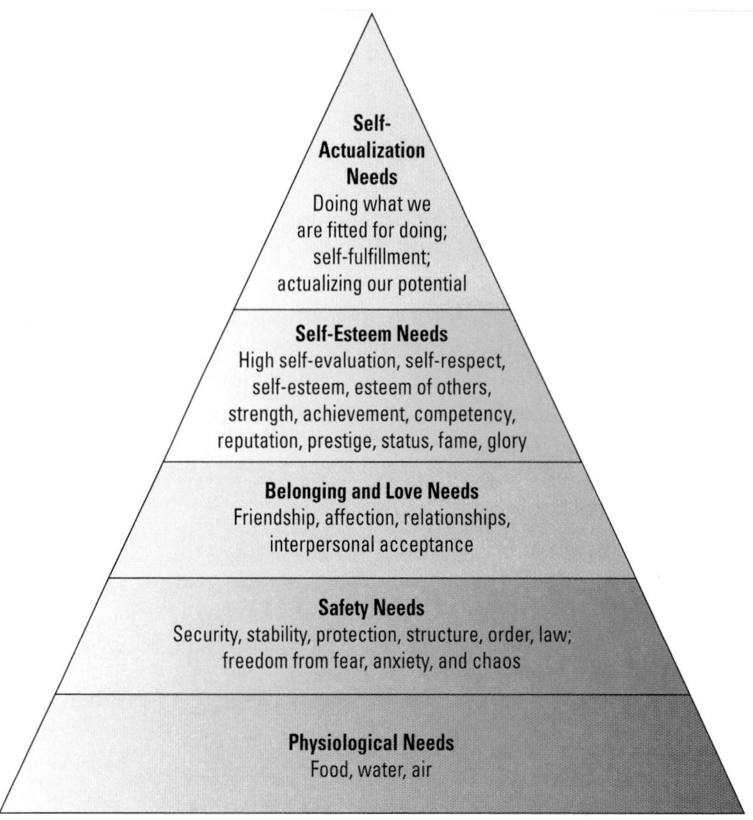

world, the speaker who promises to meet these basic physiological needs is the one the people will follow. Most college students in the United States, however, have their physiological needs for food, water, and air well satisfied—so these needs will not help motivate them. People who already have sufficient food won't be motivated to get more.

Safety Needs

Those who do not have their basic safety and freedom-from-fear needs met will be motivated by appeals to security, protection, and freedom from physical and psychological distress. You see appeals to this need in advertisements for burglar protection devices for home and car, in political speeches promising greater police protection on the streets and in schools, and in speeches by motivational gurus who promise psychological safety and freedom from anxiety. This freedom from anxiety also seems to be the motive used in the advertisements of psychic services that promise to tell you what is really going on (with, say, your romantic partner) as well as what will happen in the future. With this information, they imply, you'll be free of the anxiety that a lack of knowledge brings. You'll also learn what you should do—break off your relationship, move to the West Coast, or take that new job. The fact that this information is totally without any factual basis seems not to deter people from spending millions of dollars on psychics.

Sometimes the safety motive takes the form of a desire for order, structure, and organization—motives seen clearly in the advertisements for personal data assistants like the Palm Pilot, cell phones, and information management software. Many people fear what is unknown, and order and structure make things predictable and, hence, safe.

Belonging and Love Needs

Belonging and love needs are extremely powerful and comprise a variety of specific motives. For example, most people are motivated to love and be loved. For most persons, love and its pursuit occupy a considerable amount of time and energy. If you can teach your audience how to be loved and how to love, you'll have not only an attentive audience but a grateful one as well.

We also want affiliation—friendship and companionship. We want to be a part of a group, despite our equally potent desire for independence and individuality. Notice how advertisements for singles clubs, cruises, and dating services appeal to this need for affiliation. On this basis alone they successfully gain the attention, interest, and participation of countless people. Again, such affiliation seems to assure us that we are in fact worthy creatures. If we have friends and companions, surely we are people of some merit.

Self-Esteem Needs

"In his private heart," wrote Mark Twain, "no man much respects himself." And perhaps because of this, we need to develop a positive self-image, to see ourselves in the best possible light. We want to see ourselves as self-confident, worthy, and contributing human beings. Inspirational speeches, speeches of the "you're the greatest" type, never seem to lack receptive and suggestible audiences.

Self-esteem comes, at least in part, from the approval of others (something that is important in all cultures but especially in collectivist cultures). Most people are concerned with peer approval but also want approval from family, teachers, elders, and even children. The approval of others contributes to positive self-esteem. Approval from others also ensures the attainment of related goals. For example, if you have peer approval, you probably also have influence. If you have approval, you're likely to have status. But in relating your propositions to your audience's desire for approval, avoid being too obvious. Few people want to be told that they need or desire approval.

People also want power, control, and influence. They want power over their own lives—to be in control of their own destiny, to be responsible for their own successes. As Emerson put it, "Can anything be so elegant as to have few wants, and to serve them one's self?"

Many people also want to have power over other persons, to be influential. Similarly, they may want to increase control over the environment and over events and things in the world. Because of this you'll motivate your listeners when you make them see that they can increase their power, control, and influence as a result of their learning what you have to say or doing as you suggest.

People want to achieve in whatever they do. As a student you want to be a successful student. You also want to achieve as a friend, as a parent, as a lover. This is why books and speeches that purport to tell people how to be better achievers are so successful. At the same time of course, you also want others to recognize your achievements as real and valuable. In using the achievement motive, be explicit in stating how your speech, ideas, and recommendations will contribute to the listeners' achievements. At the same time, recognize that different cultures will view achievement very differently. To some achievement may mean financial success; to others, group popularity; to still others, security. Show your audience how what you have to say will help them achieve these goals, and you'll likely have an active and receptive audience.

Although they often deny it, most people are motivated to some extent by the desire for financial gain—for what money can buy, for what it can do. Concern for lower taxes, for higher salaries, and for fringe benefits are all related to the money motive. Show the audience that what you're saying or advocating will make them money, and they'll listen with considerable interest—much as they read the get-rich-quick books that flood the bookstores.

Self-Actualization Needs

The self-actualization motive, according to Maslow (1970), influences attitudes and behaviors only after

VIEWPOINT

As explained in the text, generally, in the United States, speakers are advised to stress their credibility—to convince their audience that they are competent, of good character, and dynamic or charismatic. In some cultures, however, this may be seen as implying that your audience members are inferior. As with any principle of communication, it helps to know something of the culture of your listeners. How would most members of your own culture weigh in on this question?

BUILDING COMMUNICATION SKILLS

Finding the Available Means of Persuasion

What persuasive strategies would you use to convince your class of the validity of either side in any of the following points of view? For example, what persuasive strategies would you use to persuade your class members that interracial adoption should be encouraged? What strategies would you use to persuade them that interracial adoption should be discouraged?

1. *Point of View: Interracial Adoption*. Those in favor of interracial adoption argue that adoption (regardless of race) is good for the child and that the welfare of the child—who might not get adopted if not by someone of another race—must be considered first. Those opposed to interracial adoption argue that children need to be raised in a family of the same race if the child is to develop self-esteem and become a functioning member of his or her own ethnic group.
2. *Point of View: Same-Sex Marriage*. Those in favor of same-sex marriage argue that gay men and lesbians should be accorded exactly the same rights and responsibilities as heterosexuals—no more, no less. Those opposed argue that same-sex marriage will undermine the concept of marriage.
3. *Point of View: Affirmative Action*. Those in favor of affirmative action argue that because of injustices in the way certain groups (racial, national, gender) were treated, they should now be given preferential treatment to correct the imbalance caused by the earlier social injustices. Those opposed argue that merit must be the sole criterion for promotion, jobs, entrance to graduate schools, and so on, and that affirmative action is just reverse discrimination.

all other needs are satisfied. And because these other needs are very rarely all satisfied, the time a speaker might spend appealing to self-actualization might be better spent on other motives. And yet, it seems that regardless of how satisfied or unsatisfied your other desires are, you have a desire to self-actualize, to become what you feel you're fit for. If you see yourself as a poet, you must write poetry. If you see yourself as a teacher, you must teach. Even if you don't pursue these as occupations, you nevertheless have a desire to write poetry or to teach. Appeals to self-actualization—"to be the best you can be"—encourage listeners to strive for their highest ideals and often are welcomed by the audience.

Use Credibility Appeals

Your **credibility** is the degree to which your audience sees you as a believable spokesperson. If your listeners see you as competent and knowledgeable, of good character, and charismatic or dynamic, they will think you credible. As a result, you'll be more effective in changing their attitudes or in moving them to do something. Credibility is not something you have or don't have in any objective sense; rather, it's what the audience thinks of you.

What makes a person credible will vary from one culture to another. In some cultures people would claim that competence is the most important factor in, say, the choice of a teacher for their preschool children. In other cultures the most important factor might be the goodness or morality of the teacher or perhaps the reputation of the teacher's family.

At the same time, each culture may define each of the characteristics of credibility differently. For example, in defining "character" some cultures may emphasize the rules of a specific religion, whereas others may stress the individual conscience. The Quran, the Torah, and the New Testament, for example, will all have very different levels of credibility ascribed to them depending on the religious beliefs of the audience. And this will be true even when all three religious books say essentially the same thing.

Before reading any further about the ways to establish your credibility, you may wish to take the self-test "How Credible Are You?"

ASK THE RESEARCHER

Age and Credibility

- *I'm a returning student and the oldest (by about 30 years) in the class. The other students seem to regard my views as outdated even before I've explained them, and I fear it's due to my being their parents' generation. What can I do to enhance my credibility with my classmates and with younger people generally?*

College classrooms in the United States are age-segregated environments. The great majority of students are between 18 and 28 and don't expect to find students from a different age group in the classroom. Therefore, numerous age-related stereotypes will exist. The good news is that time and positive interactions can change these often negative stereotypes. First, it's important to accept that you'll be perceived as significantly different from your younger classmates. Second, it's important to realize that your life experiences, learning styles, cultural likes and dislikes, and responsibilities outside the classroom will not be similar to those of the other students. But these differences can be turned into positives. Listen to the younger students, empathize with their life issues, engage their concerns, accommodate to their styles of interaction, and find interactive strategies that are far from aggressive and "all-knowing." As the course progresses, the negative stereotypes that are evident at initial encounters will disappear, and your credibility as a student will increase.

For further information: Nussbaum, J. F., Thompson, T. L., & Robinson, J. D. (2000). *Communication and aging* (2nd ed.). Mahwah, NJ: Erlbaum. And Baringer, D. K., Kundrat, A. L., & Nussbaum, J. F. Instructional communication and older adults. In J. F. Nussbaum & J. Coupland (Eds.) (2004) *Handbook of communication and aging research* (2nd ed., pp. 543–562). Mahwah, NJ: Erlbaum.

Jon F. Nussbaum (Ph.D., Purdue University) is professor of communication arts and sciences and human development and family studies at Pennsylvania State University. He conducts research and teaches courses on the communicative world of older adults across numerous social contexts. He has recently been elected president of the International Communication Association.

TEST YOURSELF

How Credible Are You?

Respond to each of the following phrases to indicate how you think members of your class see you when you deliver a public speech. Use the following scale: Definitely true = 5; probably true = 4; neither true nor untrue = 3; probably untrue = 2; and definitely untrue = 1.

____ **1.** Knowledgeable about the subject matter

____ **2.** Experienced

____ **3.** Informed about the subject matter

____ **4.** Fair in the presentation of material (evidence and argument)

____ **5.** Concerned with the audience's needs

____ **6.** Consistent over time on the issues addressed in the speech

____ **7.** Assertive in personal style

____ **8.** Enthusiastic about the topic and in general

____ **9.** Active rather than passive

HOW DID YOU DO? This test focuses on the three qualities of credibility—competence, character, and charisma—and is based on a large body of research (for example, McCroskey, 1997; Riggio, 1987). Items 1 to 3 refer to your perceived competence: How competent or capable does the audience see you when you give a public speech? Items 4 to 6 refer to your perceived character: Does the audience see you as a person of good and moral character? Items 7 to 9 refer to your perceived charisma: Does the audience see you as dynamic and active rather than as static and passive? Scores will range from a high of 45 to a low of 9. If you scored relatively high (say around 32 or higher) then you feel your audience sees you as credible. If you

UNDERSTANDING *THEORY* AND *RESEARCH*

Credibility Impressions

You form a credibility impression of a speaker on the basis of two sources of information. First, you assess the reputation of the speaker as you know it. This is initial—or what theorists call "extrinsic"—credibility. Second, you evaluate the degree to which that reputation is confirmed or refuted by what the speaker says and does during the speech. This is derived—or "intrinsic"—credibility. In other words, you merge what you know about the speaker's reputation with the more immediate information you get from present interactions in order to form a combined final assessment of credibility.

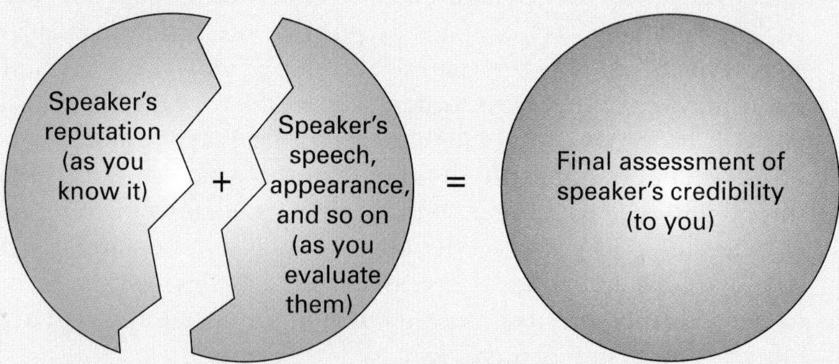

Working with Theories and Research

- *Does this model adequately explain how you form credibility impressions of others? Can you derive from this model any practical advice for increasing your own credibility?*

TEST YOURSELF, continued

scored relatively low (say below 27), then you feel your audience sees you as lacking in credibility.

WHAT WILL YOU DO? Think about how you might go about increasing your credibility. What specific steps can you take to change any audience perception with which you may be unhappy? Are there specific things you can do to strengthen your competence, character, and charisma? A good source to consult is Ronald Riggio's 1987 book *The Charisma Quotient* (New York: Dodd, Mead).

Competence

Competence includes both knowledge and expertise. The more knowledge and expertise the audience sees you as having, the more likely the audience will believe you. Similarly, you're likely to believe a teacher or doctor if you think he or she is knowledgeable on the subject. You can demonstrate your competence to your audience in a variety of ways.

Tell Listeners of Your Competence. Let the audience know of any special experience or training that qualifies you to speak on this specific topic. If you're speaking on communal living and you've lived on a commune yourself, then say so in your speech. Tell the audience of your unique and personal experiences when these contribute to your credibility.

This recommendation to tell listeners of your competence generally applies to most audiences you'll encounter in the United States. But in some cultures—notably collectivist cultures such as those of Japan, China, and Korea, for example—stressing your own competence or that of your corporation may be taken to mean that your audience members are inferior or that their corporations are not as good as yours. In other cultures—notably individualist cultures such as those of Scandinavia, the United States, and western Europe, for example—if you don't stress your competence, your listeners may assume it's because you don't have any.

Cite a Variety of Research Sources. Make it clear to your audience that you've thoroughly re-

THE *PUBLIC SPEAKING* SAMPLE ASSISTANT

A Poorly Constructed Persuasive Speech

This speech was written by the author to illustrate some really broad as well as some rather subtle errors that a beginning speaker might make in constructing a persuasive speech.

XXX Has Got to Go

You probably didn't read the papers this weekend, but there's a XXX movie, I mean video, store that moved in on Broad and Fifth Streets. My parents, who are retired teachers, are protesting it, and so am I. My parents are organizing a protest for next weekend.

What do you think of the title of the speech? Visualizing yourself as a listener, how would the opening comment make you feel? Does the speaker gain your attention? What thesis do you think the speaker will support? Does mentioning "my parents" help or hurt the speaker's credibility?

There must be hundreds of XXX video stores in the country, and they all need to be closed down. I have a lot of reasons.

What is the speaker's thesis? What impression are you beginning to get of the speaker?

First, my parents think it should be closed down. My parents are retired teachers and have organized protests over the proposed new homeless shelter and to prevent the city from making that park on Elm Street. So they know what they're doing.

How do the speaker's parents sound to you? Do they sound like credible leaders with a consistent cause? Professional protesters (with perhaps a negative agenda)? What evidence is offered to support the assertion that we should believe the speaker's parents? Is this adequate? What would you need to know about people before believing them?

The XXX video place is un-Christian. No good Christian people would ever go there. Our minister is against it and is joining in the protest.

What does this statement assume about the audience? How would this statement be responded to by your public speaking class? What are some reasons why the speaker might not have explained how XXX video stores are un-Christian?

These stores bring crime into the neighborhood. I have proof of that. Morristown's crime increased after the XXX video store opened. And in Martinsville, where they got rid of the video store, crime did not increase. If we allow the video store in our own town, then we're going to be like Morristown and our crime is going to increase.

What do you think of the reasoning used here? Are there other factors that could have influenced Morristown's crime increase? Is there any evidence that getting rid of the video store resulted in the stable crime rate in Martinsville? What assumption about the audience does the speaker make in using Martinsville and Morristown as analogies?

These stores make lots of garbage. The plastic wrappings from the videos will add to our already overextended and overutilized landfill. And a lot of them are going to wind up as litter on the streets.

Do you agree with this argument about the garbage? Is this argument in any way unique to the video store? Is it likely that people will open the wrappers and drop them on the street?

The XXX Video House stays open seven days a week, 24 hours a day. People will be forced to work at all hours and on Sunday, and that's not fair. And the store will increase the noise level at night with the cars pulling up and all.

What validity do you give to each of these arguments? Given the 24-hour policy, how might you construct an argument against the video store? Are there advantages of a neighborhood store's 24-hour policy that the audience may be thinking of and thus countering the speaker's argument? If there are, how should the speaker deal with them?

The XXX Video House—that's its name, by the way—doesn't carry regular videos that most people want. So, why do we want them?	Upon hearing this, would you be likely to extend this argument and start asking yourself, "Do we now close up all stores that most people don't want?"
The XXX Video House got a lease from an owner who doesn't even live in the community, someone by the name of, well, it's an organization called XYX Management. And their address is Carlson Place in Jeffersonville. So, they don't even live here.	Is there a connection between who the owner is and whether the video store should or shouldn't be closed? Could the speaker have effectively used this information in support of the thesis to close the video store?
A neighboring store owner says he thinks the store is in violation of several fire laws. He says they have no sprinkler system and no metal doors to prevent the spread of a fire. So, he thinks they should be closed down, too.	What credibility do you ascribe to the "neighboring store owner"? Do you begin to wonder if the speaker would simply agree to have the store brought up to the fire code laws?
Last week on *Oprah* three women were on and they were in the XXX movie business and they were all on drugs and had been in jail and they said it all started when they went into the porno business. One woman wanted to be a teacher, another wanted to be a nurse, and the other wanted to be a beautician. If there weren't any XXX video stores then there wouldn't be a porn business and, you know, pornography is part of organized crime, and so if you stop pornography you take a bite out of crime.	What is the cause and what is the effect that the speaker is asserting? How likely is it that the proposed cause actually produced the effect? Might there have been causes other than the pornography that might have led these women into drugs? What credibility do you give to people you see on talk shows? Does it vary with the specific talk show? Do you accept the argument that there would be no pornography business without video stores? What would have to be proved to you before you accepted this connection? How do you respond to the expression "Take a bite out of crime"?
One of the reasons I think it should be closed is that the legitimate video stores—the ones that have only a small selection of XXX movies somewhere in the back—will lose business. And if they continue to lose business, they'll leave the neighborhood and we'll have no video stores.	Is the speaker implying that this is the real reason against XXX video stores? Do you start wondering if the speaker is against XXX video stores—as it seemed in the last argument—or only against stores that sell XXX material exclusively? What effect does this impression have on your evaluation of the speaker's credibility and the speaker's thesis?
That's a lot of reasons against XXX movie houses. I have a quote here: Reason is "a portion of the divine spirit set in a human body." Seneca.	How do you feel about the number of "reasons"? Would you have preferred fewer reasons or reasons more fully developed or more reasons? What purpose does this quotation serve?
In conclusion and to wrap it up and close my speech, I want to repeat and say again that the XXX video stores should all be closed down. They corrupt minors. And they're offensive to men and women and especially women. I hope you'll all protest with the Marshalls—my mother and father—and there'll be lots of others there too. My minister, I think, is coming too.	Might the speaker have introduced this conclusion differently? What is the speaker's thesis now? What do you think of the arguments that XXX video stores are offensive? What is the effect of this argument's being introduced here in the conclusion? Do you think you'd go to the protest? Why or why not?

searched your topic. Do this by mentioning some of the books you've read, the persons you've interviewed, the articles you've consulted. Weave these throughout your speech. Don't bunch them together at one time.

Stress the Competencies of Your Sources. If your audience isn't aware of them, then emphasize the particular competencies of your sources. In this way it becomes clear to the audience that you've chosen your sources carefully and with a view to-

VIEWPOINT

If this speaker were addressing members of your community on the need to welcome a new homeless shelter in the neighborhood, to what motives would you advise him to appeal?

ward providing the most authoritative sources possible. For example, saying simply, "Senator Cardova thinks . . . " does nothing to establish the senator's credibility. Instead, consider saying something like "Senator Cardova, who headed the finance committee for three years and was formerly a professor of economics at MIT, thinks . . . ."

Character

An audience will see you as credible if they perceive you as having high moral **character:** as someone who is honest and someone they can trust. When an audience perceives your intentions as good for them (rather than for your own personal gain), they'll think you credible and they'll believe you. You can establish your high moral character in several ways.

Stress Fairness. In your persuasive speech, show your fairness; stress that you've examined both sides of the issue (if indeed you have). If you're presenting both sides, then make it clear that your presentation is accurate and fair. Be particularly careful not to omit any argument the audience may already have thought of—this is a sure sign that your presentation isn't fair and balanced. Tell the audience that you would not advocate a position if you did not base it on a fair evaluation of the issues.

Stress Concern for Audience. Make it clear to the audience that you're interested in their welfare rather than seeking self-gain. If the audience feels that you're "out for yourself," they'll justifiably downgrade your credibility. Make it clear that the audience's interests are foremost in your mind. Tell your audience how the new legislation will reduce *their* taxes, how recycling will improve *their* community, how a knowledge of sexual harassment will make *their* workplace more comfortable and stress free.

Stress Concern for Enduring Values. We view speakers who are concerned with small and insignificant issues as less credible than speakers who demonstrate a concern for lasting truths and general principles. Thus, make it clear to the audience that your position—your thesis—is related to higher-order values; show them exactly how this is true.

Charisma

Charisma is a combination of your personality and dynamism as seen by the audience. An audience will perceive you as credible (and believable) if they like you and if they see you as friendly and pleasant rather than aloof and reserved. Similarly, audiences favor the dynamic speaker over the hesitant, nonassertive individual. They'll perceive you as less credible if they see you as shy, introverted, and soft-spoken rather than as extroverted and forceful. Perhaps people feel that dynamic speakers are open and honest in presenting themselves whereas shy, introverted individuals may be hiding something. As a speaker there's much that you can do to increase your charisma and hence your perceived credibility.

Demonstrate a Positive Outlook. Show the audience that you have a positive orientation to the public speaking situation and to the entire speaker–audience encounter. We see positive and forward-looking people as more credible than negative and backward-looking people. Stress your pleasure at addressing the audience. Stress hope rather than despair; stress happiness rather than sadness.

Demonstrate Enthusiasm. The lethargic speaker, the speaker who somehow plods through the speech, is the very opposite of the charismatic speaker. Try viewing a film of Martin Luther King Jr. or Billy Graham speaking—they're totally absorbed with the speech and with the audience. They're excellent examples of the enthusiasm that makes a charismatic speaker.

Be Emphatic. Use language that is emphatic rather than colorless and indecisive. Use gestures that are clear and decisive rather than random and hesitant. Demonstrate a firm commitment to the position you're advocating; the audience will be much more likely to agree with a speaker who believes firmly in the thesis of the speech.

Credibility Errors

Some speakers try to raise their own credibility by unfairly attacking another's character. For example, here are three types of such attacks. You'll want to avoid using these tactics as a speaker, and you'll want to be alert for these tactics as you listen to others (Lee & Lee, 1972, 1995; Pratkanis & Aronson, 1991; Herrick, 2004).

- *Personal interest:* Personal interest attacks may take either of two forms. In one form the speaker disqualifies someone because he or she isn't directly affected by the issue or doesn't have firsthand knowledge, as would be the case if a speaker dismissed an argument on abortion because it was made by a man. In another form the speaker disqualifies someone because he or she will benefit in some way from a proposal. But arguing that, for example, someone is rich, middle class, or poor and thus will benefit from a proposed tax cut does not mean that the tax cut proposal is invalid. The legitimacy of an argument can never depend on the gender (or socioeconomic status or culture) of its proponents. Nor can it depend on any gain that a person may derive from the position advocated. The legitimacy of an argument can be judged only on the basis of the evidence and reasoning presented.
- *Character attacks:* Character attacks, often referred to as ad hominem attacks, involve accusing another person (usually an opponent) of some serious wrongdoing or of some serious character flaw. The purpose of this kind of fallacious appeal is to discredit the person or to divert attention from the issue under discussion. Remarks such as "How can we support a candidate who has smoked pot (or avoided the military)?" or "Do you want to believe someone who has been unfaithful on more than one occasion?" are often heard in political discussions but probably have little to do with the logic of the argument.
- *Name calling:* In **name calling,** often referred to as "poisoning the well," the speaker calls an idea, a group of people, or a political philosophy a bad name ("atheist," "anti-American") to try to get listeners to condemn the idea without analyzing the argument and evidence. The opposite of name calling is the use of the **glittering generality** in which the speaker tries to make listeners accept some idea by associating it with things they value highly ("democracy," "free speech," "academic freedom"). By using such "virtue words," the speaker tries to lead listeners to ignore the evidence and simply approve of the idea.

Motivate Your Listeners

If you want to persuade your listeners, you have to motivate them to believe or to act in some way. One

Table 18.1
The Motivated Sequence as a Persuasive Strategy

Step	Purpose	Audience Question Speaker Should Answer	Audience Response You Want to Avoid
Attention	Focus listeners' attention on you and your message.	Why should I listen? Why should I use my time listening?	This is boring. This is irrelevant. This is of no interest to me.
Need	Demonstrate that there is a problem that affects them.	Why do I need to know or do anything?	I don't need to hear this. Things are fine now. This won't benefit me.
Satisfaction	Show listeners how they can satisfy the need (solve the problem).	Can I do anything about this?	I really can't do anything. It's beyond my control.
Visualization	Show listeners what their lives will be like with the need satisfied.	How would anything be different or improved?	I can't see how anything would be different. Nothing's going to change.
Action	Urge listeners to do something to solve the problem.	What can I do to effect this change?	I can't do anything. I'll be wasting my time and energy.

BUILDING COMMUNICATION SKILLS

Constructing Logical, Motivational, and Credibility Appeals

Below are statements suitable as theses for a variety of persuasive speeches. Select any one statement (or its opposite) and construct *(a)* a logical appeal, *(b)* an emotional appeal, and *(c)* a credibility appeal that would prove effective in persuading your class.

1. Sports involving cruelty to animals—such as bullfighting, cockfighting, and foxhunting—should (not) be universally condemned and declared illegal.
2. Gay men and lesbians should (not) be allowed to serve in the military on the same conditions as heterosexuals.
3. Retirement should (not) be mandatory at age 65 for all government employees.
4. The death penalty is (not) morally wrong.
5. Too little (too much) government money is spent on accommodating people with disabilities.

way to motivate, as explained in Unit 15, is to use the *motivated sequence:* Gain your audience's attention, demonstrate that a need exists, demonstrate how that need can be satisfied when they believe or do what you say, show them what things will be like once the need is satisfied, and urge them to do something to solve the problem.

Table 18.1 summarizes the motivated sequence as a persuasive strategy and will help you develop your persuasive speeches, whether they deal with questions of fact, value, or policy—the topics to which we now turn.

Ideal Audience Response	Speech Materials to Use	Cautions to Observe
This sounds interesting. Tell me more.	Attention-gaining materials, p. 318.	Make attention relevant to speech topic.
OK, I understand; there's a problem.	Supporting materials (examples, statistics, testimony), pp. 301–313.	Don't overdramatize the need.
I can change things.	Supporting materials, pp. 301–313; logical, emotional, and credibility appeals, pp. 380–392.	Answer any objections listeners might have to your plan.
Wow! Things look a lot better this way.	Emotional appeals, pp. 383–386. Illustrations and language high in imagery (pp. 334–342).	Be realistic; don't visualize the world as perfect once your listeners do as you suggest.
Let me sign up. Here's my contribution. I'll participate in the effort.	Emotional appeals, pp. 383–386. Specific language, pp. 336–338.	Be specific. Ask for small attitude changes and easily performed behaviors.

GOING *ONLINE*

Great Speeches

http://www.c-span.org/classroom/lang/speeches.asp

C-Span and PBS maintain websites of both historical and contemporary speeches. Read one of the speeches and critique it.

In addition, visit the companion website for this text (www.ablongman.com/devito). Take the self-test on the ethics of persuasion, "When Is Persuasion Unethical?," read the discussion "Motivational Principles," and try the exercises "Analyzing Arguments: The Toulmin Model" and "Gender, Credibility, and the Topics of Persuasive Speaking."

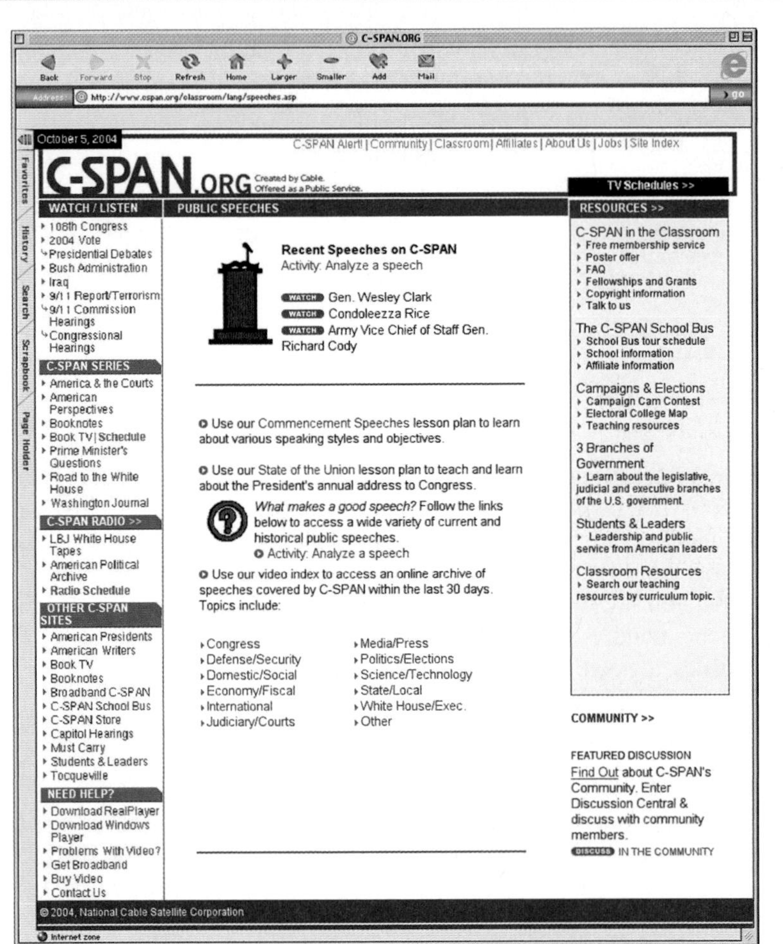

The Speech on Questions of Fact

Questions of fact concern what is or is not true, what does or does not exist, what did or did not happen. Some questions of fact are easily answered. These include the many academic questions you're all familiar with: What is philosophy? Who was Aristotle? When was the first satellite launched? Questions of fact also include more mundane questions such as What's on television? When is the meeting? What's Jenny's e-mail address? You can find the answers to these questions by looking at some reference book, finding the relevant website, or asking someone who knows the answer.

The questions of fact that we deal with in persuasive speeches are a bit different. Although these questions also have answers, the answers are not that easy to find and in fact may never be found. The questions concern controversial issues for which different people have different answers. Daily newspapers abound in questions of fact. For example, the February 29, 2004, edition of the *New York Times* raised such questions of fact as these: Was Martha Stewart guilty of lying to government investigators about a stock sale? What was causing Zimbabwe's food shortage? How did the nurse who killed some 40 people continue to get hired, and who was responsible for allowing him to work for so long in so many hospitals? Did the British spy on United Nations Secretary General Kofi Annan? What was the NFL doing to reduce steroid use among athletes?

Thesis

In a persuasive speech you'll formulate a thesis around a question of fact such as:

- This company has a glass ceiling for women.
- The plaintiff was slandered (or libeled or defamed).
- The death was a case of physician-assisted suicide.
- Gay men and lesbians make competent military personnel.
- Television violence leads to violent behavior in viewers.

If you were preparing a persuasive speech on, say, the first example given above, you might phrase your thesis as "This company discriminates against women." Whether or not the company does discriminate is a question of fact; clearly the company does discriminate or it doesn't. Whether you can prove it does or it doesn't, however, is another issue.

Main Points

Once you've formulated your thesis, you can generate your main points by asking the simple question "How do you know this?" or "Why would you believe this is true (factual)?" The answers to one of these questions will enable you to develop your main points. The bare bones of your speech might then look something like this:

General Purpose:	To persuade.
Specific Purpose:	To persuade my listeners that this company discriminates against women.
Thesis:	This company discriminates against women. (How does this company discriminate against women?)

I. Women earn less than men.
II. Women are hired less often than men.
III. Women occupy fewer managerial positions than men.

Support

Having identified your main points, you would then begin searching for information to support them. Taking the first proposition, you might develop it something like this:

I. Women earn less than men.
   A. Over the past five years, the average salary for editorial assistants was $2,000 less for women than it was for men.
   B. Over the past five years, the entry-level salaries for women were $1,500 less than the entry-level salaries for men.
   C. Over the past five years, the bonuses earned by women were 20 percent below the bonuses earned by men.

The above speech focuses entirely on a question of fact; the thesis itself is a question of fact. In other speeches, however, you may want just one of your propositions to center on a question of fact. So, for example, let's say you're giving a speech advocating that the military give gay men and lesbians full equality. In this case one of your main points might focus on a question of fact: research showing that gay men and lesbians make competent military personnel. That fact established, you'd then be in a better position to argue for equality in military policy.

Developing Speeches on Questions of Fact

In developing a persuasive speech on a question of fact, consider the following suggestions.

1. Emphasize logical proof. Facts are your best support. The more facts you have, the more persuasive you'll be in dealing with questions of fact. For example, the more evidence you can find that women earn less than men, the more convincing you will be in proving that women do in fact earn less, and ultimately, that women are discriminated against.
2. Use the most recent materials possible. The more recent your materials, the more relevant they will be to the present time and the more persuasive they're likely to be. In our example, if you had said that in 1990 women earned on average $10,000 less than men, that statistic would not have helped you prove that the company discriminates against women *now*.
3. Use highly competent sources. When you use the testimony of others or you cite research, establish the competence of the source. Let the audience see that the people you're citing know what is going on and have the competence to speak authoritatively.
4. Clearly connect your main points to your thesis in your introduction, when introducing each of the points, and again in your summary. For example, don't allow the audience to forget that the reality of women's lower salaries directly supports the thesis that this company discriminates against women.

The Speech on Questions of Value

Questions of value concern what you consider good or bad, moral or immoral, just or unjust. In the February 29, 2004, *New York Times,* for example, there were a lot of questions of value debated: Should marriage be restricted to opposite-sex couples? Should Israel build walls in the West Bank? Should Lebanon have reinstituted the death penalty? Should additional wilderness areas throughout the United States be opened for commerical logging? Should both creationism and evolution be taught in schools? Should Social Security benefits be cut?

Oftentimes speeches of value will seek to strengthen existing attitudes, beliefs, or values. Much religious and political speaking, for example, has this goal. People who listen to religious speeches usually are already believers, so these speeches strive to strengthen the beliefs and values the people already hold. Here the audience already shares the speaker's values and is willing to listen. Speeches that seek to change audience values are much more difficult to construct. Most people resist change. When you try to get people to change their values or beliefs you're fighting an uphill (though not necessarily impossible) battle.

Thesis

Theses devoted to questions of value might look something like this:

- The death penalty is unjustifiable.
- Bullfighting is inhumane.
- Discrimination on the basis of affectional orientation is wrong.
- Chemical weapons are immoral.
- Human cloning is morally justified.
- College athletics minimize the importance of academics.

Main Points

As with questions of fact, you can generate your main points by asking a strategic question of your thesis; in this case, "Why is this good?" or "Why is this immoral?" For example, you can take the first thesis given above and ask, "Why is the death penalty unjustifiable?" The answers to this question will give you the speech's main points. The body of your speech might then look something like this:

General Purpose: To persuade.
Specific Purpose: To persuade my listeners that the death penalty is unjustifiable.
Thesis: The death penalty is unjustifiable. (Why is the death penalty unjustifiable?)

I. We can make mistakes.
II. The death penalty is useless as a deterrent.
III. No one has the moral right to take another's life.

Support

You would then begin to search for evidence. For example, to show that mistakes have been made, you might itemize three or four high-profile cases in which people were put to death and later, through DNA, found to have been innocent.

At times and with certain topics, it may be useful to identify the standards you would use to judge something moral or justified or fair or good. For example, in the "bullfighting is inhumane" speech, you might devote your first main point to defining when an action can be considered inhumane. In this case the body of your speech might look like this:

I. An inhumane act has two qualities.
  A. It is cruel and painful.
  B. It serves no human necessity.
II. Bullfighting is inhumane.
  A. It is cruel and painful.
  B. It serves no necessary function.

Notice that in the example of capital punishment, the speaker aims to strengthen or change the listeners' beliefs about the death penalty. The speaker is not asking the audience to do anything about capital punishment but just to believe that it's not justified. However, you might also use this question of value as a first step toward persuading your audience to take some action. For example, once you get your audience to believe that the death penalty is unjustified, you might then ask them to take certain actions—perhaps in your next speech—to support an anti-death penalty politician, to vote for or against a particular proposition, or to join an organization fighting against the death penalty.

Developing Speeches on Questions of Value

In constructing your persuasive speech on a question of value, consider these suggestions:

1. Define clearly the specific value on which you're focusing. For example, let's say that you're de-

veloping a speech to persuade high school students to attend college and you want to stress that college is of value. But what type of value would you focus on? The financial value (college graduates earn more money than non-graduates)? The social value (college is a lot of fun and a great place to make friends)? The intellectual value (college will broaden your view of the world and make you a more critical and creative thinker)? Once you clarify the type of value on which you'll focus, you'll find it easier to develop the relevant points. You'll also find it easier to locate appropriate supporting materials.

2. Begin with shared assumptions and beliefs and then progress gradually to areas of disagreement. For example, in the death penalty speech, it's likely that even people in favor of the death penalty would agree that mistakes can be made and would be willing to accept evidence that mistakes have in fact been made, especially if you cite reliable statistical evidence and expert testimony. By starting with this point, you secure initial agreement and can use that as a basis for approaching areas where you and the audience see things differently.
3. Use sources that the audience values highly. For example, if you were addressing an audience of devout Catholics who were active participants in their church, the testimony of the pope or a cardinal would likely be influential. But if your audience were composed of Muslims, Jews, Buddhists, or atheists, then it's unlikely that these sources would be as influential. With some listeners, these sources might even have a negative effect. So do a thorough audience analysis before you select your testimonials.

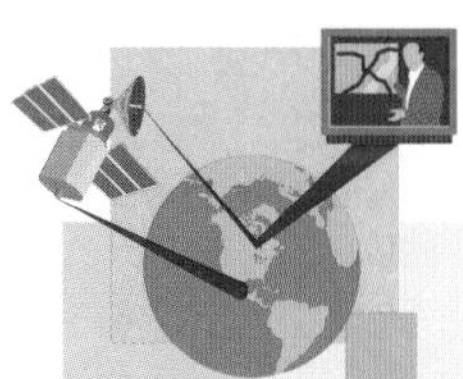

MEDIA WATCH

Reversing Media's Influence

Although you generally think of the media as exerting influence on you, you also can exert influence on the media—on radio, television, newspapers and magazines, film, and the Internet (Jamieson & Campbell, 1997; Postman & Powers, 1992):

- Register your complaints. E-mail, write letters, or call a television station or an advertiser expressing your views. Write to a public forum, such as a newspaper or newsgroup, or to the Federal Communication Commission (FCC) or other regulatory agencies. Use any of the variety of websites (www.vote.com is perhaps the most popular) that encourage users to voice their opinions and then forward these to the appropriate agencies.
- Exert group pressure. Join with others who think the same way you do. Bring group pressure to bear on television networks, newspapers, advertisers, and manufacturers.
- Protest through an established organization. There's probably an organization already established for the issue with which you're concerned. Search the Internet for relevant newsgroups, professional organizations, and chat rooms that focus on your topic.
- Protest with a social movement, a technique used throughout history to gain civil rights. Forming such movements or aligning yourself with an established movement can help you secure not only a large number of petitioners but also media coverage that may help you communicate your message to a large audience.
- Create legislative pressure. Exert influence on the state or federal level by influencing your local political representatives (through voting, calls, letters, and e-mails), who will in turn influence representatives on higher levels of the political hierarchy.

You and the Media

Let's say that you're unhappy about the way in which the national and local media (television and newspapers) have treated the abortion controversy. How would you go about exerting pressure on the media to better reflect your own position in their coverage?

THE *PUBLIC SPEAKING* SAMPLE ASSISTANT

An Excellent Persuasive Speech

Here is an excellent persuasive speech that was given by Jayme Meyer of the University of Texas at Austin at the American Forensic Association, National Individual Events tournament in 2004. The speech is used here with the permission of Jayme Meyer.

The Home of the Slaves

History books tell us that slavery ended after the Civil War. Try telling that to Andrea. At the age of four, she was sold by her mother and enslaved for 12 years. Locked in a basement with 16 other children, the *New York Times Magazine* of January 25, 2004, explains, Andrea was raped almost every night while her owner got rich. Tragically, Andrea and her companions were not victims of an inadequate third world government, but, according to September 2003 *National Geographic,* they are among the almost 150,000 slaves currently held here in the United States.

This dramatic story was designed to gain attention and to suggest the topic of the speech. Did it gain your attention? If not, what else might the speaker have done?

Is 150,000 people a lot? How might the speaker have dramatized this number and made it more significant to an audience of college students?

Unlike the slaves of our early history, these slaves are lured to America with false promises of a better life through well-paying jobs or marriage. But as the *Boston Globe* of April 17, 2003, elaborates, once they arrive, these immigrants are forced to work in "brothels, sweatshops, fields, or private homes." And the terror doesn't stop there. The *San Antonio Express News* of April 3, 2003, reveals that slavery is now the third-largest source of money for organized crime, generating $19 billion annually, money that is often used for other criminal activity, including drug trafficking and arms smuggling, producing more crime for all of us to deal with here at home.

This elaboration continues to dramatize the issue of present-day slavery in the United States and presents it as a problem for the listeners. Was the speaker successful in convincing you that this is a problem for society and for you? If not, what else might the speaker have done to convince you that this problem really affects you personally?

So in order to break this cycle of slavery, we must, first, explore the extent of slavery in the United States; next, understand why this problem keeps us in chains; and finally, implement some solutions to what John Miller of the U.S. State Department calls in the *Washington Post* of January 1, 2004, "the emerging human rights issue of the 21st century."

Here the speaker provides an excellent orientation to the speech and identifies the three main points of the speech: (1) the present state of slavery in the United States, (2) the reasons this is a problem, and (3) ways of solving the problem. The organizational pattern is also identified; the first two sections focus on the problem and the third presents the solution. In what other ways could this speech have been organized?

The 13th Amendment was supposed to end slavery in December 1865, but even today slaves are forced into the U.S. and slavery fosters additional crime. Kristiina Kangaspunta of the United Nations told the Associated Press on

Here the speaker begins to explain the current state of slavery and makes us see it as a horrendous crime.

The speaker continues to introduce current material from reliable sources and makes us feel she is

May 13, 2003, that the United States is now one of the top three human trafficking destinations in the world, with most slaves originating from Thailand, Russia, or the Ukraine. The January 25, 2004, *New York Times Magazine* explains that traffickers promise better lives in the U.S. as waiters, actors, models, or nannies. But after tricking them into paying their own way into Mexico, the traffickers smuggle them across the border and force them into a nightmare world of brutality. According to the U.S. Department of State's *Trafficking in Persons Report* of June 11, 2003, slaves are exposed to appalling working conditions, sexually transmitted diseases from rape and forced prostitution, poor nutrition, and even torture. For instance, four girls between the ages of 14 and 17 were recently discovered working in an underground brothel in Plainfield, New Jersey. The same *New York Times Magazine* described the conditions when the police found them: the emaciated girls slept on rotting mattresses, used a doorless, filthy bathroom, and were surrounded by morning-after pills and abortion-inducing medications.

extremely well prepared and knowledgeable, which adds to her credibility.

The speaker makes a great effort to give the topic of these enslaved individuals relevance for a group of listeners who are probably quite comfortable and secure. Did the speaker succeed in making you feel that this problem affects you? If not, what else might the speaker have done?

Here the speaker moves from general statements about slavery to a specific case of four girls. Moving from the abstract to the specific is a useful technique for making your listeners understand and feel the problem.

Although we may not personally be enslaved, all of us are affected by America's slave trade. According to the Summer/Fall 2003 *Brown Journal of World Affairs,* the profits made from slavery are often invested in the mainstream economy, giving criminal networks more power because of their immense wealth. And the more they make, the more we're affected. As M2 Presswire of October 14, 2003, explains, crime syndicates use the billions of dollars generated by slavery to fund other criminal activities, including drug trafficking, arms smuggling, and money laundering. While 150,000 slaves suffer the immediate evils of slavery, all of us are endangered by its long-term implications.

The speaker cleverly answers a potential audience question ("Why should this concern me?") by explaining that slavery creates additional crime, from which we all suffer. Was the speaker successful in getting you to feel that this is important to you? How much do you care about these other problems—drug trafficking, arms smuggling, and money laundering? If you don't care very much, what might the speaker have done to make you care?

We pride ourselves on our freedoms, but 150,000 people within our borders are denied theirs because of slavery's lucrative nature and ineffective legislation. The *Agence France Presse* of August 1, 2003, reports the results of an International Labour Organization study: Modern-day slavery is "more lucrative . . . than drug trafficking." As the aforementioned *Trafficking in Persons Report* reveals, slave owners make up to thousands of dollars for each child laborer and tens of thousands for each brothel worker. And, as a February 24, 2004, article on the Florida State University web page notes, "unlike drugs, humans can be recycled . . . so it's a better investment for the traffickers." And according to *National Geographic* of September 2003, countless people take ad-

Again, the speaker cleverly weaves in specific examples along with the generalizations and gives the problem a human face.

Would selective exposure play a role in this speech? If so, what could the speaker do to anticipate selective exposure?

What kinds of logical appeals does the speaker use in this speech? How effective are they?

vantage of its lucrative nature. Juan, Ramiro, and Jose Ramos forced men and women from Mexico to pick fruit in Florida. Sardar and Nadira Gasanov made women from Uzbekistan work in strip clubs in West Texas. Louisa Satia and Kevin Nanji tricked a 14-year-old girl from Cameroon into working as their private servant in Maryland after raping her and imprisoning her in their house—and the list goes on.

And unfortunately, current laws are simply not strong enough. The Trafficking Victims Protection Act of 2000 has done a good job of protecting some victims, giving former slaves temporary U.S. visas and offering protection from their traffickers. But helping victims after they are discovered doesn't get to the root of the problem; getting traffickers off the streets would. The *San Antonio Express News* of April 3, 2003, states that while $60 million per year is spent on the cause, only 75 traffickers were actually prosecuted in 2000, simply not enough for the problem that Assistant Secretary of State Richard Armitage tells the *Weekly Standard* of October 6, 2003, will "outstrip the illicit trade in guns and narcotics within a decade."

What types of emotional appeals can you find throughout this speech? How effective are they? How might they have been made even more effective?

What has the speaker done throughout this speech to identify with the audience? What else might the speaker have done?

We thought we abolished slavery in 1865, but the fight obviously is not over. Action from the UN and the United States government, as well as our own attention, can help protect those who have lost all freedom. The United Nations needs to follow through with its international database of human trafficking. As a UN press release of May 16, 2003, states, the database, now consisting of about 3,000 cases, tracks the "countries of origin, transit and destination of trafficked persons." This database needs to be continuously updated in order to give governments accurate information to prosecute those who traffic in human beings. The U.S. government needs to work in conjunction with the UN to help populate the database, and then must utilize the information once it is available. This database will help us find a way to stop the flow of slaves into the United States, allowing us to get to the root of the problem.

This first sentence is an interesting but subtle transition from the problem, already discussed, to the solution, which is about to be discussed. Would you have preferred a more obvious and direct transition?

Does the speaker convince you that the United Nations can help in combating this problem?

Once this information is acquired, United States lawmakers must also take swift action. The Trafficking Victims Protection Act of 2000 was definitely a good first step. However, Congress needs to refocus funding on the prosecution of traffickers. To reach this goal, more money obviously needs to be spent. According to Mohamed Matted, codirector of the Protection Project at Johns Hopkins University, in his testimony to the House Committee on Interna-

The second part of the solution concerns lawmakers. Does the speaker make an effective case for the role that laws and lawmakers must play in human trafficking?

What types of credibility appeals can you identify throughout this speech? Would you have used credibility appeals differently? What would you have said?

tional Relations on June 24, 2003, this can be done by confiscating traffickers' assets. This money could be used to fund prosecution of other traffickers as well as provide restitution for the victims.

Finally, you and I easily can play our part in abolishing slavery by going to the American Anti-Slavery Group's website at iAbolish.com. Next time you are online, become an e-abolitionist by signing antislavery petitions and joining the site's Freedom Action Network. The network will send you weekly e-mail newsletters to keep you informed and alert you to antislavery events in your area. We have condemned past slavery and those who allowed it to persist. But now it's our turn to stand up for what we know is right and help abolish the slavery that plagues our time.

The third part of the speaker's proposed solution is individual action, specifically participation in a particular Internet group devoted to the elimination of slavery. Might you join the effort after reading this speech? If not, what might the speaker have said to move you to action?

Is the speaker asking for reasonable amounts of change? If not, what correction would you suggest?

Even though Andrea has been free for about 5 years, so are those who tortured her for 12. Fearing retribution, she's in constant hiding, dealing with the daily trauma from her years of forced servitude. But after understanding the extent of modern-day slavery and discussing how it comes about, we can implement solutions to help people like Andrea see for themselves that we do live in the land of the free, not the home of the slave.

Here the speaker returns to the introduction, signaling that this is nearing the end of the speech.

The speaker here summarizes the main points introduced in the introduction and developed throughout the speech.

Now that you've read the entire speech, what would you have titled it if it were to be given in your public speaking class?

The Speech on Questions of Policy

When you move beyond a focus on value to urging your audience to do something about it, you're then into a question of policy. For example, in a speech designed to convince your listeners that bullfighting is inhumane, you'd be focusing on a question of value. If you were to urge that bullfighting should therefore be declared illegal, you'd be urging the adoption of a particular policy; in other words, you'd be dealing with a question of policy. Items in the same February 29, 2004, *New York Times* that focused on questions of policy included, for example, Should the United States enact a constitutional amendment to limit marriage to opposite-sex couples? Should same-sex couples have a legal right to marry? What should be done to alleviate hunger in Zimbabwe? What should the United States do in regard to the Haitian rebellion? What should Iraq's constitution look like? Who should police financial institutions holding pension funds?

Thesis

Theses on questions of policy concern what should be done, what procedures should be adopted, what laws should be changed; in short, what policy should be followed. In some speeches you may want to advocate a specific policy, whereas in others you may wish to argue that a current policy should be discontinued. Persuasive speeches frequently revolve around questions of policy. Some examples:

- Colleges should ban hate speech.
- Our community should adopt a zero tolerance policy for guns in schools.
- Abortion should be available on demand.
- Music CDs should be rated for violence and profanity.
- Medical marijuana should be legalized.
- Smoking should be banned from all public buildings and parks.

As you can tell from these examples, questions of policy almost invariably involve questions of values.

To argue, for example, that colleges should ban hate speech reflects a belief that hate speech is wrong. To argue for a zero tolerance policy on guns in schools implies that you think it's wrong for students and faculty to carry guns to school.

Main Points

You can develop your speech on a question of policy by asking a strategic question of your thesis. With policy issues the question might be "Why should the policy be adopted?" or "Why is the policy desirable?" or "Why is this policy better than what we now have?" Taking our first example, we might ask, "Why should colleges ban hate speech?" From the answers to this question, you would develop your main points, which might look something like this:

1 Hate speech encourages violence against women and minorities.
2 Hate speech denigrates women and minorities.
3 Hate speech teaches hate instead of tolerance.

Support

You would then support each of these points with a variety of supporting materials that would convince your audience that hate speech should be banned from college campuses. For example, you might cite the websites put up by certain groups that advocate violence against women and minority members or the lyrics of certain performers who came to campus. Or you might cite examples of actual violence that had been accompanied by hate speech or hate literature.

In some speeches of policy you might simply want your listeners to agree that the policy you're advocating is a good idea. In other cases you might want them to do something about the policy—to vote for a particular candidate, to take vitamin C, to diet, to write to their elected officials, to participate in the walkathon, to wear an AIDS awareness ribbon, and so on.

Generally, questions of policy are used more often as theses than as main points. Still, in some instances, you might phrase a main point around a policy issue. For example, in a speech designed to get a client off on a driving-while-intoxicated charge, a lawyer might want to argue that the blood alcohol level used to establish "drunk driving" should be much higher than it currently is.

Developing Speeches on Questions of Policy

In developing your speech on a question of policy, consider the following suggestions:

1. Prove that the policy is needed. You might, for example, show that a health care plan is needed because currently workers have no health care coverage. Or you might show that a particular policy is needed because the current policy is inadequate.
2. Emphasize that the policy you're supporting is practical and reasonable. If possible, show that the policy you're advocating has been successfully put into operation elsewhere.
3. Show your listeners how the policy will benefit them directly. Generally, listeners want to know that changes will prove beneficial to them on a personal level. The more personal you can make this policy, the better it will be received.
4. When asking for action, ask for small, easily performed, and very specific behaviors. For example, it will generally be easier to get listeners to sign a petition than to donate their Saturday afternoon to a walkathon. Similarly, it's likely to be easier to get listeners to contribute $5 to the athletic fund than $50.
5. Use the organizational pattern (see Unit 15) that best fits your topic. For example, in the speech on zero tolerance on guns in school, you might consider using a problem–solution pattern in which your speech would be divided into two basic parts:

   I. Guns are destroying our high schools. (problem)
   II. We must adopt a zero tolerance policy. (solution)

Organizational Examples

Questions of policy are especially well suited to organization with the motivated sequence and comparison-and-contrast patterns (Unit 15).

The Motivated Sequence

For example, in the hate speech example mentioned above, you might use a motivated sequence and develop the speech somewhat as follows:

Attention
I. Here are just a few examples of the hate speech I collected right here on campus.
[Show slides 1–7]

Need
II. Hate speech creates all sorts of problems.
  A. Hate speech encourages violence.
  B. Hate speech denigrates women and minorities.
  C. Hate speech teaches intolerance.

Satisifaction

III. If we're to build an effective learning environment, hate speech must go.

Visualization

IV. Banning hate speech will help us build an environment conducive to learning.
   A. Students will not fear violence.
   B. Women and minorities will not feel as if they are second-class citizens.
   C. Tolerance can replace intolerance.

Action

V. Sign my petition urging the administration to take action, to ban hate speech.

Comparison and Contrast

If you're seeking to persuade your listeners that one policy will be more effective than another (say, the present policy), then a comparison-and-contrast order might work best. Here you might divide each of your main points into two parts—the present plan and the proposed plan—so as to effectively compare and contrast them on each issue. The body of your speech might look something like this:

I. The plans are different in their coverage for psychiatric problems.
   A. The present plan offers nothing for such problems.
   B. The proposed plan provides the same coverage for psychiatric problems as for physical problems.

II. The plans differ in their deductibles.
   A. The present plan has a $2,000 deductible.
   B. The proposed plan has a $500 deductible.

III. The plans differ in the hospitalization allowances.
   A. In the present plan two days are allowed for child birth; in the proposed plan four days are allowed.
   B. In the present plan all patients are assigned to large wards; in the proposed plan all patients are assigned to semi-private rooms.

The Ethics of Emotional Appeals

Emotional appeals are all around. Persons who want to restrict the media's portrayal of violence may appeal to your fear of increased violence in your community; the real estate broker may appeal to your desire for status; the friend who wants a favor may appeal to your desire for social approval; the salesperson may appeal to your desire for sexual rewards. But are such appeals ethical?

- Most communication theorists would argue that emotional appeals are ethical when, for example, they are used in combination with logical appeals, used in moderation, and directed at our better selves.
- Emotional appeals are considered unethical when, for example, they're used instead of logical evidence, directed at our baser selves, or aimed at children.

The distinction between the ethical and unethical use of emotional appeals, however, often can be difficult to draw.

WHAT WOULD YOU DO? You want to dissuade your teenaged sons and daughter from engaging in sexual relationships. Would it be ethical to use emotional appeals to scare them so that they'll avoid sexual relationships? Would it be ethical to use the same appeals to get them to avoid associating with teens of other races? More generally, does the persuader's goal have anything to do with whether emotional appeals are ethical or unethical?

SUMMARY

This unit focused on persuasive speeches and examined several principles of persuasion and three types of persuasive speeches.

1. Among the guidelines for preparing persuasive speeches are the following:
   - Anticipate selective exposure.
   - Ask for reasonable amounts of change.
   - Identify with your audience.
   - Use logical appeals.
   - Use emotional appeals.
   - Use credibility appeals.
   - Motivate your listeners.
2. Persuasive speeches can be classified in various ways. One way is in terms of the major question dealt with:
   - Questions of fact focus on what is or is not.
   - Questions of value focus on what is good or bad.
   - Questions of policy focus on what should be done.
3. Several logical fallacies are especially widespread and should be avoided by speakers and recognized by listeners: anecdotal evidence, straw man, appeal to tradition, bandwagon, testimonial, transfer, plain folks, card stacking, thin entering wedge, and agenda setting.

4. Attacks on another's credibility also should be avoided; these include attacks on the grounds of personal interest, character attacks, and name calling.

KEY TERMS

persuasion
selective exposure
foot-in-the-door technique
door-in-the-face technique
identification
logical appeals
reasoning from specific instances
reasoning from causes and effects
reasoning from sign
anecdotal evidence
straw man
appeal to tradition
bandwagon
testimonial
transfer
plain folks
card stacking
thin entering wedge
agenda setting
emotional appeals
hierarchy of needs
physiological needs
safety needs
belonging and love needs
self-esteem needs
self-actualization needs
credibility
competence
character
charisma
personal interest
character attacks
name calling
motivated sequence strategy
questions of fact
questions of value
questions of policy

THINKING CRITICALLY ABOUT

Persuasive Speaking

1. You're planning to give a speech urging more conscientious recycling to two separate audiences. One audience will be composed solely of women and the other audience solely of men. Otherwise the audience members will be similar: college-educated professionals about 30 years old. In what ways would you make the two speeches differ? What general principles or assumptions about gender are you making as you differentiate these two speeches?
2. You want to get your listeners to contribute one hour a week to your college's program of helping high school students prepare for college. You're considering using the foot-in-the-door or the door-in-the-face technique. How would you develop each of these strategies? Which would you eventually use?
3. Read a persuasive speech, focusing on the principles of persuasion covered in the first section of this unit. Does the speaker make use of any of these principles? What persuasive principles can you identify from reading the speech?
4. Examine a speech for questions of fact, value, and policy. How are these issues used in the speech?
5. Visit the National Press Club website at http://npc.press.org/ for complete texts of speeches from the National Press Club's luncheons. Read one of the speeches and evaluate it in terms of the principles of persuasion discussed in this unit. This is also an excellent research website; it provides guides that will prove useful for just about any topic.
6. Prepare and deliver a two-minute speech in which you do one of the following:
   - explain an interesting attitude, belief, or value that you have come across
   - explain how a speech strengthened or changed one of your attitudes or beliefs
   - explain an advertisement in terms of the principles of persuasion
   - explain cultural differences in popularly held beliefs regarding such concepts as God, life, death, family, happiness, education, law, or men and women

Glossary of Human Communication Concepts

abstraction process The process by which a general concept is derived from specifics; the process by which some (never all) characteristics of an object, person, or event are perceived by the senses or included in some term, phrase, or sentence.

abstraction A general concept derived from a class of objects; a partial representation of some whole.

accent The stress or emphasis placed on a syllable when it is pronounced.

acculturation The processes by which a person's culture is modified or changed through contact with or exposure to another culture.

active listening A process of putting together into some meaningful whole the listener's understanding of the speaker's total message—the verbal and the nonverbal, the content and the feelings.

adaptors Nonverbal behaviors that satisfy some personal need and usually occur without awareness; for example, scratching to relieve an itch or moistening your lips to relieve dryness. Three types of adaptors are often distinguished: **self-adaptors, alter-adaptors,** and **object-adaptors.**

adjustment The principle of verbal interaction that claims that communication takes place only to the extent that the parties communicating share the same system of signals.

affect displays Movements of the facial area that convey emotional meaning—for example, expressions showing anger, fear, or surprise.

affinity-seeking strategies Behaviors designed to increase our interpersonal attractiveness.

affirmation The communication of support and approval.

ageism Discrimination based on age, usually against the elderly.

agenda A list of the items that a small group must deal with in the order in which they should be covered.

agenda setting A persuasive technique in which the speaker states or implies that XYZ is the issue and that all others are unimportant.

aggressiveness See **verbal aggressiveness.**

allness A language distortion; the assumption that all can be known or is known about a given person, issue, object, or event.

alter-adaptors Body movements you make in response to your current interactions; for example, crossing your arms over your chest when someone unpleasant approaches or moving closer to someone you like.

altercasting Placing the listener in a specific role for a specific purpose and asking that the listener approach the question or problem from the perspective of this specific role.

ambiguity Uncertainty of meaning; the possibility of interpreting a message in more than one way.

analogy, reasoning from A type of reasoning in which you compare like things and conclude that since they are alike in so many respects that they are also alike in some previously unknown respect.

apology A type of excuse in which you acknowledge responsibility for the behavior, generally ask forgiveness, and claim that this will not happen again.

apprehension See **communication apprehension.**

arbitrariness The feature of human language that reflects the absence of a real or inherent relationship between the form of a word and its meaning. If we do not know anything of a particular language, we cannot examine the form of a word and thereby discover its meaning.

argument Evidence (for example, facts or statistics) and a conclusion drawn from the evidence.

argumentativeness Willingness to argue for a point of view, to speak your mind. Distinguished from **verbal aggressiveness.**

articulation The physiological movements of the speech organs as they modify and interrupt the air stream emitted from the lungs.

artifactual communication Communication that takes place through the wearing and arrangement of various items made by human hands—for example, clothing, jewelry, buttons, or the furniture in your house and its arrangement.

assertiveness Willingness to stand up for your own rights while respecting the rights of others.

assimilation A process of distortion in which messages are reconstructed to conform to our own attitudes, prejudices, needs, and values.

attack A persuasive technique that involves accusing another person (usually an opponent) of some serious wrongdoing so that the issue under discussion never gets examined.

attention The process of responding to a stimulus or stimuli; usually involves some consciousness of responding.

attitude A predisposition to respond for or against an object, person, or position.

attraction The state or process by which one individual is drawn to another and forms a highly positive evaluation of that other person.

attraction theory A theory holding that we form relationships on the basis of our attraction to another person.

attractiveness The degree to which a person is perceived to be physically appealing and to possess a pleasing personality.

attribution A process through which we attempt to understand the behaviors of others (as well as our own), particularly the reasons or motivations for these behaviors.

attribution theory A theory concerned with the processes through which we attempt to understand the behaviors of others (as well as our own), particularly the reasons or motivations for those behaviors.

audience participation principle A principle of persuasion stating that persuasion is achieved more effectively when the audience participates actively.

authoritarian leader A group leader who determines group policies or makes decisions without consulting or securing agreement from group members.

avoidance An unproductive **conflict** strategy in which a person takes mental or physical flight from the actual conflict.

backchanneling cues Listener responses to a speaker that do not ask for the speaking role.

bandwagon A persuasive technique in which the speaker tries to gain compliance by saying that "everyone is doing it" and urging listeners to jump on the bandwagon.

barriers to communication Factors (physical or psychological) that prevent or hinder effective communication.

behavioral synchrony The similarity in the behavior, usually nonverbal, of two persons. Generally, it is taken as an index of mutual liking.

belief Confidence in the existence or truth of something; conviction.

beltlining An unproductive **conflict** strategy in which one person hits at the level at which the other person cannot withstand the blow.

blame An unproductive **conflict** strategy in which we attribute the cause of the conflict to the other person or devote our energies to discovering who is the cause and avoid talking about the issues causing the conflict.

boundary marker An object that divides one person's territory from another's—for example, a fence.

brainstorming A technique for generating ideas either alone or, more usually, in a small group.

breadth The number of topics about which individuals in a relationship communicate.

card stacking A persuasive technique in which the speaker selects only the evidence and arguments that build his or her case and omits or distorts any contradictory evidence.

causes and effects, reasoning from A form of reasoning in which you conclude that certain effects are due to specific causes or that specific causes produce certain effects.

censorship Restriction on people's rights to produce, distribute, and/or receive various communications.

central marker An item that is placed in a territory to reserve it for a specific person—for example, the sweater thrown over a library chair to signal that the chair is taken.

certainty An attitude of closed-mindedness that creates a defensiveness among communication participants; opposed to **provisionalism.**

channel The vehicle or medium through which signals are sent.

character An individual's honesty and basic nature; moral qualities that contribute to **credibility.**

charisma An individual's dynamism or forcefulness; one of the qualities that contribute to **credibility.**

cherishing behaviors Small behaviors we enjoy receiving from others, especially from our relational partner—for example, a kiss, a smile, or a gift of flowers.

chronemics The study of the communicative nature of time—the way you treat time and use it to communicate. Two general areas of chronemics are **cultural time** and **psychological time.**

civil inattention Polite ignoring of others so as not to invade their privacy.

cliché An overused expression that has lost its novelty and part of its meaning and that calls attention to itself because of its overuse, such as "tall, dark, and handsome" as a description of a man.

closed-mindedness An unwillingness to receive certain communication messages.

code A set of symbols used to translate a message from one form to another.

coercive power Power derived from an individual's ability to punish or to remove rewards from another person.

cognitive restructuring A theory for substituting logical and realistic beliefs for unrealistic ones; used in reducing communication apprehension and in raising self-esteem.

cohesiveness The property of togetherness. In group communication situations, cohesiveness has to do with the mutual attraction among members; it's a measure of the extent to which individual group members work together as a group.

collectivist culture A culture in which the group's goals are given greater importance than the individual's and in which, for example, benevolence, tradition, and conformity are given special emphasis. Opposed to **individualist culture.**

color communication The meanings that different colors communicate in various cultures.

communication (1) The process or act of communicating; (2) the actual message or messages sent and received; (3) the study of the processes involved in the sending and receiving of messages. (The term *communicology* is suggested for the third definition.)

communication accommodation theory Theory holding that speakers adjust their speaking style to their listeners to gain social approval and achieve greater communication effectiveness.

communication apprehension Fear or anxiety over communicating; may be "trait apprehension" (fear of communication generally, regardless of the specific situation) or "state apprehension" (fear that is specific to a given communication situation).

communication competence A knowledge of the rules and skills of communication; the term often refers to the qualities that make for effectiveness in communication.

communication network The pathways of messages; the organizational structure through which messages are sent and received.

communicology The study of communication, particularly the subsection concerned with human communication.

competence A person's ability and knowledge; one of the qualities that contribute to **credibility.**

complementarity A principle of **attraction** stating that we are attracted by qualities that we do not possess or that we wish to possess and to people who are opposite or different from ourselves; opposed to **similarity.**

complementary relationship A relationship in which the behavior of one person (e.g., energetic activity) serves as the stimulus for the complementary behavior of the other (e.g., laziness); in complementary relationships behavioral differences are maximized.

compliance-gaining strategies Behaviors that are directed toward gaining the agreement of others; behaviors designed to persuade others to do as we wish.

compliance-resisting strategies Behaviors directed at resisting the persuasive attempts of others.

confidence A quality of interpersonal effectiveness; a comfortable, at-ease feeling in interpersonal communication situations.

confirmation A communication pattern that acknowledges another person's presence and also indicates an acceptance of this person, this person's definition of self, and the relationship as defined or viewed by this other person; opposed to **disconfirmation.**

conflict An extreme form of competition in which interdependent persons perceive their respective goals to be incompatible and see each other as interfering with their own attainment of desired goals.

congruence A condition in which both verbal and nonverbal behaviors reinforce each other.

connotation The feeling or emotional aspect of meaning, generally viewed as consisting of the evaluative (for example, good–bad), potency (strong–weak), and activity (fast–slow) dimensions; the associations of a term. See also **denotation.**

consensus A principle of attribution through which we attempt to establish whether other people react or behave in the same way as the person on whom we are now focusing. If the person is acting in accordance with the general consensus, then we seek reasons for the behavior outside the individual; if the person is not acting in accordance with the general consensus, then we seek reasons that are internal to the individual.

consistency A perceptual process that influences us to maintain balance among our perceptions; a process that makes us tend to see what we expect to see and to be uncomfortable when our perceptions run contrary to our expectations.

contact The first stage of an interpersonal relationship, in which perceptual and interactional contact occurs.

contamination A form of territorial encroachment that renders another's territory impure.

content and relationship dimensions A principle of communication stating that messages refer both to content (the world external to both speaker and listener) and to the relationship existing between the individuals who are interacting.

content message Communication message relating to the objective world—the world external to both speaker and listener.

context The physical, psychological, social, and temporal environment in which communication takes place.

contrast, principle of Often followed rule of perception: messages or people who are very different from each other probably don't belong together and do not constitute a set or group.

controllability One of the factors considered in judging whether or not a person is responsible for his or her behavior. If the person was in control, then you judge that he or she was responsible. A principle in **attribution theory.**

conversation Communication engaged in by two or three people and usually including an opening, feedforward, a business stage, feedback, and a closing.

conversational management The conduct of a conversation by means of **conversational turns.**

conversational maxims Principles that are followed in conversation to ensure that the goal of the conversation is achieved.

conversational turns The process of exchanging the speaker and listener roles during conversation.

cooperation An interpersonal process by which individuals work together for a common end; the pooling of efforts to produce a mutually desired outcome. In communication, an implicit agreement that calls for speaker and listener to work together to achieve mutual comprehension.

credibility The degree to which a speaker is perceived to be believable; **competence, character,** and **charisma** (dynamism) are its major dimensions.

critical thinking The process of logically evaluating reasons and evidence and reaching a judgment on the basis of this analysis.

critical thinking hats technique Technique developed by Edward deBono in which a problem or issue is viewed from six distinct perspectives: facts, feelings, negative arguments, positive benefits, creative new ideas, and control of thinking.

criticism The reasoned judgment of some work; although often equated with fault finding, criticism can involve both positive or negative evaluations.

cultural display Signs that communicate one's cultural identification, for example, clothing or religious jewelry.

cultural rules Rules that are specific to a given cultural group.

cultural time The perspective on time shared by members of a particular culture.

culture The relatively specialized lifestyle of a group of people—consisting of their values, beliefs, artifacts, ways of behaving, and ways of communicating—that is passed on from one generation to the next.

culture shock The psychological reaction we experience at being placed in a culture very different from our own or from what we are used to.

date An **extensional device** used to emphasize the notion of constant change and symbolized by a subscript: for example, John Smith $_{1992}$ is not John Smith $_{2005}$.

deception cues Verbal or nonverbal cues that reveal the person is lying.

decoder Something that takes a message in one form (for example, sound waves) and translates it into another form (for example, nerve impulses) from which meaning can be formulated (for example, in vocal–auditory communication). In human communication the decoder is the auditory mechanism; in electronic communication the decoder is, for example, the telephone earpiece. See also **encoder.**

decoding The process of extracting a message from a code—for example, translating speech sounds into nerve impulses. See also **encoding.**

defensiveness An attitude of an individual or an atmosphere in a group characterized by threats, fear, and domination; messages evidencing evaluation, control, strategy, neutrality, superiority, and certainty are assumed to lead to defensiveness; opposed to **supportiveness.**

delayed reactions Reactions that are consciously delayed while a situation is analyzed.

Delphi method A type of problem-solving group in which questionnaires are used to poll members (who don't interact among themselves) on several occasions so as to arrive at a group decision on, for example, the most important problems a company faces or activities a group might undertake.

democratic leader A group leader who stimulates self-direction and self-actualization on the part of the group members.

denial One of the obstacles to the expression of emotion; the process by which we deny our emotions to ourselves or to others.

denotation Referential meaning; the objective or descriptive meaning of a word. See also **connotation.**

depenetration A reversal of penetration; a condition in which the **breadth** and **depth** of a relationship decrease. See **social penetration theory.**

depth In interpersonal relationships, the degree to which the inner personality—the inner core—of an individual is penetrated in interpersonal interaction.

deterioration A stage in an interpersonal relationship in which the bonds holding the individuals together are weakened.

determinism The principle of verbal interaction that holds that all verbalizations are to some extent purposeful—that there is a reason for every verbalization.

dialogue A form of **communication** in which each person is both speaker and listener; communication characterized by involvement, concern, and respect for the other person; opposed to **monologue.**

direct speech Speech in which the speaker states his or her intentions clearly and forthrightly.

disclaimer Statement that asks the listener to receive what the speaker says as intended and not to interpret it as reflecting negatively on the image of the speaker.

disconfirmation The process by which one person ignores or denies the right of another person even to define himself or herself; opposed to **confirmation.**

dissolution The breaking of the bonds holding an interpersonal relationship together.

downward communication Communication in which messages are sent from higher to lower levels of an organization or hierarchy.

dyadic communication Two-person communication.

dyadic consciousness An awareness of an interpersonal relationship or pairing of two individuals; distinguished from situations in which two individuals are together but do not perceive themselves as being a unit or twosome.

dyadic effect The process by which one person in a dyad imitates the behavior of the other person, usually used to refer to the tendency of one person's self-disclosures to prompt the other to also self-disclose.

earmarker A physical sign that identifies an item as belonging to a specific person—for example, a nameplate on a desk or initials on an attaché case.

effect The outcome or consequence of an action or behavior; communication is assumed always to have some effect.

emblems Nonverbal behaviors that directly translate words or phrases—for example, the signs for "OK" and "peace."

emotion The feelings we have—for example, our feelings of guilt, anger, or sorrow.

empathy Feeling another person's feeling; feeling or perceiving something as does another person.

encoder Something that takes a message in one form (for example, nerve impulses) and translates it into another form (for example, sound waves). In human communication the encoder is the speaking mechanism; in electronic communication the encoder is, for example, the telephone mouthpiece. See also **decoder.**

encoding The process of putting a message into a code—for example, translating nerve impulses into speech sounds. See also **decoding.**

enculturation The process by which culture is transmitted from one generation to another.

E-prime A form of the English language that omits the verb *to be* except when used as an auxiliary or in statements of existence; also called E'. Designed to eliminate the tendency toward **projection.**

equality An attitude that recognizes that each individual in a communication interaction is equal, that no one is superior to any other; encourages supportiveness; opposed to **superiority.**

equilibrium theory A theory of proxemics holding that intimacy and physical closeness are positively related; as relationship becomes more intimate, the individuals will use shorter distances between them.

equity theory A theory of interpersonal relationships claiming that we experience relational satisfaction when there is an equal distribution of rewards and costs between the two persons in the relationship.

et cetera An **extensional device** used to emphasize the notion of infinite complexity; because we can never know all about anything, we should end any statement about the world or an event with an explicit or implicit "etc."

ethics The rightness or wrongness of actions; the branch of philosophy that studies moral values.

ethnic identity A commitment to the beliefs and philosophy of your culture.

ethnocentrism The tendency to see others and their behaviors through our own cultural filters, often as distortions of our own behaviors; the tendency to evaluate the values and beliefs of our own culture more positively than those of another culture.

euphemism A polite word or phrase used to substitute for some taboo or otherwise offensive term.

excluding talk Talk about a subject or in a vocabulary that only certain people understand, often in the presence of someone who does not belong to this group and therefore does not understand; use of terms unique to a specific culture as if they were universal.

excuse An explanation designed to lessen the negative consequences of something done or said.

expectancy violations theory A theory of proxemics holding that people have a certain expectancy for space relationships. When that expectancy is violated (for example, when a person stands too close to you or a romantic partner maintains abnormally large distances from you), the relationship comes into clearer focus and you wonder why this "normal distance" is being violated.

experiential limitation The limit of an individual's ability to communicate, as set by the nature and extent of that individual's experiences.

expert power Power that a person possesses because others believe the individual to have expertise or knowledge.

expressiveness A quality of interpersonal effectiveness that consists of genuine involvement in speaking and listening, conveyed verbally and nonverbally.

extemporaneous speech A speech that is thoroughly prepared and organized in detail and in which certain aspects of style are predetermined.

extensional device Linguistic device to help make language a more accurate means for talking about the world. Proposed by Alfred Korzybski, the extensional devices include **et cetera, date,** and **index,** among others.

extensional orientation A tendency to give primary consideration to the world of experience and only secondary consideration to labels. Opposed to **intensional orientation.**

face-saving Maintaining a positive public self-image in the minds of others.

facial feedback hypothesis The theory that your facial expressions can produce physiological and emotional effects.

facial management techniques Techniques used to mask certain emotions and to emphasize others; for example, intensifying your expression of happiness to make a friend feel good about a promotion.

fact–inference confusion A misevaluation in which a person makes an inference, regards it as a fact, and acts upon it as if it were a fact.

factual statement A statement made after observation and limited to what is observed. Opposed to **inferential statement.**

family A group of people who consider themselves related and connected to one another and among whom the actions of one have consequences for others.

fear appeal The appeal to fear to persuade an individual or group of individuals to believe or to act in a certain way.

feedback Information that is given back to the source. Feedback may come from the source's own messages (as when we hear what we are saying) or may come from the receiver(s) in the form of applause, yawning, puzzled looks, questions, letters to the editor of a newspaper, increased or decreased subscriptions to a magazine, and so forth. See also **negative feedback; positive feedback.**

feedforward Information that is sent prior to a regular message telling the listener something about what is to follow.

field of experience The sum total of an individual's experiences, which influences his or her ability to communicate. In some views of communication, two people can communicate only to the extent that their fields of experience overlap.

flexibility The ability to adjust communication strategies on the basis of the unique situation.

focus group A group designed to explore the feelings and attitudes of its individual members; usually follows a question-and-answer format.

force An unproductive **conflict** strategy in which a person attempts to win an argument by physical force or threats of force.

forum A small group format in which members of the group answer questions from the audience; often follows a symposium.

free information Information that is revealed implicitly and that may be used as a basis for opening or pursuing conversations.

friendship An interpersonal relationship between two persons that is mutually productive, established and maintained through perceived mutual free choice, and characterized by mutual positive regard.

fundamental attribution error The tendency to attribute a person's behavior to the kind of person he or she is (to the person's personality, perhaps) and to give too little importance to the situation the person is in.

game A simulation of some situation with rules governing the behaviors of the participants and with some payoff for winning; in transactional analysis, "game" refers to a series of ulterior transactions that lead to a payoff; the term also refers to a basically dishonest kind of transaction in which participants hide their true feelings.

General Semantics The study of the relationships among language, thought, and behavior.

glittering generality Attempt by a speaker to gain listeners' acceptance of an idea by associating it with things they value highly; the opposite of **name calling.**

gossip Communication about someone not present, some third party; usually concerns matters that are private to this third party.

grapevine The informal lines through which messages in an organization may travel; these informal routes resemble a physical grapevine, with its twists and turns and its unpredictable pattern of branches.

group norms Rules or expectations of appropriate behavior for members of groups.

group A collection of individuals connected to one another by some common purpose and with some structure among them.

group self-esteem A person's positive (or negative) evaluation of himself or herself as a member of a particular cultural group.

groupthink A tendency observed in some groups in which agreement among members becomes more important than the exploration of the issues at hand.

gunnysacking An unproductive **conflict** strategy of storing up grievances—as if in a gunnysack—and holding them in readiness to dump on the opponent in a disagreement.

halo effect The tendency to generalize an individual's positive or negative qualities from one area to another.

haptics The study of touch communication.

heterosexist language Language that assumes all people are heterosexual and thereby denigrates lesbians and gay men.

high-context culture A culture in which much of the information in communication is in the context or in the person rather than explicitly coded in the verbal messages. **Collectivist cultures** are generally high context. Opposed to **low-context** culture.

high-power-distance culture A culture in which there is a great difference in power between groups, for example, between teachers and students or managers and workers.

home-field advantage The increased power that comes from being in your own territory.

home territories Territories about which individuals have a sense of intimacy and over which they exercise control—for example, a professor's office.

hyphen An **extensional device** used to illustrate that what may be separated verbally may not be separable on the event level or on the nonverbal level; although one may talk about body and mind as if they were separable, in reality they are better referred to as body-mind.

idea-generation group A group whose purpose is to generate ideas. See also **brainstorming.**

illustrators Nonverbal behaviors that accompany and literally illustrate verbal messages—for example, an upward gesture accompanying the verbalization "It's up there."

I-messages Messages in which the speaker accepts responsibility for his or her own thoughts and behaviors; messages in which the speaker's point of view is acknowledged explicitly. Opposed to **you-messages.**

immediacy A quality of interpersonal effectiveness that creates a sense of contact and togetherness and conveys interest in and liking for the other person.

implicit personality theory A theory of personality, complete with rules or systems, that each individual maintains and through which the individual perceives others.

impromptu speech A speech given without any explicit prior preparation.

inclusion principle In verbal interaction, the principle that all members should be a part of (included in) the interaction.

inclusive talk Communication that includes all people; communication that does not exclude certain groups, for example, women, lesbians and gays, or members of certain races or nationalities.

index An **extensional device** used to emphasize the notion of nonidentity (no two things are the same) and symbolized by a mental subscript—for example, $politician_1$ is not $politician_2$.

indirect speech Speech that may hide the speaker's true intentions or that may be used to make requests and observations in a roundabout way.

indiscrimination A misevaluation caused by categorizing people, events, or objects into a particular class and responding to them only as members of the class; a failure to recognize that each individual is unique; a failure to apply the **index.**

individualist culture A culture in which the individual's goals and preferences are given greater importance than the group's. Opposed to **collectivist culture.**

inevitability A principle of communication stating that communication cannot be avoided; all behavior in an interactional setting is communication.

inferential statement A statement that can be made by anyone, is not limited to what is observed, and can be made at any time. Opposed to **factual statement.**

informal time Approximate rather than exact time, denoted in terms such as, "soon," "early," and "in a while."

information That which reduces uncertainty.

information overload A condition in which the amount of information is too great to be dealt with effectively or the number or complexity of messages is so great that an individual or organization is not able to deal with them.

information power Power that a person possesses because others see that individual as having signficant information and the ability to communicate logically and persuasively. Also called "persuasion power."

inoculation principle A principle stating that persuasion will be more difficult to achieve when beliefs and attitudes that have already been challenged previously are attacked, because the individual has built up defenses against such attacks in a manner similar to inoculation.

insulation A reaction to **territorial encroachment** in which you erect some sort of barrier between yourself and the invaders.

intensional orientation A point of view in which primary consideration is given to the way things are labeled and only secondary consideration (if any) to the world of experience. Opposed to **extensional orientation.**

interaction management A quality of interpersonal effectiveness; the control of interaction to the satisfaction of both parties. Includes managing conversational turns, fluency, and message consistency.

interaction process analysis A content analysis method that classifies messages into four general categories: social emotional positive, social emotional negative, attempted answers, and questions.

intercultural communication Communication that takes place between or among persons of different cultures or persons who have different cultural beliefs, values, or ways of behaving.

interpersonal communication Communication between two persons or among a small group of persons and distinguished from public or mass communication; communication of a personal nature and distinguished from impersonal communication; communication between or among intimates or those involved in a close relationship; often, dyadic and small group communication in general.

interpersonal conflict A conflict or disagreement between two persons.

interpersonal perception Our perception of people; the processes through which we interpret and evaluate people and their behavior.

interview A particular form of interpersonal communication in which two persons interact largely by question-and-answer format for the purpose of achieving specific goals.

intimacy The closest interpersonal relationship; usually, a close **primary relationship.**

intimacy claims Obligations incurred by virtue of being in a close and intimate relationship.

intimate distance The closest **proxemic distance,** ranging from touching to 18 inches. See also **proxemics.**

intrapersonal communication Communication with yourself.

invasion The unwarranted entrance into another's territory that changes the meaning of the territory. See also **territorial encroachment.**

involvement stage The stage in an interpersonal relationship that normally follows contact; in this stage the individuals get to know each other better and explore the potential for greater intimacy.

irreversibility A principle of communication holding that communication cannot be reversed; once something has been communicated, it cannot be uncommunicated.

jargon The technical language of any specialized group, often a professional class, that is unintelligible to individuals not belonging to the group; "shop talk."

Johari window A diagram of the four selves (open, blind, hidden, and unknown) that details the different kinds of information in each self.

kinesics The study of the communicative dimensions of facial and bodily movements.

laissez-faire leader A group leader who allows the group to develop and progress (or make mistakes) on its own.

lateral communication Communication among equals—for example, manager to manager, worker to worker.

leadership That quality by which one individual directs or influences the thoughts and/or the behaviors of others. See also **laissez-faire leader, democratic leader,** and **authoritarian leader.**

leave-taking cues Verbal and nonverbal cues that indicate a desire to terminate a conversation.

legitimate power Power that a person possesses because others believe that the individual has a right, by virtue of position, to influence or control their behavior.

level of abstraction The relative distance of a term or statement from an actual perception. A low-order abstraction would be a description of the perception, whereas a high-order abstraction would consist of inferences about descriptions of the perception.

leveling A process of message distortion in which a message is repeated but the number of details is reduced, some details are omitted entirely, and some details lose their complexity.

listening An active process of receiving messages sent orally; this process consists of five stages: receiving, understanding, remembering, evaluating, and responding.

logic The science of reasoning; the study of the principles governing the analysis of inference making.

looking-glass self The self-concept that results from the image of yourself that others reveal to you.

loving An interpersonal process in which one feels a closeness, a caring, a warmth, and an excitement for another person.

low-context culture A culture in which most of the information in communication is explicitly stated in the verbal messages. **Individualist cultures** are usually low-context cultures. Opposed to **high-context culture.**

low-power-distance culture A culture in which there is little difference in power between groups, for example, between doctors and patients or men and women.

magnitude of change principle A principle of persuasion stating that the greater and more important the change desired by the speaker, the more difficult its achievement will be.

maintenance A stage of relationship stability at which the relationship does not progress or deteriorate significantly; a continuation as opposed to a dissolution of a relationship.

maintenance strategies Specific behaviors designed to preserve an interpersonal relationship. Compare to **relationship repair.**

manipulation An unproductive **conflict** strategy in which a person avoids open conflict but instead attempts to divert the conflict by being especially charming and getting the opponent into a noncombative frame of mind.

manuscript speech A speech designed to be read verbatim from a script.

markers Devices that signify that a certain territory belongs to a particular person. See also **boundary marker, central marker,** and **earmarker.**

mass communication Communication addressed to an extremely large audience, mediated by audio and/or visual transmitters, and processed by gatekeepers before transmission.

matching hypothesis An assumption that we date and mate with people who are similar to ourselves—who match us—in physical attractiveness.

meaningfulness A perception principle that refers to your assumption that people's behavior is sensible, stems from some logical antecedent, and is consequently meaningful rather than meaningless.

mediated communication Messages sent by a source through some electronic device to a receiver; includes both mass media and computer communication.

mere exposure hypothesis The theory that repeated or prolonged exposure to a stimulus may result in a change in attitude toward the stimulus object, generally in the direction of increased positiveness.

message Any signal or combination of signals transmitted to a **receiver.**

metacommunication Communication about communication.

metalanguage Language used to talk about language.

metamessage A message that makes reference to another message; for example, comments like "Did I make myself clear?" or "That's a lie" refer to other messages and are therefore considered metamessages.

metaskills Skills for regulating more specific skills; for example, interpersonal communication skills such as **openness** and **empathy** must be regulated by the metaskills of **flexibility, mindfulness,** and **metacommunication.**

mindfulness A state of awareness in which we are conscious of the logic and rationality of our behaviors and the logical connections existing among elements. In a mindless state we are unaware of this logic and rationality.

mixed messages Messages that contradict themselves, messages that ask for two different (often incompatible) responses.

model A representation of an object or process.

monochronic time orientation A view of time in which things are done sequentially; one thing is scheduled at a time. Opposed to **polychronic time orientation.**

monologue A form of **communication** in which one person speaks and the other listens; there is no real interaction among participants. Opposed to **dialogue.**

motivated sequence An organizational pattern for arranging the information in a speech to motivate an audience to respond positively to the speaker's purpose.

name calling A persuasive technique in which the speaker gives an idea a derogatory name.

negative feedback Feedback that serves a corrective function by informing the source that his or her message is not being received in the way intended. Negative feedback serves to redirect the source's behavior. Looks of boredom, shouts of disagreement, letters critical of newspaper policy, and teachers' instructions on how better to approach a problem are examples of negative feedback. See also **positive feedback.**

noise Anything that interferes with a person's receiving a message as the source intended the message to be received. Noise is present in a communication system to the extent that the message received is not the message sent.

nominal group A collection of individuals who record their thoughts and opinions, which are then distributed to others. Without direct interaction, the thoughts and opinions are gradually pared down until a manageable list (of solutions or decisions) is produced. When this occurs, the nominal group (a group in name only) may restructure itself into a problem-solving group that analyzes the final list.

nonallness An attitude or point of view in which it is recognized that one can never know all about anything and that what we know, say, or hear is only a part of what there is to know, say, or hear.

nondirective language Language that does not direct or focus our attention on certain aspects; neutral language.

nonnegotiation An unproductive **conflict** strategy in which the individual refuses to discuss the conflict or to listen to the other person.

nonverbal communication Communication without words; communication by means of space, gestures, facial expressions, touching, vocal variation, and silence, for example.

nonverbal dominance Nonverbal behavior through which one person exercises psychological dominance over another.

norm See **group norms.**

object language Language used to communicate about objects, events, and relations in the world; the structure of the object language is described in a **metalanguage;** the display of physical objects—for example, flower arranging and the colors of the clothes we wear.

object-adaptors Movements that involve manipulation of some object; for example, punching holes in or drawing on a Styrofoam coffee cup, clicking a ballpoint pen, or chewing on a pencil.

olfactory communication Communication by smell.

openness A quality of interpersonal effectiveness encompassing (1) willingness to interact openly with others, to self-disclose as appropriate; (2) willingness to react honestly to incoming stimuli; and (3) willingness to own our own feelings and thoughts.

oral style The style of spoken discourse; when compared with written style, consists of shorter, simpler, and more familiar words; more qualification, self-reference terms, allness terms, verbs and adverbs; and more concrete terms and terms indicative of consciousness of projection—for example, "as I see it."

other-orientation A quality of interpersonal effectiveness involving attentiveness, interest, and concern for the other person.

other talk Talk about the listener or some third party.

owning feelings The process by which you take responsibility for your own feelings instead of attributing them to others.

panel A small group format in which "expert" participants speak without any set pattern and respond to questions from an audience.

paralanguage The vocal but nonverbal aspect of speech. Paralanguage consists of voice qualities (for example, pitch range, resonance, tempo); vocal characterizers (laughing or crying, yelling or whispering); vocal qualifiers (intensity, pitch height); and vocal segregates ("uh-uh," meaning "no," or "sh" meaning "silence").

parasocial relationships Relationships between a real person and an imagined or fictional character; after, relationships between a viewer and a real or fictional television personality.

pauses Silent periods in the normally fluent stream of speech. Pauses are of two major types: filled pauses (interruptions in speech that are filled with such vocalizations as "er" or "um") and unfilled pauses (silences of unusually long duration).

perception The process of becoming aware of objects and events from the senses. See also **interpersonal perception.**

perception checking The process of verifying your understanding of some message or situation or feeling to reduce uncertainty.

perceptual accentuation A process that leads you to see what you expect to see and what you want to see—for example, seeing people you like as better looking and smarter than people you do not like.

personal distance The second-closest **proxemic distance,** ranging from 18 inches to four feet. See also **proxemics**.

personal rejection An unproductive **conflict** strategy in which one individual withholds love and affection and seeks to win the argument by getting the other person to break down under this withdrawal.

persuasion The process of influencing attitudes and behavior.

phatic communication Communication that is primarily social; communication designed to open the channels of communication rather than to communicate something about the external world. "Hello" and "How are you?" in everyday interaction are examples.

pitch The highness or lowness of the vocal tone.

plagiarism The act of passing off the work of someone else as your own without acknowledging the source.

plain folks A persuasive strategy in which the speaker seeks to identify himself or herself (and his or her proposal) with the audience.

polarization A form of fallacious reasoning in which only two extremes are considered; also referred to as "black-or-white" or "either/or" thinking or as a two-valued orientation.

politeness Good communication manners; a way of interacting that is considerate and respectful.

polychronic time orientation A view of time in which several things may be scheduled or engaged in at the same time. Opposed to **monochronic time orientation.**

positive feedback Feedback that supports or reinforces the continuation of behavior along the same lines in which it is already proceeding—for example, applause during a speech. See also **negative feedfack.**

positiveness A characteristic of effective communication involving positive attitudes toward the self and toward the interpersonal interaction. Also can mean complimenting another and expressing acceptance and approval.

power The ability to control the behaviors of others.

power play A consistent pattern of behavior in which one person tries to control the behavior of another.

pragmatic implication An assumption that seems logical but is not necessarily true.

premature self-disclosures Disclosures that are made before the relationship has developed sufficiently.

primacy–recency Processes of perception in which we give more credence to that which occurs first (primacy) or to that which occurs last or most recently (recency).

primacy effect The condition in which what comes first exerts greater influence in our perceptions than what comes later. See also **recency effect.**

primary relationship The relationship between two people that they consider their most (or one of their most) important; for example, the relationship between spouses or domestic partners.

primary territories Areas that a person can consider his or her own exclusive preserve—for example, someone's room or office.

problem-solving group A group whose primary task is to solve a problem or, perhaps more often, to reach a decision.

problem-solving sequence A logical step-by-step process for solving a problem that is frequently used by groups; consists of defining and analyzing the problem, establishing criteria for evaluating solutions, identifying possible solutions, evaluating solutions, selecting the best solution(s), and testing the selected solution(s).

process Ongoing activity; by thinking of communication as a process, we emphasize that it is always changing, always in motion.

productivity The feature of language that makes possible the creation and understanding of novel utterances. With human language we can talk about matters that have never been talked about before, and we can understand utterances we have never heard before. Also referred to as **openness.**

progressive differentiation A relational problem caused by the exaggeration or intensification of differences or similarities between individuals.

projection A psychological process whereby we attribute characteristics or feelings of our own to others; often, the process whereby we attribute our own faults to others.

pronunciation The production of syllables or words according to some accepted standard, as presented, for example, in a dictionary.

protection theory A theory of proxemics referring to the fact that people establish a body-buffer zone to protect themselves from unwanted closeness, touching, or attack.

provisionalism An attitude of open-mindedness that leads to the creation of supportiveness; opposed to **certainty.**

proxemic distances The spatial distances that people maintain in communication and social interaction.

proxemics The study of the communicative function of space; the study of how people unconsciously structure their space—the distances between people in their interactions, the organization of spaces in homes and offices, and even the design of cities.

proximity Physical closeness; one of the qualities influencing **attraction.** Also, as a principle of perception, the tendency to perceive people or events that are physically close as belonging together or representing some unit.

psychological time The importance you place on past, present, or future time.

public communication Communication in which the source is one person and the receiver is an audience of many persons.

public distance The longest **proxemic distance,** ranging from 12 to more than 25 feet. See also **proxemics.**

public speaking Comunication in which a speaker presents a relatively continuous message to a relatively large audience in a unique context.

public territory Areas that are open to all people—for example, restaurants or parks.

punctuation of communication The breaking up of continuous communication sequences into short sequences with identifiable beginnings and endings or stimuli and responses.

punishment Noxious or aversive stimulation.

pupillometrics The study of communication through changes in the size of the pupils of the eyes.

purr words Highly positive words that express the speaker's feelings rather than referring to any objective reality; opposite of **snarl words.**

quality circle Group of workers whose task it is to investigate and make recommendations for improving the quality of some organizational function.

quotes An **extensional device** to emphasize that a word or phrase is being used in a special sense and should therefore be given special attention.

racist language Language that denigrates or is derogatory toward members of a particular race.

rate The speed with which you speak, generally measured in words per minute.

reasoning from causes and effects See **causes and effects.**

reasoning from sign See **sign.**

reasoning from specific instances See **specific instances.**

receiver Any person or thing that takes in messages. Receivers may be individuals listening to or reading a message, a group of persons hearing a speech, a scattered television audience, or machines that store information.

recency effect The condition in which what comes last (that is, most recently) exerts greater influenc in our perceptions than what comes first. See also **primacy effect.**

redundancy The quality of a message that makes it totally predictable and therefore lacking in information. A message of zero redundancy would be completely unpredictable; a message of 100% redundancy would be completely predictable. All human languages contain some degree of built-in redundancy, generally estimated to be about 50%.

referent power Power that a person possesses because others desire to identify with or be like that individual.

reflexiveness The feature of human language that makes it possible for that language to be used to refer to itself; that is, we can talk about our talk and create a **metalanguage**—a language for talking about language.

regulators Nonverbal behaviors that regulate, monitor, or control the communications of another person, such as nods or changes in body posture.

reinforcement theory A theory of behavior that when applied to relationships would hold (essentially) that relationships develop because they are rewarding or end because they are punishing.

rejection A response to an individual that rejects or denies the validity of that individual's ideas or actions.

relational communication Communication between or among intimates or those in close relationships; used by some theorists as synonymous with **interpersonal communication.**

relationship deterioration The stage of a relationship during which the connecting bonds between the partners weaken and the partners begin drifting apart; can lead to **dissolution.**

relationship development The stages of a relationship that lead up to **intimacy;** in the model of relationships presented here, relationship development includes the **contact** and **involvement** stages.

relationship dialectics theory A theory that describes relationships in terms of the tensions between a series of competing opposite desires or motivations, such as the desire for autonomy versus the desire to belong to someone, desires for novelty versus predictability, and desires for closedness versus openness.

relationship maintenance The processes by which individuals attempt to keep an interpersonal relationship stable and satisfying.

relationship message Message that comments on the relationship between the speakers rather than on matters external to them.

relationship repair Efforts to reverse the process of **relationship deterioration.**

response Any overt or covert behavior.

reward power Power derived from an individual's ability to reward another person.

rigid complementarity The inability to break away from a **complementary relationship** that once was appropriate but is no longer.

role The part an individual plays in a group; an individual's function or expected behavior.

round table A small group format in which members arrange themselves in a circular or semicircular pattern and interact informally, with or without a moderator.

rules theory A theory that describes relationships as interactions governed by series of rules that couples agree to follow. When the rules are followed, a relationship is maintained; when they are broken, the relationship experiences difficulty.

schemata Mental templates or structures that help us organize the millions of items of information we come into contact with every day (singular: *schema*).

script A general idea of how an event should unfold; a rule governing the sequence of occurrences in some activity A type of **schema.**

secondary territory Areas that do not belong to a particular person but that have been occupied by that person and are therefore associated with her or him—for example, the seat you normally take in class.

selective attention A principle of perception that states that listeners attend to those things that they anticipate will fulfill their needs or will prove enjoyable.

selective exposure A principle of perception and persuasion that states that listeners actively seek out information that supports their opinions and actively avoid information that contradicts their existing opinions, beliefs, attitudes, and values.

self-acceptance Being satisfied with ourselves, our virtues and vices, and our abilities and limitations.

self-adaptors Movements that usually satisfy a physical need, especially a need to be more comfortable; for example, scratching your head to relieve an itch, moistening your lips because they feel dry, or pushing your hair out of your eyes.

self-attribution A process through which we seek to account for and understand the reasons and motivations for our own behaviors.

self-awareness The degree to which a person knows himself or herself.

self-concept An individual's self-evaluation; an individual's self-appraisal.

self-disclosure The process of revealing something about ourselves to another; usually, revealing information that would normally be kept hidden.

self-esteem The value you place on yourself; your self-evaluation; usually, the positive value you place on yourself.

self-fulfilling prophecy The situation in which we make a prediction or prophecy and fulfill it ourselves—for example, expecting a class to be boring and then fulfilling this expectation by perceiving it as boring.

self-monitoring The manipulation of the image one presents to others in interpersonal interactions so as to give the most favorable impression of oneself.

self-serving bias A bias that operates in the **self-attribution** process and leads us to take credit for the positive consequences and to deny responsibility for the negative consequences of our behaviors.

self-talk Talk about oneself.

semantics The area of language study concerned with meaning.

sexist language Language derogatory to one sex, usually women; also, language that seems to prefer one gender over the other, as in the use of "man" for "humankind."

sexual harassment Unsolicited and unwanted sexual messages.

shyness The condition of discomfort and uneasiness in interpersonal situations.

sign, reasoning from A form of reasoning in which the presence of certain signs (clues) are interpreted as leading to a particular conclusion.

signal-to-noise ratio In verbal interaction, the relative amounts of signal (meaningful) and noise (interference); this ratio itself is relative to the communication analyst, the participants, and the context.

signal reaction A conditioned response to a signal; a response to some signal that is immediate rather than delayed.

silence The absence of vocal communication. Often misunderstood to refer to the absence of any and all communication, silence actually can communicate feelings or can serve to prevent communication about certain topics.

similarity A principle of **attraction** holding that we are attracted to qualities similar to those we possess and to people who are similar to ourselves; opposed to **complementarity.**

slang Language used by particular groups that is highly informal, nonstandard, and often considered improper.

small group communication Communication among a collection of individuals small enough in number that all members may interact with relative ease as both senders and receivers, the members being connected to one another by some common purpose and with some degree of organization or structure.

snarl words Highly negative words that express the feelings of the speaker rather than referring to any objective reality; opposite to **purr words.**

social clock An internalized schedule—based on cultural teachings—for when important events should be done, for example, the approximate time for getting married or for buying a house.

social comparison processes The processes by which you compare yourself (for example, your abilities, opinions, and values) with others and then assess and evaluate yourself; one of the sources of **self-concept.**

social distance The third **proxemic distance,** ranging from 4 to 12 feet; the distance at which business is usually conducted. See also **proxemics.**

social exchange theory A theory hypothesizing that we develop relationships in which our rewards or profits will be greater than our costs and that we avoid or terminate relationships in which the costs exceed the rewards.

social penetration theory A theory describing how relationships develop from the superficial to the intimate level and from few to many areas of interpersonal interaction.

source Any person or thing that creates messages. A source may be an individual speaking, writing, or gesturing or a computer sending an error message.

spatial distance Physical distance that signals the type of relationship you are in: intimate, personal, social, or public.

specific instances, reasoning from A form of reasoning in which several specific instances are examined and then a conclusion about the whole is formed.

speech Messages utilizing a vocal-auditory channel.

spontaneity Communication pattern in which a person verbalizes what he or she is thinking without attempting to develop strategies for control; encourages **supportiveness;** opposed to **manipulation.**

stability The principle of perception that refers to the fact that our perceptions of things and of people are relatively consistent with our previous perceptions.

static evaluation An orientation that fails to recognize that the world is characterized by constant change; an attitude that sees people and events as fixed rather than as constantly changing.

status The relative level a person occupies in a hierarchy; because status always involves a comparison, one individual's status is only relative to the status of another.

stereotype In communication, a fixed impression of a group of people through which we then perceive specific individuals; stereotypes are most often negative but also may be positive.

stimuli External or internal changes that impinge on or arouse an organism (singular: *stimulus*).

subjectivity The principle of perception that refers to the fact that one's perceptions are not objective but are influenced by one's wants and needs and one's expectations and predictions.

supportiveness An attitude of an individual or an atmosphere in a group that is characterized by openness, absence of fear, and a genuine feeling of equality.

symmetrical relationship Relationship between two or more persons in which one person's behavior prompts the same type of behavior in the other person(s). For example, anger in one person may encourage or serve as a stimulus for anger in another person, or a critical comment by one person may lead the other person to criticize in return.

symposium A small group format in which each member of the group delivers a relatively prepared talk on some aspect of the topic. Often combined with a **forum.**

systematic desensitization A theory and technique for dealing with fears (such as communication apprehension) in which you gradually expose yourself to and develop a comfort level with the fear-causing stimulus.

taboo Forbidden; culturally censored. Taboo language is language that is frowned on by "polite society." Topics and specific words may be considered taboo—for example, death, sex, certain forms of illness, and various words denoting sexual activities and excretory functions.

temporal communication The messages communicated by a person's time orientation and treatment of time.

territoriality A possessive or ownership reaction to an area of space or to particular objects.

testimonial A persuasive technique in which the speaker uses the authority or image of some positively evaluated person to try to gain your approval—or the image of some negatively evaluated person to gain your rejection.

theory A general statement or principle applicable to related phenomena.

thesis The main assertion of a message—for example, the theme of a public speech.

touch avoidance The tendency to avoid touching and being touched by others.

touch communication Communication through tactile means.

transactional Characterizing the relationship among elements whereby each influences and is influenced by each other element; communication is such a process where no element is independent of any other element.

transfer A persuasive technique in which a speaker associates an idea with something you respect to gain your approval or with something you dislike to gain your rejection.

uncertainty reduction strategies Passive, active, and interactive ways of increasing your accuracy in interpersonal perception.

uncertainty reduction theory The theory holding that as relationships develop, uncertainty is reduced; relationship development is seen as a process of reducing uncertainty about one another.

universal of communication A feature of communication common to all communication acts.

unrepeatability Principle of communication stating that no communication can ever be re-created in quite the same way, because circumstances are never the same.

upward communication Communication in which the messages originate from the lower levels of an organization or hierarchy and are sent to upper levels—for example, from line worker to management.

value Relative worth; a quality that makes something desirable or undesirable; an ideal or custom about which we have emotional responses, whether positive or negative.

verbal aggressiveness An unproductive **conflict** strategy that involves trying to win an argument by attacking the other person's **self-concept.** Often considered opposed to **argumentativeness.**

visual dominance The use of the eyes to maintain a superior or controlling position; for example, when making an especially important point, you might look intently at the other person.

voice qualities Aspects of **paralanguage**—specifically, pitch range, vocal lip control, glottis control, pitch control, articulation control, rhythm control, resonance, and tempo.

volume The relative loudness of the voice.

withdrawal (1) A reaction to territorial encroachment in which we leave the territory. (2) A tendency to close oneself off from conflicts rather than confront the issues.

you-messages Messages in which you deny responsibility for your own thoughts and behaviors; messages that attribute your perception to another person; messages of blame. Opposed to **I-messages.**

Glossary of Human Communication Skills

abstractions Use both abstract and specific terms when describing or explaining.

accommodation Accommodate to the speaking style of your listeners with moderation: Too much mirroring of the other person's manner of communicating may appear too obvious and even manipulative.

active interpersonal conflict Engage in interpersonal conflict actively; generally, don't rely on silence as a way of avoiding the issues.

active listening To listen actively, paraphrase the speaker's meaning, express understanding of the speaker's feelings, and ask questions when you need something clarified.

advantages and disadvantages of relationships In evaluating your own relationship choices, consider both the advantages and the disadvantages of relationships generally and of your specific relationships.

allness Avoid allness statements (for example, statements containing such words as *all, never,* or *always*); they invariably misstate the reality and often will offend other people.

amplifying informative speeches For an informative speech, select a variety of amplifying materials: examples, illustrations, and narratives; testimony, definitions, statistics, and visual aids.

amplifying persuasive speeches Support the main points of a persuasive speech with amplifying materials such as examples, statistics, and visual aids and with logical, emotional, and ethical proofs.

analyze your perceptions Increase accuracy in interpersonal perception by (1) identifying the influence of your physical and emotional state; (2) making sure that you're not drawing conclusions from too little information; and (3) identifying any perceptions that may be the result of your mindreading.

anger management Manage your anger by calming down as best you can and then reflecting on the fact that communication is irreversible, reviewing your communication options, and considering the relevant communication skills for expressing your feelings.

appreciating cultural differences Look at cultural differences not as deviations from the norm or as deficiencies but simply as the differences they are. At the same time, remember that recognizing differences and considering these as you communicate does not necessarily mean accepting them.

appropriateness of self-disclosure In self-disclosure consider the legitimacy of your motives, the appropriateness of the disclosure, the listener's responses (is the dyadic effect operating?), and the potential burdens such disclosures might impose.

argumentativeness During conflict aim for argumentativeness, not aggressiveness. That is, avoid attacking the other person's self-concept; instead focus logically on the issues; emphasize finding solutions; and work to ensure that what is said will result in positive self-feelings for both individuals.

articulation and pronunciation Avoid the articulation and pronunciation errors of omission, substitution, addition, accent, and pronouncing sounds that should be silent.

artifactual communication Use artifacts (such as color, clothing, body adornment, of space decoration) to communicate your desired messages. But check that the messages you think are being communicated are the same that others see.

audience analysis Analyze your audience in terms of its sociological and psychological characteristics and adapt your speech based on these findings.

before and after the conflict Prepare for interpersonal conflict by arranging to fight in private, knowing what you're fighting about, and fighting about things that can be solved. After the conflict, profit from it by learning what worked and what didn't, by keeping the conflict in perspective, and by increasing the exchange of rewards.

body movements Use body and hand gestures to reinforce your communication purposes.

brainstorming In brainstorming follow these general rules: Avoid negative criticism, strive for quantity, combine and extend the contributions of others, and contribute ideas that are as wild as possible.

channel Assess your communication channel options (such as face-to-face conversation, e-mail, or leaving a voice mail message when you know the person won't be home) before communicating important messages.

checking perceptions Increase accuracy in perception by (1) describing what you see or hear and the meaning you assign to it and (2) asking the other person if your perceptions and meanings are accurate.

communicating appropriately interculturally Communicate interculturally with appropriate openness, empathy, positiveness, immediacy, interaction management, expressiveness, and other-orientation.

communicating assertively To use an assertive approach, describe the problem, say how the problem affects you, propose solutions, confirm your understanding, and reflect on your own assertiveness.

communicating power Communicate power by avoiding mannerisms such as hesitations, too many intensifiers, disqualifiers, tag questions, one-word answers, self-critical statements, overly polite statements, and vulgar and slang expressions.

communicating with the grief-stricken With someone who is grieving, use confirming messages, give the person permission to grieve, avoid directing the person, encourage the expression of feelings, and communicate empathy and support.

communication apprehension management To manage apprehension acquire communication skills and experiences, focus on your prior successes, reduce unpredictability, and put apprehension in perspective.

communication options Assess your communication options before communicating, remembering that communication is inevitable, irreversible, and unrepeatable.

conclusions Conclusions to speeches should summarize the main points and bring the speech to a crisp close.

confirmation When you wish to be confirming, acknowledge (verbally and/or nonverbally) others in your group and their contributions.

conflict, culture, and gender Approach conflict with an understanding of cultural and gender differences in what constitutes conflict and in how it should be pursued.

conflict styles Adjust your conflict style to the specific conflict in which you find yourself.

connotative meanings As a speaker, clarify your connotative meanings if you have any doubts that your listeners might misunderstand you; as a listener, ask questions if you have doubts about the speaker's connotations.

content and relationship Listen to both the content and the relationship aspects of messages, distinguish between them, and respond to both.

content and relationship conflicts Analyze conflict messages in terms of content and relationship dimensions and respond to each accordingly.

context adjustment Adjust your messages to the unique communication context, taking into consideration its physical, cultural, social-psychological, and temporal aspects.

conversational maxims Follow (generally) the basic maxims of conversation, such as those governing quantity, quality, relations, manner, and politeness.

conversational rules Observe the general rules for conversation (for example, using relatively short speaking turns and avoiding interruptions), but break them when there seems logical reason to do so.

conversational turns Maintain relatively short conversational turns; when appropriate, pass the speaker's turn to another person nonverbally or verbally.

credibility appeals Seek to establish credibility by displaying competence, high moral character, and dynamism or charisma.

critical analysis Critically analyze reasoning from specific instances to generalizations, causes and effects, and sign.

critical thinking Use Edward deBono's critical thinking hats technique: Evaluate problems in terms of facts, feelings, negative arguments, positive benefits, creative ideas, and control of thinking.

cultural differences in listening When listening in multicultural settings, realize that people from different cultures may give very different listening cues and may operate with different rules for listening.

cultural identifiers Use cultural identifiers that are sensitive to the desires of others; when appropriate, make clear the cultural identifiers you prefer.

cultural influences Communicate with an understanding that culture influences communication in all its forms.

cultural sensitivity Increase your cultural sensitivity by learning about different cultures, recognizing and facing your own fears of intercultural interaction, recognizing differences between yourself and others, and becoming conscious of the cultural rules and customs of other cultures.

culture and groups Recognize and appreciate cultural differences in relation to aspects of group membership and leadership.

culture and perception Increase accuracy in perception by learning as much as you can about the cultures of those with whom you interact.

dating statements Mentally date your statements to avoid thinking and communicating that the world is static and unchanging. Be sure that your messages reflect the inevitability of change.

deciding to self-disclose In deciding to self-disclose, consider the potential benefits (for example, self-knowledge) as well as the potential personal, relationship, and professional risks.

delivery During the presentation of a speech, maintain eye contact with the entire audience, allow facial expressions to convey feelings, gesture naturally, and incorporate purposeful body movements.

delivery method In general, use the extemporaneous method of delivery for speeches.

Delphi method Use the Delphi method (polling by questionnaire) to solve problems when members are separated geographically.

dialogic conversation Treat conversation as a dialogue rather than a monologue; show concern for the other person, and for the relationship between you, with other-orientation.

disclaimers Preface your comments with disclaimers if you feel you might be misunderstood. But avoid disclaimers when they aren't necessary; too many disclaimers can make you appear unprepared or unwilling to state an opinion.

disconfirming language Avoid sexist, heterosexist, racist, and ageist language, which is disconfirming and insulting, and invariably contributes to communication barriers.

emotional appeals In persuasive speaking use emotional appeals—for example, appeals to fear; power, control, and influence; safety; achievement; and financial gain—as appropriate to the speech and the audience.

emotional communication To communicate emotions effectively, (1) describe feelings, (2) identify the reasons for the feelings, (3) anchor feelings to the present, and (4) own your feelings and messages.

emotional display Express your emotions and interpret the emotions of others in light of the cultural rules dictating what is and what isn't "appropriate" emotional expression.

emotionality in interpersonal communication Include the inevitable emotionality of your thoughts and feelings in your interpersonal communication, verbally and nonverbally.

emotional understanding Be able to identify and describe emotions (both positive and negative) clearly and specifically. Learn the vocabulary of emotional expression.

empathic and objective listening To listen empathically, punctuate the interaction from the speaker's point of view, engage in dialogue, and understand the speaker's thoughts and feelings. To listen objectively, be careful that you don't hear what you want to hear.

empathic conflict Engage in interpersonal conflict with empathy rather than with blame. And express this empathy ("I can understand how you must have felt").

empathy When appropriate, communicate empathy: Resist evaluating the person's behaviors, focus concentration on the person, express active involvement through facial expressions and gestures, reflect back the feelings you think are being expressed, self-disclose, and address any mixed messages.

ethnocentric thinking Recognize your own ethnocentric thinking and how it influences your verbal and nonverbal messages.

evaluating In evaluating messages, try first to understand fully what the speaker means; also try to identify any biases and self-interests that may lead the speaker to give an unfair presentation of the material.

expressiveness Expressiveness means communicating active involvement in the interaction: Use active listening, address mixed messages, use I-messages, and use appropriate variations in paralanguage and gestures.

eye movements Use eye movements to seek feedback, exchange conversational turns, signal the nature of your relationship with others, and compensate for increased physical distance. As the same time, look for such meanings in the eye movements of others.

face-saving strategies In a conflict use strategies that allow your opponent to save face; for example, avoid beltlining (hitting your opponent with attacks that he or she will have difficulty absorbing and will resent).

facial messages Use facial expressions to communicate that you're involved in the interaction. As a listener, look to the emotional expressions of others as additional cues to their meaning.

facts and inferences Distinguish facts (verifiably true past events) from inferences (guesses, hypotheses, hunches), and act on inferences with tentativeness.

fallacy identification When listening to a persuasive speech, detect such fallacies as name calling, transfer, testimonial, plain folks, card stacking, bandwagon, and character attacks; avoid using these in your own speeches.

feedback Be alert to both verbal and nonverbal feedback—from yourself and from others—and use these cues to adjust your messages for greatest effectiveness.

feedforward Preface your messages with some kind of feedforward when you feel your listener needs some background or when you want to ease into a particular topic, such as bad news.

flexibility Because no two communication situations are identical, because everything is in a state of flux, and because everyone is different, cultivate flexibility and adjust your communication to the unique situation.

friendships Establish friendships to help serve such needs as utility, ego support, stimulation, and security. At the same time, seek to serve your friends' similar needs.

fundamental attribution error Avoid the fundamental attribution error, whereby you attribute someone's behavior solely to internal factors, by focusing on possible situational influences.

gaining perspective on problems and solutions To gain perspective on problems and solutions, analyze them in terms of facts, feelings, negative arguments, positive benefits, creative new ideas, and control of thinking.

gender differences in listening Communicate with men and women with an understanding that women give more cues that they're listening and appear more supportive in their listening than men.

giving space Give others the amount of space they need, which will vary on the basis of culture, gender, and emotional state. Look to the other person for any signs of spatial discomfort.

group norms Actively seek to discover the norms of the group, and take these norms into consideration when interacting in the group.

group participation Be group—rather than individually—oriented, center any conflict on issues rather than on personalities, be critically open-minded, and make sure that group members' meanings are clearly understood.

groupthink Recognize the symptoms of groupthink and actively counter any groupthink tendencies evidenced in groups you participate in.

high- and low-context cultures Adjust your messages and your listening in light of the differences between high- and low-context cultures.

I-messages Use I-messages when communicating your feelings; take responsibility for your own feelings ("I get angry when you . . .") rather than attributing them to others ("You make me angry").

immediacy Maintain nonverbal immediacy through close physical distances, eye contact, and smiling; maintain verbal immediacy by using the other person's name and focusing on the other's remarks.

implicit personality theory Bring to your mindful state your implicit personality theory to subject your perceptions and conclusions to logical analysis.

increasing assertiveness Increase your own assertiveness by analyzing the assertive messages of others, rehearsing assertive messages, and communicating assertively.

indirect messages Use indirect messages when a more direct style might prove insulting or offensive; but be aware that indirectness can create communication problems, because indirect statements are easier to misunderstand than direct ones.

indiscrimination Avoid indiscrimination; that is, treat each situation and each person as unique (when possible) even when they're covered by the same label or name. "Index" your key concepts.

individualist and collectivist cultures Adjust your messages and your listening on the basis of the differences between individualist and collectivist cultures.

individual roles In a small group, avoid playing the popular but dysfunctional individual roles—the roles of aggressor, blocker, recognition seeker, self-confessor, or dominator.

informative speaking Follow the principles of informative speaking: Stress the information's usefulness, relate new information to information the audience already knows, present information through several senses, adjust the level of complexity, vary the levels of abstraction, avoid information overload, and recognize cultural variations.

initial impressions Guard against drawing impressions too quickly or on the basis of too little information; initial impressions can function as filters and prevent you from forming more accurate perceptions on the basis of more information.

intensional orientation Avoid intensional orientation. This is, respond to things first and to labels second; for example, the way a person is talked about is not the best measure of who that person really is.

interaction management Speak in relatively short conversational turns, avoid long and frequent pauses, and use verbal and nonverbal messages that are consistent.

intercultural communication When communicating interculturally, become mindful of (1) the differences between yourself and the member of a different culture, (2) the differences within every cultural group, (3) the differences in meanings for both verbal and nonverbal signals that you and the other person may have, and (4) the differences in cultural rules and customs.

introductions Introductions to speeches should gain attention and preview what is to follow.

leadership style Adjust your leadership style to the task at hand and the needs of group members.

leading a group It is a leader's responsibility to start group interaction, maintain effective interaction throughout the discussion, keep members on track, ensure member satisfaction, encourage ongoing evaluation and improvement, and prepare members for the discussion as necessary.

listening to the feelings of others In listening to the feelings of others, avoid the tendency to try to solve their problems; instead, listen, empathize, focus on the other person, and encourage the person to explore his or her feelings.

making excuses Repair conversational problems by offering excuses (apologies) that (1) demonstrate that you understand the problem, (2) acknowledge your responsibility, (3) acknowledge your displeasure at what you did, (4) request forgiveness, and (5) make it clear that this will never happen again.

managing relationship deterioration When a relationship ends, break the loneliness-depression cycle, take time out, bolster your self-esteem, seek the support of nourishing others, and avoid repeating negative patterns.

markers Become sensitive to the markers (central, boundary, and ear) of others, and learn to use these markers to define your own territories and to communicate the desired impression.

masculine and feminine cultures Adjust your messages and your listening to differences in cultural "masculinity" and "femininity."

meanings depend on context When deciphering messages, look at the context for cues as to how you should interpret the meanings.

meanings in people When you are deciphering meaning, the best source is the person; meanings are in people. So, when in doubt, find out—from the source.

message overload Combat message overload by using and disposing of messages as they come to you, organizing your messages, getting rid of extra copies, and distinguishing between messages you should save and messages you should throw away.

metacommunication Metacommunicate when you want to clarify the way you're talking or what you're talking about; for example, give clear feedforward and paraphrase your own complex messages.

mindfulness Increase your mindfulness by creating and recreating categories, being open to new information and points of view, and avoiding excessive reliance on first impressions.

mixed messages Avoid emitting mixed messages by focusing clearly on your purposes when communicating and by increasing conscious control over your verbal and nonverbal behaviors.

negatives and positives of conflict Approach conflict to minimize negative outcomes and to maximize the positive benefits of conflict and its resolution.

networking Establish a network of relationships to provide insights into issues relevant to your personal and professional life, and be willing to lend your expertise to the networks of others.

noise management Reduce the influence of physical, physiological, psychological, and semantic noise to the extent that you can; use repetition and restatement and, when in doubt, ask if you're being clear.

nominal group Use the nominal group technique (compilation of unsigned written opinions) to solve problems when anonymity may be desirable.

nonjudgmental and critical listening To listen nonjudgmentally, keep an open mind, avoid filtering out difficult messages, and recognize your own biases. When listening to evaluate, listen extra carefully, ask questions if in doubt, and check your perceptions before offering criticism.

nonverbal communication and culture As far as possible, interpret the nonverbal cues of others not with the meanings assigned by your culture but with the meanings assigned by the speaker's culture.

online conflict Avoid common causes of online conflict such as sending out unsolicited commercial messages, spamming, and flaming.

open expression in conflict In interpersonal conflict try to facilitate open expression on the part of your combatant. Avoid power tactics that inhibit expression; these not only will not help resolve the conflict but also may have lasting negative effects on the relationship.

openness Increase openness when appropriate by self-disclosing, responding spontaneously and honestly to those with whom you're interacting, and owning your own feelings and thoughts.

organizing a speech To organize the main points of a speech; select a thought pattern appropriate to the subject matter, the purpose of the speech, and the audience.

organizing learning discussions In educational or learning groups, use an organizational structure—chronological or spatial, for example—to give order to the discussion.

other-orientation Demonstrate other-orientation by acknowledging the importance of the other person; using focused eye contact and appropriate facial expressions; smiling, nodding, and leaning toward the other person; and expressing agreement when appropriate.

overattribution Avoid overattribution; rarely is any one factor an accurate explanation of complex human behavior.

packaging Make your verbal and nonverbal messages consistent; inconsistencies between, say, verbal and nonverbal messages, often create uncertainty and misunderstanding.

paralanguage Vary paralinguistic features such as rate, pauses, pitch, and volume to communicate your meanings and to add interest and color to your messages.

pauses Use pauses to signal transitions, to allow listeners time to think, and to signal the approach of a significant idea.

perceptual shortcuts Be mindful of your perceptual shortcuts (for example, rules, schemata, and scripts) so that they don't mislead you and result in inaccurate perceptions.

persuasive speaking Apply (where relevant) the principles of persuasion, including selective exposure, audience participation, and magnitude of change.

polarization Avoid thinking and talking in extremes by using middle terms and qualifiers. At the same time, remember that using too many qualifiers may make you appear unsure of yourself.

positiveness Communicate positiveness: Express your own satisfaction with the interaction and compliment others by expressing your positive thoughts and feelings about and to the other person.

power distance Adjust your messages and listening based on the power-distance orientation of the culture in which you find yourself.

power communication Communicate power through forceful speech; avoidance of weak modifiers and excessive body movement; and demonstration of your knowledge, preparation, and organization relative to the matters at hand.

power plays Respond to power plays with cooperative strategies: (1) Express your feelings, (2) describe the behavior to which you object, and (3) state a cooperative response.

present-focus conflict Focus conflict resolution messages on the present; avoid dredging up old grievances and unloading them on the other person (gunnysacking).

problem solving Follow these six steps in group problem-solving situations: (1) Define and analyze the problem, (2) establish the criteria for evaluating solutions, (3) identify possible solutions, (4) evaluate solutions, (5) select the best solution(s), and (6) test selected solution(s).

problem-solving conflicts Treat interpersonal conflicts as problems to be solved systematically: (1) Define the problem, (2) examine possible solutions, (3) test the solution, (4) evaluate the solution, and (5) accept or reject the solution.

quality circles Use the quality circle technique to improve organizational functions.

receiving In receiving messages, focus your attention on both the verbal and the nonverbal messages, because both communicate meaning.

reducing uncertainty To increase accuracy in perception, reduce your uncertainty, using passive, active, and interactive strategies.

rehearsal Rehearsal guidelines for speeches are the following: Rehearse often, perfect delivery, rehearse the speech as a whole, time the speech at each rehearsal, approximate the specific speech situation as much as possible, see and think of yourself as a public speaker, and incorporate any delivery notes that may be of value during the actual speech presentation.

relationship messages Formulate messages that are appropriate to the stage of the relationship. Also, listen to messages from relationship partners that may reveal differences in perception about your relationship stage.

relationship repair To repair a deteriorating relationship, recognize the problem, engage in productive conflict resolution, pose possible solutions, affirm each other, integrate solutions into normal behavior, and take risks as appropriate.

relationship rules Follow the rules for maintaining relationships (such as sharing activities, sharing values, being faithful, and communicating openly and positively) when you do in fact wish to maintain and even strengthen a relationship.

remembering To enhance your ability to remember messages, identify the central ideas, summarize the message in an easy-to-retain form, and repeat (aloud or to yourself) key terms and names.

research Research topics effectively and efficiently, and critically evaluate the reliability of the research material.

responding In responding to messages, express support for the speaker using I-messages ("I didn't understand the point about . . .") instead of you-messages ("You didn't clarify what you meant about . . .").

responding to others' disclosures Respond appropriately to the disclosures of others by listening actively, supporting the discloser, and keeping the disclosures confidential.

responding to questions Frame and respond appropriately to questions varying in terms of openness-closedness, primary-follow up, direct-indirect, and neutral-biased.

restimulating brainstorming If appropriate, restimulate a brainstorming group that has lost its steam by asking for additional contributions or for further extensions of previously contributed ideas.

romantic workplace relationships Approach any romantic relationship at work with a clear understanding of the potential problems.

selecting main points After generating the possible main points for a speech, eliminate those that seem least important to the thesis, combine those that have a common focus, and select those most relevant to the purpose of the speech and the audience.

self-awareness Increase self-awareness: Listen to others, increase your open self as appropriate, and seek out information (discreetly) to reduce any blind spots.

self-concept Learn who you are: See yourself through the eyes of others; compare yourself to similar (and admired) others; examine the influences of culture; and observe, interpret, and evaluate your own message behaviors.

self-esteem Raise your self-esteem: Challenge self-destructive beliefs, seek out nurturing people with whom to interact, work on projects that will result in success, and seek affirmation.

self-fulfilling prophecy Take a second look at your perceptions when they correspond very closely to your initial expectations; the self-fulfilling prophecy may be at work.

self-serving bias Become mindful of any self-serving bias—any tendency to give too much weight to internal factors when explaining your positives but too much weight to external factors when explaining your negatives.

sentence style In preparing a speech construct sentences that are short, direct, active, and positive, and vary the type and length of sentences.

sexual harassment management First, talk to the harasser; if this doesn't stop the behavior, then consider collecting evidence, using appropriate channels within the organization, and filing a complaint. Do not blame yourself.

sexual harassment messages Avoid behaviors that could be interpreted as sexual harassment: behavior that's sexual in nature, that might be considered unreasonable, that is severe or pervasive, and that is unwelcome and offensive.

silence Silence can communicate lots of different meanings (e.g., anger or a need for time to think), so examine silence for meanings just as you would eye movements or body gestures.

spatial and proxemic conversational distances Let your spatial relationships reflect your interpersonal relationships. Maintain spatial distances that are comfortable (neither too close nor too far apart) and that are appropriate to the situation and to your relationship with the other person.

speech of definition For a speech of definition, consider using a variety of definitions, choose credible sources, and proceed from the known to the unknown.

speech of demonstration For a speech of demonstration, consider using a temporal pattern, employ transitions to connect the steps, present a broad overview and then the specific steps, and incorporate visual aids.

speech of description For a speech of description, consider using a spatial, topical, or 5W organizational pattern, a variety of descriptive categories, and visual aids.

speech rate Use variations in rate to increase communication efficiency and persuasiveness as appropriate.

stereotypes Be careful of thinking and talking in stereotypes; recognize that members of all groups are different, and focus on the individual rather than on the individual's membership in one group or another.

surface and depth listening To listen in depth: Focus on both verbal and nonverbal messages and on both content and relationship messages, and take special note of statements that refer back to the speaker. At the same time, do not avoid the surface or literal meaning.

talk versus force Talk about your problems rather than trying to use physical or emotional force.

thesis and main points Expand the thesis or main assertion of the speech by asking strategic questions to develop the main points or propositions.

time cues Interpret time cues from the perspective of the person with whom you're interacting. Be especially sensitive to leave-taking cues such as comments that "it's getting late" or glances at the person's watch.

topic and purpose Select speech topics and purposes that are appropriate to speaker, audience, and occasion, and narrow them to manageable proportions.

touch and touch avoidance Respect the touch-avoidance tendencies of others; pay special attention to cultural and gender differences in touch preferences and touch avoidance.

transitions Use transitions and internal summaries to connect the parts of a speech and to help listeners remember the speech.

turn-taking cues Respond to both the verbal and the nonverbal conversational turn-taking cues given to you by others, and make your own cues clear to others.

understanding To enhance your ability to understand messages, relate new information to what you already know, ask questions, and paraphrase what you think the speaker said.

vocal variation Vary vocal volume and rate to reflect and reinforce verbal messages. Avoid a volume that is too low to understand and rates that are monotonous, too slow, or too fast.

win–win solutions In interpersonal conflict strive for win–win solutions rather than solutions in which one person wins and the other loses.

word style Word your speeches so they are clear, vivid, appropriate, and personal.

Bibliography

Acor, A. A. (2001). Employers' perceptions of persons with body art and an experimental test regarding eyebrow piercing. (Doctoral dissertation, Marquette University, 2001). *Dissertation Abstracts International, 61,* 3885B.

Adler, R. B. (1977). *Confidence in communication: A guide to assertive and social skills.* New York: Holt, Rinehart & Winston.

Adrianson, L. (2001). Gender and computer-mediated communication: Group processes in problem solving. *Computers in Human Behavior, 17,* 71–94.

Aiex, N. K., & Aiex, P. (1992). *Health communication in the 90s.* ERIC Clearing House on Reading, English, and Communication Digest #76 (EDO-CS-92-09 October 1992).

Akert, R. M., & Panter, A. T. (1988). Extraversion and the ability to decode nonverbal communication. *Personality & Individual Differences, 9,* 965–972.

Akinnaso, F. N. (1982). On the differences between spoken and written language. *Language and Speech, 25* (Part 2), 97–125.

Albas, D. C., McCluskey, K. W., & Albas, C. A. (1976). Perception of the emotional content of speech: A comparison of two Canadian groups. *Journal of Cross-Cultural Psychology, 7* (December), 481–490.

Alessandra, T. (1986). *How to listen effectively, speaking of success* (Video Tape Series). San Diego, CA: Levitz Sommer Productions.

Al-Simadi, F. A. (2000). Detection of deception behavior: A cross-cultural test. *Social Behavior & Personality, 28,* 455–461.

Altman, I. (1975). *The environment and social behavior.* Monterey, CA: Brooks/Cole.

Altman, I., & Taylor, D. (1973). *Social penetration: The development of interpersonal relationships.* New York: Holt, Rinehart & Winston.

Amato, P. R. (1994). The impact of divorce on men and women in India and the United States. *Journal of Comparative Family Studies, 25,* 207–221.

Andersen, P. (1991). Explaining intercultural differences in nonverbal communication. In L. A. Samovar & R. E. Porter (Eds.), *Intercultural communication: A reader* (6th ed., pp. 286–296). Belmont, CA: Wadsworth.

Andersen, P. A., & Leibowitz, K. (1978). The development and nature of the construct touch avoidance. *Environmental Psychology and Nonverbal Behavior, 3,* 89–106.

Anderson, K. J. (1998). Meta-analysis of gender effects on conversational interruption: Who, what, when, where, and how. *Sex Roles, 39* (August), 225–252.

Angier, N. (1995a, February 14). Powerhouse of senses: Smell, at last, gets its due. *New York Times,* pp. C1, C6.

Angier, N. (1995b, May 9). Scientists mull role of empathy in man and beast. *New York Times,* pp. C1, C6.

Angier, N. (2003, July 8). Opposites attract? Not in real life. *New York Times,* pp. F1, F6.

Argyle, M. (1986). Rules for social relationships in four cultures. *Australian Journal of Psychology, 38* (December), 309–318.

Argyle, M. (1988). *Bodily communication* (2nd ed.). New York: Methuen.

Argyle, M., & Henderson, M. (1984). The rules of friendship. *Journal of Social and Personal Relationships, 1* (June), 211–237.

Argyle, M., & Ingham, R. (1972). Gaze, mutual gaze, and distance. *Semiotica, 1,* 32–49.

Arliss, L. P. (1991). *Gender communication.* Englewood Cliffs, NJ: Prentice-Hall.

Armstrong, C. B., & Rubin, A. M. (1989). Talk radio as interpersonal communication. *Journal of Communication, 39* (Spring), 84–94.

Aronson, E., Wilson, T. D., & Akert, R. M. (1999). *Social psychology: The heart and the mind* (3rd ed.). New York: Longman.

Asch, S. (1946). Forming impressions of personality. *Journal of Abnormal and Social Psychology, 41,* 258–290.

Aspinwall, L. G., & Taylor, S. E. (1993). Effects of social comparison direction, threat, and self-esteem on affect, evaluation, and expected success. *Journal of Personality and Social Psychology, 64,* 708–722.

Aune, K.-S., Buller, D. B., & Aune, R. K. (1996). Display rule development in romantic relationships: Emotion management and perceived appropriateness of emotions across relationship stages. *Human Communication Research, 23* (September), 115–145.

Aune, R. K., & Kikuchi, T. (1993). Effects of language intensity similarity on perceptions of credibility, relational attributions, and persuasion. *Journal of Language and Social Psychology, 12* (September), 224–238.

Authier, J., & Gustafson, K. (1982). Microtraining: Focusing on specific skills. In E. K. Marshall, P. D. Kurtz, and Associates (Eds.), *Interpersonal helping skills: A guide to training methods, programs, and resources* (pp. 93–130). San Francisco: Jossey-Bass.

Axtell, R. E. (1990). *Do's and taboos of hosting international visitors.* New York: Wiley.

Axtell, R. E. (1992). *Do's and taboos of public speaking: How to get those butterflies flying in formation.* New York: Wiley.

Axtell, R. E. (1993). *Do's and taboos around the world* (3rd ed.). New York: Wiley.

Ayres, J. (1983). Strategies to maintain relationships: Their identification and perceived usage. *Communication Quarterly, 31,* 62–67.

Ayres, J. (1986). Perceptions of speaking ability: An explanation for stage fright. *Communication Education, 35,* 275–287.

Ayres, J., Ayres, D. M., & Sharp, D. (1993). A progress report on the development of an instrument to measure communication apprehension in employment interviews. *Communcation Research Reports, 10,* 87–94.

Ayres, J., & Hopf, T. S. (1992). Visualization: Reducing speech anxiety and enhancing performance. *Communication Reports, 5,* 1–10.

Ayres, J., & Hopf, T. S. (1993). *Coping with speech anxiety.* Norwood, NJ: Ablex.

Ayres, J., Hopf, T. S., & Ayres, D. M. (1994). An examination of whether imaging ability enhances the effectiveness of an intervention designed to reduce speech anxiety. *Communication Education, 43* (July), 252–258.

Ayres, J., Hopf, T., & Ayres, D. M. (1997). Visualization and performance visualization: Applications, evidence, and speculation. In J. A. Daly, J. C. McCroskey, J. Ayres, T. S. Hopf, & D. M. Ayres, *Avoiding communication: Shyness, reticence, and communication apprehension* (2nd ed., pp. 401–419). Cresskill, NJ: Hampton Press.

Bach, G. R., & Wyden, P. (1968). *The intimate enemy.* New York: Avon.

Bailey, B. (1997). Communication of respect in interethnic service encounters. *Language in Society, 26* (September), 327–356.

Bailey, G., & Pownell, D. (1998). Technology staff-development and support programs: Applying Abraham Maslow's hierarchy of needs. *Learning and Leading with Technology, 26* (November), 47–51.

Bales, R. F. (1950). *Interaction process analysis: A method for the study of small groups.* Cambridge, MA: Addison-Wesley.

Balswick, J. O., & Peck, C. (1971). The inexpressive male: A tragedy of American society? *The Family Coordinator, 20,* 363–368.

Banks, J. (1995, April). *MTV as gatekeeper and censor: A survey of the program service's attempts to impose its standards on U.S. popular music.* Paper presented at the Eastern Communication Association Convention, Pittsburgh, PA.

Barbato, C. A., & Perse, E. M. (1992). Interpersonal communication motives and the life position of elders. *Communication Research, 19,* 516–531.

Barge, J. K. (1994). *Leadership: Communication skills for organizations and groups.* New York: St. Martin's.

Baringer, D. K., & McCroskey, J. C. (2000). Immediacy in the classroom: Student immediacy. *Communication Education, 49,* 178–186.

Barker, D. C. (1998). The talk radio community: Nontraditional social networks and political participation. *Social Science Quarterly, 79* (June), 261–272.

Barker, L. L., Edwards, R., Gaines, C., Gladney, K., & Holley, F. (1980). An investigation of proportional time spent in various communication activities by college students. *Journal of Applied Communication Research, 8,* 101–109.

Barker, L. L., & Gaut, D. (2002). *Communication* (8th ed.). Boston: Allyn & Bacon.

Barna, L. M. (1985). Stumbling blocks in intercultural communication. In L. A. Samovar & R. E. Porter (Eds.), *Intercultural communication: A reader* (4th ed., pp. 330–338). Belmont, CA: Wadsworth.

Barnlund, D. C. (1970). A transactional model of communication. In J. Akin, A. Goldberg, G. Myers, & J. Stewart (Eds.), *Language behavior: A book of readings in communication.* The Hague: Mouton.

Barnlund, D. C. (1989). *Communicative styles of Japanese and Americans: Images and realities.* Belmont, CA: Wadsworth.

Baron, R. A. (1990). Countering the effects of destructive criticism: The relative efficacy of four interventions. *Journal of Applied Psychology, 75* (June), 235–245.

Baron, R. A., & Byrne, D. (1984). *Social psychology: Understanding human interaction* (4th ed.). Boston: Allyn & Bacon.

Barr, M. J. (2000). Mentoring relationships: A study of informal/formal mentoring, psychological type of mentors, and mentor/protégé type combinations. *Dissertation Abstracts International, 60,* 2568A.

Barrett, L., & Godfrey, T. (1988). Listening. *Person-Centered Review, 3* (November), 410–425.

Barron, J. (1995, January 11). It's time to mind your e-manners. *New York Times,* p. C1.

Basso, K. H. (1972). To give up on words: Silence in Apache culture. In P. P. Giglioli (Ed.), *Language and social context.* New York: Penguin.

Baxter, L. A. (1983). Relationship disengagement: An examination of the reversal hypothesis. *Western Journal of Speech Communication, 47,* 85–98.

Baumeister, R. F., Bushman, B. J., & Campbell, W. K. (2000). Self-esteem, narcissism, and aggression: Does violence result from low self-esteem or from threatened egotism? *Current Directions in Psychological Science, 9* (February), 26–29.

Baxter, L. A. (1984). An investigation of compliance-gaining as politeness. *Human Communication Research, 10,* 427–456.

Baxter, L. A. (1986). Gender differences in the heterosexual relationship rules embedded in break-up accounts. *Journal of Social and Personal Relationships, 3,* 289–306.

Baxter, L. A. (1988). A dialectical perspective on communication strategies in relationship development. In S. Duck (Ed.), *Handbook of Personal Relationships.* New York: Wiley.

Baxter, L. A. (1990). Dialectical contradictions in relationship development. *Journal of Social and Personal Relationships, 7* (February), 69–88.

Baxter, L. A., & Simon, E. P. (1993). Relationship maintenance strategies and dialectical contradictions in personal relationships. *Journal of Social and Personal Relationships, 10* (May), 225–242.

Beach, W. A. (1990–91). Avoiding ownership for alleged wrongdoings. *Research on Language and Social Interaction, 24,* 1–36.

Beatty, M. J. (1988). Situational and predispositional correlates of public speaking anxiety. *Communication Education, 37,* 28–39.

Bechler, C., & Johnson, S. D. (1995). Leadership and listening: A study of member perceptions. *Small Group Research, 26,* 77–85.

Becker, S. L., & Roberts, C. L. (1992). *Discovering mass communication* (3rd ed.). New York: HarperCollins.

Beebe, S. A., & Masterson, J. T. (2000). *Communicating in small groups: Principles and practices* (6th ed.). Boston: Allyn & Bacon.

Behzadi, K. G. (1994). Interpersonal conflict and emotions in an Iranian cultural practice: QAHR and ASHTI. *Culture, Medicine, and Psychiatry, 18* (September), 321–359.

Beier, E. (1974). How we send emotional messages. *Psychology Today, 8* (October), 53–56.

Bell, R. A., & Daly, J. A. (1984). The affinity-seeking function of communication. *Communication Monographs, 51,* 91–115.

Bell, S. T., Kuriloff, P. J., & Lottes, I. (1994). Understanding attributions of blame in stranger rape and date rape situations: An examination of gender, race, identification, and students' social perceptions of rape victims. *Journal of Applied Social Psychology, 24* (October), 1719–1734.

Benne, K. D., & Sheats, P. (1948). Functional roles of group members. *Journal of Social Issues, 4,* 41–49.

Bennett, M. (1990). Children's understanding of the mitigating function of disclaimers. *Journal of Social Psychology, 130* (February), 29–37.

Bennis, W., & Nanus, B. (1985). *Leaders: The strategies for taking charge.* New York: Harper & Row.

Berg, J. H., & Archer, R. L. (1983). The disclosure-liking relationship. *Human Communication Research, 10,* 269–281.

Berger, C. R., & Bradac, J. J. (1982). *Language and social knowledge: Uncertainty in interpersonal relations.* London: Edward Arnold.

Bernstein, W. M., Stephan, W. G., & Davis, M. H. (1979). Explaining attributions for achievement: A path analytic approach. *Journal of Personality and Social Psychology, 37,* 1810–1821.

Berry, J. W., Poortinga, Y. H., Segall, M. H., & Dasen, P. R. (1992). *Cross-cultural psychology: Research and applications.* New York: Cambridge University Press.

Blake, R. R., & Mouton, J. S. *The managerial grid III* (3rd ed.). Houston, TX: Gulf Publishing, 1984.

Blanchard, K. (1992). One-minute management. *Emergency Librarian, 19,* 37–38.

Blieszner, R., & Adams, R. G. (1992). *Adult friendship.* Thousand Oaks, CA: Sage.

Blumstein, P., & Schwartz, P. (1983). *American couples: Money, work, sex.* New York: Morrow.

Bochner, A. (1984). The functions of human communication in interpersonal bonding. In C. C. Arnold & J. W. Bowers (Eds.), *Handbook of rhetorical and communication theory* (pp. 544–621). Boston: Allyn & Bacon.

Bochner, A., & Kelly, C. (1974). Interpersonal competence: Rationale, philosophy, and implementation of a conceptual framework. *Communication Education, 23,* 279–301.

Bochner, A. P., & Yerby, J. (1977). Factors affecting instruction in interpersonal competence. *Communication Education, 26,* 91–103.

Bochner, S., & Hesketh, B. (1994). Power, distance, individualism/collectivism, and job-related attitudes in a culturally diverse work group. *Journal of Cross-Cultural Psychology, 25* (June), 233–257.

Bodon, J., Powell, L., & Hickson, M., III. (1999). Critiques of gatekeeping in scholarly journals: An analysis of perceptions and data. *Journal of the Association for Communication Administration, 28* (May), 60–70.

Bok, S. (1978). *Lying: Moral choice in public and private life.* New York: Pantheon.

Bok, S. (1983). *Secrets.* New York: Vintage.

Bok, S. (1998). *Mayhem: Violence as public entertainment.* Reading, MA: Perseus Books.

Bond, Jr., C. F., & Atoum, A. O. (2000). International deception. *Personality & Social Psychology Bulletin, 26* (March), 385–395.

Borden, G. (1991). *Cultural orientation: An approach to understanding intercultural communication.* Englewood Cliffs, NJ: Prentice-Hall.

Bosmajian, H. (1974). *The language of oppression.* Washington, D.C.: Public Affairs Press.

Bourland, D. D., Jr. (1965–66). A linguistic note: Writing in E-prime. *General Semantics Bulletin, 32–33,* 111–114.

Bower, B. (2001). Self-illusions come back to bite students. *Science News, 159,* 148.

Brauer, M., Judd, C. M., & Gliner, M. D. (1995). The effects of repeated expressions on attitude polarization during group discussions. *Journal of Personality and Social Psychology, 68* (June), 1014–1029.

Bravo, E., & Cassedy, E. (1992). *The 9 to 5 guide to combating sexual harassment.* New York: Wiley.

Brennan, M. (1991). Mismanagement and quality circles: How middle managers influence direct participation. *Employee Relations, 13,* 22–32.

Bridges, C. R. (1996). The characteristics of career achievement perceived by African American college administrators. *Journal of Black Studies, 26* (July), 748–767.

Brilhart, J., & Galanes, G. (1992). *Effective group discussion* (7th ed.). Dubuque, IA: Brown & Benchmark.

Brody, J. E. (1991, April 28). How to foster self-esteem. *New York Times Magazine,* pp. 26–27.

Brody, J. E. (1994, March 21). Notions of beauty transcend culture, new study suggests. *New York Times,* p. A14.

Brody, L. R. (1985). Gender differences in emotional development: A review of theories and research. *Journal of Personality, 53* (June), 102–149.

Brooks, B. (2003). Active listening. *Advisor Today, 98* (June), 82.

Brown, J. D., & Schulze, L. (1990). The effects of race, gender, and fandom on audience interpretations of Madonna's music videos. *Journal of Communication, 40* (Spring), 88–102.

Brown, P., & Levinson, S. C. (1988). *Politeness: Some universals of language usage.* NY: Cambridge University Press.

Brown, P. (1980). How and why are women more polite: Some evidence from a Mayan community. In S. McConnell-Ginet, R. Borker, & M. Furman (Eds.), *Women and language in literature and society* (pp. 111–136). New York: Praeger.

Brownell, J. (1987). Listening: The toughest management skill. *Cornell Hotel and Restaurant Administration Quarterly, 27,* 64–71.

Brownell, J. (2002). *Listening: Attitudes, principles, and skills* (2nd ed.). Boston: Allyn & Bacon.

Bruneau, T. (1985). The time dimension in intercultural communication. In L. A. Samovar & R. E. Porter (Eds.), *Intercultural communication: A reader* (4th ed., pp. 280–289). Belmont, CA: Wadsworth.

Bruneau, T. (1990). Chronemics: The study of time in human interaction. In J. A. DeVito & M. L. Hecht (Eds.), *The nonverbal communication reader* (pp. 301–311). Prospect Heights, IL: Waveland Press.

Bugental, J., & Zelen, S. (1950). Investigations into the "self-concept": I. The W-A-Y technique. *Journal of Personality, 18,* 483–498.

Bull, R., & Rumsey, N. (1988). *The social psychology of facial appearance.* New York: Springer-Verlag.

Buller, D. B., & Aune, R. K. (1992). The effects of speech rate similarity on compliance: Application of communication accommodation theory. *Western Journal of Communication, 56* (Winter), 37–53.

Buller, D. B., LePoire, B. A., Aune, K., & Eloy, S. (1992). Social perceptions as mediators of the effect of speech rate similarity on compliance. *Human Communication Research, 19* (December), 286–311.

Bullock, C., McCluskey, M., Stamm, K., Tanaka, K., Torres, M. & Scott, C. (2002). Group affiliations, opinion polarization, and global organization: Views of the World Trade Organization before and after Seattle. *Mass Communication & Society, 5*(4), 433–450.

Burgoon, J. K. (1978). A communication model of personal space violations: Explication and an initial test. *Human Communication Research, 4,* 129–142.

Burgoon, J. K. (1991). Relational message interpretations of touch, conversational distance, and posture. *Journal of Nonverbal Behavior, 15* (Winter), 233–259.

Burgoon, J. K., & Bacue, A. E. (2003). Nonverbal communication skills. In J. O. Greene & B. R. Burleson (Eds.), *Handbook of communication and social interaction skills* (pp. 179–220). Mahwah, NJ: Lawrence Erlbaum.

Burgoon, J. K., Berger, C. R., & Waldron, V. R. (2000). Mindfulness and interpersonal communication. *Journal of Social Issues, 56,* 105–127.

Burgoon, J. K., Buller, D. B., & Woodall, W. G. (1996). *Nonverbal communication: The unspoken dialogue* (2nd ed.). New York: McGraw-Hill.

Burgoon, J. K., & Hoobler, G. D. (2002). Nonverbal signals. In M. L. Knapp & J. A. Daly (Eds.), *Handbook of interpersonal communication* (3rd ed., pp. 240–299). Thousand Oaks, CA: Sage.

Burgoon, M. (1971). The relationship between willingness to manipulate others and success in two different types of basic speech communication courses. *Communication Education, 20,* 178–183.

Burke, N. D. (1993). Restricting gang clothing in the public schools. *West's Education Law Quarterly, 2* (July), 391–404.

Burleson, B. R., Kunkel, A. W., & Birch, J. D. (1994). Thoughts about talk in romantic relationships: Similarity makes for attraction (and happiness, too). *Communication Quarterly, 42* (Summer), 259–273.

Burleson, B. R., Samter, W., & Luccetti, A. E. (1992). Similarity in communication values as a predictor of friendship choices: Studies of friends and best friends. *Southern Communication Journal, 57,* 260–276.

Bushman, B. J., & Baumeister, R. F. (1998). Threatened egotism, narcissism, self-esteem, and direct and displaced aggression: Does self-love or self-hate lead to violence? *Journal of Personality and Social Psychology, 75,* 219–229.

Busse, W. M., & Birk, J. M. (1993). The effects of self-disclosure and competitiveness on friendship for male graduate students over 35. *Journal of College Student Development, 34* (May), 169–174.

Butler, P. E. (1981). *Talking to yourself: Learning the language of self-support.* New York: Harper & Row.

Byers, E. S., & Demmons, S. (1999). Sexual satisfaction and sexual self-disclosure within dating relationships. *Journal of Sex Research, 36,* 180–189.

Cai, D. A., & Fink, E. L. (2002). Conflict style differences between individualists and collectivists. *Communication Monographs, 69* (March), 67–87.

Callan, V. J. (1993). Subordinate-manager communication in different sex dyads: Consequences for job satisfaction. *Journal of Occupational & Organizational Psychology, 66* (March), 1–15.

Canary, D. J., Cody, M. J., & Manusov, V. L. (2000). *Interpersonal communication: A goals-based approach* (2nd ed.). Boston: Bedford/St. Martins.

Canary, D. J., Cupach, W. R., & Messman, S. J. (1995). *Relationship conflict.* Thousand Oaks, CA: Sage.

Canary, D. J., & Hause, K. S. (1993). Is there any reason to research sex differences in communication? *Communication Quarterly, 41* (Spring), 129–144.

Canary, D. J., & Stafford, L. (1994a). *Communication and relational maintenance.* San Diego, CA: Academic Press.

Canary, D. J., & Stafford, L. (1994b). Maintaining relationships through strategic and routine interaction. In D. J. Canary & L. Stafford (Eds.), *Communication and relational maintenance.* San Diego, CA: Academic Press.

Canary, D. J., Stafford, L., Hause, K. S., & Wallace, L. A. (1993). An inductive analysis of relational maintenance strategies: Comparisons among lovers, relatives, friends, and others. *Communication Research Reports, 10* (June), 5–14.

Cappella, J. N. (1993). The facial feedback hypothesis in human interaction: Review and speculation. *Journal of Language and Social Psychology, 12* (March–June), 13–29.

Carducci, B. J., with P. G. Zimbardo (1995). Are you shy? *Psychology Today, 28* (November–December), pp. 34–41, 64–70, 78–82.

Carle, G. (1995, Spring). 10 reasons why talk shows are good for you. *All Talk,* p. 27.

Cassell, M. M., Jackson, C., & Cheuvront, B. (1998). Health communication on the Internet: An effective channel for health behavior change? *Journal of Health Communication, 3* (January–March), 71–79.

Castleberry, S. B., & Shepherd, D. D. (1993). Effective interpersonal listening and personal selling. *Journal of Personal Selling and Sales Management, 13,* 35–49.

Cate, R., Henton, J., Koval, J., Christopher, R., & Lloyd, S. (1982). Premarital abuse: A social psychological perspective. *Journal of Family Issues, 3,* 79–90.

Cathcart, D., & Cathcart, R. (1985). Japanese social experience and concept of groups. In L. A. Samovar & R. E. Porter (Eds.), *Intercultural communication: A reader* (4th ed., pp. 190–197). Belmont, CA: Wadsworth.

Cawthon, S. W. (2001). Teaching strategies in inclusive classrooms with deaf students. *Journal of Deaf Studies and Deaf Education, 6,* 212–225.

Cegala, D. J., Savage, G. T., Brunner, C. C., & Conrad, A. B. (1982). An elaboration of the meaning of interaction involvement. *Communication Monographs, 49,* 229–248.

Chadwick-Jones, J. K. (1976). *Social exchange theory: Its structure and influence in social psychology.* New York: Academic Press.

Chaney, R. H., Givens, C. A., Aoki, M. F., & Gombiner, M. L. (1989). Pupillary responses in recognizing awareness in persons with profound mental retardation. *Perceptual and Motor Skills, 69* (October), 523–528.

Chang, H.-C., & Holt, G. R. (1996). The changing Chinese interpersonal world: Popular themes in interpersonal communication books in modern Taiwan. *Communication Quarterly, 44* (Winter), 85–106.

Chanowitz, B., & Langer, E. (1981). Premature cognitive commitment. *Journal of Personality and Social Psychology, 41,* 1051–1063.

Chen, G.-M. (1990). Intercultural communication competence: Some perspectives of research. *The Howard Journal of Communication, 2* (Summer), 243–261.

Chen, G.-M. (1992). *Differences in self-disclosure patterns among Americans versus Chinese: A comparative study.* Paper presented at the annual meeting of the Eastern Communication Association, Portland, ME.

Cheney, G., & Tompkins, P. K. (1987). Coming to terms with organizational identification and commitment. *Central States Speech Journal, 38* (Spring), 1–15.

Cherulnik, P. D. (1979). Sex differences in the expression of emotion in a structured social encounter. *Sex Roles, 5* (August), 413–424.

Cho, H. (2000). Asian in America: Cultural shyness can impede Asian Americans' success. *Northwest Asian Weekly, 19* (December 8), 6.

Christie, R. (1970a). The Machiavellis among us. *Psychology Today, 4* (November), pp. 82–86.

Christie, R. (1970b). Scale construction. In R. Christie & F. L. Geis (Eds.), *Studies in Machiavellianism* (pp. 35–52). New York: Academic Press.

Chung, L. C., & Ting-Toomey, S. (1999). Ethnic identity and relational expectations among Asian Americans. *Communication Research Reports, 16* (Spring), 157–166.

Cialdini, R. T. (1984). *Influence: How and why people agree to things.* New York: Morrow.

Cialdini, R. T., & Ascani, K. (1976). Test of a concession procedure for inducing verbal, behavioral, and further compliance with a request to give blood. *Journal of Applied Psychology, 61,* 295–300.

Coates, E. J., & Feldman, R. S. (1996). Gender differences in nonverbal correlates of social status. *Personality and Social Psychology Bulletin, 22* (October), 1014–1022.

Coates, J. (1986). *Women, men and language.* New York: Longman.

Coates, J., & Sutton-Spence, R. (2001). Turn-taking patterns in deaf conversation. *Journal of Sociolinguistics, 5* (November), 507–529.

Cohen, C. E. (1983). Inferring the characteristics of other people: Categories and attribute accessibility. *Journal of Personality and Social Psychology, 44,* 34–44.

Cohen, J. (2001, January 18). On the Internet, love really is blind. *New York Times,* pp. G1, G9.

Cohen, J. (2002, May 9). An e-mail affliction: The long goodbye. *New York Times,* p. G6.

Cole, T., & Leets, L. (1999). Attachment styles and intimate television viewing: Insecurely forming relationships in a parasocial way. *Journal of Social and Personal Relationships, 16* (August), 495–511.

Coleman, P. (2002). *How to say it for couples: Communicating with tenderness, openness, and honesty.* Paramus, NJ: Prentice-Hall.

Collier, M. J. (1991). Conflict competence within African, Mexican, and Anglo-American friendships. In S. Ting-Toomey & F. Korzenny (Eds.), *Cross-cultural interpersonal communication* (pp. 132–154). Thousand Oaks, CA: Sage.

Collins, C. L., & Gould, O. N. (1994). Getting to know you: How own age and other's age relate to self-disclosure. *International Journal of Aging and Human Development, 39,* 55–66.

Comadena, M. E. (1984). Brainstorming groups: Ambiguity tolerance, communication apprehension, task attraction, and individual productivity. *Small Group Behavior, 15,* 251–254.

Comer, L. B., & Drollinger, T. (1999). Active emphatic listening and selling success: A conceptual framework. *Journal of Personal Selling and Sales Management, 19,* 15–29.

Cook, M. (1971). *Interpersonal perception.* Baltimore, MD: Penguin.

Cooley, C. H. (1922). *Human nature and the social order* (Rev. ed.). New York: Scribners.

Coombes, A. (2003). E-termination: Employees are getting fired for e-mail infractions. CBSMarketWatch.Com (accessed 9/3/04).

Cooper, A., & Sportolari, L. (1997). Romance in cyberspace: Understanding online attraction. *Journal of Sex Education and Therapy, 22,* 7–14.

Coover, G. E., & Murphy, S. T. (2000). The communicated self: Exploring the interaction between self and social context. *Human Communication Research, 26,* 125–147.

Copeland, L., & Griggs, L. (1985). *Going international: How to make friends and deal effectively in the global marketplace.* New York: Random House.

Cornwell, B., & Lundgren, D. C. (2001). Love on the Internet: Involvement and misrepresentation in romantic relationships in cyberspace vs. realspace. *Computers in Human Behavior, 17,* 197–211.

Coupland, N., Coupland, J., Giles, H., Henwood, K., et al. (1988). Elderly self-disclosure: Interactional and intergroup issues. *Language & Communication, 8,* 109–133.

Cragan, J. F., & Wright, D. W. (1990). Small group communication research of the 1980s: A synthesis and critique. *Communication Studies, 41* (Fall), 212–236.

Crampton, S. M., Hodge, J. M., & Mishra, J. M. (1998). The informal communication network: Factors influencing grapevine activity. *Public Personnel Management, 27* (Winter), 569–584.

Crohn, J. (1995). *Mixed matches.* New York: Fawcett.

Crown, C. L., & Cummins, D. A. (1998). Objective versus perceived vocal interruptions in the dialogues of unacquainted pairs, friends, and couples. *Journal of Language and Social Psychology, 17* (September), 372–389.

Crusco, A. H., & Wetzel, C. G. (1984). The Midas touch: The effects of interpersonal touch on restaurant tipping. *Personality and Social Psychology Bulletin, 10* (December), 512–517.

Dainton, M., & Stafford, L. (1993). Routine maintenance behaviors: A comparison of relationship type, partner similarity, and sex differences. *Journal of Social and Personal Relationships, 10,* 255–272.

Daly, J. A., McCroskey, J. C., Ayres, J., Hopf, T., & Ayres, D. M. (1997). *Avoiding communication: Shyness, reticence, and communication apprehension* (2nd ed.). Cresskill, NJ: Hampton Press.

Darley, J. M., & Oleson, K. C. (1993). Introduction to research on interpersonal expectations. In P. D. Blanck (Ed.), *Interpersonal expectations: Theory, research, and applications. Studies in emotion and social interaction* (pp. 45–63). New York: Cambridge University Press.

Davis, K. (1977). The care and cultivation of the corporate grapevine. In R. Huseman, C. Logue, & D. Freshley (Eds.), *Readings in interpersonal and organizational communication* (3rd ed., pp. 131–136). Boston: Holbrook.

Davis, K. (1980). Management communication and the grapevine. In S. Ferguson & S. D. Ferguson (Eds.), *Intercom: Readings in organizational communication* (pp. 55–66). Rochelle Park, NJ: Hayden Books.

Davis, M. S. (1973). *Intimate relations.* New York: Free Press.

Davison, W. P. (1983). The third-person effects and the differential impact in negative political advertising. *Journalism Quarterly, 68,* 680–688.

Davitz, J. R. (Ed.). (1964). *The communication of emotional meaning.* New York: McGraw-Hill.

Deal, J. E., & Wampler, K. S. (1986). Dating violence: The primacy of previous experience. *Journal of Social and Personal Relationships, 3,* 457–471.

deBono, E. (1976). *Teaching thinking.* New York: Penguin.

deBono, E. (1987). *The six thinking hats.* New York: Penguin.

DeFrancisco, V. (1991). The sound of silence: How men silence women in marital relations. *Discourse and Society, 2,* 413–423.

DeGroot, T., & Motowidlo, S. J. (1999). Why visual and vocal interview cues can affect interviewers' judgments and predict job performance. *Journal of Applied Psychology, 84* (December), 986–993.

DeJong, W. (1979). An examination of self-perception mediation of the foot-in-the-door effect. *Journal of Personality and Social Psychology, 37,* 2221–2239.

DePaulo, B. M. (1992). Nonverbal behavior and self-presentation. *Psychological Bulletin, 111,* 203–212.

Derlega, V. J., Winstead, B. A., Wong, P. T. P., & Greenspan, M. (1987). Self-disclosure and relationship development: An attributional analysis. In M. E. Roloff & G. R. Miller (Eds.), *Interpersonal processes: New directions in communication research* (pp. 172–187). Thousand Oaks, CA: Sage.

Derlega, V. J., Winstead, B. A., Wong, P. T. P., & Hunter, S. (1985). Gender effects in an initial encounter: A case where men exceed women in disclosure. *Journal of Social and Personal Relationships, 2,* 25–44.

Derne, S. (1999). Making sex violent: Love as force in recent Hindi films. *Violence against Women, 5* (May), 548–575.

DeStephen, R., & Hirokawa, R. (1988). Small group consensus: Stability of group support of the decision, task process, and group relationships. *Small Group Behavior 19,* 227–239.

DeTurck, M. A. (1987). When communication fails: Physical aggression as a compliance-gaining strategy. *Communication Monographs, 54,* 106–112.

DeVito, J. A. (1974). *General semantics: Guide and workbook* (Rev. ed.). DeLand, FL: Everett/Edwards.

DeVito, J. A. (1989). *The nonverbal communication workbook.* Prospect Heights, IL: Waveland Press.

DeVito, J. A. (1996). *Brainstorms: How to think more creatively about communication (or about anything else).* New York: Longman.

DeVito, J. A. (2000). *The elements of public speaking* (7th ed.). New York: Longman.

Dewey, J. (1910). *How we think.* Boston: Heath.

DeZoysa, R., & Newman, O. (2002). Globalization, soft power and the challenge of Hollywood. *Contemporary Politics, 8,* 185–202.

Dickenson-Hazard, N. (1998, June 1). Nursing: The next millennium. *Vital Speeches of the Day,* 493–495.

Dietz, T. L. (1998). An examination of violence and gender role portrayals in video games: Implications for gender socialization and aggressive behavior. *Sex Roles, 38* (March), 425–442.

Dindia, K., & Baxter, L. A. (1987). Strategies for maintaining and repairing marital relationships. *Journal of Social and Personal Relationships, 4,* 143–158.

Dindia, K., & Fitzpatrick, M. A. (1985). Marital communication: Three approaches compared. In S. Duck & D. Perlman (Eds.), *Understanding personal relationships: An interdisciplinary approach* (pp. 137–158). Thousand Oaks, CA: Sage.

Dindia, K., & Timmerman, L. (2003). Accomplishing romantic relationships. In J. O. Greene & B. R. Burleson (Eds.), *Handbook of communication and social interaction skills* (pp. 685–722). Mahwah, NJ: Lawrence Erlbaum.

Dodd, C. H. (1995). *Dynamics of intercultural communication* (4th ed.). Dubuque, IA: William C. Brown.

Dolgin, K. G., Meyer, L., & Schwartz, J. (1991). Effects of gender, target's gender, topic, and self-esteem on disclosure to best and middling friends. *Sex Roles, 25,* 311–329.

Dominick, J. R. (2000). *The dynamics of mass communication* (6th ed.). New York: McGraw-Hill.

Donaldson, S. (1992). Gender and discourse: The case of interruptions. *Carleton Papers in Applied Language Studies, 9,* 47–66.

Donohue, W. A., with Kolt, R. (1992). *Managing interpersonal conflict.* Thousand Oaks, CA: Sage.

Dovidio, J. F., Gaertner, S. E., Kawakami, K., & Hodson, G. (2002). Why can't we just get along? Interpersonal biases and interracial distrust. *Cultural Diversity and Ethnic Minority Psychology, 8,* 88–102.

Dresser, N. (1996). *Multicultural manners: New rules of etiquette for a changing society.* New York: Wiley.

Drews, D. R., Allison, C. K., & Probst, J. R. (2000). Behavioral and self-concept differences in tattooed and nontattooed college students. *Psychological Reports, 86,* 475–481.

Dreyfuss, H. (1971). *Symbol sourcebook.* New York: McGraw-Hill.

Driskell, J., Olmstead, B., & Salas, E. (1993). Task cues, dominance cues, and influence in task groups. *Journal of Applied Psychology, 78* (February), 51–60.

Drucker, S. J., & Gumpert, G. (1991). Public space and communication: The zoning of public interaction. *Communication Theory, 1* (November), 294–310.

Dsilva, M. U., & Whyte, L. O. (1998). Cultural differences in conflict styles: Vietnamese refugees and established residents. *The Howard Journal of Communications, 9* (January–March), 57–68.

Duncan, S. D., Jr. (1972). Some signals and rules for taking speaking turns in conversation. *Journal of Personality and Social Psychology, 23,* 283–292.

Duran, R. L., & Kelly, L. (1988). The influence of communicative competence on perceived task, social, and physical attractiveness. *Communication Quarterly, 36,* 41–49.

Eagly, A. H., & Crowley, M. (1986). Gender and helping behavior: A meta-analytic review of the social psychological literature. *Psychological Bulletin, 100* (November), 283–308.

Eakins, B., & Eakins, R. G. (1978). *Sex differences in communication.* Boston: Houghton Mifflin.

Edelstein, A. S. (1993). Thinking about the criterion variable in agenda-setting research. *Journal of Communication, 43,* 85–99.

Eden, D. (1992). Leadership and expectations: Pygmalion effects and other self-fulfilling prophecies in organizations. *Leadership Quarterly, 3* (Winter), 271–305.

Eder, D., & Enke, J. L. (1991). The structure of gossip: Opportunities and constraints on collective expression among adolescents. *American Sociological Review, 56,* 494–508.

Ehrenhaus, P. (1988). Silence and symbolic expression. *Communication Monographs, 55* (March), 41–57.

Einstein, E. (1995). Success or sabotage: Which self-fulfilling prophecy will the stepfamily create? In D. K. Huntley (Ed.), *Understanding stepfamilies: Implications for assessment and treatment.* Alexandria, VA: American Counseling Association.

Eisenberger, N. I., Liberman, M. D., & Williams, K. D. (2003). Does rejection hurt? An fMRI study of social exclusion. *Science, 302* (October), 290–292.

Ekman, P. (1985). *Telling lies: Clues to deceit in the marketplace, politics, and marriage.* New York: Norton.

Ekman, P., & Friesen, W. V. (1969). The repertoire of nonverbal behavior: Categories, origins, usage, and coding. *Semiotica, 1,* 49–98.

Ekman, P., Friesen, W. V., & Ellsworth, P. (1972). *Emotion in the human face: Guidelines for research and an integration of findings.* New York: Pergamon Press.

Elfenbein, H. A., & Ambady, N. (2002). Is there an in-group advantage in emotion recognition? *Psychological Bulletin, 128,* 243–249.

Ellis, A. (1988). *How to stubbornly refuse to make yourself miserable about anything, yes anything.* Secaucus, NJ: Lyle Stuart.

Ellis, A., & Harper, R. A. (1975). *A new guide to rational living.* Hollywood, CA: Wilshire Books.

Elmes, M. B., & Gemmill, G. (1990). The psychodynamics of mindlessness and dissent in small groups. *Small Group Research, 21,* 28–44.

Emmers-Sommer, T. M., & Allen, M. (1999). Surveying the effect of media effects: A meta-analytic summary of the media effects research in *Human Communication Research. Human Communication Research, 25* (June), 478–497.

Epley, N., & Dunning, D. (2000). Feeling "holier than thou": Are self-serving assessments produced by errors in self- or social prediction? *Journal of Personality and Social Psychology, 79* (December), 861–875.

Esten, G., & Willmott, L. (1993). Double-bind messages: The effects of attitude towards disability on therapy. *Women and Therapy, 14,* 29–41.

Exline, R. V., Ellyson, S. L., & Long, B. (1975). Visual behavior as an aspect of power role relationships. In P. Pliner, L. Krames, & T. Alloway (Eds.), *Nonverbal communication of aggression.* New York: Plenum Press.

Felson, R. B. (2002). Violence and gender reexamined. *Law and public policy.* Washington, DC: American Psychological Association.

Fernald, C. D. (1995). When in London . . . : Differences in Disability Language Preferences Among English-Speaking Countries. *Mental Retardation, 33* (April), 99–103.

Festinger, L. (1954). A theory of social comparison processes. *Human Relations, 7,* 117–140.

Field, R. H. G. (1989). The self-fulfilling prophecy leader: Achieving the Metharme Effect. *Journal of Management Studies, 26* (March), 151–175.

Fiol, C. M., & O'Connor, E. J. (2003). Waking up! Mindfulness in the face of bandwagons. *Academy of Management Review, 28* (January), 54–70.

Fischer, A. H. (1993). Sex differences in emotionality: Fact or stereotype? *Feminism & Psychology, 3,* 303–318.

Fiske, S. T., & Taylor, S. E. (1984). *Social cognition.* Reading, MA: Addison-Wesley.

Fitzpatrick, M. A. (1983). Predicting couples' communication from couples' self-reports. In R. N. Bostrom (Ed.), *Communication Yearbook 7* (pp. 49–82). Thousand Oaks, CA: Sage.

Fitzpatrick, M. A. (1988). *Between husbands and wives: Communication in marriage.* Thousand Oaks, CA: Sage.

Fitzpatrick, M. A. (1991). Sex differences in marital conflict: Social psychophysiological versus cognitive explanations. *Text, 11,* 341–364.

Foddy, M., & Crundall, I. (1993). A field study of social comparison processes in ability evaluation. *British Journal of Social Psychology, 32* (December), 287–305.

Fodor, I. G., & Collier, J. C. (2001). Assertiveness and conflict resolution: An integrated Gestalt/cognitive behavioral model for working with urban adolescents. In M. McConville & G. Wheeler (Eds.), *The heart of development: Vol. II: Adolescence: Gestalt approaches to working with children, adolescents and their worlds* (pp. 214–252). Cambridge, ME: Analytic Press.

Folger, J. P., Poole, M. S., & Stutman, R. K. (1997). *Working through conflict: A communication perspective* (3rd ed.). New York: Longman.

Folkerts, J., & Lacy, S. (2001). *The media in your life: An introduction to mass communication* (2nd ed.). Boston: Allyn & Bacon.

Forbes, G. B. (2001). College students with tattoos and piercings: Motives, family experiences, personality factors, and perception by others. *Psychological Reports, 89,* 774-786.

Franklin, C. W., & Mizell, C. A. (1995). Some factors influencing success among African-American men: A preliminary study. *Journal of Men's Studies, 3,* 191-204.

Fraser, B. (1990). Perspectives on politeness. *Journal of Pragmatics, 14* (April), 219-236.

Fraser, Christopher O. (2000). The social goals of excuses: Self-serving attributions or politeness strategies. *Journal of Applied Social Psychology, 30* (March), 599-611.

Frederikse, M. E., Lu, A., Aylward, E., Barta, P., & Pearlson, G. (1999). Sex differences in the inferior parietal lobule. *Cerebral Cortex, 9,* 869-901.

Freedman, J., & Fraser, S. (1966). Compliance without pressure: The foot-in-the-door technique. *Journal of Personality and Social Psychology, 4,* 195-202.

French, J. R. P., Jr., & Raven, B. (1968). The bases of social power. In D. Cartwright & A. Zander (Eds.), *Group dynamics: Research and theory* (3rd ed., pp. 259-269). New York: Harper & Row.

Frentz, T. (1976). *A general approach to episodic structure.* Paper presented at the Western Speech Association Convention, San Francisco, CA. Cited in Reardon (1987).

Frey, K. J., & Eagly, A. H. (1993). Vividness can undermine the persuasiveness of messages. *Journal of Personality and Social Psychology, 65* (July), 32-44.

Friedkin, N. E. (1999). Choice shift and group polarization. *American Sociological Review, 64* (December), 856-875.

Frieze, I. H. (2000). Violence in close relationships—development of a research area: Comment on Archer (2000). *Psychological Bulletin, 126* (September), 681-684.

Frymier, A. B., & Shulman, G. M. (1995). "What's in it for me?": Increasing content relevance to enhance students' motivation. *Communication Education, 44* (January), 40-50.

Frymier, A. B., & Thompson, C. A. (1992). Perceived teacher affinity-seeking in relation to perceived teacher credibility. *Communication Education, 41* (October), 388-399.

Furlow, F. B. (1996). The smell of love. *Psychology Today* (March/April), 38-45.

Furnham, A., & Bitar, N. (1993). The stereotyped portrayal of men and women in British television advertisements. *Sex Roles, 29* (August), 297-310.

Furnham, A., & Bochner, S. (1986). *Culture shock: Psychological reactions to unfamiliar environments.* New York: Methuen.

Gabriel, Y. (1998). An introduction to the social psychology of insults in organizations. *Human Relations, 51* (November), 1329-1354.

Gabrielides, C., Stephan, W. G., Ybarra, O., Pearson, V. M. D. S., & Villareal, L. (1997). Preferred styles of conflict resolution: Mexico and the United States. *Journal of Cross-Cultural Psychology, 28* (November), 661-677.

Galvin, K., Bylund, C., & Brommel, B. J. (2004). *Family communication: Cohesion and change* (6th ed.). Boston: Allyn & Bacon.

Gamson, J. (1998). Publicity traps: Television talk shows and lesbian, gay, bisexual, and transgender visibility. *Sexualities, 1* (February), 11-41.

Gao, G. (1991). Stability of romantic relationships in China and the United States. In S. Ting-Toomey & F. Korzenny (Eds.), *Cross-cultural interpersonal communication* (pp. 99-115). Thousand Oaks, CA: Sage.

Gaziano, C., & McGrath, K. (1986). Measuring the concept of credibility. *Journalism Quarterly, 63,* 451-462.

Gelfand, M. J., Nishii, L. H., Holcombe, K. M., Dyer, N., Ohbuchi, K., & Fukuno, M. (2001). Cultural influences on cognitive representations of conflict: Interpretations of conflict episodes in the United States and Japan. *Journal of Applied Psychology, 86,* 1059-1074.

Gelles, R., & Cornell, C. (1985). *Intimate violence in families.* Thousand Oaks, CA: Sage.

Gerbner, G., Gross, L. P., Morgan, M., & Signorielli, N. (1980). The "mainstreaming" of America: Violence profile no. 11. *Journal of Communication, 30,* 10-29.

Gergen, K. J., Greenberg, M. S., & Willis, R. H. (1980). *Social exchange: Advances in theory and research.* New York: Plenum Press.

Giles, D. C. (2001). Parasocial interaction: A review of the literature and a model for future research. *Media Psychology, 4,* 279-305.

Giles, H., Mulac, A., Bradac, J. J., & Johnson, P. (1987). Speech accommodation theory: The first decade and beyond. In M. L. McLaughlin (Ed.), *Communication yearbook 10* (pp. 13-48). Thousand Oaks, CA: Sage.

Giordano, J. (1989). *Telecommuting and organizational culture: A study of corporate consciousness and identification.* Unpublished doctoral dissertation, University of Massachusetts, Amherst.

Gladstone, G. L., & Parker, G. B. (2002). When you're smiling, does the whole world smile for you? *Australasian Psychiatry, 10* (June), 144-146.

Glucksberg, S., & Danks, J. H. (1975). *Experimental psycholinguistics: An introduction.* Hillsdale, NJ: Erlbaum.

Goffman, E. (1971). *Relations in public: Microstudies of the public order.* New York: HarperCollins.

Goldin-Meadow, S., Nusbaum, H., Kelly, S. D., & Wagner, S. (2001). Gesture—Psychological aspects. *Psychological Science, 12,* 516-522.

Goldsmith, D. J., & Fulfs, P. A. (1999). "You just don't have the evidence": An analysis of claims and evidence. In M. E. Roloff (Ed.), *Communication yearbook, 22* (pp. 1-49). Thousand Oaks, CA: Sage.

Goleman, D. (1995, February 14). For man and beast, language of love shares many traits. *New York Times,* pp. C1, C9.

Gonzalez, A., & Zimbardo, P. G. (1985). Time in perspective. *Psychology Today, 19,* 20-26.

Gonzenbach, W. J., King, C., & Jablonski, P. (1999). Homosexuals and the military: An analysis of the spiral of silence. *Howard Journal of Communication, 10* (October-December), 281-296.

Goode, E. (2000, August 8). How culture molds habits of thought. *New York Times,* pp. F1, F8.

Goode, E. (2003, September 2). Power of positive thinking may have a health benefit, study says. *New York Times,* p. F5.

Gorden, W. I., & Nevins, R. J. (1993). *We mean business: Building communication competence in business and professions.* New York: Longman.

Gordon, T. (1975). *P.E.T.: Parent effectiveness training.* New York: New American Library.

Gorham, B. W. (1999). Stereotypes and the media: So what? *Howard Journal of Communications, 10* (October-December), 229-247.

Gosling, S. D., Ko, S. J., Mannarelli, T., & Morris, M. E. (2002). A room with a cue: Personality judgments based on offices and bedrooms. *Journal of Personality and Social Psychology, 82* (March), 379-398.

Goss, B., Thompson, M., & Olds, S. (1978). Behavioral support for systematic desensitization for communication apprehension. *Human Communication Research, 4,* 158-163.

Gottman, J. M., & Carrere, S. (1994). Why can't men and women get along? Developmental roots and marital inequities. In D. J. Canary & L. Stafford (Eds.), *Communication and relational maintenance* (pp. 203-229). San Diego, CA: Academic Press.

Gottman, J. M., & Levenson, R. W. (1999). Dysfunctional marital conflict: Women are being unfairly blamed. *Journal of Divorce and Remarriage, 31,* 1-17.

Gould, S. J. (1995, June 7). No more "wretched refuse." *New York Times,* p. A27.

Gouran, D. S., & Hirokawa, R. Y. (1986). Counteractive functions of communication in effective group decision-making. In R. Y. Hirokawa & M. S. Poole (Eds.), *Communication and group decision-making* (pp. 81-90). Thousand Oaks, CA: Sage.

Graham, E. E. (1994). Interpersonal communication motives scale. In R. B. Rubin, P. Palmgreen, & H. E. Sypher (Eds.), *Communication research measures: A sourcebook* (pp. 211-216). New York: Guilford.

Graham, E. E., Barbato, C. A., & Perse, E. M. (1993). The interpersonal communication motives model. *Communication Quarterly, 41,* 172-186.

Graham, J. A., & Argyle, M. (1975). The effects of different patterns of gaze, combined with different facial expressions, on impression formation. *Journal of Human Movement Studies, 1* (December), 178-182.

Graham, J. A., Bitti, P. R., & Argyle, M. (1975). A Cross-cultural study of the communication of emotion by facial and gestural cues. *Journal of Human Movement Studies, 1* (June), 68-77.

Grandey, A. A. (2000). Emotion regulation in the workplace: A new way to conceptualize emotional labor. *Journal of Occupational Health and Psychology, 5* (January), 95-110.

Grant, A. E., Guthrie, K. K., & Ball-Rokeach, S. J. (1991). Television shopping: A media system dependency perspective. *Communication Research, 18* (December), 773-798.

Greene, J. O., & Burleson, B. R. (Eds.). (2003). *Handbook of communication and social interaction skills.* Mahwah, NJ: Lawrence Erlbaum.

Grice, G. L., & Skinner, J. F. (2004). *Mastering public speaking* (5th ed.). Boston: Allyn & Bacon.

Grice, H. P. (1975). Logic and conversation. In P. Cole and J. L. Morgan (Eds.), *Syntax and semantics: Vol. 3. Speech Acts* (pp. 41-58). New York: Seminar Press.

Griffin, E. (1991). *A first look at communication theory.* New York: McGraw-Hill.

Gross, L. (1991). The contested closet: The ethics and politics of outing. *Critical Studies in Mass Communication, 8* (September), 352-388.

Grossin, W. (1987). Monochronic time, polychronic time and policies for development. *Studi di Sociologia, 25* (January-March), 18-25.

Gudykunst, W. B. (1994). *Bridging differences: Effective intergroup communication* (2nd ed.). Thousand Oaks, CA: Sage.

Gudykunst, W. B., & Kim, Y. Y. (1992). *Communicating with strangers: An approach to intercultural communication* (2nd ed.). New York: Random House.

Gudykunst, W., & Nishida, T. (1984). Individual and cultural influence on uncertainty reduction. *Communication Monographs, 51,* 23-36.

Gudykunst, W. B., & Ting-Toomey, S., with Chua, E. (1988). *Culture and interpersonal communication.* Thousand Oaks, CA: Sage.

Gudykunst, W., Yang, S., & Nishida, T. (1985). A cross-cultural test of uncertainty reduction theory: Comparisons of acquaintance, friend, and dating relationships in Japan, Korea, and the United States. *Human Communication Research, 11,* 407-454.

Gudykunst, W. B. (Ed.). (1983). *Intercultural communication theory: Current perspectives.* Thousand Oaks, CA: Sage.

Gueguen, N. (2003). Help on the Web: The effect of the same first name between the sender and the receptor in a request made by e-mail. *Psychological Record, 53* (Summer), 459-466.

Guerrero, L. K., & Andersen, P. A. (1991). The waxing and waning of relational intimacy: Touch as a function of relational stage, gender and touch avoidance. *Journal of Social and Personal Relationships, 8,* 147-165.

Guerrero, L. K., Eloy, S. V., & Wabnik, A. I. (1993). Linking maintenance strategies to relationship development and disengagement: A reconceptualization. *Journal of Social and Personal Relationships, 10,* 273-282.

Guerrero, L. K., & Andersen, P. A. (1994). Patterns of matching and initiation: Touch behavior and touch avoidance across romantic relationship stages. *Journal of Nonverbal Behavior, 18* (Summer), 137-153.

Guerrero, L. K., DeVito, J. A., & Hecht, M. L. (Eds.). (1999). *The nonverbal communication reader: Class and contemporary readings* (2nd ed.). Prospect Heights, IL: Waveland Press.

Gumpert, G., & Drucker, S. J. (1995). Place as medium: Exegesis of the cafe drinking coffee, the art of watching others, civil conversation—with excursions into the effects of architecture and interior design. *The Speech Communication Annual, 9* (Spring), 7-32.

Guo-Ming, C., & Starosta, W. J. (1995). Intercultural communication competence: A synthesis. In B. R. Burleson (Ed.), *Communication Yearbook 19.* Thousand Oaks, CA: Sage.

Haar, B. F., & Krahe, B. (1999). Strategies for resolving interpersonal conflicts in adolescence: A German-Indonesian comparison. *Journal of Cross-Cultural Psychology, 30* (November), 667-683.

Hackman, M. Z., & Johnson, C. E. (1991). *Leadership: A communication perspective.* Prospect Heights, IL: Waveland Press.

Haferkamp, C. J. (1991-92). Orientations to conflict: Gender, attributions, resolution strategies, and self-monitoring. *Current Psychology Research and Reviews, 10* (Winter), 227-240.

Haga, Y. (1988). Traits de langage et caractere Japonais. *Cahiers de Sociologie Economique et Culturelle, 9,* 105-109.

Hall, E. T. (1959). *The silent language.* Garden City, NY: Doubleday.

Hall, E. T. (1963). A system for the notation of proxemic behavior. *American Anthropologist, 65,* 1003-1026.

Hall, E. T. (1976). *Beyond culture.* Garden City, NY: Doubleday.

Hall, E. T., & Hall, M. R. (1987). *Hidden differences: Doing business with the Japanese.* New York: Doubleday.

Hall, J. A. (1998). How big are nonverbal sex differences? The case of smiling and sensitivity to nonverbal cues. In D. J. Canary & K. Dindia (Eds.), *Sex differences and similarities in communication: Critical essays and empirical investigations of sex and gender in interaction* (pp. 155-178). Mahwah, NJ: Lawrence Erlbaum.

Hall, J. K. (1993). Tengo una bomba: The paralinguistic and linguistic conventions of the oral practice Chismeando. *Research on Language and Social Interaction, 26,* 55-83.

Halmari, H. (1995). The organization of episode structure in Finnish/Finnish and Finish/Anglo-American business telephone conversations: An intercultural perspective. ERIC Clearinghouse: FL022794 (Accession No. ED386914).

Hambrick, R. S. (1991). *The management skills builder: Self-directed learning strategies for career development.* New York: Praeger.

Haney, W. (1973). *Communication and organizational behavior: Text and cases* (3rd ed.). Homewood, IL: Irwin.

Haridakis, P. M., & Rubin, A. M. (2003). Motivation for watching television violence and viewer aggression. *Mass Communication and Society, 6* (February), 29-56.

Harmon, M. D. (2001). Affluenza: Television use and cultivation of materialism. *Mass Communication & Society, 4* (November), 405-418.

Harnack, A., & Kleppinger, E. (1997). *Online! The Internet guide for students and writers.* New York: St. Martin's.

Hart, R. P., Carlson, R. E., & Eadie, W. F. (1980). Attitudes toward communication and the assessment of rhetorical sensitivity. *Communication Monographs, 47,* 1-22.

Hatfield, E., & Rapson, R. L. (1996). *Love and sex: Cross-cultural perspectives.* Boston: Allyn & Bacon.

Havlena, W. J., Holbrook, M. B., & Lehmann, D. R. (1989). Assessing the validity of emotional typologies. *Psychology and Marketing, 6* (Summer), 97-112.

Hayakawa, S. I., & Hayakawa, A. R. (1990). *Language in thought and action* (5th ed.). New York: Harcourt Brace Jovanovich.

Hays, R. B. (1989). The day-to-day functioning of close versus casual friendships. *Journal of Social and Personal Relationships, 6,* 21-37.

Heap, J. L. (1992). Seeing snubs: An introduction to sequential analysis of classroom interaction. *Journal of Classroom Interaction, 27,* 23-28.

Heasley, J. B., Babbitt, C. E., & Burbach, H. J. (1995). Gender differences in college students' perceptions of "fighting words." *Sociological Viewpoints, 11* (Fall), 30-40.

Hecht, M. L. (1978a). The conceptualization and measurement of interpersonal communication satisfaction. *Human Communication Research, 4,* 253-264.

Hecht, M. L. (1978b). Toward a conceptualization of communication satisfaction. *Quarterly Journal of Speech, 64,* 47-62.

Hecht, M. L., Collier, M. J., & Ribeau, S. (1993). *African American communication: Ethnic identity and cultural interpretation.* Thousand Oaks, CA: Sage.

Heenehan, M. (1997). *Networking.* New York: Random House.

Heiskell, T. L., & Rychiak, J. F. (1986). The therapeutic relationship: Inexperienced therapists' affective preference and empathic communication. *Journal of Social and Personal Relationships, 3,* 267-274.

Hellweg, S. A. (1992). Organizational grapevines. In K. L. Hutchinson (Ed.), *Readings in organizational communication* (pp. 159-172). Dubuque, IA: William C. Brown.

Hendrick, C., & Hendrick, S. (1990). A relationship-specific version of the love attitudes scale. In J. W. Heulip (Ed.), *Handbook of replication research in the behavioral and social sciences* [Special issue]. *Journal of Social Behavior and Personality, 5,* 239-254.

Henley, N. M. (1977). *Body politics: Power, sex, and nonverbal communication.* Englewood Cliffs, NJ: Prentice-Hall.

Herrick, J. A. (2004). *Argumentation: Understanding and shaping arguments* (updated edition). State College, PA: Strata.

Hersey, P., Blanchard, K. H., & Johnson, D. E. (2001). *Management of organizational behavior: Leading human resources* (8th ed.). Upper Saddle River, NJ: Prentice-Hall.

Hess, E. H. (1975). *The tell-tale eye.* New York: Van Nostrand Reinhold.

Hess, E. H., Seltzer, A. L., & Schlien, J. M. (1965). Pupil response of hetero- and homosexual males to pictures of men and women: A pilot study. *Journal of Abnormal Psychology, 70,* 165-168.

Hess, U., Kappas, A., McHugo, G. J., Lanzetta, J. T., et al. (1992). The facilitative effect of facial expression on the self-generation of emotion. *International Journal of Psychophysiology, 12* (May), 251-265.

Hewitt, J. P. (1998). *The myth of self-esteem: Finding happiness and solving problems in America.* New York: St. Martin's Press.

Hewitt, J., & Stokes, R. (1975). Disclaimers. *American Sociological Review, 40,* 1-11.

Hickson, M. L., Stacks, D. W., & Moore, N. J. (2003). *Nonverbal communication: Studies and applications.* Los Angeles: Roxbury.

Hilton, L. (2000). They heard it through the grapevine. *South Florida Business Journal, 21* (August), 53.

Himle, J. A., Abelson, J. L, & Haghightgou, H. (1999). Effect of alcohol on social phobic anxiety. *American Journal of Psychiatry, 156* (August), 1237-1243.

Hirokawa, R. Y., & Wagner, A. E. (2004). Superior-subordinate influence in organizations. In J. S. Seiter & R. H. Gass (Eds.), *Perspectives on persuasion, social influence, and compliance gaining* (pp. 337-351). Boston: Allyn & Bacon.

Hirokawa, R. Y., & Miyahara, A. (1986). A comparison of influence strategies utilized by managers in American and Japanese organizations. *Communication Quarterly, 34,* 250-265.

Hocker, J. L., & Wilmot, W. W. (1985). *Interpersonal conflict* (2nd ed.). Dubuque, IA: William C. Brown.

Hoffner, C., et al. (2001). The third-person effect in perceptions of the influence of television violence. *Journal of Communication, 51* (June), 283-299.

Hofstede, G. (1984). *Culture's consequences: International differences in work-related values.* Thousand Oaks, CA: Sage.

Hofstede, G. (1997). *Cultures and organizations: Software of the mind.* New York: McGraw-Hill.

Hofstede, G. (Ed.). (1998). *Masculinity and femininity: The taboo dimension of national cultures.* Thousand Oaks, CA: Sage.

Hofstetter, C. R., & Gianos, C. L. (1997). Political talk radio: Actions speak louder than words. *Journal of Broadcasting and Electronic Media, 41* (Fall), 501-515.

Hoft, N. L. (1995). *International technical communication: How to export information about high technology.* New York: Wiley.

Holden, J. M. (1991). The most frequent personality priority pairings in marriage and marriage counseling. *Individual Psychology Journal of Adlerian Theory, Research, and Practice, 47* (September), 392-398.

Holmes, J. (1986). Compliments and compliment responses in New Zealand English. *Anthropological Linguistics, 28,* 485-508.

Holmes, J. (1995). *Women, men and politeness.* New York: Longman.

Hosman, L. A. (1989). The evaluative consequences of hedges, hesitations, and intensifiers: Powerful and powerless speech styles. *Human Communication Research, 15,* 383-406.

Hui, H., & Luk, C. L. (1997). Industrial/organizational psychology. In J. W. Berry, M. H. Segall, & C. Kagitcibasi (Eds.), *Handbook of cross-cultural psychology: Vol. 3. Social behavior and applications* (pp. 371-411). Boston: Allyn & Bacon.

Hunt, M. O. (2000). Status, religion, and the "belief in a just world": Comparing African Americans, Latinos, and whites. *Social Science Quarterly, 81* (March), 325-343.

Iizuka, Y. (1993). Regulators in Japanese conversation. *Psychological Reports, 72* (February), 203-209.

Imahori, T. T., & Cupach, W. R. (1994). A cross-cultural comparison of the interpretation and management of face: U.S. American and Japanese responses to embarrassing predicaments. *International Journal of Intercultural Relations, 18* (Spring), 193-219.

Infante, D. A. (1988). *Arguing constructively.* Prospect Heights, IL: Waveland Press.

Infante, D. A., & Rancer, A. S. (1982). A conceptualization and measure of argumentativeness. *Journal of Personality Assessment, 46,* 72-80.

Infante, D. A., & Rancer, A. S. (1995). Argumentativeness and verbal aggressiveness: A review of recent theory and research. In B. R. Burleson (Ed.), *Communication Yearbook 19.* Thousand Oaks, CA: Sage.

Infante, D. A., Rancer, A. S., & Womack, D. F. (2002). *Building communication theory* (4th ed.). Prospect Heights, IL: Waveland Press.

Infante, D. A., & Wigley, C. J. (1986). Verbal aggressiveness: An interpersonal model and measure. *Communication Monographs, 53,* 61–69.

Ingram, M. P. B. (1998). A study of transformative aspects of career change experiences and implications for current models of career development. (Doctoral dissertation, Texas A&M University, 1998). *Dissertation Abstracts International, 58,* 4156A.

Insel, P. M., & Jacobson, L. F. (Eds.). (1975). *What do you expect? An inquiry into self-fulfilling prophecies.* Menlo Park, CA: Cummings.

Jablin, F. M. (1981). Cultivating imagination: Factors that enhance and inhibit creativity in brainstorming groups. *Human Communication Research, 7,* 245–258.

Jacobs, A. J. (1995, December 8). Talkin' trash. *Entertainment Weekly,* pp. 42–43.

Jacobson, D. (1999). Impression formation in cyberspace: Online expectations and offline experiences in text-based virtual communities. *Journal of Computer-Mediated Communication, 5,* n.p.

Jaffe, C. (1998). *Public speaking: Concepts and skills for a diverse society* (2nd ed.). Belmont, CA: Wadsworth.

Jaksa, J. A., & Pritchard, M. S. (1994). *Communication ethics: Methods of analysis* (2nd ed.). Belmont, CA: Wadsworth.

James, D. L. (1995). *The executive guide to Asia-Pacific communications.* New York: Kodansha International.

James, P., & Weingarten, J. (1995). *Internet guide for windows 95.* Research Triangle Park, NC: Ventana.

James-Catalano, C. N. (1996). *Researching on the World Wide Web.* Rocklin, CA: Prima.

Jamieson, K. H., & Campbell, K. K. (1992). *The interplay of influence* (3rd ed.). Belmont, CA: Wadsworth.

Jandt, F. E. (2004). *Intercultural communication* (4th ed.). Thousand Oaks, CA: Sage.

Janis, I. (1983). *Victims of group thinking: A psychological study of foreign policy decisions and fiascoes* (2nd ed.). Boston: Houghton Mifflin.

Jaworski, A. (1993). *The power of silence: Social and pragmatic perspectives.* Thousand Oaks, CA: Sage.

Jecker, J., & Landy, D. (1969). Liking a person as a function of doing him a favor. *Human Relations, 22,* 371–378.

Jeffres, L. W., Neuendorf, K. A., & Atkin, D. (1999). Spirals of silence: Expressing opinions when the climate of opinion is unambiguous. *Political Communication, 16* (April–June), 115–131.

Jessmer, S. L., & Anderson, D. (2001). The effect of politeness and grammar on user perceptions of electronic mail. *North American Journal of Psychology, 3,* 331–346.

Johannesen, R. L. (1974). The functions of silence: A plea for communication research. *Western Speech, 38* (Winter), 25–35.

Johannesen, R. L. (2001). *Ethics in human communication* (6th ed.). Prospect Heights, IL: Waveland Press.

Johansson, W., & Percy, W. A. (1994). *Outing: Shattering the conspiracy of silence.* New York: Harrington Park Press.

Johnson, K. (1998, May 5). Self-image is suffering from lack of esteem. *New York Times,* p. F7.

Johnson, M. P. (1973). Commitment: A conceptual structure and empirical application. *Sociological Quarterly, 14,* 395–406.

Johnson, M. P. (1982). Social and cognitive features of the dissolution of commitment to relationships. In S. Duck (Ed.), *Personal Relationships: 4. Dissolving personal relationships* (pp. 51–73). New York: Academic Press.

Johnson, M. P. (1991). Commitment to personal relationships. In W. H. Jones & D. Perlman (Eds.), *Advances in personal relationships* (Vol. 3, pp. 117–143). London: Jessica Kingsley.

Johnson, S. A. (1993). *When "I love you" turns violent: Emotional and physical abuse in dating relationships.* Far Hills, NJ: New Horizon Press.

Johnson, S. D., & Bechler, C. (1998). Examining the relationships between listening effectiveness and leadership emergence: Perceptions, behaviors, and recall. *Small Group Research, 29* (August), 452–471.

Joiner, T. E. (1994). Contagious depression: Existence, specificity to depressed symptoms, and the role of reassurance seeking. *Journal of Personality and Social Psychology, 67,* 287–296.

Joinson, A. N. (2001). Self-disclosure in computer-mediated communication. The role of self-awareness and visual anonymity. *European Journal of Social Psychology, 31* (March–April), 177–192.

Jones, E. E., et al. (1984). *Social stigma: The psychology of marked relationships.* New York: W. H. Freeman.

Jones, E. E., & Davis, K. E. (1965). From acts to dispositions: The attribution process in person perception. In L. Berkowitz (Ed.), *Advances in experimental social psychology* (Vol. 2, pp. 219–266). New York: Academic Press.

Jones, S. (1986). Sex differences in touch communication. *Western Journal of Speech Communication, 50,* 227–241.

Jones, S., & Yarbrough, A. E. (1985). A naturalistic study of the meanings of touch. *Communication Monographs, 52,* 19–56. A version of this paper appears in DeVito and Hecht (1990).

Jourard, S. M. (1968). *Disclosing man to himself.* New York: Van Nostrand Reinhold.

Jourard, S. M. (1971a). *Self-disclosure.* New York: Wiley.

Jourard, S. M. (1971b). *The transparent self* (Rev. ed.). New York: Van Nostrand Reinhold.

Joyner, R. (1993). An auto-interview on the need for E-prime. *Etc.: A Review of General Semantics, 50* (Fall), 317–325.

Kanner, B. (1989, April 3). Color schemes. *New York Magazine,* pp. 22–23.

Kanter, A. B. (1995). *The essential book of interviewing: Everything you need to know from both sides of the table.* New York: Random House.

Kapoor, S., Wolfe, A., & Blue, J. (1995). Universal values structure and individualism–collectivism: A U.S. test. *Communication Research Reports, 12* (Spring), 112–123.

Kealey, D. J., & Ruben, B. D. (1983). Cross-cultural personnel selection criteria, issues, and methods. In D. Landis & R. W. Brislin (Eds.), *Handbook of intercultural training. Vol. 1: Issues in theory and design* (pp. 155–175). NY: Pergamon.

Kearney, P., Plax, T. G., Richmond, V. P., & McCroskey, J. C. (1984). Power in the classroom IV: Alternatives to discipline. In R. B. Bostrom (Ed.), *Communication Yearbook* (8th ed., pp. 724–746). Thousand Oaks, CA: Sage.

Kelley, H. H. (1979). *Personal relationships: Their structures and processes.* Hillsdale, NJ: Erlbaum.

Kelly, P. K. (1994). *Team decision-making techniques.* Irvine, CA: Richard Chang Associates.

Kennedy, C. W., & Camden, C. T. (1988). A new look at interruptions. *Western Journal of Speech Communication, 47,* 45–58.

Kennedy, J. L. (1996). *Job interviews for dummies.* New York: Hungry Minds.

Ketcham, H. (1958). *Color planning for business and industry.* New York: Harper.

Keyes, R. (1980). *The height of your life.* New York: Warner Books.

Kiel, J. M. (1999). Reshaping Maslow's hierarchy of needs to reflect today's education and managerial philosophies. *Journal of Instructional Psychology, 26* (September), 167–168.

Kim, H. J. (1991). Influence of language and similarity on initial intercultural attraction. In S. Ting-Toomey & F. Korzenny (Eds.), *Cross-cultural interpersonal communication* (pp. 213–229). Thousand Oaks, CA: Sage.

Kim, M.-S., & Sharkey, W. F. (1995). Independent and interdependent construals of self: Explaining cultural patterns of interpersonal communication in multi-cultural organizational settings. *Communication Quarterly, 43* (Winter), 20–38.

Kim, S. H., & Smith, R. H. (1993). Revenge and conflict escalation. *Negotiation Journal, 9* (January), 37–43.

Kim, Y. Y. (1988). Communication and acculturation. In L. A. Samovar & R. E. Porter (Eds.), *Intercultural communication: A reader* (4th ed., pp. 344–354). Belmont, CA: Wadsworth.

Kindler, H. S. (1996). *Managing disagreement constructively* (Rev. ed.). Menlo Park, CA: Crisp Publications.

Kiraly, Z. (2000). The relationship between emotional self-disclosure of male and female adolescents' friendship. *Dissertation abstracts international: Section B. The Sciences and Engineering, 60* (February), 3619.

Kirby, D. (2001, January 30). Finessing interviews: Don't ask, do tell. *New York Times,* p. G2.

Klein, J. (Ed.). (1992). The E-prime controversy: A symposium [Special issue]. *Etc.: A Review of General Semantics, 49*(2).

Kleinfeld, N. R. (1992, October 25). The smell of money. *New York Times,* Section 9, pp. 1, 8.

Kleinke, C. L. (1986). *Meeting and understanding people.* New York: W. H. Freeman.

Kleinke, C. L., & Dean, G. O. (1990). Evaluation of men and women receiving positive and negative responses with various acquaintance strategies. *Journal of Social Behavior and Personality, 5,* 369–377.

Klineberg, O., & Hull, W. F. (1979). *At a foreign university: An international study of adaptation and coping.* New York: Praeger.

Knapp, M. L., & Hall, J. (1997). *Nonverbal behavior in human interaction* (4th ed.). New York: Holt, Rinehart & Winston.

Knapp, M. L., Hart, R. P., Friedrich, G. W., & Shulman, G. M. (1973). The rhetoric of goodbye: Verbal and nonverbal correlates of human leave-taking. *Communication Monographs, 40,* 182–198.

Knapp, M. L., & Taylor, E. H. (1995). Commitment and its communication in romantic relationships. In A. L. Weber & J. H. Harvey (Eds.), *Perspectives on close relationships* (pp. 153–175). Boston: Allyn & Bacon.

Knapp, M. L., & Vangelisti, A. L. (2000). *Interpersonal communication and human relationships* (4th ed.). Boston: Allyn & Bacon.

Knobloch, L. K., & Solomon, D. H. (1999). Measuring the sources and content of relational uncertainty. *Communication Studies, 50* (Winter), 261–278.

Kochman, T. (1981). *Black and white: Styles in conflict.* Chicago, IL: University of Chicago Press.

Kohn, A. (1989). Do religious people help more? Not so you'd notice. *Psychology Today* (December), 66–68.

Korda, M. (1975). *Power! How to get it, how to use it.* New York: Ballantine.

Korzybski, A. (1933). *Science and sanity.* Lakeville, CT: International Non-Aristotelian Library.

Kposowa, A. J. (2000). Marital status and suicide in the National Longitudinal Mortality Study. *Journal of Epidemiology and Community Health, 54* (April), 254–261.

Kramarae, C. (1981). *Women and men speaking.* Rowley, MA: Newbury House.

Kramarae, C. (1999). The language and nature of the Internet: The meaning of Global English. *New Media & Society, 1* (April), 47–53.

Kramer, R. (1997). Leading by listening: An empirical test of Carl Rogers's theory of human relationship using interpersonal assessments of leaders by followers. *Dissertation Abstracts International: Section A. Humanities and Social Sciences, 58* (August), 0514.

Krebs, G. L. (1990). *Organizational communication* (2nd ed.). New York: Longman.

Krivonos, P. D., & Knapp, M. L. (1975). Initiating communication: What do you say when you say hello? *Central States Speech Journal, 26,* 115–125.

Kurdek, L. A. (1994). Areas of conflict for gay, lesbian, and heterosexual couples: What couples argue about influences relationship satisfaction. *Journal of Marriage and the Family, 56* (November), 923–934.

Kurdek, L. A. (1995). Developmental changes in relationship quality in gay and lesbian cohabiting couples. *Developmental Psychology, 31* (January), 86–93.

Labott, S. M., Martin, R. B., Eason, P. S., & Berkey, E. Y. (1991). Social reactions to the expression of emotion. *Cognition and Emotion, 5* (September–November), 397–417.

Laing, M. (1993). Gossip: Does it play a role in the socialization of nurses? *Journal of Nursing Scholarship, 25* (Spring), 37–43.

Laing, R. D., Phillipson, H., & Lee, A. R. (1966). *Interpersonal perception.* New York: Springer.

Lamm, K., & Lamm, K. (1999). *10,000 ideas for term papers, projects, reports, and speeches* (5th ed.). New York: Arco.

Langer, E. J. (1989). *Mindfulness.* Reading, MA: Addison-Wesley.

Lantz, A. (2001). Meetings in a distributed group of experts: Comparing face-to-face, chat and collaborative virtual environments. *Behaviour and Information Technology, 20,* 111–117.

Lanzetta, J. T., Cartwright-Smith, J., & Kleck, R. E. (1976). Effects of nonverbal dissimulations on emotional experience and autonomic arousal. *Journal of Personality and Social Psychology, 33,* 354–370.

Larsen, R. J., Kasimatis, M., & Frey, K. (1992). Facilitating the furrowed brow: An unobtrusive test of the facial feedback hypothesis applied to unpleasant affect. *Cognition and Emotion, 6* (September), 321–338.

Lauer, C. S. (2003). Listen to this. *Modern Healthcare, 33* (February 10), 34.

Lawlor, J. (1998, August 27). Videoconferencing: From stage fright to stage presence. *New York Times,* p. G6.

Lazarsfeld, P. F., & Merton, R. K. (1951). Mass communication, popular taste, and organized social action. In L. Bryson (Ed.), *The communication of ideas* (pp. 95–118). New York: Harper & Row.

Lea, M., & Spears, R. (1995). Love at first byte? Building personal relationships over computer networks. In J. T. Wood & S. Duck (Eds.), *Under-studied relationships: Off the beaten track* (pp. 197–233). Thousand Oaks, CA: Sage.

Leaper, C., & Holliday, H. (1995). Gossip in same-gender and cross-gender friends' conversations. *Personal Relationships, 2* (September), 237–246.

Leathers, D. G. (1997). *Successful nonverbal communication: Principles and applications* (3rd ed.). New York: Macmillan.

Lebow, J. (1998). Not just talk, maybe some risk: The therapeutic potentials and pitfalls of computer-mediated conversation. *Journal of Marital and Family Therapy, 24* (April), 203–206.

Lederer, W. J. (1984). *Creating a good relationship.* New York: Norton.

Lee, A. M., & Lee, E. B. (1972). *The fine art of propaganda.* San Francisco: International Society for General Semantics.

Lee, A. M., & Lee, E. B. (1995). The iconography of propaganda analysis. *Etc.: A Review of General Semantics, 52* (Spring), 13–17.

Lee, C., & Gudykunst, W. B. (2001). Attraction in initial interethnic interactions. *International Journal of Intercultural Relations, 25* (July), 373-387.

Lee, F. (1993). Being polite and keeping MUM: How bad news is communicated in organizational hierarchies. *Journal of Applied Social Psychology, 23,* 1124-1149.

Lee, H. O., & Boster, F. J. (1992). Collectivism-individualism in perceptions of speech rate: A cross-cultural comparison. *Journal of Cross-Cultural Psychology, 23,* 377-388.

Lee, J. A. (1976). *The colors of love.* New York: Bantam.

Lee, K. (2000, November 1). Information overload threatens employee productivity. *Employee Benefit News* (Securities Data Publishing, Inc.), p. 1.

Lee, R. L. M. (1984). Malaysian queue culture: An ethnography of urban public behavior. *Southeast Asian Journal of Social Science, 12,* 36-50.

Leung, K. (1987). Some determinants of reactions to procedural models for conflict resolution: A cross-national study. *Journal of Personality and Social Psychology, 53,* 898-908.

Leung, K. (1988). Some determinants of conflict avoidance. *Journal of Cross-Cultural Psychology, 19* (March), 125-136.

Leung, S. A. (2001). Editor's introduction. *Asian Journal of Counseling, 8,* 107-109.

Lever, J. (1995, August 22). The 1995 *Advocate* survey of sexuality and relationships: The women, lesbian sex survey. *The Advocate, 687/688,* pp. 22-30.

Levesque, M. J. (1995). Excuses as a method of impression management: Toward an understanding of the determinants of excuse effectiveness. *Dissertation Abstractions International Section B: The Sciences and Engineering, 56* (August), 1150.

Levine, D. (2000). Virtual attraction: What rocks your boat. *CyberPsychology & Behavior, 3* (August), 565-573.

LeVine, R., & Bartlett, K. (1984). Pace of life, punctuality, and coronary heart disease in six countries. *Journal of Cross-Cultural Psychology, 15,* 233-255.

Lewin, K. (1947). *Human relations.* New York: Harper & Row.

Lewis, D. (1989). *The secret language of success.* New York: Carroll & Graf.

Lewis, M. (2001, July 15). Faking it. *The New York Times Magazine,* pp. 32-37, 44, 61-63.

Lewis, P. H. (1995, November 13). The new Internet gatekeepers. *New York Times,* pp. D1, D6.

Li, C., & Shi, K. (2003). Transformational leadership and its relationship with leadership effectiveness. *Psychological Science, 26* (January), 115-117.

Li, H. Z. (1999). Communicating information in conversations: A cross-cultural comparison. *International Journal of Intercultural Relations, 23* (May), 387-409.

Lindeman, M., Harakka, T., & Keltikangas-Jarvinen, L. (1997). Age and gender differences in adolescents' reactions to conflict situations: Aggression, prosociality, and withdrawal. *Journal of Youth and Adolescence, 26* (June), 339-351.

Lloyd, S. R. (2001). *Developing positive assertiveness* (3rd ed.). Menlo Park, CA: Crisp Publications.

Loden, M. (1986, May 15). Feminine leadership. *Vital Speeches of the Day,* 472-475.

Lu, S. (1998, October 9). *Critical reflections on phatic communication research: schematizations, limitations and alternatives.* Paper delivered at the New York State Speech Communication Association, Monticello, New York.

Lucas, S. (2004). *The art of public speaking* (8th ed.). New York: McGraw-Hill.

Luft, J. (1969). *Of human interaction* (3rd ed.). Palo Alto, CA: Mayfield.

Luft, J. (1984). *Group processes: An introduction to group dynamics* (3rd ed.). Palo Alto, CA: Mayfield.

Lukens, J. (1978). Ethnocentric speech. *Ethnic Groups, 2,* 35-53.

Lumsden, G., & Lumsden, D. (1996). *Communicating in groups and teams* (2nd ed.). Belmont, CA: Wadsworth.

Lustig, M. W., & Koester, J. (2003). *Intercultural competence: Interpersonal communication across cultures* (4th ed.). New York: Longman.

Ma, K. (1996). *The modern Madame Butterfly: Fantasy and reality in Japanese cross-cultural relationships.* Rutland, VT: Charles E. Tuttle.

Ma, R. (1992). The role of unofficial intermediaries in interpersonal conflicts in the Chinese culture. *Communication Quarterly, 40* (Summer), 269-278.

MacLachlan, J. (1979). What people really think of fast talkers. *Psychology Today, 13* (November), 113-117.

Maggio, R. (1997). *Talking about people: A guide to fair and accurate language.* Phoenix, AZ: Oryx Press.

Main, F., & Oliver, R. (1988). Complementary, symmetrical, and parallel personality priorities as indicators of marital adjustment. *Individual Psychology Journal of Adlerian Theory, Research, and Practice, 44* (September), 324-332.

Malandro, L. A., Barker, L., & Barker, D. A. (1989). *Nonverbal communication* (2nd ed.). New York: Random House.

Malinowski, B. (1923). The problem of meaning in primitive languages. In C. K. Ogden & I. A. Richards, *The meaning of meaning* (pp. 296-336). New York: Harcourt Brace Jovanovich.

Mallen, M. J., Day, S. X., & Green, M. A. (2003). Online versus face-to-face conversation: An examination of relational and discourse variables. *Psychotherapy: Theory, Research, Practice, Training, 40* (Spring-Summer), 155-163.

Manes, J., & Wolfson, N. (1981). The compliment formula. In F. Coulmas (Ed.), *Conversational routines* (pp. 115-132). The Hague: Mouton.

Mao, L. R. (1994). Beyond politeness theory: "Face" revisited and renewed. *Journal of Pragmatics, 21* (May), 451-486.

Marien, M. (1992). *Vital Speeches of the Day* (March 15), 340-344.

Markman, H. J., Silvern, L., Clements, M., & Kraft-Hanak, S. (1993). Men and women dealing with conflict in heterosexual relationships. *Journal of Social Issues, 49* (Fall), 107-125.

Marsh, P. (1988). *Eye to eye: How people interact.* Topfield, MA: Salem House.

Marshall, E. (1983). *Eye language: Understanding the eloquent eye.* New York: New Trend.

Marshall, L. L., & Rose, P. (1987). Gender, stress, and violence in the adult relationships of a sample of college students. *Journal of Social and Personal Relationships, 4,* 299-316.

Martin, G. N. (1998). Human electroencephalographic (EEG) response to olfactory stimulation: Two experiments using the aroma of food. *International Journal of Psychophysiology, 30,* 287-302.

Martin, M. M., & Anderson, C. M. (1995). Roommate similarity: Are roommates who are similar in their communication traits more satisfied? *Communication Research Reports, 12* (Spring), 46-52.

Martin, M. M., & Rubin, R. B. (1994). Development of a communication flexibility measure. *The Southern Communication Journal, 59* (Winter), 171-178.

Martin, S. L., & Klimoski, R. J. (1990). Use of verbal protocols to trace cognitions associated with self- and supervisor evaluations of performance. *Organizational Behavior and Human Decision Processes, 46,* 135-154.

Maslow, A. (1970). *Motivation and personality.* New York: HarperCollins.

Mastin, T. (1998). Employees' understanding of employer-sponsored retirement plans: A knowledge gap perspective. *Public Relations Review, 24* (Winter), 521-534.

Matsumoto, D. (1991). Cultural influences on facial expressions of emotion. *Southern Communication Journal, 56* (Winter), 128–137.

Matsumoto, D. (1994). *People: Psychology from a cultural perspective.* Pacific Grove, CA: Brooks/Cole.

Matsumoto, D. (1996). *Culture and psychology.* Pacific Grove, CA: Brooks/Cole.

Matsumoto, D., & Kudoh, T. (1993). American-Japanese cultural differences in attributions of personality based on smiles. *Journal of Nonverbal Behavior, 17,* 231–243.

May, R. A. B. (1999). Tavern culture and television viewing: The influence of local viewing culture on patron's reception of television programs. *Journal of Contemporary Ethnography, 28* (February), 69–99.

McAuley, E., Blissmer, B., Katula, J., Duncan, T. E., & Mihalko, S. L. (2000). Physical activity, self-esteem, and self-efficacy relationships in older adults: A randomized controlled trial. *Annals of Behavioral Medicine, 22* (Spring), 131–139.

McCall, D. L., & Green, R. G. (1991). Symmetricality and complementarity and their relationship to marital stability. *Journal of Divorce and Remarriage, 15,* 23–32.

McCombs, M. E., Lopez-Escobar, E., & Llamas, J. P. (2000). Setting the agenda of attributes in the 1996 Spanish general election. *Journal of Communication, 50* (Spring), 77–92.

McCombs, M. E., & Shaw, D. L. (1972). The agenda-setting function of mass media. *Public Opinion Quarterly, 36,* 176–185.

McCombs, M. E., & Shaw, D. L. (1993). The evolution of agenda-setting research: Twenty-five years in the marketplace of ideas. *Journal of Communication, 43,* 58–67.

McCroskey, J. C. (1997). *Introduction to rhetorical communication* (7th ed.). Englewood Cliffs, NJ: Prentice-Hall.

McCroskey, J. C., & Richmond, V. P. (1995). Correlates of compulsive communication: Quantitative and qualitative characteristics. *Communication Quarterly, 43* (Winter), 39–52.

McCroskey, J., & Wheeless, L. (1976). *Introduction to human communication.* Boston: Allyn & Bacon.

McGill, M. E. (1985). *The McGill report on male intimacy.* New York: Harper & Row.

McGuire, W. J. (1964). Inducing resistance to persuasion: Some contemporary approaches. In L. Berkowitz (Ed.), *Advances in experimental social psychology* (Vol. 1, pp. 191–229). New York: Academic Press.

McKerrow, R. E., Gronbeck, B. E., Ehninger, D., & Monroe, A. H. (2000). *Principles and types of speech communication* (14th ed.). Boston: Allyn & Bacon.

McLaughlin, M. L. (1984). *Conversation: How talk is organized.* Thousand Oaks, CA: Sage.

McLean, P. A., & Jones, B. D. (1992). Machiavellianism and business education. *Psychological Reports, 71* (August), 57–58.

McLoyd, V., & Wilson, L. (1992). Telling them like it is: The role of economic and environmental factors in single mothers' discussions with their children. *American Journal of Community Psychology, 20* (August), 419–444.

McNatt, D. B. (2001). Ancient Pygmalion joins contemporary management: A meta-analysis of the result. *Journal of Applied Psychology, 85,* 314–322.

Medora, N. P., Larson, J. H., Hortacsu, N., & Dave, P. (2002). Perceived attitudes towards romanticism: A cross-cultural study of American, Asian-Indian, and Turkish young adults. *Journal of Comparative Family Studies, 33* (Spring), 155–178.

Mehrabian, A. (1976). *Public places and private spaces.* New York: Basic Books.

Meier, A. (2000). Offering social support via the Internet: A case study of an online support group for social workers. *Journal of Technology in Human Services, 1,* 237–267.

Meier, A. (2002). An online stress management support group for social workers. *Journal of Technology in Human Services, 20,* 107–132.

Merton, R. K. (1957). *Social theory and social structure.* New York: Free Press.

Messick, R. M., & Cook, K. S. (Eds.). (1983). *Equity theory: Psychological and sociological perspectives.* New York: Praeger.

Metts, S. (1989). An exploratory investigation of deception in close relationships. *Journal of Social and Personal Relationships, 6* (May), 159–179.

Metts, S., & Grohskopf, E. (2003). Impression management: Goals, strategies, and skills. In J. O. Greene & B. R. Burleson (Eds.), *Handbook of communication and social interaction skills* (pp. 357–399). Mahwah, NJ: Lawrence Erlbaum.

Metts, S., & Planalp, S. (2002). Emotional communication. In M. L. Knapp & J. A. Daly (Eds.), *Handbook of interpersonal communication* (3rd ed., pp. 339–373). Thousand Oaks, CA: Sage.

Meyer, J. R. (1994). Effect of situational features on the likelihood of addressing face needs in requests. *Southern Communication Journal, 59* (Spring), 240–254.

Midooka, K. (1990). Characteristics of Japanese style communication. *Media, Culture and Society, 12* (October), 477–489.

Miller, D. T., Turnbull, W., & McFarland, C. (1988). Particularistic and universalistic evaluation in the social comparison process. *Journal of Personality and Social Psychology, 55* (December), 908–917.

Miller, G. R. (1978). The current state of theory and research in interpersonal communication. *Human Communication Research, 4,* 164–178.

Miller, G. R., & Burgoon, J. (1990). Factors affecting assessments of witness credibility. In J. A. DeVito & M. L. Hecht (Eds.), *The nonverbal communication reader* (pp. 340–357). Prospect Heights, IL: Waveland Press.

Miller, G. R., & Parks, M. R. (1982). Communication in dissolving relationships. In S. Duck (Ed.), *Personal relationships. 4: Dissolving personal relationships.* New York: Academic Press.

Miller, J. G. (1984). Culture and the development of everyday social explanation. *Journal of Personality and Social Psychology, 46,* 961–978.

Miller, M. J., & Wilcox, C. T. (1986). Measuring perceived hassles and uplifts among the elderly. *Journal of Human Behavior and Learning, 3,* 38–46.

Moghaddam, F. M., Taylor, D. M., & Wright, S. C. (1993). *Social psychology in cross-cultural perspective*. New York: W. H. Freeman.

Mok, T. A. (1998a). Asian Americans and standards of attractiveness: What's in the eye of the beholder? *Cultural Diversity & Mental Health, 4,* 1–18.

Mok, T. A. (1998b). Getting the message: Media images and stereotypes and their effect on Asian Americans. *Cultural Diversity and Ethnic Minority Psychology, 4,* 185–202.

Molloy, J. (1975). *Dress for success.* New York: P. H. Wyden.

Molloy, J. (1977). *The woman's dress for success book.* New York: Warner Books.

Molloy, J. (1981). *Molloy's live for success.* New York: Bantam.

Monin, B. (2003). The warm glow heuristic: When liking leads to familiarity. *Journal of Personality and Social Psychology, 85* (December), 1035–1048.

Montagu, A. (1971). *Touching: The human significance of the skin.* New York: Harper & Row.

Moon, D. G. (1996). Concepts of "culture": Implications for intercultural communication research. *Communication Quarterly, 44* (Winter), 70–84.

Moore, A., Masterson, J. T., Christophel, D. M., & Shea, K. A. (1996). College teacher immediacy and student ratings of instruction. *Communication Education, 45,* 29–39.

Morales, J. (1995, May 2). London: Death by outing. *The Advocate, 680,* pp. 20–22.

Morgan, M., & Shanahan, J. (1991). Television and the cultivation of political attitudes in Argentina. *Journal of Communication, 41* (Winter), 88–103.

Morreale, S. P., Osborn, M. M., & Pearson, J. C. (2000). Why communication is important: A rationale for the centrality of the study of communication. *Journal of the Association for Communication Administration, 29* (January), 1–25.

Morris, D. (1977). *Manwatching: A field guide to human behavior.* New York: Abrams.

Mullen, B., Tara, A., Salas, E., & Driskell, J. E. (1994). Group cohesiveness and quality of decision making: An integration of tests of the groupthink hypothesis. *Small Group Research, 25,* 189–204.

Mullen, B., Salas, E., & Driskell, J. (1989). Salience, motivation, and artifact as contributions to the relation between participation rate and leadership. *Journal of Experimental Social Psychology, 25* (November), 545–559.

Murata, K. (1994). Intrusive or co-operative? A cross-cultural study of interruption. *Journal of Pragmatics, 21* (April), 385–400.

Murphy, R. (1958). The speech as literary genre. *Quarterly Journal of Speech, 44* (April), 117–127.

Naifeh, S., & Smith, G. W. (1984). *Why can't men open up? Overcoming men's fear of intimacy.* New York: Clarkson N. Potter.

Naisbitt, J. (1984). *Megatrends: Ten new directions transforming our lives.* New York: Warner.

Nakanishi, M. (1986). Perceptions of self-disclosure in initial interaction: A Japanese sample. *Human Communication Research, 13* (Winter), 167–190.

Napier, R. W., & Gershenfeld, M. K. (1992). *Groups: Theory and experience* (5th ed.). Boston: Houghton Mifflin.

National Institute of Mental Health. (1982). *Television and behavior: Ten years of scientific progress and implications for the eighties.* Rockville, MD: National Institute of Mental Health.

Neff, K. D., & Harter, S. (2002). The authenticity of conflict resolutions among adult couples: Does women's other-oriented behavior reflect their true selves? *Sex Roles, 47* (November), 403–417.

Neugarten, B. (1979). Time, age, and the life cycle. *American Journal of Psychiatry, 136,* 887–894.

Neuliep, J. W., & Grohskopf, E. L. (2000). Uncertainty reduction and communication satisfaction during initial interaction: An initial test and replication of a new axiom. *Communication Reports, 13,* 67–77.

Ng, S. H., Loong, C. S. F., He, A. P., Liu, J. H., & Weatherall, A. (2000). Communication correlates of individualism and collectivism: Talk directed at one or more addressees in family conversations. *Journal of Language and Social Psychology, 19* (March), 26–45.

Nice, M. L., & Katzev, R. (1998). Internet romantics: The frequency and nature of romantic on-line relationships. *CyberPsychology and Behavior, 1* (Fall), 217–223.

Nicotera, A. M., & Rancer, A. S. (1994). The influence of sex on self-perceptions and social stereotyping of aggressive communication predispositions. *Western Journal of Communication, 58* (Fall), 283–307.

Noble, B. P. (1994, August 14). The gender wars: Talking peace. *New York Times,* p. 21.

Noelle-Neumann, E. (1973). Return to the concept of powerful mass media. In H. Eguchi & K. Sata (Eds.), *Studies in broadcasting: An international annual of broadcasting science* (pp. 67–112). Tokyo: Nippon Hoso Kyokai.

Noelle-Neumann, E. (1980). Mass media and social change in developed societies. In G. C. Wilhoit & H. de Bock (Eds.), *Mass communication review yearbook* (Vol. 1, pp. 657–678). Thousand Oaks, CA: Sage.

Noelle-Neumann, E. (1991). The theory of public opinion: The concept of the spiral of silence. In J. A. Anderson (Ed.), *Communication yearbook 14* (pp. 256–287). Thousand Oaks, CA: Sage.

Noller, P. (1993). Gender and emotional communication in marriage: Different cultures or differential social power? In *Emotional communication, culture, and power* [Special issue]. *Journal of Language and Social Psychology, 12* (March–June), 132–152.

Noller, P., & Fitzpatrick, M. A. (1993). *Communication in family relationships.* Englewood Cliffs, NJ: Prentice-Hall.

Northouse, P. G. (1997). *Leadership: Theory and practice.* Thousand Oaks, CA: Sage.

Oatley, K., & Duncan, E. (1994). The experience of emotions in everyday life. *Cognition and Emotion, 8,* 369–381.

Ober, C., Weitkamp, L. R., Cox, N., Dytch, H., Kostyu, D., & Elias, S. (1977). HLA and mate choice in humans. *American Journal of Human Genetics, 61,* 494–496.

Oberg, K. (1960). Culture shock: Adjustment to new cultural environments. *Practical Anthropology, 7,* 177–182.

Offerman, L. R., & Hellman, P. S. (1997). Culture's consequences for leadership behavior: National values in action. *Journal of Cross-Cultural Psychology, 28* (May), 342–351.

Oggins, J., Veroff, J., & Leber, D. (1993). Perceptions of marital interaction among black and white newlyweds. *Journal of Personality and Social Psychology, 65* (September), 494–511.

O'Hair, D., Cody, M. J., Goss, B., & Krayer, K. J. (1988). The effect of gender, deceit orientation and communicator style on macro-assessments of honesty. *Communication Quarterly, 36,* 77–93.

O'Hair, D., Cody, M. J., & McLaughlin, M. L. (1981). Prepared lies, spontaneous lies, Machiavellianism, and nonverbal communication. *Human Communication Research, 7,* 325–339.

O'Keefe, D. J. (1999). How to handle opposing arguments in persuasive messages: A meta-analytic review of the effects of one-sided and two-sided messages. In M. E. Roloff (Ed.), *Communication yearbook 22* (pp. 209–249). Thousand Oaks, CA: Sage.

Olday, D., & Wesley, B. (1990). Intimate relationship violence among divorcees. *Free Inquiry in Creative Sociology, 18* (May), 63–71.

O'Neill, R. M., & Sankowsky, D. (2001). The Caligula Phenomenon: Mentoring relationships and theoretical abuse. *Journal of Management Inquiry, 10,* 206–216.

Osborn, A. (1957). *Applied imagination* (Rev. ed.). New York: Scribners.

Osborn, M., & Osborn, S. (2000). *Speaking in public* (5th ed.). Boston: Houghton Mifflin.

Oswald, R. F. (2000). A member of the wedding? Heterosexism and family ritual. *Journal of Social and Personal Relationships, 17* (June), 349–368.

Page, R. A., & Balloun, J. L. (1978). The effect of voice volume on the perception of personality. *Journal of Social Psychology, 105,* 65–72.

Parks, M. R. (1995). Webs of influence in interpersonal relationships. In C. R. Berger & M. E. Burgoon (Eds.), *Communication and social influence processes* (pp. 155–178). East Lansing: Michigan State University Press.

Parks, M. R., & Floyd, K. (1996). Making friends in cyberspace. *Journal of Communication, 46* (Winter): 80–97.

Parks, M. R., & Roberts, L. D. (1998). "Making MOOsic": The development of personal relationships online and a comparison to their off-line counterparts. *Journal of Social and Personal Relationships, 15,* 517–537.

Parsons, C. K., Liden, R. C., & Bauer, T. N. (2001). Personal perception in employment interviews. In M. London (Ed.), *How people evaluate others in organizations* (pp. 67–90). Mahwah, NJ: Lawrence Erlbaum.

Patton, B. R., Giffin, K., & Patton, E. N. (1989). *Decision-making group interaction* (3rd ed.). New York: HarperCollins.

Paul, A. M. (2001). Self-help: Shattering the myths. *Psychology Today, 34,* 60ff.

Pearson, J. C. (1980). Sex roles and self-disclosure. *Psychological Reports, 47,* 640.

Pearson, J. C. (1993). *Communication in the family* (2nd ed.). New York: Harper & Row.

Pearson, J. C., & Spitzberg, B. H. (1990). *Interpersonal communication: Concepts, components, and contexts* (2nd ed.). Dubuque, IA: William C. Brown.

Pearson, J. C., West, R., & Turner, L. H. (1995). *Gender and communication* (3rd ed.). Dubuque, IA: William C. Brown.

Peck, J. (1995). TV talk shows as therapeutic discourse: The ideological labor of the televised talking cure. *Communication Theory, 5* (February), 58–81.

Penfield, J. (Ed.). (1987). *Women and language in transition*. Albany, NY: State University of New York Press.

Pennebaker, J. W. (1991). *Opening up: The healing power of confiding in others*. New York: Avon.

Peplau, L. A., & Perlman, D. (Eds.). (1982). *Loneliness: A sourcebook of current theory, research, and therapy*. New York: Wiley/Interscience.

Perlman, D., & Peplau, L. A. (1981). Toward a social psychology of loneliness. In S. Duck & R. Gilmour (Eds.), *Personal Relationships. 3: Personal Relationships in Disorder* (pp. 31–56). New York: Academic Press.

Perse, E. M., & Rubin, R. B. (1989). Attribution in social and parasocial relationhips. *Communication Research, 16* (February), 59–77.

Peters, R. (1987). *Practical intelligence: Working smarter in business and the professions*. New York: HarperCollins.

Peterson, C. C. (1996). The ticking of the social clock: Adults' beliefs about the timing of transition events. *International Journal of Aging and Human Development, 42,* 189–203.

Peterson, R. W. (1985). *Vital speeches of the day* (July), 549.

Petrocelli, W., & Repa, B. K. (1992). *Sexual harassment on the job.* Berkeley, CA: Nolo Press.

Petronio, S. (Ed.). (2000). *Balancing the secrets of private disclosures*. Mahwah, NJ: Erlbaum.

Petronio, S., & Bantz, C. (1991). Controlling the ramifications of disclosure: "Don't tell anybody but. . . ." *Journal of Language and Social Psychology, 10,* 263–269.

Petty, R. E., & Wegener, D. T. (1998). Attitude change: Multiple roles for persuasion variables. In D. T. Gilbert, S. T. Fiske, & G. Lindzey (Eds.), *The handbook of social psychology* (4th ed., Vol. 1, pp. 323–390). New York: McGraw-Hill.

Pierce, C. A., & Aquinis, H. (2001). A framework for investigating the link between workplace romance and sexual harassment. *Group and Organization Management, 26* (June), 206–229.

Pilkington, C. J., & Richardson, D. R. (1988). Perceptions of risk in intimacy. *Journal of Social and Personal Relationships, 5,* 503–508.

Pilkington, C., & Woods, S. P. (1999). Risk in intimacy as a chronically accessible schema. *Journal of Social and Personal Relationships, 16,* 249–263.

Piot, C. D. (1993). Secrecy, ambiguity, and the everyday in Kabre culture. *American Anthropologist, 95* (June), 353–370.

Pittenger, R. E., Hockett, C. F., & Danehy, J. J. (1960). *The first five minutes*. Ithaca, NY: Paul Martineau.

Place, K. S., & Becker, J. A. (1991). The influence of pragmatic competence on the likeability of grade school children. *Discourse Processes, 14* (April–June), 227–241.

Plutchik, R. (1980). *Emotion: A psycho-evolutionary synthesis*. New York: Harper & Row.

Pollack, A. (1995, August 7). A cyberspace front in a multicultural war. *New York Times*, pp. D1, D4.

Pornpitakpan, C. (2003). The effect of personality traits and perceived cultural similarity on attraction. *Journal of International Consumer Marketing, 15,* 5–30.

Porter, J. R., & Washington, R. E. (1993). Minority identity and self-esteem. *Annual Review of Sociology, 19,* 139–161.

Porter, R. H., & Moore, J. D. (1981). Human kin recognition by olfactory cues. *Physiology and Behavior, 27,* 493–495.

Porter, S., Brit, A. R., Yuille, J. C., & Lehman, D. R. (2000). Negotiating false memories: Interviewer and rememberer characteristics relate to memory distortion. *Psychological Science, 11* (November), 507–510.

Postman, N., & Powers, S. (1992). *How to watch TV news*. New York: Penguin.

Potter, W. J. (1986). Perceived reality and the cultivation hypothesis. *Journal of Broadcasting and Electronic Media, 30,* 159–174.

Potter, W. J., & Chang, I. C. (1990). Television exposure measures and the cultivation hypothesis. *Journal of Broadcasting and Electronic Media, 34,* 313–333.

Pratkanis, A. R. (2000). Altercasting as an influence tactic. In D. J. Terry & M. A. Hogg (Eds.), *Attitudes, behavior, and social context: The role of norms and group membership* (pp. 201–226). Mahwah, NJ: Erlbaum.

Pratkanis, A. R., & Aronson, E. (1991). *Age of propaganda: The everyday use and abuse of persuasion*. New York: W. H. Freeman.

Prisbell, M. (1994). Students' perceptions of teachers' use of affinity-seeking and its relationship to teachers' competence. *Perceptual and Motor Skills, 78* (April), 641–642.

Proctor, R. F. (1991). *An exploratory analysis of responses to owned messages in interpersonal communication*. Unpublished doctoral dissertation, Bowling Green University.

Prosky, P. S. (1992). Complementary and symmetrical couples. *Family Therapy, 19,* 215–221.

Prusank, D. T., Duran, R. L., & DeLillo, D. A. (1993). Interpersonal relationships in women's magazines: Dating and relating in the 1970s and 1980s. *Journal of Social and Personal Relationships, 10* (August), 307–320.

Pullum, Stephen J. (1991). Illegal questions in the selection interview: Going beyond contemporary business and professional communication textbooks. *Bulletin of the Association for Business Communication, 54* (September), 36–43.

Rabinowitz, F. E. (1991). The male-to-male embrace: Breaking the touch taboo in a men's therapy group. *Journal of Counseling and Development, 69* (July–August), 574–576.

Radford, M. L. (1998). Approach or avoidance? The role of nonverbal communication in the academic library user's decision to initiate a reference encounter. *Library Trends, 46* (Spring), 699–717.

Radford, M. L., Barnes, S. B., & Barr, L. R. (2002). *Web research: Selecting, evaluating and citing*. Boston: Allyn & Bacon.

Ramsey, S. J. (1981). The kinesics of femininity in Japanese women. *Language Sciences, 3,* 104–123.

Rancer, A. S. (1998). Argumentativeness. In J. C. McCroskey, J. A. Daly, M. M. Martin, & M. J. Beatty (Eds.), *Communication and personality: Trait perspectives* (pp. 149–170). Cresskill, NJ: Hampton Press.

Rancer, A. S., Kosberg, R. L., & Baukus, R. A. (1992). Beliefs about arguing as predictors of trait argumentativeness: Implications for training in argument and conflict management. *Communication Education, 41* (October), 375–387.

Raney, R. F. (2000, May 11). Study finds Internet of social benefit to users. *New York Times*, p. G7.

Rankin, P. (1929). Listening ability. *Proceedings of the Ohio State Educational Conference's Ninth Annual Session*.

Raven, R., Centers, C., & Rodrigues, A. (1975). The bases of conjugal power. In R. E. Cromwell & D. H. Olson (Eds.), *Power in families* (pp. 217–234). New York: Halsted Press.

Rawlins, W. K. (1989). A dialectical analysis of the tensions, functions, and strategic challenges of communication in young adult friendships. In J. A. Andersen (Ed.), *Communication yearbook 12* (pp. 157–189). Thousand Oaks, CA: Sage.

Rawlins, W. K. (1992). *Friendship matters: Communication, dialectics, and the life course*. Hawthorne, NY: Aldine DeGruyter.

Regan, P. C., Kocan, E. R., & Whitlock, T. (1998). Ain't love grand! A prototype analysis of the concept of romantic love. *Journal of Social and Personal Relationships, 15,* 411–420.

Reardon, K. K. (1987). *Where minds meet: Interpersonal communication*. Belmont, CA.: Wadsworth.

Rector, M., & Neiva, E. (1996). Communication and personal relationships in Brazil. In W. B. Gudykunst, S. Ting-Toomey, & T. Nishida, *Communication in personal relationships across cultures* (pp. 156–173). Thousand Oaks, CA: Sage.

Reisman, J. M. (1979). *Anatomy of friendship*. Lexington, MA: Lewis.

Reisman, J. M. (1981). Adult friendships. In S. Duck & R. Gilmour (Eds.), *Personal relationships. 2: Developing personal relationships* (pp. 205–230). New York: Academic Press.

Reynolds, C. L., & Schnoor, L. G. (Eds.). (1991). *1989 championship debates and speeches*. Normal, IL: American Forensic Association.

Rich, A. L. (1974). *Interracial communication*. New York: Harper & Row.

Richards, I. A. (1951). Communication between men: The meaning of language. In H. von Foerster (Ed.), *Cybernetics, transactions of the eighth conference*.

Richmond, V. P., & McCroskey, J. C. (1998). *Communication: Apprehension, avoidance, and effectiveness* (5th ed.). Boston: Allyn & Bacon.

Riggio, R. E. (1987). *The charisma quotient*. New York: Dodd, Mead.

Roach, D. K. (1991). The influence and effects of gender and status on university instructor affinity-seeking behavior. *Southern Communication Journal, 57* (Fall), 73–80.

Roberts, W. (1987). *Leadership secrets of Attila the Hun*. New York: Warner.

Robinson, J., & McArthur, L. Z. (1982). Impact of salient vocal qualities on casual attribution for a speaker's behavior. *Journal of Personality and Social Psychology, 43,* 236–247.

Robinson, W. P. (1993). Lying in the public domain. *American Behavioral Scientist, 36* (January), 359–382.

Rodman, G. (2001). *Making sense of media: An introduction to mass communication*. Boston: Allyn & Bacon.

Rodman, G., & Adler, R. (1997). *The new public speaking*. Fort Worth, TX: Harcourt Brace.

Rodriguez, M. (1988). Do Blacks and Hispanics evaluate assertive male and female characters differently? *Howard Journal of Communication, 1,* 101–107.

Roebuck, C. (1999). *Effective leadership: The essential guide to thinking and working smarter.* New York: American Management Association.

Rogers, C. (1970). *Carl Rogers on encounter groups*. New York: Harrow Books.

Rogers, C., & Farson, R. (1981). Active listening. In J. A. DeVito (Ed.), *Communication: Concepts and processes* (3rd ed., pp. 137–147). Englewood Cliffs, NJ: Prentice-Hall.

Rogers-Millar, E., & Millar, F. E. (1979). Domineeringness and dominance: A transactional view. *Human Communication Research* (Spring), 238–246.

Rollman, J. B., Krug, K., & Parente, F. (2000). The chat room phenomenon: Reciprocal communication in cyberspace. *CyberPsychology and Behavior, 3* (April), 161–166.

Ronfeldt, H. M., Kimerling, R., & Arias, I. (1998). Satisfaction with relationship power and the perpetration of dating violence. *Journal of Marriage & the Family, 60* (February), 70–78.

Rosenbaum, M. E. (1986). The repulsion hypothesis: On the nondevelopment of relationships. *Journal of Personality and Social Psychology, 51,* 1156–1166.

Rosenfeld, L. B. (1979). Self-disclosure avoidance: Why I am afraid to tell you who I am. *Communication Monographs, 46* (1979), 63–74.

Rosenfeld, L. B., & Bowen, G. L. (1991). Marital disclosure and marital satisfaction: Direct-effect versus interaction-effect models. *Western Journal of Speech Communication, 55* (Winter), 69–84.

Rosenthal, R. (2002). Covert communication in classrooms, clinics, courtroom, and cubicles. *American Psychologist, 57,* 839–849.

Rosenthal, R., & DePaulo, B. M. (1979). Sex differences in accommodation in nonverbal communication. In R. Rosenthal (Ed.), *Skill in nonverbal communication: Individual differences* (pp. 68–103). Cambridge, MA: Oelgeschlager, Gunn & Hain.

Rosenthal, R., & Jacobson, L. (1992). *Pygmalion in the classroom*. New York: Holt, Rinehart & Winston.

Rosnow, R. L. (1977). Gossip and marketplace psychology. *Journal of Communication, 27* (Winter), 158–163.

Ross, J. L. (1995). Conversational pitchbacks: Helping couples bat 1000 in the game of communications. *Journal of Family Psychotherapy, 6,* 83–86.

Rotello, G. (1995, April 18). The inning of outing. *The Advocate, 679,* p. 80.

Rothwell, J. D. (1992). *In mixed company: Small group communication*. Fort Worth, TX: Harcourt Brace Jovanovich.

Rowland-Morin, P. A., & Carroll, J. G. (1990). Verbal communication skills and patient satisfaction: A study of doctor-patient interviews. *Evaluation and the Health Professions, 13,* 168–185.

Ruben, B. D. (1985). Human communication and cross-cultural effectiveness. In L. A. Samovar & R. E. Porter (Eds.), *Intercultural communication: A reader* (4th ed., pp. 338–356). Belmont, CA: Wadsworth.

Rubenstein, C. (1993, June 10). Fighting sexual harassment in schools. *New York Times*, p. C8.

Rubenstein, C., & Shaver, P. (1982). *In search of intimacy*. New York: Delacorte.

Rubin, A. M. (1994). News credibility scale. In R. B. Rubin, P. Palmgreen, & H. E. Sypher (Eds.), *Communication research measures: A source book*. New York: Guilford.

Rubin, A. M., Perse, E., & Powell, R. (1985). Loneliness, parasocial interaction, and local television news viewing. *Human Communication Research, 12,* 155–180.

Rubin, R. B. (1982). Assessing speaking and listening competence at the college level: The communication competency assessment instrument. *Communication Education, 31* (January), 19–32.

Rubin, R. B. (1985). The validity of the communication competency assessment instrument. *Communication Monographs, 52,* 173–185.

Rubin, R. B., Fernandez-Collado, C., & Hernandez-Sampieri, R. (1992). A cross-cultural examination of interpersonal communication motives in Mexico and the United States. *International Journal of Intercultural Relations, 16,* 145-157.

Rubin, R. B., & Graham, E. E. (1988). Communication correlates of college success: An exploratory investigation. *Communication Education, 37,* 14-27.

Rubin, R. B., & Martin, M. M. (1994). Development of a measure of interpersonal communication competence. *Communication Research Reports, 11,* 33-44.

Rubin, R. B., & Martin, M. M. (1998). Interpersonal communication motives. In J. C. McCroskey, J. A. Daly, M. M. Martin, & M. J. Beatty (Eds.), *Communication and personality: Trait perspectives* (pp. 287-307). Cresskill, NJ: Hampton Press.

Rubin, R. B., & McHugh, M. (1987). Development of parasocial interaction relationships. *Journal of Broadcasting and Electronic Media, 31,* 279-292.

Rubin, R. B., Perse, E. M., & Barbato, C. A. (1988). Conceptualization and measurement of interpersonal communication motives. *Human Communication Research, 14,* 602-628.

Rubin, R. B., & Rubin, A. M. (1992). Antecedents of interpersonal communication motivation. *Communication Quarterly, 40,* 315-317.

Rubin, Z. (1973). *Liking and loving: An invitation to social psychology*. New York: Holt.

Rubin, Z., & McNeil, E. B. (1985). *Psychology: Being human* (4th ed.). New York: Harper & Row.

Ruggiero, T. E. (2000). Uses and gratifications theory in the 21st century. *Mass Communication & Society, 3* (Winter), 3-37.

Rundquist, S. (1992). Indirectness: A gender study of Fluting Grice's maxims. *Journal of Pragmatics, 18* (November), 431-449.

Rusbult, C. E., & Buunk, B. P. (1993). Commitment processes in close relationships: An interdependence analysis. *Journal of Social and Personal Relationships, 10* (May), 175-204.

Ruscher, J. B. (2001). *Prejudiced communication: A social psychological perspective*. New York: Guilford.

Rutledge, T., & Linden, W. (2000). Self-deception predicts the development of hypertension. *Journal of Hypertension, 16,* 1-7.

Sabatelli, R. M., & Pearce, J. (1986). Exploring marital expectations. *Journal of Social and Personal Relationships, 3,* 307-321.

Salekin, R. T., Ogloff, J. R. P., McGarland, C., & Rogers, R. (1995). Influencing jurors' perceptions of guilt: Expression of emotionality during testimony. *Behavioral Sciences and the Law, 13* (Spring), 293-305.

Samovar, L. A., & Porter, R. E. (1995). *Communication between cultures* (2nd ed.). Belmont, CA: Wadsworth.

Sayre, S. (1992). T-shirt messages: Fortune or folly for advertisers? In S. R. Danna (Ed.), *Advertising and popular culture* (pp. 73-82). Bowling Green, OH: Bowling Green State University Popular Press.

Scandura, T. (1992). Mentorship and career mobility: An empirical investigation. *Journal of Organizational Behavior, 13,* 169-174.

Schaap, C., Buunk, B., & Kerkstra, A. (1988). Marital conflict resolution. In P. Noller & M. A. Fitzpatrick (Eds.), *Perspectives on marital interaction* (pp. 203-244). Philadelphia: Multilingual Matters.

Schachter, S. (1964). The interaction of cognitive and physiological determinants of emotional state. In L. Berkowitz (Ed.), *Advances in experimental social psychology,* Vol. 1. New York: Academic Press.

Schaefer, C. M., & Tudor, T. R. (2001). Managing workplace romances. *SAM Advanced Management Journal* (Summer), 4-10.

Schafer, M., & Crichlow, S. (1996). Antecedents of groupthink. *Journal of Conflict Resolution, 40* (September), 415-435.

Scherer, K. R. (1986). Vocal affect expression. *Psychological Bulletin, 99,* 143-165.

Scheufele, D. A., & Moy, P. (2000). Twenty-five years of the spiral of silence: A conceptual review and empirical outlook. *International Journal of Public Opinion Research, 12* (Spring), 3-28.

Schlenker, B. R., Pontari, B. A., & Christopher, A. N. (2001). Excuses and character: Personal and social implications of excuses. *Personality and Social Psychology Review, 5,* 15-32.

Schnoor, L. G. (Ed.). (1997). *Winning orations of the interstate oratorical association*. Mankato, MN: Interstate Oratorical Association.

Schnoor, L. G. (Ed.). (1999). *Winning orations of the interstate oratorical association*. Mankato, MN: Interstate Oratorical Association.

Schott, G., & Selwyn, N. (2000). Examining the "male, antisocial" stereotype of high computer users. *Journal of Educational Computing Research, 23,* 291-303.

Schramm, W., & Porter, W. E. (1982). *Men, women, messages and media: Understanding human communication*. New York: Harper & Row.

Schultz, B. G. (1996). *Communicating in the small group: Theory and practice* (2nd ed.). New York: HarperCollins.

Schwartz, M., and the Task Force on Bias-Free Language of the Association of American University Presses. (1995). *Guidelines for bias-free writing*. Bloomington, IN: Indiana University Press.

Seidman, I. E. (1991). *Interviewing as qualitative research: A guide for researchers in education and the social sciences*. New York: Teachers College, Columbia University.

Seiter, J. S., & Sandry, A. (2003). Pierced for success?: The effects of ear and nose piercing on perceptions of job candidates' credibility, attractiveness, and hirability. *Communication Research Reports, 20* (Fall), 287-298.

Severin, W. J., with Tankard, J. W., Jr. (1988). *Communication theories* (2nd ed.). New York: Longman.

Shaffer, D. R., Pegalis, L. J., & Cornell, D. P. (1991). Interactive effects of social context and sex role identity on female self-disclosure during the acquaintance process. *Sex Roles, 24* (January), 1-19.

Shaffer, D. R., Pegalis, L. J., & Cornell, D. P. (1992). Gender and self-disclosure revisited: Personal and contextual variations in self-disclosure to same-sex acquaintances. *Journal of Social Psychology, 132* (June), 307-315.

Shanahan, J., & Morgan, M. (1999). *Television and its viewers: Cultivation theory and research*. New York: Cambridge University Press.

Shannon, C. E., & Weaver, W. (1949). *The mathematical theory of communication*. Urbana, IL: University of Illinois Press.

Shannon, J. (1987). Don't smile when you say that. *Executive Female, 10,* 33, 43.

Shaw, L. H., & Grant, L. M. (2002). Users divided? Exploring the gender gap in Internet use. *CyberPsychology & Behavior, 5* (December), 517-527.

Shaw, M. E., & Gouran, D. S. (1990). Group dynamics and communication. In G. Dahnke & G. W. Clatterbuck (Eds.), *Human communication: Theory and research.* Belmont, CA: Wadsworth.

Shea, V. (1994). *Netiquette.* San Rafael, CA: Albion Books.

Shimanoff, S. (1980). *Communication rules: Theory and research.* Thousand Oaks, CA: Sage.

Shimanoff, S. B. (1985). Rules governing the verbal expression of emotions between married couples. *Western Journal of Speech Communication, 49* (Summer), 147-165.

Shiraev, E., & Levy, D. (2001). *Introduction to cross-cultural psychology: Critical thinking and contemporary applications.* Boston: Allyn & Bacon.

Siegert, J. R., & Stamp, G. H. (1994). "Our first big fight" as a milestone in the development of close relationships. *Communication Monographs, 61* (December), 345–360.

Signorile, M. (1993). *Queer in America: Sex, the media, and the closets of power.* New York: Random House.

Signorielli, N., & Lears, M. (1992). Children, television, and concepts about chores: Attitudes and behaviors. *Sex Roles, 27* (August), 157–170.

Silverman, T. (2001). Expanding community: The Internet and relational theory. *Community, Work and Family, 4,* 231–237.

Skinner, M. (2002). In search of feedback. *Executive Excellence* (June), 18.

Slade, M. (1995, February 19). We forgot to write a headline. But it's not our fault. *New York Times*, p. 5.

Smith, B. (1996). Care and feeding of the office grapevine. *Management Review, 85* (February), 6.

Smith, D. (2003, December 2). Doctors cultivate a skill: Listening. *New York Times,* p. 6.

Smith, P. B., Dugan, S., Peterson, M. F., & Leung, K. (1998). Individualism: Collectivism and the handling of disagreement. *International Journal of Intercultural Relations, 22* (August), 351–367.

Smith, S. M., & Shaffer, D. R. (1991). Celerity and cajolery: Rapid speech may promote or inhibit persuasion through its impact on message elaboration. *Personality and Social Psychology Bulletin, 17* (December), 663–669.

Smith, S. M., & Shaffer, D. R. (1995). Speed of speech and persuasion: Evidence for multiple effects. *Personality and Social Psychology Bulletin, 21* (October), 1051–1060.

Smith-Lovin, L., & Brody, C. (1989). Interruptions in group discussions: The effects of gender and group composition. *American Sociological Review, 54* (June), 424–435.

Smoreda, Z., & Licoppe, C. (2000). Gender-specific use of the domestic telephone. *Social Psychology Quarterly, 63,* 238–252.

Snyder, C. R. (1984). Excuses, excuses. *Psychology Today, 18,* 50–55.

Snyder, C. R., Higgins, R. L., & Stucky, R. J. (1983). *Excuses: Masquerades in search of grace.* New York: Wiley.

Snyder, M. (1987). *Public appearances, private realities.* New York: W. H. Freeman.

Snyder, M. (1992). A gender-informed model of couple and family therapy: Relationship enhancement therapy. *Contemporary Family Therapy: An International Journal, 14* (February), 15–31.

Solomon, G. B., Striegel, D. A., Eliot, J. F., Heon, S. N., et al. (1996). The self-fulfilling prophecy in college basketball: Implications for effective coaching. *Journal of Applied Sport Psychology, 8* (March), 44–59.

Sommer, R. (1969). *Personal space: The behavioral basis of design.* Englewood Cliffs, NJ: Prentice-Hall.

Sorenson, P. S., Hawkins, K., & Sorenson, R. L. (1995). Gender, psychological type and conflict style preferences. *Management Communication Quarterly, 9* (August), 115–126.

Spiers, C. J. (1998). Commitment and stability in lesbian relationships. *Dissertation Abstracts International Section B: The Sciences and Engineering, 59,* 3076.

Spitzberg, B. H. (1991). Intercultural communication competence. In L. A. Samovar & R. E. Porter (Eds.), *Intercultural communication: A reader* (pp. 353–365). Belmont, CA: Wadsworth.

Spitzberg, B. H., & Cupach, W. R. (1984). *Interpersonal communication competence.* Beverly Hills, CA: Sage.

Spitzberg, B. H., & Cupach, W. R. (1989). *Handbook of interpersonal competence research.* New York: Springer.

Spitzberg, B. H., & Cupach, W. R. (2002). Interpersonal skills. In M. L. Knapp and J. A. Daly (Eds.), *Handbook of interpersonal communication* (3rd ed., pp. 564–611). Thousand Oaks, CA: Sage.

Spitzberg, B. H., & Hecht, M. L. (1984). A component model of relational competence. *Human Communication Research,* 10, 575–599.

Sprecher, S., & Metts, S. (1989). Development of the "romantic beliefs scale" and examination of the effects of gender and gender-role orientation. *Journal of Social and Personal Relationships, 6,* 387–411.

Staines, G. L., Pottick, K. J., & Fudge, D. A. (1986). Wives' employment and husbands' attitudes toward work and life. *Journal of Applied Psychology,* 71, 118–128.

Steil, L. K., Barker, L. L., & Watson, K. W. (1983). *Effective listening: Key to your success.* Reading, MA: Addison-Wesley.

Stein, M. M., & Bowen, M. (2003). Building a customer satisfaction system: Effective listening when the customer speaks. *Journal of Organizational Excellence, 22* (Summer), 23–34.

Steinfatt, T. M. (1987). Personality and communication: Classic approaches. In J. C. McCroskey & J. A. Daly (Eds.), *Personality and interpersonal communication* (pp. 42–126). Thousand Oaks, CA: Sage.

Stephan, W. G., & Stephan, C. W. (1985). Intergroup anxiety. *Journal of Social Issues, 41,* 157–175.

Stephan, W. G., & Stephan, C. W. (1992). *Improving intergroup relations.* Thousand Oaks, CA: Sage.

Stephan, W. G., Stephan, C. W., Wenzel, B., & Cornelius, J. (1991). Intergroup interaction and self-disclosure. *Journal of Applied Social Psychology, 21* (August), 1370–1378.

Stephen, R., & Zweigenhaft, R. L. (1986). The effect on tipping of a waitress touching male and female customers. *Journal of Social Psychology, 126* (February), 141–142.

Stewart, C. J., & Cash, W. B., Jr. (1997). *Interviewing: Principles and practices* (8th ed.). Dubuque, IA: William C. Brown.

Stratford, J. (1998). Women and men in conversation: A consideration of therapists' interruptions in therapeutic discourse. *Journal of Family Therapy, 20* (November), 383–394.

Strecker, I. (1993). Cultural variations in the concept of "face." *Multilingua 12,* 119–141.

Swim, J. K., & Hyers, L. L. (1999). Excuse me—what did you say?!: Women's public and private responses to sexist remarks. *Journal of Experimental Social Psychology, 35* (January), 68–88.

Tanaka, K. (1999). Judgments of fairness by just world believers. *Journal of Social Psychology, 139* (October), 631–638.

Tang, S., & Zuo, J. (2000). Dating attitudes and behaviors of American and Chinese college students. *The Social Science Journal, 37* (January), 67–78.

Tannen, D. (1990). *You just don't understand: Women and men in conversation.* New York: Morrow.

Tannen, D. (1994a). *Gender and discourse.* New York: Oxford University Press.

Tannen, D. (1994b). *Talking from 9 to 5: How women's and men's conversational styles affect who gets heard, who gets credit, and what gets done at work.* New York: Morrow.

Tannen, D. (2001). *I only say this because I love you: How the way we talk can make or break family relationships throughout our lives.* New York: Random House.

Taub, M. (1997). *Interviews.* Princeton, NJ: Princeton Review.

Tersine, R. J., & Riggs, W. E. (1980). The Delphi technique: A long-range planning tool. In S. Ferguson & S. D. Ferguson (Eds.), *Intercom: Readings in organizational communication* (pp. 366–373). Rochelle Park, NJ: Hayden Books.

Thibaut, J. W., & Kelley, H. H. (1986). *The social psychology of groups.* New Brunswick, NJ: Transaction.

Thompson, C. A., & Klopf, D. W. (1991). An analysis of social style among disparate cultures. *Communication Research Reports, 8,* 65–72.

Thompson, C. A., Klopf, D. W., & Ishii, S. (1991). A comparison of social style between Japanese and Americans. *Communication Research Reports, 8,* 165–172.

Thorne, B., Kramarae, C., & Henley, N. (Eds.). (1983). *Language, gender and society.* Rowley, MA: Newbury House.

Tichenor, P. J., Donohue, G. A., & Olien, C. N. (1970). Mass media flow and differential growth in knowledge. *Public Opinion Quarterly, 34,* 159–170.

Ting-Toomey, S. (1981). Ethnic identity and close friendship in Chinese-American college students. *International Journal of Intercultural Relations, 5,* 383–406.

Ting-Toomey, S. (1985). Toward a theory of conflict and culture. *International and Intercultural Communication Annual, 9,* 71–86.

Ting-Toomey, S. (1986). Conflict communication styles in black and white subjective cultures. In Y. Y. Kim (Ed.), *Interethnic communication: Current research* (pp. 75–88). Thousand Oaks, CA: Sage.

Torbiorn, I. (1982). *Living abroad.* New York: Wiley.

Trager, G. L. (1958). Paralanguage: A first approximation. *Studies in Linguistics, 13,* 1–12.

Trager, G. L. (1961). The typology of paralanguage. *Anthropological Linguistics, 3,* 17–21.

Traxler, A. J. (1980). Let's get gerontologized: Developing a sensitivity to aging. Springfield, IL: Illinois Department of Aging.

Trower, P. (1981). Social skill disorder. In S. Duck & R. Gilmour (Eds.), *Personal relationships 3* (pp. 97–110). New York: Academic Press.

Turner, M. M., Mazur, M. A., Wendel, N., & Winslow, R. (2003). Relational ruin or social glue? The joint effect of relationship type and gossip valence on liking, trust, and expertise. *Communication Monographs, 70* (June), 129–141.

UCLA Internet report: Surveying the digital future (2000). Los Angeles: UCLA Center for Communication Policy.

Ueleke, W., et al. (1983). Inequity resolving behavior as a response to inequity in a hypothetical marital relationship. *A Quarterly Journal of Human Behavior, 20,* 4–8.

Ulfelder, S. (1997, July 14). Lies, damn lies and the Internet. *Computerworld, 31,* pp. 75ff.

UNESCO [United Nations Educational, Scientific, and Cultural Organization]. (1993). *World education report.* Paris: UNESCO Publishing.

Unger, F. L. (2001). Speech directed at able-bodied adults, disabled adults, and disabled adults with speech impairments. (Doctoral dissertation, Hofstra University, 2001). *Dissertation Abstracts International, 62,* 1146B.

Uris, A. (1986). *101 of the greatest ideas in management.* New York: Wiley.

Valenti, J. (1982). *Speaking up with confidence: How to prepare, learn, and deliver effective speeches.* New York: Morrow.

Veenendall, T. L., & Feinstein, M. C. (1995). *Let's talk about relationships: Cases in Study* (2nd ed.). Prospect Heights, IL: Waveland Press.

Velting, D. M. (1999). Personality and negative expectations: Trait structure of the Beck Hopelessness Scale. *Personality and Individual Differences, 26,* 913–921.

Verderber, R. (2000). *The challenge of effective speaking* (11th ed.). Belmont, CA: Wadsworth.

Vergeer, M., Lubbers, M., & Scheepers, P. (2000). Exposure to newspapers and attitudes toward ethnic minorities: A longitudinal analysis. *Howard Journal of Communication, 11* (April–June), 127–143.

Vernon, J. A., Williams, J. A., Phillips, T., & Wilson, J. (1990). Media stereotyping: A comparison of the way elderly women and men are portrayed on prime-time television. *Journal of Women and Aging, 4,* 55–68.

Victor, D. (1992). *International business communication.* New York: HarperCollins.

Viswanath, K., & Finnegan, J. R., Jr. (1995). The knowledge-gap hypothesis: Twenty-five years later. In B. R. Burleson (Ed.), *Communication yearbook 19.* Thousand Oaks, CA: Sage.

von Tetzchner, S., & Jensen, K. (1999). Interacting with people who have severe communication problems: Ethical considerations. *International Journal of Disability, Development and Education, 46* (December), 453–462.

Vrij, A., & Mann, S. (2001). Telling and detecting lies in a high-stake situation: The case of a convicted murderer. *Applied Cognitive Psychology, 15* (March–April), 187–203.

Wade, Carole, & Tavris, Carol (1998). *Psychology* (5th ed.). New York: Longman.

Wade, N. (2002, January 22). Scent of a man is linked to a woman's selection. *New York Times*, p. F2.

Wallace, K. (1955). An ethical basis of communication. *Communication Education, 4* (January), 1–9.

Walster, E., & Walster, G. W. (1978). *A new look at love.* Reading, MA: Addison-Wesley.

Walster, E., Walster, G. W., & Berscheid, E. (1978). *Equity: Theory and research.* Boston: Allyn & Bacon.

Walters, A. S., & Curran, M. C. (1996). "Excuse me, sir? May I help you and your boyfriend?": Salespersons' differential treatment of homosexual and straight customers. *Journal of Homosexuality, 31,* 135–152.

Watson, A. K., & Cadey, H. D. (1984). Alleviating communication apprehension through rational emotive therapy: A comparative evaluation. *Communication Education, 33,* 257–266.

Watzlawick, P. (1977). *How real is real? Confusion, disinformation, communication: An anecdotal introduction to communications theory.* New York: Vintage.

Watzlawick, P. (1978). *The language of change: Elements of therapeutic communication.* New York: Basic Books.

Watzlawick, P., Beavin, J. H., & Jackson, D. D. (1967). *Pragmatics of human communication: A study of interactional patterns, pathologies, and paradoxes.* New York: Norton.

Weathers, M. D., Frank, E. M., & Spell, L. A. (2002). Differences in the communication of affect: Members of the same race versus members of a different race. *Journal of Black Psychology, 28,* 66–77.

Weinberg, H. L. (1958). *Levels of knowing and existence.* New York: Harper & Row.

Weiner, B., Russell, D., & Lerman, D. (1979). "Affective consequences of causal ascriptions." In J. H. Harvey, W. J. Ickes, & R. F. Kidd (Eds.), *New directions in attribution research,* Vol. 2. Hillsdale, NJ: Erlbaum.

Weinstein, E. A., & Deutschberger, P. (1963). Some dimensions of altercasting. *Sociometry, 26,* 454–466.

Weinstein, F. (1995, April). Professionally speaking. *Profiles: The Magazine of Continental Airlines,* pp. 50–55.

Weitzman, P. F., & Weitzman, E. A. (2000). Interpersonal negotiation strategies in a sample of older women. *Journal of Clinical Geropsychology, 6,* 41–51.

Weitzman, P. F. (2001). Young adult women resolving interpersonal conflicts. *Journal of Adult Development, 8,* 61–67.

Wennerstrom, A., & Siegel, A. F. (2003). Keeping the floor in multiparty conversation: Intonation, syntax, and pause. *Discourse Processes, 36* (September), 77–107.

Werner, E. K. (1975). *A study of communication time.* Unpublished master's thesis, University of Maryland, College Park. Cited in Wolvin and Coakley (1982).

Werrbach, G. B., Grotevant, H. D., & Cooper, C. R. (1990). Gender differences in adolescents' identity development in the domain of sex role concepts. *Sex Roles, 23* (October), 349–362.

Westwood, R. I., Tang, F. F., & Kirkbride, P. S. (1992). Chinese conflict behavior: Cultural antecedents and behavioral consequences. *Organizational Development Journal, 10* (Summer), 13-19.

Wetzel, P. J. (1988). Are "powerless" communication strategies the Japanese norm? *Language in Society, 17,* 555-564.

Wheeless, L. R., & Grotz, J. (1977). The measurement of trust and its relationship to self-disclosure. *Human Communication Research, 3,* 250-257.

Whitty, M., & Gavin, J. (2001). Age/sex/location: Uncovering the social cues in the development of online relationships. *CyberPsychology and Behavior, 4,* 623-630.

Wiemann, J. M. (1977). Explication and test of a model of communicative competence. *Human Communication Research, 3,* 195-213.

Wigley, C. J., III. (1998). Verbal aggressiveness. In J. C. McCroskey, J. A. Daly, M. M. Martin, & M. J. Beatty (Eds.), *Communication and personality: Trait perspectives* (pp. 191-214). Cresskill, NJ: Hampton Press.

Wilkins, B. M., & Andersen, P. A. (1991). Gender differences and similarities in management communication: A meta-analysis. *Management Communication Quarterly, 5* (August), 6-35.

Wilmot, W. W. (1987). *Dyadic communication* (3rd ed.). New York: Random House.

Wilson, A. P., & Bishard, T. G. (1994). Here's the dirt on gossip. *American School Board Journal, 181* (December), 27-29.

Wilson, J. H., & Taylor, K. W. (2001). Professor immediacy as behaviors associated with liking students. *Teaching of Psychology, 28,* 136-138.

Wilson, K. G., & Hayes, S. C. (2000). Why it is crucial to understand thinking and feeling: An analysis and application to drug abuse. *Behavior Analyst, 23* (Spring), 25-43.

Wilson, R. A. (1989). Toward understanding E-prime. *Etc.: A Review of General Semantics, 46,* 316-319.

Wimmer, R. D., & Dominick, J. R. (2003). *Mass media research: An introduction* (7th ed.). Belmont, CA: Wadsworth.

Windahl, S., & Signitzer, B., with Olson, J. T. (1992). *Using communication theory: An introduction to planned communication.* Thousand Oaks, CA: Sage.

Winquist, L. A., Mohr, C. D., & Kenny, D. A. (1998). The female positivity effect in the perception of others. *Journal of Research in Personality, 32* (September), 370-388.

Wispé, L. G., & Drambarean, N. C. (1953). Physiological need, word frequency, and visual duration thresholds. *Journal of Experimental Psychology, 46,* 25-31.

Withecomb, J. L. (1997). Causes of violence in children. *Journal of Mental Health, 5* (October), 433-442.

Witt, P. L., & Wheeless, L. R. (2001). An experimental study of teachers' verbal and nonverbal immediacy and students' affective and cognitive learning. *Communication Education, 50,* 327-342.

Wolfson, N. (1988). The bulge: A theory of speech behaviour and social distance. In J. Fine (Ed.), *Second language discourse: A textbook of current research* (pp. 21-38). Norwood, NJ: Ablex.

Wolfson, S. (2000). Students' estimates of the prevalence of drug use: Evidence for a false consensus effect. *Psychology of Addictive Behaviors, 14* (September), 295-298.

Wolpe, J. (1957). *Psychotherapy by reciprocal inhibition.* Stanford, CA: Stanford University Press.

Wolvin, A. D., & Coakley, C. G. (1982). *Listening.* Dubuque, IA: William C. Brown.

Won-Doornink, M.-J. (1985). Self-disclosure and reciprocity in conversation: A cross-national study. *Social Psychology Quarterly, 48,* 97-107.

Wood, W. (2000). Attitude change: Persuasion and social influence. *Annual Review of Psychology, 51,* 539-570.

Woodward, K. L. (1998, June 22). Religion: Using the bully pulpit? *Time,* p. 69.

Wrench, J. S., & McCroskey, J. C. (2003). A communibiological examination of ethnocentrism and homophobia. *Communication Research Reports, 20,* 24-33.

Wright, J. W., & Hosman, L. W. (1983). Language style and sex bias in the courtroom: The effects of male and female use of hedges and intensifiers on impression formation. *Southern Speech Communication Journal, 48,* 137-152.

Young, K. S., et al. (2000). Online infidelity: A new dimension in couple relationships with implications for evaluation and treatment. *Sexual Addiction and Compulsivity, 7,* 59-74.

Yun, H. (1976). The Korean personality and treatment considerations. *Social Casework, 57,* 173-178.

Zane, N., & Yeh, M. (2002). The use of culturally-based variables in assessment: Studies on loss of face. In K. S. Kurasaki (Ed.), *Asian American mental health: Assessment theories and methods* (pp. 123-138). New York: Kluwer Academic/Plenum Publishers.

Zimmerman, A. (2000, November 10). If boys just want to have fun, this may bring them down. *Wall Street Journal,* pp. A1, A12.

Zincoff, M. Z., & Goyer, R. S. (1984). *Interviewing.* New York: Macmillan.

Zuckerman, M., Klorman, R., Larrance, D. T., & Spiegel, N. H. (1981). Facial, autonomic, and subjective components of emotion: The facial feedback hypothesis versus the externalizer-internalizer distinction. *Journal of Personality and Social Psychology, 41,* 929-944.

Credits

Text and Illustrations

Page 47: Reprinted from *International Journal of Intercultural Relations,* Vol. 5, 1981, pp. 383–406, Ting-Toomey: "Ethnic identity and close friendship in Chinese-American college students." Used with permission from Elsevier.

Page 116: Figure 7.1, Nessa Wolfson (1988). The bulge: A theory of speech behaviour and social distance. In J. Fine (Ed.), Second language discourse: A textbook of current research (pp. 21–38). Used with permission of Greenwood Publishing.

Page 195: Scale "Intimacy and Risk" from "Perceptions of risk in intimacy" by Pilkington, C., & Richardson, D., in *Journal of Social and Personal Relationships,* Vol. 5, pp. 503–508, Sage Publications, 1989. Used by permission.

Page 255: Figure 13.1, An adaptation of Blake and Mouton's approach to managerial leadership conflict from THE MANAGERIAL GRID III, 3rd Edition by Blake & Mouton (Authors). Grid International Inc., copyright owners. Reprinted by permission.

Pages 370–373: "The Electric Heart" by Steve Zammit. Used by permission of the author.

Pages 398–401: "The Home of the Slaves." Used by permission of the author

Page 16: Screen shot reprinted by permission of Allyn & Bacon.

Page 24: Screen shot reprinted by permission of Pearson Education.

Page 43: Screen shot reprinted by permission of DiversityInc.com.

Page 59: Screen shots reprinted by permission of National Communication Association and International Communication Association.

Page 87: Screen shot reprinted by permission of International Listening Association.

Page 97: Screen shot reprinted by permission of *Psychology Today Magazine*.

Page 128: Screen shot reprinted by permission of Institute of General Semantics.

Page 140: Screen shot reprinted by permission of University of Salamanca.

Page 162: Screen shot reprinted by permission of Allyn & Bacon.

Page 184: Screen shot reprinted by permission of Terrence A. Doyle.

Page 210: Screen shot reprinted by permission of Allyn & Bacon.

Page 235: Screen shot reprinted by permission of The Academy of Leadership, University of Maryland.

Page 253: Screen shot reprinted by permission of The Center for Human Services, U.C. Davis.

Page 270: Screen shot reprinted by permission of Allyn & Bacon.

Page 303: Screen shot reprinted by permission of FedStats.gov.

Page 327: Screen shot reprinted by permission of Douglass Archives.

Page 369: Screen shot reprinted by permission of Sweet Briar College.

Page 394: Screen shots reprinted by permission of PBS and C-Span.

Photos

Page 2: Photographer's Choice/Getty Images; Page 7: Bob Daemmrich/The Image Works; Page 17: Sotograph/Getty Images; Page 21: Lara Jo Regan/Getty Images; Page 26: Kathy McLaughlin/The Image Works; Page 32: CBS Photo Archive; Page 36: Steve Niedorf/Getty Images; Page 48: AP/Wide World Photos; Page 52: Steve Niedorf/Getty Images; 57: The Kobal Collection; 71: HBO/MPTV; 72: R. W. Jones/Corbis; 77: Stone/Getty Images; Page 83: Bob Daemmrich Photo, Inc.; Page 90: Felicia Martinez/PhotoEdit, Inc.; Page 95: Richard Lord/PhotoEdit, Inc.; Page 100: AP/Wide World Photos; Page 109: Richard Lord/PhotoEdit, Inc.; Page 112: Gary Conner/PhotoEdit, Inc.; Page 125: Michael Newman/PhotoEdit, Inc.; Page 127: Chuck Savage/Corbis; Page 133: Stuart Cohen/The Image Works; Page 146: Walter Hodges/Corbis; Page 154: Pictor/Image-State; Page 159: AP/Wide World Photos; Page 167: Bob Daemmrich/The Image Works; Page 173: Yellow Dog Productions/Getty Images; Page 182: Royalty Free/Corbis; Page 192: Jim Whitmer; Page 198: Andrew Lichtenstein/The Image Works; Page 208: Photodisc Green/Getty Images; Page 221: David Young-Wolff/PhotoEdit, Inc.; Page 213: Charles Gupton/Stock Boston;; Page 228: Photodisc Green/Getty Images; Page 239: an Bosler/Getty Images; Page 242: Michael Newman/PhotoEdit, Inc.; Page 245: Digital Vision/Getty Images; Page 257: Jim Whitmer; Page 259: Bob Daemmrich Photo, Inc.; Page 266: Barbara Stitzer/PhotoEdit, Inc.; Page 276: Michael Newman/PhotoEdit, Inc.; Page 284: Bob Daemmrich Photography; Page 297: Bill Aaron/PhotoEdit, Inc.; Page 317: Walter Hodges/Getty Images; Page 321: Barbara Stitzer/PhotoEdit, Inc.; Page 325: Bob Daemmrich Photography, Inc.; Page 345: Dratch/The Image Works; Page 348: Mary Kate Denny/PhotoEdit, Inc.; Page 356: Richard Hutchings/PhotoEdit, Inc.; Page 360: K. Shamsi-Basha/The Image Works; Page 367: Frank Micelotta/Getty Images; Page 377: Stone/Getty Images; Page 385: Bob Daemmrich/Stock Boston; Page 391: Pictor/ImageState.

Index

The letters b, f, and t following page numbers indicate boxes, figures, and tables, respectively. G indicates a glossary entry. Entries in blue appear in the CD-ROM units.